NOTICE: If any part of these contents is lost or damaged, the Patron will be charged for the total cost of all i̶

_____ Disk   _____

_____ Cassette   _____

_____1____ Text   _1_ DVD___ Other

P9-EDG-899

CompTIA® A+ 220-701 and 220-702 Cert Guide

Mark Edward Soper
Scott Mueller
David L. Prowse

Pearson
800 East 96th Street
Indianapolis, Indiana 46240 USA

CompTIA® A+ 220-701 and 220-702 Cert Guide

Copyright © 2011 by Pearson Education, Inc.

ISBN-13: 978-0-7897-4790-7
ISBN-10: 0-7897-4790-1
Library of Congress Cataloging-in-Publication Data
Soper, Mark Edward.
  CompTIA A+ 220-701 and 220-702 cert guide / Mark Edward Soper, David L. Prowse, Scott Mueller. -- 2nd ed.
      p. cm.
  Includes index.
  ISBN 978-0-7897-4790-7 (hardcover)
 1. Microcomputers--Maintenance and repair--Examinations--Study guides.
 2. Computer technicians--Certification--Study guides. 3. Computing Technology Industry Association--Examinations--Study guides. I. Prowse, David L. II. Mueller, Scott. III. Title.
  TK7887.S565 2011
  004.16--dc22
                                    2011000316
Printed in the United States of America
First Printing: February 2011

Trademarks

All terms mentioned in this book that are known to be trademarks or service marks have been appropriately capitalized. Pearson Education, Inc. cannot attest to the accuracy of this information. Use of a term in this book should not be regarded as affecting the validity of any trademark or service mark.

Warning and Disclaimer

Bulk Sales

Pearson Education, Inc. offers excellent discounts on this book when ordered in quantity for bulk purchases or special sales. For more information, please contact

U.S. Corporate and Government Sales

1-800-382-3419

corpsales@pearsontechgroup.com

For sales outside of the United States, please contact

International Sales

international@pearson.com

Associate Publisher
David Dusthimer

Executive Editor
Rick Kughen

Acquisitions Editor
Betsy Brown

Development Editor
Dayna Isley

Managing Editor
Sandra Schroeder

Project Editor
Mandie Frank

Indexer
Cheryl Lenser

Proofreaders
Dan Knott,
Jovana Shirley

Technical Editor
Chris Crayton

Publishing Coordinator
Vanessa Evans

Multimedia Developer
Dan Scherf

Book Designer
Louisa Adair

Composition
Studio GaLou, LLC

Contents at a Glance

Table of Contents

About the Authors

Mark Edward Soper has been working with PCs since the days of the IBM PC/XT and AT as a sales person, technology advisor, consultant, experimenter, and technology writer. Since 1992, he's taught thousands of students across the country how to repair, manage, and troubleshoot the hardware, software, operating systems, and firmware inside their PCs. He's created many versions of his experimental computer known as "FrankenPC" for this and previous books. Mark earned his CompTIA A+ Certification in 1999 and has written two other A+ Certification books covering previous versions of the A+ Certification exams for Que Publishing.

Mark has contributed to many editions of *Upgrading and Repairing PCs*, working on the 11th through 18th editions, coauthored *Upgrading and Repairing Networks*, Fifth Edition, and written two books about digital photography, *Easy Digital Cameras* and *The Shot Doctor: The Amateur's Guide to Taking Great Digital Photos.*

In addition, Mark has contributed to Que's Special Edition *Using* series on Windows Me, Windows XP, and Windows Vista, Que's *Windows 7 In Depth*, contributed to *Easy Windows Vista*, has written two books about Windows Vista, including *Maximum PC Microsoft Windows Vista Exposed* and *Unleashing Microsoft Windows Vista Media Center*, and two books about Windows 7, *Easy Microsoft Windows 7* and *Sams Teach Yourself Microsoft Windows 7 in 10 Minutes.*

Mark also stays busy on the Web, posting many blog entries and articles at MaximumPC.com, as well as writing articles for *Maximum PC* magazine. He has taught A+ Certification and other technology-related subjects at Ivy Tech Community College in Evansville, Indiana.

David L. Prowse is a computer network specialist, author, and technical trainer. As a consultant, he installs and secures the latest in computer and networking technology. Over the past several years, he has authored and co-authored a number of networking and computer titles for Pearson Education. In addition, over the past decade, he has taught CompTIA A+, Network+, and Security+ certification courses to more than 2,000 students, both in the classroom and via the Internet.

Dedication

From Mark Edward Soper:

For Paul and Maggie, with love, always.

Acknowledgments

From Mark Edward Soper:

As always, I want to thank God for the wonderful world He created and for giving mankind the ability to discover and share knowledge and wisdom with others.

I'm once again grateful for the opportunity to work with Scott Mueller, dean of PC technology books, on another project. Scott's *Upgrading and Repairing PCs* continues to be one of my most significant hardware references now as it was more than 20 years ago. I also want to thank David L. Prowse for helping make sure this new edition reflects the continuing improvements and changes in the CompTIA A+ Certification exams, and Chris Crayton for checking the contents for accuracy.

I've always been blessed with a supportive family, which continues to grow in numbers as well as technology diversity (some of them even use Macs!). Thanks, as always, to Cheryl, who has helped me find the humor in high tech; our children and their spouses and families, who have entertained us with vigorous discussions on software, hardware, firmware, and retro gaming and music; my parents and parents-in-law, my brother and sister, my brothers- and sisters-in-law—all of whom have provided me with various opportunities to keep their PCs running.

This book would not have been possible without the help of the first-class publishing team provided by Pearson Education. As you review their names on the copyright page, join me in thanking them for their achievement in seeing this book from conception to the moment you open it and begin your journey to A+ Certification.

From David L. Prowse:

Thanks to Pearson Education and Mark for letting me be a part of this project.

About the Reviewer

Chris Crayton is an author, technical editor, technical consultant, and trainer. Formerly, he worked as a computer and networking instructor at Keiser University; as network administrator for Protocol, a global electronic customer relationship management (eCRM) company; and at Eastman Kodak Headquarters as a computer and network specialist. Chris has authored several print and online books on PC Repair, CompTIA A+, CompTIA Security+, and Microsoft Windows Vista. Chris has also served as technical editor and contributor on numerous technical titles for many of the leading publishing companies. He holds MCSE, A+, and Network+ certifications.

We Want to Hear from You!

As the reader of this book, *you* are our most important critic and commentator. We value your opinion and want to know what we're doing right, what we could do better, what areas you'd like to see us publish in, and any other words of wisdom you're willing to pass our way.

As an associate publisher for Pearson IT Certification, I welcome your comments. You can email or write me directly to let me know what you did or didn't like about this book—as well as what we can do to make our books better.

Please note that I cannot help you with technical problems related to the topic of this book. We do have a User Services group, however, where I will forward specific technical questions related to the book.

When you write, please be sure to include this book's title and author as well as your name, email address, and phone number. I will carefully review your comments and share them with the author and editors who worked on the book.

Email: feedback@pearsonitcertification.com

Mail: David Dusthimer
                Associate Publisher
                Pearson IT Certification
                800 East 96th Street
                Indianapolis, IN 46240 USA

Reader Services

Visit our website and register this book at www.informit.com/title/9780789747907 for convenient access to any updates, downloads, or errata that might be available for this book.

Introduction

CompTIA A+ Certification is widely recognized as the first certification you should receive in an information technology (IT) career. Whether you are planning to specialize in PC hardware, Windows operating system management, or network management, the CompTIA A+ Certification exams measure the baseline skills you need to master to begin your journey toward greater responsibilities and achievements in IT.

CompTIA A+ Certification is designed to be a "vendor-neutral" exam that measures your knowledge of industry-standard technology.

Goals and Methods

The number one goal of this book is a simple one: to help you pass the 2011 version of the CompTIA A+ Certification Essentials Exam (number 220-701) and the Practical Application Exam (number 220-702) and thereby earn your CompTIA A+ Certification. Although the 2011 versions of these exams have the same numbers as the 2009 versions, the 2011 versions now include Windows 7-specific content.

Because CompTIA A+ Certification exams now stress problem-solving abilities and reasoning more than memorization of terms and facts, our goal is to help you master and understand the required objectives for each exam.

To aid you in mastering and understanding the A+ Certification objectives, this book uses the following methods:

- **Opening topics list**—This defines the topics to be covered in the chapter; it also lists the corresponding CompTIA A+ objective numbers.

- **"Do I Know This Already Quizzes?"**—At the beginning of each chapter is a quiz. The quizzes and answers/explanations (found in Appendix A, "Answers to the 'Do I Know This Already?' Quizzes and Troubleshooting Scenarios"), are meant to gauge your knowledge of the subjects. If the answers to the questions don't come readily to you, be sure to read the entire chapter.

- **Foundation Topics**—This is heart of the chapter that explains the topics from a hands-on and a theory-based standpoint. This includes in-depth descriptions, tables, and figures that are geared to build your knowledge so that you can pass the exam. The chapters are broken down into several topics each.

- **Key Topics**—The key topics indicate important figures, tables, and lists of information that you should know for the exam. They are interspersed throughout the chapter and are listed in table format at the end of the chapter.

- **Memory Tables**—These can be found on the DVD within Appendix B, "Memory Tables." Use them to help memorize important information.

- **Key Terms**—Key terms without definitions are listed at the end of each chapter. Write down the definition of each term and check your work against the complete key terms in the glossary.

- **Troubleshooting Scenarios**—Most chapters conclude with a troubleshooting scenario. Imagine possible solutions and check your work in Appendix A.

For a number of years, the CompTIA A+ Certification objectives were divided into a hardware exam and an operating systems exam. Starting with the 2006 exam, the exams were restructured so that knowledge of hardware and operating systems were needed for both exams. This design continues with the current 2009 and 2011 objectives with the addition of:

- Windows Vista has been incorporated into the 2009 objectives with Windows 7 incorporated into the 2011 objectives.

- Older operating systems, such as Windows 95, 98, Me, and NT, have been removed.

- Newer multicore processor technologies, such as Core 2 Duo and Phenom II, have been added.

- Newer hard drive and memory technologies have been added.

- The A+ troubleshooting process has been updated.

- Increased amount of networking and security topics with increased difficulty.

We'll cover all these changes and more within these chapters.

For more information about how the A+ certification can help your career, or to download the latest official objectives, access CompTIA's A+ webpage at http://www.comptia.org/certifications/listed/a.aspx.

One method used by many A+ certification authors is to simply follow the objectives step by step. The problem is that because different parts of the computer—such as hard disk, display, Windows, and others—are covered in many different objectives, this approach creates a lot of overlap between chapters and does not help readers to understand exactly how a particular part of the computer fits together with the rest.

In this book, we have used a subsystem approach. Each chapter is devoted to a particular part of the computer so you understand how the components of each part work together and how each part of the computer works with other parts. To make sure you can relate the book's contents to the CompTIA A+ Certification objectives, each chapter contains cross-references to the appropriate objectives as needed, and we provide a master cross-reference list later in this introduction.

Who Should Read This Book?

The CompTIA A+ exams measure the necessary competencies for an entry-level IT professional with the equivalent knowledge of at least 500 hours of hands-on experience in the lab or field. This book is written for people who have that amount of experience working with desktop PCs and laptops. Average readers will have attempted in the past to replace a hardware component within a PC; they should also understand how to navigate through Windows and access the Internet.

Readers will range from people who are attempting to attain a position in the IT field to people who want to keep their skills sharp or perhaps retain their job due to a company policy that mandates that they take the new exams.

This book is also aimed at the reader who wants to acquire additional certifications beyond the A+ certification (Network+, Security+, and so on). The book is designed in such a way to offer easy transition to future certification studies.

Strategies for Exam Preparation

Strategies for exam preparation will vary depending on your existing skills, knowledge, and equipment available. Of course, the ideal exam preparation would consist of building a PC from scratch and installing and configuring the operating systems covered including Windows 7 (Ultimate edition is recommended), Windows Vista (Ultimate edition is preferred), and Windows XP Professional. To make things easier for the reader, we recommend that you use Microsoft's Windows Virtual PC (which works with Windows 7 Professional, Ultimate, and Enterprise) or Virtual PC 2007 (which works with other Windows 7 editions, Windows Vista, and Windows XP). Either program allows you to run virtual operating systems from within your current operating system without the need for an additional computer, and they can be downloaded for free from Microsoft's website. It is also recommended that the reader get access to a laptop, a laser printer, and as many peripheral PC devices as possible. This hands-on approach will really help to reinforce the ideas and concepts expressed in the book. However, not everyone has access to this equipment, so the next best step you can take is to read through the chapters in this book, jotting notes down with key concepts or configurations on a separate notepad. Each chapter begins with a "Do I Know This Already?" quiz designed to give you a good idea of the chapter's content and your current understanding of it. In some cases, you might already know most of or all the information covered in a given chapter.

After you have read through the book, have a look at the current exam objectives for the CompTIA A+ Certification Exams listed at http://www.comptia.org/certifications/listed/a.aspx. If there are any areas shown in the certification exam outline that you would still like to study, find those sections in the book and review them.

When you feel confident in your skills, attempt the practice exam included on the DVD with this book. As you work through the practice exam, note the areas where you lack confidence and review those concepts or configurations in the book. After you have reviewed the areas, work through the practice exam a second time and rate your skills. Keep in mind that the more you work through the practice exam, the more familiar the questions will become, and the practice exam will become a less accurate judge of your skills.

After you have worked through the practice exam a second time and feel confident with your skills, schedule the real CompTIA A+ Essentials exam (220-701) and Practical Application Exam (220-702), through either Sylvan Prometric (www.2test.com) or Pearson Vue (www.vue.com). To prevent the information from evaporating out of your mind, you should typically take the exam within a week of when you consider yourself ready to take the exam.

The CompTIA A+ Certification credential for those passing the certification exams is now valid for three years (effective January 1, 2011). To renew your certification without retaking the exam, you need to participate in continuing education (CE) activities and pay an annual maintenance fee of $25.00 ($75.00 for three years). To learn more about the certification renewal policy, see http://www.comptia.org/certifications/listed/renewal.aspx.

CompTIA A+ Exam Topics

Table I-1 lists the exam topics for the CompTIA A+ exams. This table also lists the book parts in which each exam topic is covered.

Table I-1 CompTIA A+ Exam Topics

Chapter	Topics	CompTIA A+ Exam Objectives Covered
1	PC Tools; Preventing Electrostatic Discharge; The Six-Step CompTIA Troubleshooting Process; Numbering Systems Used in Computers; Measuring Data Transfer and Frequency; Important Websites	n/a
2	The Essential Parts of Any Computer; Points of Failure; Hardware, Software, and Firmware; Working Inside Your PC; Hardware Resources	CompTIA A+ 220-701 objectives 1.1 and 1.2 and CompTIA A+ 220-702 objectives 1.1 and 1.2
3	Motherboards and Their Components; Processors and CPUs; Installing Adapter Cards	CompTIA A+ 220-701 objectives 1.2, 1.4, and 1.5 and CompTIA A+ 220-702 objectives 1.1 and 1.2
4	Understanding BIOS, CMOS, and Firmware; Configuring the System BIOS; Power-On Self-Test and Error Reporting; BIOS Upgrades	CompTIA A+ 220-701 objective 1.2 and CompTIA A+ 220-702 objective 1.2.
5	Power Supplies; Power Protection Types; Troubleshooting Power Problems	CompTIA A+ 220-701 objectives 1.3 and 2.5 and CompTIA A+ 220-702 objectives 1.1, 1.2, and 1.4
6	RAM Basics; RAM Types; Operational Characteristics; Installing Memory Modules; Troubleshooting Memory; Preventative Maintenance for Memory	CompTIA A+ 220-701 objectives 1.2 and 1.6 and CompTIA A+ 220-702 objectives 1.1 and 1.2
7	Understanding I/O Ports; Understanding Input Devices; Understanding Multimedia Devices; Installing Input and Multimedia Devices; Troubleshooting Input and Multimedia Devices; Troubleshooting I/O Ports; Maintaining Input Devices	CompTIA A+ 220-701 objectives 1.1, 1.2, 1.8, and 1.9 and CompTIA A+ 220-702 objectives 1.1 and 1.2

Table I-1 CompTIA A+ Exam Topics

Chapter	Topics	CompTIA A+ Exam Objectives Covered
8	Video (Graphics) Cards Types; Installing a Video Card; Display Types; Video Connector Types; Display Settings; Installing a Monitor; Troubleshooting Displays and Video Cards; Preventative Maintenance for Displays	CompTIA A+ 220-701 objectives 1.7 and 1.9 and CompTIA A+ 220-702 objectives 1.1 and 1.2
9	Fundamental Features of Laptops and Portable Devices; Configuring Power Management; Applications for Portable and Laptop Hardware; Safe Removal of Laptop-Specific Hardware; Portable and Laptop Diagnostics; Preventative Maintenance for Laptops and Portable Devices	CompTIA A+ 220-701 objectives 1.10 and 2.4 and CompTIA A+ 220-702 objective 1.3
10	Security Fundamentals; Securing Wireless Networks; Data and Physical Security; Access Control Purposes and Principles; Installing, Configuring, and Troubleshooting; Security Features	CompTIA A+ 220-701 objectives 5.1, and 5.2 and CompTIA A+ 220-702 objectives 4.1 and 4.2
11	Printing Fundamentals; Printer and Scanner Control; Print Processes; Interface Types; Printer and Scanner Installation; Optimizing Printer Performance; Optimizing Scanner Performance; Installing and Configuring Printer Upgrades; Printer and Scanner Troubleshooting Tools and Techniques	CompTIA A+ 220-701 objectives 1.11 and 2.3 and CompTIA A+ 220-702 objective 1.5
12	Floppy Disk Drives; Hard Disk Drives; CD and DVD Optical Drives; Removable Storage; Tape Drives; Flash Memory and Card Readers; USB Flash Memory Drives; External Hard Disks; Troubleshooting Storage	CompTIA A+ 220-701 objectives 1.1, 1.2, and 2.5 and CompTIA A+ 220-702 objectives 1.1 and 1.2
13	Differences in Windows Versions; Primary Windows Components; Windows Interfaces; Essential Operating System Files; Disk Partition, File and Folder Management; Command-Line Functions; Optimizing Windows	CompTIA A+ 220-701 objectives 3.2 and 3.3 and CompTIA A+ 220-702 objectives 2.2 and 2.3
14	Installing Operating Systems; Upgrading Operating Systems	CompTIA A+ 220-701 objectives 3.1 and 3.3

Table I-1 CompTIA A+ Exam Topics

Chapter	Topics	CompTIA A+ Exam Objectives Covered
15	Troubleshooting Windows; Maintaining Windows	CompTIA A+ 220-701 objectives 2.2, 2.5, and 3.4 and CompTIA A+ 220-702 objectives 2.1, 2.3, and 2.4
16	Network Models; Internet Connectivity Technologies; Network Protocols; TCP/IP Applications and Technologies; Network Topologies; Network Types; Cable and Connector Types; Installing Network Interface Cards; Switches and Hubs; Beyond LANs; Networking Configuration; Setting Up Shared Resources; Setting Up the Network Client; Using Shared Resources; Browser Installation and Configuration; Using Network Command-Line Tools; Network and Internet Troubleshooting	CompTIA A+ 220-701 objectives 4.1, 4.2, and 4.3 and CompTIA A+ 220-702 objectives 3.1 and 3.2
17	Recycling and Disposal Issues; Using an MSDS (Material Safety Data Sheet); Electrostatic Discharge; Hazards; Environmental and Accident Handling	CompTIA A+ 220-701 objective 6.1
18	Troubleshooting Methods Overview; Determining Whether a Problem Is Caused by Hardware or Software; Where to Go for More Information; Useful Hardware and Software Tools; Professional Behavior	CompTIA A+ 220-701 objectives 2.1, 2.2, and 6.2

How This Book Is Organized

Although this book could be read cover-to-cover, it is designed to be flexible and allow you to easily move between chapters and sections of chapters to cover just the material that you need more work with. If you do intend to read all the chapters, the order in the book is an excellent sequence to use.

Chapter 1, "PC Technician Essentials," is an introductory chapter that is designed to ease readers that are new to computers into this book. It covers foundation concepts such as PC tools, ESD, basic troubleshooting, and numbering systems. The experienced computer technician might opt to skip this chapter and start with Chapter 2, "PC Anatomy," but it is not recommended for most readers.

The core chapters, Chapters 2 through 18, cover the following topics:

- **Chapter 2, "PC Anatomy 101"**—This chapter focuses on the components of a computer, inside and outside, and describes the common points of failure in a computer. It also describes how to work inside a desktop PC and defines the hardware resources that the reader should know.

- **Chapter 3, "Motherboards, Processors, and Adapter Cards"**—This chapter discusses some of the core components of the computer, including the motherboard, processor, and adapter cards. Everything connects to the motherboard, so it stands to reason that proper planning and design of a PC, to a certain degree, starts with this component.

- **Chapter 4, "BIOS"**—This chapter explains the motherboard's firmware, known as the BIOS. It also describes the relationship between the CMOS and the BIOS and demonstrates how to configure and update the BIOS.

- **Chapter 5, "Power Supplies and System Cooling"**—This chapter describes the device that transforms AC power from the wall outlet into DC power that a computer can use. The chapter also walks through how to troubleshoot power problems and describes the various power protection types.

- **Chapter 6, "RAM"**—This chapter examines random access memory (RAM), delving into the RAM types and operational characteristics. It also demonstrates how to install and troubleshoot RAM and how to prevent memory issues from occurring.

- **Chapter 7, "I/O and Multimedia Ports and Devices"**—Input/output (I/O) devices allow a user to control the computer and display information. This chapter focuses on the many types of input devices, I/O ports, and multimedia devices that a technician sees in the field.

- **Chapter 8, "Video Displays and Graphics Cards"**—This chapter describes the different types of video cards including PCI, AGP, and PCIe, and the various methods of cooling video cards. It also delves into the different types of displays including LCD, CRT, and projectors.

- **Chapter 9, "Laptops and Portable Devices"**—This chapter dives into the components of a laptop and their locations and what makes a laptop different from a PC. Within these pages are techniques for the safe removal of hardware and diagnostic procedures.

- **Chapter 10, "Security"**—This chapter discusses security from personal computer and basic networking standpoints. The chapter also describes how to secure basic wireless networks and how to control access to data.

- **Chapter 11, "Printers"**—This chapter focuses on laser, inkjet, thermal, and impact printers, as well as image scanners. From printing and scanning fundamentals to installation to troubleshooting, this chapter covers everything a technician needs to know for the exam and for the field.

- **Chapter 12, "Storage Devices"**—This chapter discusses magnetic disks such as hard drives and floppy drives, optical discs such as CD and DVD, and solid state media such as USB flash drives.

- **Chapter 13, "Using and Managing Windows"**—This chapter demonstrates how to configure and manage Windows 7, Vista, and XP. It discusses how to use the graphical user interface (GUI) and the command-line effectively to have an efficient operating system.

- **Chapter 14, "Installing and Upgrading Windows Operating Systems"**— This chapter discusses how to install Windows 7, Windows Vista, and Windows XP. It also demonstrates how to upgrade a system from Windows 2000/XP to Vista, how to upgrade to Windows 7, and how to upgrade from 2000 to XP.

- **Chapter 15, "Troubleshooting and Maintaining Windows"**—This chapter demonstrates how to troubleshoot Windows effectively. It covers common problems you might encounter in Windows: how to troubleshoot boot up errors, how to fix application issues, and how to decipher error codes and messages. Finally, it shows how to maintain and update a Windows system.

- **Chapter 16, "Networking"**—This chapter discusses network models, Internet connectivity, TCP/IP, topologies, cabling, networking devices, and much more. It also delves into how to troubleshoot a malfunctioning network connection.

- **Chapter 17, "Safety and Environmental Issues"**—This chapter explains how to properly recycle and dispose of computer components. It also discusses material safety data sheets (MSDS) and describes how to avoid and manage hazards in the workplace.

- **Chapter 18, "Troubleshooting and Communications Methods and Professional Behavior"**—This chapter discusses the two factors that make for a successful troubleshooter: extensive computer knowledge and an understanding of human psychology. The chapter delves into how to troubleshoot a computer or other device. It also covers the proper way to treat customers.

In addition to the 18 main chapters, this book includes tools to help you verify that you are prepared to take the exam. The DVD includes the glossary, practice test, and memory tables that you can work through to verify your knowledge of the subject matter. The DVD also contains sample videos from *CompTIA A+ Video Mentor*, which is available as part of the *CompTIA A+ Cert Kit* (ISBN-13: 9780789742438).

This chapter covers the following subjects:

- **PC Tools**—This section describes the basic tools that should be part of every PC technician's toolkit.

- **Preventing Electrostatic Discharge**—This section describes damages that can result from electrostatic discharge (ESD) and ways to prevent it.

- **The CompTIA Six-Step Troubleshooting Process**—This section describes the six-step troubleshooting process, which you should memorize. You will need to know it for the exam and for the real world.

- **Numbering Systems Used in Computers**—This section defines common terms and numbering systems and how they relate to PC technologies.

- **Measuring Data Transfer and Frequency**—This section describes the concepts of bandwidth and hertz.

- **Important Websites**—This section lists websites you might find helpful as you prepare for the exams.

Before you can open a computer to work on it, it's important to have the proper PC tools and to know how to eliminate electrostatic discharge (ESD). When working with computers it is also important to understand some fundamentals about computer terms and technologies. This chapter provides you with the foundation needed for the chapters that follow by making sure you understand the basic tools, computer terms, and concepts.

This chapter touches on several fundamental computer concepts, most of which are covered in more depth later in the book. Having a good grasp of these fundamentals is essential for fully understanding the concepts discussed in this book and for putting them into practice in the real world. If you feel you have sufficient understanding of these essential topics, you may choose to skip ahead to Chapter 2, "PC Anatomy 101."

CHAPTER 1

PC Technician Essentials

PC Tools

A technician's best tools are his or her senses and hands. However, a technician needs hardware tools to open the personal computer (PC) and to install and replace components. There are several PC tools that should be a part of every technician's toolkit including

- **Phillips and straight-blade screwdrivers**—Used when hex drivers are not compatible; non-magnetic preferred

- **Torx drivers**—Required for some Compaq models; non-magnetic preferred

- **Hex drivers**—Used for opening and closing cases and securing and removing cards and motherboards; non-magnetic preferred

- **3-claw parts retrieval tool**—Retrieves loose parts from computer interior; prevents lost parts, which can lead to dead shorts

- **Hemostat clamps**—Replaces tweezers for inserting and removing jumper blocks and cables

- **Needle-nose pliers**—Straightens bent pins

- **Eyebrow tweezers**—Replaces normal tweezers in toolkit for removing and replacing jumpers

- **Penlight**—Illuminates dark cases

- **Magnifier**—Makes small parts and markings easier to read

- **Jeweler's screwdriver set**—Enables repairs to devices that use small screws

You can buy toolkits that contain many of these items, but don't hesitate to supplement a kit you already have with additional items from this list or other items you find useful. Figure 1-1 illustrates some important tools.

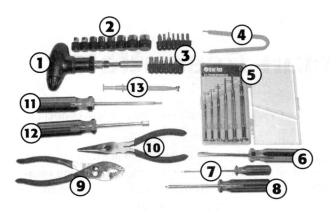

1. Screwdriver with removable tips (shown in #2 and #3)
2. Hex driver tips
3. Screw and Torx tips
4. Chip puller (also useful for removing keytops)
5. Jeweler's screwdriver set
6. Flat-blade screwdriver
7. Small Phillips-head screwdriver
8. Phillips-head screwdriver
9. Pliers
10. Needle-nose pliers
11. Torx driver
12. Hex driver
13. 3-claw parts retrieval tool

Figure 1-1 Typical tools used by computer technicians.

Preventing Electrostatic Discharge

Electrostatic discharge (ESD) occurs when two objects of different voltages come into contact with each other. The human body is always gathering static electricity, more than enough to damage a computer component. ESD is a silent killer. If you were to touch a component without proper protection, the static electricity could discharge from you to the component, most likely damaging it, but with no discernable signs of damage. Worse yet, it is possible to discharge a small amount of voltage to the device and damage it to the point where it works intermittently, making it tough to troubleshoot. It only takes 30 volts or so to damage a component. On a dry winter day, you could gather as much as 20,000 volts when walking across a carpeted area! Ouch! There are several ways to equalize the electrical potentials, allowing you to protect components from ESD:

■ **Use an antistatic wrist strap**—The most common kind is inexpensive and only takes a moment to put on and connect to the chassis of the computer (an unpainted portion of the frame inside the case). By using an antistatic wrist strap, you are constantly discharging to the case's metal frame instead of to the components that you handle. Of course, the chassis of the computer can only absorb so much ESD, so consider another earth-bonding point to connect to or try to implement as many other antistatic methods as possible. Most wrist straps come equipped with a resistor (often 1 megaohm) that protects the user from shock hazards when working with low-voltage components.

More advanced types of wrist straps are meant to connect to an actual *ground*; a ground strip or the ground plug of a special dedicated AC outlet. These are used in more sophisticated repair labs. Do not attempt to connect the alligator clip of a basic wrist strap (purchased at an office store), to the ground plug of an outlet in your home.

- **Touch the chassis of the computer**—Do this to further discharge yourself before handling any components. This is also a good habit to get into for those times when an anti-static strap is not available.

- **Use an antistatic mat**—Place the computer on top of the antistatic mat and connect the alligator clip of the mat to the computer's chassis in the same manner that you did with the wrist strap. (Some people stand on the mat and connect it to the computer.)

- **Use antistatic bags**—Adapter cards, motherboards, and so on are normally shipped in antistatic bags. Hold on to them! When installing or removing components, keep them either inside or on top of the bag until you are ready to work with them.

Remember: ESD need only happen once, and that $500 video card you are trying to install is toast!

The CompTIA Six-Step Troubleshooting Process

It is necessary to approach computer problems from a logical standpoint. To best accomplish this, PC technicians will implement a troubleshooting methodology (or maybe more than one). CompTIA has included a six-step process within the 2011 A+ objectives. Memorize the steps listed in Table 1-1.

Table 1-1 The Six-Step CompTIA A+ Troubleshooting Methodology

Step	Description
Step 1	Identify the problem
Step 2	Establish a theory of probable cause (question the obvious)
Step 3	Test the theory to determine the cause
Step 4	Establish a plan of action to resolve the problem and implement the solution
Step 5	Verify full system functionality and, if applicable, implement preventative measures
Step 6	Document findings, actions, and outcomes

As you attempt to troubleshoot computer issues, think in terms of this six-step process. Plug the problem directly into these steps. If you test a theory in Step 3, and the theory is disproved, return to Step 2 and develop another theory. Continue in this manner until you have found a theory that is plausible.

Numbering Systems Used in Computers

Since the development of the first PCs more than 30 years ago, many terms such as bits, bytes, decimal, binary, and hexadecimal have become part of common language. However, these terms are not always used correctly. This section helps you understand what these terms and numbering systems mean and how they relate to the PC technologies you will be studying in future chapters.

Three numbering systems are used in computers: decimal, binary, and hexadecimal. You already are familiar with the decimal system: Look at your hands. Now, imagine your fingers are numbered from 0–9, for a total of 10 places. Decimal numbering is sometimes referred to as base 10.

The binary system doesn't use your fingers; instead, you count your hands: One hand represents 0, and the other 1, for a total of two places. Thus, binary numbering is sometimes referred to as base 2.

The hexadecimal system could be used by a pair of spiders who want to count: One spider's legs would be numbered 0–7, and the other spider's legs would be labeled 8, 9, A–F to reach a total of 16 places. Hexadecimal numbering is sometimes referred to as base 16.

TIP Although all data in the computer is stored as a stream of binary values (0s and 1s), most of the time you will use decimal ("512 MB of RAM") or hexadecimal ("memory conflict at C800 in upper memory") measurements. The typical rule of thumb is to use the system that produces the smallest *meaningful* number. If you need to convert between these systems, you can use any scientific calculator, including the Windows Calculator program (select View, Scientific from the menu).

Decimal Numbering System

We use the decimal or base 10 system for everyday math. A variation on straight decimal numbering is to use "powers of 2" as a shortcut for large values. For example, drive storage sizes often are defined in terms of decimal bytes, but the number of colors that a video card can display can be referred to as "24-bit" (or 2^{24}), which is the same as 16,777,216 colors.

Binary Numbering System

All data is stored in computers in a stream of 1s (on) and 0s (off). Because only two characters (0 and 1) are used to represent data, this is called a "binary" numbering system. Text is converted into its numerical equivalents before it is stored, so binary coding can be used to store all computer data and programs.

Table 1-2 shows how you would count from 1 to 10 (decimal) in binary.

Table 1-2   Decimal Numbers 1–10 and Binary Equivalents

Decimal	0	1	2	3	4	5	6	7	8	9	10
Binary	0	1	10	11	100	101	110	111	1000	1001	1010

Because even a small decimal number occupies many places if expressed in binary, binary numbers are usually converted into hexadecimal or decimal numbers for calculations or measurements. Binary numbers are also the basis for bits and bytes: a single binary value is represented by a bit, and eight bits equals a byte.

NOTE   Once you understand how binary numbering works, you can appreciate the joke going around the Internet and showing up on T-shirts near you:

"There are 10 kinds of people in the world—those who understand binary and those who don't."

T-shirts are available from ThinkGeek (www.thinkgeek.com).

There are several ways to convert a decimal number into binary:

■   Use a scientific calculator with conversion

■   Use the division method

■   Use the subtraction method

To use the division method, follow these steps:

Step 1.   Divide the number you want to convert by 2.

Step 2.   Record the remainder: If there's no remainder, enter 0. If there's any remainder, enter 1.

Step 3.   Divide the resulting answer by 2.

Step 4.   Repeat the process, recording the remainder each time.

Step 5.   Repeat the process until you divide 0 by 2. This is the last answer.

Step 6.   When the last answer is divided, the binary is recorded from Least Significant Bit (LSB) to Most Significant Bit (MSB). Reverse the order of bit numbers so that MSB is recorded first and the conversion is complete. For example, to convert the decimal number 115 to binary using the division method, follow the procedure shown in Figure 1-2.

If you use a scientific calculator (such as the scientific mode of the Windows Calculator) to perform the conversion, keep in mind that any leading zeros will be suppressed. For example, the calculation in Figure 1-2 indicates the binary equivalent of 115 decimal is 01110011. However, a scientific calculator will drop the leading zero and display the value as 1110011.

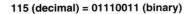

115 (decimal) = 01110011 (binary)

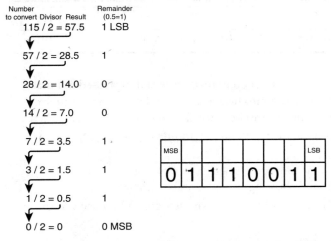

Figure 1-2   Converting decimal 115 to binary with the division method.

To use the subtraction method, follow these steps:

Step 1.   Look at the number you want to convert and determine the smallest power of two that is greater than or equal to the number you want to subtract. Table 1-3 lists powers of two from 2^0 through 2^{17}. For example, 115 decimal is less than 2^7 (128) but greater than 2^6 (64).

Step 2.   Subtract the highest power of two from the value you want to convert. Record the value and write down binary 1.

Table 1-3   Powers of 2

Power of 2	Decimal Value	Power of 2	Decimal Value
2^0	1	2^9	512
2^1	2	2^{10}	1024
2^2	4	2^{11}	2048
2^3	8	2^{12}	4096
2^4	16	2^{13}	8192
2^5	32	2^{14}	16384
2^6	64	2^{15}	32768
2^7	128	2^{16}	65536
2^8	256	2^{17}	131072

Step 3.   Move to the next lower power of two. If you can subtract it, record the result and also write down binary 1. If you cannot subtract it, write down binary 0.

Step 4.   Repeat Step 3 until you attempt to subtract 2^0 (1). Again, write down binary 1 if you can subtract it or binary 0 if you cannot. The binary values (0 and 1) you have recorded are the binary conversion for the decimal number. Unlike the division method, this method puts them in the correct order; there's no need to write them down in reverse order.

For example, to convert 115 decimal to binary using the subtraction method, see Figure 1-3.

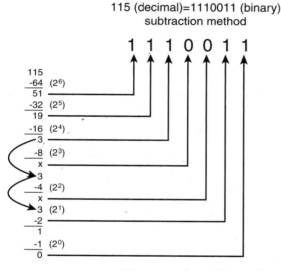

X = can't subtract (enter 0)
Enter 1 when you can subtract

Figure 1-3   Converting 115 decimal to binary with the subtraction method.

TIP   Table 1-3 provides a listing of powers of 2, but you can use the Windows Calculator in scientific view mode to calculate any power of two you want. To open the Windows Calculator click **Start**, then **Run** and type **calc.exe**. (If you cannot see the Run option in Windows Vista or Windows 7, press the **Windows key** and **R** simultaneously.) Just enter **2**, click the **x^y** button, and enter the value for the power of 2 you want to calculate (such as 24). The results are displayed instantly (you add the commas). Use the Edit menu to copy the answer to the Windows Clipboard, and use your program's Paste command to bring it into your document. Sure beats counting on your fingers!

CAUTION   You might need to convert decimal to binary numbers for the A+ Certification exam, so try both pencil and paper methods (division and subtraction) and get comfortable with one of them.

Binary Versus Decimal MB/GB

Although a byte represents the basic "building block" of storage and RAM calculation, most measurements are better performed with multiples of a byte. All calculations of the capacity of RAM and storage are done in *bits* and *bytes*. Eight bits is equal to one byte.

Table 1-4 provides the most typical values and their relationship to the byte.

Table 1-4   Decimal and Binary Measurements

Measurement	Type D=Decimal B=Binary	Number of Bytes/Bits
Bit	D, B	1/8 of a byte
Nibble	D, B	1/2 of a byte
Byte	D, B	8 bits
Kilobit (Kb)	D	1,000 bits
	B	1,024 bits (128 bytes)
Kilobyte (KB)	D	1,000 bytes
	B	1,024 bytes
Megabit (Mb)	D	1,000,000 bits
	B	1,048,576 bits (131,072 bytes)
Megabyte (MB)	D	1,000,000 bytes
	B	1,048,576 bytes
Gigabit (Gb)	D	1,000,000,000 bits
	B	1,073,741,824 bits
Gigabyte (GB)	D	1,000,000,000 bytes
	B	1,073,741,824 bytes

DECIMAL VERSUS BINARY NUMBERING CONFUSION

The use of the terms kilobit, kilobyte, megabit, megabyte, gigabit, and gigabyte to refer both to decimal and binary values has caused widespread confusion about the capacities of magnetic, optical, and flash memory storage. Storage device manufacturers almost always rate drives and media in decimal megabytes (multiples of 1 million bytes) or decimal gigabytes (multiples of 1 billion bytes), which is also the standard used by disk utilities such as CHKDSK, ScanDisk, and FORMAT. However, most BIOS programs and Windows Disk Management utilities list drive sizes in binary megabytes or binary gigabytes.

The differences in numbering between the decimal and binary versions of a numbering system often leads to a perception that device vendors are not properly describing the capacities of their drives or media. An attempt was made in late 1998 to use the prefixes kibi, mebi, and gibi to refer to binary numbers in place of kilo, mega, and giga. However, this numbering system has not been adopted by the industry. The A+ Certification exams might use KB, MB, and GB to refer to either type of numbering system.

Consider a hard disk rated by its maker as 160 GB (decimal). This is 160,000,000,000 bytes (decimal). However, when the drive is detected and configured by the BIOS and partitioned with FDISK, its size is listed as only 149.01 GB (binary GB). At first glance, you might believe you've lost some capacity (see Figure 1-4).

However, as you've already seen, there is a substantial difference between the number of bytes in a binary gigabyte and one billion bytes. This different numbering system, not any loss of bytes, accounts for the seeming discrepancy. Use this information to help explain to a customer that the "missing" capacity of the hard disk isn't really missing (see Figure 1-5).

Data Storage and Overhead

As you learned earlier in this chapter, bits and bytes are the building blocks of measuring storage and memory capacities. However, why is it that when the same information is stored in different ways that the size of the file changes so much?

If you are storing text-only information in the computer, each character of that text (including spaces and punctuation marks) equals a byte. Thus, to calculate the number of bytes in the following sentence, count the letters, numbers, spaces, and punctuation marks:

```
"This book is published by Pearson."
12345678901234567890123456789012345678901234
        |             |         |         |
       10            20        30        40
```

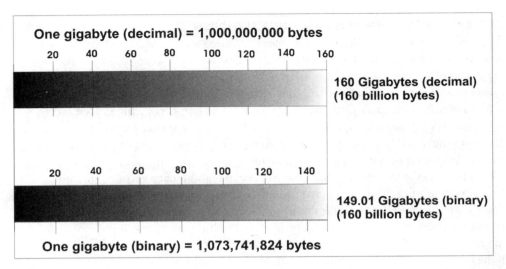

Figure 1-4 The capacity of 160 GB hard disk size is 160 billion bytes (top bar), but most BIOS programs and Windows FDISK/Disk Management measure drives in binary gigabytes (bottom bar) and report a capacity of 149.01GB.

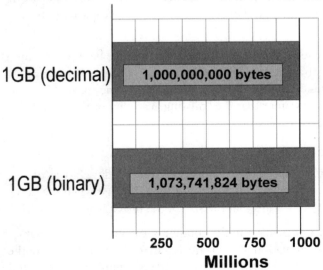

Figure 1-5 A binary gigabyte has over 73 million more bytes than a decimal gigabyte (1 billion bytes).

From the scale you can see that the sentence uses 36 bytes. You can prove this to yourself by starting Windows Notepad and entering the text just as you see it printed here. Save the text as EXAMPLE.TXT and view the File properties. You'll see that the text is exactly 36 bytes.

Do most computer programs store just the text when you write something? To find out, start a word-processing program, such as Windows WordPad or Microsoft Word. Enter the same sentence again, and save it as EXAMPLE. If you use Word-Pad, save the file as a Rich Text Format (.RTF) file. Depending upon whether you use WordPad or Microsoft Word, the file will take up a different amount of space. For example, WordPad for Windows XP saves text as an RTF file, using 193 bytes to store the file. The same sentence takes approximately 24 kilobytes (kB) when saved as a .DOC file by Microsoft Word!

When data you create is stored in a computer, it must be stored in a particular arrangement suitable for the program that created the information. This arrangement of information is called the *file format*.

A few programs, such as Windows Notepad, store only the text you create. What if you want to boldface a certain word in the text? A text-only editor can't do it. All that Edit and Notepad can store is text. As you have seen, in text-only storage, a character equals a byte.

In computer storage, however, pure text is seldom stored alone. WordPad and other word-processing programs such as Microsoft Word, OpenOffice Writer, and Corel WordPerfect enable you to **boldface**, <u>underline</u>, *italicize*, and make text larger or smaller. You can also use different fonts in the same document.

Most modern programs also enable you to insert tables, create columns of text, and insert pictures into the text. Some, such as Microsoft Word, have provisions for tracking changes made by different users. In other words, there's a whole lot more than text in a document.

To keep all this non-text information arranged correctly with the text, WordPad and other programs must store references to these additional features along with the text, making even a sentence or two into a relatively large file, even if none of the extra features is actually used in that particular file. Thus, for most programs, the bytes used by the data they create are the total of the bytes used by the text or other information created by the program and the additional bytes needed to store the file in a particular file format.

Because different programs store data in different ways, it's possible to have an apparent software failure take place because a user tries to use program B to open a file made with program A. Unless program B contains a converter that can understand and translate how program A stores data, program B can't read the file, and might even crash. To help avoid problems, Windows associates particular types of data files with matching programs, enabling you to open the file with the correct program by double-clicking the file in Windows Explorer.

Hexadecimal Numbering System

A third numbering system used in computers is hexadecimal. Hexadecimal numbering is also referred to as base 16, a convenient way to work with data because 16 is also the number of bits in 2 bytes or 4 nibbles (a nibble being 4 bits). Hexadecimal numbers use digits 0–9 and letters A–F to represent the 16 places (0–15 decimal). Hexadecimal numbers are used to represent locations in data storage, data access, and RAM. Table 1-5 shows how decimal numbers are represented in hex.

Table 1-5 Decimal and Hexadecimal Equivalents

Decimal	0	1	2	3	4	5	6	7	8	9	10	11	12	13	14	15
Hexadecimal	0	1	2	3	4	5	6	7	8	9	A	B	C	D	E	F

The most typical uses for hexadecimal numbering are

- Upper memory addresses
- I/O port addresses
- MAC addresses and IPv6 addresses

Measuring Data Transfer and Frequency

Data is constantly being transferred within a computer and between computers. But how much data, and how fast is it being computed? Data transfer is known as bandwidth, which specifies how much data is being sent per second. The speed at which data is computed is known as Hertz, which also dictates the frequency used to transfer data.

Bandwidth

Other than bits and bytes and their multiples, probably the second most significant concept to understand about computer measurements is bandwidth, also known as data transfer rate. Bandwidth refers to the amount of information that can be sent or received through a computer or network connection in one second. This can be measured in bits (with a lowercase b) or bytes (with an uppercase B). For example, the bandwidth of a USB 1.1 port running at full speed transfers a maximum of 12 megabits per second (12 Mbps, notice the lowercase b), while the bandwidth of a USB 2.0 port running at high speed is 480 Mbps, and a user might download 300 kilobytes (300 KB/s, notice the uppercase B) of data per second. Or an expansion card that goes into a PCI slot could transfer a maximum of 266 MB/s.

Bandwidth measurements like this are used for measuring the performance of serial, parallel, wired and wireless network connections, expansion slots (PCI, PCIe, and AGP), hard disk interfaces (PATA and SATA), and multipurpose device interfaces (SCSI, USB, and FireWire). It defines the amount of information that can flow through the computer.

Information flows through the computer in many ways. The CPU is the central point for most information. When you start a program, the CPU instructs the storage device to load the program into RAM. When you create data and print it, the CPU instructs the printer to output the data.

Because of the different types of devices that send and receive information, two major types of data transfers take place within a computer: parallel and serial. These terms are used frequently, but if you're not familiar with the differences between them, check out Figure 1-6.

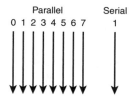

Figure 1-6   Parallel data transfers move data 8 bits at a time, whereas serial data transfers move 1 bit at a time.

Parallel Information Transfers

Parallel transfers use multiple "lanes" for data and programs, and in keeping with the 8 bits = 1 byte nature of computer information, most parallel transfers use multiples of 8. Parallel transfers take place between the following devices:

- Processor (CPU) and RAM

- Processor (CPU) and interface cards

- LPT (printer) port and parallel printer

- SCSI port and SCSI devices

- PATA /IDE host adapter and PATA/IDE drives

- RAM and interface cards, either via the CPU or directly with direct memory access (DMA)

Before the development of high-speed interfaces such as serial ATA (SATA), universal serial bus (USB), and FireWire (IEEE 1394), parallel interfaces were the most common types of interfaces between peripherals and PC components. There were two reasons for this:

- Multiple bits of information are sent at the same time.

- At identical clock speeds, parallel transfers are faster than serial transfers because more data is being transferred.

However, parallel transfers also have problems:

- Many wires or traces (wire-like connections on the motherboard or expansion cards) are needed, leading to interference concerns and thick, expensive cables.

- Excessively long parallel cables or traces can cause data to arrive at different times. This is referred to as *signal skew* (see Figure 1-7).

Figure 1-7   Parallel cables that are too long can cause signal skew, allowing the parallel signals to become "out of step" with each other.

- Differences in voltage between wires or traces can cause *jitter*.

As a result of these problems some compromises have had to be included in computer and system design:

- Short maximum lengths for parallel, PATA/IDE, and SCSI cables

- Dual-speed motherboards (running the CPU internally at much faster speeds than the motherboard or memory)

Fortunately, there is a second way to transmit information: serial transfers.

Serial Transfers

A *serial transfer* uses a single "lane" in the computer for information transfers. This sounds like a recipe for slowdowns, but it all depends on how fast the speed limit is on the "data highway."

The following ports and devices in the computer use serial transfers:

- Serial (also called RS-232 or COM) ports and devices

- Modems (which can be internal devices or can connect to serial or USB ports)

- USB (Universal Serial Bus) 1.1 and 2.0 ports and devices

- IEEE 1394 (FireWire, i.Link) ports and devices

- Serial ATA (SATA) host adapters and drives

Serial transfers have the following characteristics:

- One bit at a time is transferred to the device.

- Transmission speeds can vary greatly, depending on the sender and receiver.

- Very few connections are needed in the cable and ports (one transmit, one receive, and a few control and ground wires).

- Cable lengths can be longer with serial devices. For example, an UltraDMA/133 PATA/IDE cable can be only 18 inches long for reliable data transmission, whereas a Serial ATA cable can be almost twice as long.

Although RS-232 serial ports are much slower than any parallel interface, newer types of devices using serial transfers such as USB, SATA, and FireWire are much faster than parallel devices. The extra speed is possible because serial transfers don't have to worry about interference or other problems caused by running so many data lines together. As a result, parallel interfacing is used primarily for some types of internal connections between motherboard devices, while USB, SATA, and FireWire have almost completely replaced serial, parallel, PATA/IDE, and SCSI interfaces.

TIP   Parallel data transfers are measured in bytes; serial data transfers are measured in bits.

Hertz (Hz)

Hertz (Hz) measures the transmission frequency of radio and electrical signals in cycles per second. For example, the common 115V alternating current (AC) electrical standard used in North America is transmitted at 60 cycles per second, or 60 Hz; thus, 115V/60Hz AC.

Megahertz (MHz) is equal to 1000 Hz; Gigahertz (GHz) is equal to 1000 MHz or one million Hz. An example of a device that runs in the GHz speeds is the processor or CPU; a typical CPU might run at 2.4 GHz. Table 1-6 shows the most common multiples for Hertz.

Table 1-6   Multiples for Hertz

Symbol	Name	Amount of cycles per second
Hz	Hertz	1
kHz	Kilohertz	1,000
MHz	Megahertz	1,000,000
GHz	Gigahertz	1,000,000,000

At this point you should have a nice little foundation of knowledge concerning PC tools, electrostatic discharge, troubleshooting, numbering systems, and data transfer. Memorize and use these concepts as you read through the upcoming chapters to help you understand the more in-depth concepts that you will encounter.

Important Websites

There are several websites that we will be referring to within this book; you will be accessing these websites quite frequently when working in the field. They include

- **Microsoft's TechNet**—http://technet.microsoft.com. This site includes highly technical information about all of Microsoft's products.

- **Microsoft Help and Support**—http://support.microsoft.com (previously known as the Microsoft Knowledge Base or MSKB). This site has thousands of articles that show how to configure and troubleshoot Windows.

- **CompTIA's A+ webpage**—http://www.comptia.org/certifications/listed/a.aspx. This site describes the CompTIA A+ certification and how the exam works, and it has downloadable objectives that show exactly what is on the exam.

This chapter covers the following subjects:

■ **The Essential Parts of Any Computer**—This section lists the vital components of a PC, for example motherboards, CPUs, video cards, and more. It also shows how to identify those components.

■ **Points of Failure**—In this section you'll learn about possible issues that could cause the computer to fail; for example overheating, hard drive failure, or loose adapter cards.

■ **Hardware, Software, and Firmware**—This section explains how hardware, software and firmware interact and defines the major types of software and utility programs.

■ **Working Inside Your PC**—This section demonstrates how to assemble/disassemble the computer. It shows how to connect cables, replace components, add adapter cards, and protect your equipment from electrostatic discharge.

■ **Hardware Resources**—In this last section you'll learn about interrupt requests (IRQs), input/output port addresses, direct memory access channels, and memory addresses, and how each is assigned to the components of your computer.

This chapter covers a portion of the CompTIA A+ 220-701 objectives 1.1 and 1.2 and CompTIA A+ 220-702 objectives 1.1 and 1.2.

CHAPTER 2

PC Anatomy 101

To really know a computer you have to get inside it. By disassembling and reassembling a PC you learn the inner workings, or the *anatomy*, of the PC. This chapter demonstrates how to open a computer and identify all the components inside. It also shows how to identify all the ports, switches, and buttons on the back and front of the computer. You learn how to protect the computer from electrostatic discharge (ESD) and the proper way to add and remove components. This chapter also describes the types of problems that can cause a computer to fail and which components might be the cause of those failures.

Of course, the anatomy of the PC goes far beyond this. Not only do you need to know about the hardware in your PC, but also the software (for example, Windows 7) and firmware (BIOS) that your computer uses. There are also the assigned resources that a PC uses, such as IRQs (interrupt requests) and I/O (input/output) settings. This chapter covers all these concepts and more.

"Do I Know This Already?" Quiz

The "Do I Know This Already?" quiz allows you to assess whether you should read this entire chapter or simply jump to the "Exam Preparation Tasks" section for review. If you are in doubt, read the entire chapter. Table 2-1 outlines the major headings in this chapter and the corresponding "Do I Know This Already?" quiz questions. You can find the answers in Appendix A, "Answers to the 'Do I Know This Already?' Quizzes and Troubleshooting Scenarios."

Table 2-1   "Do I Know This Already?" Foundation Topics Section-to-Question Mapping

Foundations Topics Section	Questions Covered in This Section
The Essential Parts of Any Computer	1, 2
Points of Failure	3
Hardware, Software, and Firmware	4, 5
Working Inside Your PC	6–10
Hardware Resources	11, 12

1. You are working on a computer. Which of the following are considered essential? (Choose all correct answers.)

   a.   Motherboard

   b.   CPU

   c.   Memory

   d.   Video card

   e.   A scanner

2. Which of the following devices might be found on the front or back of a computer? (Choose all correct answers.)

   a.   Activity lights

   b.   Power switch

   c.   USB ports

   d.   None of these options are correct

3. Which of the following can cause a desktop computer to fail? (Choose all that apply.)

   a. Overheating

   b. Loose add-on cards

   c. Drive failures

   d. Adding more memory

4. Which of the following are the most commonly used Windows operating systems? (Choose the three best answers.)

   a. Windows XP

   b. Windows 7

   c. Windows Vista

   d. Windows 98

5. Which of the following can be used in your day-to-day work on a standard Windows computer? (Choose the two best answers.)

   a. CHKDSK

   b. toopath

   c. Disk Defragmenter

   d. ifconfig

6. Which of the following is the first thing you should do when replacing a PCI card?

   a. Shut down the system and unplug the power

   b. Open the case

   c. Open the package and set it beside the computer

   d. Purchase the device

7. Which of the following steps is important to perform when opening the case to access the internal parts of a computer?

   a. Check your system manual

   b. Get out the screwdriver

   c. Check for ESD

   d. None of these options are correct

8. Which of the following can help in preventing ESD? (Choose two.)

    a. Touch the unpainted metal of the chassis

    b. Wear sneakers

    c. Remove the power supply

    d. Wear an antistatic wrist strap

9. How do you identify the cable that connects to the floppy drive?

    a. It is flat.

    b. It is the longest cable.

    c. There is a twist at one end.

    d. None of these options are correct.

10. How do you attach the VGA cable to the video card to prevent it from losing connection?

    a. By snapping it into the video port with both thumbs

    b. By using the locking arm mechanism

    c. By using a torx screwdriver

    d. By turning the thumbscrews

Foundation Topics

The Essential Parts of Any Computer

What makes a computer a computer? After all, some furniture stores put 3D cardboard facsimile computers on computer desks so you can see that the furniture really will hold a computer. But, what is it about a real computer that makes it different than the cardboard phony?

Real computers contain a variety of components and subsystems, including

- Storage devices

- Motherboards

- Power supplies

- Processors/CPUs

- Memory

- Display devices

- Input, multimedia, and biometric devices

- Adapter cards

- Ports and cables

- Cooling systems

This section describes the components of a desktop PC and contrasts the feature of a desktop with those of a laptop, or notebook, computer.

Front and Rear Views of a Desktop PC

Many of these components are visible in the front and rear views of a desktop computer. Figure 2-1 shows the front view of a typical desktop computer, and Figure 2-2 shows the rear view of the same computer.

NOTE   The system shown in Figure 2-2 lacks legacy ports such as serial and parallel ports. For a look at a system with these ports, refer to Figure 7-1 in Chapter 7, "I/O and Multimedia Ports and Devices."

Some components, such as RAM, disk drives, and the CPU, are only visible when you remove part of the cover. Figure 2-3 shows the interior of a typical desktop computer, which, as you can see, is a pretty crowded place.

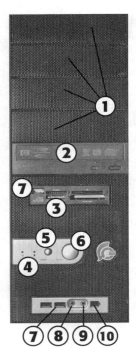

1. Empty 5.25-inch drive bay
2. Rewritable DVD drive
3. Flash memory card reader
4. Activity lights
5. Reset switch
6. Power switch
7. USB port
8. Microphone jack
9. Speaker/headset jack
10. IEEE-1394a (FireWire 400) port

Figure 2-1   The front of a typical desktop computer.

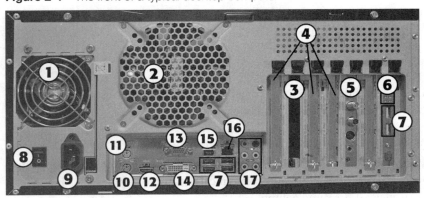

1. Power supply fan
2. Case fan
3. Empty expansion slot without slot cover
4. Empty expansion slot with slot cover
5. TV tuner card
6. Motherboard diagnostic lights
7. USB port
8. Power supply on/off switch
9. AC power connector

10. PS/2 keyboard port
11. PS/2 mouse port
12. HDMI audio/video port
13. VGA video port
14. DVI-D video port
15. IEEE-1394a (FireWire 400) port
16. Ethernet (RJ-45) port
17. 1/8-inch mini-jack audio port cluster

Figure 2-2   The rear of a typical desktop computer.

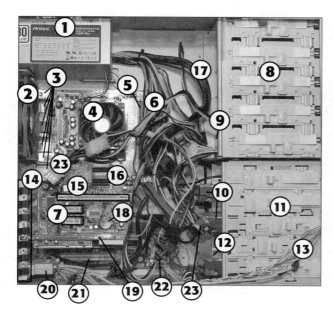

1. Power supply
2. Case fan
3. Rear port cluster
4. Active heatsink over CPU
5. Memory modules
6. Power cables for drives and fans
7. PCI Express x1 expansion slots
8. Empty 5.25-inch drive bay
9. Rewritable DVD drive in
   5.25-inch drive bay
10. PATA drive in 3.5-inch drive bay
11. Empty 3.5-inch drive bay
12. SATA hard disk in 3.5-inch
    drive bay
13. Front panel cables
14. Expansion slot covers
15. PCI Express x16 video card slot
16. Passive heatsink over
    North Bridge chip
17. Power cable to motherboard
18. CMOS battery (CR-2032)
19. TV tuner card
20. Rear header cable
21. PCI expansion slot
22. Front header cable
23. Unused drive/fan power
    connector

Figure 2-3 The interior of a typical desktop computer.

All Around a Notebook (Laptop) Computer

Notebook computers use the same types of peripherals, operating system, and application software as desktop computers use. However, notebook computers vary in several ways from desktop computers:

■ Most notebook computers feature integrated ports similar to those found in recent desktop computers (such as USB 2.0 ports and 10/100 or Gigabit Ethernet network ports) as well as one or more PC Card (PCMCIA) or ExpressCard slots and a 56 kilobits per second (Kbps) modem.

■ Some notebook computers support swappable drives, but less-expensive models require a trip to the service bench for a drive upgrade.

■ Most notebook computers don't have an internal floppy drive, but rely on rewriteable DVD, combo CD-RW/DVD-ROM, or USB drives to transfer or back up data.

■ Notebook computers have integrated pointing devices built into their keyboards; most use a touchpad, but a few (primarily Lenovo and some Toshiba models) have a pointing stick (which type is better is a matter of personal preference).

Figure 2-4 shows you the ports on a typical notebook computer, an HP dv5000 series. Note that this computer has ports on the left and right sides only, while some other portable computers have ports on the rear as well.

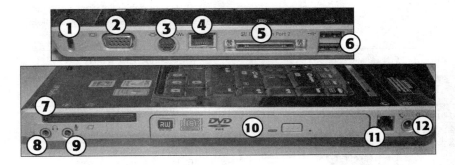

1. Security cable connector	7. Express Card slot
2. VGA video port	8. Headphone jack
3. S-Video (TV out) port	9. Microphone jack
4. Ethernet (RJ-45) port	10. Rewriteable DL DVD
5. Proprietary expansion port	11. 56Kbps modem port
6. USB port	12. AC power jack

Figure 2-4   Left and right views of an HP dv5000 series notebook computer.

Quick Reference to PC Components

Use Table 2-2 to learn more about many of the components and devices shown in Figures 2-1–2-4.

Table 2-2   Where to Learn More About PC Components and Devices

Component/Device	Chapter
Audio jacks (microphone, speaker, headphone, and so on)	7
Case fan	5
CMOS battery	4
Drive bay	12
DVD drive	12
DVI-D video port	8
Ethernet network port	16
Express Card slot	9

Table 2-2   Where to Learn More About PC Components and Devices

Component/Device	Chapter
Flash memory card reader	12
IEEE-1394 port	7
Memory module	6
Modem port	16
Motherboard and its components	3
PATA hard disk drive and interface	12
PC Card/CardBus slot	12
PCI Express x1 slot	3
PCI Express x16 slot	3
PCI slot	3
Power supply	5
PS/2 keyboard and mouse ports	7
SATA hard disk drive and interface	12
S-video port	8
TV tuner card	7
USB port	7
VGA video port	8
Video card	8

Points of Failure

The phrase *point of failure* identifies components and accessories that can fail on a desktop or portable computer. This section describes points of failure on desktop and laptop computers.

Points of Failure on a Desktop Computer

A desktop computer can fail for a variety of reasons, including

- **Overheating**—Failure of the fans in the power supply or those attached to the processor, northbridge chip, or video card can cause overheating and can lead to component damage. Some fans plug into the motherboard, while others plug into a lead from the power supply.

- **Loose add-on cards**—A loose add-on card might not be detected by plug-and-play or the Windows Add New Hardware wizard, or might have intermittent failures after installation.

- **Inability to start the computer**—A loose processor or memory module can prevent the computer from starting.

- **Drive failures**—If drives are not properly connected to power or data cables, or are not properly configured with jumper blocks, they will not work properly.

- **Front panel failures**—The tiny cables that connect the case power switch, reset switch, and status lights are easy to disconnect accidentally if you are working near the edges of the motherboard.

- **Battery failure**—The battery maintains the system settings that are configured by the system BIOS. The settings are stored in a part of the computer called the CMOS, more formally known as the non-volatile RAM/real-time clock (NVRAM/RTC). If the battery dies (average life is about two to three years), these settings will be lost. After you replace the battery, you must re-enter the CMOS settings and save the changes to the CMOS before you can use the system.

- **BIOS chip failure**—The system BIOS chip can be destroyed by ESD or lightning strikes. However, BIOS chips can also become outdated. Although some systems use a rectangular socketed BIOS chip, others use a square BIOS chip which might be socketed or surface-mounted. In both cases, software BIOS upgrades are usually available to provide additional BIOS features, such as support for newer processors and hardware.

Points of Failure on a Notebook Computer

As with desktop computers, cabling can be a major point of failure on notebook computers. However, notebook computers also have a few unique points of failure. PC Card (PCMCIA card) or Express Card slots represent a significant potential point of failure for the following reasons:

- If a PC Card or Express Card is not completely pushed into its slot, it will not function.

- If a PC Card or Express Card is ejected without being stopped by using the Safely Remove Hardware system tray control, it could be damaged.

- Some older PC Cards designed as 10/100 Ethernet network adapters or 56Kbps modems use dongles (refer to Figure 16-5 in Chapter 16, "Networking"). If the dongle is damaged, the card is useless until you get a replacement dongle.

Replacing Internal Drives and Displays on Notebook Computers

Although a notebook computer's drives are much more rugged than those found in desktop computers, they are more expensive to replace with an equivalent or larger sized drive if damaged. Although some mid-range and high-end notebook computers offer swappable drives, most lower-priced models do not. Depending upon the specific notebook computer model, you can often perform an upgrade to a hard disk without special tools, but replacement of other types of drives on systems that don't support swappable drive bays can be expensive.

Drives are expensive to replace on notebook computers, but the biggest potential expense is the LCD display. Although some vendors provide user-replaceable LCD display modules, you should carefully consider the cost of replacing the LCD versus replacing the entire computer if the display is damaged. If an equivalent notebook computer is available new for less than twice the cost of replacing the display on an existing notebook computer, it usually makes sense to replace the computer instead of the display module.

Hardware, Software, and Firmware

The components seen in Figures 2-1–2-4 represent the hardware portion of the computer. Of these, the processor, or central processing unit (CPU), is king: Other components interact with the processor to create and modify information. However, the processor relies on other components to receive instructions, store new and updated information, and send information to output or display devices. These essential parts can be broken down into three categories: hardware, software, and firmware. Components in all three categories are necessary to the operation of any computer.

Hardware

Hardware is the part of computing you can pick up, move around, open, and close. Although hardware might represent the glamorous side of computing—whose computer is faster, has a larger hard disk, more memory, and so on—a computer can do nothing without software and firmware to provide instructions. Hardware failures can take place because of loose connections, electrical or physical damage, or incompatible devices.

Software

Software provides the instructions that tell hardware what to do. The same computer system can be used for word processing, gaming, accounting, or Web surfing by installing and using new software. Software comes in various types, including operating systems, application programs, and utility programs.

Operating systems provide standard methods for saving, retrieving, changing, printing, and transmitting information. The most common operating systems today are various versions of Microsoft Windows. The 2011 version of the A+ Certification exams focuses on recent 32-bit and 64-bit desktop versions of Windows (for example, Windows XP, Windows Vista, and Windows 7). Because operating systems provide the "glue" that connects hardware devices and applications, they are written to work on specified combinations of CPUs and hardware.

Operating system commands come in two major types: internal and external. Internal commands are those built into the operating system when it starts the computer. External commands require that you run a particular program that is included with the operating system.

Application programs are used to create, store, modify, and view information you create, also called data. Because an operating system provides standard methods for using storage, printing, and network devices to work with information, applications must be written to comply with the requirements of an operating system and its associated CPUs. A+ Certification does not require specific knowledge of application programs, but to provide the best technical support, you should learn the basics of the major applications your company supports, such as Microsoft Office, Corel WordPerfect Suite, OpenOffice, Adobe Photoshop, and many others.

Certifications are available for major operating systems and applications, and seeking certifications in these areas can further improve your chances of being hired and promoted.

Utility programs are used to keep a computer in good working condition or to set up new devices. In the chapters related to operating systems, you'll learn how to use the major utilities that are included with Windows.

Because utilities included in Windows have limited capabilities, you might also want to invest in other utility programs, such as disk imaging, file backup, partition management, and others, for use in your day-to-day work; however, only standard Windows utilities, such as CHKDSK, Disk Management, Defrag, and others, are covered on the A+ Certification Exams.

Firmware

Firmware represents a middle ground between hardware and software. Like hardware, firmware is physical: a chip or chips attached to devices such as motherboards, video cards, network cards, modems, and printers. However, firmware is also software: Firmware chips (such as the motherboard BIOS) contain instructions for hardware testing, hardware configuration, and input/output routines. In essence, firmware is "software on a chip," and the software's job is to control the device to which the chip is connected. Because firmware works with both hardware and software, changes in either one can cause firmware to become outdated. Outdated firmware can lead to device or system failure or even data loss. Most firmware today is "flashable," meaning that its contents can be changed through software. You'll learn more about the most common type of firmware, the motherboard's BIOS, in Chapter 4, "BIOS."

Why Hardware, Software, and Firmware Are Important to Understand

As a computer technician, you will be dealing on a day-to-day basis with the three major parts of any computing environment. Whether you're working on a computer, printer, or component such as a video card, you must determine whether the problem involves hardware, software, firmware, or a combination of these three.

Working Inside Your PC

If you've never opened a computer before, it can be pretty overwhelming. This section helps you get started with practical advice on how to

- Open the case
- Protect your system against electrostatic discharge (ESD)
- Connect internal and external data cables
- Install a PCI card

Opening the Case of a Desktop PC

Look at your system manual for case opening instructions, particularly if you have a retail-store system made by HP, Dell, or other major vendors. Depending upon the type of case you have, you might need to remove just one or two screws, or maybe a handful. If you're opening the case to gain access to the motherboard, you might need to do more than just take the cover off the system.

So-called "white box" systems are usually fairly straightforward to open because they use case designs made for user access instead of low cost. Figure 2-5 shows the rear of two typical cases used by white-box computer dealers or as replacement cases. The computer on the left has a single screw holding the covers in place. After this screw is removed, the top panel must be removed before the side panels can be removed. The computer on the right uses four screws per side to hold the side panels in place, but the side panels can be removed without removing the top cover. The right-hand side panel can even be swung out and latched back into place for faster card and drive installation.

Retail-store systems often use a single-piece molding that slips off the rear of the chassis. It can be held in place by several screws.

Figure 2-5 Two generic cases compared to each other.

> **CAUTION**   Check your warranty and system manual to make sure that you can open the case without voiding your system warranty.
>
> Be sure to unplug the system before you open the case.
>
> Don't mix up the screws used for the case with screws used for holding expansion cards or drives in place. Keep them separate. Label empty film or medicine containers and use one for each type of screw you remove.

Taking ESD Precautions

After you open your PC, what should you do next? Ideally, you should wear a commercial wrist strap made for ESD protection and clip it to an unpainted metal part on the computer you are servicing, as in Figure 2-6, before you touch any other part of the interior of your computer.

When you put the wrist strap on, make sure the metal plate on the inside of the strap touches bare skin; don't wear it over a shirt or sweater, and make sure it's comfortably snug. When the wrist strap is connected to a metal part of the chassis with the alligator clip on the end of the cable that snaps onto the wrist strap, it equalizes the electrical potential of your body and the computer to prevent ESD discharge.

Attaching cable with alligator
(grounding) clip to wrist strap

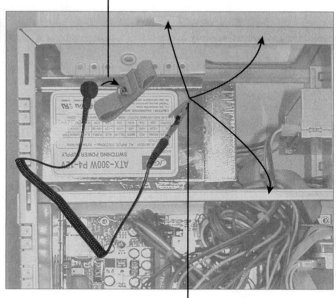

Bare metal parts of chassis that are suitable
locations to attach the grounding clip

Figure 2-6   A wrist strap and some suitable places to clip it inside the system.

If you don't have a wrist strap, touch unpainted metal on the chassis or the power supply before you touch or remove any cables or other parts. If possible, keep touching the chassis or power supply while you work. For more details on ESD protection, see Chapter 17, "Safety and Environmental Issues."

Connecting Internal and External Data Cables

Connecting internal and external drives and devices is critical if you want to have reliably working PCs. Here are a couple of examples of how to do it properly.

Attaching Cables to the Floppy Drive and Controller

The floppy drive uses a 34-pin cable that has a twist at one end. This end of the cable connects to the floppy drive (A:) drive. The middle connector is used for the B: drive (if one is present; it's not supported on some machines). The connector with the untwisted end plugs into the floppy controller on the motherboard. The colored marking on the cable and the twist indicate the pin 1 side of the cable. This is important to note because floppy drives and controllers are not always keyed to prevent incorrect installation.

The floppy drive is powered by a small four-pin power cable. There is a small cutout in the center of the connector on the drive that corresponds to a projection on the cable.

Figure 2-7 shows how the floppy drive cable and power cable connect to the rear of a typical floppy drive and to the floppy controller.

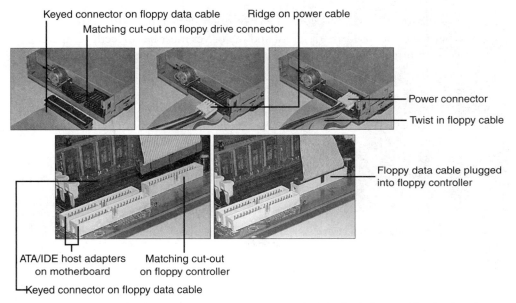

Figure 2-7   Connecting data and power cables to a typical 3.5-inch floppy drive (top) and floppy controller on a motherboard (bottom).

To install the cables, follow these steps:

Step 1.   Take the ESD precautions discussed in the "Taking ESD Precautions" section earlier in this chapter after you open the case and before you touch the cables or other components.

Step 2.   Be sure to line up the keying on the cable (if any) with the cutout on the floppy drive and controller connectors.

Step 3.   Push the cable firmly but gently into place.

Step 4.   Make sure the ridge on the power cable connector faces away from the drive; the power cable can be forced into place upside down, but this will destroy the drive when the power is turned on.

Step 5.   Push the power cable connector firmly but gently into place. If you don't have a spare four-wire connector for the floppy drive, you can purchase an adapter that converts the large Molex connector used for hard disks into a floppy drive power connector. You can also purchase a Y-splitter that can power a floppy drive and a hard drive.

CAUTION   If any pins are bent on the floppy drive or controller data or power connectors, straighten them before installing the cables.

The installation of an ATA/IDE hard disk or other drive type is similar in many ways, but the cables used are different and the drives must be correctly jumpered. For more information on floppy drives and hard drives, cables, and floppy media, see Chapter 12, "Storage Devices."

Attaching the VGA Cable to a Video Card or Port

The VGA cable has as many as fifteen wires that are routed into a connector the same size as a serial (COM) port. Consequently, it is one of the heaviest cables you need to connect to a PC. If you don't attach it correctly, you could have poor-quality images on your monitor, and if the cable falls off, you won't have any picture at all.

Depending upon the computer, the VGA port might be located on a card built into an expansion slot, or it might be clustered with other ports at the rear of the computer. In either case, the port and the cable are the same.

Figure 2-8 shows how the VGA cable should be connected to the VGA port.

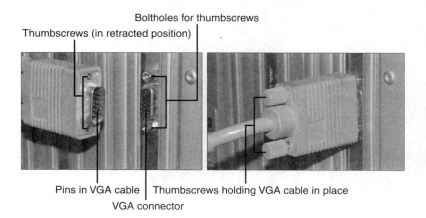

Figure 2-8   Connecting a VGA cable to a VGA port.

To connect the VGA cable to the VGA port, follow these steps:

Step 1.   Turn the thumbscrews so they are completely retracted. If they are not completely retracted, they could prevent proper connection.

Step 2.   Check the VGA cable for bent pins, but don't panic if you see a few pins that appear to be missing. Most VGA monitors don't use all fifteen pins. Carefully straighten any bent pins you find.

Step 3.   Line up the cable with the port and carefully push the cable into the port.

Step 4.   Fasten the thumbscrews tightly but evenly to hold the cable in place.

For more information about graphics cards and cables, including installing and configuring cards that support multiple displays, see Chapter 8, "Video Displays and Graphics Cards."

Installing a PCI Card

Most desktop systems have at least one open PCI card slot; it's the standard card type used for most devices. If you need to add an internal modem, wired or wireless network adapter, USB 2.0, IEEE-1394a, hard disk, or SCSI host adapter to a desktop PC, you will add a PCI or PCIe card that includes the necessary port.

Figure 2-9 shows a PCI card (specifically, a Serial ATA hard disk host adapter) being added to a typical system. The procedure for installing other types of cards into AGP or PCI Express slots is similar.

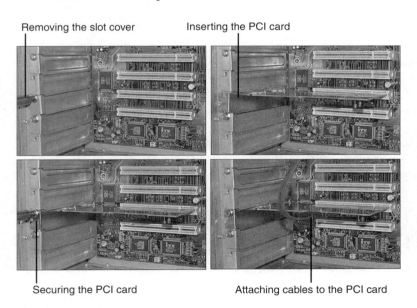

Removing the slot cover   Inserting the PCI card

Securing the PCI card   Attaching cables to the PCI card

Figure 2-9   Installing a Serial ATA card into a PCI slot.

To add a PCI card, follow these steps:

Step 1.   Shut down the system and unplug it.

Step 2.   Open the system.

Step 3.   Follow the ESD precautions discussed in "Taking ESD Precautions," earlier in this chapter.

Step 4.   Remove the slot cover behind the PCI slot you want to use.

Step 5.   Line up the connector on the bottom of the card with the slot.

Step 6.   Carefully push the card until it locks into place. Make sure the bracket on the card fits between the rear edge of the motherboard and the outer wall of the case.

Step 7.   Fasten the card into place using the screw you removed from the slot cover in Step 4.

Step 8.   Attach any cables required between the card and other devices.

Step 9.   Double-check your work, close your system, and then follow the instructions provided with the card for driver installation and card configuration.

Hardware Resources

There are four types of hardware resources used by both onboard and add-on card devices:

- IRQ
- I/O port address
- DMA channel
- Memory address

Each device needs its own set of hardware resources or needs to be a device that can share IRQs (the only one of the four resources that can be shared). Resource conflicts between devices can prevent your system from starting, lock up your system, or even cause data loss.

Although today's computers use Plug and Play (PnP) configuration of hardware resources to assure that conflicts are rare, you still need to understand how these resources function—and, after you join the computer workforce, you might still run into an older system that has resource conflicts. For more information, refer to Appendix D, "Hardware Resources."

Exam Preparation Tasks

Review All the Key Topics

Review the most important topics in the chapter, noted with the key topics icon in the outer margin of the page. Table 2-5 lists a reference of these key topics and the page numbers on which each is found.

Table 2-5   Key Topics for Chapter 2

Key Topic Element	Description	Page Number
Figure 2-6	An anti-static wrist strap and common places to put it	35
List	Adding a PCI card	38

Definitions of Key Terms

Define the following key terms from this chapter, and check your answers in the glossary.

Hardware, software, firmware, electrostatic discharge

This chapter covers the following subjects:

- **Motherboards and Their Components**—This section talks about the foundation of the computer, form factors, integrated ports and interfaces, memory slots, and expansion slots, and demonstrates how to install and troubleshoot motherboards.

- **Processors and CPUs**—In this section you'll learn about the various types of processors available, their architecture and technologies, and installing and troubleshooting processors.

- **Installing Adapter Cards**—This section demonstrates how to install video and sound cards, and how to troubleshoot common adapter card issues.

This chapter covers a portion of CompTIA A+ 220-701 objectives 1.2, 1.4, and 1.5, and CompTIA A+ 220-702 objectives 1.1 and 1.2.

CHAPTER 3

Motherboards, Processors, and Adapter Cards

In this chapter we'll talk about some of the core components of the computer—the guts of the computer—including the motherboard, processor, and adapter cards. Everything connects to the motherboard, so it stands to reason that proper planning and design of a PC, to a certain degree, starts with this component. Just as important is the processor. The processor (or CPU) is the "brain" of the computer and takes care of the bulk of the PC's calculations. Deciding on a CPU and motherboard should be the first tasks at hand when building a PC. Adapter cards are vital because they allow video, audio, and network capabilities. It is important to know how many and what type of adapter card slots are available on your motherboard before selecting specific adapter cards.

Within these pages you will learn how to install and troubleshoot motherboards, processors, and adapter cards and discover some of the considerations to take into account when building the core of a PC.

"Do I Know This Already?" Quiz

The "Do I Know This Already?" quiz allows you to assess whether you should read this entire chapter or simply jump to the "Exam Preparation Tasks" section for review. If you are in doubt, read the entire chapter. Table 3-1 outlines the major headings in this chapter and the corresponding "Do I Know This Already?" quiz questions. You can find the answers in Appendix A, "Answers to the 'Do I Know This Already?' Quizzes and Troubleshooting Scenarios."

Table 3-1   "Do I Know This Already?" Foundation Topics Section-to-Question Mapping

Foundations Topics Section	Questions Covered in This Section
Motherboards and Their Components	1–5
Processors and CPUs	6–10
Installing Adapter Cards	11

1. The system bus and I/O bus carry four different types of signals throughout the computer. Which of the following are the signals? (Choose all that apply.)

    a. Data

    b. Power

    c. Control

    d. Adapters

    e. Address

2. Which of the following are considered expansion slots? (Choose all that apply.)

    a. PCI

    b. FireWire

    c. AGP

    d. USB

3. Which of the following can you use with SCSI (Small Computer Systems Interface)? (Choose all that apply.)

    a. Hard drives

    b. Scanners

    c. Laser printers

    d. DVD-ROMs

    e. A dot-matrix printer

4. Which of the following are in the ATX family of motherboards? (Choose all that apply.)

    a. ATX

    b. Mini-ATX

    c. FlexATX

    d. ATX and Mini-ATX only

    e. None of the options provided is correct

5. Which of the following are considered integrated I/O ports?

    a. Serial port

    b. Parallel port

    c. USB port

    d. PS/2 mouse and keyboard

    e. Audio port

    f. Ethernet port

    g. All of these options are correct

6. Which one of the listed processors was the last slot-based processor designed by Intel?

   a. Celeron

   b. Core 2 Duo

   c. Pentium D

   d. Pentium III

7. Which of the following processors was the first dual-core design by AMD?

   a. Athlon 64 X2

   b. Athlon

   c. Duron

   d. Sempron

8. Which of the following best describes hyperthreading?

   a. Overclocking your CPU

   b. Processing two execution threads simultaneously

   c. Having more than one processor

   d. None of these options is correct

9. Before you remove the processor from the motherboard, what device should you remove first?

   a. Power supply

   b. RAM chip

   c. Heat sink

   d. Thermal compound

10. You have been dispatched to a client's computer. You have decided that the processor is overheating. Which of the following steps can you take to help with the air flow around the processor?

   a. Blow it out with compressed air

   b. Remove the heat sink from the CPU

   c. Place it on a surface covered with old newspapers or waste paper

   d. Clean off the old thermal paste and reapply a small amount to the processor

   e. All of these options are correct

11. Which of the following are causes of overheating? (Choose all that apply.)

   a. Fan failure

   b. The power supply fan is too large

   c. Incorrect heat sink

   d. Incorrect processor

12. To connect speakers to the sound card, which of the following must you use?

   a. 1/2-inch jack

   b. 1 1/4-inch jack cable

   c. 2/3-inch jack cable

   d. 1/8-inch mini-jack cable

   e. None of these options is correct

Foundation Topics

Motherboards and Their Components

The motherboard represents the logical foundation of the computer. In other words, everything that makes a computer a computer must be attached to the motherboard. From the CPU to storage devices, from RAM to printer ports, the motherboard provides the connections that help them work together. Figure 3-1 shows an example of a typical motherboard. The various components of the motherboard are called out in the figure. We will be referring to this figure throughout the chapter.

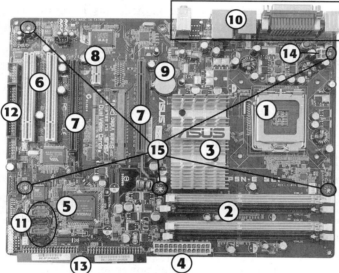

1. Socket 775 processor socket
2. Dual-channel DDR2 memory slots
3. Heat sink over North Bridge
4. 24-pin ATX v2.0 power connector
5. South Bridge chip
6. PCI slot (2)
7. PCI Express x16 slot (2)
8. PCI Express x1 slot
9. CMOS battery
10. Port cluster
11. SATA host adapter (4)
12. Floppy drive controller
13. PATA host adapter (2)
14. 4-pix ATX12 power connector
15. Mounting holes

Figure 3-1 A typical motherboard.

The motherboard is essential to computer operation in large part because of the two major buses it contains: the system bus and the I/O bus. Together, these buses carry all the information between the different parts of the computer. The location and orientation of these busses will vary depending on the type of form factor used. The form factor is the design of the motherboard, which the case and power supply must comply with. Motherboards can come with integrated I/O ports; these are usually found as a rear port cluster. The motherboard will also have memory slots, which allow a user to add sticks of RAM, thus increasing the computer's total resources. Of course, the motherboard also has expansion slots most commonly used by audio and video cards, although the slots can be used by many other types of cards as well. You will also find mass storage ports for hard drives, CD-ROMs, and DVD-ROMs on the motherboard. After we cover all of these concepts, we'll show how to select, install, and troubleshoot the motherboard. As you can see, the motherboard is the central meeting point of all technologies in the computer. There is a lot to cover concerning motherboards. Let's begin by discussing the system and I/O busses.

The System Bus and I/O Bus

The system bus carries four different types of signals throughout the computer:

- Data
- Power
- Control
- Address

To help you understand this concept, let's take an imaginary trip to Chicago and compare the city to a typical motherboard. If you were on the Willis Tower observation deck overlooking downtown Chicago one evening, you would first notice the endless stream of cars, trucks, and trains carrying people and goods from everywhere to everywhere else along well-defined surface routes (the expressways and tollways, commuter railroads, Amtrak, and airports). You can compare these routes to the data bus portion of the system bus, which carries information between RAM and the CPU. If you've ever listened to the traffic reports on a radio station such as Chicago's WBBM (780 AM), you've heard how traffic slows down when expressway lanes are blocked by construction or stalled traffic. In your computer, wider data buses that enable more "lanes" of data to flow at the same time promote faster system performance.

Now, imagine that you've descended to street level, and you've met with a local utility worker for a tour of underground Chicago. On your tour, you will find an elaborate network of electric and gas lines beneath the street carrying the energy needed to power the city. You can compare these to the power lines in the system bus, which transfer power from the motherboard's connection to the power supply to the integrated circuits (ICs or chips) and expansion boards connected to the motherboard.

Go back to street level, and notice the traffic lights used both on city streets and on the entrance ramps to busy expressways, such as the Eisenhower and the Dan Ryan. Traffic stops and starts in response to the signals. Look at the elevated trains or at the Metra commuter trains and Amtrak intercity trains; they also move as directed by signal lights. These signals, which control the movement of road and rail traffic, can be compared to the control lines in the system bus, which control the transmission and movement of information between devices connected to the motherboard.

Finally, as you look around downtown, take a close look at the men and women toting blue bags around their shoulders or driving electric vans and Jeeps around the city. As these mail carriers deliver parcels and letters, they must verify the correct street and suite addresses for the mail they deliver. They correspond to the address bus, which is used to "pick up" information from the correct memory location among the gigabytes of RAM in computer systems and "deliver" new programs and changes back to the correct memory locations.

The I/O bus connects storage devices to the system bus and can be compared to the daily flow of commuters and travelers into the city in the morning, and out again in the evening. Between them, the system and I/O buses carry every signal throughout the motherboard and to every component connected to the motherboard.

Form Factors

Although all motherboards have some features in common, their layout and size vary a great deal. The most common motherboard designs in current use include ATX, Micro ATX, BTX, and NLX. Some of these designs feature riser cards and daughterboards. The following sections cover the details of these designs.

ATX and Micro ATX

The ATX family of motherboards has dominated desktop computer designs since the late 1990s. ATX stands for "Advanced Technology Extended," and it replaced the AT and Baby-AT form factors developed in the mid 1980s for the IBM PC AT and its rivals. ATX motherboards have the following characteristics:

- A rear port cluster for I/O ports
- Expansion slots that run parallel to the short side of the motherboard
- Left side case opening (as viewed from the front of a tower PC)

There are four members of the ATX family, listed in Table 3-2. In practice, though, the Mini-ATX design is not widely used.

Table 3-2 ATX Motherboard Family Comparison

Motherboard Type	Maximum Width	Maximum Depth	Maximum Number of Expansion Slots	Typical Uses
ATX	12 in	9.6 in	Seven	Full tower
Mini-ATX	11.2 in	8.2 in	Seven	Full tower
microATX	9.6 in	9.6 in	Four	Mini tower
FlexATX	9.0 in	7.5 in	Four	Mini tower, small form factor

BTX

One problem with the ATX design has been the issue of system cooling. Because ATX was designed more than a decade ago, well before the development of today's faster components, it's been difficult to properly cool the hottest-running components in a typical system: the processor, memory modules, and the processor's voltage regulator circuits.

To enable better cooling for these devices, and to promote better system stability, the BTX family of motherboard designs was introduced in 2004. Compared to ATX motherboards, BTX motherboards have the following:

- Heat-producing components such as the process, memory, chipset, and voltage regulator are relocated to provide straight-through airflow from front to back for better cooling.
- The processor socket is mounted at a 45-degree angle to the front of the motherboard to improve cooling.
- A thermal module with a horizontal fan fits over the processor for cooling.
- The port cluster is moved to the rear left corner of the motherboard.
- BTX cases include multiple rear and side air vents for better cooling.
- Because of the standardization of processor and memory locations, it's easy to use the same basic design for various sizes of BTX motherboards; the designer can just add slots.
- BTX tower cases use a right-opening design as viewed from the front.

Although BTX designs are easier to cool than ATX designs, the development of cooler-running processors has enabled system designers to continue to favor ATX. There are relatively few BTX-based motherboards and systems currently on the market.

Figure 3-2 compares typical ATX and BTX motherboard layouts to each other.

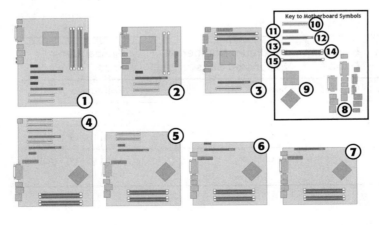

Key to Motherboard Symbols

1. ATX motherboard
2. microATX motherboard
3. FlexATX motherboard
4. BTX motherboard
5. microBTX motherboard
6. nanoBTX motherboard
7. picoBTX motherboard
8. Port cluster (at rear of system)
9. Processor (CPU) socket
10. PCI 32-bit slot
11. Motherboard power connector
12. PCI Express x16 slot
13. PCI Express x1 slot
14. Pair of memory sockets
15. Single memory sockets

Figure 3-2   The ATX motherboard family includes ATX (largest), microATX, and flexATX (smallest). The BTX motherboard family includes BTX, microBTX, nanoBTX, and picoBTX (smallest).

NOTE The motherboard examples shown in Figure 3-2 are simplified examples of actual motherboards. Onboard ports, port headers, and additional motherboard power connectors are not shown. Also, motherboards using a particular design might have components in slightly different positions than shown here.

NLX

NLX motherboards are designed for quick replacement in corporate environments. They use a riser card that provides power and expansion slots that connect to the right edge of the motherboard (as viewed from the front). NLX motherboards have a two-row cluster of ports along the rear edge of the motherboard.

Most systems that use NLX motherboards are considered obsolete. Figure 3-3 illustrates a typical NLX motherboard and riser card.

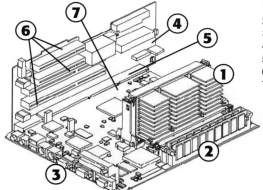

1. Processor and passive heat sink
2. Memory modules
3. Port cluster
4. Riser card
5. Connection to motherboard
6. Expansion slots
7. Motherboard

Figure 3-3 A typical NLX motherboard and riser card.

Riser Cards and Daughterboards

Riser cards and daughterboards provide two different methods for providing access to motherboard–based resources. In current slimline or rackmounted systems based on ATX or BTX technologies, riser cards are used to make expansion slots usable that would otherwise not be available because of clearances inside the case. Riser card designs can include one or more expansion slots, and are available in PCI, PCI-X (used primarily in workstation and server designs), and PCI-Express designs. Figure 3-4 shows two typical implementations of riser card designs.

The term *daughterboard* is sometimes used to refer to riser cards, but daughterboard can also refer to a circuit board that plugs into another board to provide extra functionality. For example, some small form factor motherboards support daughterboards that add additional serial or Ethernet ports, and some standard-size motherboards use daughterboards for their voltage regulators.

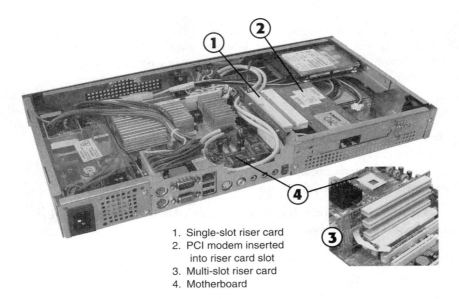

1. Single-slot riser card
2. PCI modem inserted
   into riser card slot
3. Multi-slot riser card
4. Motherboard

Figure 3-4   Examples of single-slot and multi-slot riser cards.

Integrated I/O Ports

Motherboards in both the ATX and BTX families feature a variety of integrated I/O ports. These are found in as many as three locations: all motherboards feature a rear port cluster (see Figure 3-5 for a typical example), and many motherboards also have additional ports on the top of the motherboard that are routed to header cables accessible from the front and rear of the system.

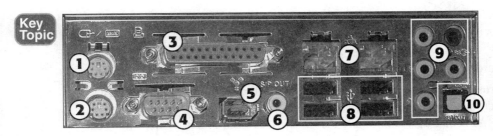

1. PS/2 mouse port
2. PS/2 keyboard port
3. Parallel (LPT) port
4. Serial (COM) port
5. FireWire 400 (IEEE-1394a) port
6. Coaxial SPDIF (digital audio) port
7. RJ-45 Ethernet port
8. Hi-Speed USB port
9. 5.1 surround audio ports
10. Fiber Optic SPDIF port

Figure 3-5   A port cluster on a late-model ATX system.

Most recent motherboards include the following ports in their port cluster:

■   Serial (COM)

- Parallel (LPT)

- PS/2 mouse

- PS/2 keyboard

- USB 2.0 (Hi-Speed USB)

- 10/100 or 10/100/1000 Ethernet (RJ-45)

- Audio

So-called "legacy-free" motherboards might omit some or all of the legacy ports (serial, parallel, PS/2 mouse and keyboard), a trend that will continue as devices using these ports have been replaced by devices that plug into USB ports.

Some high-end systems might also include one or more FireWire (IEEE-1394a) ports, and systems with integrated video include a VGA or DVI-I video port and an S-Video or HDMI port for TV and home theater use.

Figure 3-5 illustrates a port cluster from a typical ATX system, but note that BTX systems use similar designs.

Some integrated ports use header cables to provide output. Figure 3-6 shows an example of 5.1 surround audio ports on a header cable. The header cable plugs into the motherboard and occupies an empty expansion slot.

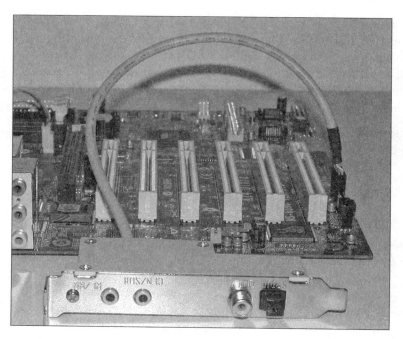

Figure 3-6   This header cable provides support for 5.1 surround analog audio and digital audio.

INTEGRATED PORT CONSIDERATIONS

Why integrated ports? They provide clear benefits to both users and technicians who set up a system. For users, integrated ports provide lower system purchase prices, faster component performance, centralized control of components through the ROM BIOS and CMOS, and an interior that is less crowded with add-on cards. In other words, you might have a slot or two available in a brand-new system for future upgrades.

For technicians, the greatest benefits of integrated components come during initial setup. Fewer components need to be installed to make a system meet standard requirements and components can be enabled or disabled through the BIOS setup program. Very handy!

However, when systems must be repaired or upgraded, integrated components can be troublesome. If an integrated component that is essential to system operation fails, you must either replace the motherboard or disable the component in question (if possible) and replace it with an add-on card. To learn more about these ports and their uses, see Chapter 7, "I/O and Multimedia Ports and Devices."

Memory Slots

Modern motherboards include two or more memory slots, as seen in Figures 3-1 and 3-2. At least one memory slot must contain a memory module, or the system cannot start or function.

Memory slots vary in design according to the type of memory the system supports. Older systems that use SDRAM use three-section memory slots designed for 168-pin memory modules. Systems that use DDR SDRAM use two-section memory slots designed for 240-pin modules. DDR3 SDRAM also uses two-section 240-pin memory slots, but the arrangement of the pins and the keying of the slot are different than in DDR2. DDR2 and DDR3 modules cannot be interchanged.

Each memory slot includes locking levers that secure memory in place. When memory is properly installed, the levers automatically swivel into place (see Figure 3-7).

To learn more about memory types and slots, see Chapter 6, "RAM."

Expansion Slots

Motherboards use expansion slots to provide support for additional I/O devices and high-speed video/graphics cards. The most common expansion slots on recent systems include peripheral component interconnect (PCI), advanced graphics port (AGP), and PCI-Express (also known as PCIe). Some systems also feature audio modem riser (AMR) or communications network riser (CNR) slots for specific purposes.

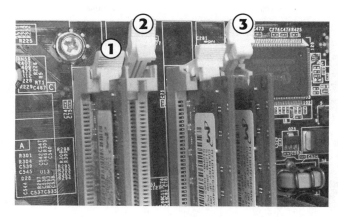

1. Installed module
   (locking lever closed)
2. Empty slot
   (locking lever open)
3. Module being installed
   (locking lever open)

Figure 3-7   Installing memory modules.

PCI Slots

The PCI slot can be used for many types of add-on cards, including network, video, audio, I/O and storage host adapters for SCSI, PATA, and SATA drives. There are several types of PCI slots, but the one found in desktop computers is the 32-bit slot running at 33MHz (refer to Figure 3-8 in the next section).

AGP

The AGP slot was introduced as a dedicated slot for high-speed video (3D graphics display) in 1996. Since 2005, the PCI Express x16 slot (described in the next section) has replaced it in most new systems. There have been several versions of the AGP slot, reflecting changes in the AGP standard, as shown in Figure 3-8. Note that all types of AGP slots can temporarily "borrow" system memory when creating 3D textures.

Note that the AGP 1x/2x and AGP 4x/8x slots have their keys in different positions. This prevents installing the wrong type of AGP card into the slot. AGP 1x/2x cards use 3.3V, whereas most AGP 4x cards use 1.5V. AGP 8x cards use 0.8 or 1.5V. The AGP Pro/Universal slot is longer than a normal AGP slot to support the greater electrical requirements of AGP Pro cards (which are used in technical workstations). The protective cover over a part of the slot is intended to prevent normal AGP cards from being inserted into the wrong part of the slot. The slot is referred to as a *universal* slot because it supports both 3.3V and 1.5V AGP cards.

CAUTION   An AGP Pro slot cover might be removed after a system has been in service for awhile, even if an AGP Pro card wasn't inserted in a computer. If you see an AGP Pro slot without a cover and you're preparing to install an AGP card, cover the extension with a sticker to prevent damaging a standard AGP card by inserting it improperly.

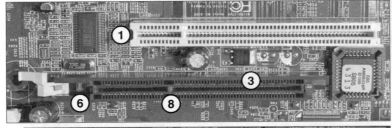

1. PCI slots
2. AGP 1x/2x (3.3v) slot
3. AGP 4x/8x (1.5v) slot
4. AGP Pro/Universal slot
5. AGP Pro slot cover
6. AGP 4x/8x retaining latch
7. AGP 1x/2x key
8. AGP 4x/8x key

Figure 3-8 PCI slots compared to an AGP 1x/2x slot (top), an AGP 4x/8x slot (middle), and an AGP Pro/Universal slot (bottom).

PCIe (PCI Express) Slots

PCI Express (often abbreviated as PCIe or PCIE) began to replace both PCI and AGP slots in new system designs starting in 2005. PCIe slots are available in four types:

■ x1

■ x4

■ x8

■ x16

The most common versions include the x1, x4, and x16 designs, as shown in Figure 3-9.

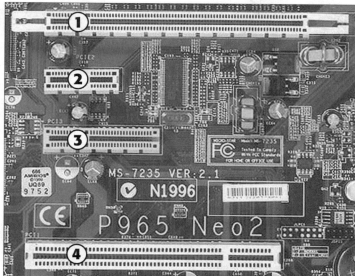

1. PCI Express x16 slot
2. PCI Express x1 slot
3. PCI Express x4 slot
4. PCI slot (32-bit, 33MHz)

Figure 3-9   PCI Express slots compared to a PCI slot.

PCI Express x1 and x4 slots are designed to replace the PCI slot, and x8 and x16 are designed to replace the AGP slot. Table 3-3 compares the performance of PCI, AGP, and PCI Express slots.

Table 3-3   Technical Information About Expansion Slot Types

Slot Type	Performance	Suggested Uses
PCI	133MBps	Video, network, SCSI, sound card
AGP 1x	266MBps	Video
AGP 2x	533MBps	Video
AGP 4x	1,066MBps	Video
AGP 8x	2,133MBps	Video
PCIe x1	500MBps*	Network, I/O
PCIe x2	1,000MBps*	Network
PCIe x8	4,000MBps*	SLI video
PCIe x16	8,000MBps*	Video (including SLI, CrossFire)

NOTE   At the time of publication of this book, there are three versions of PCI Express. V1.0 is rated at 250MB/s per lane, V2.0 at 500 MB/s, and V3.0 at 1GB/s with a maximum of 32 lanes. All three versions use the same slot designs but run at different speeds due to internal differences.

*The data rates listed in Table 3-3 are the bidirectional (simultaneous send/receive) throughput amounts you should know for the exam (these reflect PCIe V1.0). Unidirectional data rates (send or receive) are one-half of the bidirectional data rates.

SLI is the NVIDIA method for using two or more graphics cards to render 3D game graphics

CrossFire is the ATI/AMD method for using two or more graphics cards to render 3D game graphics.

AMR and CNR Slots

Some motherboards have one of two specialized expansion slots in addition to the standard PCI, PCI Express, or AGP slots. The audio modem riser (AMR) slot enables motherboard designers to place analog modem and audio connectors and the codec chip used to translate between analog and digital signals on a small riser card. AMR slots are frequently found on older systems with chipsets that integrate software modems and audio functions.

The AMR was replaced by the communications network riser (CNR) slot, a longer design that can support up to six-channel audio, S/PDIF digital audio, and home networking functions. Some vendors have used the CNR slot to implement high-quality integrated audio. Very few AMR riser cards were ever sold, but some motherboard vendors have bundled CNR riser cards with their motherboards to provide six-channel audio output and other features.

Figure 3-10 compares the AMR, PCI, and CNR slots. Figure 3-11 illustrates the AMR and CNR riser cards.

The AMR or CNR slot, when present, is usually located on the edge of the motherboard. The AMR slot was often found on Pentium III or AMD Athlon-based systems, while the CNR slot was used by some Pentium 4-based systems. Current systems integrate network and audio features directly into the motherboard and its port cluster, making both types of slots obsolete.

NOTE   AMR and CNR riser cards were generally provided by motherboard makers because they are customized to the design of particular motherboards. Although some parts suppliers have sold AMR and CNR cards separately, it's best to get the riser card from the same vendor as the motherboard to ensure proper hardware compatibility and driver support.

To learn more about PCI, PCIe, and AGP slots when used for graphics cards, see Chapter 8, "Video Displays and Graphics Cards." To learn more about installing adapter cards, see "Installing Adapter Cards," later in this chapter.

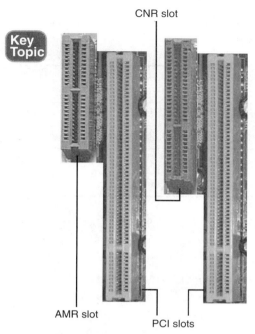

Figure 3-10 An AMR slot and PCI slot (left) compared to a CNR slot and PCI slot (right).

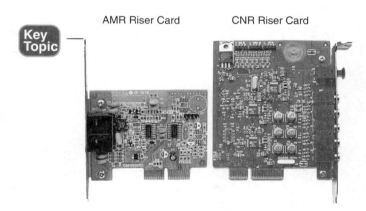

Figure 3-11 An AMR riser card used for soft modem support (left) and a CNR riser card used for six-channel (5.1) analog and digital audio support (right).

Mass Storage Interfaces

Motherboards also include mass storage interfaces such as PATA/IDE, SATA, and SCSI. The following sections compare and contrast the appearance and functionality of these interfaces. Table 3-4 provides a quick overview of technical information about these interfaces.

Table 3-4   Technical Information About Mass Storage Interfaces

Interface	Performance	Suggested Uses
SATA 1st generation	1.5Gbps	Hard disk, rewritable DVD
SATA 2nd generation	3.0Gbps	Hard disk, rewritable DVD
PATA/IDE	1.0–1.3Gbps	Rewritable DVD, rewritable CD, Zip, JAZ, REV, tape
SCSI	1.6–3.2Gbps*	Hard disk, tape backup

Note: *Current Ultra 160 and Ultra 320 SCSI standards; older standards are much slower.

The following sections describe each of these interfaces in greater detail.

PATA/IDE

Until recently, most motherboards included two or more PATA/IDE (also known as ATA/IDE) host adapters for PATA devices such as hard disks, CD or DVD drives, tape backups, and removable-media drives. Each host adapter uses a 40-pin interface similar to the one shown in Figure 3-12, and can control up to two drives.

Figure 3-12   PATA and SATA host adapters on a typical motherboard.

Most recent systems use a plastic skirt around the PATA connector with a notch on one side. This prevents improper insertion of a keyed PATA (ATA/IDE) cable. However, keep in mind that some older systems have unskirted connectors and some older ATA/IDE cables are not keyed. To avoid incorrect cable connections, be sure to match pin 1 on the PATA host adapter to the red-striped edge of the PATA ribbon cable.

On systems with a third PATA/IDE host adapter, the additional host adapter is typically used for a RAID 0 or RAID 1 drive array. See your system or motherboard
documentation for details. Most current systems now have only one PATA/IDE host
adapter, as the industry is transitioning away from PATA/IDE to SATA interfaces
for both hard disk and DVD drives.

SATA

Most recent systems have anywhere from two to as many as eight Serial ATA (SATA)
host adapters. Each host adapter controls a single SATA drive, such as a hard disk or
rewritable DVD drive.

The original SATA host adapter design did not have a skirt around the connector,
making it easy for the cable to become loose. Many late-model systems now use a
skirted design for the host adapter (see Figure 3-13).

SATA host adapters

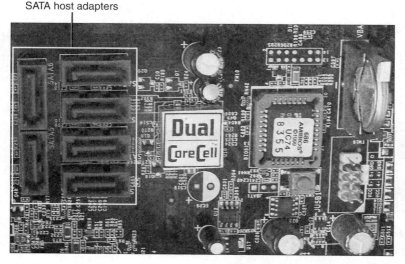

Figure 3-13   Most late model systems include multiple SATA host adapters with skirted connectors.

SCSI

SCSI (Small Computer Systems Interface) is a more flexible drive interface than
PATA (ATA/IDE) because it can accommodate many devices that are not hard disk
drives. The fastest versions of SCSI are comparable in speed to today's SATA. However, SCSI systems are usually used in servers and power workstations, as opposed to
regular PCs. The following have been common uses for SCSI:

- High-performance and high-capacity hard drives
- Image scanners

■ Removable-media drives such as Zip, Jaz, and Castlewood Orb

■ High-performance laser printers

■ High-performance optical drives, including CD-ROM, CD-R, CD-RW, DVD-ROM, and others

So-called Narrow SCSI host adapters (which use an 8-bit data channel) can accommodate up to seven devices of different varieties on a single connector on the host adapter through daisy-chaining. Wide SCSI host adapters use a 16-bit data channel and accommodate up to 15 devices on a single connector on the host adapter through daisy-chaining. Narrow SCSI devices and host adapters use a 50-pin or (rarely) a 25-pin cable and connector, while Wide SCSI devices use a 68-pin cable and connector.

Several years ago, SCSI host adapters were found on some high-end desktop and workstation motherboards. However, most recent systems use SATA in place of SCSI, and SCSI host adapters and devices are now primarily used by servers. Currently, SCSI is used primarily for high-performance hard disks and tape backups.

Systems with onboard SCSI host adapters might have one or more 50-pin or 68-pin female connectors similar to those shown in Figure 3-14.

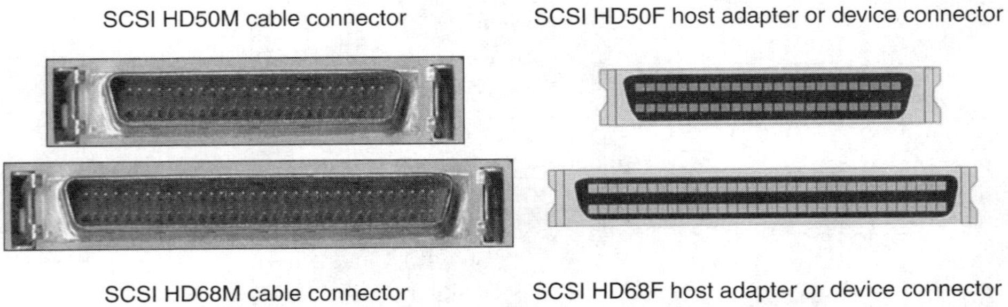

SCSI HD50M cable connector   SCSI HD50F host adapter or device connector

SCSI HD68M cable connector   SCSI HD68F host adapter or device connector

Figure 3-14   SCSI HD50 and HD68 cables and connectors are typically used on systems with onboard SCSI host adapters.

To learn more about storage devices, see Chapter 12, "Storage Devices."

Choosing the Best Motherboard for the Job

So, how do you go about choosing the best motherboard for the job? Follow this process:

Step 1.   Decide what you want the motherboard (system) to do. Because most of a computer's capabilities and features are based on the motherboard, you need to decide this first.

Some examples:

If you need high CPU performance, you must choose a motherboard that supports the fastest dual-core or multi-core processors available. If you want to run a 64-bit (x64) operating system, you need a motherboard that supports 64-bit processors and more than 4GB of RAM. If you want to run fast 3D gaming graphics, you need a motherboard that supports NVIDIA's SLI or ATI's CrossFire multi-GPU technologies. If you want to support multimedia uses such as video editing, you'll prefer a motherboard with onboard IEEE-1394a (FireWire 400). If you are building a system for use as a home theater, a system with HDMI graphics might be your preferred choice.

Step 2. Decide what form factor you need to use. If you are replacing an existing motherboard, the new motherboard must fit into the case (chassis) being vacated by the old motherboard and (ideally) be powered by the existing power supply. If you are building a new system, though, you can choose the form factor needed.

Some examples:

Full-size ATX or BTX motherboards provide the most room for expansion but require mid-size or full-size tower cases. If no more than three expansion slots are needed, micro ATX or micro BTX systems fit into mini-tower cases that require less space and can use smaller, less-expensive power supplies. If only one slot (or no slots) are needed, picoATX or picoBTX systems that fit into small form factor cases require very little space.

Installing Motherboards

What keeps a motherboard from sliding around inside the case? If you look at an unmounted motherboard from the top, you can see that motherboards have several holes around the edges and one or two holes toward the middle of the motherboard. Most ATX-family and BTX-family motherboards are held in place by screws that are fastened to brass spacers that are threaded into holes in the case or a removable motherboard tray. Before you start working with motherboards or other static-sensitive parts, see the section "Electrostatic Discharge (ESD)," in Chapter 17, "Safety and Environmental Issues," for ESD and other precautions you should follow.

Step-by-Step Motherboard Removal (ATX and BTX)

Removing the motherboard is an important task for the computer technician. For safety's sake, you should remove the motherboard before you install a processor upgrade as well as if you need to perform a motherboard upgrade.

To remove ATX or BTX-family motherboards from standard cases, follow these steps:

Step 1.   Turn off the power switch and disconnect the AC power cable from the power supply.

Step 2.   Disconnect all external and internal cables attached to add-on cards after labeling them for easy reconnection.

Step 3.   Disconnect all ribbon cables attached to built-in ports on the motherboard (I/O, storage, and so on) after labeling them for easy reconnection.

Step 4.   Disconnect all cables leading to internal speakers, key locks, speed switches, and other front-panel cables. Most recent systems use clearly marked cables as shown in Figure 3-15, but if the cables are not marked, mark them before you disconnect them so you can easily reconnect them later.

Figure 3-15   Front-panel cables attached to a typical motherboard, which control system power to the motherboard, case speaker, drive and power lights, and so on.

TIP   You can purchase premade labels for common types of cables, but if these are not available, you can use a label maker or blank address labels to custom-make your own labels.

Step 5.   Remove all add-on cards and place them on an antistatic mat or in (not on top of) antistatic bags.

Step 6.   Disconnect header cables from front- or rear-mounted ports and remove them from the system (see Figure 3-16).

Step 7.   Disconnect the power-supply leads from the motherboard. The new motherboard must use the same power-supply connections as the current motherboard. See Chapter 5, "Power Supplies and System Cooling," for details about power supply connections.

Expansion slot bracket

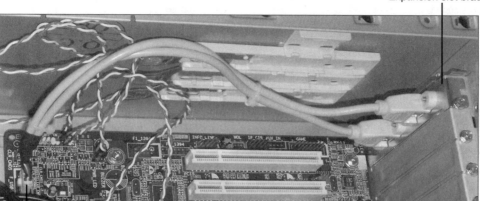

USB header cable connected to motherboard

Figure 3-16 A typical dual-USB header cable that uses an expansion slot bracket.

Step 8. Remove the heat sink and the processor before you remove the motherboard and place them on an anti-static mat. Removing these items before you remove the motherboard helps prevent excessive flexing of the motherboard and makes it easier to slip the motherboard out of the case. However, skip this step if the heat sink requires a lot of downward pressure to remove and if the motherboard is not well supported around the heat sink/processor area.

Step 9. Unscrew the motherboard mounting screws (refer to Figure 3-1) and store for reuse; verify that all screws have been removed.

CAUTION Easy does it with the screwdriver! Whether you're removing screws or putting them back in, skip the electric model and do it the old-fashioned way to avoid damaging the motherboard. If your motherboard is held in place with hex screws, use a hex driver instead of a screwdriver to be even more careful.

Step 10. Lift the motherboard and plastic stand-off spacers out of the case and place them on an antistatic mat. Remove the I/O shield (the metal plate on the rear of the system which has cutouts for the built-in ports; refer to Figure 3-17) and store it with the old motherboard.

Step-by-Step Motherboard Removal (NLX)

NLX motherboards are designed for fast, easy removal. Follow this procedure:

Step 1. As described earlier, disconnect cables from any installed add-on cards.

Step 2. Remove any add-on cards, remembering to handle the cards by their edges.

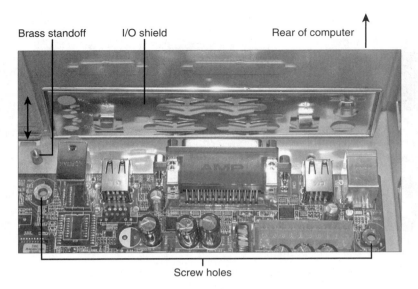

Figure 3-17   An ATX I/O shield and motherboard during installation.

Step 3.   Pull the motherboard release lever to disconnect the motherboard from the NLX riser.

Step 4.   Slide the motherboard out of the case.

Preparing the Motherboard for Installation (ATX/BTX)

Before you install the new motherboard into the computer, perform the following steps:

Step 1.   Review the manual supplied with the new motherboard to determine correct sizes of memory supported, processor types supported, and configuration information.

Step 2.   Install the desired amount of memory. See Chapter 6 for details.

Step 3.   Install the processor (CPU) and heat sink as described later in this chapter.

Step 4.   Configure CPU speed, multiplier, type, and voltage settings on the motherboard if the motherboard uses jumpers or DIP (Dual Inline Pin) switches. Note that many recent motherboards use BIOS configuration options instead.

To learn more about configuring the motherboard for a particular CPU, see the section "Processors and CPUs" later in this chapter.

Making these changes after the motherboard is installed in the computer is normally very difficult.

Step-by-Step Motherboard Installation (ATX/BTX)

After you have prepared the motherboard for installation, follow these steps to install the motherboard:

Step 1.   Place the new motherboard over the old motherboard to determine which mounting holes should be used for standoffs (if needed) and which should be used for brass spacers. Matching the motherboards helps you determine that the new motherboard will fit correctly in the system.

Step 2.   Move brass spacers as needed to accommodate the mounting holes in the motherboard.

Step 3.   Place the I/O shield and connector at the back of the case. The I/O shield is marked to help you determine the port types on the rear of the motherboard. If the port cutouts on some I/O shields are not completely removed, remove them before you install the shield.

Step 4.   Determine which holes in the motherboard have brass stand-off spacers beneath them and secure the motherboard using the screws removed from the old motherboard (see Figure 3-17).

Step 5.   Reattach the wires to the speaker, reset switch, IDE host adapter, and power lights.

Step 6.   Reattach the ribbon cables from the drives to the motherboard's IDE and floppy disk drive interfaces. Match the ribbon cable's colored side to pin 1 on the interfaces.

Step 7.   Reattach cables from the SATA drives to the SATA ports on the motherboard. Use SATA port 1 for the first SATA drive, and so on.

Step 8.   Reattach the power supply connectors to the motherboard.

Step 9.   Insert the add-on cards you removed from the old motherboard; make sure your existing cards don't duplicate any features found on the new motherboard (such as sound, ATA/IDE host adapters, and so on). If they do, and you want to continue to use the card, you must disable the corresponding feature on the motherboard.

Step 10.   Mount header cables that use expansion card slot brackets into empty slots and connect the header cables to the appropriate ports on the motherboard.

Step 11.   Attach any cables used by front-mounted ports such as USB, serial, or IEEE-1394 ports to the motherboard and case.

Step-by-Step Motherboard Installation (NLX)

After you have prepared the motherboard for installation, follow these steps to install the motherboard:

Step 1. Line up the replacement motherboard with the motherboard rails located at the bottom of the case.

Step 2. Slowly push the motherboard into place. After the motherboard is connected to the riser card, it stops moving.

Step 3. Lift and push the motherboard release lever to lock the motherboard into place.

Step 4. Replace the side panel. If the side panel cannot be replaced properly, the motherboard is not installed properly.

Troubleshooting Motherboards

When you're troubleshooting a computer, there is no shortage of places to look for problems. However, because the motherboard is the "home" for the most essential system resources, it's often the source of many problems. If you see the following problems, consider the motherboard as a likely place to look for the cause:

■ **System will not start**—When you push the power button on an ATX or BTX system, the computer should start immediately. If it doesn't, the problem could be motherboard–related.

■ **Devices connected to the port cluster don't work**—If ports in the port cluster are damaged or disabled in the system BIOS configuration (CMOS setup), any devices connected to the port cluster will not work.

■ **Devices connected to header cables don't work**—If ports connected to the header are not plugged into the motherboard, are damaged, or are disabled in the system BIOS configuration (CMOS setup), any devices connected to these ports will not work.

■ **Mass storage drives are not recognized or do not work**—If mass storage ports on the motherboard are not properly connected to devices, are disabled, or are not configured properly, drives connected to these ports will not work.

■ **Memory failures**— Memory failures could be caused by the modules themselves, or they could be caused by the motherboard.

■ **Problems installing aftermarket processor heat sinks or replacement cards**—You cannot assume that every device fits every system.

The following sections help you deal with these common problems.

System Will Not Start

If the computer will not start, check the following:

- Incorrect front panel wiring connections to the motherboard

- Loose or missing power leads from power supply

- Loose or missing memory modules

- Loose BIOS chips

- Incorrect connection of EIDE/PATA cables to onboard host adapter

- Dead short in system

- Incorrect positioning of a standoff

- Loose screws or slot covers

The following sections describe each of these possible problems.

Incorrect Front Panel Wiring Connections to the Motherboard   The power switch is wired to the motherboard, which in turn signals the power supply to start. If the power lead is plugged into the wrong pins on the motherboard, or has been disconnected from the motherboard, the system will not start and you will not see an error message.

Check the markings on the front panel connectors, the motherboard, or the motherboard/system manual to determine the correct pinouts and installation. Figure 3-18 shows typical motherboard markings for front panel connectors (refer to Figure 3-15 for typical markings on front-panel wires).

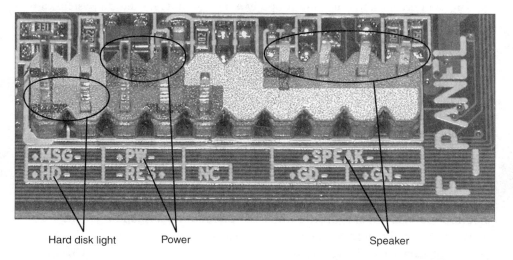

Hard disk light   Power   Speaker

Figure 3-18   A typical two-row front panel connector on a motherboard.

Loose or Missing Power Leads from Power Supply   Modern power supplies often have both a 20- or 24-pin connection and a four- or eight-pin connection to the motherboard. If either or both connections are loose or not present, the system cannot start and you will not see an error message.

For details, see Chapter 5.

Loose or Missing Memory Modules   If the motherboard is unable to recognize any system memory, it will not start properly. Unlike the other problems, you will see a memory error message.

Make sure memory modules are properly locked into place, and that there is no corrosion on the memory contacts on the motherboard or on the memory modules themselves. To remove corrosion from memory module contacts, remove the memory modules from the motherboard and gently wipe the contacts off to remove any built-up film or corrosion. An Artgum eraser (but *not* the conventional rubber or highly abrasive ink eraser) can be used for stubborn cases. Be sure to rub in a direction away from the memory chips to avoid damage. Reinsert the modules and lock them into place.

CAUTION   Never mix tin memory sockets and gold memory module connectors, or vice versa. Using different metals for memory socket and module connectors has been a leading cause of corrosion.

Loose BIOS Chips   Socketed motherboard chips that don't have retaining mechanisms, such as BIOS chips, can cause system failures if the chips work loose from their sockets. The motherboard BIOS chip (see Figure 3-19) is responsible for displaying boot errors, and if it is not properly mounted in its socket, the system cannot start and no error messages will be produced (note that many recent systems have surface-mounted BIOS chips).

The cycle of heating (during operation) and cooling (after the power is shut down) can lead to *chip creep*, in which socketed chips gradually loosen in the sockets. To cure chip creep, push the chips back into their sockets. Use even force to press a square BIOS chip into place. On older systems that use rectangular BIOS chips, alternately push on each end of the chip until the chip is securely mounted.

NOTE   Check your system or motherboard documentation to determine the location of the BIOS chip.

Incorrect Connection of PATA/IDE Cables to Onboard Host Adapter   Many systems are designed to wait for a response from a device connected to a PATA/IDE host adapter on the motherboard before continuing to boot. If the PATA/IDE cable is plugged in incorrectly, the system will never get the needed response, and some systems will not display an error message.

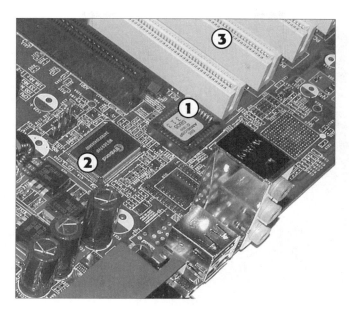

1. System BIOS chip
2. LPC I/O chip (for comparison)
3. PCI slots (for comparison)

Figure 3-19   If a socketed BIOS chip like this one becomes loose, the system will not boot.

Make sure pin 1 on the cable is connected to pin 1 on the EIDE/PATA device and the corresponding host adapter on the system. Check the motherboard manual for the position of pin 1 on the motherboard's host adapter if the host adapter is not marked properly.

Dead Short (Short Circuit) in System   A dead short (short circuit) in your system will prevent a computer from showing any signs of life when you turn it on. Some of the main causes for dead shorts that involve motherboards include

■ Incorrect positioning of a standoff

■ Loose screws or slot covers

The following sections describe both possible causes.

Incorrect positioning of a standoff
Brass standoffs should be lined up with the mounting holes in the motherboard (refer to Figure 3-1 for typical locations). Some motherboards have two types of holes: plain holes that are not intended for use with brass standoffs (they might be used for heat sink mounting or for plastic standoffs) and reinforced holes used for brass standoffs. Figure 3.20 compares these hole types.

If a brass standoff is under a part of the motherboard not meant for mounting, such as under a plain hole or under the solder connections, the standoff could cause a dead short that prevents the system from starting.

Plain hole (not used for motherboard installation)

Metal-reinforced hole designed to ground the motherboard when mounted with brass standoffs

Figure 3-20   Mounting holes compared to other holes on a typical motherboard.

Loose screws or slot covers

Leaving a loose screw inside the system and failing to fasten a slot cover or card in place are two common causes for dead shorts, because if these metal parts touch live components on the motherboard, your system will short out and stop working.

The solution is to open the case and remove or secure any loose metal parts inside the system. Dead shorts also can be caused by power supply–related problems.

For more about the power supply and dead shorts, see Chapter 5.

Devices Connected to the Port Cluster Don't Work

The port cluster (refer to Figure 3-5) provides a "one–stop shop" for most I/O devices, but if devices plugged into these ports fail, check the disabled ports and possible damage to a port in the port cluster, as described in the following sections.

Disabled Port   If a port hasn't been used before, and a device connected to it doesn't work, be sure to check the system's BIOS configuration to determine if the port is disabled. This is a particularly good idea if the port is a legacy port (serial/COM, parallel/LPT) or is the second network port. Ports can also be disabled using Windows Device Manager.

To learn how to manage integrated ports using the system BIOS setup, see Chapter 4 "BIOS." To learn how to manage hardware using Windows Device Manager, see Chapter 15, "Troubleshooting and Maintaining Windows."

Damage to a Port in the Port Cluster If a port in the port cluster has missing or bent pins, it's obvious that the port is damaged, but don't expect all types of damage to be obvious. The easiest way to see if a port in the port cluster is damaged is to follow these steps:

Step 1. Verify that the port is enabled in the system BIOS and Windows Device Manager.

Step 2. Make sure the device cable is connected tightly to the appropriate port. Use the thumbscrews provided with serial/COM, parallel/LPT, and VGA or DVI video cables to assure a proper connection.

Step 3. If the device fails, try the device on another port or another system. If the device works, the port is defective. If the device doesn't work, the device or the device's cable is defective.

To solve the problem of a defective port, use one of these solutions:

- **Replace the motherboard with an identical model**—This is the best solution for long-term use. Note that if you replace the motherboard with a different model you might need to reinstall Windows, or, at a minimum, reinstall drivers and reactivate Windows and some applications.

- **Install an add-on card to replace the damaged port**—This is quicker than replacing the motherboard, but if you are replacing a legacy port such as serial/COM or parallel/LPT, it can be expensive. If the device that plugged into a legacy port can also use a USB port, use a USB port instead.

- **Use a USB/legacy port adapter**—Port adapters can be used to convert serial/COM or parallel/LPT devices to work on USB ports. However, note that some limitations might be present. Generally, this is the least desirable solution.

Devices Connected to Header Cables Don't Work

Before assuming that a port that uses a header cable is defective or disabled, make sure the header cable is properly connected to the motherboard. If the system has just been assembled, or if the system has recently undergone internal upgrades or servicing, it's possible the header cable is loose or disconnected.

If the header cable is properly connected to the motherboard, follow the steps in the previous section to determine the problem and solution.

NOTE Check system or motherboard documentation to determine how to properly connect header cables to the motherboard.

Mass Storage Devices Do Not Work Properly

Mass storage devices that connect to SATA, PATA/IDE, or SCSI host adapters on the motherboard will not work if either of the following are true, as described in the next sections:

- Mass storage ports are disabled in system BIOS or Windows
- Data or power cables are not properly connected to the motherboard or drives

Mass Storage Ports Disabled in System BIOS or Windows   Before assuming a mass storage device is defective, be sure to verify whether the port has been disabled in the system BIOS configuration (CMOS setup or in Windows Device Manager). If you cannot connect the device to another port, enable the port and retry the device. To learn how to manage integrated ports using the system BIOS setup, see Chapter 4. To learn how to manage hardware using the Windows Device Manager, see Chapter 15.

Data or Power Cables Are Not Properly Connected to the Motherboard or Drives   If internal upgrades or servicing has taken place recently, it's possible that data or power cables have become loose or disconnected from the mass storage host adapters on the motherboard or the drives themselves. Before reconnecting the cables, shut down the computer and disconnect it from AC power.

For more about mass storage devices and cabling, see Chapter 12.

Memory Failures

Memory failures could be caused by the modules themselves, or they could be caused by the motherboard. For more information on memory problems and motherboards, see the section "Loose or Missing Memory Modules," earlier in this chapter.

Card, Memory, or Heat Sink Blocked by Motherboard Layout

Internal clearances in late-model systems are very tight, and if you attempt to install some types of hardware in some systems, such as an oversized processor heat sink or a very large video card, it might not be possible because of the motherboard's layout.

Before purchasing an aftermarket heat sink, check the clearances around the processor. Be especially aware of the location of capacitors and the voltage regulator; if the heat sink is too large, it could damage these components during installation. To help verify that an aftermarket heat sink will fit properly, remove the original heat sink from the processor and take it with you to compare its size to the aftermarket models you are considering.

Before purchasing an expansion card, check the slot clearance to be sure the card will fit into the desired expansion slot. In some cases, you might need to move a card from a neighboring slot to make room for the cooling fan shroud on some high-performance graphics cards.

Processors and CPUs

To do well on A+ Certification exams, you must understand the major types of processors available for recent systems, their technologies, how to install them, and how to troubleshoot them.

Overview of Processor Differences

Although Intel and AMD processors share two common architectures, x86 (used for 32-bit processors and for 64-bit processors running in 32-bit mode) and x64 (an extension of x86 that enables larger files, larger memory sizes, and more complex programs), these processor families differ in many ways from each other, including:

- Different processor sockets

- Different types of microcode

- Differences in dual-core, triple-core, and quad-core designs (two or more processor cores help run multiple programs and programs with multiple execution threads more efficiently)

- Cache sizes (cache memory stores a copy of recently-read memory locations to help improve system performance; L1 cache is in the processor core; L2 and L3 cache are in the processor module but outside the core)

- Performance versus clock speed

Intel Processors

Intel processors developed from 2000 to the present include the following product families:

- Pentium III

- Pentium 4

- Pentium D

- Celeron

- Core 2 Duo

- Core 2 Quad

- Core i3

- Core i5

- Core i7

NOTE   Intel's Centrino technology refers to a combination of the Core 2 Duo and certain Intel chipsets made for mobile computers.

The Pentium III processor was the last Intel processor produced in both a slot-based and socket-based design. Slot-based versions use Slot 1, the same slot design used by the Pentium II and slot-based Celeron processors. Socketed versions use Socket 370, which is mechanically the same as the socket used by the first socketed Celeron processors. However, some early Socket 370 motherboards are not electrically compatible with the Pentium III.

The Pentium 4 replaced the Pentium III and ran at much higher clock speeds. Early versions used Socket 423, a socket used by no other Intel processor. Most Pentium 4 designs used Socket 478, while late-model Pentium 4 designs used Socket 775, which is also used by current Intel processors. The different sockets used by the Pentium 4 were necessary because of substantial design changes throughout the processor's lifespan, including the introduction of 64-bit extensions (x64).

The Pentium 4's successor was the Pentium D, which is essentially two Pentium 4 processor cores built into a single physical processor. Although it used the same Socket 775 as late-model Pentium 4 processors, it required support from different chipsets because data was transferred between processor cores via the Memory Controller Hub (North Bridge) component. The Pentium D was Intel's first dual-core processor. The Pentium Extreme Edition is a faster version of the Pentium D designed for gaming or other high-performance tasks. The Pentium D and Pentium Extreme Edition both support x64 extensions, as does the Core 2 Duo.

The Pentium D was replaced by the Core and Core 2 families of processors. The Core and Core 2 families use processor architectures that emphasize real-world performance over clock speed. The first Core 2 processors were the Core 2 Duo (featuring two processor cores), followed by the Core 2 Quad models (with four processor cores). Although Core 2 processors run at much slower clock speeds than the fastest Pentium 4 or Pentium D processors, they perform much better in real-world operations. Core processors are single-core, while Core Duo and Core 2 Duo are dual-core. Core, Core Solo, and Core Duo processors are x86 (32-bit), while Core 2 Duo, Quad, and Extreme processors are x64 (64-bit).

The most recent processors in the Core family include the Core i7, Core i5, and Core i3, all of which support x64 (64-bit) processing. The Core i7 features quad core or six core designs with Intel HT Technology (hyperthreading, which supports two processor threads per core), Intel VT-x hardware-assisted virtualization, and Intel Turbo Boost overclocking. Core i5 is a simplified version of the Core i7, with only a few dual-core models supporting HT Technology (quad-core Core i5 does not support HT Technology); however, all Core i5 desktop processors include VT-x and Turbo Boost and some also include integrated graphics. Core i3 processors are dual-core with support for HT Technology, VT-x, and integrated graphics, but lack Turbo Boost. Note that mobile processors with these same model numbers differ in some details.

Celeron is actually a brand name rather than a specific processor design. Celeron processors have been based on the Pentium II, Pentium III, Pentium 4, and Core 2 processors. However, they feature lower clock speeds, slower front side bus speeds (the clock speed of the memory bus), and smaller L2 caches, making them less powerful (and less expensive) processors than the designs they're based on. Very few Celeron models support x64 extensions.

Because most Intel processor families have gone through many changes during their lifespans, specific models are sometimes referred to by their code names. In an attempt to make it easier to understand the performance and feature differences of models in a particular processor family, Intel has assigned processor numbers to recent versions of the Pentium 4, as well as all more recent processors.

Table 3-5 provides a brief summary of Intel desktop processors produced from 1998 to mid 2010. For additional details, see *Upgrading and Repairing PCs*, 19th Edition by Scott Mueller (Que Publishing).

Table 3-5   Intel Desktop Processors from Pentium III through Core i7

Processor	Code Names	Clock Speed Range	FSB Speed	Processor Socket or Slot	L2 Cache Sizes	Based On or Notes
Pentium III	Katmai, Coppermine, Coppermine-T, Tualatin	450MHz–1.3GHz	100MHz, 133MHz	Slot 1, Socket 370	256KB or 512KB	—
Celeron	Coppermine-128, Tualatin 256	533MHz–1.4GHz	66MHz, 100MHz	Slot 1, Socket 370	128KB, 256KB	Pentium III
Pentium 4	Willamette, Northwood, Prescott, Cedar Mill	1.4GHz–3.8 GHz	400MHz, 533MHz, 800MHz	Socket 423, Socket 478, Socket 775	256KB, 512KB, 1MB, 2MB	—
Pentium 4 Extreme Edition	Gallatin, Prescott 2M	3.2GHz–3.733GHz	800MHz	Socket 775	512KB+2 MB L3 or 2MB	Pentium 4 Prescott
Celeron	Willamette-128, Northwood-128	1.7GHz–2.8 GHz	400MHz	Socket 478	128KB	Pentium 4 Willamette, Northwood
Celeron D	Prescott-256, Cedar Mill-512	2.13GHz–3.6GHz	533MHz	Socket 478, Socket 775	256KB, 512KB	Pentium 4 Prescott, Cedar Mill

Table 3-5 Intel Desktop Processors from Pentium III through Core i7

Processor	Code Names	Clock Speed Range	FSB Speed	Processor Socket or Slot	L2 Cache Sizes	Based On or Notes
Pentium D	Smithfield	2.66GHz–3.66GHz	533MHz, 800MHz	Socket 775	1MB×2 or 2MB ×2	Dual-core version of Pentium 4 Prescott
Pentium Extreme Edition	Smithfield	3.73GHz	800MHz	Socket 775	2MB×2	Pentium 4 Prescott
Core 2 Duo	Conroe, Wolfdale, Allendale	1.80GHz–3.33GHz	800MHz, 1066MHz, 1333MHz	Socket 775	2MB, 4MB, 6MB	Dual-core version of Core (notebook processor)
Core 2 Extreme	Conroe XE	2.93GHz	1066MHz	Socket 775	4MB	Core 2 Duo Conroe
Celeron	Conroe L	1.2–2.2GHz	800MHz	Socket 775	512KB	Single-core version of Core 2 Duo Conroe
Celeron	Allendale-512	1.6–2.4GHz	800MHz	Socket 775	512KB	Core 2 Duo Allendale
Core 2 Quad	Kentsfield	2.4–2.6GHz	1066MHz	Socket 775	4MB×2	Two Core 2 Duo Conroe cores
Core 2 Quad	Yorkfield	2.26–3.0 GHz	1333MHz	Socket 775	3MB×2, 6MB×2	Integrated quad-core design
Core 2 Extreme	Kentsfield XE	2.66–3.0 GHz	1066MHz, 1333MHz	Socket 775	4MB×2	Core 2 Quad Kentsfield
Core 2 Extreme	Yorkfield XE	3.0–3.2GHz	1333MHz, 1600MHz	LGA-771	6MB×2	Core 2 Quad Yorkfield
Core i3	Clarkdale	2.93–3.33GHz	1066MHz, 1333MHz	FCLGA-1156	4MB	Clarkdale used for Core i3, Core i5

Table 3-5   Intel Desktop Processors from Pentium III through Core i7

Processor	Code Names	Clock Speed Range	FSB Speed	Processor Socket or Slot	L2 Cache Sizes	Based On or Notes
Core i5	Clarkdale	2.4–3.46GHz	1066MHz, 1333MHz	FCLGA-1156	4MB	Clarkdale used for Core i3, Core i5
Core i7	Lynnfield, Bloom-field, Gulftown	2.66–3.2GHz	800MHz–1066MHz; 1066MHz–1333MHz	FCLGA-1156	8MB–12MB	Gulftown is a six-core processor; others quad-core

Socket 775 is also referred to as LGA-775 because the socket contains leads that connect with solder balls on the bottom of the processor.

FCLGA-1156 is also known as LGA-1156

The processor code names and performance in this table are effective as of mid 2010.

AMD Processors

AMD processors contemporary with the Intel Pentium III and its successors include the following processor families as of mid 2010:

- Athlon
- Duron
- Athlon XP
- Sempron
- Athlon 64
- Athlon 64 FX
- Athlon 64 X2
- Phenom X3
- Phenom X4
- Phenom II X2
- Phenom II X3
- Phenom II X4
- Phenom II x6

The Athlon processor was the first (and last) AMD processor produced in a slot-based design. It uses Slot A, which physically resembled Slot 1 used by Intel Pentium II and Pentium III models, but was completely different in its pinout. Later versions of the Athlon switched to Socket A, a 462-pin socket, which was also used by the Duron, Athlon XP, and Socket A versions of the Sempron.

The Athlon XP replaced the Athlon, and featured higher clock speeds and larger L2 cache. The lower-performance counterpart of the Athlon and Athlon XP was the Duron, which featured a smaller L2 cache and slower FSB speed.

The Athlon XP design was used for the Socket A versions of the Sempron when AMD moved to 64-bit processing with the introduction of the Athlon 64, AMD's first x64 64-bit desktop processor.

The Athlon 64 family initially used Socket 754, but because the memory controller is built into the processor, rather than into the North Bridge as on conventional processors, it was necessary to develop a new Socket 939 to support dual-channel memory.

The Athlon 64 FX is a faster performance–oriented version of the Athlon 64. Initial versions were based on the Opteron workstation and server processor, and thus used Socket 940. Later versions used Socket 939 and its successor, Socket AM2.

AMD's first dual-core processor was the Athlon 64 X2, which uses a design that permits both processor cores to communicate directly with each other, rather than using the North Bridge (Memory Controller Hub) as in the Intel Pentium D. This enabled upgrades from Socket 939 Athlon 64 to the X2 version after performing a BIOS upgrade.

AMD's economy version of the Athlon 64 is also called the Sempron, various versions of which have used Socket 754 and Socket 939.

AMD's Phenom series is based on the AMD K10 processor architecture, and all Phenoms include multiple processor cores that are built as a single unit. Phenom II is an improved version of Phenom, featuring a smaller process, more cache, and better cache management. The Phenom II series uses a more efficient socket and increases the total possible amount of processor cores to 6. Processor speeds are also increased in this series. These processors use a more powerful chipset. The chipset is the main controller of the motherboard. When selecting an AMD processor, the motherboard's chipset should be taken into account to ensure compatibility.

AMD's Athlon II series is available in dual-core, triple-core, quad-core, and six-core versions (X2, X3, X4, and X6).

Because most AMD processor families have gone through many changes during their lifespans, specific models are sometimes referred to by their code names.

Table 3-6 provides a brief summary of AMD desktop processors produced over the last decade. For additional details, see *Upgrading and Repairing PCs*, 19th Edition.

Table 3-6 AMD Desktop Processors from Athlon through Phenom II

Processor	Code Names	Clock Speed Range	FSB Speed	Processor Socket or Slot	L2 Cache Sizes	Based On
Athlon	K7, K75, Thunderbird	500MHz–1.4GHz	200–266 MHz	Slot A, Socket A (aka Socket 462)	256–512KB	—
Athlon XP	Palomino, Thoroughbred, Thorton	1.333–2.2 GHz	266–400 MHz	Socket A	256–512 KB	—
Duron	Spitfire, Morgan, Applebred, Appaloosa	550MHz–1.8GHz	200–266 MHz	Socket A	64KB	Athlon Socket A
Sempron	Thorton, Barton	1.5–2.2GHz	166–200 MHz	Socket A	256KB (Thorton), 512KB (Barton)	Athlon XP
Sempron	Paris, Palermo	1.4–2.0 GHz	800MHz–1GHz	Socket 754	128–256 KB	Athlon 64 (Socket 754 versions)
Athlon 64	ClawHammer, Newcastle, San Diego, Venice, Orleans	1–2.6GHz	800MHz–1GHz	Socket 754, Socket 939, Socket 940, Socket AM2	512KB–1MB	—
Sempron	Palermo	1.8–2.0GHz	800MHz	Socket 939	128KB–256KB	Athlon 64
Athlon 64 FX	See Athlon 64 code names; also Windsor	2.2–2.8GHz	800MHz–1GHz	Socket 939, Socket 940	1MB	Athlon 64
Sempron	Manila, Sparta	1.6–2.3GHz	800MHz	Socket AM2	128-256-512KB	Athlon 64

Table 3-6   AMD Desktop Processors from Athlon through Phenom II

Processor	Code Names	Clock Speed Range	FSB Speed	Processor Socket or Slot	L2 Cache Sizes	Based On
Athlon 64 X2	Manchester, Toledo, Windsor, Brisbane	1.9–3.2GHz	1GHz	Socket 939 (Manchester, Toledo), Socket AM2 (Windsor, Brisbane)	256KB×2; 512KB×2; 1MB×2	Dual-core version of Athlon 64
Athlon 64 FX	Toledo, Windsor	2.0–3.2GHz	1GHz	Socket 939 (Toledo), Socket AM2 (Brisbane)	1MB×2	Dual-core version of Athlon 64 FX
Phenom X4	Agena	1.8–2.6 GHz	1.6-2GHz	Socket AM2	512KB×4 + 2MB L3	K10 microarchitecture
Phenom X3	Toliman	2.1–2.5GHz	1.6-1.8GHz	Socket AM2	512KB×3 + 2MB L3	K10 microarchitecture
Phenom X2	Kuma	2.3–2.8GHz	1.8GHz	Socket AM2+	512KB×2 + 2MB L3	K10 microarchitecture
Athlon X2	Kuma	2.3–2.8GHz	1.8GHz	Socket AM2+	512KB×2 + 2MB L3	Phenom X2
Phenom II X2	Callisto	2.8–3.3GHz	2GHz, 2.2GHz	Socket AM3	512KB×2 + 6MB L3	Deneb with two cores disabled
Phenom II X3	Heka	2.4–3.2GHz	2GHz	Socket AM3	512KB×3 +6MB L3	Deneb with one core disabled
Phenom II X4	Deneb	2.5–3.5GHz	1.8GHz, 2GHz	Socket AM2+, AM3	512KB×4 + 4MB or 6MB L3	DDR3 memory supported on Socket AM3 only

Table 3-6   AMD Desktop Processors from Athlon through Phenom II

Processor	Code Names	Clock Speed Range	FSB Speed	Processor Socket or Slot	L2 Cache Sizes	Based On
Phenom II X6	Thuban	2.7–3.2GHz	2GHz	Socket AM3	512KB×6 +6MB L3	Includes Turbo Core overclock support
Athlon II	Regor	1.8–2.0GHz	1.8GHz	Socket AM3	1MB	Single-core version of Regor (X2)
Athlon II	Regor (X2)	1.6–3.3GHz	2GHz	Socket AM3	512KB×2 or 1024KB×2	Phenom II without L3 cache
Athlon II	Rana (X3)	2.2–3.2GHz	2GHz	Socket AM3	512KB×3	Phenom II without L3 cache
Athlon II	Propus (X4)	2.2–3.1GHz	2GHz	Socket AM3	512KB×4	Phenom II without L3 cache

The processor code names and performance in this table are effective as of mid 2010.

Processor Sockets and Packaging

Most processors listed in the previous sections use some form of the pin grid array (PGA) package, in which pins on the bottom of the processor plug into holes in the processor socket. The exceptions include slot-mounted processors (Slot 1 and Slot A) and the current LGA and FCLGA sockets, which use a different type of processor package called the land grid array (LGA). LGA packaging uses gold pads on the bottom of the processor package to connect with raised leads in the processor socket.

Figure 3-21 compares processor packages and sockets to each other.

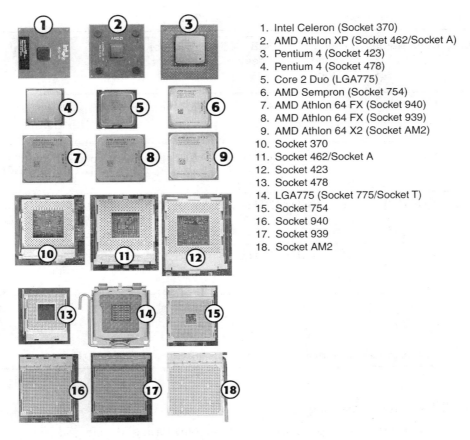

1. Intel Celeron (Socket 370)
2. AMD Athlon XP (Socket 462/Socket A)
3. Pentium 4 (Socket 423)
4. Pentium 4 (Socket 478)
5. Core 2 Duo (LGA775)
6. AMD Sempron (Socket 754)
7. AMD Athlon 64 FX (Socket 940)
8. AMD Athlon 64 FX (Socket 939)
9. AMD Athlon 64 X2 (Socket AM2)
10. Socket 370
11. Socket 462/Socket A
12. Socket 423
13. Socket 478
14. LGA775 (Socket 775/Socket T)
15. Socket 754
16. Socket 940
17. Socket 939
18. Socket AM2

Figure 3-21   Intel and AMD processors and sockets.

CPU Technologies

Processor technologies in the following sections might be used by AMD only, by Intel only, or by both vendors. These technologies are used to help distinguish different processors from each other in terms of performance or features.

Hyperthreading (HT Technology)

Hyperthreading (HT Technology) is a technology developed by Intel for processing two execution threads within a single processor. Essentially, when HT Technology is enabled in the system BIOS and the processor is running a multithreaded application, the processor is emulating two physical processors. The Pentium 4 was the first desktop processor to support HT Technology, which Intel first developed for its Xeon workstation and server processor family.

Pentium 4 processors with processor numbers all support HT Technology, as do older models with 800MHz FSB and a clock speed of 3.06GHz or higher. HT

Technology is also incorporated in a number of more recent dual-core, quad-core, and six-core processors in the Core 2, Core i5, and i7 series to further improve the execution of multithreaded applications.

Dual-Core and Multi-Core

Two or more physical processors in a system enable it to perform much faster when multitasking or running multithreaded applications. However, systems with multiple processors are very expensive to produce and some operating systems cannot work with multiple processors. Dual core processors, which combine two processor cores into a single physical processor, provide virtually all of the benefits of two physical processors, and are lower in cost and work with any operating system that supports traditional single-core processors.

The first dual-core desktop processors were introduced by Intel (Pentium D) and AMD (Athlon 64 X2) in 2005. Athlon 64 X2's processor cores communicate directly with each other, enabling systems running single-core Athlon 64 processors to swap processors after a simple BIOS upgrade. The Pentium D, on the other hand, required new chipsets to support it. Core 2 Duo, Core i3, and some versions of the Core i5 represent major current dual-core processor families. Like the AMD Athlon 64 X2 and newer AMD dual-core processors, these processors' cores communicate directly with each other.

Both Intel and AMD have released processors that include more than two cores. Intel's Core 2 Quad, Core i7, and some versions of the Core 2 Extreme contain four or more processor cores, while AMD's Phenom and Phenom II are available in versions with two, three, four, or more processor cores.

Processor Throttling

Processors do not need to run at full speed when they have little, or no, work to perform. By slowing down—or throttling—the processor's clock speed when the workload is light, the processor runs cooler, the system uses less energy, and—in the case of mobile systems—the computer enjoys a longer battery life. Throttling, sometimes referred to as thermal throttling, can also take place when a processor gets too hot for the computer's cooling system to work properly.

Intel uses the terms SpeedStep or Enhanced SpeedStep for its throttling technologies. AMD uses the term Cool'n'Quiet for its throttling technology.

Microcode (MMX)

All Intel and AMD processors in current use include various types of microcode instructions for boosting multimedia performance. The first processor to include this type of microcode was the Pentium MMX, which included 57 new instructions (known as MMX) for working with multimedia. MMX was the first example of what is known as single instruction, multiple data (SIMD) capability.

Later Intel processors included enhanced versions of MMX known as SSE (MMX+70 additional instructions, introduced with the Pentium III), SSE2 (MMX+SSE+144 new instructions, introduced with the Pentium 4), SSE3 (MMX+SSE+SSE2+13 new instructions, introduced with the Pentium 4 Prescott), and, most recently, SSSE3 (MMX+SSE+SSE2+SSE3+32 new instructions, introduced with the Core 2 Duo). The SSE4 instruction set, which adds 51 new instructions, was introduced with the introduction of 45nm processor technology in the Penryn versions of the Core 2 Duo and subsequent processors. SSE4.1 is a subset of SSE4, containing 47 instructions. SSE4.2 includes the seven remaining instructions and was introduced with the Core i7. The term "HD Boost" refers to SSE4 support.

AMD also provides multimedia-optimized microcode in its processors, starting with 3DNow! (introduced by the K6, which was roughly equivalent to the Pentium MMX). However, AMD's version differs in details from Intel's, offering 21 new instructions. The AMD Athlon introduced 3DNow! Enhanced (3DNow!+24 new instructions), while the Athlon XP introduced 3DNow! Professional (3DNow!+Enhanced+51). 3DNow! Professional is equivalent to Intel's SSE. Starting with the Athlon 64 family, AMD now supports SSE2, and it added SSE3 support to the Athlon 64 X2 and newer versions of the Athlon 64 family. AMD also supports four SSE4 instructions as well as two SSE instructions known as SSE4a.

Overclocking

Overclocking refers to the practice of running a processor or other components, such as memory or the video card's graphics processing unit (GPU) at speeds higher than normal. Overclocking methods used for processors include increasing the clock multiplier or running the front side bus (FSB) at faster speeds than normal. These changes are performed by altering the normal settings in the system BIOS setup for the processor's configuration. Figure 3-22 is a typical BIOS processor configuration screen.

Most processors feature locked clock multipliers. That is, the clock multiplier frequency cannot be changed. In such cases, the only way to overclock the processor is to increase the front side bus speed, which is the speed at which the processor communicates with system memory. Increasing the FSB speed can lead to greater system instability than changing the clock multipliers.

Some processors from Intel and AMD feature unlocked clock multipliers, so that the user can choose the best method for overclocking the system. Overclocked processors and other components run hotter than normal, so techniques such as using additional cooling fans, replacing standard active heat sinks with models that feature greater cooling, and adjusting processor voltages are often used to help maintain system stability at faster speeds.

Intel's Core i7, Core i5, and AMD's Phenom II series support automatic overclocking according to processor load. Intel refers to this feature as Turbo Boost, while AMD's term is Turbo Core.

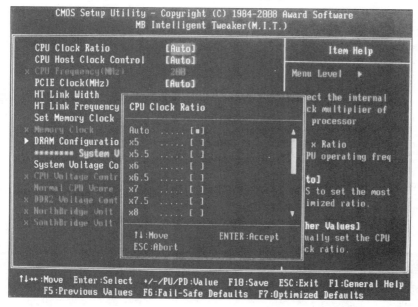

Figure 3-22   Preparing to overclock a system running an AMD Athlon 64 X2 processor.

Cache

Cache memory, as mentioned previously, improves system performance by enabling the processor to reuse recently retrieved memory locations without needing to fetch them from main memory. Processors from AMD and Intel feature at least two levels of cache:

- Level 1 (L1) cache is built into the processor core. L1 cache is relatively small (8KB–64KB). When the processor needs to access memory it checks the contents of L1 cache first.

- Level 2 (L2) cache is also built into the processor. On older slot-mounted processors, L2 cache was external to the processor die, and ran at slower speeds than the processor. On socketed processors, L2 cache is built into the processor die. If the processor does not find the desired memory locations in L1 cache, it checks L2 cache next.

- Level 3 (L3) cache is found on some very high-performance processors from Intel (such as the Core i7 series) and on several high-performance and mid-level processors from AMD. L3 is also built into the processor die. On systems with L3 cache, the processor checks L3 cache after checking L1 and L2 caches.

If cache memory does not contain the desired information, the processor retrieves the desired information from main memory, and stores copies of that information in its cache memory (L1 and L2, or L1, L2, and L3). Processors with larger L2 caches (or L2 and L3 caches) perform most tasks much more quickly than processors that have smaller L2 caches for two reasons. Cache memory is faster than main memory, and the processor checks cache memory for needed information before checking main memory.

VRM

Starting with Socket 7 versions of the Intel Pentium, processors have not received their power directly from the power supply. Instead, a device called a voltage regulator module (VRM) has been used to reduce 5V or 12V DC power from the power supply to the appropriate power requested by the processor through its voltage identification (VID) logic.

Although some motherboards feature a removable VRM, most motherboards use a built-in VRM that is located next to the processor socket, as shown in Figure 3-23.

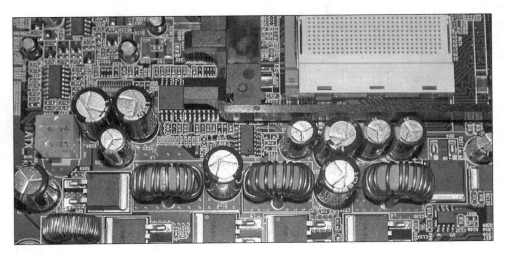

Figure 3-23 A portion of the VRM on an Athlon 64 motherboard.

NOTE Be sure to determine the free space around a processor before ordering or installing a third-party active heat sink. Some motherboards have VRM components located so close to the processor that some heat sinks will not fit.

Speed (Real Versus Actual): Clock Speed Versus Performance

A common measurement of processor performance has been clock speed. However, clock speed can be misleading. For example, the Intel Core 2 Duo and AMD Athlon 64 X2 processors perform computing tasks much more quickly than the Pentium D, even though the Pentium D runs at a much higher clock speed.

To determine the actual performance of a processor, you should use benchmark tests such as Futuremark's SYSmark, PCMark, and 3DMark.

32-bit Versus 64-bit

Processors developed before the AMD Athlon 64 were designed only for 32-bit operating systems and applications. 32-bit software cannot access more than 4GB of RAM (in fact, 32-bit Windows programs can use only 3.25GB of RAM), which makes working with large data files difficult, as only a portion of a file larger than the maximum memory size can be loaded into memory at one time.

The Athlon 64 was the first desktop processor to support 64-bit extensions to the 32-bit x86 architecture. These 64-bit extensions, commonly known as x64, enable processors to use more than 4GB of RAM and run 64-bit operating systems, but maintain full compatibility with 32-bit operating systems and applications.

Late-model Pentium 4 processors from Intel also support x64, as do subsequent processors such as the Pentium 4 Extreme Edition, Pentium D, Pentium Extreme Edition, Core 2 Duo, Core 2 Quad, Core 2 Extreme, Core i3, Core i5, and Core i7. Subsequent AMD processors including the Athlon X2, Athlon II, Phenom, and Phenom II also support x64. Most processors made today support x64 operation.

NOTE To learn more about a particular processor's support for x64 operation, hardware virtualization, and other features, look up the processor specifications at the manufacturer's website.

Choosing the Best Processor for the Job

If you are buying or building a new system, you have free rein in the choice of a processor to build the system around. This section describes important considerations.

Performance

If you need a system that can handle high-resolution graphics and video, and can perform heavy-duty number crunching, get the fastest dual-core or multi-core processor you can afford. However, if your requirements are less extreme, you can save money for your clients by opting for a processor from the same family with slower clock speed or less cache memory.

Thermal Issues

Many processor models are available in two or more versions that differ in their thermal requirements; that is, the type of active heat sink necessary to cool them and the amount of power (in watts) needed to operate them. This figure is often referred to as Max TDP (maximum thermal design power). In a mid-tower or full tower system, these considerations might be less important than in a micro-tower or small form factor system, or a system that might need to run as quietly as possible.

32-bit Versus 64-bit (x64) Compatibility

Unless you are trying to build the least-expensive system possible, you will find it difficult to find 32-bit only processors today. However, if you are repurposing existing systems, you might need to determine which systems include processors with support for 64-bit operation, and which support only 32-bit operation.

Other Processor Features

Processor features such as NX (no execute, which provides hardware-based protection against some types of viruses and malware) and hardware-based virtualization (which enables a single processor to be split into multiple virtual machines with little or no slowdown) are also important to consider in business environments. Check the specification sheets provided by processor vendors to determine the exact features supported by a particular processor.

TIP   To help determine detailed information for current and late-model installed Intel processors (Pentium 4, Celerons based on the Pentium 4 and newer), use the Intel Processor Identification Utility available from the Intel website (www.intel.com). For older Intel processors, use the Intel Processor Frequency ID Utility, also available from the Intel website.

To help determine detailed information for installed AMD and Intel processors, download and install CPU-Z from the CPUID website (www.cpuid.com).

Installing Processors

Processors are one of the most expensive components found in any computer. Because a processor can fail, or more likely, might need to be replaced with a faster model, knowing how to install and remove processors is important. On the A+ Certification exams, you should be prepared to answer questions related to the safe removal and replacement of socketed processors.

The methods used for CPU removal vary according to two factors: the processor type and the socket/slot type.

As you saw in Tables 3-5 and 3-6, most recent processors are socketed. Before the development of the ZIF socket, the processor was held in place by tension on the chip's legs, pins, or leads. Thus, to remove these chips, you must pull the chip out of the socket. Because the chip's legs, pins, or leads are fragile, special tools are strongly recommended for removing chips that are not mounted in ZIF sockets.

Before removing and installing any CPU or other internal component, be sure to review and follow the ESD precautions discussed in Chapter 17.

Removing the Heat Sink

ZIF sockets are used on almost all desktop systems using Pentium III-class or newer socketed processors (except for processors using LGA sockets). They allow easy installation and removal of the processor.

What makes ZIF sockets easy to work with? They have a lever that, when released, loosens a clamp that holds the processor in place.

If the processor has a removable heat sink, fan, or thermal duct that is attached to the motherboard, you must remove these components before you can remove the processor.

Heat sinks used on Socket 370 and Socket A processors have a spring-loaded clip on one side and a fixed lug on the other side. To release this clip, press down on it using a screwdriver, as shown in Figure 3-24.

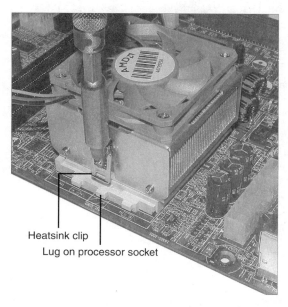

Heatsink clip
Lug on processor socket

Figure 3-24 Releasing the spring clip on a Socket A processor's heat sink.

Most newer processors use heat sinks that are attached to a frame around the processor or are mounted through the motherboard. To release these heat sinks, you might need to flip up a lever on one side of the heat sink or release the locking pins. Figure 3-25 illustrates a typical installation on an Athlon 64 processor, and Figure 3-26 illustrates the components of a typical heat sink for LGA 775 processors.

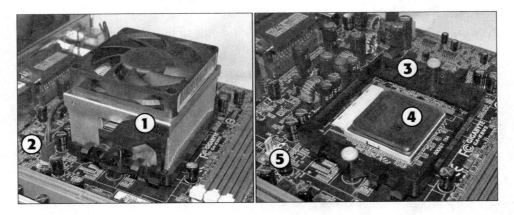

1. Locking lever
2. Power lead for heat sink fan
3. Heat sink frame
4. Processor
5. Motherboard power connector for heat sink fan

Figure 3-25   Typical heat sink assembly on Athlon 64 processor.

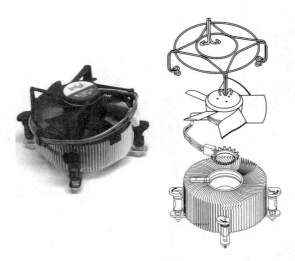

Figure 3-26   Stock heat sink assembly for Intel Core 2 Duo LGA 775 processor.

BTX systems use a horizontally mounted thermal module that is equipped with a fan. The thermal module also helps cool other components such as the motherboard chipset and memory. Figure 3-27 illustrates a typical thermal module installed on a motherboard. Note that the front of the thermal module extends below the edge of the motherboard to provide cooling for both top and bottom.

To remove a thermal module from a BTX motherboard, follow these steps:

Step 1.   Remove the screws that attach the module to the retention bracket on the underside of the motherboard.

Step 2.   Disconnect the thermal module's fan power lead.

Step 3.   Lift the thermal module off the processor.

Be careful when removing head sinks or thermal modules. Be careful not to drop the heat sink or thermal module on the CPU or on the motherboard. Heat sinks and thermal modules are bulky and heavy and can easily damage the expensive parts of the your computer.

Removing the Processor

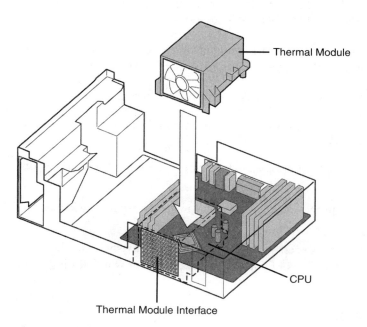

Figure 3-27   Thermal module placement on a typical BTX motherboard. Figure courtesy of www.Formfactors.org.

After removing the heat sink, follow these instructions to complete the processor removal process.

Step 1.   Disconnect the active heat sink (if included) from its power source and lift the assembly away.

Step 2.   Push the lever on the ZIF socket slightly to the outside of the socket to release it.

Step 3.   Lift the end of the lever until it is vertical (see Figure 3-28). This releases the clamping mechanism on the processor's pins.

Figure 3-28   After the heat sink fan is disconnected from power (left) to reveal the processor (center), the lever on the ZIF socket (right) can be lifted to release the processor.

Step 4.   Grasp the processor on opposite sides, making sure not to touch the pins, and remove it from the socket. Put it into antistatic packaging.

The process of removing an LGA-based processor is a bit different:

Step 1.   Disconnect the active heat sink (if included) from its power source and lift the assembly away.

Step 2.   Lift the locking lever to release the load plate, which holds the processor in place.

Step 3.   Carefully lift the processor away and place in into antistatic packaging.

Be careful when removing the processor and when unlocking any sockets. These components are very delicate. Think of yourself as a watchmaker when dealing with these parts!

Installing a New Processor

Before installing a new processor, verify that the processor you plan to install is supported by the motherboard. Even though a particular combination of processor and motherboard might use the same socket, issues such as BIOS, voltage, memory support, or chipset considerations can prevent some processors from working on particular motherboards. You can destroy a processor or motherboard if you install a processor not suitable for a particular motherboard.

After verifying compatibility by checking the system or processor manual (and installing any BIOS updates required for processor compatibility), check a PGA-type processor for bent pins, and the socket of an LGA processor for bent leads. Correct these problems before continuing.

To insert a PGA-type CPU into a ZIF socket, find the corner of the chip that is marked as pin 1 (usually with a dot or triangle). The underside of some chips might be marked with a line pointing toward pin 1. Then follow these steps:

Step 1.   Line up the pin 1 corner with the corner of the socket also indicated as pin 1 (look for an arrow or other marking on the motherboard). If you put the chip in with pin 1 aligned with the wrong corner and apply the power, you will destroy the chip.

Step 2.   Make sure the lever on the ZIF socket is vertical; insert the CPU into the socket and verify that the pins are fitting into the correct socket holes.

Step 3.   Lower the lever to the horizontal position and snap it into place to secure the CPU.

Step 4.   Before attaching the heat sink or fan, determine if the heat sink has a thermal pad (also called a phase-change pad) or if you need to apply thermal compound to the processor core (refer to Figure 3-27). Remove the protective tape from the thermal pad or apply thermal compound as needed. Attach the heat sink or fan. You must use some type of thermal compound between the processor and the bottom of the heat sink.

Step 5.   Attach the heat sink to the processor as directed by the processor vendor (for heat sinks supplied with the processor) or heat sink vendor (for aftermarket heat sinks). In some cases, you might need to attach mounting hardware to the motherboard before you can attach the heat sink.

Step 6.   If you are installing an active heat sink (a heat sink with a fan), plug the fan into the appropriate connector on the motherboard.

To insert an LGA processor, locate the notches on each side of the processor. These correspond with key tabs in the processor socket. Then follow these steps:

Step 1.   Make sure the load plate assembly is completely open. It has a plastic cover that can be removed at the end of Step 5.

Step 2.   Line up the notches in the processor with the key tabs in the processor socket. This assures that the processor's Pin 1 is properly aligned with the socket.

Step 3.   Lower the processor into place, making sure the metal heat spreader plate faces up and the gold pads face down. Do not drop the processor, as the lands in the processor socket could be damaged.

Step 4.   Push down the load plate and close the load plate assembly cam lever.

Step 5.   Lock the lever in place on the side of the socket. Remove the plastic cover and save it for future use.

Step 6.   Before attaching the heat sink or fan, determine if the heat sink has a thermal pad (also called a phase-change pad) or if you need to apply thermal compound to the processor core (refer to Figure 3-27). Remove the protective tape from the thermal pad or apply thermal compound as needed. Attach the heat sink or fan. You must use some type of thermal compound between the processor and the bottom of the heat sink.

Step 7.   Attach the heat sink to the processor as directed by the processor vendor (for heat sinks supplied with the processor) or heat sink vendor (for aftermarket heat sinks). In some cases, you might need to attach mounting hardware to the motherboard before you can attach the heat sink.

Step 8.   If you are installing an active heat sink (a heat sink with a fan), plug the fan into the appropriate connector on the motherboard.

Check the processor installation by booting the computer and by checking the speed of the processor in the BIOS and in Windows.

Slot-Type CPU (early Pentium III, early AMD Athlon, and Others)

You won't see many slot-type CPUs anymore, but if you need to install one on a motherboard, make sure the motherboard has a retention mechanism attached. If the motherboard doesn't have one, you will need to remove the motherboard from the case to attach a retention mechanism if it is not already attached.

To remove a slot-type CPU, follow these steps:

Step 1.   Push down on the retainers at each end of the CPU to release the CPU from the retention mechanism.

Step 2.   Disconnect the power lead to the CPU fan (if present).

Step 3.   Remove the CPU and fan/heat sink from the retention mechanism. The CPU slides straight up from the slot.

To attach a slot-type CPU, follow these steps

Step 1.   Attach the CPU retention mechanism to the motherboard. Leave the foam backing on the bottom of the motherboard while pushing the supports into place. Lift up the motherboard and secure the retention mechanism with the screws supplied.

Some motherboards are shipped with the retention mechanism already installed, so this step might not apply to you. If the retention mechanism is folded against the motherboard, unfold it so the supports stand straight up.

Step 2.   Attach the fan and heat sink to the CPU if it is not already attached; some CPUs have a factory-attached heat sink/fan, whereas others require you to add it in the field.

Step 3.   Match the pinouts on the bottom of the CPU to the motherboard's slot; note that the slot has two sides of unequal length, making it easy to match the slot with the CPU.

Step 4.   Insert the CPU into the retention mechanism; push down until the retaining clips lock the CPU into place. Figure 3-29 shows the CPU in place.

Step 5.   Connect the power lead from the fan (if present) to the motherboard or drive power connector as directed.

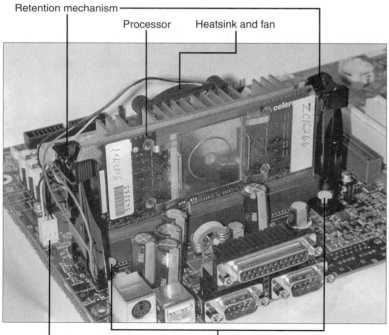

Figure 3-29   A Slot 1–based Celeron CPU after installation. The heat sink and fan are attached to the rear of the CPU.

Troubleshooting Processors

Keeping the processor running reliably is vital to correct system operation. This section focuses on some common problems and solutions.

System Runs Slower Than Rated Speed

A system running slower than its rated speed might do so because of processor throttling due to overheating, less than optimal settings in the Windows Power Options in Control Panel, or because of incorrect BIOS timing.

Overheating of the Processor or System   A system that overheats will stop operating, and with some older processors serious damage can result. Most processors today are fitted with active heat sinks that contain a fan. If the fan stops working, the process will overheat.

Fan Failure

Heat sink fans don't have to stop turning to fail; if they turn more slowly than they are specified to run, they can cause processor overheating.

Fan failures can be caused by dirt in the fan, worn-out bearings, or a bad connection to the motherboard or drive-cable power. In most cases, it's better to replace the heat sink fan than to try to clean it. If you must clean it, follow these steps:

Step 1.   Remove the heat sink from the CPU.

Step 2.   Place it on a surface covered with old newspapers or waste paper.

Step 3.   Blow it out with compressed air.

Before reattaching the heat sink, clean the old thermal material from the processor and the heat sink and reapply a small amount of thermal material to the top center of the processor cap. For specific thermal material installation recommendations for a particular processor, check the processor manufacturer's website.

If you opt for a replacement fan, improve reliability and life by specifying a ball-bearing fan rather than the typical (and cheap) sleeve-bearing units. Overheating can also be caused by a dirty power supply or case fan, or by missing slot covers. Clean or replace the fans, and replace the slot covers. Don't overlook cleaning out the inside of the case, because a dirty case interior will eventually clog other components due to the system's airflow.

Incorrect Heat Sink for Processor Type/Speed

If the processor overheats and the heat sink is properly attached and the fan is running, make sure the heat sink is designed for the processor type and speed in use. Heat sinks made for lower speed processors might not provide adequate cooling for faster processors, which often run at higher temperatures.

Use the heat sink provided by the processor vendor, or, if you are using a separately purchased heat sink, make sure the heat sink is designed for the processor type and speed in use.

The hardware monitor feature in the system BIOS can warn of overheating or fan failure. This is most effective if the motherboard or system vendor's monitoring software is also installed so you can be warned of problems while Windows is running.

Windows Power Options in Control Panel

Computers which are configured to use power settings other than High Performance will run more slowly at times to help save power and reduce heat. Systems using settings other than High Performance might also go into sleep mode more quickly, which can reduce system responsiveness. For maximum performance, use the High Performance power management setting (known as power scheme in some versions of Windows). Note that some older laptop computers use a special keystroke to activate or manage proprietary power management software.

Underclocked System   Some systems revert to a "fail-safe" setting in which the CPU frequency and/or clock multiplier default to low-speed settings if the system fails to boot properly or is shut off before starting. Check the system speed reported on the System properties sheet in Windows XP/Vista/7 or the CPU frequency/ multiplier values in the BIOS. If these values are incorrect, set the CPU frequency and multiplier values according to the processor manufacturer's guidelines. See Chapter 4 for details.

If the system is configured to automatically detect the correct values for CPU frequency and clock multiplier but will not report the correct speed, the system might need a BIOS upgrade to properly support the processor, or you might be using a re-marked processor (one that has had its original model number and technical information altered to make it appear as if it's a faster processor).

Processor Failure

If the processor is not locked into place, you will not be able to attach the heat sink. Never run the system if the processor is not properly installed, including heat sink installation.

Installing Adapter Cards

Although most desktop systems are equipped with a wide variety of I/O ports and integrated adapters, it is still often necessary to install adapter cards to enable the system to perform specialized tasks or to achieve higher performance. The following sections show you how to perform typical installations.

General Installation

Before installing an adapter card, you should determine the following:

■ **Does the adapter card perform the same task as an integrated adapter?**—
For example, if you are installing a display adapter (also called a graphics card
or video card), does the system already have an integrated adapter? If you are
installing a sound card, does the system already have a sound card? Depending
upon the type of card you are installing, it might be necessary to disable the
comparable onboard feature first to avoid hardware resource conflicts.

■ **What type(s) of expansion slots are available for expansion cards?**—A typical
system today might have two or three different types of expansion slots, such
as PCI Express x16, PCI Express x1 and PCI, or PCI and AGP, as shown in
Figure 3-30. PCI Express x1 and PCI slots can be used for a variety of adapter
cards, while PCI Express and AGP slots are designed for display adapters. The
adapter card you select must fit into an available slot.

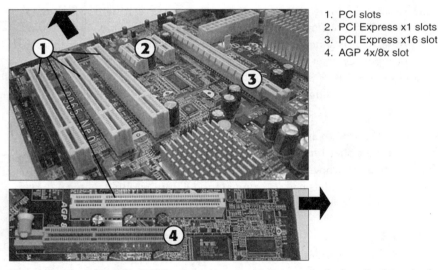

1. PCI slots
2. PCI Express x1 slots
3. PCI Express x16 slot
4. AGP 4x/8x slot

Figure 3-30 AGP, PCI, PCI Express x1 and x16 slots on typical motherboards. Arrow indicates rear of motherboard.

■ **When PCI and PCI Express x1 slots are available, which slot should be used?**—
PCI Express x1 slots provide higher performance than PCI slots, and should be
used whenever possible. Use PCI cards if PCIe cards are not available.

To learn how to change BIOS configuration settings to disable onboard ports, see
Chapter 4.

The general process of installing an adapter card works like this:

Step 1. Shut down the system.

Step 2.   Disconnect it from AC power, either by unplugging the system or by turning off the power supply with its own on/off switch.

Step 3.   Remove the system cover. Depending upon the motherboard design and case design, the exact method varies:

■ If the case has a one-piece design, remove the entire case.

■ If the case is a tower design with removable side panels, remove the left side panel (as seen from the front) to install cards into an ATX system. Remove the right side panel to install cards into a BTX system.

Step 4.   Locate the expansion slot you want to use. If the slot has a header cable installed in the slot cover, you will need to move the header cable to a different slot. Figure 3-31 illustrates a typical system that has some available slots.

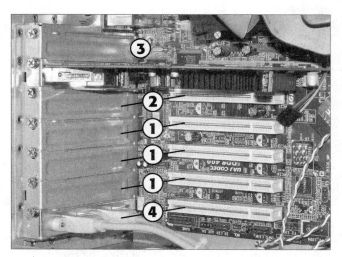

1. Available slots and slot covers
2. Not available; too close to neighboring card
3. Available for header cable only; no matching slot
4. Not available; header cable blocks slot

Figure 3-31   A typical system has some available slots and some that are not available for various reasons.

Step 5.   Remove the slot cover corresponding to the slot you want to use for the adapter card. Most slot covers are held in place by set screws that fasten the slot cover to the rear of the case, as shown in Figure 3-31. However, some systems use different methods.

TIP   If you are unable to remove the slot cover after removing the set screw, loosen the set screw on the adjacent slot cover. Sometimes the screw head overlaps the adjacent slot cover.

Step 6.   Remove the card from its antistatic packaging. Hold the card by the bracket, not by the circuit board, chips, or card connector. Figure 3-32 illustrates a typical card and where to hold it safely.

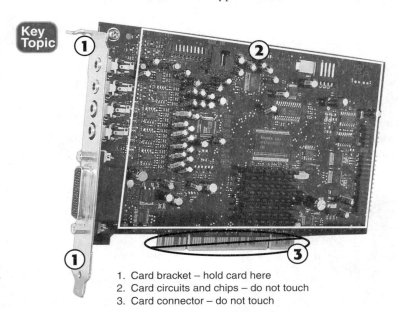

1. Card bracket – hold card here
2. Card circuits and chips – do not touch
3. Card connector – do not touch

Figure 3-32   A typical adapter card. Callouts indicate where it is safe and not safe to hold the card.

Step 7.   Insert the card into the expansion slot, lining up the connector on the bottom.

Step 8.   Push the card connector firmly into the slot.

Step 9.   Secure the card bracket; on most systems, you will secure the card bracket by replacing the set screw. See Figure 3-33.

Step 10.   Connect any cables required for the card.

Step 11.   Reconnect AC power and restart the system.

A Incorrect installation   B Correct installation

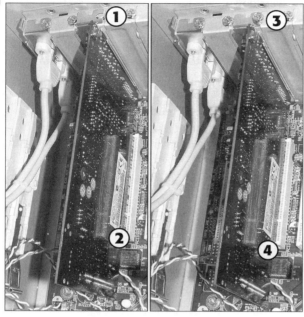

1. Bracket not secured to rear of system
2. Card connector not completely inserted
3. Bracket secured
4. Card connector completely inserted

Figure 3-33   An improperly installed card compared with a properly installed card.

Step 12.   When the system restarts, provide drivers as prompted.

The following sections discuss some special installation considerations that apply to some types of adapter cards.

Display Adapters

Before installing a display adapter in a working system, you should open Device Manager and uninstall the current display adapter. To learn more about using Device Manager, see Chapter 13 "Using and Managing Windows".

Display adapters are available for PCI Express x16, AGP, and PCI expansion slots. Display adapters in PCI form factor are intended for use in systems that don't have PCI Express or AGP slots, or to provide support for additional displays on systems that already have PCI Express or AGP cards installed.

When you install a card into an AGP slot, make sure the card locking mechanism on the front of the slot is open before you install the card. Locking mechanisms sometimes use a lever that is moved to one side, flips up and down, or has a locking tab that is pulled to one side.

After installing the display adapter, install the drivers provided by the graphics card vendor. If possible, use updated drivers downloaded from the vendor's website rather than the ones provided on CD.

When connecting the monitor(s) to the display adapter, keep in mind that CRT and some LCD monitors use the 15-pin VGA connector, while many LCD monitors use the larger DVI connector or the compact HDMI adapter that supports home theater systems (HDTVs and audio amplifiers). You can use an adapter to enable a DVI-I connector on a display adapter to connect to a monitor that uses the VGA connector and a DVI to HDMI adapter to connect a DVI port to a display or HDTV with an HDMI connector. To learn more about display adapters and graphics cards, see Chapter 8.

Sound Cards

After installing a sound card, you must connect 1/8-inch mini-jack cables from speakers and the microphone to the sound card. Most sound cards use the same PC99 color-coding standards for audio hardware that are used by onboard audio solutions, as described in Table 3-7.

Table 3-7   PC99 Color Coding for Audio Jacks

Usage	Color	Jack Type
Microphone input (mono)	Pink	Mini-jack
Line in (stereo)	Light blue	Mini-jack
Speaker or headphone (front/stereo)	Lime green	Mini-jack
Speaker out/subwoofer	Orange	Mini-jack
Game port/MIDI out	Gold	15-pin DIN

After installing the sound card, you are prompted to install drivers when you restart the system. The driver set might also include a customized mixer program that is used to select speaker types, speaker arrangement (stereo, 5.1, and so on), and provides speaker testing and diagnostics. Be sure to test the speakers to assure they are plugged into the correct jack(s) and are working properly.

Video Capture Cards

Video capture cards are used to capture video from analog or digital video sources. Video capture card types include

- **IEEE 1394 (FireWire) cards**—These capture video from DV camcorders and can also be used for other types of 1394 devices, such as hard disks and scanners. An onboard IEEE 1394 port can also be used for video capture.

- **Analog video capture cards**—These capture video from analog sources, such as cable or broadcast TV, composite video, or S-video. Many of these cards also include TV tuners. Examples include the Hauppauge WinTV PVR series and the ATI Theater Pro series.

- **Digital video capture card**—These capture digital video from HDMI sources, such as HDTV.

- **The ATI All-in-Wonder series**—These cards incorporate accelerated 3D video display output to monitors, video capture, and TV tuner support.

After installing any type of video capture card, you need to install the drivers provided with the card, connect the card to video sources, and, in the case of cards with onboard TV tuners, set up the TV tuner feature.

Troubleshooting Adapter Cards

Adapter card problems can be detected in the following ways:

- A device connected to the adapter card doesn't work.

- The adapter card listing in Device Manager indicates a problem.

To solve these problems, see the following sections.

Device Connected to Adapter Card Doesn't Work

If a device connected to an adapter card doesn't work, it could indicate a variety of issues. After verifying that the device works on another system, check the following:

Step 1.   Check Device Manager and make sure the adapter card is listed as working. Windows XP uses the yellow ! symbol to indicate devices that are not working, and the red X mark to indicate devices that have been disabled. Windows Vista and Windows 7 also use a yellow ! mark for non-working devices, but use a down-arrow icon for disabled devices. In some cases, an adapter card will work after you install a driver upgrade. To learn more about driver and firmware upgrades, see "Performing Driver and Firmware Upgrades," in this chapter. To learn more about using Device Manager, see Chapter 13.

Step 2.   Check the system BIOS setup to ensure that any onboard devices that might interfere with the adapter card's operation have been disabled.

Step 3.   Make sure the adapter card is properly secured in the expansion slot. Refer to Figure 3-33.

Step 4.   If the adapter card requires additional power, make sure an appropriate power cable is connected from the power supply to the card. Some IEEE-1394 and display adapter cards require additional power to operate properly.

Performing Driver and Firmware Upgrades

A device is only as good as the software that makes it work. Device drivers are found in two forms:

- Driver files
- Firmware

The drivers for most devices installed in Windows can be updated through the Update Driver wizard found in the properties sheet for the device in Device Manager. The wizard can locate updated drivers on the Internet or can be directed to install drivers from a location you provide, such as drivers on a floppy disk, CD, or a particular folder on a hard disk.

To learn more about using Device Manager, see Chapter 13.

Firmware, which is software stored on a flash memory chip, can also be upgraded, although most adapter cards don't use upgradeable firmware. If a firmware upgrade is available from the adapter card vendor, follow the vendor's instructions for installing the upgrade.

Some upgrades are installed by creating a special boot disk from the downloaded file provided by the vendor, while others are installed from within Windows. Regardless of how firmware is upgraded, it's very important to keep in mind that the upgrade process can take two or three minutes and must not be interrupted. If the firmware process is interrupted, the card will no longer function, and it must be repaired or replaced.

Exam Preparation Tasks

Review All the Key Topics

Review the most important topics in the chapter, noted with the key topics icon in the outer margin of the page. Table 3-8 lists a reference of these key topics and the page numbers on which each is found.

Table 3-8   Key Topics for Chapter 3

Key Topic Element	Description	Page Number
Figure 3-1	A typical ATX motherboard with support for NVIDIA's scalable link interface (SLI) technology.	47
Figure 3-5	A port cluster on a late ATX system model.	52
Figure 3-8	PCI slots compared to AGP slots.	56
Figure 3-9	PCI Express slots compared to a PCI slot.	57
Figures 3-10 and 3-11	AMR slots and risers.	59
Table 3-4	Technical Information About Mass Storage Interfaces.	60
Figure 3-12	PATA and SATA host adapters on a typical motherboard.	60
Figure 3-32	How to safely hold an adapter card.	102
Figure 3-33	Proper and improper adapter card installations.	103
Table 3-7	PC99 Color Coding for Audio Jacks.	104

Complete the Tables and Lists from Memory

Print a copy of Appendix B, "Memory Tables," (found on the CD), or at least the section for this chapter, and complete the tables and lists from memory. Appendix C, "Memory Tables Answer Key," also on the CD, includes completed tables and lists to check your work.

Definitions of Key Terms

Define the following key terms from this chapter, and check your answers in the glossary.

Motherboard, CPU, system bus, I/O bus, integrated circuits, PCI, AGP, PCI Express, PATA, SATA, SCSI

Troubleshooting Scenario

You have recently purchased a 500GB storage device. You plug it in to your system and nothing happens. What could be the cause of the problem, and how would you correct this?

Refer to Appendix A for the answer.

This chapter covers the following subjects:

- **Understanding BIOS, CMOS, and Firmware**—This section explains the motherboard's firmware, known as the BIOS. It also describes the relationship between the CMOS and the BIOS.

- **Configuring the System BIOS**—This section demonstrates how to access the BIOS and modify settings, for example, RAM, processor, and video settings.

- **Power-On Self-Test and Error Reporting**—This section describes the POST and audible and visible errors that the POST reports.

- **BIOS Updates**—In this section you will learn how to upgrade the BIOS through a process known as *flashing*.

This chapter covers a portion of the CompTIA A+ 220-701 objective 1.2 and CompTIA A+ 220-702 objective 1.2.

BIOS

The basic input/output system (BIOS) is an essential component of the motherboard. This boot firmware, also known as *System BIOS*, is the first code run by a computer when it is booted. It prepares the machine by testing it during boot-up and paves the way for the operating system to start. It tests and initializes components such as the processor, RAM, video card, magnetic disks, and optical disks. If any errors occur, the BIOS will report them as part of the testing stage, known as the power-on self test (POST). The BIOS resides on a ROM chip and stores a setup program that you can access when the computer first boots up. From this program, a user can change settings in the BIOS and upgrade the BIOS as well. Within this chapter you will find out about how the BIOS, CMOS, and batteries on the motherboard interact, and will learn how to configure and upgrade the BIOS.

"Do I Know This Already?" Quiz

The "Do I Know This Already?" quiz allows you to assess whether you should read this entire chapter or simply jump to the "Exam Preparation Tasks" section for review. If you are in doubt, read the entire chapter. Table 4-1 outlines the major headings in this chapter and the corresponding "Do I Know This Already?" quiz questions. You can find the answers in Appendix A, "Answers to the 'Do I Know This Already?' Quizzes and Troubleshooting Scenarios."

Table 4-1 "Do I Know This Already?" Foundation Topics Section-to-Question Mapping

Foundations Topics Section	Questions Covered in This Section
Understanding BIOS, CMOS, and Firmware	1, 2
Configuring the System BIOS	3–10
Power-On Self-Test and Error Reporting	11, 12
BIOS Updates	13, 14

1. What is the CMOS memory used for?

    a.   Keeping the time

    b.   To store BIOS settings

    c.   To boot the computer

    d.   None of these options is correct

2. What happens when the CMOS battery fails?

    a.   All the CMOS configuration information is lost

    b.   The computer won't boot

    c.   The computer is destroyed

    d.   The motherboard is dead

3. To make changes to the default settings in the BIOS, what must you do at startup?

    a.   Press the F2 key

    b.   Press Enter

    c.   Press the F8 key

    d.   Hold down the shift key

4. What BIOS settings will allow you to automatically configure your system? (Choose all that apply.)

    a.   BIOS Defaults

    b.   Setup Defaults

    c.   Turbo

    d.   Function

5. Which of the following will not work when configuring or viewing BIOS settings?

    a.   Esc Key

    b.   Enter Key

    c.   The + key

    d.   The mouse

6. Of the following system information, which can be viewed in the BIOS? (Choose all that apply.)

a. Installed Memory (RAM)

b. BIOS Information

c. Processor Type

d. Processor Speed

e. L2 cache memory

f. Feature settings

7. What features can be found in the advanced BIOS settings? (Choose two.)

a. Enable quick boot

b. Change the clock

c. View information

d. Enable boot sector protection

8. In today's most recent systems, what common feature is used to help prevent excessive heat from damaging your computer?

a. Task Manager

b. System Monitor

c. Hardware Monitor

d. Drive Lock

9. Which of the following security features are included in most of the currently used BIOSs programs?

a. BIOS Password

b. Power on password

c. Chassis Intrusion

d. Boot sector protection

e. All these options are correct

10. What option would you use if you are in the BIOS of your computer and you want to exit without making any changes? (Choose all that apply.)

a. Save Configuration

b. Discard Changes

c. Hit the ESC key

d. Press F8 to return to desktop

11. When you start your computer, it performs an important test. What is this test known as?

   a.   CPU Processing

   b.   POST

   c.   A CMOS test

   d.   Hard drive test

12. What are BIOS beep codes used for? (Choose two.)

   a.   A fatal error

   b.   A system message

   c.   A serious error

   d.   A warning message

13. If you are installing a new drive in your computer and it is not recognized, what can you do to fix the problem?

   a.   Update the BIOS

   b.   Call the manufacturer of the new drive

   c.   Search for problems on the Internet

   d.   Refer to the information that came with the drive

14. What is the process called when upgrading the BIOS?

   a.   Putting a new BIOS chip on the motherboard

   b.   Removing the CMOS battery

   c.   Flashing the BIOS

   d.   Windows Update

Foundation Topics

Understanding BIOS, CMOS, and Firmware

You know what the CPU does—it does the "thinking" for the computer. But, how does the CPU "know" what kinds of drives are connected to the computer? What tells the CPU when the memory is ready to be read or written to? What turns on the USB ports or turns them off? The answer to all these questions is the BIOS. Next to the CPU, the BIOS chip is the most important chip found on the motherboard. Figure 4-1 illustrates the location of the BIOS chip on some typical systems.

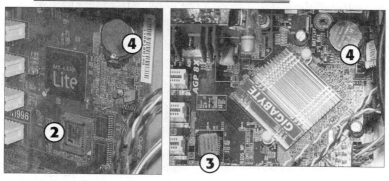

1. DIP-Type socketed BIOS chip
2. PLCC-type socketed BIOS chip
3. Surface-mounted BIOS chip
4. CR2032 CMOS batteries

Figure 4-1   BIOS chips and CMOS batteries on typical motherboards.

The BIOS is a complex piece of firmware ("software on a chip") that provides support for the following devices and features of your system:

■ Selection and configuration of storage devices connected to the motherboard's host adapters, such as hard drives, floppy drives, and CD-ROM drives

■ Configuration of main and cache memory

■ Configuration of built-in ports, such as PATA and SATA hard disk, floppy disk, serial, parallel, PS/2 mouse, USB, and IEEE-1394 ports

■ Configuration of integrated (built into the motherboard chipset) audio, network, and graphics features when present

- Selection and configuration of special motherboard features, such as memory error correction, antivirus protection, and fast memory access

- Support for different CPU types, speeds, and special features

- Support for advanced operating systems, including networks and plug-and-play versions of Windows

- Power management

- Hardware monitoring (processor temperature, voltage levels, and fan performance)

Without the BIOS, your computer would be a collection of metal and plastic parts that couldn't interact with one another or do much of anything but gather dust.

The BIOS also performs two other important tasks:

- It runs the power-on self test (POST) when the system is started.

- It establishes a list of locations that can be used by an operating system to boot the computer (hard disk, CD or DVD drive, USB drive, floppy drive, network) and turns over control of the system by using the Bootstrap loader after completing its startup tasks.

The BIOS doesn't do its job alone. It works with two other important components:

- CMOS memory

- Motherboard battery (also called the CMOS battery; refer to Figures 4-1 and 4-2)

In the following sections, you'll learn more about how these components work together to control system startup and onboard hardware.

NOTE   For much more information about BIOS functions, beep codes, and upgrades, see the BIOS chapter in the 19th edition of *Scott Mueller's Upgrading and Repairing PCs*.

Standard settings are configured by the motherboard or system vendor, but can be overridden by the user to enable the system to work with different types of hardware or to provide higher performance. CMOS memory, also referred to as nonvolatile memory, is used to store BIOS settings. CMOS memory should not be confused with system memory (RAM); CMOS memory is built into the motherboard and cannot be removed by the user.

The contents of CMOS memory are retained as long as a constant flow of DC current from a battery on the motherboard is provided. Some typical CMOS batteries are shown in Figure 4-2.

When the battery starts to fail, the clock will start to lose time. Complete battery failure causes the loss of all CMOS configuration information (such as drive types,

Figure 4-2   The CR2032 lithium watch battery (center) is the most common battery used to maintain CMOS settings in recent systems, but other batteries such as the Dallas Semiconductor DS12887A clock/battery chip (left) and the AA-size 3.6 volt (V) Eternacell (right) have also been used in older systems.

settings for onboard ports, CPU and memory speeds, and much more). When this takes place, the system cannot be used until you install a new battery and re-enter all CMOS configuration information by using the CMOS configuration program.

Because the battery that maintains settings can fail at any time, and viruses and power surges can also affect the CMOS configuration, you should record important information before it is lost.

TIP   At one time, many system BIOS programs supported printing BIOS screens to a printer connected to the parallel port. Those days are gone (in fact, so are parallel printers, as well as printer ports!). However, you can still document BIOS screens the easy way: use a digital camera set for macro (close-up) mode. That's the method I used to record BIOS screens for this chapter, and it works very well.

Configuring the System BIOS

The system BIOS has default settings provided by the system or motherboard maker, but as a system is built up with storage devices, memory modules, adapter cards, and other components, it is usually necessary to alter the standard settings.

To perform this task, the system assembler must use the BIOS setup program to make changes and save them to the CMOS. Originally, the BIOS setup program was run from a bootable floppy disk, but for many years most system BIOS chips have included the setup program.

Accessing the BIOS Setup Program

On most systems built since the late 1980s, the BIOS configuration program is stored in the BIOS chip itself. Just press the key or key combination displayed on-screen (or described in the manual) to get started.

Although these keystrokes vary from system to system, the most popular keys on current systems include the escape (Esc) key, the Delete (Del) key, the F1 key, the F2 key, the F10 key, and various combinations of Ctrl+Alt+ another specified key.

Most recent systems display the key(s) necessary to start the BIOS setup program at startup, as in Figure 4-3. However, if you don't know which key to press to start your computer's BIOS setup program, check the system or motherboard manual for the correct key(s).

1 Keystroke to start the BIOS setup program

Figure 4-3   The splash screens used by many recent systems display the keystrokes needed to start the BIOS setup program.

NOTE   Because the settings you make in the BIOS setup program are stored in the non-volatile CMOS, the settings are often called CMOS settings or BIOS settings.

In the following sections, we will review the typical setup process, looking at each screen of a typical desktop system with an Athlon 64 x2 processor.

Table 4-2   Common Keystrokes Used to Start the BIOS Setup Program

BIOS	Keystrokes	Notes
Phoenix BIOS	Ctrl+Alt+Esc	—
—	Ctrl+Alt+F1	—
—	Ctrl+Alt+S	—
—	Ctrl+Alt+Enter	—
—	Ctrl+Alt+F11	—
—	Ctrl+Alt+Ins	—
Award BIOS	Ctrl+Alt+Esc	—
—	Esc	—
—	Del	—
AMI BIOS	Del	—
IBM BIOS	Ctrl+Alt+Ins* F1	*Early notebook models; press when cursor is in upper-right corner of screen.
Compaq & HP BIOS	F10	Depending upon the model, the keystroke might load the Compaq or HP setup program from hard disk partition or start the setup program from the BIOS chip; press when cursor is in upper-right corner of screen.
Dell	F2	Keystroke actually loads Dell BIOS from hard disk partition.

CAUTION   BIOS programs vary widely, but the screens used in the following sections are representative of the options available on typical recent systems; your system might have similar options, but place the settings on different screens than those shown here. Laptop and corporate desktop systems generally offer fewer options than those shown here.

Be sure to consult the manual that came with your computer or motherboard before toying with the settings you find here. Monkeying with the settings can improve performance, but it can also wreak havoc on an otherwise healthy PC if you don't know what you're doing. Be warned!

BIOS Settings Overview

Table 4-3 provides a detailed discussion of the most important CMOS/BIOS settings. Use this table as a quick reference to the settings you need to make or verify in any system. Examples of these and other settings are provided in the following sections.

Table 4-3   Major CMOS/BIOS Settings

A+ Topic	Option	Setting	Notes
Advanced	CHIP (Chipset Configuration)	Set AGP card speed and memory speed to match device speed	Nonstandard AGP or memory settings could cause instability.
Boot Sequence	Boot Sequence	Adjust as desired	To boot from bootable Windows or diagnostic CDs or DVDs, place CD or DVD (optical) drive before hard drive; to boot from USB device, place USB device before hard drive.
Memory Configuration	Memory Configuration	By SPD	Provides stable operation using the settings stored in memory by the vendor.
		Manual settings (Frequency, CAS Latency [CL], Fast R-2-R turnaround, and so on)	Use for overclocking (running memory at faster than normal speeds) or to enable memory of different speeds to be used safely by selecting slower settings.
Processor	CPU Clock and Frequency	Set to correct settings for your processor (see Chapter 3, "Motherboards, Processors, and Adapter Cards")	Faster or higher settings overclock the system but could cause instability; some systems default to low values if system doesn't start properly.
	CPU/Memory Cache	Enabled	Disable only if you are running memory testing software.
Hardware Monitor	Hardware Monitor	Enable display for all fans plugged into the motherboard	Some systems, such as the example in this chapter, primarily report settings with very few options.
Integrated Peripherals	Onboard Audio, Modem, or Network	Varies	Enable if you don't use add-on cards for these functions; disable each setting before installing a replacement card.

Table 4-3 Major CMOS/BIOS Settings

A+ Topic	Option	Setting	Notes
	PS/2 Mouse	Varies with mouse type	Disable if you use USB mouse; some systems use a motherboard jumper.
	USB Legacy	Enable if USB keyboard is used	Enables USB keyboard to work outside of Windows.
	Serial Ports	Disable unused ports; use default settings for port you use	Avoid setting two serial ports to use the same IRQ.
	Parallel Port	Disable unused port; use EPP/ECP mode with default IRQ/DMA if parallel port or device is connected	Compatible with almost any recent parallel printer or device; be sure to use an IEEE-1284-compatible printer cable.
	USB Function	Enable	If motherboard supports USB 2.0 (Hi-Speed USB) ports, be sure to enable USB 2.0 function and load USB 2.0 drivers in Windows.
Misc	Keyboard	Numlock, auto-repeat rate/delay	Leave at defaults (NumLock On) unless keyboard has problems.
	PCI IRQs	Use Auto unless Windows Device Manager indicates conflict or Windows can't configure the device	Sound cards should be installed in a PCI slot that doesn't share IRQs with another slot.
	PCI/PnP IRQ, DMA, I/O Port Address Configuration (Exclusion)	Leave at defaults unless you have non-PnP ISA cards installed	No changes required on systems without ISA cards (motherboard-integrated serial, parallel, and PS/2 mouse ports are ISA but support PnP).
	Plug-and-Play OS	Enable for all except some Linux distributions, Windows NT, MS-DOS	When enabled, Windows configures devices.

Table 4-3   Major CMOS/BIOS Settings

A+ Topic	Option	Setting	Notes
	Primary VGA BIOS	Varies	Select the primary graphics card type (PCIe or AGP) unless you have PCIe or AGP and PCI graphics (video) cards installed that won't work unless PCI is set as primary.
	Shadowing	Varies	Enable shadowing for video BIOS; leave other shadowing disabled.
	Quiet Boot	Varies	Disable to display system configuration information at startup.
	Boot-Time Diagnostic Screen	Varies	Enable to display system configuration information at startup.
Power Manage-ment	Power Man-agement (Menu)	Enable unless you have problems with devices	Enable CPU fan settings to receive warnings of CPU fan failure.
	AC Pwr Loss Restart	Enable restart	Prevents system from staying down if power failure takes place.
	Wake on LAN (WOL)	Enable if you use WOL-compatible network card or modem	WOL-compatible cards use a small cable between the card and ; some integrated network ports also support WOL.
Security	User/ Power-On Password	Blocks system from starting if password not known	Enable for security but be sure to record password in a secure place.
	Setup Pass-word	Blocks access to setup if password not known	Both passwords can be cleared on both systems if CMOS RAM is cleared.
	Write-Protect Boot Sector	Varies	Enable for normal use, but disable when in-stalling drives or using a multiboot system; helps prevent accidental formatting, but might not stop third-party disk prep software from working.

Table 4-3 Major CMOS/BIOS Settings

A+ Topic	Option	Setting	Notes
	Boot Virus Detection (Antivirus Boot Sector)	Enable	Stops true infections but allows multiboot configuration.
Storage	Floppy Drive	Usually 3.5-inch 1.44MB	Set to actual drive type/capacity; some systems default to other sizes.
	PATA (IDE), SATA Drives	Varies	Auto-detects drive type and settings at startup time; select CD/DVD for CD or DVD drive; select None if drive not present or to disable an installed drive.
	LBA Mode	Enable	Disable would prevent MS-DOS or Windows from using more than 504MiB (528.5MB) of a PATA/IDE drive's capacity. Some older systems put this setting in various locations away from the standard setup screen.

Automatic Configuration of BIOS/CMOS Settings

Let's be frank—after reading Table 4-3, you might be wondering, "Isn't there an easier way to configure the BIOS?" Well, actually there is, in a way.

Many BIOS versions enable you to automatically configure your system with a choice of these options from the main menu:

- BIOS defaults (also referred to as Original/Fail-Safe on some systems)
- Setup defaults (also referred to as Optimal on some systems)
- Turbo

These options primarily deal with performance configuration settings in the BIOS, such as memory timings, memory cache, and the like. The settings used by each BIOS setup option are customized by the motherboard or system manufacturer.

Use BIOS defaults to troubleshoot the system because these settings are very conservative in memory timings and other options. Normally, the Setup defaults provide better performance. Turbo, if present, speeds the memory refresh rate used by the system. As you view the setup screens in this chapter, you'll note these options are listed.

CAUTION   If you use automatic setup after you make manual changes, all your manual changes will be overridden. Use one of these settings first (try Turbo or Setup Defaults) and then make any other changes you want.

With many recent systems, you can select Optimal or Setup defaults, save your changes, and exit, and the system will work acceptably. However, you might want more control over your system. In that case, look at the following screens and make the necessary changes.

Selecting Options

On typical systems, you set numerical settings, such as date and time, by scrolling through allowable values with keys such as + and - or page up/page down. However, you select settings with a limited range of options, such as enable/disable or choices from a menu, by pressing the Enter key on the keyboard and choosing the option desired from the available choices.

Main Menu

When you start the BIOS configuration program for your system, you might see a menu similar to the CMOS Setup Utility menu shown in Figure 4-4. From this menu, you can go to any menu, select default settings, save changes, or exit the CMOS setup menu.

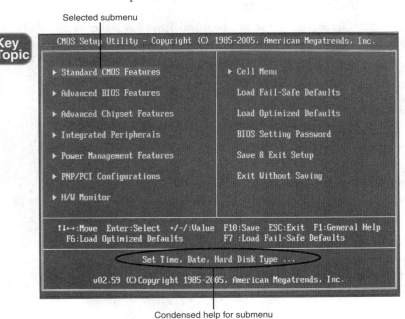

Figure 4-4   A typical CMOS Setup utility main menu.

TIP If you need to quickly find a particular BIOS setting and you don't have the manual for the system or the motherboard, visit the system or motherboard vendor's website and download the manual. In most cases, especially with a motherboard-specific manual, the BIOS screens are illustrated. Most vendors provide the manuals in Adobe Reader (PDF) format.

Standard Features/Settings

The Standard Features/Settings menu (Figure 4-5 shows an example) is typically used to configure the system's date and time as well as drives connected to PATA (ATA/IDE), SATA, and floppy drive interfaces on the motherboard.

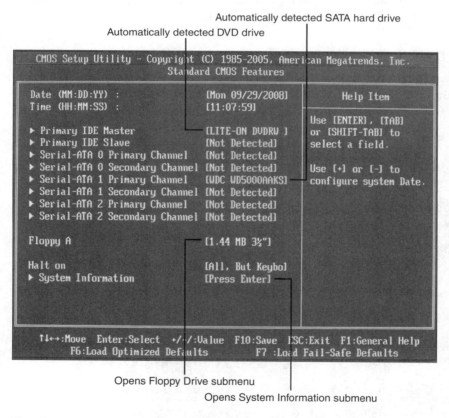

Figure 4-5 A typical CMOS Standard Features/Settings menu.

NOTE Some BIOS setup programs open this menu and provide access to other menus with a top-level menu bar.

PATA and SATA BIOS Configuration

Most recent systems automatically detect the drive connected to each PATA and SATA host adapter, as shown earlier in Figure 4-5. However, some systems might use manual entry of the correct settings instead. These are usually listed on the drive's faceplate or in the instruction manual. See Chapter 12, "Storage Devices," for details.

CAUTION   Although some users recommend that you configure the settings for hard drives to user-defined, which will list the exact settings for each hard drive, this can cause a major problem in case your BIOS settings are lost due to a virus, battery failure, or other causes. If you are not an experienced user, I highly recommend you let your computer do the work by using the Auto feature.

Floppy Drive BIOS Configuration

On systems that have an onboard floppy drive, the floppy drive must be selected manually if a different type of floppy drive is installed, or if the floppy drive is not present (see Figure 4-6).

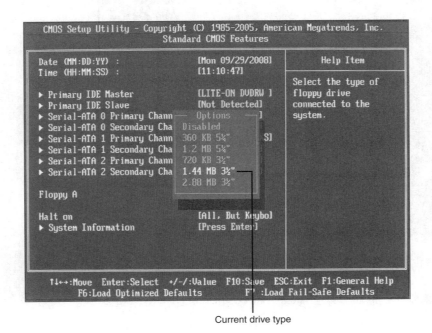

Current drive type

Figure 4-6   Viewing available floppy disk drive types.

TIP   If your system supports an internal floppy drive, but you don't use the drive, you might be able to disable the floppy controller. In such cases, you will no longer need to select Disabled from the menu shown in Figure 4-6.

System Information

Some systems display system information such as processor type, clock speed, cache memory size, installed memory (RAM), and BIOS information on the standard menu or a submenu, as shown in Figure 4-7. Use this information to help determine if a system needs a processor, memory, or BIOS update.

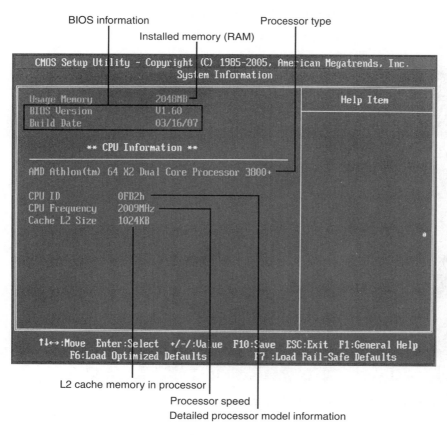

Figure 4-7   Viewing system information.

Advanced BIOS Settings/Features

The Advanced BIOS Settings/Features menu typically includes settings that control how the system boots, as shown in Figure 4-8. Enabling Quick Boot skips memory and drive tests to enable faster startup. Enabling Boot Sector Protection provides some protection against boot sector computer viruses. Enabling Boot Up Num-Lock LED turns on the keyboard's Num Lock option.

The Boot Sequence submenu shown in Figure 4-9 is used to adjust the order that drives are checked for bootable media. For everyday use, follow this order:

- First drive—Hard disk

- Second—Floppy (if present) or CD/DVD drive

- Third—CD/DVD drive or USB device

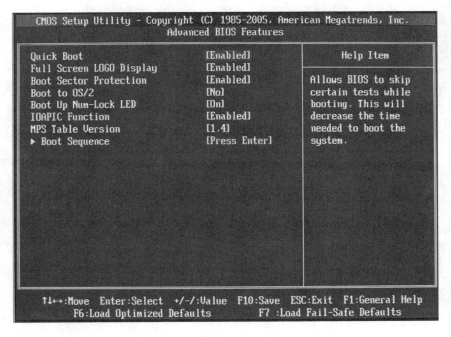

Figure 4-8 A typical Advanced BIOS Features menu.

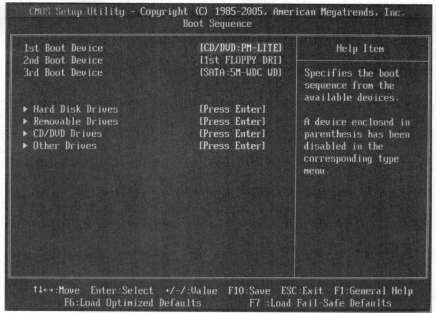

Figure 4-9 A typical Boot Sequence submenu configured to permit booting from a CD/DVD or floppy disk.

NOTE Even when the first boot drive is set up as CD/DVD, some discs will prompt the user to press a key in order to boot from the CD/DVD drive when a bootable disk is found. Otherwise, the system checks the next available device for boot files.

The order shown in Figure 4-9 is recommended for situations in which you need to boot from a CD/DVD or floppy disk drive (installing a new operating system or booting diagnostic software).

Note that if you have more than one drive in any category that you can select the boot drive from the submenus below the boot device listing.

Integrated Peripherals

The typical system today is loaded with onboard ports and features, and the Integrated Peripherals menu shown in Figure 4-10 and its submenus are used to enable, disable, and configure them.

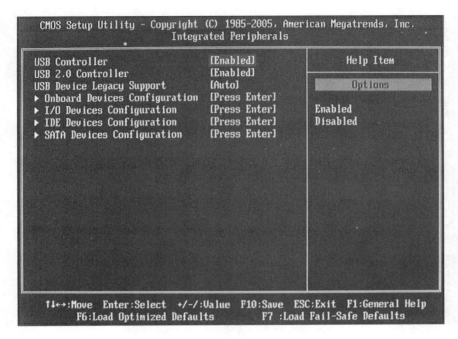

Figure 4-10   A typical Integrated Peripherals menu.

Note that most systems have separate settings for USB controller and USB 2.0 controller. If you connect a USB 2.0 device to a USB port on your system and you see a "This device can perform faster" error message in Windows, make sure the USB 2.0 controller or USB 2.0 mode is enabled. If USB 2.0 features are disabled in the BIOS, all of your system's USB ports will run in USB 1.1 mode only.

Onboard Devices

The Onboard Devices submenu on this system, shown in Figure 4-11, is used to enable or disable newer types of ports, such as IEEE-1394 (FireWire), audio, and Ethernet LAN ports (this system has two). The onboard LAN option ROM is disabled on this system, but should be enabled if you want to boot from an operating system that is stored on a network drive.

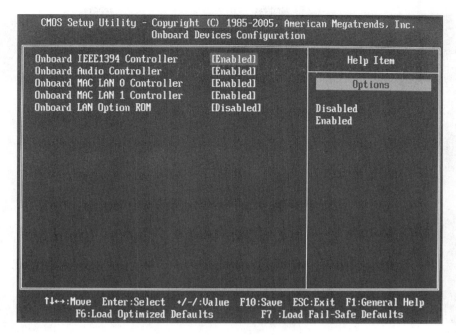

Figure 4-11   A typical Onboard Devices submenu.

I/O Devices

Most systems separate legacy ports such as floppy, serial (COM), and parallel port (LPT) into their own submenus, as in the I/O Devices submenu in Figure 4-12. Some systems might also have a setting for the PS/2 mouse port on this or another CMOS/BIOS menu.

The COM (serial) port is disabled on this system because there are no devices connected to it (most devices that formerly used COM ports, such as modems, pointing devices, and printers, now use USB ports; similarly, most mice that formerly used PS/2 ports now use USB ports). The parallel (LPT) port is enabled because it is used by a printer.

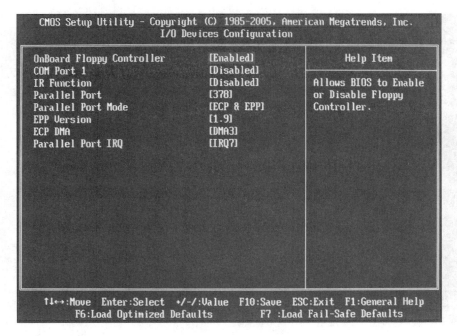

```
CMOS Setup Utility - Copyright (C) 1985-2005, American Megatrends, Inc.
                      I/O Devices Configuration

  OnBoard Floppy Controller      [Enabled]              Help Item
  COM Port 1                     [Disabled]
  IR Function                    [Disabled]       Allows BIOS to Enable
  Parallel Port                  [378]            or Disable Floppy
  Parallel Port Mode             [ECP & EPP]      Controller.
  EPP Version                    [1.9]
  ECP DMA                        [DMA3]
  Parallel Port IRQ              [IRQ7]




  ↑↓←→:Move  Enter:Select  +/-/:Value  F10:Save  ESC:Exit  F1:General Help
         F6:Load Optimized Defaults        F7 :Load Fail-Safe Defaults
```

Figure 4-12   A typical I/O Devices submenu.

NOTE   You should disable ports that are not used to make it easier for the system to assign other ports, such as the ones in the Onboard Devices menu, their own hardware resources.

To learn more about ECP, EPP, IRQ, and DMA settings for parallel ports, see Chapter 7, "I/O and Multimedia Ports and Devices."

PATA/IDE and SATA Configuration

The PATA/IDE and SATA configuration menus usually don't need adjustment, except when you need to create a redundant array of inexpensive drives (RAID) array from two or more drives. Figure 4-13 shows the SATA configuration menu, and Figure 4-14 shows the PATA/IDE configuration menu.

Use the SATA configuration menu to enable, disable, or specify how many SATA host adapters to make available; to enable or disable SATA RAID; and to configure SATA host adapters to run in compatible (emulating PATA) or native (AHCI) mode. AHCI permits hot-swapping of eSATA drives, and the system shown in Figure 4-13 does not list this option. To learn more about RAID configuration, see "Creating an ATA or SATA RAID Array," in Chapter 12.

Use the PATA configuration menu to enable or disable PATA/IDE host adapters and to enable or disable bus-mastering. Bus-mastering should be enabled, as disabling it

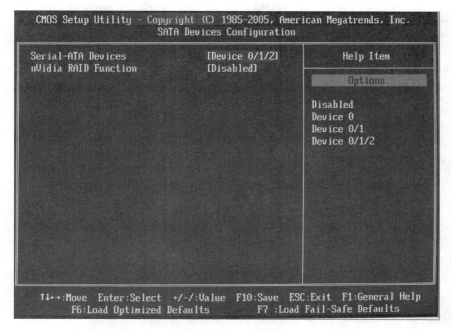

Figure 4-13 Typical SATA configuration menu.

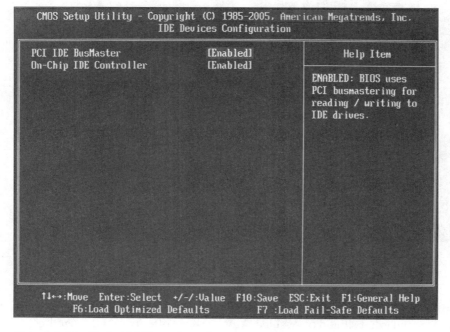

Figure 4-14 Typical PATA configuration menu.

causes drive access to be very slow. When bus-mastering (the default on most systems) is enabled, the operating system must load chipset-specific drivers to permit this option to work. Many systems (but not the one shown in Figure 4-14) have two or more PATA host adapters and support RAID functions with PATA drives.

TIP   To assure that the PATA/IDE bus-mastering feature works properly, install the most up-to-date drivers available for the motherboard. Check the motherboard or system vendor's website for the latest drivers for the version of Windows or other operating system in use.

Power Management

Although Windows includes power management features, the BIOS controls how any given system responds to standby or power-out conditions. Figure 4-15 illustrates a typical power management menu.

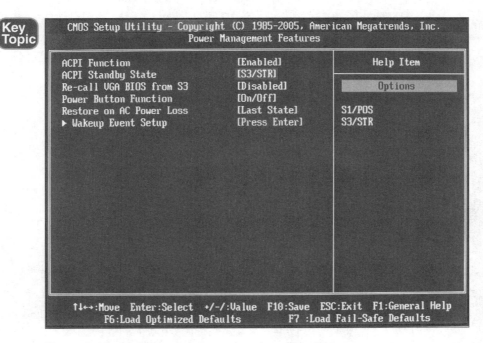

Figure 4-15   Typical power management configuration menu.

ACPI is the power management function used in modern systems, replacing the older APM standard; it should be enabled. Most systems offer two ACPI standby states: S1/POS (power on standby) and S3/STR (suspend to RAM). Use S3/STR whenever possible, as it uses much less power when the system is idle than S1/POS.

You can also configure your system power button, specify how to restart your system if AC power is lost, and specify how to wake up a system from standby, sleep, or hibernation modes as shown in Figure 4-16.

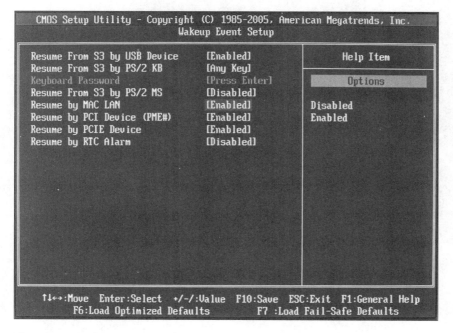

CMOS Setup Utility - Copyright (C) 1985-2005, American Megatrends, Inc.
Wakeup Event Setup

		Help Item
Resume From S3 by USB Device	[Enabled]	
Resume From S3 by PS/2 KB	[Any Key]	
Keyboard Password	[Press Enter]	Options
Resume From S3 by PS/2 MS	[Disabled]	
Resume by MAC LAN	[Enabled]	Disabled
Resume by PCI Device (PME#)	[Enabled]	Enabled
Resume by PCIE Device	[Enabled]	
Resume by RTC Alarm	[Disabled]	

↑↓↔:Move Enter:Select +/-/:Value F10:Save ESC:Exit F1:General Help
F6:Load Optimized Defaults   F7 :Load Fail-Safe Defaults

Figure 4-16 Configuring Wakeup Events.

PnP/PCI Configurations

The PnP/PCI Configuration dialog shown in Figure 4-17 is used to specify which graphics adapter is primary (PCI Express versus PCI or AGP versus PCI), the IRQ settings to use for PCI slots, the settings for the PCI latency timer, and which IRQ and DMA hardware resources to set aside for use by non-PnP devices.

Generally, the default settings do not need to be changed. However, if you need to make a PCI graphics adapter card—rather than a PCI Express or AGP card—the primary graphics adapter, be sure to select **PCI->PCIe** or **PCI->AGP** as appropriate.

NOTE   Most systems have options, as this one does, to reserve IRQ and DMA hardware resources for use by non-PnP adapters, but unless you are managing a system that has non-PnP cards installed (primarily ISA cards, which are now obsolete), there is no need to set aside those resources. If you do set them aside, you must determine the IRQs and DMAs used by these cards and reserve those settings; otherwise, non-PnP cards would not work.

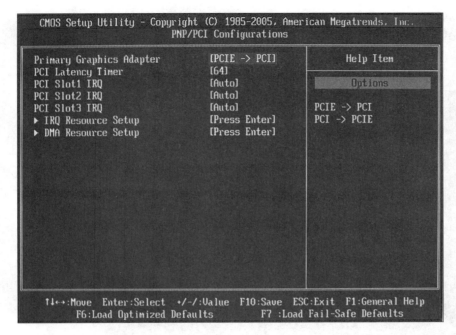

Figure 4-17   Configuring PnP/PCI settings.

Hardware Monitor

As hot as a small room containing a PC can get, it's a whole lot hotter inside the PC itself. Excessive heat is the enemy of system stability and shortens the life of your hardware. Adding fans can help, but if they fail, you have problems. See Chapter 5, "Power Supplies and System Cooling," for more information.

The Hardware Monitor screen (sometimes referred to as PC Health) is a common feature in most recent systems. It helps you make sure that your computer's temperature and voltage conditions are at safe levels for your computer (see Figure 4-18), and it sometimes also includes the Chassis Intrusion feature.

Although it is useful to view temperature and voltage settings in the BIOS setup program, temperature values are usually higher after the computer has been working for awhile (after you've booted to Windows and no longer have access to this screen). Generally, the major value of this screen is that its information can be detected by Windows-based motherboard or system monitoring programs like the one shown in Figure 4-19. These programs enable you to be warned immediately if there are any heat- or fan-related problems with your system.

NOTE   Overheating can be caused by improper airflow through the system, a very hot room, or by a power supply that has too low a wattage rating for the devices attached to the power supply (internally or externally).

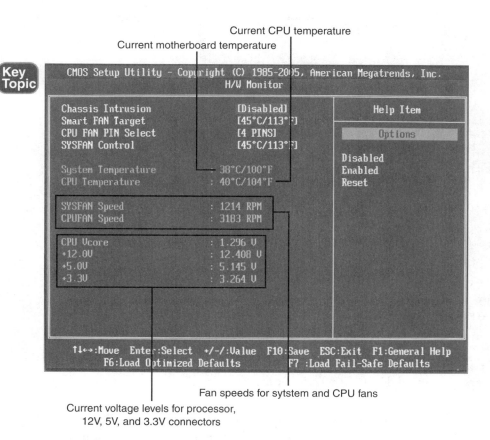

Figure 4-18   A typical Hardware Monitor screen.

Processor and Memory Configuration

Some older processors, such as the Athlon XP, do not automatically configure the system BIOS settings for processor clock multiplier and frequency, while newer processors typically do. However, the processor configuration dialog shown in Figure 4-20 is found in performance-oriented systems and displays current settings and enables the user to adjust these and other settings to overclock the system (running its components at faster than normal settings).

TIP   Some BIOS programs "hide" the processor dialog; you must press a keystroke combination (Control+F1 is a popular choice) to reveal it. BIOS programs in laptops and corporate systems typically don't include a processor configuration dialog.

Generally, you should not adjust processor or memory timings unless you are trying to overclock a system, or if the system does not properly configure your processor or memory.

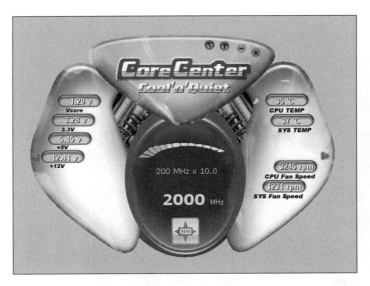

Figure 4-19   A typical Windows-based hardware monitoring program that displays information from the Hardware Monitor feature in the system BIOS.

CAUTION   If you make changes to processor or memory settings, and your system no longer boots or is unstable after booting, restart your system, restart the BIOS setup program, and load default or failsafe settings.

Figure 4-21 shows two views of a typical memory configuration screen. The default Auto MCT Timing Mode (Figure 4-21a) offers limited memory adjustments, while changing the mode to Manual (Figure 4-21b) enables many more settings and is useful primarily for overclocking and maximum-performance situations.

NOTE   Before making any changes to memory timing, you should find out what memory modules are installed in the system and check the technical specifications at the memory vendor's website.

TIP   It is not necessary to understand the intricacies of processor and memory overclocking for the A+ Certification exams. If you want to learn more about this topic, some useful websites include Overclockers (www.overclockers.com), Extreme Overclocking (www.extremeoverclocking.com), Maximum PC (www.maximumpc. com; www.maximumpc.com/forums/), and Tom's Hardware Guide (www. tomshardware.com).

Security Features

Security features of various types are scattered around the typical system BIOS dialogs. These include

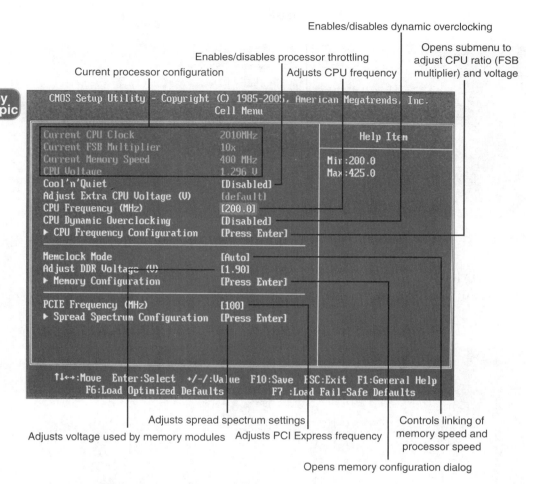

Figure 4-20 A typical processor configuration screen.

- **BIOS password**—BIOS Settings Password or Security dialogs

- **Power-on password**—Configured through the Security dialog

- **Chassis Intrusion**—Various locations

- **Boot sector protection**—Advanced BIOS Features dialog

For more information about other security features covered on the A+ Certification exams, see Chapter 10, "Security."

Exiting the BIOS and Saving/Discarding Changes

When you exit the BIOS setup program, you can elect to save configuration changes or discard changes. Choose the option to save changes (Figure 4-22a) if you made changes you want to keep. Choose the option to discard changes (Figure

A   B

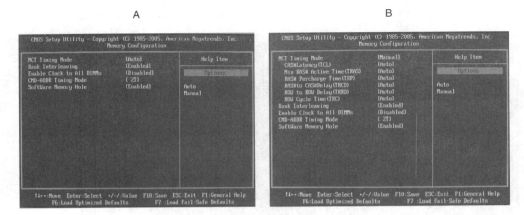

Figure 4-21   A typical memory configuration dialog in auto mode (a) and manual mode (b).

4-22b) if you were "just looking" and did not intend to make any changes. When you exit the BIOS setup program with either option, the system restarts.

A   B

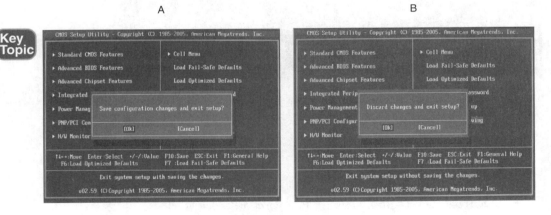

Figure 4-22   Typical exit dialogs: saving changes (a) and discarding changes (b).

Power-On Self-Test and Error Reporting

Every time you turn on your PC, the BIOS performs one of its most important jobs: the POST. The POST portion of the BIOS enables the BIOS to find and report errors in the computer's hardware.

The POST checks the following parts of the computer:

■   The CPU and the POST ROM portion of the BIOS

■   The system timer

- Video display (graphics) card

- Memory

- The keyboard

- The disk drives

You hope the POST always checks out OK. But what happens if the POST encounters a problem? The system will stop the boot process if it encounters a serious or fatal error (see the following "Beep Codes" section). During the POST process, the BIOS uses any one of several methods to report problems:

- Beep codes

- POST error messages (displayed on the monitor)

- POST (hex) error codes

The next sections describe each method in detail.

Beep Codes

Beep codes are used by most BIOS versions to indicate either a fatal error or a serious error. A *fatal error* is an error that is so serious that the computer cannot continue the boot process. A fatal error would include a problem with the CPU, the POST ROM, the system timer, or memory. The *serious error* that beep codes report is a problem with your video display card or circuit. Although systems can boot without video, seldom would you want to because you can't see what the system is doing.

Beep codes vary by the BIOS maker. Some companies, such as IBM, Acer, and Compaq, create their own BIOS chips and firmware. However, most other major brands of computers and virtually all "clones" use a BIOS made by one of the "Big Three" BIOS vendors: American Megatrends (AMI), Phoenix Technologies, and Award Software (now owned by Phoenix Technologies).

As you might expect, the beep codes and philosophies used by these three companies vary a great deal. AMI, for example, uses beep codes for more than ten fatal errors. It also uses eight beeps to indicate a defective or missing video card. Phoenix uses beep codes for both defects and normal procedures (but has no beep code for a video problem), and the Award BIOS has only a single beep code (one long, two short), indicating a problem with video.

TIP You can download and play actual audio samples of several beep codes by visiting the official website for this book and registering your book copy. Go to www.informit.com/title/9780789740472 to get started. Check them out!

Because beep codes do not report all possible problems during the startup process, you can't rely exclusively on beep codes to help you detect and solve system problems.

The most common beep codes you're likely to encounter are listed in Table 4-4.

Table 4-4   Common System Errors and Their Beep Codes

| Problem | Beep Codes by BIOS Version | | | |
	Phoenix BIOS	Award BIOS	AMI BIOS	IBM BIOS
Memory	Beep sequences: 1-3-4-1 1,3,4,3 1,4,1,1	Beeping (other than 2 long, 1 short)	1 or 3 or 11 beeps 1 long, 3 short beeps	(None)
Video	(none)	2 long, 1 short beep	8 beeps 1 long, 8 short beeps	1 long, 3 short beeps, or 1 beep
Processor or mother-board	Beep sequence: 1-2-2-3	(none)	5 beeps or 9 beeps	1 long, 1 short beep

NOTE   For additional beep codes, see the following resources:

- **AMI BIOS**—http://www.ami.com/support/bios.cfm
- **Phoenix BIOS**—http://www.phoenix.com/
- **IBM, Dell, Acer, other brands**—http://www.bioscentral.com

NOTE   Don't mix up your boops and beeps! Many systems play a single short boop (usually a bit different in tone than a beep) when the system boots successfully. This is normal.

POST Error Messages

Most BIOS versions do an excellent job of displaying POST error messages indicating what the problem is with the system. These messages can indicate problems with memory, keyboards, hard disk drives, and other components. Some systems document these messages in their manuals, or you can go to the BIOS vendors' website for more information.

NOTE   Keep in mind that the system almost always stops after the first error, so if a system has more than one serious or fatal error, the first problem will stop the boot process before the video card has been initialized to display error messages.

POST Hex Codes

There are beep codes and text messages to tell you that there's a problem with your computer, but there's also a third way your PC can let you know it needs help: by transmitting hexadecimal codes to an I/O port address (usually 80h) that indicate the progress of testing and booting. The hexadecimal codes output by the BIOS change rapidly during a normal startup process as different milestones in the boot process are reached. These codes provide vital clues about what has gone wrong when your system won't boot and you don't have a beep code or onscreen message to help you. It would be handy if systems included some way to view these codes, but most do not (a few systems include a four-LED header cable that displays boot progress, but this is only a partial solution for a system that won't start properly).

To monitor these codes, you need a POST card such as the one shown in Figure 4-23, available from a variety of vendors, including JDR Microdevices (www.jdr.com) and Ultra-X (www.ultra-x.com). These cards are available in versions that plug into either the now-obsolete ISA slot or into PCI or PCI Express x1 expansion slots. The simplest ones have a two-digit LED area that displays the hex codes, whereas more complicated (and expensive) models also have additional built-in tests. Some vendors also offer POST display devices that plug into parallel ports; these are useful for monitoring system startup without opening the case on both desktop and portable systems that include parallel ports.

The same hex code has different meanings to different BIOS versions. For example, **POST code** 31h means "display (video) memory read/write test" on an AMI BIOS, but it means "test base and extended memory" on the Award BIOS, and it is not used on Phoenix BIOS. As with other types of error messages, check your manual or the BIOS manufacturer's website for the meaning of any given code.

TIP   The worst time to learn how to interpret a POST card is when your system's sick. On the other hand, the best way to learn to use a POST card is to plug it into a healthy system and watch the codes change during a normal system startup. Typically, the codes change very quickly until the final code (often "FF") is reached and the system starts. On a defective system, the codes will pause or stop when a defective item on the system is tested. The cards don't need to be left in systems routinely.

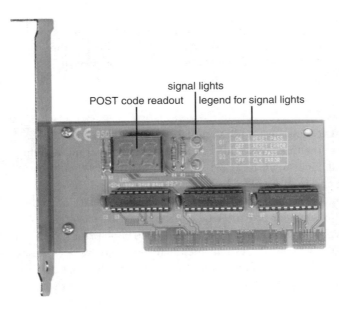

Figure 4-23   This POST card plugs into a PCI slot.

BIOS Updates

The BIOS chip can be regarded as the "glue" that binds the hardware to the operating system. If the BIOS doesn't recognize the operating system or the hardware it communicates with, you're sure to have problems.

Because the BIOS chip bridges hardware to the operating system, you will need to update the BIOS whenever your current BIOS version is unable to properly support

- New hardware, such as large SATA and PATA/IDE hard drives and different types of removable-storage drives

- Faster CPUs

- New operating systems and features

- New BIOS options

Although software drivers can be used as workarounds for hard drive BIOS limitations, a true BIOS update is the best solution for hard disk control, and the only solution if your BIOS can't handle new processors or operating systems.

If you keep your computer for more than a year or so, or if you decide to install a new processor, you might need to upgrade the BIOS. Back in the 1980s into the early 1990s, a BIOS update required a physical chip swap and, sometimes, reprogramming the chip with a device called an electrically erasable programmable read only memory (EEPROM) burner. If the replacement or reprogrammed BIOS chip was installed incorrectly into the socket, it could be destroyed.

Fortunately, since the mid-1990s, a BIOS update can now be performed with software. The Flash BIOS chips in use on practically every recent system contain a special type of memory that can be changed through a software download from the system or motherboard maker.

Although Flash BIOS updates are easier to perform than the older replace-the-chip style, you still need to be careful. An incomplete or incorrect BIOS update will prevent your system from being accessed. No BIOS, no boot! Regardless of the method, for maximum safety, I recommend the following initial steps:

Step 1.   Back up important data.

Step 2.   Record the current BIOS configuration, especially hard disk settings as discussed earlier in this chapter.

CAUTION   BIOS configuration information might need to be re-entered after a BIOS update, especially if you must install a different chip.

Flash BIOS Update

So, you've decided you need a Flash BIOS update. Where do you get it? Don't ask the BIOS manufacturers (Phoenix, AMI, and Award/Phoenix). They don't sell BIOS updates because their basic products are modified by motherboard and system vendors.

Here are the general steps for performing a Flash BIOS update:

Step 1.   For major brands of computers, go to the vendor's website and look for "downloads" or "tech support" links. The BIOS updates are listed by system model and by version; avoid beta (pre-release) versions.

TIP   If your system is a generic system (that is, it came with a "mainboard" or "motherboard" manual and other component manuals rather than a full system manual), you need to contact the motherboard maker. Some systems indicate the maker during bootup. Others display only a mysterious series of numbers. You can decode these numbers to get the motherboard's maker. See the following websites for details:

- Wim's BIOS page (www.wimsbios.com)

- eSupport (www.biosagentplus.com)

- American Megatrend's BIOS Support page (www.ami.com/support/bios.cfm)

You can also buy replacement flash BIOS code from eSupport if you are unable to get updated BIOS code from your system or motherboard vendor.

Step 2.   Download the correct BIOS update for your system or motherboard. For generic motherboards, Wim's BIOS page also has links to the motherboard vendors' websites.

Step 3.   You might also need to download a separate loader program, or the download might contain both the loader and the BIOS image. If the website has instructions posted, print or save them to a floppy disk for reference.

Step 4.   Next, install the BIOS update loader and BIOS image to a floppy disk. Follow the vendor's instructions.

NOTE   Some BIOS updates can be done within Windows XP and Vista. If this is the case, just double-click the BIOS executable to begin the upgrade; a system restart will be necessary.

Step 5.   After installation is complete, restart your system with the floppy disk containing the upgrade; make sure the floppy disk is the first item in the BIOS boot sequence. Press a key if necessary to start the upgrade process.

Some upgrades run automatically; others require that you choose the image from a menu, and still others require the actual filename of the BIOS. The BIOS update might also prompt you to save your current BIOS image to a floppy disk. Choose this option if possible so you have a copy of your current BIOS in case there's a problem.

Step 6.   After the update process starts, it takes about three minutes to rewrite the contents of the BIOS chip with the updated information.

CAUTION   While performing a Flash upgrade, make sure that you don't turn off the power to your PC and that you keep children or pets away from the computer to prevent an accidental shutdown (read: your four-year-old decides to unplug the computer). Wait for a message indicating the BIOS update has been completed before you even *think* about touching the computer. If the power goes out during the Flash update, the BIOS chip could be rendered useless.

Step 7.   Remove the floppy disk and restart the system to use your new BIOS features. Reconfigure the BIOS settings if necessary.

TIP   Some motherboards have a jumper on the motherboard that can be set to write-protect the Flash BIOS. Take a quick look at your documentation before you start the process and disable this jumper first. Then, re-enable the write-protect jumper after you're done with the upgrade.

RECOVERING FROM A FAILED BIOS UPDATE

In the event that the primary system BIOS is damaged, keep in mind that some motherboard vendors offer dual BIOS chips on some products. You can switch to the secondary BIOS if the primary BIOS stops working.

If you use the wrong Flash BIOS file to update your BIOS, or if the update process doesn't finish, your system can't start. You might need to contact the system or motherboard maker for service or purchase a replacement BIOS chip.

Some BIOSs contain a "mini-BIOS" that can be reinstalled from a reserved part of the chip. Systems with this feature have a jumper on the motherboard called the *Flash recovery jumper*.

To use this feature, download the correct Flash BIOS, make the floppy disk, and take it to the computer with the defective BIOS. Set the jumper to Recovery, insert the floppy disk, and rerun the setup process. Listen for beeps and watch for the drive light to run during this process, because the video won't work. Turn off the computer, reset the jumper to Normal, and restart the computer.

If the update can't be installed, your motherboard might have a jumper that write-protects the Flash BIOS. Check the manual to see if your system has this feature. To update a BIOS on a system with a write-protected jumper, you must follow these steps:

Step 1. Disable the write-protection.

Step 2. Perform the update.

Step 3. Re-enable the write-protection to keep unauthorized people from changing the BIOS.

BIOS Chip Replacement

On motherboards whose BIOS programs can't be upgraded with software, you might be able to purchase a replacement BIOS from vendors such as eSupport or BIOSMAN (www.biosman.com). Before you order a BIOS chip replacement, consider the following:

- BIOS chip upgrades cost about $30–40 each.

- Although the BIOS will be updated, the rest of the system might still be out of date. If your system is more than two years old and is not fast enough for your needs, you might be better off buying a replacement motherboard or system.

- A replacement BIOS enables you to improve system operation without reinstalling Windows.

If you still need to update the BIOS chip itself, first verify that the vendor has the correct BIOS chip replacement. The replacement needs to

- Plug into your current motherboard; as you saw in Figure 4-1, some BIOS chips are square, while others are rectangular.

- Support your motherboard/chipset.

- Provide the features you need (such as support for larger hard disks, particular processor speeds, and so on).

It might be a different brand of BIOS than your current BIOS. If so, make sure that you have recorded your hard drive information. You will need to re-enter this and other manually configured options into the new BIOS chip's setup program.

How does the BIOS vendor know what your system uses? The vendor will identify the BIOS chip you need by the motherboard ID information displayed at bootup. eSupport offers a free download utility to display this information for you. To re-place the chip, follow these steps:

Step 1.   Locate the BIOS chip on your motherboard after you open the case to perform the upgrade. It sometimes has a sticker listing the BIOS maker and model number. If not, go to Step 2.

Step 2.   Socketed BIOS chips might be in a DIP-type package (rectangular with legs on two sides) or in a PLCC (Plastic Leaded Chip Carrier; square with connectors on four sides). Refer to Figure 4-1. The vendor typically supplies a chip extraction tool to perform the removal.

Step 3.   Use the chip extraction tool to remove the BIOS chip. Don't try to remove the chip all at once; gently loosen each connected side until the chip can be lifted free.

Step 4.   Remove the existing BIOS chip carefully and put it on antistatic material in case you need to reuse it in that system.

Step 5.   Align the new BIOS chip with the socket. Note that a DIP-type BIOS can be installed backward (which will destroy the chip when power is turned on), so be sure to align the dimpled end of the chip with the cutout end of the socket. PLCC BIOS chips have one corner cut out.

Step 6.   Adjust the legs on a new DIP-type BIOS chip so it fits into the sockets, and press it down until the legs on both sides are inserted fully. Press the PLCC BIOS chip into the socket.

Step 7.   Double-check the alignment and leg positions on the BIOS chip before you start the system; if the chip is aligned with the wrong end of the socket, you'll destroy it when the power comes on.

Step 8.   Turn on the system, and use the new BIOS's keystroke(s) to start the setup program to re-enter any information. You might get a "CMOS" error at startup, which is normal with a new BIOS chip. After you re-enter the BIOS data from your printout and save the changes, the system will run without error messages.

NOTE   A "CMOS Checksum" error is normal after you replace the BIOS chip. However, after you run the BIOS setup program and save the settings, this error should go away. If you continue to see this error, test the motherboard battery. If the battery checks out okay, contact the motherboard or system vendor for help.

Exam Preparation Tasks

Review All the Key Topics

Review the most important topics in the chapter, noted with the key topics icon in the outer margin of the page. Table 4-4 lists a reference of these key topics and the page numbers on which each is found.

Table 4-5   Key Topics for Chapter 4

Key Topic Element	Description	Page Number
Figure 4-1	BIOS chip and CMOS battery on a typical motherboard.	115
Figure 4-2	The CR2032 lithium battery.	117
Table 4-2	Common Keystrokes Used to Start the BIOS Setup Program.	119
Figure 4-4	A typical CMOS Setup utility main menu.	124
Figures 4-9	A typical Boot Sequence submenu.	129
Figure 4-15	Typical power management configuration menu.	134
Figure 4-18	A typical Hardware Monitor screen.	137
Figure 4-20	A typical processor configuration screen.	139
Figure 4-22	Typical exit dialogs: saving changes (a) and discarding changes (b).	140
Table 4-4	Common System Errors and Their Beep Codes.	142

Complete the Tables and Lists from Memory

Print a copy of Appendix B, "Memory Tables," (found on the CD), or at least the section for this chapter, and complete the tables and lists from memory. Appendix C, "Memory Tables Answer Key," also on the CD, includes completed tables and lists to check your work.

Definitions of Key Terms

Define the following key terms from this chapter, and check your answers in the glossary.

BIOS, POST, CMOS

Troubleshooting Scenario

You have just started up your computer. It gives off a series of loud beeps and will not boot. What would you need to do to determine what the beeps mean and how to fix the problem?

Refer to Appendix A for the answer.

This chapter covers the following subjects:

- **Power Supplies**—This section describes the device that transforms AC power from the wall outlet into DC power that your computer can use. It also describes the various form factors and voltage levels, and how to protect your power supply.

- **Power Protection Types**—In this section you'll learn about devices that can protect your computer from over and under voltage issues. These include surge protectors, uninterruptible power supplies, and line conditioners.

- **Troubleshooting Power Problems**—This section demonstrates how to troubleshoot complete failure and intermittent power supply problems that you might encounter.

- **System Cooling**—This last section describes the various ways to cool your system, including fans and liquid cooling, and demonstrates how to monitor the system temperature.

This chapter covers a portion of CompTIA A+ 220-701 objectives 1.3 and 2.5 and CompTIA A+ 220-702 objectives 1.1, 1.2, and 1.4.

Clean, well-planned power is imperative, from the AC outlet to the electrical protection equipment to the power supply. Many of the issues that you will see concerning power are due to lack of protection or improper planning, and as such you will see several questions on the A+ exams regarding this subject.

In this chapter we'll delve into how power is conveyed to the computer, which power supply to select depending on your configuration and needs, how to install and troubleshoot power supplies, and how to cool the system.

CHAPTER 5

Power Supplies and System Cooling

"Do I Know This Already?" Quiz

The "Do I Know This Already?" quiz allows you to assess whether you should read this entire chapter or simply jump to the "Exam Preparation Tasks" section for review. If you are in doubt, read the entire chapter. Table 5-1 outlines the major headings in this chapter and the corresponding "Do I Know This Already?" quiz questions. You can find the answers in Appendix A, "Answers to the 'Do I Know This Already?' Quizzes and Troubleshooting Scenarios."

Table 5-1 "Do I Know This Already?" Foundation Topics Section-to-Question Mapping

Foundations Topics Section	Questions Covered in This Section
Power Supplies	1–8
Power Protection Types	9–11
Troubleshooting Power Problems	12
System Cooling	13, 14

1. Which of the following would you use to keep the power supply working properly? (Choose two.)

   a. Surge protector

   b. Extra power supply

   c. UPS units

   d. Multimeter

2. Power supplies are rated using which of the following units?

   a. Amps

   b. Volts

   c. Watts

   d. Output

3. Newer desktop tower-case computers' power supplies typically have which of the following power output ratings?

   a. 300 watts

   b. 400 watts

   c. 250 watts

   d. 500 watts or higher

4. Most power supplies in use today are designed to handle which two voltage ranges? (Choose two.)

   a. 115

   b. 300

   c. 230

   d. 450

5. Which of the following are causes of power supply overheating?

   a. Overloading the power supply

   b. Fan failure

   c. Dirt or dust

   d. All of these options are correct

6. How many pins are used for the main power connection by recent ATX/BTX motherboards with ATX12V 2.2 power supplies?

   a. 24

   b. 48

   c. 32

   d. 16

7. Which of the following steps would you use to remove a power supply?

   a. Shut down the computer. If the power supply has an on-off switch, turn it off as well

   b. Disconnect the AC power cord from the computer

   c. Disconnect power connections from the motherboard, hard drives, and optical drives

   d. All of these options are correct

8. To avoid power supply hazards you must never do which of the following? (Choose two.)

    a. Disassemble the power supply

    b. Put metal tools through the openings

    c. Switch the voltage to 220

    d. Put a smaller power supply in the computer

9. What device provides emergency power to a computer in case of a complete power failure?

    a. UTP

    b. UPS

    c. Power strip

    d. Surge protector

10. What is the minimum time recommendation for a UPS to supply power for an individual workstation?

    a. 30 minutes

    b. 45 minutes

    c. 1 hour

    d. 15 minutes

11. What is the major difference between a UPS and an SPS? (Choose all that apply.)

    a. The battery is only used when the AC power fails

    b. They are on all the time

    c. A momentary gap in power occurs between loss of AC power

    d. They are far less expensive

12. If a system is dead and gives no signs of life when you turn on the computer, which of the following might be the cause? (Choose all that apply.)

    a. Defects in AC power to the system

    b. Power supply failure or misconfiguration

    c. Temporary short circuits in internal or external components

    d. Power button or other component failure

13. All processors require a finned metal device to help with cooling. What is this device called? (Choose two.)

    a. Passive heat sink

    b. Thermal compound

    c. Active heat sink

    d. Chassis heat sink

14. What is the purpose of thermal compound?

    a. Provides the best possible thermal transfer between a component and its heat sink

    b. Provides the best possible thermal transfer between a component's heat sink and its fan

    c. To negate the effects of thermal contraction and expansion in adapter cards

    d. Provides the best possible thermal transfer between the northbridge and its fan

Foundation Topics

Power Supplies

Power issues are largely ignored by most computer users, but a properly working power supply is the foundation to correct operation of the system. When the power supply stops working, the computer stops working, and when a power supply stops functioning properly—even slightly—all sorts of computer problems can take place. From unexpected system reboots to data corruption, from unrecognized bus-powered USB devices to system overheating, a bad power supply is bad news. The power supply is vital to the health of the computer. So, if your computer is acting "sick," you should test the power supply to see if it's the cause. To keep the power supply working properly, use surge suppression and battery backup (UPS) units.

The power supply is really misnamed: It is actually a power converter that changes high-voltage alternating current (AC) to low-voltage direct current (DC). There are lots of wire coils and other components inside the power supply that do the work, and during the conversion process, a great deal of heat is produced. Most power supplies include one or two fans to dissipate the heat created by the operation of the power supply; however, a few power supplies designed for silent operation use passive heat sink technology instead of fans. On power supplies that include fans, fans also help to cool the rest of the computer. Figure 5-1 shows a typical desktop computer's power supply.

Power Supply Ratings

Power supply capacity is rated in watts, and the more watts a power supply provides, the more devices it can safely power.

You can use the label attached to the power supply, shown in Figure 5-2, to determine its wattage rating and see important safety reminders.

NOTE   The power supply shown in Figure 5-2 is a so-called "split rail" design with two separate 12V outputs ($+12V_1$ and $+12V_2$). This type of design is frequently used today to provide separate 12V power sources for processors (which reduce 12V power to the power level needed) and other devices such as PCI Express video cards, fans, and drive). Add the values together to get the total 12V output in amps (36A).

Figure 5-1 A typical ATX power supply.

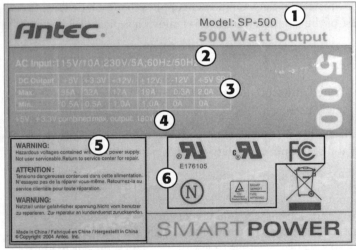

1. Power supply rating
2. AC input voltage levels
3. DC output levels by type
4. 3.3V and 5V output and peak output
5. Hazard warnings
6. Product certifications

Figure 5-2 A typical power supply label.

How can you tell if a power supply meets minimum safety standards? Look for the appropriate safety certification mark for your country or locale. For example, in the U.S. and Canada, the backward UR logo is used to indicate the power supply has the UL and UL Canada safety certifications as a component (the familiar circled UL logo is used for finished products only).

CAUTION   Power supplies that do not bear the UL or other certification marks should not be used, as their safety is unknown. For a visual guide to electrical and other safety certification marks in use around the world, visit the Standard Certification Marks page at www.technick.net/public/code/cp_dpage.php?aiocp_dp=guide_safetymarks.

Typically, power supplies in recent tower-case (upright case) machines use 500-watt or larger power supplies, reflecting the greater number of drives and cards that can be installed in these computers. Power supplies used in smaller desktop computers have typical ratings of around 300 to 400 watts. The power supply rating is found on the top of the power supply, along with safety rating information and amperage levels produced by the power supply's different DC outputs.

What happens if you connect devices that require more wattage than a power supply can provide? This is a big problem called an *overload*. An overloaded power supply has two major symptoms:

■ Overheating

■ Spontaneous rebooting (cold boot with memory test) due to incorrect voltage on the Power Good line running from the power supply to the motherboard

Here's a good rule of thumb: If your system starts spontaneously rebooting, replace the power supply as soon as possible. However, power supply overheating can have multiple causes; follow the steps listed in the section "Causes and Cures of Power Supply Overheating," later in this chapter, before replacing an overheated power supply.

To determine whether Power Good or other motherboard voltage levels are within limits, perform the measurements listed in the section "Determining Power Supply DC Voltage Levels" later in this chapter.

Multivoltage Power Supplies

Most power supplies are designed to handle two different voltage ranges:

■ 110–120V/60Hz

■ 220–240V/50Hz

Standard North American power is now 115–120V/60Hz-cycle AC (the previous standard was 110V). The power used in European and Asian countries is typically 230–240V/50Hz AC (previously 220V). Power supplies typically have a slider switch with two markings: 115 (for North American 110–120V/60HzAC) and 230 (for European and Asian 220–240V/50Hz AC). Figure 5-3 shows a slider switch set for correct North American voltage. If a power supply is set to the wrong input voltage, the system will not work. Setting a power supply for 230V with 110–120V current is harmless; however, feeding 220–240V into a power supply set for 115V will destroy the power supply.

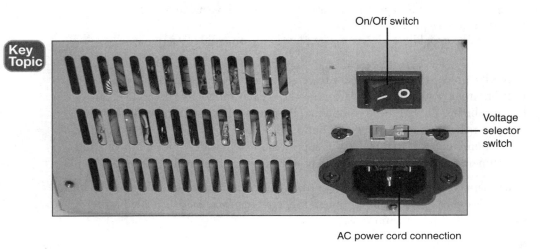

Figure 5-3   A typical power supply's sliding voltage switch set for correct North American voltage (115V). Slide it to 230V for use in Europe and Asia.

NOTE   Note that some power supplies for desktop and notebook computers can automatically determine the correct voltage level and cycle rate. These are referred to as *autoswitching power supplies*, and lack the voltage/cycle selection switch shown in Figure 5-3.

The on/off switch shown in Figure 5-3 controls the flow of current into the power supply. It is not the system power switch, which is located on the front of most recent systems and is connected to the motherboard. When you press the system power switch, the motherboard signals the power supply to provide power.

CAUTION   Unless the power supply is disconnected from AC current or is turned off, a small amount of power can still be flowing through the system, even when it is not running. Do not install or remove components or perform other types of service to the inside of a PC unless you disconnect the AC power cord or turn off the power supply. Wait a few seconds afterward to assure that the power is completely off. Some desktop motherboards have indicator lights that turn off when the power has completely drained from the system.

Causes and Cures of Power Supply Overheating

Got an overheated power supply? Not sure? If you touch the power supply case and it's too hot to touch, it's overheated. Overheated power supplies can cause system failure and possible component damage, due to any of the following causes:

- Overloading

- Fan failure

- Inadequate air flow outside the system

- Inadequate air flow inside the system

- Dirt and dust

Use the following sections to figure out the possible effects of these problems in any given situation.

Overloading

An overloaded power supply is caused by connecting devices that draw more power (in watts) than the power supply is designed to handle. As you add more card-based devices to expansion slots and install more internal drives in a system, the odds of having an overloaded power supply increase.

If a power supply fails or overheats, check the causes listed in the following sections before determining whether you should replace the power supply. If you determine that you should replace the power supply, purchase a unit that has a higher wattage rating.

Use the following methods to determine the wattage rating needed for a replacement power supply:

- Whip out your calculator and add up the wattage ratings for everything connected to your computer that uses the power supply, including the motherboard, processor, memory, cards, drives, and bus-powered USB devices. If the total wattage used exceeds 70% of the wattage rating of your power supply, you should upgrade to a larger power supply. Check the vendor spec sheets for wattage ratings.

- If you have amperage ratings instead of wattage ratings, multiply the amperage by the volts to determine wattage and then start adding. If a device uses two or three different voltage levels, be sure to carry out this calculation for each voltage level, and add up the figures to determine the wattage requirement for the device. Table 5-2 provides calculations for typical AMD and Intel–based systems.

Table 5-2   Calculating Power Supply Requirements

MicroATX system with integrated video		Full-size ATX system with SLI (dual graphics cards)	
Components	**Wattage**	**Components**	**Wattage**
AMD Athlon 64 X2 4000+ Socket AM2	65	Intel Core 2 Quad Q6700 Socket 775	95
microATX motherboard	60	ATX motherboard	100
2GB RAM	30	3GB RAM	45
Rewritable DVD drive	30	Rewritable DVD drive	30
SATA hard disk	20	SATA hard disk	20
Two case fans	6	Three case fans	9
CPU fan	3	CPU fan	3
Integrated Video	—	High-end SLI video cards (2)	210 (105×2)
Estimated Wattage	214	Estimated Wattage	472
Minimum Power Supply Size Recommended (70% efficiency assumed)	300	Minimum Power Supply Size Recommended (70% efficiency assumed)	700

■ Use an interactive power supply sizing tool such as the calculators provided by eXtreme Outervision (www.extreme.outervision.com) or PC Power and Cooling (www.pcpower.com).

Note that the recommended power supply shown for each example in Table 5-2 is considerably larger than the estimated wattage rating to make up for the reduced efficiency of some power supplies.

NOTE   The 80 PLUS certification standard is an industry standard for evaluating power supply efficiency. 80 PLUS certified power supplies achieve 80% efficiency at up to 100% of rated load. Higher standards (80 PLUS Bronze, Silver, Gold, and Platinum) achieve up to 89% efficiency at 100% of rated load on 115V power and up to 91% on 230V power. For more information, see the Ecos Plug Load Solutions website at http://www.plugloadsolutions.com/.

Fan Failure

The fan inside the power supply cools it and is partly responsible for cooling the rest of the computer. If the fan fails, the power supply and the entire computer are at risk of damage. The fan also might stop turning as a symptom of other power problems.

A fan that stops immediately after the power comes on usually indicates incorrect input voltage or a short circuit. If you turn off the system and turn it back on again under these conditions, the fan will stop each time.

To determine whether the fan has failed, listen to the unit; it should make less noise if the fan has failed. You can also see the fan blades spinning rapidly on a power supply fan that is working correctly. If the blades aren't turning, the fan has failed or is too clogged with dust to turn.

NOTE   Note that if the fan has failed because of a short circuit or incorrect input voltage, you will not see any picture onscreen because the system cannot operate.

If the system starts normally but the fan stops turning later, this indicates a true fan failure instead of a power problem.

CAUTION   Should you try to replace a standard power supply fan? No. Because the power supply is a sealed unit, you would need to remove the cover from most power supplies to gain access to the fan. The capacitors inside a power supply retain potentially *lethal* electrical charges. Instead, scrap the power supply and replace it with a higher-rated unit. See the section "Removing and Replacing the Power Supply" later in this chapter.

Inadequate Air Flow Outside the System

The power supply's capability to cool the system depends in part on free airflow space outside the system. If the computer is kept in a confined area (such as a closet or security cabinet) without adequate ventilation, power supply failures due to overheating are likely.

Even systems in ordinary office environments can have airflow problems; make sure that several inches of free air space exist behind the fan output for any computer.

Inadequate Air Flow Inside the System

As you have seen in previous chapters, the interior of the typical computer is a messy place. Wide ribbon cables used for hard and floppy drives, drive power cables, and expansion cards create small air dams that block air flow between the heat sources—such as the motherboard, CPU, drives, and memory modules—and the fan in the power supply.

You can do the following to improve air flow inside the computer:

- Use cable ties to secure excess ribbon cable and power connectors out of the way of the fans and the power supply.

- Replace any missing slot covers.

- Make sure that auxiliary case fans and CPU fans are working correctly.

- Use Serial ATA drives in place of conventional ATA hard drives (assuming the system supports Serial ATA); Serial ATA drives use very narrow data cables.

For more information about cooling issues, see the section "System Cooling," later in this chapter for details.

Dirt and Dust

Most power supplies, except for a few of the early ATX power supplies, use a cooling technique called *negative pressure*; in other words, the power supply fan works like a weak vacuum cleaner, pulling air through vents in the case, past the components, and out through the fan. Vacuum cleaners are used to remove dust, dirt, cat hairs, and so on from living rooms and offices, and even the power supply's weak impression of a vacuum cleaner works the same way.

When you open a system for any kind of maintenance, look for the following:

- Dirt, dust, hair, and gunk clogging the case vents

- A thin layer of dust on the motherboard and expansion slots

- Dirt and dust on the power supply vent and fans

Yuck! You never know what you'll find inside of a PC that hasn't been cleaned out for a year or two. So how can you get rid of the dust and gunk? You can use either a vacuum cleaner specially designed for computer use or compressed air to remove dirt and dust from inside the system. If you use compressed air, be sure to spread newspapers around the system to catch the dirt and dust. If possible, remove the computer from the computer room so the dust is not spread to other equipment.

Replacing Power Supply Form Factors and Connectors

When you shop for a power supply, you also need to make sure it can connect to your motherboard. There are two major types of power connectors on motherboards:

- 20-pin, used by older motherboards in the ATX family

- 24-pin, used by recent ATX/BTX motherboards requiring the ATX12V 2.x power supply standard

Some high-wattage power supplies with 20-pin connectors might also include a 20-pin to 24-pin adapter.

Some motherboards use power supplies that feature several additional connectors to supply added power, as follows:

- The four-wire ATX12V connector provides additional 12V power to the motherboard; this connector is sometimes referred to as a "P4" or "Pentium 4" connector.

- Many recent high-end power supplies use the eight-wire EPS12V connector instead of the ATX12V power connector.

- Some older motherboards use a six-wire AUX connector to provide additional power.

Figure 5-4 illustrates most of these connectors.

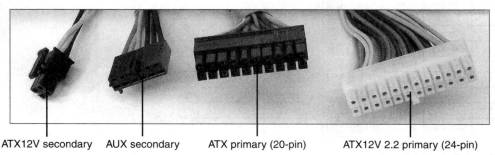

ATX12V secondary   AUX secondary   ATX primary (20-pin)   ATX12V 2.2 primary (24-pin)

Figure 5-4   Typical power supply connectors to the motherboard.

Figure 5-5 lists the pinouts for the 20-pin and 24-pin ATX power supply connectors shown in Figure 5-4.

ATX 20-pin power connector (top view)

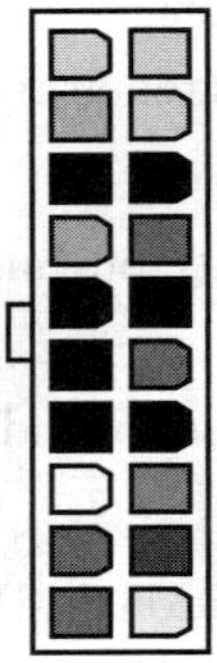

11	+3.3v	Orange		Orange	+3.3v	1
12	-12v	Blue		Orange	+3.3v	2
13	Ground	Black		Black	Ground	3
14	PS-On	Green		Red	+5v	4
15	Ground	Black		Black	Ground	5
16	Ground	Black		Red	+5v	6
17	Ground	Black		Black	Ground	7
18	-5v	White		Gray	Power Good	8
19	+5v	Red		Purple	+5v Standby	9
20	+5v	Red		Yellow	+12v	10

ATX 12V version 2.x 24-pin power connector (top view)

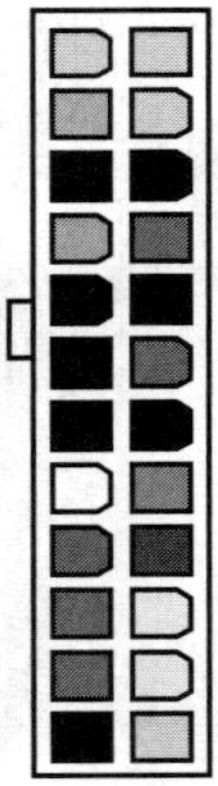

13	+3.3v	Orange		Orange	+3.3v	1
14	-12v	Blue		Orange	+3.3v	2
15	Ground	Black		Black	Ground	3
16	PS-On	Green		Red	+5v	4
17	Ground	Black		Black	Ground	5
18	Ground	Black		Red	+5v	6
19	Ground	Black		Black	Ground	7
20	NC	White		Gray	Power Good	8
21	+5v	Red		Purple	+5v Standby	9
22	+5v	Red		Yellow	+12v	10
23	+5v	Red		Yellow	+12v	11
24	Ground	Black		Orange	+3.3v	12

Figure 5-5   Pinout for standard ATX 20-pin and 24-pin power connectors.

The power supply also powers various peripherals, such as the following:

- PATA hard disks, CD and DVD optical drives, and case fans that do not plug into the motherboard use a four-pin Molex power connector.

- 3.5-inch floppy drives use a reduced-size version of the Molex power supply connector.

- Serial ATA (SATA) hard disks use an L-shaped thinline power connector.

- High-performance PCI Express x16 video cards that require additional 12V power use a PCI Express six-pin power cable.

Figure 5-6 illustrates these connectors compared to the 20- and 24-pin ATX primary motherboard power connectors.

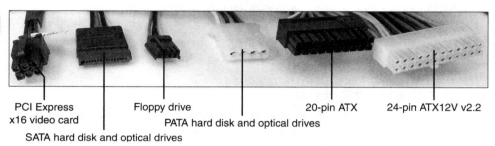

PCI Express   Floppy drive   20-pin ATX   24-pin ATX12V v2.2
x16 video card
              PATA hard disk and optical drives
SATA hard disk and optical drives

Figure 5-6   Typical peripheral power connectors.

If your power supply doesn't have enough connectors, you can add Y-splitters to divide one power lead into two, but these can short out and can also reduce your power supply's efficiency. You can also convert a standard Molex connector into an SATA or floppy drive power connector with the appropriate adapter.

CAUTION   Many recent and older Dell computers use proprietary versions of the 20-pin or 24-pin ATX power supply connectors. Dell's versions use a different pinout that routes voltages to different wires than in standard power supplies. Consequently, if you plug a standard power supply into a Dell PC that uses the proprietary version, or use a regular motherboard as an upgrade for a model that has the proprietary power supply, stand by for smoke and fire! To determine if a particular Dell computer model requires a proprietary power supply, check the PC Power and Cooling PSU recommendation for your Dell system at http://www.pcpower.com/Dell.html.

If your wattage calculations or your tests (covered later in this chapter) agree that it's time to replace the power supply, make sure the replacement will meet the following criteria:

- Have the same power supply connectors and the same pinout as the original.

- Have the same form factor (shape, size, and switch location).

- Have the same or higher wattage rating; a higher wattage rating is highly desirable.

■   Support any special features required by your CPU, video card, and motherboard, such as SLI support (support for PCI Express 6-pin connectors to
power dual high-performance PCI Express x16 video cards), high levels of
+12V power, and so on.

TIP   To assure form factor connector compatibility, consider removing the old
power supply and taking it with you if you plan to buy a replacement at retail. If
you are buying a replacement online, measure the dimensions of your existing
power supply to assure that a new one will fit properly in the system.

Removing and Replacing the Power Supply

If you have done your homework (checked compatibility and size and dug up the
case-opening instructions for your PC), installing a new power supply is one of the
easier repairs to make. You don't need to fiddle with driver CDs or Windows Update to get the new one working. But, you do need to be fairly handy with a screwdriver or nut driver.

Typical power supplies are held in place by several screws that attach the power
supply to the rear panel of the computer. The power supply also is supported by a
shelf inside the case, and screws can secure the power supply to that shelf. To remove a power supply, follow these steps:

Step 1.   Shut down the computer. If the power supply has an on-off switch, turn
it off as well.

Step 2.   Disconnect the AC power cord from the computer.

Step 3.   Open the case to expose the power supply, which might be as simple as
removing the cover on a desktop unit, or as involved as removing both
side panels, front bezel, and case lid on a tower PC. Consult the documentation that came with your computer to determine how to expose
the power supply for removal.

Step 4.   Disconnect the power supply from the motherboard (refer to Figure 5-
7). The catch securing the power supply connector must be released to
permit the connector to be removed.

Step 5.   Disconnect the power supply from all drives.

Step 6.   Disconnect the power supply from the case and CPU fans.

Step 7.   Remove the power supply screws from the rear of the computer case
(see Figure 5-8).

Step 8.   Remove any screws holding the power supply in place inside the case.
(Your PC might not use these additional screws.)

Step 9.   Disconnect the power supply switch from the case front (if present).

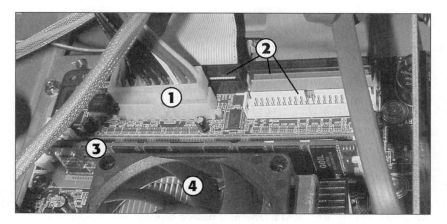

1. Catch securing power supply connector
2. PATA/IDE drive connectors
3. Memory module
4. Active heat sink for processor

Figure 5-7   Disconnecting the power supply from the motherboard.

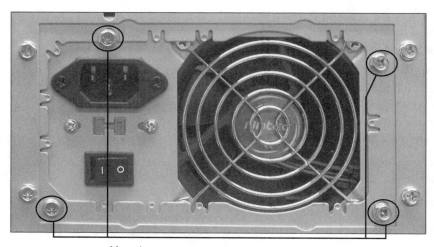

Mounting screws

Figure 5-8   Removing the mounting screws from a typical power supply.

Step 10.   Lift or slide the power supply from the case.

Before installing the replacement power supply, compare it to the original, making sure the form factor, motherboard power connectors, and switch position match the original.

To install the replacement power supply, follow these steps:

Step 1.   Lower the power supply into the case.

Step 2.   Attach the power supply to the shelf with screws if required.

Step 3.   Attach the power supply to the rear of the computer case; line up the holes in the unit carefully with the holes in the outside of the case.

Step 4.   Connect the power supply to the case, CPU fans, drives, and motherboard. Note that some power supplies provide a two-wire cable for use by motherboards that can monitor the power supply fan speed. Be sure to connect this cable as well as the main power cable and additional power cables as required.

Step 5.   Check the voltage setting on the power supply. Change it to the correct voltage for your location.

Step 6.   Attach the AC power cord to the new power supply.

Step 7.   Turn on the computer.

Step 8.   Boot the system normally to verify correct operation, and then run the normal shutdown procedure for the operating system. If necessary, turn off the system with the front power switch only.

Step 9.   Close the case and secure it.

Testing Power Supplies with a Multimeter

How can you find out that a defective power supply is really defective? How can you make sure that a cable has the right pinouts? Use a multimeter. A *multimeter* is one of the most flexible diagnostic tools around. It is covered in this chapter because of its usefulness in testing power supplies, but it also can be used to test coaxial, serial, and parallel cables, as well as fuses, resistors, and batteries.

Multimeters are designed to perform many different types of electrical tests, including the following:

- DC voltage and polarity
- AC voltage and polarity
- Resistance (Ohms)
- Diodes
- Continuity
- Amperage

All multimeters are equipped with red and black test leads. When used for voltage tests, the red is attached to the power source to be measured, and the black is attached to ground.

Multimeters use two different readout styles: digital and analog. Digital multimeters are usually *autoranging*, which means they automatically adjust to the correct range for the test selected and the voltage present. Analog multimeters, or non-autoranging digital meters, must be set manually to the correct range and can be damaged more easily by overvoltage. Figure 5-9 compares typical analog and digital multimeters.

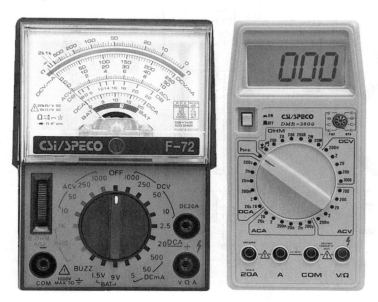

Figure 5-9   Typical analog (left) and digital (right) multimeters. Photos courtesy of Colacino Electric Supply (www.colacinoelectric.com/).

Multimeters are designed to perform tests in two ways: in series and in parallel. Most tests are performed in parallel mode, in which the multimeter is not part of the circuit but runs parallel to it. On the other hand, amperage tests require that the multimeter be part of the circuit, so these tests are performed in series mode. Many low-cost multimeters do not include the ammeter feature for testing amperage (current), but you might be able to add it as an option.

Figure 5-10 shows a typical parallel mode test (DC voltage for a motherboard CMOS battery) and the current (amperage) test, which is a serial-mode test.

Table 5-3 summarizes the tests you can perform with a multimeter.

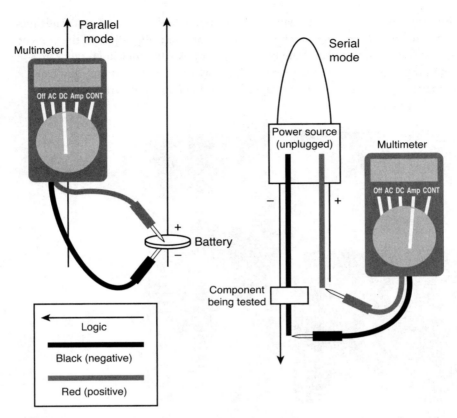

Figure 5-10   A parallel-mode (DC current) test setup (left) and an amperage (current) serial-mode test setup (right).

The following section covers the procedure for using a multimeter to diagnose a defective power supply.

Determining Power Supply DC Voltage Levels

You can use a multimeter to find out if a power supply is properly converting AC power to DC power. Here's how: Measure the DC power going from the power supply to the motherboard. A power supply that does not meet the measurement standards listed in Table 5-4 should be replaced.

You can take the voltage measurements directly from the power supply connection to the motherboard. Both 20-pin and 24-pin power connectors are designed to be back-probed as shown in Figure 5-11; you can run the red probe through the top of the power connector to take a reading (the black probe uses the power supply enclosure or metal case frame for ground).

Table 5-3 Using a Multimeter

Test to Perform	Multimeter Setting	Probe Positions	Procedure
AC voltage (wall outlet)	AC	Red to hot, black to ground.	Read voltage from meter; should be near 115V in North America
DC voltage (power supply outputs to motherboard, drives, batteries)	DC	Red to hot, black to ground (see next section for details).	Read voltage from meter; compare to default values
Continuity (cables, fuses)	CONT	Red to lead at one end of cable; black to corresponding lead at other end.	No CONT signal indicates bad cable or bad fuse
		For a straight-through cable, check the same pin at each end. For other types of cables, consult a cable pinout to select the correct leads.	Double-check leads and retest to be sure
Resistance (Ohms)	Ohms	Connect one lead to each end of resistor.	Check reading; compare to rating for resistor
			A fuse should have no resistance
Amperage (Ammeter)	Ammeter	Red probe to positive lead of circuit (power disconnected!); black lead to negative lead running through component to be tested.	Check reading; compare to rating for component tested

Table 5-4 Acceptable Voltage Levels

Rated DC Volts	Acceptable Range
+5.0	+4.8–5.2
-5.0	-4.8–5.2
-12.0	-11.4–12.6
+12.0	+11.4–12.6
+3.3	+3.14–3.5
Power Good	+3.0–6.0

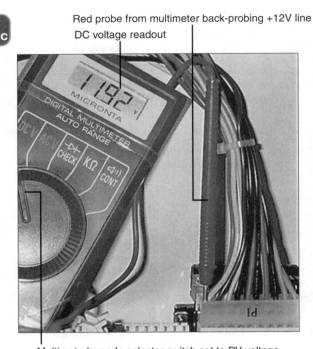

Red probe from multimeter back-probing +12V line

DC voltage readout

Multimeter's mode selector switch set to DV voltage

Figure 5-11   Testing the +12V line on an ATX power supply. The voltage level indicated (+11.92V) is well within limits.

The multimeter also can be used to check the Power Good or Power OK line by pushing the red lead through the open top of the power connector. See Table 5-4 for the acceptable voltage levels for each item.

If a power supply fails any of these measurements, replace it and retest the new unit.

Avoiding Power Supply Hazards

To avoid shock and fire hazards when working with power supplies, follow these important guidelines:

- **Never disassemble a power supply or push metal tools through the openings in the case**—Long after you shut off the system, the wire coils inside the power supply retain potentially fatal voltage levels. If you want to see the interior of a power supply safely, check the websites of leading power supply vendors such as PC Power and Cooling.

- **If you are replacing the power supply in a Dell desktop computer, determine whether the computer uses a standard ATX or Dell proprietary ATX power supply**—Many Dell computers built from September 1998 to the present use a nonstandard version of the ATX power supply with a different pinout for the power connector. Install a standard power supply on a system built to use a Dell proprietary model, or upgrade from a Dell motherboard that uses the Dell proprietary ATX design to a standard motherboard, and you can literally cause a power supply and system fire!

The proprietary Dell version of the 20-pin ATX connector has no 3.3V (orange) lines, and its Power Good (gray wire) line is pin 5, not pin 8 as with a standard ATX power supply. The 3.3V (orange) wires are routed to the 6-pin Dell proprietary auxiliary connector. The proprietary Dell version of the 24-pin ATX connector also uses pin 5 for Power Good, and provides 3.3V power (blue/white) through pins 11, 12, and 23, rather than through 1, 2, 12, and 13 as with a standard 24-pin ATX power supply. Make sure you buy a power supply made specifically for your Dell model.

- **Always use a properly wired and grounded outlet for your computer and its peripherals**—You can use a plug-in wiring tester to quickly determine if a three-prong outlet is properly wired; signal lights on the tester indicate the outlet's status (see Figure 5-12).

Power Protection Types

How well can a power supply work if it has poor-quality AC power to work with? Answer. Not very well. Because computers and many popular computer peripherals run on DC power that has been converted from AC power, it's essential to make sure that proper levels of AC power flow to the computer and its peripherals. There are four problems you might run into:

- Overvoltages (spikes and surges)

- Undervoltages (brownouts)

- Power failure (blackouts)

- Noisy power (interference)

Extremely high levels of transient or sustained overvoltages can damage the power supply of the computer and peripherals, and voltage that is significantly lower than required will cause the computer and peripherals to shut down. Shutdowns happen immediately when all power fails. A fourth problem with power is interference; "noisy" electrical power can cause subtle damage, and all four types of problems put the most valuable property of any computer, the data stored on the computer, at risk. Protect your computer's power supply and other components with appropriate devices:

- Surge suppressors, which are also referred to as surge protectors

- Battery backup systems, which are also referred to as uninterruptible power supply (UPS) or standby power supply (SPS) systems

- Power conditioning devices

Figure 5-12   An outlet tester like this one can find wiring problems quickly. This outlet is wired correctly.

Surge Suppressors

Stop that surge! While properly designed surge suppressors can prevent power surges (chronic overvoltage) and spikes (brief extremely high voltage) from damaging your computer, low-cost ones are often useless because they lack sufficient components to absorb dangerous surges. Surge suppressors range in price from under $10 to close to $100 per unit.

Both spikes and surges are overvoltages: voltage levels higher than the normal voltage levels that come out of the wall socket. *Spikes* are momentary overvoltages, whereas *surges* last longer. Both can damage or destroy equipment and can come through data lines (such as RJ-11 phone or RJ-45 network cables) as well as through power lines. In other words, if you think of your PC as a house, spikes and surges can come in through the back door or the garage as well as through the front door. Better "lock" (protect) all the doors. Many vendors sell data-line surge suppressors.

How can you tell the real surge suppressors from the phonies? Check for a TVSS (transient voltage surge suppressor) rating on the unit. Multi-outlet power strips do not have a TVSS rating.

Beyond the TVSS rating, look for the following features to be useful in preventing power problems:

- A low TVSS let-through voltage level (400V AC or less). This might seem high compared to the 115V standard, but power supplies have been tested to handle up to 800V AC themselves without damage.

- A covered-equipment warranty that includes lightning strikes (one of the biggest causes of surges and spikes).

- A high Joule rating. Joules measure electrical energy, and surge suppressors with higher Joule ratings can dissipate greater levels of surges or spikes.

- Fusing that will prevent fatal surges from getting through.

- Protection for data cables such as telephone/fax (RJ-11), network (RJ-45), or coaxial (RG6).

- EMI/RFI noise filtration (a form of line conditioning).

- Site fault wiring indicator (no ground, reversed polarity warnings).

- Fast response time to surges. If the surge suppressor doesn't clamp fast enough, the surge can get through.

- Protection against surges on hot, neutral, and ground lines.

If you use surge protectors with these features, you will minimize power problems. The site-fault wiring indicator will alert you to wiring problems that can negate grounding and can cause serious damage in ordinary use.

A surge suppressor that meets the UL 1449 or ANSI/IEEE C62.41 Category A (formerly IEEE 587 Category A) standards provides protection for your equipment. You might need to check with the vendor to determine if a particular unit meets one of these standards.

NOTE To learn more about UL 1449 and the other UL standards it incorporates, see ulstandardsinfonet.ul.com/scopes/scopes.asp?fn=1449.html.

In preparing for the A+ Certification exam, you should pay particular attention to the UL standard for surge suppressors and the major protection features just listed.

CAUTION If you're looking for a way to negate the protection provided by high-quality surge protectors, plug them into an ungrounded electrical outlet. You'll still find them in older homes and buildings.

The two- to three-prong adapter you use to make grounded equipment plug into an ungrounded outlet is designed to be attached to a ground such as a metal water pipe (that's what the metal loop is for). If you can't ground the adapter, don't use a computer or other electronic device with it. If you do, sooner or later you'll be sorry.

Battery Backup Units (UPS and SPS)

A UPS is another name for a battery backup unit. A UPS provides emergency power when a power failure strikes (a blackout) or when power falls below minimum levels (a brownout).

There are two different types of UPS systems: true UPS and SPS systems. A true UPS runs your computer from its battery at all times, isolating the computer and monitor from AC power. There is no switchover time with a true UPS when AC power fails because the battery is already running the computer. A true UPS inherently provides power conditioning (preventing spikes, surges, and brownouts from reaching the computer) because the computer receives only battery power, not the AC power coming from the wall outlet. True UPS units are sometimes referred to as line-interactive battery backup units because the battery backup unit interacts with the AC line, rather than the AC line going directly to the computer and other components.

An SPS is also referred to as a UPS, but its design is quite different. Its battery is used only when AC power fails. A momentary gap in power (about 1ms or less) occurs between the loss of AC power and the start of standby battery power; however, this switchover time is far faster than is required to avoid system shutdown because computers can coast for several milliseconds before shutting down. SPS-type battery backup units are far less expensive than true UPSs, but work just as well as true UPSs when properly equipped with power-conditioning features.

NOTE In the rest of this section, the term *UPS* refers to both true UPS or SPS units except as noted, because most backup units on the market technically are SPS but are called UPS units by their vendors.

Make sure you understand the differences between these units for the exam.

Battery backup units can be distinguished from each other by differences in the following:

- **Run times**—The amount of time a computer will keep running on power from the UPS. A longer runtime unit uses a bigger battery and usually will cost more than a unit with a shorter run time. Fifteen minutes is a minimum recommendation for a UPS for an individual workstation; much larger systems are recommended for servers that might need to complete a lengthy shutdown procedure.

- **Network support**—Battery backup units made for use on networks are shipped with software that broadcasts a message to users about a server shutdown so that users can save open files and close open applications and then shuts down the server automatically before the battery runs down.

- **Automatic shutdown**—Some low-cost UPS units lack this feature, but it is essential for servers or other unattended units. The automatic shutdown feature requires an available USB (or RS-232 serial) port and appropriate software from the UPS maker. If you change operating systems, you will need to update the software for your UPS to be supported by the new operating system.

- **Surge suppression features**—Virtually all UPS units today have integrated surge suppression, but the efficiency of integrated surge suppression can vary as much as separate units. Look for UL-1449 and IEEE-587 Category A ratings to find reliable surge suppression in UPS units.

Figure 5-13 illustrates the rear of a typical UPS unit.

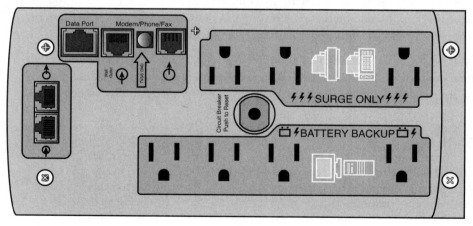

Figure 5-13 A typical UPS with integrated surge suppression for printers and other AC powered devices, 10/100/1000 Ethernet (including VoIP), and conventional telephony devices.

NOTE Always plug a UPS directly into a wall outlet, not into a power strip or surge suppressor.

Buying the Correct-Sized Battery Backup System

Battery backups can't run forever. But then, they're not supposed to. This section describes how you can make sure you get enough time to save your files and shut down your computer.

UPS units are rated in VA (volt-amps), and their manufacturers have interactive buying guides you can use online or download to help you select a model with adequate capacity. If you use a UPS with an inadequate VA rating for your equipment, your runtime will be substantially shorter than it should be.

Here's how to do the math: You can calculate the correct VA rating for your equipment by adding up the wattage ratings of your computer and monitor and multiplying the result by 1.4. If your equipment is rated in amperage (amps), multiply the amp rating by 120 (volts) to get the VA rating.

For example, my computer has a 450W power supply, which would require a 630VA-rated UPS (450×1.4) and a 17-inch monitor that is rated in amps, not watts. The monitor draws 0.9A, which would require a 108VA-rated UPS (0.9×120). Add the VA ratings together, and my computer needs a 750VA-rated battery backup unit or larger. Specifying a UPS with a VA rating at least twice what is required by the equipment attached to the UPS (for example, a 1500VA or higher rating, based on a minimum requirement of 750VA) will greatly improve the runtime of the battery.

In this example, a typical 750VA battery backup unit would provide about five minutes of runtime when used with my equipment. However, if I used a 1500VA battery backup, I could increase my runtime to more than 15 minutes because my equipment would use only about half the rated capacity of the UPS unit.

If you need a more precise calculation, for example, if you will also power an additional monitor or other external device, use the interactive sizing guides provided by battery backup vendors, such as American Power Conversion (www.apc.com).

CAUTION   You should *not* attach laser printers to a UPS because their high current draw will cause the runtime of the battery to be very short. In most cases, only the computer and monitor need to be attached to the UPS. However, inkjet printers and external modems have low current draw and can be attached to the UPS with little reduction in runtime.

Power Conditioning Devices

Although power supplies are designed to work with voltages that do not exactly meet the 115V or 230V standards, power that is substantially higher or lower than what the computer is designed for can damage the system. Electrical noise on the power line, even with power at the correct voltage, also causes problems because it disrupts the correct sinewave alternating-current pattern the computer, monitor, and other devices are designed to use.

Better-quality surge protectors often provide power filtration to handle electromagnetic interference (EMI)/radio frequency interference (RFI) noise problems from laser printers and other devices that generate a lot of electrical interference. However, to deal with voltage that is too high or too low, you need a true power conditioner.

These units take substandard or overstandard power levels and adjust them to the correct range needed by your equipment. Some units also include high-quality surge protection features.

To determine whether you need a power-conditioning unit, you can contact your local electric utility company to see if it loans or rents power-monitoring devices. Alternatively, you can rent them from power consultants. These units track power level and quality over a set period of time (such as overnight or longer) and provide reports to help you see the overall quality of power on a given line.

Moving surge- and interference-causing devices such as microwaves, vacuum cleaners, refrigerators, freezers, and furnaces to circuits away from the computer circuits will help minimize power problems. However, in older buildings, or during times of peak demand, power conditioning might still be necessary. A true (line-interactive) UPS provides built-in power conditioning by its very nature (see the previous discussion).

Troubleshooting Power Problems

A dead system that gives no signs of life when turned on can be caused by the following:

- Defects in AC power to the system

- Power supply failure or misconfiguration

- Temporary short circuits in internal or external components

- Power supply or other component failure

With four suspects, it's time to play detective. Use the procedure outlined next to find the actual cause of a dead system. If one of the test procedures in the following list corrects the problem, the item that was changed is the cause of the problem. Power supplies have a built-in safety feature that shuts down the unit immediately in case of short circuit. The following steps are designed to determine whether the power problem is caused by a short circuit or another problem:

Step 1.   Check the AC power to the system; a loose or disconnected power cord, a disconnected surge protector, a surge protector that has been turned off, or a dead AC wall socket will prevent a system from receiving power.

If the wall socket has no power, reset the circuit breaker in the electrical service box for the location.

Step 2. Check the AC voltage switch on the power supply; it should be set to 115V for North America. Turn off the power, reset the switch, and restart the system if the switch was set to 230V. Note that many desktop computer power supplies no longer require a switch selection, because they are autoranging.

Step 3. Check the keyboard connector; a loose keyboard connector could cause a short circuit.

Step 4. Open the system and check for loose screws or other components such as loose slot covers, modem speakers, or other metal items that can cause a short circuit. Correct them and retest.

Step 5. Verify that the cable from the front-mounted power switch is properly connected to the motherboard.

Step 6. Check for fuses on the motherboard (mainly found in very old systems). Turn off the power, replace any blown fuse on the motherboard with a fuse of the correct rating, and retest. Never try to short-circuit or bypass fuses on the motherboard or anywhere else.

Step 7. Remove all expansion cards and disconnect power to all drives; restart the system and use a multimeter to test power to the motherboard and expansion slots per Table 5-4, earlier in this chapter.

Step 8. If the power tests within accepted limits with all peripherals disconnected, reinstall one card at a time and check the power. If the power tests within accepted limits, reattach one drive at a time and check the power.

Step 9. If a defective card or drive has a dead short, reattaching the defective card or drive should stop the system immediately upon power-up. Replace the card or drive and retest.

Step 10. Test the Power Good line at the power supply motherboard connector with a multimeter.

It's a long list, but chances are you will track down the offending component before you reach the end of it.

System Cooling

Today's computers often run much hotter than systems of a few years ago, so it's important to understand how to keep the hottest-running components running cooler. The following sections discuss the components that are most in need of cooling and how to cool them.

Passive and Active Heat Sinks

All processors require a heat sink. A heat sink is a finned metal device that radiates heat away from the processor. In almost all cases, an *active heat sink* (a heat sink with a fan) is required for adequate cooling, unless the system case (chassis) is specially designed to move air directly over the processor and a passive heat sink.

Although aluminum has been the most common material used for heat sinks, copper has better thermal transfer properties, and many designs mix copper and aluminum components. Traditional active heat sinks include a cooling fan that rests on top of the heat sink and pulls air past the heat sink in a vertical direction. However, many aftermarket heat sinks use a horizontally mounted cooling fan and heat pipes to cool the process. Figure 5-14 compares typical examples of passive and active processor heat sinks used in ATX chassis.

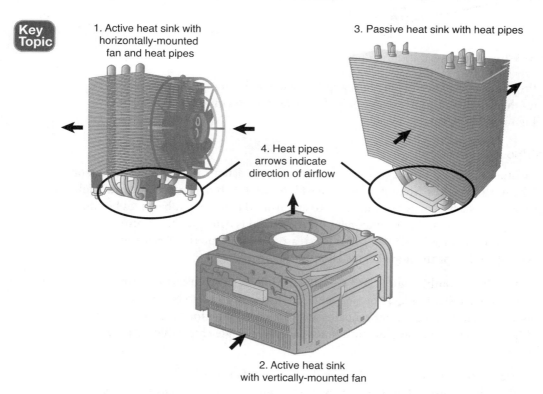

Figure 5-14   Active and passive processor heat sinks. Note that the passive heat sink has more fins than the active heat sinks to enable it to provide adequate cooling.

The infrequently-encountered BTX chassis use a different approach to processor cooling. These chassis use a thermal duct that fits over the processor and its heat sink. A cooling fan at one end of the duct directs air past the processor. Figure 5-15 illustrates this type of processor cooler.

Figure 5-15   A typical BTX thermal duct.

Processor fans typically plug into a specially marked three-prong jack on the motherboard that provides power and fan speed monitoring capabilities (see Figure 5-16).

North/Southbridge Cooling

Most motherboards use a two-chip chipset to route data to and from the processor. The northbridge or Memory Controller Hub (MCH) chip, because it carries high-speed data such as memory and video to and from the processor, becomes hot during operation, and, if the component overheats and is damaged, the entire motherboard must be replaced. For this reason, most motherboards feature some type of cooler for the northbridge chip.

Although the southbridge or I/O Controller Hub (ICH) chip carries lower-speed traffic, such as hard disk, audio, and network traffic, it can also become overheated. As a result, most recent motherboards also feature cooling for the southbridge chip. Some chipsets combine both functions into a single chip, which also requires cooling.

Three methods have been used for cooling the motherboard chipset. Passive heat sinks are inexpensive, but do not provide sufficient cooling for high-performance systems. Active heat sinks provide better cooling than passive heat sinks, but low-quality sleeve-bearing fans can cause premature fan failure and lead to overheating. The latest trend in chipset cooling uses heat pipes, which draw heat away from the chipset and dissipates it through high-performance, very large passive heat sinks located away from the chipset itself.

Figure 5-17 illustrates passive and active heat sinks for north and southbridge chips.

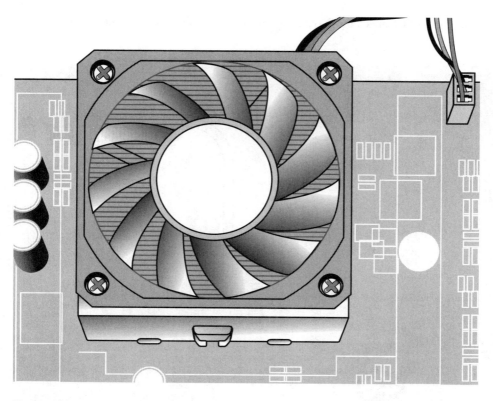

Figure 5-16   A typical processor active heat sink plugged into the motherboard.

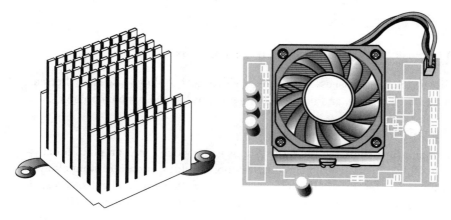

Figure 5-17   Passive and active heat sinks for chipsets.

Figure 5-18 illustrates a motherboard that uses heat pipes for chipset cooling.

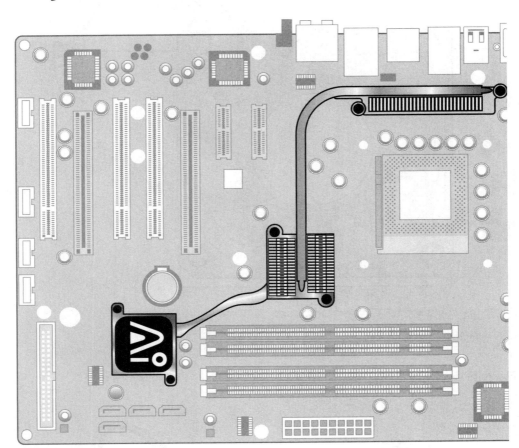

Figure 5-18   Motherboard with heat pipe cooling for the chipset.

The following sections discuss the role that video card cooling, case fans, thermal compound for heat sinks, and liquid cooling systems have in system cooling.

Video Card Cooling

Another major heat source in modern systems is the video card's graphics processing unit (GPU) chip, which renders the desktop, graphics, and everything else you see on your computer screen. With the exception of a few low-end video cards, almost all video cards use active heat sinks to blow hot air away from the GPU.

However, the memory chips on a video card can also become very hot. To cool both the GPU and video memory, most recent mid-range and high-end video card designs use a fan shroud to cool both components. Fan shrouds often require enough space to prevent the expansion slot next to the video card from being used.

Figure 5-19 illustrates a typical video card with a two-slot fan shroud.

Figure 5-19   The EVGA GeForce GTX 580 is a high-performance PCI Express x16 video card that requires a two-slot fan shroud. Image courtesy of EVGA Corporation.

Case Fans

Most ATX chassis have provisions for at least two case fans: one at the front of the system, and one at the rear of the system. Case fans can be powered by the motherboard or by using a Y-splitter connected to a four-pin Molex power connector. Case fans at the front of the system should draw air into the system, while case fans at the rear of the system should draw air out of the system.

Figure 5.20 shows a typical rear case fan. You can plug fans like this into the three-prong chassis fan connection found on many recent motherboards or into the 4-pin Molex drive power connector used by hard drives. If the motherboard power connector is used, the PC Health or hardware monitor function found in many recent system BIOS setup programs can monitor fan speed. See Chapter 4, "BIOS," for a typical example.

NOTE   Some case fans that can be powered by a Molex power connector include a special power cable that permits the fan speed to be monitored by the motherboard, even though the motherboard is not used to power the fan.

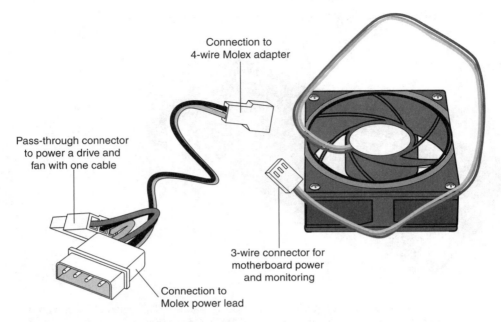

Connection to
4-wire Molex adapter

Pass-through connector
to power a drive and
fan with one cable

3-wire connector for
motherboard power
and monitoring

Connection to
Molex power lead

Figure 5-20   A rear case fan that can be plugged into the motherboard or into a Molex power connector.

Rear case fans are available in various sizes up to 120mm. The fan shown in Figure 5-20 is an 80mm model; measure the opening at the rear of the case to determine which fan size to purchase. Some recent systems, such as the one shown in Figure 5-21, might feature two rear fans. The system shown in Figure 5-21 also has a video card that uses a two-slot fan shroud.

Case fans as well as processor fans and other fans that are connected to the motherboard can be monitored by the hardware monitor display in the system BIOS as shown in Figure 5-22 or by system monitoring software running after system startup. If a case fan fails or runs too slowly, it can cause the system to overheat.

Thermal Compound

When passive or active heat sinks are installed on a processor, north or southbridge chip, GPU or other component, thermal compound (also known as thermal transfer material, thermal grease, or phase change material) must be used to provide the best possible thermal transfer between the component and the heat sink.

Heat sinks supplied with boxed processors might use a preapplied phase-change material on the heat sink, whereas OEM processors with third-party heat sinks usually require the installer to use a paste or thick liquid thermal grease or silver-based compound. Coolers for northbridge or southbridge chips might use thermal grease or a phase-change pad.

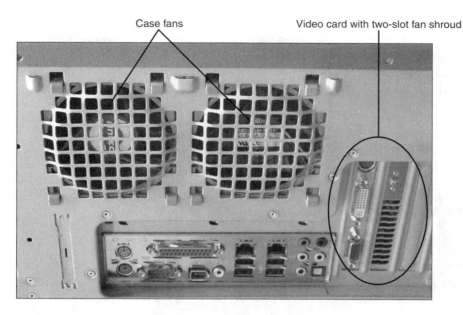

Figure 5-21   A system with two rear case fans.

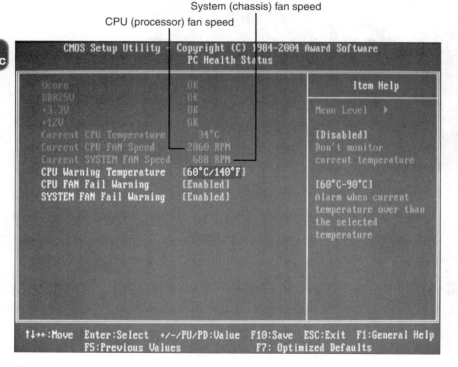

Figure 5-22   The PC Health (system monitor) dialog in a typical system BIOS.

If the thermal material is preapplied to the heat sink, make sure you remove the protective tape before you install the heat sink. If a third-party heat sink is used, or if the original heat sink is removed and reinstalled, carefully remove any existing thermal transfer material from the heat sink and processor die surface. Then, apply new thermal transfer material to the processor die before you reinstall the heat sink on the processor.

Figure 5-23 illustrates the application of thermal compound to a northbridge chip before attaching a heat sink.

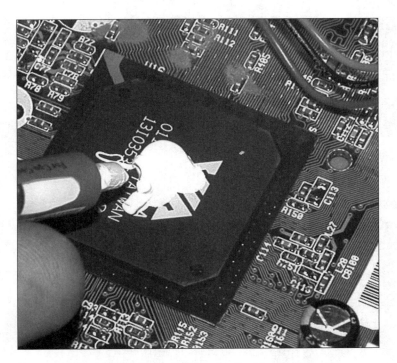

Figure 5-23   Applying thermal grease to the Northbridge chip.

CAUTION   Never operate a system before attaching the heat sink to the processor with the appropriate thermal transfer material. The processor could be destroyed by overheating in just a few moments. Most recent systems have thermal safeguards that shut down the system in the event of processor overheating, but if these safeguards fail, there could also be damage to the processor.

Liquid Cooling Systems

Liquid cooling systems for processors, motherboard chipsets, and GPUs are now available. Some are integrated into a custom case, whereas others can be retrofitted into an existing system that has openings for cooling fans.

Liquid cooling systems attach a liquid cooling unit instead of an active heat sink to the processor and other supported components. A pump moves the liquid (which might be water or a special solution, depending upon the cooling system) through the computer to a heat exchanger, which uses a fan to cool the warm liquid before it is sent back to the processor. Liquid cooling systems are designed primarily for very high-performance systems, especially overclocked systems. It's essential that only approved cooling liquids and hoses be used in these systems (check with cooling system vendors for details); unauthorized types of liquids or hoses could leak and corrode system components.

Figure 5-24 illustrates a typical liquid cooling system for cooling the processor.

Figure 5-24   A typical liquid cooling system.

Exam Preparation Tasks

Review All the Key Topics

Review the most important topics in the chapter, noted with the key topics icon in the outer margin of the page. Table 5-5 lists a reference of these key topics and the page numbers on which each is found.

Table 5-5   Key Topics for Chapter 5

Key Topic Element	Description	Page Number
Figure 5-2	A typical power supply label.	158
Figure 5-3	A typical power supply's sliding voltage switch set for North American voltage (115V).	160
Figure 5-4	Typical power supply connectors to the motherboard.	165
Figure 5-6	Typical peripheral power connectors.	167
Table 5-3	Using a Multimeter.	173
Figure 5-11 and Table 5-4	Testing the +12V line on an ATX power supply, and acceptable voltage levels.	173-174
Figure 5-12	An outlet tester can find wiring problems quickly.	176
List	This list of features is useful in preventing power problems.	177
Figure 5-14	Active and passive processor heat sinks.	183
Figure 5-22	The PC Health (system monitor) dialog in a typical system BIOS.	189

Definitions of Key Terms

Define the following key terms from this chapter, and check your answers in the glossary.

AC, DC, power supply, surge protector, UPS

Troubleshooting Scenario

You are working on a computer that is overheating. What steps should you take to make sure the power supply is not being overloaded?

Refer to Appendix A for the answer.

This chapter covers the following subjects:

- **RAM Basics**—This section talks about what RAM does, how it works, and how it relates to the rest of the computer system.

- **RAM Types**—In this section you learn about the various types of RAM available, including SDRAM, DDR, and Rambus. Their architecture, capacity, and speed will also be described.

- **Operational Characteristics**—This section describes the features of memory modules and types of memory like ECC, EDO, registered, and unbuffered.

- **Installing Memory Modules**—This section demonstrates how to install SIMMs and DIMMs properly.

- **Troubleshooting Memory**—This section covers some issues you might encounter with RAM due to incompatible memory speeds and types.

- **Preventative Maintenance for Memory**—Due to the possibility of memory overheating, this section describes some measures you can take to keep your memory modules clean and protected.

This chapter covers a portion of the CompTIA A+ 220-701 objectives 1.2 and 1.6 and CompTIA A+ 220-702 objectives 1.1 and 1.2

CHAPTER 6

RAM

When it's time for the CPU to process something, RAM (random access memory) is the workspace it uses. RAM is one of two types of memory found in your computer; the other type of memory is ROM (read-only memory). What's the difference? RAM's contents can be changed at any time, while ROM's contents require special procedures to change. Think of RAM as a blank sheet of paper and a pencil: you can write on it, erase what you've done, and keep making changes. On the other hand, ROM is like a newspaper. If you want to change what's printed on the newspaper, you must recycle it so it can be reprocessed back into newsprint and sent through the newspaper's printing presses again. This chapter focuses on the types, installation, and troubleshooting of RAM.

"Do I Know This Already?" Quiz

The "Do I Know This Already?" quiz allows you to assess whether you should read this entire chapter or simply jump to the "Exam Preparation Tasks" section for review. If you are in doubt, read the entire chapter. Table 6-1 outlines the major headings in this chapter and the corresponding "Do I Know This Already?" quiz questions. You can find the answers in Appendix A, "Answers to the 'Do I Know This Already?' Quizzes and Troubleshooting Scenarios."

Table 6-1 "Do I Know This Already?" Foundation Topics Section-to-Question Mapping

Foundations Topics Section	Questions Covered in This Section
RAM Basics	1
RAM Types	2–4
Operational Characteristics	5–7
Installing Memory Modules	8
Troubleshooting Memory	9–11
Preventative Maintenance for Memory	12–13

1. Which of the following loses its contents when you shut down the computer?

   a.   Hard disk drive

   b.   USB flash drive

   c.   RAM

   d.   ROM

2. Which type of memory chip is much bulkier and more expensive than DRAM?

   a.   SDRAM

   b.   SRAM

   c.   DRAM

   d.   DDR

3. What type of RAM must be installed in pairs?

   a.   DDR

   b.   SDRAM

   c.   DDR2

   d.   Rambus

4. Which type of memory was the first to run in sync with the memory bus?

   a.   DDR2

   b.   SDRAM

   c.   SRAM

   d.   Rambus

5. Name the two methods that are used to protect the reliability of memory.

   a.   Parity-Checking

   b.   System checking

   c.   ECC (error-correcting code)

   d.   Smart checking

6. Most types of desktop memory modules use which kind of memory?

   a.   Unbuffered memory

   b.   No memory

   c.   SIMM module

   d.   Stable memory

7. Critical applications and network servers have a special type of memory. What is it called?

    a. ECC memory

    b. unbuffered memory

    c. static memory

    d. desktop memory

8. To correctly install a DIMM or Rambus module, what should you do? (Choose all that apply.)

    a. Line up the module connectors with the socket

    b. Verify that the locking tabs on the socket are swiveled to the outside (open) position

    c. Verify that the module is lined up correctly with the socket. Then, push the module straight down until the locks on each end of the socket snap into place at the top corners of the module.

    d. None of these options is correct

9. Which of the following is the name for running the processor or memory at speeds faster than what is recommended?

    a. CPU tweaking

    b. Overclocking

    c. Memory leak

    d. CPU duplicating

10. Which of the following are types of metal used for contacts on SIMMs? (Choose two.)

    a. Tin

    b. Copper

    c. Zinc

    d. Gold

11. Which of the following are utilities that are used to check memory? (Choose all that apply.)

    a. CheckIT

    b. AMIDiag

    c. RAMExam

    d. All of these options are correct

12. To prevent overheating memory modules, which of the following tasks should you perform? (Choose all that apply.)

    a. Keep the surfaces of the modules clean. You can use compressed air or a data-rated vacuum cleaner to remove dust.

    b. Make sure you are using the recommended voltage level for the memory installed if your system's BIOS setup permits voltage adjustments.

    c. Install additional case fans over or behind the location of memory modules to pull hot air out of the system.

    d. All these options are correct.

13. Which of the following statements are correct about DDR3 memory? (Choose all that apply.)

    a. DDR3 has the same pinouts as DDR2.

    b. DDR3 and DDR2 both use 240-pin connectors.

    c. DDR3 uses higher voltages than DDR2.

    d. All these options are correct.

RAM Basics

RAM is used for programs and data, and by the operating system for disk caching (using RAM to hold recently accessed disk sectors). Thus, installing more RAM improves transfers between the CPU and both RAM and disk drives. If your computer runs short of RAM, Windows can also use the hard disk as a very slow substitute for RAM. The swapfile (Windows 9x/Me) or paging file (Windows NT/2000/XP/Vista/7) is a file on the hard disk used to hold part of the contents of memory if the installed RAM on the system isn't large enough for the tasks currently being performed.

Although the hard disk can substitute for RAM in a pinch, don't confuse RAM with magnetic storage devices such as hard disks. Although the contents of RAM and magnetic storage can be changed freely, RAM loses its contents as soon as you shut down the computer, while magnetic storage can hold data for years. Although RAM's contents are temporary, RAM is much faster than magnetic storage: RAM speed is measured in nanoseconds (billionths of a second), while magnetic storage is measured in milliseconds (thousandths of a second).

Even though every computer ever made is shipped with RAM, you will probably need to add more RAM to a computer as time passes. Ever-increasing amounts of RAM are needed as operating systems and applications get more powerful and add more features. Because RAM is one of the most popular upgrades to add to any system during its lifespan, you need to understand how RAM works, what types of RAM exist, and how to add it to provide the biggest performance boost to the systems you maintain.

When you must specify memory for a given system, there are several variables you need to know:

- **Memory module type (240-pin DIMM, 184-pin DIMM, 168-pin DIMM, and so on)**—The module type your system can use has a great deal to do with the memory upgrade options you have with any given system. Although a few systems can use more than one memory module type, in most cases if you want to change to a faster type of memory module, such as from 184-pin DIMM (used by DDR SDRAM) to 240-pin DIMM (such as DDR2 or DDR3 SDRAM), you need to upgrade the motherboard first.

- **Memory chip type used on the module (SDRAM, DDR SDRAM, RDRAM, and so on)**—Today, a particular memory module type uses only one type of memory. However, older memory module types such as 72-pin SIMM and early 168-pin DIMMs were available with different types of memory chips. You need to specify the right memory chip type in such cases to avoid conflicts with onboard memory and provide stable performance.

■ **Memory module speed (60ns, PC-133, PC800, PC2700, and so on)**—There are three ways to specify the speed of a memory module: the actual speed in ns (nanoseconds) of the chips on the module (60ns), the clock speed of the data bus (PC-133 is 133MHz; PC800 is 800MHz), or the throughput (in MBps) of the memory (for example, PC2700 is 2,700MBps or 2.7GBps DDR; PC2-2 6400 is 6,400MBps or 6.4GBps). The throughput method is used by current memory types.

■ **Error checking (parity, non-parity, ECC)**—Most systems don't perform parity checking (to verify the contents of memory) or correct errors, but some motherboards and systems support these functions. Although parity-checked memory mainly slows down the system, ECC memory can detect memory errors as well as correct them. If a system is performing critical work (high-level mathematics or financial functions, departmental or enterprise-level server tasks), ECC support in the motherboard and ECC memory are worthwhile options to specify. Some systems also support registered or non-registered modules. Registered modules are more reliable, but are slower because they include a chip that boosts the memory signal.

■ **Allowable module sizes and combinations**—Some motherboards insist you use the same speeds and sometimes the same sizes of memory in each memory socket, while others are more flexible. To find out which is true about a particular system, check the motherboard or system documentation before you install memory or add more memory.

■ **The number of modules needed per bank of memory**—Systems address memory in banks, and the number of modules per bank varies with the processor and the memory module type installed. If you need more than one module per bank, as with SIMM memory on a Pentium-class system, and only one module is installed, the system will ignore it. Systems that require multiple modules per bank require that modules be the same size and speed.

■ **Whether the system requires or supports dual-channel memory (two identical memory modules instead of one at a time) or triple-channel memory (three identical memory modules)**—Dual-channel memory and triple-channel memory are accessed in an interleaved manner to improve memory latency (the time required between memory accesses). As a result, systems running dual-channel memory offer faster memory performance than systems running single-channel memory. Intel's Core i7 processor is the first processor to use triple-channel memory (which runs even faster than dual-channel memory), although it can also use dual-channel memory if only two identical modules are installed.

■ **The total number of modules that can be installed**—The number of sockets on the motherboard determines the number of modules that can be installed. Very small-footprint systems (such as those which use microATX, flexATX, or Mini-ITX motherboards) often support only one or two modules, but systems that use full-size ATX motherboards often support three or more modules, especially those designed for dual-channel or triple-channel memory.

When it comes to memory, compatibility is important. The memory module type must fit the motherboard; speed must be compatible, and the module storage size/combination must match your computer system as well. To find out exactly what type of memory modules are compatible with your motherboard, visit a memory manufacturer's website and check within their database. Be sure to have the model number of the motherboard, or the model of the computer handy.

RAM Types

While today's systems use memory modules built from a combination of chips, rather than individual chips plugged into the motherboard as with early PC systems, it's still necessary to understand the different types of memory chips that have been and are used to build memory modules.

DRAM

Virtually all memory modules use some type of *dynamic* RAM, or DRAM chips. DRAM requires frequent recharges of memory to retain its contents. Early types of DRAM, including variations such as fast-page mode (FPM) and extended data-out (EDO), were speed rated by access time, measured in nanoseconds (ns; smaller is faster). Typical speeds for regular DRAM chips were 100ns or slower; FPM memory, used primarily in 30-pin and 72-pin SIMM modules, ran at speeds of 70ns, 80ns, and 100ns. EDO DRAM, which was used primarily in 72-pin SIMM modules and a few 168-pin DIMM modules, typically ran at 60ns.

While these types of DRAM are long obsolete, other types of DRAM, including SDRAM, DDR SDRAM, DDR2 SDRAM, DDR3 SDRAM, and Rambus, are used in more recent systems.

SRAM

Static random-access memory (SRAM) is RAM that does not need to be periodically refreshed. Memory refreshing is common to other types of RAM and is basically the act of reading information from a specific area of memory and immediately rewriting that information back to the same area without modifying it. Due to SRAM's architecture, it does not require this refresh. You will find SRAM being used as cache memory for CPUs, as buffers on the motherboard or within hard drives, and as temporary storage for LCD screens. Normally, SRAM is soldered directly to a printed circuit board (PCB) or integrated directly to a chip. This means that you probably won't be replacing SRAM. SRAM is faster than, and is usually found in smaller quantities than its distant cousin DRAM.

SDRAM

Synchronous DRAM (SDRAM) was the first type of memory to run in sync with the processor bus (the connection between the processor, or CPU, and other components on the motherboard). Most 168-pin DIMM modules use SDRAM memory. To determine if a DIMM module contains SDRAM memory, check its speed markings. SDRAM memory is rated by bus speed (PC66 equals 66MHz bus speed; PC100 equals 100MHz bus speed; PC133 equals 133MHz bus speed).

Depending upon the specific module and motherboard chipset combination, PC133 modules can sometimes be used on systems that are designed for PC100 modules.

DDR SDRAM

The second generation of systems running synchronous DRAM use double-data-rate SDRAM (DDR SDRAM). DDR SDRAM performs two transfers per clock cycle, instead of one as with regular SDRAM. 184-pin DIMM memory modules use DDR SDRAM chips.

While DDR SDRAM is sometimes rated in MHz, it is more often rated by throughput (MBps). Common speeds for DDR SDRAM include PC1600 (200 MHz/1600 MBps), PC2100 (266 MHz/2100 MBps), PC2700 (333 MHz/2700 MBps), and PC3200 (400 MHz/3200 MBps), but other speeds are available from some vendors.

DDR2 SDRAM

Double-double data rate SDRAM (DDR2 SDRAM) is the successor to DDR SDRAM. DDR2 SDRAM runs its external data bus at twice the speed of DDR SDRAM, enabling faster performance. However, DDR2 SDRAM memory has greater latency than DDR SDRAM memory. Latency is a measure of how long it takes to receive information from memory; the higher the number, the greater the latency. Typical latency values for mainstream DDR2 memory are CL=5 and CL=6, compared to CL=2.5 and CL=3 for DDR memory. 240-pin memory modules use DDR2 SDRAM.

DDR2 SDRAM memory might be referred to by the effective memory speed of the memory chips on the module (the memory clock speed ×4 or the I/O bus clock speed ×2), for example DDR2-533 (133 MHz memory clock×4 or 266 MHz I/O bus clock ×2)=533 MHz) or by module throughput (DDR2-533 is used in PC2-4200 modules, which have a throughput of more than 4200 MBps). PC2- indicates the module uses DDR2 memory, while PC- indicates the module uses DDR memory.

Other common speeds for DDR2 SDRAM modules include PC2-3200 (DDR2-400; 3200 MBps throughput); PC2-5300 (DDR2-667); PC2-6400 (DDR2-800).

DDR3 SDRAM

Double data Rate 3 SDRAM (DDR3 SDRAM) is the latest generation of SDRAM. Compared to DDR2, DDR3 runs at lower voltages, has twice the internal banks, and most versions run at faster speeds than DDR2. As with DDR2 versus DDR, DDR3 has greater latency than DDR2. Typical latency values for mainstream DDR3 memory are CL7, compared to CL5 or CL6 for DDR2. Although DDR3 modules use 240 pins, their layout and keying are different than DDR2, and they cannot be interchanged.

DDR3 SDRAM memory might be referred to by the effective memory speed of the memory chips on the module (the memory clock speed ×4 or the I/O bus clock speed ×2), for example DDR3-1333 (333 MHz memory clock×4 or 666 MHz I/O bus clock×2)=1333 MHz) or by module throughput (DDR3-1333 is used in PC3-10600 modules, which have a throughput of more than 10,600 MBps or 10.6GBps). PC3- indicates the module uses DDR3 memory.

Other common speeds for DDR3 SDRAM modules include PC3-8500 (DDR3-1066; 8500 MBps throughput); PC3-12800 (DDR3-1600); PC3-17000 (DDR3-2133).

Rambus

Rambus Direct RAM (RDRAM) memory was used by early Pentium 4-based chipsets from Intel, including the i820, i840, and E7205 Granite Bay workstation chipset, but has not been used by more recent systems. RDRAM modules are known as RIMMs and were produced in 16-bit and 32-bit versions.

16-bit RIMMs use a 184-pin connector, while 32-bit RIMMs use a 232-pin connector. 32-bit motherboards that use RIMMs must use pairs of 16-bit modules. Empty RIMM sockets must be occupied by a continuity module (resembles a RIMM but without memory; also known as a CRIMM).

Common Rambus 16-bit module speeds include PC600 (1200 MBps bandwidth); PC700 (1420 MBps bandwidth); PC800 (1600 MBps bandwidth); PC1066 (also known as RIMM 2100; 2133 MBps bandwidth); and PC1200 (also called RIMM 2400; 2400 MBps bandwidth).

32-bit (dual-channel) RIMM modules use the RIMM xxxx identifier, listing the throughput in MBps as part of the name, for example, RIMM 3200 (3200 MBps bandwidth); RIMM 4200 (4200 MBps bandwidth); RIMM 4800 (4800 MBps bandwidth); and RIMM 6400 (6400 MBps bandwidth).

Table 6-2 shows a comparison of the types of RAM you need to know for the exam.

Table 6-2   RAM Comparisons

RAM Type	Pins	Common Type and Speed	Defining Characteristic
DRAM	30 and 72	33 or 66 MHz	Obsolete.
SDRAM	168	PC133 = 133 MHz	This original version of SDRAM is now obsolete and has given way to DDR, DDR2, and DDR3 memory.
DDR SDRAM	184	PC3200 = 400 MHz/3200 MBps	Double the transfers per clock cycle compared to regular SDRAM.
DDR2 SDRAM	240	DDR2-800 (PC2-6400) = 800 MHz/6400 MBps	External data bus speed (I/O bus clock) is 2x faster than DDR SDRAM.
DDR3 SDRAM	240 (the keying on DDR3 is offset to one side compared to DDR2)	DDR3-1333 (PC3-10600) =1333MHz/10,600MBps	External data bus speed (I/O bus clock) is 2x faster than DDR2 SDRAM (4x faster than DDR SDRAM).
Rambus (RDRAM)	184 and 232	PC800 = 1600 MBps	Not used in new computers, but you still might see existing systems using Rambus memory modules.

Operational Characteristics

Memory modules can be classified in various ways, including:

- The amount of memory (in bits) found on the module
- The differences between parity and non-parity memory
- The differences between ECC and non-ECC memory
- The differences between registered and unbuffered memory
- The differences between single-sided and double-sided memory

The following sections deal with these operational characteristics.

Comparison of Memory Modules

All systems built since the early 1990s have used some form of memory module, and most of these systems have used standard versions of these modules. These modules come in these major types:

- **Single Inline Memory Module (SIMM)** — Has a single row of 30 or 72 edge connectors on the bottom of the module. *Single* refers to both sides of the module having the same pinout.

- **Single Inline Pin Package (SIPP)** — A short-lived variation on the 30-pin SIMM, which substituted pins for the edge connector used by SIMM modules.

- **Dual Inline Memory Module (DIMM)** — These are available in 168-pin, 184-pin, and 240-pin versions. *Dual* refers to each side of the module having a different pinout.

- **Small Outline DIMM (SODIMM)** — A compact version of the standard DIMM module, available in various pinouts for use in notebook computers and laser/LED printers. To learn more about SODIMM modules, see Chapter 9, "Laptops and Portable Devices."

- **Rambus RDRAM Module** — A memory module using Direct Rambus memory (RDRAM) chips. Kingston Technology has copyrighted the name RIMM for its Rambus RDRAM modules, but Rambus RDRAM modules are often referred to as RIMMs, regardless of their actual manufacturer.

- **Small Outline Rambus Module** — A compact version of the standard Rambus module for use in notebook computers.

> **NOTE** To see a comparison of DDR, DDR2, and DDR3 keying, see http://www.intel.com/support/motherboards/desktop/sb/CS-012038.htm.

Figure 6-1 illustrates SIMM, SIPP, and DIMM modules used in desktop computers.

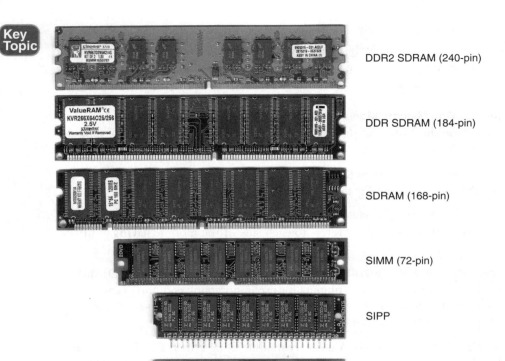

DDR2 SDRAM (240-pin)

DDR SDRAM (184-pin)

SDRAM (168-pin)

SIMM (72-pin)

SIPP

SIMM (30-pin)

Figure 6-1   Desktop memory modules (SIMM, SIPP, and DIMM) compared.

Memory Module Width

Memory modules are classified in a variety of ways, including size, speed, memory type, and width in bits. A byte is the basic building block used to determine storage and RAM capacity, and eight bits make a byte. Memory module widths (in bits) have become wider as the memory bus sizes of processors have increased.

Memory must be added in banks, and a bank of memory refers to a memory module, or modules, whose width in bits add up to the width of the memory bus and are identical in other characteristics, such as size and speed.

Table 6-3 lists memory bus sizes, memory module bus sizes, and the number of identical modules needed to make a bank of memory for processors from the 386 to today's Core 2 Duo/Core 2 Quad and Athlon 64 X2 and Phenom processors.

Table 6-3   Processor Memory Banks and Module Bus Size Comparisons

Processor	Memory Bus Size	Number of Memory Modules to Make a Bank		
		8-bit module (30-pin SIMM)	32-bit module (72-pin SIMM)	64-bit module (DIMM)
386, 486	32-bit	Four	One	—
Pentium, Pentium II, Pentium III, Pentium 4, Pentium D, Celeron, Core 2 Duo, Core 2 Quad, Core i7, Core i5, Core i3	64-bit	Eight*	Two	One
AMD Athlon, Athlon XP, Sempron, Duron, Athlon 64, Athlon 64 X2, Phenom, Phenom II	64-bit	Eight*	Two	One

*Listed for comparison only

Parity and Non-Parity Memory

There are two methods that have been used to protect the reliability of memory:

- Parity-checking

- ECC (error-correcting code)

Both of these methods depend upon the presence of an additional memory chip over the chips required for the data bus of the module. For example, a module that uses eight chips for data would use a ninth chip to support parity or ECC.

Parity checking, which goes back to the original IBM PC, works like this: Whenever memory is accessed, each data bit has a value of 0 or 1. When these values are added to the value in the parity bit, the resulting checksum should be an odd number. This is called *odd parity*. A memory problem will typically cause the data bit values plus the parity bit value to total an even number. This triggers a parity error, and your system halts with a parity error message. Note that parity checking requires parity-enabled memory and support in the motherboard. On modules that support parity-checking, there's a parity bit for each group of eight bits.

The method used to fix this type of error varies with the system. On museum-piece systems that use individual memory chips, you must open the system, push all memory chips back into place, and test the memory thoroughly if you have no spares (using memory testing software), or replace the memory if you have spare memory chips. If the computer uses memory modules, replace one module at a time, test the memory (or at least run the computer for awhile) to determine if the problem has gone away. If the problem recurs, replace the original module, swap out the second module and repeat.

TIP   Some systems' error message tells you the logical location of the error so you can take the system documentation and determine which module or modules to replace.

NOTE   Parity checking has always cost more because of the extra chips involved and the additional features required in the motherboard and chipset, and it fell out of fashion for PCs starting in the mid-1990s. Systems that lack parity checking freeze up when a memory problem occurs, and do not display any message onscreen.

Because parity-checking "protects" you from bad memory by shutting down the computer (which can cause you to lose data), vendors have created a better way to use the parity bits to solve memory errors using a method called ECC.

ECC and Non-ECC Memory

For critical applications, network servers have long used a special type of memory called *error-correcting code (ECC)*. This memory enables the system to correct single-bit errors and notify you of larger errors.

Although most desktops do not support ECC, some workstations and most servers do offer ECC support. On systems that offer ECC support, ECC support might be enabled or disabled through the system BIOS, or it might be a standard feature. The parity bit in parity memory is used by the ECC feature to determine when the contents of memory is corrupt and to fix single-bit errors. Unlike parity checking, which only warns you of memory errors, ECC memory actually corrects errors.

ECC is recommended for maximum data safety, although parity and ECC do provide a small slowdown in performance in return for the extra safety. ECC memory modules use the same types of memory chips used by standard modules, but they use more chips and might have a different internal design to allow ECC operation. ECC modules, like parity-checked modules, have an extra bit for each group of eight data bits.

To determine if a system supports parity-checked or ECC memory, check the system BIOS memory configuration (typically on the Advanced or Chipset screens). Systems that support parity or ECC memory can use non-parity checked memory if parity checking and ECC are disabled. Another name for ECC is *EDAC (Error Detection and Correction)*.

Registered and Unbuffered Memory

Most types of desktop memory modules use unbuffered memory. However, many servers and some desktop or workstation computers use a type of memory module called *registered memory*. Registered memory modules contain a register chip that enables the system to remain stable with large amounts of memory installed. The register chip acts as a buffer, which slightly slows down memory access.

Registered memory modules can be built with or without ECC support. However, most registered memory modules are used by servers and include ECC support. Figure 6-2 compares a standard (unbuffered) memory module with a registered memory module that also supports ECC.

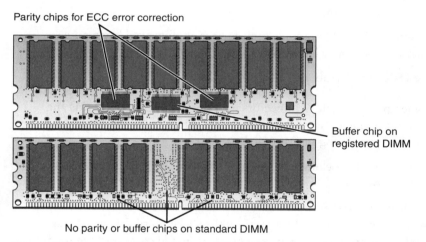

Figure 6-2 A registered module with ECC (top) compared to a standard unbuffered module (bottom).

Single-Sided and Double-Sided Memory

A double-sided SIMM acts like two conventional SIMMs in one, and can be recognized by having data chips on both sides of the module. Some systems work with both double-sided and single-sided SIMM memory modules, while others restrict the number of double-sided modules you can use or won't let you use them at all. Read the manual for the system or motherboard to determine if you can use double-sided SIMMs.

On modern systems that use DIMMs, the term "double-sided" refers to a module that contains two memory banks. On systems that restrict the number of banks that can be installed, you can install more single-sided DIMMs than double-sided DIMMs. To determine if a particular system (motherboard) has this type of restriction, see its documentation.

Installing DIMMs and Rambus RDRAM Modules

Memory modules are the memory "sticks" that are installed into the slots of a motherboard. Installing memory modules is fairly easy, and can be a fun initial task for people who have never worked on a computer before. However, precautions must be taken not to damage the memory module or the motherboard. Before working with any memory modules, turn the computer off, and unplug it from the AC outlet. Be sure to employ electrostatic discharge (ESD) protection in the form of an antistatic strap and antistatic mat. Use an antistatic bag to hold the memory modules while you are not working with them. Before actually handling any components, touch an unpainted portion of the case chassis in a further effort to ground yourself. Try not to touch any of the chips, connectors, or circuitry of the memory module; instead hold them from the sides.

DIMM and Rambus RDRAM module sockets have an improved keying mechanism and a better locking mechanism compared to SIMMs.

To install the DIMM or Rambus RDRAM module, follow these steps:

Step 1.   Line up the modules' connectors with the socket. Both DIMMs and Rambus modules have connections with different widths, preventing the module from being inserted backwards.

Step 2.   Verify that the locking tabs on the socket are swiveled to the outside (open) position.

Step 3.   After verifying that the module is lined up correctly with the socket, push the module straight down into the socket until the swivel locks on each end of the socket snap into place at the top corners of the module (see Figure 6-3). A fair amount of force is required to engage the locks. Do not touch the gold-plated connectors on the bottom of the module; this can cause corrosion or ESD.

For clarity, the memory module installation pictured in Figure 6-3 was photographed with the motherboard out of the case. However, the tangle of cables around and over the DIMM sockets in Figure 6-4 provides a much more realistic view of the challenges you face when you install memory in a working system.

Locking clips not engaged

Locking clips engaged; module locked in place

Figure 6-3   A DIMM partly inserted (top) and fully inserted (bottom). The memory module must be pressed firmly into place before the locking tabs will engage.

When you install memory on a motherboard inside a working system, use the following tips to help your upgrade go smoothly and the module to work properly:

■   If the system is a tower system, consider placing the system on its side to make the upgrade easier. Doing this also helps to prevent tipping the system over by accident when you push on the memory to lock it into the socket.

■   Move the locking mechanisms on the DIMM sockets to the open position before you try to insert the module. In Figure 6-4, the locks on the empty socket are in the closed position. Figure 6-3 shows open and closed locks for comparison.

■   Move power and drive cables away from the memory sockets so you can access the sockets. Disconnect drive cables if necessary.

■   Use a flashlight to shine light into the interior of the system so you can see the memory sockets and locking mechanisms clearly; this enables you to determine the proper orientation of the module and to make sure the sockets' locking mechanisms are open.

■   Use a flashlight to double-check your memory installation to make sure the module is completely inserted into the slot and locked into place.

- Replace any cables you moved or disconnected during the process before you close the case and restart the system.

> **TIP**   Note the positions of any cables you need to remove before you remove them to perform an internal upgrade. I like to use self-stick colored dots on a drive and its matching data and power cables. You can purchase sheets of colored dots at most office-supply and discount stores.

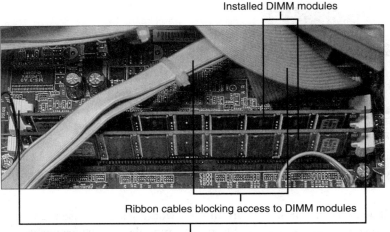

Installed DIMM modules

Ribbon cables blocking access to DIMM modules

Locking mechanism on empty DIMM socket in closed position;
must be opened before another module can be installed

Figure 6-4   DDR DIMM sockets in a typical system are often surrounded and covered up by drive and power cables, making it difficult to properly install additional memory.

Troubleshooting Memory

Because all information you create with a computer starts out in RAM, keeping RAM working properly is very important. This section describes troubleshooting problems that might affect memory.

Verifying RAM Compatibility

Because of the wide range of speeds, latencies (CL ratings), and other performance factors, it's easier than ever before to install a memory module that will fit into a system but is not compatible with the system. Incompatible memory modules can cause system lockups or crashes or corrupted data.

To determine whether a particular module will work in a particular system or motherboard, check the module for brand and model number markings, then use a lookup or system analysis tool provided by the memory module vendor to determine which modules are recommended for a particular system or motherboard. Most memory vendors provide these tools on their websites. If the module is not recommended for the system or motherboard, don't install it.

Overclocking Can Lead to System Instability

If you run the processor or memory at speeds faster than those recommended, a process called *overclocking*, you could cause components to overheat and the system to crash. If your system crashes after overclocking, return the settings to standard values and restart the system. If the system is now stable, don't overclock it until you can add adequate cooling to the system. Overclocking is not recommended for business uses or for beginners.

CAUTION   Overclocking generates excess heat, which alone can cause damage to components. To make matters worse, one of the favorite ways that overclockers have to improve system stability is to slightly increase the voltage going to the processor core (Vcore) or to the memory modules, which further increases heat.

Don't even *think* about overclocking unless you study overclocking-oriented websites such as www.overclockers.com or publications such as *MaximumPC* (www.maximumpc.com). A careful perusal of these and other resources will tell you that successful overclocking requires a lot of time, a fair amount of cash, a lot of tolerance for damaged components, frequent rebooting, crashes, voided warranties, and so on.

Avoid Mixing Metals in RAM and Sockets

Two types of metal are used for contacts on SIMMs: gold and tin. Putting gold-tipped SIMMs in tin sockets or tin-tipped SIMMs in gold sockets is asking for corrosion and eventual system lockups. Match the metal to avoid problems. If you have systems that have mixed metals and you can't change them, periodically remove the memory modules, wipe off the contacts carefully, and reinstall them.

Use Caution When Mismatching RAM Speeds

Motherboards are designed to use particular speeds of memory modules, and all memory modules installed in a computer should meet or exceed the memory speed required by the system. Depending on the system, memory might be rated in nanoseconds (ns), by the bus speed of the CPU (such as PC-133), or by their throughput (such as DDR2-6400).

Newer systems are generally more tolerant of differences in memory timing. Some systems can access each module at its maximum speed, whereas others might slow down automatically to adjust to the slower access time. Some older systems might crash if additional memory is a different speed than the memory originally installed. Adjusting BIOS settings for memory timing might improve reliability in such cases.

Memory speeds can be determined from the memory chips themselves on SIMMs or from the markings on DIMMs or Rambus RDRAM modules (see Figure 6-5).

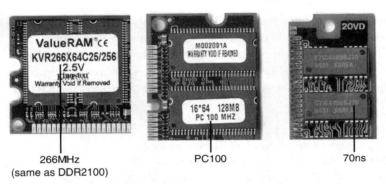

266MHz   PC100   70ns
(same as DDR2100)

Figure 6-5 Memory-speed markings on a DDR DIMM module (left), a standard SDRAM DIMM module (center), and a 72-pin SIMM (right).

As you can see from Figure 6-5, newer DIMM modules often have more informative markings than old modules. If you need to read the memory speed directly from the chips on the module, use these rules of thumb:

■ Generally, the speed (in nanoseconds) is the last two numbers (often following a dash or alphanumerics) on the memory module: xxxxx - 15 (15ns) yyyyyyyy - 60 (60ns).

■ Some memory chips use an abbreviated marking: xxxxx - 7 (70ns) yyyyy - 10 (100ns).

To verify speeds, you can use a standalone RAM tester, a small device that has connectors for different types of memory and a readout indicating actual speed, size, and other information.

For more information about testing RAM with both diagnostics software and hardware testing devices, see "Other Methods for RAM Testing," later in this chapter.

EDO Compatibility with Other RAM Types

Although 168-pin DIMM modules are available in both SDRAM and EDO types (EDO is rare), and some older motherboards can use one or the other, don't mix them. Their timings aren't compatible; EDO RAM has an access speed of 60ns, whereas SDRAM has access speeds of 15ns or less, depending on whether it is PC-66, PC-100, or PC-133 compatible.

EDO memory can be used with FPM memory on systems using 72-pin SIMMs if the memory is in separate banks. EDO will be forced to slow down to match FPM's slower access. Some systems require that you enable EDO support in the BIOS setup.

If you are adding memory to older systems that use SIMMs, don't mix 60ns (EDO) with 70ns or slower FP memory unless the system can be configured to provide separate timing settings for each bank. Keep in mind that you must use two identical 72-pin SIMMs to provide a memory bank for a 64-bit system that uses SIMMs.

"Parity Error - System Halted" Message

Parity errors halt your system and require you to restart your computer. To use parity checking, you must be using parity-checked RAM (x9, x36, or x72 module types) and your computer must support parity checking and have this feature enabled. Parity error can result from

- Mixing parity and non-parity RAM on parity-checked systems
- Mixing slow and fast RAM in the same bank or on the same motherboard
- Loose or corroded chip and module connectors
- Memory module/chip failure

If you enable parity checking in the BIOS setup and don't have parity modules, you'll have immediate errors. You can use parity memory along with non-parity memory by disabling parity checking in the system BIOS. Refer to Chapter 4, "BIOS," for more information about BIOS.

RAM-Sizing Errors at Bootup

Most systems test memory, and some will alert you to a change in the memory size detected compared to the BIOS value. This is normal if you have just added memory. In such cases, enter the system BIOS setup program, exit and save changes, and restart the computer. However, a memory size error that occurs later indicates a memory problem. To determine which module is affected, follow these steps:

Step 1.   Note the memory count reached onscreen when the memory error is detected.

Step 2.   Check the motherboard documentation to see which modules must be installed first.

Step 3.   Change one module at a time, starting with the one you think is defective, until the error goes away.

Step 4.   Disable cache RAM in the BIOS setup when testing memory.

A memory-sizing error that won't go away after all memory is changed might indicate a defective motherboard or defective cache memory.

Determining Whether Cache RAM Is the Source of a Memory Problem

Because cache RAM holds a copy of the information in main memory, errors in cache RAM can appear to be errors in system RAM. Use the following procedure to determine whether cache RAM is the cause of a memory problem:

Step 1.   Disable L2 cache first.

Step 2.   If the memory problem goes away, determine where L2 cache is located (processor or motherboard). If the motherboard uses removable cache chips or a cache module (some very old systems used cache chips or modules), replace the cache memory. If the motherboard uses non-removable cache chips, replace the motherboard. If L2 cache is built into the processor, replace the processor.

Step 3.   If the system runs normally, the replacement is successful. If the problem persists after replacing the component containing cache RAM, return the original component(s) to the system.

Step 4.   Disable L1 cache.

Step 5.   If the system runs normally, replace the CPU and retest.

Step 6.   If the system runs normally after replacement, the CPU's L1 cache is faulty.

NOTE   If the processor includes both L2 and L3 cache, disable both in Step 1. Check the system BIOS for an option such as CPU Internal cache. Some memory testing programs can be configured to bypass cache memory when testing main memory. See the documentation or help system for your memory testing program for details.

Other Methods for RAM Testing

Many utility programs, including CheckIt, AMIDiag, RAMExam, and others feature powerful memory-testing programs that can run continuously and use many more testing options than the fast POST test performed by the computer at startup. Most of these programs are run from bootable floppy or CD media, so they bypass the normal operating system.

If you install or replace a large number of memory modules, a dedicated RAM tester provides the most accurate and complete method for finding RAM problems. RAM testers can be used to do the following:

- Determine memory type, size, and true speed

- Separate good RAM from bad RAM when all RAM is removed from a system

- Heat test and stress test RAM independently of the motherboard or operating system

Preventative Maintenance for Memory

The contents of memory are sensitive to overheating. To avoid overheated memory modules, perform the following tasks as needed.

- Keep the surfaces of the modules clean. You can use compressed air or a data-rated vacuum cleaner to remove dust.

- Make sure you are using the recommended voltage level for the memory installed if your system's BIOS setup permits voltage adjustments.

- Install additional case fans over or behind the location of memory modules to pull hot air out of the system.

- Keep air intake vents in the front of the system clean.

- Replace any defective cooling fans.

To learn more about system cooling issues, see Chapter 5, "Power Supplies and System Cooling." To learn more about BIOS configuration issues, see Chapter 4.

Exam Preparation Tasks

Review All the Key Topics

Review the most important topics in the chapter, noted with the key topics icon in the outer margin of the page. Table 6-4 lists a reference of these key topics and the page numbers on which each is found.

Table 6-4 Key Topics for Chapter 6

Key Topic Element	Description	Page Number
Table 6-2	RAM Comparisons.	204
Figure 6-1	Desktop memory modules (SIMM, SIPP, and DIMM) compared.	206
Figure 6-3	A DIMM partly inserted (top) and fully inserted (bottom).	211
Figure 6-5	Memory-speed markings.	214

Complete the Tables and Lists from Memory

Print a copy of Appendix B, "Memory Tables," (found on the CD), or at least the section for this chapter, and complete the tables and lists from memory. Appendix C, "Memory Tables Answer Key," also on the CD, includes completed tables and lists to check your work.

Definitions of Key Terms

Define the following key terms from this chapter, and check your answers in the glossary.

RAM, Paging, Paging file, SRAM, DRAM, SDRAM, DDR SDRAM, DDR2 SDRAM, DDR3 SDRAM, Rambus, SIMM, SIPP, DIMM, SODIMM, SIMM, SIPP, Rambus RDRAM Module, Small Outline Rambus Module, ECC, EDO

Troubleshooting Scenario

You are asked to help someone overclock their system memory. What should you tell them?

Refer to Appendix A for the answer.

This chapter covers the following subjects:

- **Understanding I/O Ports**—This section describes the types of I/O ports used to send information to and from the processor and memory.

- **Understanding Input Devices**—This section describes the important characteristics of keyboards, mice, biometric readers, and other input devices.

- **Understanding Multimedia Devices**—This section covers the basics of multimedia devices such as webcams, digital cameras, MIDI ports, microphones, sound cards, and video capture cards.

- **Installing Input and Multimedia Devices**—This section demonstrates how to install keyboards, mice, webcams, digital cameras, and other input and multimedia devices.

- **Troubleshooting Input and Multimedia Devices**—This section describes how you troubleshoot the input and multimedia devices covered in the chapter.

- **Troubleshooting I/O Ports**—This section demonstrates how to fix common issues that may affect PS/2, LPT, Serial, and USB ports.

- **Maintaining Input Devices**—This section talks about how to take care of keyboards, mice, and other devices with cleaning and proper tools.

This chapter covers a portion of the CompTIA A+ 220-701 objectives 1.1, 1.2, 1.8, and 1.9, and CompTIA A+ 220-702 objectives 1.1 and 1.2

CHAPTER 7

I/O and Multimedia Ports and Devices

Input/output (I/O) devices allow us to control the computer and display information in a variety of ways. There are a plethora of ports that connect these devices to the computer, for example, the well-known USB port. To fully understand how to install, configure, and troubleshoot input, output, and multimedia devices, you need to know the ports like the back of your hand. In this chapter you will learn about serial, parallel, SCSI, USB, sound, and FireWire ports; the goal is to make you proficient with the various interfaces you will see in the IT field.

"Do I Know This Already?" Quiz

The "Do I Know This Already?" quiz allows you to assess whether you should read this entire chapter or simply jump to the "Exam Preparation Tasks" section for review. If you are in doubt, read the entire chapter. Table 7-1 outlines the major headings in this chapter and the corresponding "Do I Know This Already?" quiz questions. You can find the answers in Appendix A, "Answers to the 'Do I Know This Already?' Quizzes and Troubleshooting Scenarios."

Table 7-1   "Do I Know This Already?" Foundation Topics Section-to-Question Mapping

Foundations Topics Section	Questions Covered in This Section
Understanding I/O Ports	1–9
Understanding Input Devices	10, 11
Understanding Multimedia Devices	12, 13
Installing Input and Multimedia Devices	14
Troubleshooting Input and Multimedia Devices	15
Troubleshooting I/O Ports	16
Maintaining Input Devices	17

1. Which of the following can be used with the SCSI- (Small Computer Systems Interface) based technology? (Choose two.)

   a. High-performance and high-capacity hard drives

   b. Image scanners

   c. Hubs

   d. Switches

2. When daisy-chaining SCSI devices, what must each device have? (Choose two.)

   a. Each device must have a unique SCSI device ID.

   b. They must have a separate bus.

   c. Each end of the daisy-chain must be terminated.

   d. They require their own adapter.

3. A serial port can hook up devices such as external modems and label printers. What is this port usually called?

   a. SCSI port

   b. COM port

   c. PS/2 ports

   d. Parallel port

4. Which of the following devices can be used for a printer port, scanner, or re-movable media?

   a. PS/2 port

   b. Parallel port

   c. NIC card

   d. I/O port

5. Which device is known as IEEE 1394?

   a. USB

   b. Parallel port

   c. FireWire

   d. PS/2

6. Some desktop systems and many of the older laptop and portable systems include a port to connect a mouse or keyboard. What is this port called?

   a. USB

   b. FireWire

   c. BIOS

   d. PS/2

7. What is the standard size of the audio mini-jack used by sound cards?

  a. 1 1/2 inch

  b. 1/8 inch

  c. 2 1/2 inch

  d. 1 inch

8. There are two standards for USB ports. What are they? (Choose two.)

  a. USB 1.1

  b. USB 3.2

  c. USB 1.0

  d. USB 2.0

9. If you run out of USB ports and need more, which of the following devices are available? (Choose all that apply.)

  a. Motherboard connectors

  b. USB hubs

  c. Add-on cards

  d. Extra PCI slots

10. Which device still remains the primary method used to enter data and send commands to the computer?

  a. Mouse

  b. Gamepad

  c. Stylus

  d. Keyboard

11. Which of the following is used to transfer data into a computer by pressing on screen icons?

  a. Touch screen monitors

  b. CRT monitors

  c. LCD monitors

  d. Serial ports

12. Which of the following are considered multimedia devices? (Choose all that apply.)

  a. Webcam

  b. Sound card

  c. Microphone

  d. All of these options are correct

13. You have just attached speakers to a sound card that you know to be working. After you restart the computer you notice that no sound is coming out. Which of the following could be the problem? (Choose two.)

   a. The sound card was not seated properly.

   b. The sound card is defective.

   c. The speakers are turned off.

   d. The speakers are plugged into the wrong jack.

14. You are in the process of installing a new keyboard to a new PC. Which of the following is the most common type of connector to use?

   a. Blu-ray connector

   b. PS/2 connector

   c. USB connector

   d. PS/3 connector

15. Which of the following can cause problems with keyboards? (Choose all that apply.)

   a. A damaged keyboard connector on the computer

   b. A damaged keyboard cable

   c. Dirt, dust, or gunk in the keyboard

   d. None of these apply

16. Which of the following would you check first when troubleshooting multiple USB devices that are not recognized by Windows?

   a. Disable the device in Windows

   b. Reinstall the driver

   c. Enable USB ports in the BIOS

   d. Flash the BIOS

17. You have been informed by a user that his mouse is not working correctly. After asking some questions you have discovered that he is using a ball and roller design. Which of the following steps can you take to correct the problem? (Choose all that apply.)

   a. Open the access cover to release the ball

   b. Shake loose any dust

   c. Turn the rollers until you see the grime or dirt

   d. Wipe the rollers clean

Foundation Topics

Understanding I/O Ports

I/O ports are used to send information to and from the processor and memory. While the most important I/O port on recent systems is the USB port, you might also encounter other ports, including legacy ports such as serial and parallel. The following sections explain the major features of each port type covered by the A+ Certification exams.

USB

Universal Serial Bus (USB) ports have largely replaced PS/2 (mini-DIN) mouse and keyboard, serial (COM), and parallel (LPT) ports on recent systems. Most recent desktop systems have at least four USB ports, and many systems support as many as eight or more front- and rear-mounted USB ports. Figure 7-1 shows the rear panel of a typical ATX system, including USB and other port types discussed in this chapter.

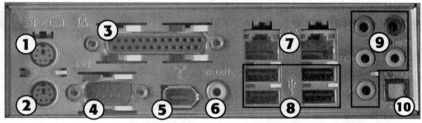

1. PS/2 mouse port   6. SPDIF coaxial digital audio port
2. PS/2 keyboard port   7. Ethernet ports
3. Parallel port   8. USB ports
4. Serial port   9. 1/8-inch mini-jack audio ports
5. IEEE 1394a port   10. SPDIF optical digital audio port

Figure 7-1   A typical ATX motherboard's I/O ports, complete with legacy (serial, parallel, PS/2 mouse and keyboard), four USB, one IEEE 1394, two Ethernet, and audio ports.

The following sections describe USB port types and how to add more USB ports.

USB Port Types, Speeds, and Technical Details

There are two standards of USB ports you need to know for the exam:

- USB 1.1

- USB 2.0 (also called Hi-Speed USB)

Both standards use the same cable and connector types, which are shown in Figure 7-2.

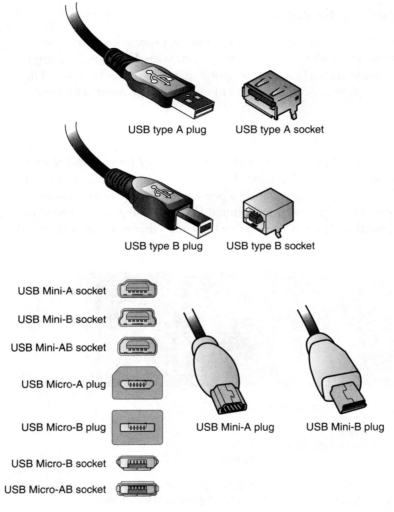

Figure 7-2 USB plugs and sockets.

USB cables use two different types of connectors: Series A (also called Type A) and Series B (also called Type B). Series A connectors are used on USB root hubs (the USB ports in the computer) and USB external hubs to support USB devices. Series B connectors are used for devices that employ a removable USB cable, such as a USB printer or a generic (external) hub. Generally, you need a Series A–to–Series B cable to attach most devices to a USB root or external hub. Cables that are Series

A–to–Series A or Series B–to–Series B are used to extend standard cables, and can cause problems if the combined length of the cables exceeds recommended distances. Adapters are available to convert Series B cables into Mini-B cables, which support the Mini-B port design used on many recent USB devices.

TIP I don't recommend using extension cables or cables that are longer than 6 feet (especially with USB 1.1 ports or with any type of hub-powered device); I've seen some devices stop working when longer-than-normal cables were used. If you need a longer cable run, use a self-powered hub between the PC and the device. The self-powered hub provides the power needed for any USB device and keeps the signal at full strength.

USB 1.1 ports run at a top speed (full-speed USB) of 12 megabits per second (Mbps), low-speed USB devices such as a mouse or a keyboard run at 1.5Mbps, and USB 2.0 (Hi-Speed USB) ports run at a top speed of 480Mbps. USB 2.0 ports are backward-compatible with USB 1.1 devices and speeds, and manage multiple USB 1.1 devices better than a USB 1.1 port does.

USB packaging and device markings frequently use the official logos shown in Figure 7-3 to distinguish the two versions of USB in common use. Note that the industry is shifting from using the term "USB 2.0" to "Hi-Speed USB."

Figure 7-3 The USB logo (left) is used for USB 1.1–compatible devices, whereas the Hi-Speed USB logo (right) is used for USB 2.0–compatible devices. Devices bearing these logos have been certified by the USB Implementers Forum, Inc.

With either version of USB, a single USB port on an add-on card or motherboard is designed to handle up to 127 devices through the use of multiport hubs and daisy-chaining hubs. Starting with Windows 98, USB devices are Plug and Play (PnP) devices that are hot swappable (can be connected and disconnected without turning off the system). The USB ports (each group of two ports is connected to a root hub) in the computer use a single IRQ and a single I/O port address, regardless of the number of physical USB ports or devices attached to those ports.

The maximum length for a cable attached to 12Mbps or 480Mbps USB devices is 5 meters, whereas the maximum length for low-speed (1.5Mbps) devices such as mice and keyboards is 3 meters. When a USB root hub is enabled in a computer running Windows, two devices will be visible in the Windows Device Manager: a USB root hub and a PCI-to-USB universal host controller (USB 1.1) or advanced host controller (USB 2.0), which uses the single IRQ and I/O port address required by USB hardware. If an external USB hub is attached to the computer, a generic hub also will be listed in the Windows Device Manager (see Figure 7-4). A root hub supports two USB ports. In Figure 7-4, there are two root hubs listed, indicating that the system has four USB ports.

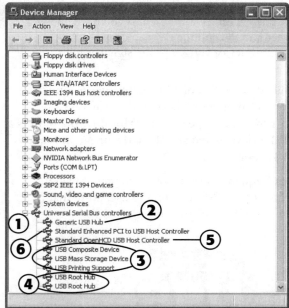

1. USB category
2. Generic (external) USB hub
3. Device-specific USB support
4. USB root hubs
5. USB universal host controller (USB 1.1 support)
6. USB enhanced host controller (USB 2.0 support)

Figure 7-4   The USB section of the Windows XP Device Manager on a typical system. Note the fork-shaped USB logo next to the category and each device.

Adding USB Ports

Need more USB ports? You can add USB ports with any of the following methods:

- Motherboard connectors for USB header cables
- Hubs
- Add-on cards

Some motherboards have USB header cable connectors, which enable you to make additional USB ports available on the rear or front of the computer. Some motherboard vendors include these header cables with the motherboard, whereas others require you to purchase them separately. Some recent case designs also include front-mounted USB ports, which can also be connected to the motherboard. Because of vendor-specific differences in how motherboards implement header cables, the header cable might use separate connectors for each signal instead of the more common single connector for all signals.

USB generic hubs enable you to connect multiple devices to the same USB port and to increase the distance between the device and the USB port. There are two types of generic hubs:

- Bus-powered
- Self-powered

Bus-powered hubs might be built into other devices, such as monitors and keyboards, or can be standalone devices. A bus-powered hub distributes both USB signals and power via the USB bus to other devices. Different USB devices use different amounts of power, and some devices require more power than others do. A bus-powered hub provides no more than 100 milliamps (mA) of power to each device connected to it. Thus, some devices fail when connected to a bus-powered hub.

A self-powered hub, on the other hand, has its own power source; it plugs into an AC wall outlet. It can provide up to 500mA of power to each device connected to it. A self-powered hub supports a wider range of USB devices, and I recommend using it instead of a bus-powered hub whenever possible.

SCSI

SCSI (Small Computer Systems Interface) is a very flexible interface because it can accommodate many devices in addition to hard disk drives. Currently, SCSI interfaces, either on the motherboard or as add-on cards, are found primarily in servers and are used for mass storage (hard disk, tape backup), although you might encounter workstations and PCs that use SCSI interfaces for devices such as

- High-performance and high-capacity hard drives
- Image scanners
- Removable-media drives such as Zip, Jaz, and Castlewood Orb
- High-performance laser printers
- Optical drives
- Tape backups

So-called Narrow SCSI host adapters (which use an 8-bit data channel) can accommodate up to seven devices of different varieties on a single connector. Wide SCSI host adapters use a 16-bit data channel and accommodate up to 15 devices on a single connector.

Multiple Device Support with SCSI Host Adapters

All true SCSI host adapters are designed to support multiple devices, although some low-cost SCSI host adapters made especially for scanners and Zip drives might not support multiple devices (also known as daisy-chaining). Several SCSI features permit daisy-chaining:

- External SCSI peripherals have two SCSI ports, enabling daisy-chaining of multiple devices.

- Internal SCSI ribbon cables resemble IDE data cables, only wider.

- Both internal and external SCSI peripherals enable the user to choose a unique device ID number for each device to distinguish one peripheral from another in the daisy-chain (see Figure 7-5).

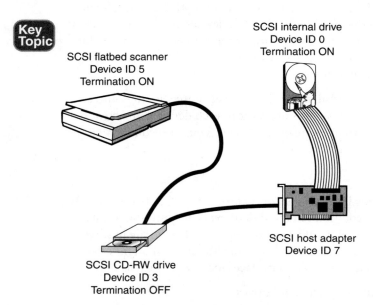

Key Topic

SCSI flatbed scanner
Device ID 5
Termination ON

SCSI internal drive
Device ID 0
Termination ON

SCSI host adapter
Device ID 7

SCSI CD-RW drive
Device ID 3
Termination OFF

Figure 7-5   When a SCSI host adapter card with internal and external connectors is used, the SCSI daisy-chain can extend through the card. Note that the devices on each end of the chain are terminated, and each device (including the host adapter) has a unique device ID number.

Multiple device support enables the different types of devices listed previously to work on a single SCSI host adapter. To determine which device IDs are in use, you can

- Physically examine each SCSI device's device ID settings.

- Scan the SCSI bus with a software program such as Adaptec's SCSI Interrogator or with the BIOS routines built into some SCSI host adapters.

- View the properties for each SCSI device in the Windows Device Manager.

Jumper Block and DIP Switch Settings for Device IDs

Each SCSI device must have a unique device ID to distinguish itself from other SCSI devices connected to the same SCSI channel. Narrow SCSI (50-pin data cable) devices use a set of three jumpers or DIP switches to set the device ID. Wide SCSI (68-pin data cable) devices use a set of four jumpers or DIP switches to set the device ID.

The device ID is set in binary (base 2) values in order from bit 0 (least significant bit or LSB) to the most significant bit or MSB. Table 7-2 lists the settings for narrow SCSI devices (IDs 0–7); Table 7-3 lists the settings for wide SCSI devices (IDs 0–15).

Table 7-2   Narrow SCSI LSB-to-MSB Device ID Settings

Device ID	Bit 0 (LSB)	Bit 1	Bit 2 (MSB)
0	0	0	0
1	1	0	0
2	0	1	0
3	1	1	0
4	0	0	1
5	1	0	1
6	0	1	1
7	1	1	1

Table 7-3   Wide SCSI LSB-to-MSB Device ID Settings

Device ID	Bit 0 (LSB)	Bit 1	Bit 2	Bit 3 (MSB)
0	0	0	0	0
1	1	0	0	0
2	0	1	0	0
3	1	1	0	0
4	0	0	1	0
5	1	0	1	0
6	0	1	1	0
7	1	1	1	0
8	0	0	0	1
9	1	0	0	1
10	0	1	0	1
11	1	1	0	1

Table 7-3   Wide SCSI LSB-to-MSB Device ID Settings

Device ID	Bit 0 (LSB)	Bit 1	Bit 2	Bit 3 (MSB)
12	0	0	1	1
13	1	0	1	1
14	0	1	1	1
15	1	1	1	1

In the following tables, 1 means jumper block on or DIP switch set to ON; 0 means jumper block off or DIP switch set to OFF.

Device ID 7 is usually reserved for use by the SCSI host adapter.

Tables 7-2 and 7-3 assume that the jumper blocks or DIP switches place bit 0 at the left. If the device places bit 0 at the right, reverse the order in the preceding list when setting the configuration.

TIP   The jumper blocks or DIP switches used to configure the device ID might be part of a larger array of jumper blocks or DIP switches used to set all drive features. Check the documentation for the drive to determine which jumper blocks or DIP switches to use.

SCSI Standards

SCSI actually is the family name for a wide range of standards, which differ from each other in the speed of devices, number of devices, and other technical details. The major SCSI standards are listed in Table 7-4.

Table 7-4   Popular SCSI Standards

Popular Name	Speed	Number of Devices	Data Bus	Signal Type
Fast	10MBps	7	8-bit	SE[1]
Fast-Wide	10MBps	15	16-bit	SE
Ultra	20MBps	7	8-bit	SE
Ultra-Wide	20MBps	15	16-bit	SE
Ultra2	40MBps	7	8-bit	LVD[2]
Ultra2Wide	80MBps	15	16-bit	LVD
Ultra 160	160MBps	15	16-bit	LVD
Ultra 320	320MBps	15	16-bit	LVD

[1]Single-ended
[2]Low-voltage differential

8-bit versions of SCSI use a 50-pin cable or a 25-pin cable; wide (16-bit) versions use a 68-pin cable.

SCSI host adapters are generally backward compatible, enabling older and newer SCSI standards to be mixed on the same host adapter. However, mixing slower and faster devices can cause the faster devices to slow down unless you use a host adapter with dual buses that can run at different speeds.

SCSI Cables

Just as no single SCSI standard exists, no single SCSI cabling standard exists. In addition to the 50-pin versus 68-pin difference between standard and wide devices, differences also appear in the Narrow SCSI external cables. Figure 7-6 compares internal SCSI cables for wide and narrow applications, and Figure 7-7 compares various types of external SCSI cables and ports.

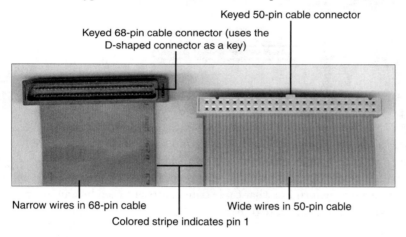

Figure 7-6 A wide (68-pin) SCSI ribbon cable (left) compared to a narrow (50-pin) SCSI ribbon cable (right).

Compare Figure 7-6 to Figure 12-8 to see the resemblance between SCSI 50-pin ribbon cables and PATA (ATA/IDE) cables: SCSI 50-pin cables resemble PATA cables but are wider. However, three different types of Narrow SCSI external connectors are available (see Figure 7-7):

- **50-pin Centronics**—Similar to, but wider than, the 36-pin Centronics port used for parallel printers. Also called LD50.

- **50-pin high-density connector (HD50)**—The Wide SCSI 68-pin connector (HD68) uses the same design but with 34 pins per row instead of 25 pins per row.

- **25-pin DB-25F**—Physically, but not electronically, similar to the DB-25F parallel printer port.

Most recent external 8-bit (narrow) SCSI devices use the HD50 connector, whereas older models use the LD50 (Centronics) connector. However, a few low-

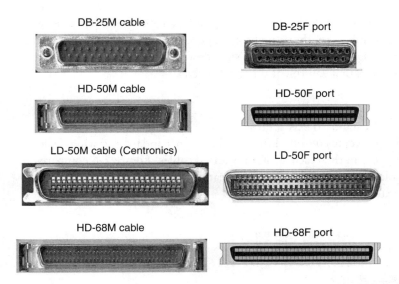

DB-25M cable

DB-25F port

HD-50M cable

HD-50F port

LD-50M cable (Centronics)

LD-50F port

HD-68M cable

HD-68F port

Figure 7-7   Wide (68-pin) and narrow (50-pin, 25-pin) SCSI cable connectors (left) and the corresponding SCSI port connectors (right).

cost SCSI devices such as the Iomega Zip-100 drive and some SCSI scanners use only the 25-pin connector, which lacks much of the grounding found on the 50-pin cable. Some SCSI devices provide two different types of SCSI connectors. Consequently, you need to determine what cable connectors are used by any external SCSI devices you wish to connect together.

SCSI Signaling Types

In Table 7-3 (previously shown), SE stands for single-ended, a SCSI signaling type that runs at speeds of up to 20MBps only. SE signaling enables relatively inexpensive SCSI devices and host adapters to be developed, but it reduces the length of cables and the top speed possible.

Ultra2, Ultra2Wide, Ultra 160, and Ultra 320 devices all use a signaling standard called low-voltage differential (LVD), which enables longer cable runs and faster, more reliable operation than the single-ended (SE) standard allows. Some LVD devices can also be used on the same bus with SE devices, but these multimode, or LVD/SE devices, will be forced to slow down to the SE maximum of 20MBps when mixed with SE devices on the same bus. Some advanced SCSI host adapters feature both an SE and an LVD bus to enable the same adapter to control both types of devices at the correct speeds.

Daisy-Chaining SCSI Devices

When you create a SCSI daisy-chain, you must keep all these factors in mind:

- Each device must have a unique SCSI device ID (refer to Table 7-2 and Table 7-3).

- Each end of the daisy-chain must be terminated. Some devices have an integral switch or jumper block for termination (see Figures 7-8 and 7-9), whereas some external devices require that you attach a terminator (which resembles the end of a SCSI cable) to the unused SCSI connector.

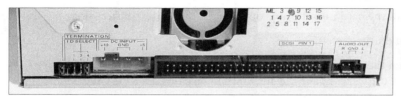

Figure 7-8   A SCSI-based internal CD-R drive with (left to right) well-marked jumpers for termination and device ID, power connector, data cable pin 1, and CD-audio cable.

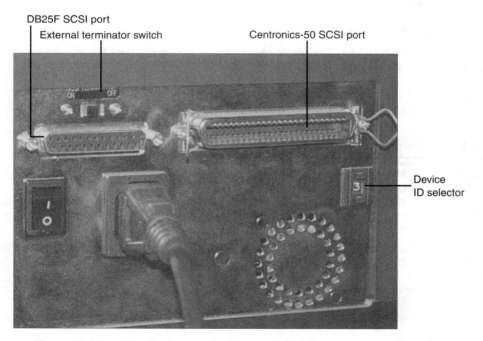

Figure 7-9   External termination and device ID selector switches on a SCSI-based scanner. This scanner has both DB25-F and Centronics-50 (also called LD50-F) SCSI ports.

- When daisy-chaining external devices, double-check the cable connector type and purchase appropriate cables. You will often need SCSI cables that have different connectors at each end because of the different connector types used (see Figure 7-9).

SCSI Host Adapter Card Installation

Follow these steps to install a PnP SCSI host adapter card:

Step 1. Check the card's documentation and make any required adjustments in the PnP configuration in the BIOS before installing the card. You might need to change the type of IRQ setting used or reserve a particular IRQ for the card.

Step 2. Install the card into the appropriate ISA or PCI expansion slot.

Step 3. Turn on the system.

Step 4. When the card is detected by the system, you'll be prompted for installation software. Insert the appropriate disk or CD-ROM and follow the prompt to complete the installation.

Step 5. Reboot the system and use the Windows Device Manager to view the card's configuration.

SCSI Daisy-Chain Maximum Length

The maximum length of a SCSI daisy-chain depends upon the speed of the devices used and the type of signaling in use.

Single-ended (SE) signaling requires a shorter bus length as transmission speed increases. See Table 7-5 for details.

Table 7-5   Single-Ended SCSI Maximum Bus Length

SCSI Type	Maximum Length with Four Devices or Less	Maximum Length with More Than Four Devices
Fast SCSI (10Mbps)	3 meters	3 meters
Fast SCSI (20Mbps)	3 meters	3 meters
Ultra/Wide Ultra SCSI (20Mbps and faster)	3 meters	1.5 meters

The now-obsolete high-voltage differential (HVD) SCSI signaling standard supports a maximum bus length of 25 meters with any number of devices.

Low-voltage differential (LVD) SCSI signaling (supported on Ultra2 SCSI and faster versions) supports cabling length of 12 meters with any number of devices.

CAUTION   If you mix single-ended and LVD devices on the same SCSI bus, you limit the length of the bus as shown in Table 7-5. Use separate host adapters or a multichannel adapter to avoid this problem.

Figure 7-10 shows you the standard markings used to identify SE, LVD, and LVD-SE SCSI devices. LVD-SE devices can be used with either SE or LVD devices on the same daisy-chain.

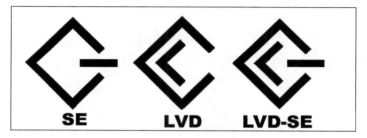

Figure 7-10   SE, LVD, and LVD-SE SCSI device markings.

SCSI Termination Methods

Both ends of a SCSI daisy-chain need to be terminated for proper operation. Although SCSI host adapters are designed to provide automatic termination, you must terminate other types of devices manually.

Low-speed external SCSI devices such as scanners and Zip drives often feature internal termination, which is configured with a switch on the unit. Some internal SCSI devices use a jumper block or DIP switch to configure termination; others use a terminating resistor pack.

Terminators are connected to the unused port on an external SCSI device or inline with the ribbon cable on an internal SCSI device if built-in termination is not available or is not used. There are two types of external termination:

- Passive
- Active

Passive terminators use no power. Passive terminators are not recommended if more than two SE devices are on a SCSI daisy-chain and are not recommended with LVD or LVD-SE devices.

Active terminators use an external power source to provide a voltage regulator for better termination. They can be used with LVD, LVD-SE, and SE-based SCSI daisy-chains.

> **TIP** Make sure you know the connector type, speed, and termination type appropriate for your SCSI device before you order a terminator. Ask the vendor for help if you aren't sure what you need. There are many varieties to choose from.

Serial (COM)

The serial port, also known as an RS-232 or COM (communication) ports historically has rivaled the parallel port in versatility (see Figure 7-11). Serial ports have been used to connect the following:

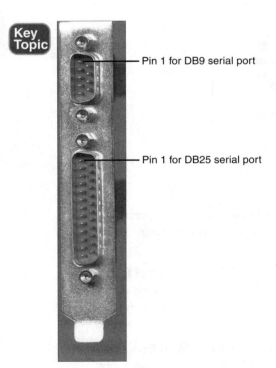

— Pin 1 for DB9 serial port

— Pin 1 for DB25 serial port

Figure 7-11 A 9-pin serial port (DB-9M connector, top) and a 25-pin serial port (DB-25M connector, bottom) on a typical extension bracket from a multi-I/O card. The ribbon cables used to connect the ports to the card can be seen in the background.

- External modems
- Serial mouse or pointing devices such as trackballs or touchpads
- Plotters
- Label printers
- Serial printers

- PDA docking stations

- Digital cameras

- PC-to-PC connections used by file transfer programs such as Direct Cable Connection, LapLink, and Interlink

NOTE   The DB-9 is actually a DE-9 connector, but is colloquially known as "DB-9" and will most likely be referred to as such on the exam. The smaller the D-sub connector, the higher the letter.

How do serial ports compare in speed with parallel ports? Serial ports transmit data one bit at a time (parallel ports send and receive data eight bits at a time), and their maximum speeds are far lower than parallel ports. However, serial cables can carry data reliably at far greater distances than parallel cables. Serial ports, unlike parallel ports, have no provision for daisy-chaining; only one device can be connected to a serial port. Because USB ports provide greater speed than both serial and parallel ports and support multiple devices connected to a single port via hubs, it's no wonder that a lot of devices that formerly plugged into the serial port are now calling the USB port "home port."

Serial ports come in two forms:

- **DB-9M** (male)

- **DB-25M** (male)

Either type can be adapted to the other connector type with a low-cost adapter (see Figure 7-12). The difference is possible because serial communications need only a few wires. Unlike parallel printers, which use a standard cable, each type of serial device uses a specially wired cable. DB-9M connectors are used on all but the oldest systems.

Figure 7-12   A typical DB-25F to DB-9M serial port converter. The DB-25F connector (lower left) connects to the 25-pin serial port and converts its signals for use by devices attaching to the DB-9M port at the other end (upper right).

Serial Port Pinouts

At a minimum, a serial cable must use at least three wires, plus ground:

- A transmit data wire

- A receive data wire

- A signal wire

Tables 7-6 and 7-7 can be used to determine the correct pinout for any specified serial cable configuration. Unlike parallel devices, which all use the same standard cable wiring, serial devices use differently wired cables. A modem cable, for example, will be wired much differently than a serial printer cable. And different serial printers might each use a unique pinout.

Table 7-6   9-Pin Serial Port Pinout

Use	Pin	Direction
Carrier Detect	1	In
Receive Data	2	In
Transmit Data	3	Out
Data Terminal Ready	4	Out
Signal Ground	5	—
Data Set Ready	6	In
Request to Send	7	Out
Clear to Send	8	In
Ring Indicator	9	In

Table 7-7   25-Pin Serial Port Pinout

Use	Pin	Direction
Transmit Data	2	Out
Receive Data	3	In
Request to Send	4	Out
Clear to Send	5	In
Data Set Ready	6	In
Signal Ground	7	—
Received Line Signal Indicator	8	In
+ Transmit Current Loop Data	9	Out

Table 7-7   25-Pin Serial Port Pinout

Use	Pin	Direction
- Transmit Current Loop Data	11	Out
+ Receive Current Loop Data	18	In
Data Terminal Ready	20	Out
Ring Indicator	22	In
- Receive Current Loop Return	25	In

NOTE   The DB-9 (9-pin male) connector is the more common of the two serial port connector types. The 25-pin serial port has many additional pins but is seldom used today. The major difference between it and the 9-pin serial interface is the 25-pin port's support for current loop data, a type of serial communications primarily used for data collection in industrial uses.

Table 7-7 lists the pinouts for the 25-pin connector; unused pins are omitted.

When a 9-pin to 25-pin serial port adapter is used (see Figure 7-12), the pins are converted to the more common 25-pin connector (see Table 7-8).

Table 7-8   9-Pin to 25-Pin Serial Port Converter/Serial Modem Pinout

Use	Pin #(9-Pin)	Pin #(25-Pin)
Carrier Detect (CD)	1	8
Receive Data (RD)	2	3
Transmit Data (TD)	3	2
Data Terminal Ready (DTR)	4	20
Signal Ground (SG)	5	7
Data Set Ready (DSR)	6	6
Request to Send (RTS)	7	4
Clear to Send (CTS)	8	5
Ring Indicator (RI)	9	22

Serial ports assume that one end of the connection transmits and the other end receives.

Types of Serial Cables

Serial cables, unlike parallel cables, can be constructed in many different ways. In fact, cables for serial devices are usually specified by device type rather than port type. This is because different devices use different pinouts.

Some of the most common examples of serial cables include

■ Null-modem (data transfer) cable

■ Modem cable

A null-modem cable enables two computers to communicate directly with each other by crossing the receive and transmit wires (meaning that two computers can send and receive data, much like a computer network, though much slower). The best known of these programs is LapLink, but the Windows Direct Cable Connection/Direct Serial Connection utilities can also use this type of cable. Although these programs support serial cable transfers, parallel port transfers are much faster and USB transfers are much faster than parallel; these methods for direct connection are recommended for most versions of Windows. However, Windows NT 4.0 and earlier do *not* support using the parallel port for file transfers, so you must use a null-modem cable such as the one shown in Figure 7-13.

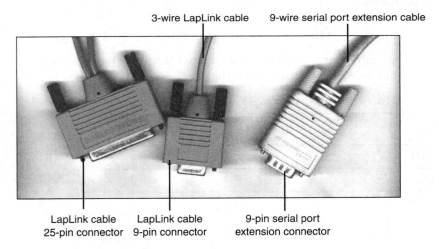

Figure 7-13   A LapLink serial cable with connectors for either 25-pin or 9-pin serial ports. Only three wires are needed, enabling the cable to be much thinner than the 9-pin serial extension cable also shown.

A modem cable is used to connect an external modem to a serial port. Some modems include a built-in cable, but others require you to use a DB-9F to DB-25M cable from the 9-pin connector on the serial port to the 25-pin port on the modem. This cable typically uses the same pinout shown in Table 7-8.

What about serial printers? These printers are used primarily with older terminals rather than with PCs, and because different printers use different pinouts, their cables must be custom-made. In fact, I've built a few myself. Fortunately, most recent terminals use parallel or USB printers.

Standard IRQ and I/O Port Addresses

Serial ports require two hardware resources: IRQ and I/O port address. Table 7-9 lists the standard IRQ and I/O port addresses used for COM ports 1–4. Some systems and add-on cards enable alternative IRQs to be used, either through jumper blocks (older cards) or via software/Device Manager configuration (newer cards).

Table 7-9   Standard Settings for COM (Serial) Ports 1–4

COM Port #	IRQ	I/O Port Address
1	4	3F8-3FFh
2	3	2F8-2FFh
3	4	3E8-3EFh
4	3	2E8-2EFh

Note that serial ports never require a DMA channel (and thus can't have DMA conflicts with other devices). However, there's another way to stumble when working with serial ports: IRQ conflicts. IRQ 4 is shared by default between COM 1 and COM 3; IRQ 3 is shared by default between COM 2 and COM 4. However, with serial ports that use the same IRQ, sharing does *not* mean that both serial ports can be used at the same time. If a device on COM 1 and a device on COM 3 that share the same IRQ are used at the same time, both devices will stop working and they might shut down the system.

How to Configure or Disable Serial Ports

Depending on the location of the serial port, there are several ways to configure the port settings to select different IRQ and I/O port addresses for a serial port, or to disable the serial port. These include

■   BIOS setup program for built-in ports

■   PnP mode for use with Windows

To adjust the configuration of a serial port built into the system's motherboard, follow these steps:

Step 1.   Start the BIOS setup program.

Step 2.   Go to the peripherals configuration screen.

Step 3.   Select the serial port you want to adjust.

Step 4.   To change the port's configuration, choose the IRQ and I/O port address you want to use, or select Disabled to prevent the system from detecting and using the serial port (see Figure 7-14).

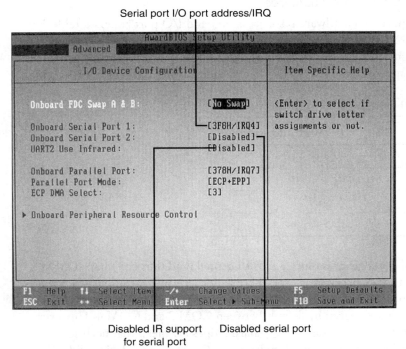

Serial port I/O port address/IRQ

Disabled IR support   Disabled serial port
for serial port

Figure 7-14   A typical BIOS I/O device configuration screen with the first serial port enabled, the second port disabled, and IR (infrared) support disabled.

Step 5.   Save changes and exit; the system reboots.

Serial ports on PCI or PCI Express cards are configured by the PnP BIOS. In some cases, you can use the Windows Device Manager to change the port configuration (see Chapter 15, "Troubleshooting and Mainaining Windows," for details).

Serial Port Software Configuration

Unlike parallel ports, serial ports have many different configuration options, making successful setup more challenging. Through software settings at the computer end, and by hardware or software settings at the device end, serial devices can use

■ A wide variety of transmission speeds, from as low as 300 bps to as high as 115,200 bps or faster

■ Different word lengths (7 bit or 8 bit)

- Different methods of flow control (XON/XOFF or DTR/DSR)

- Different methods of ensuring reliable data transmission (even parity, odd parity, no parity, 1-bit or 2-bit parity length)

Although simple devices such as a mouse or a label printer don't require that these settings be made manually (the software drivers do it), serial printers used with PCs running terminal-emulation software, PCs communicating with mainframe computers, serial pen plotters, serial printers, and PCs using modems often do require that these options be set correctly. Both ends of a serial connection must have these configurations set to identical values, or the communications between your computer and the other device will fail.

Figure 7-15 illustrates how Windows XP configures the port speed, flow control, and hardware settings for a serial port connected to an external modem.

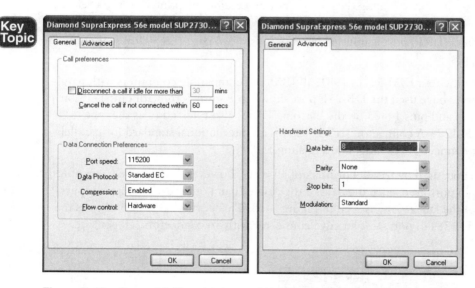

Figure 7-15   General (left) and Advanced (right) dialog boxes used in Windows XP to configure a serial port connected to an external modem.

Adding Additional Serial Ports

You can add additional serial ports to a system with any of the following:

- PCI-based serial or multi-I/O card

- PCI Express-based serial or multi-I/O card

- USB-to-serial-port adapter

Parallel (LPT)

The parallel port, also known as the LPT (Line Printer) port, was originally designed for use with parallel printers. However, don't let the name "LPT port" fool you. Historically, the parallel port has been among the most versatile of I/O ports in the system because it was also used by a variety of devices, including tape backups, external CD-ROM and optical drives, scanners, and removable-media drives such as Zip drives. Although newer devices in these categories are now designed to use USB or IEEE 1394 ports, the parallel port continues to be an important external I/O device for older systems.

> **CAUTION**   Devices other than printers that plug into the parallel (LPT) port have two connectors: one for the cable that runs from the device to the parallel port, and another for the cable that runs from the device to the printer. Although it's theoretically possible to create a long daisy-chain of devices ending with a printer, in practice you should have no more than one device plus a printer plugged into a parallel port. If you use more than one device, you could have problems getting the devices (not to mention the printer) to work reliably.

The parallel (LPT) port is unusual because it uses two completely different connector types:

- Since the first IBM PC of 1981, all IBM and compatible computers with parallel ports have used the DB-25F port shown in Figure 7-16, with pins 1–13 on the top and pins 14–25 on the bottom. This is also referred to as the type IEEE-1284-A connector. (IEEE 1284 is an international standard for parallel port connectors, cabling, and signaling.)

- The port used by parallel printers of all types, however, is the same Centronics 36-pin port used since the days of the Apple II and other early microcomputers of the late 1970s, as seen in Figure 7-16. This port is also referred to as the IEEE-1284-B port. It is an edge connector with 36 connectors, 18 per side.

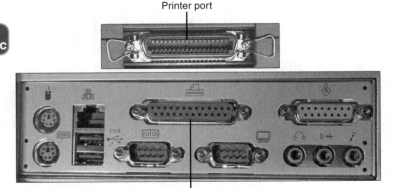

Printer port

Parallel port on computer

Figure 7-16   Parallel devices use the Centronics port (top) for printers and some other types of parallel devices, whereas the DB-25F port (bottom) is used for the computer's parallel port. Some external devices also use a DB-25F port.

Some Hewlett-Packard LaserJet printers also use a miniature version of the Centronics connector known as the IEEE-1284-C, which is also a 36-pin edge connector. The 1284-C connector doesn't use wire clips.

Accordingly, a parallel printer cable also has different connectors at each end, as seen in Figure 7-17.

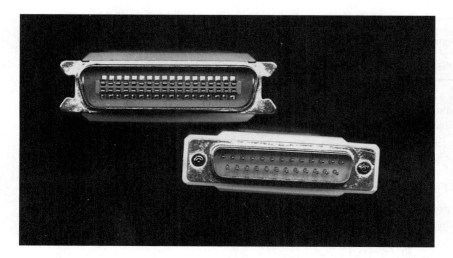

Figure 7-17　The ends of a typical IBM-style parallel cable. The Centronics 36-pin connector (upper left) connects to the printer; the DB-25M connector (lower right) connects to the computer's DB-25F parallel port.

Parallel cables have the pinout described in Table 7-10.

Table 7-10　Parallel Port Pinout (DB-25F Connector)

Pin #	Description	I/O	Pin #	Description	I/O
1	-Strobe	Out	8	+Data bit 6	Out
2	+Data bit 0	Out	9	+Data bit 7	Out
3	+Data bit 1	Out	10	-Acknowledge	In
4	+Data bit 2	Out	11	+Busy	In
5	+Data bit 3	Out	12	+Paper End	In
6	+Data bit 4	Out	13	+Select	In
7	+Data bit 5	Out	14	-Auto Feed	Out

Table 7-10   Parallel Port Pinout (DB-25F Connector)

Pin #	Description	I/O	Pin #	Description	I/O
15	-Error	In	21	-Ground (Data bit 3 Return)	In
16	-Initialize Printer	Out	22	-Ground (Data bit 4 Return)	In
17	-Select Input	Out	23	-Ground (Data bit 5 Return)	In
18	-Ground (Data bit 0 Return)	In	24	-Ground (Data bit 6 Return)	In
19	-Ground (Data bit 1 Return)	In	25	-Ground (Data bit 7 Return)	In
20	-Ground (Data bit 2 Return)	In			

NOTE   Note that the parallel designation for the LPT port comes from its use of eight data lines (pins 2–9) and that the port has provisions for printer status messages (pins 10–12).

Parallel Port Configuration

The configuration of the LPT port consists of the following:

■ Selecting the port's operating mode

■ Selecting the IRQ, I/O port address, and DMA channel (for certain modes)

The LPT port can be configured for a variety of operating modes. The options available for a particular port depend on the capabilities of the system. Most systems you're likely to work with should offer all of these modes, although a few digital dinosaurs still kicking around in some offices might not have the IEEE-1284 modes.

These modes differ in several ways, including port performance, whether the port is configured for output only or for bidirectional (input-output) operation, and the types of hardware resources such as IRQ, DMA, and I/O port addresses used.

Standard Mode   The standard mode of the LPT port is the configuration first used on PCs, and it is the only mode available on very old systems. On some systems, this is also known as *compatible mode*. Although configuration for this mode typically includes both the IRQ and I/O port address, only the I/O port address is actually used for printing. If the parallel port is used in standard/compatible mode, IRQ 7 can be used for another device. The standard mode is the slowest mode (150 kilobytes per second [KBps] output/50KBps input), but it is the most suitable mode for very old printers. In this mode, eight lines are used for output, but only four lines are used for input. The port can send or receive, but only in one direction at a time.

This mode will work with any parallel cable.

PS/2—Bidirectional   The next mode available on most systems is the PS/2 or bidirectional mode. This mode was pioneered by the old IBM PS/2 computers and is the simplest mode available on some computer models.

Bidirectional mode is more suitable for use with devices other than printers because eight lines are used for both input and output, and it uses only I/O port addresses. This mode is no faster than compatible mode for printing but accepts incoming data at a faster rate than compatible mode; the port sends and transmits data at 150KBps.

This mode requires a bidirectional printer cable or IEEE-1284 printer cable.

IEEE-1284 High-Speed Bidirectional Modes   Three modes that are fully *bidirectional* (able to send and receive data 8 bits at a time) and are also much faster than the original PS/2-style bidirectional port include

- **EPP (Enhanced Parallel Port)**—Uses both an IRQ and an I/O port address. This is the mode supported by most high-speed printers and drives attached to the parallel port.

- **ECP (Enhanced Capabilities Port)**—Designed for daisy-chaining different devices (such as printers and scanners) to a single port. It uses an IRQ, an I/O port address, and a DMA channel, making it the most resource hungry of all the different parallel port modes.

- **EPP/ECP**—Many recent systems support a combined EPP/ECP mode, making it possible to run devices preferring either mode on a single port.

These modes, which transmit data at up to 2 megabytes per second (MBps) and receive data at 500KBps, have all been incorporated into the IEEE-1284 parallel port standard. Most Pentium-based and newer systems have ports that comply with at least one of these standards. All of these require an IEEE-1284–compliant parallel cable.

These modes are suitable for use with

- High-speed laser and inkjet printers

- External tape-backup drives, optical drives, and Zip drives

- Scanners

- Data-transfer programs such as Direct Cable Connection, Direct Parallel Connection, LapLink, Interlink, and others

Basically, the list includes all of the most recent printers and peripherals that plug into the parallel port.

Types of Parallel Cables   There are three major types of parallel cables:

- **Printer**—Uses the DB-25M connector on one end, and the Centronics connector on the other.

- **Switchbox/Device**—Most use the DB-25M connector on both ends.

- **Data transfer**—Uses the DB-25M connector at both ends and crosses the transmit and receive wires at one end (meaning that two computers can send and receive data, much like a computer network, though much slower).

CAUTION   If you use a switchbox or device cable in place of a data transfer cable, or vice-versa, your device or your data transfer process won't work. Fortunately, data transfer cables are usually thinner than switchbox or device cables because only a few of the wire pairs are required for data transfer. However, you might want to label the different types of cables to avoid mixing them up.

Printer and switchbox/device cables can support the IEEE-1284 or earlier bidirectional standards. Here's how they differ internally:

- IEEE-1284 cables feature several types of shielding in both the cable and at the printer end of the cable. This shielding is designed to minimize interference from outside sources. Normal cables have minimal shielding.

- IEEE-1284 cables use a twisted wire-pair construction internally, running 18 wire pairs to the printer. The wire pairs help minimize *crosstalk* (interference between different wires in the cable). Standard (compatible) cables don't use as many wire pairs, and bidirectional cables use less shielding. As a result, IEEE-1284 cables are both a good deal thicker and more expensive than ordinary or bidirectional printer cables.

TIP   When purchasing or selecting parallel cables, IEEE-1284–compatible cables can be used with any parallel port mode and provide superior signal quality. New cables are clearly marked as IEEE-1284 compliant on the package. Existing cables often have IEEE-1284 marked on the rubberized outer shield of the cable.

Standard and Optional Parallel Port Settings   Parallel ports can be configured as LPT1, LPT2, and LPT3. When a single parallel port is found in the system, regardless of its configuration, it is always designated as LPT1. The configurations for LPT2 and LPT3, shown in Table 7-11, apply when you have a computer with more than one parallel port.

Table 7-11   Typical Parallel Port Hardware Configuration Settings

LPT Port #	IRQ	I/O Port Address Range
LPT1	7	378-37Fh or 3BC-38Fh
LPT2	5	278-27Fh or 378-37Fh
LPT3	5	278-27Fh

If one of the ports is an ECP or EPP/ECP port, DMA 3 is normally used on most systems along with the IRQ and I/O port address ranges listed here. Some computers default to DMA 1 for an ECP or EPP/ECP parallel port, but DMA 1 will conflict with most sound cards running in Sound Blaster emulation mode.

PCI or PCI Express-based multi-I/O cards can place the parallel port at any available IRQ. PCI parallel port or multi-I/O (parallel and serial ports and possibly others on the same card) cards can share IRQs with other PCI cards. However, ISA parallel ports, including those built into the motherboard, cannot share IRQs when used in EPP, ECP, or EPP/ECP mode (these modes use an IRQ).

How to Configure or Disable Parallel Ports   Depending on the location of the parallel port, there are a couple of ways to configure the port settings in recent systems. These include

- BIOS setup program for built-in ports
- PnP mode for use with Windows

Follow these steps to adjust the configuration of a parallel port built into the system's motherboard:

Step 1.   Start the BIOS setup program.

Step 2.   Change to the I/O device or peripheral configuration screen (see Figure 7-18).

Step 3.   Select the mode, IRQ, I/O port address, and DMA channel if required.

Step 4.   Save changes and exit; the system reboots.

PCI-based parallel ports are configured by the PnP BIOS. In some cases, you can adjust the settings used by a PnP parallel port or a motherboard-based parallel port with Windows Device Manager. See Chapter 15 for details.

Parallel port I/O port address/IRQ

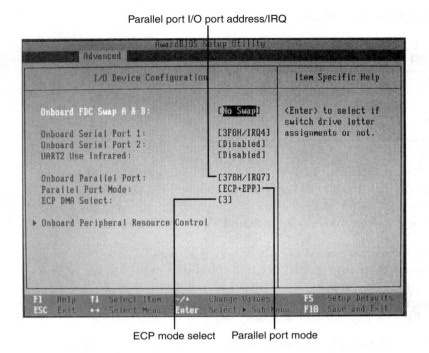

ECP mode select   Parallel port mode

Figure 7-18   A typical BIOS I/O device configuration screen with the parallel port configured for EPP/ECP mode with default settings.

Adding Parallel Ports   Although you can daisy-chain a printer and another parallel-port device to a single parallel port, you can't connect two printers to the same port unless you use a switchbox. If you want to have two parallel printers that can be used at the same time, or if you want to provide different parallel-port devices with their own ports, you need to add a parallel port. What are your options?

You can add additional parallel ports to a system with any of the following:

■   PCI-based parallel or multi-I/O card

■   PCI Express-based parallel or multi-I/O card

■   USB-to-parallel-port adapter

TIP   A USB-to-parallel-port adapter has a USB Type A connection at one end and a Centronics connection at the other end. This adapter enables you to connect a parallel printer to your USB port so you can use the parallel port for other devices. However, this type of adapter isn't designed to support other types of parallel port devices. If you want to connect a parallel port drive or scanner, you must use a real parallel port.

IEEE 1394 (FireWire)

IEEE 1394 is a family of high-speed bidirectional serial transmission ports that can connect PCs to each other, digital devices to PCs, or digital devices to each other.

The most common version of IEEE 1394 is known as IEEE 1394a, and is also known as FireWire 400. Sony's version is known as i.LINK. At 400Mbps, IEEE 1394a is one of the fastest and most flexible ports used on personal computers. IEEE 1394a can be implemented either as a built-in port on the motherboard (refer to Figure 7-1) or as part of an add-on card (see Figure 7-19).

1. External IEEE 1394a ports
2. Internal IEEE 1394a port
3. Four-pin hard disk-type power connector

Figure 7-19   A typical IEEE 1394a host adapter card with three external and one internal ports.

IEEE 1394 Ports and Cables

Standard IEEE 1394a ports and cables use a 6-pin interface (four pins for data, two for power), but some digital camcorders and all i.LINK ports use the alternative 4-pin interface, which supplies data and signals but no power to the device. Six-wire to four-wire cables enable these devices to communicate with each other.

A faster version of the IEEE 1394 standard, IEEE 1394b (also known as FireWire 800), runs at 800Mbps. IEEE 1394b ports use a 9-pin interface. There are two versions of the IEEE 1394b port: The Beta port and cable are used only for 1394b-to-1394b connections, whereas the Bilingual cable and port are used for 1394b-to-1394a or 1394b-to-1394b connections. Beta cables and ports have a wide notch at the top of the cable and port, whereas Bilingual cables and ports have a narrow notch at the 1394b end, and use either the 4-pin or 6-pin 1394a connection at the other end of the cable. All four cable types are shown in Figure 7-20.

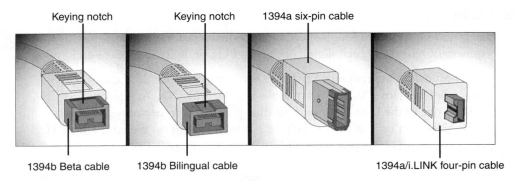

Figure 7-20   1394b and 1394a cable connectors compared.

IEEE 1394–Compatible Devices and Technical Requirements

IEEE 1394–compatible devices include internal and external hard drives, digital camcorders (also referred to as DV camcorders), web cameras, MP3 players (such as older models of Apple's iPod) and high-performance scanners and printers, as well as hubs, repeaters, and SCSI to IEEE 1394 converters. IEEE 1394 ports support hot-swapping, enabling you to add or remove a device from an IEEE 1394 port without shutting down the system. 1394 ports can also be used for networking with Windows XP (but not Vista).

Up to 16 IEEE 1394 devices can be connected to a single IEEE 1394 port through daisy-chaining. Most external IEEE 1394 devices have two ports to enable daisy-chaining.

Windows 98 was the first version of Windows to include IEEE 1394 support. IEEE 1394 cards can use PCI or PCI Express buses (versions for laptops use ExpressCard or CardBus designs) and require the following hardware resources:

- One IRQ (it can be shared on systems that support IRQ sharing by PCI devices)

- One memory address range (must be unique)

The exact IRQ and memory address range used by a particular IEEE 1394 card can be determined by using the Windows Device Manager. When an IEEE 1394 card is installed, a device category called 1394 Bus Controller is added to the Device Manager, and the particular card installed is listed beneath that category.

Installing an IEEE 1394 Card

To install and configure an IEEE 1394 card, follow this procedure:

Step 1.   Turn off the computer and remove the case cover.

Step 2.   Locate an available PCI or PCI Express expansion slot.

Step 3.   Remove the slot cover and insert the card into the slot. Secure the card in the slot.

Step 4. Some IEEE 1394 cards are powered by the expansion slot, whereas others require a 4-pin connector for power. Connect a power lead if the card requires it; you can use a Y-splitter to free up a power lead if necessary (see Figure 7-21).

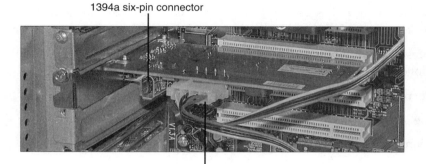

1394a six-pin connector

4-wire Molex power cable

Figure 7-21 A typical IEEE 1394a card after installation. This card requires a four-wire power cable and also includes an internal port.

Step 5. Close the system, restart it, and provide the driver disk or CD-ROM when requested by the system.

Step 6. The IRQ and memory address required by the card will be assigned automatically.

PS/2 (Mini-DIN)

PS/2 ports (also referred to as Mini-DIN ports) are used by PS/2 keyboards, mice, and pointing devices. Most desktop systems, and many older laptop and portable systems, include PS/2 ports.

In a typical ATX/BTX port cluster, the bottom PS/2 port is used for keyboards, and the top PS/2 port is used for mice and pointing devices. On systems and devices that use the standard PC99 color coding for ports, PS/2 keyboard ports (and cables) are purple, and PS/2 mouse ports (and cables) are green. Refer to Figure 7-1 for the location of these ports.

Centronics

Centronics ports are used by parallel (LPT) printers and by some older narrow SCSI devices. Centronics parallel ports use a 36-pin edge connector (refer to Figure 7-17), while Centronics SCSI ports use a 50-pin edge connector (refer to Figure 7-7).

For more information about parallel (LPT) ports, see the section "Parallel (LPT)," earlier in this chapter. For more information about SCSI ports, see the section "SCSI," earlier in this chapter.

1/8-inch Audio Mini-Jack

The 1/8-inch audio mini-jack is used by sound cards and motherboard-integrated sound for speakers, microphone, and line-in jacks, as shown in Figure 7-1.

To avoid confusion, most recent systems and sound cards use the PC99 color coding listed as follows:

- **Pink**—Microphone in

- **Light Blue**—Line in

- **Lime Green**—Stereo/headphone out

- **Brown**—Left to right speaker

- **Orange**—Subwoofer

SPDIF Digital Audio

Many systems include both analog audio (delivered through 1/8-inch audio mini-jacks) and digital audio. Sony/Philips Digital Interconnect Format (SPDIF) ports output digital audio signals to amplifiers, such as those used in home theater systems, and come in two forms: optical and coaxial.

Optical SPDIF uses a fiber optic cable, while coaxial SPDIF uses a shielded cable with an RCA connector. The cables are shown in Figure 7-22. To see SPDIF ports, refer to Figure 7-1.

Sound cards might incorporate SPDIF ports into the card itself or into drive bay or external extension modules.

TIP   By default, systems with both analog and digital output use analog output. To enable digital output, use the Sounds and Audio Devices dialog in Windows Control Panel or the proprietary mixer provided with some sound cards or onboard audio devices.

Figure 7-22   SPDIF optical (top) and coaxial (bottom) cables.

MIDI Port

Some sound cards feature MIDI ports. MIDI ports are used to communicate with MIDI keyboards. Older devices with MIDI support use MIDI ports that use a five-pin DIN design similar to the original IBM PC keyboard jack, while newer devices use the smaller Mini-DIN design, but with five pins instead of the six pins used by PS/2 keyboards and mice.

Figure 7-23 illustrates a drive bay-mounted module that contains MIDI ports. Note that some older sound cards use adapters that connect to the joystick port.

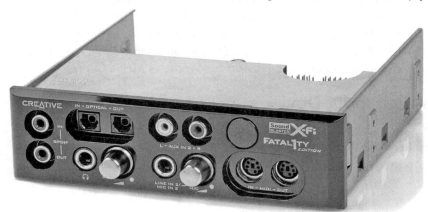

Figure 7-23   MIDI ports in a Creative Labs add-on module for sound cards.

RG-6 Coaxial

RG-6 coaxial connections are used by TV and FM radio tuners to receive signals from broadcast and cable TV and radio. Figure 7-24 illustrates a typical TV tuner card with an F-connector and an RG-6 cable.

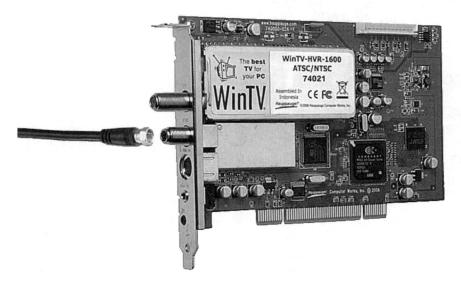

Figure 7-24   TV tuner cards use RG-6 cables for video sources such as broadcast and cable TV.

To enjoy TV broadcasts on your PC, you must also use software that can tune in the appropriate station, display the video, and play back the audio. To enjoy FM radio broadcasts on your PC, you must also use software that can tune in the appropriate station and play back the audio. Most recent TV and radio tuner cards and devices are bundled with suitable software and drivers for Windows Media Center.

Understanding Input Devices

Modern PCs use many different types of input devices, including keyboards and mice, bar code readers, biometric devices, and touch screens. The following sections cover the important characteristics of each of these devices.

Keyboard

The keyboard remains the primary method used to send commands to the computer and enter data. You can even use it to maneuver around the Windows Desktop if your mouse or other pointing device stops working.

Keyboards can be connected through dedicated keyboard connectors or through the USB port. Extremely old systems use the 5-pin DIN connector, whereas newer systems use the smaller 6-pin mini-DIN connector (also called the PS/2 keyboard connector) shown in Figure 7-1.

Some recent systems use the USB port for the keyboard, and any system with USB ports can be equipped with a USB keyboard if the system BIOS supports USB Legacy mode and if the system runs an operating system that supports USB ports (Windows 98 or newer).

Most recent systems use the 104-key keyboard layout, which includes Windows keys on each side of the space bar and a right-click key next to the right Ctrl key. Otherwise, the 104-key keyboard's layout is the same as the older 101-key keyboard.

Mouse and Pointing Devices

Next to the keyboard, the mouse is the most important device used to send commands to the computer. For Windows users who don't perform data entry, the mouse is even more important than the keyboard. Mouse alternatives, such as trackballs or touchpads, are considered mouse devices because they install and are configured the same way.

Current mice and pointing devices use the USB 1.1 or USB 2.0 port, but older models used the 6-pin PS/2 (mini-DIN), serial (COM) ports, or 8–pin bus mouse port.

Some mice sold at retail work with either the USB port or the PS/2 port and include a PS/2 adapter. This adapter and others are shown in Figure 7-25.

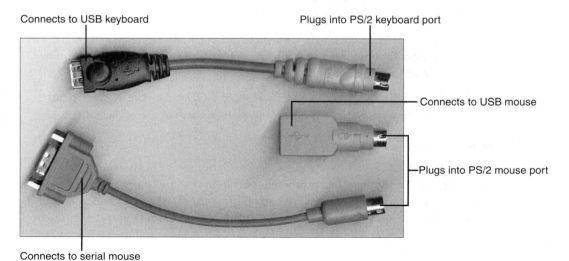

Figure 7-25 A USB keyboard–to–PS/2 keyboard port adapter (top) compared to a USB mouse–to–PS/2 mouse port adapter (middle) and serial mouse–to–PS/2 mouse port adapter (bottom).

> **NOTE**   Adapters cannot be used successfully unless the mouse (or keyboard) is designed to use an adapter. A mouse designed to use an adapter is sometimes called a hybrid mouse.

Mouse Resource Usage

A USB mouse uses the IRQ and I/O port address of the USB port to which it is connected. Because a single USB port can support up to 127 devices through the use of hubs, a USB mouse doesn't tie up hardware resources the way other mouse types do.

A PS/2 mouse uses IRQ 12; if IRQ 12 is not available, the device using that IRQ must be moved to another IRQ to enable IRQ 12 to be used by the mouse. A serial mouse uses the IRQ and I/O port address of the serial port to which it is connected.

Bar Code Reader

Bar code readers are used in a variety of point-of-sale retail, library, industrial, medical, and other environments to track inventory.

Bar code readers use one of the following technologies:

- Pen-based readers use a pen-shaped device that includes a light source and photo diode in the tip. The point of the pen is dragged across the bar code to read the varying thicknesses and positions of the bars in the bar code and translate them into a digitized code that is transmitted to the POS or inventory system.

- Laser scanners are commonly used in grocery and mass-market stores. They use a horizontal-mounted or vertical-mounted prism or mirror and laser beam protected by a transparent glass cover to read bar codes.

- CCD or CMOS readers use a hand-held gun-shaped device to hold an array of light sensors mounted in a row. The reader emits light that is reflected off the bar code and is detected by the light sensors.

- Camera-based readers contain many rows of CCD sensors that generate an image of the sensor that is processed to decode the barcode information.

Biometric Devices

A biometric device is used to prevent access to a computer or other electronic device by anyone other than the authorized user. It does so by comparing the fingerprint or other biometric marker of the prospective user to the information stored by the authorized user during initial setup. Some keyboards and laptop computers include built-in fingerprint readers, and some vendors also produce USB-based fingerprint readers.

To learn more about fingerprint readers and other biometric devices, see Chapter 10, "Security."

Touch Screens

Touch screen (or touchscreen) monitors enable the user to transfer data into the computer by pressing onscreen icons. Touch screen monitors are very popular in public-access and point-of-sale installations.

Touch screen monitors use CRT or LCD technology and also incorporate one of the following surface treatments to make the monitor touch sensitive:

- **Four-wire resistive technology**—Uses a glass panel coated with multiple layers that conduct and resist electricity. A flexible polyester cover sheet fits over the glass panel and is separated from the panel with insulating separator dots. The outer side of the cover has a durable coating; the inner side has a conductive coating. When the cover is pressed, an electrical signal is generated and is sent through the interface to the computer. The lowest-cost touchscreen technology, this type of screen is designed for public use.

- **Five-wire resistive technology**—A more sensitive and more accurate version of four-wire resistive technology suitable for use by trained personnel (offices, point-of-sale, and so on).

- **Surface wave**—Uses horizontal and vertical piezoelectric transducers to create ultrasonic waves. Touching the screen overlay disrupts the waves and the coordinates of the touch determine what signal is sent to the computer. It's a durable surface able to compensate for surface damage and dirt and is suitable for self-service applications such as banking or information kiosks.

- **Touch-on-tube**—Combines surface wave technology with direct touch contact to the CRT; no overlay is necessary. LCDs use an overlay with a simple air gap between the overlay and the panel surface. Suitable for self-service applications.

- **Scanning infrared**—A light grid created by infrared (IR) signals is used to sense touches. Works with plasma as well as other types of displays.

Touch screens are available in freestanding versions similar to normal desktop CRT and LCD displays as well as in kiosk and built-in designs.

Touch Screen Interfacing to the Computer

Touch screens, like ordinary LCD and CRT monitors, use standard VGA analog or DVI digital interfaces to the video card. However, the touch signals are transmitted to the computer through a separate interface known as the touch screen controller. Touch screen controllers can use either of the following interfaces:

- **Serial (RS-232)**—Some touch screen monitors have an internal serial controller; others use an external serial controller. The internal serial controller might use a standard 9-pin serial cable or a special PS/2–to–9-pin serial cable to connect the controller to a serial (COM) port on the computer, depending upon the monitor model. The external serial controller uses a controller with a built-in serial cable.

■ **USB**—A touch screen monitor with an internal USB interface uses a standard USB cable to connect to a USB port on the computer.

Understanding Multimedia Devices

Multimedia devices such as webcams, digital cameras, MIDI ports, microphones, sound cards, and video capture cards are used by both home and business-oriented PCs. The following sections discuss the characteristics of each of these devices.

Webcam

A webcam is a simple digital camera capable of taking video or still images for transmission over the Internet. Unlike digital cameras (next section), webcams don't include storage capabilities.

Most webcams plug into a USB port, but a few have used IEEE 1394 or parallel ports.

Webcams are generally used in live chat situations, such as with AOL Instant Messenger or other IM clients. They offer resolutions ranging from sub-VGA to as high as 2 million pixels (2 megapixels). Some offer autofocus and zoom features for better image clarity, and some have built-in microphones.

Digital Camera

Digital cameras have largely replaced film cameras for both amateur and professional photography. They use CMOS or CCD image sensors to record images onto internal or card-based flash memory form factors such as Compact Flash, SD, Memory Stick, xD-Picture Card, and Smart Media.

Digital cameras transfer images to computers for emailing, printing, or storage via either flash memory card readers or direct USB port connections.

MIDI Music and MIDI Ports

Musical instrument digital interface (MIDI) music is created from digitized samples of musical instruments that are stored in the ROM or RAM of a MIDI device (such as a sound card) and played under the command of a MIDI sequencer. MIDI sequences can be stored as files for future playback, and can be transferred between sound cards and MIDI-enabled devices such as keyboards via the MIDI port. To learn more about MIDI ports, see the section "MIDI Port," earlier in this chapter.

Sound Card

Sound cards are used to record and play back analog audio, and most can also play back digital audio sources as well. When recording analog audio sources such as CDs, line in or microphone in, sound cards digitize the audio at varying sample rates and store files in either uncompressed forms such as WAV or compressed forms such as WMA or MP3.

Most recent sound cards support 5.1 or 7.1 surround audio, and many sound cards also support digital stereo or surround audio playback standards via SPDIF ports. In recent years, sound cards have become less popular due to the popularity of on-board audio, but sound cards are preferred by users who create audio recordings.

Figure 7-26 illustrates a typical soundcard.

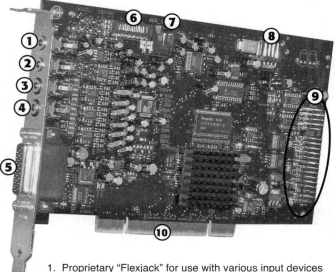

1. Proprietary "Flexjack" for use with various input devices
2. Line out 1 (front left/right, stereo, and headphone jack)
3. Line out 2 (rear and side speakers in home theater systems)
4. Line out 3 (center, subwoofer, and side speakers in home theater systems)
5. Proprietary connector to external I/O breakout box
6. Proprietary connector
7. Aux-In from internal analog audio (CD/DVD drives, TV tuners)
8. Power connector for internal I/O breakout box
9. Data connector for internal I/O breakout box
10. 32-bit PCI slot connector

Figure 7-26   Typical input and output jacks on a typical sound card (the Creative Labs X-Fi Xtreme Gamer).

Microphone

Microphones plug into the 1/8-inch mini-jack microphone jack on a sound card or integrated motherboard audio. The most common microphones used on PCs include those built into headsets (Figure 7-27) or those which use a stand.

Microphone volume is controlled by the Windows Sounds and Audio Devices applet's mixer control. Open the Recording tab to adjust volume, to mute or unmute the microphone, or to adjust microphone boost.

Figure 7-27   A typical PC stereo headset with microphone.

NOTE   The microphone jack is monaural, whereas the line-in jack supports stereo. Be sure to use the line-in jack to record from a stereo audio source.

Video Capture Card

As the name suggests, video capture cards are used to capture live video from various sources, including analog camcorders, VCRs, analog output from DV camcorders, broadcast TV, and cable TV. Most recent cards with video capture capabilities are actually multi-purpose cards that include other functions. These include ATI's All-in-Wonder series of video (graphics) cards with onboard TV tuner and video capture functions, video (graphics) cards with VIVO (video-in/video-out) S-video or composite video ports, and TV tuner cards and USB devices. Video can be stored in a variety of formats, including MPEG, AVI, and others for use in video productions.

Installing Input and Multimedia Devices

The installation processes for the most common input and multimedia devices are covered in the following sections.

Installing a Keyboard

To install the keyboard using a DIN or mini-DIN jack, turn off the power and insert the connector end of the keyboard cable into the keyboard connector (usually on the back of the computer). No special drivers are required unless the keyboard has special keys, a programmable feature, or is a wireless model that uses a receiver. Note that systems with a PS/2 keyboard port usually also have a PS/2 mouse port. Be sure to use the PS/2 keyboard port; check the color code or the keyboard icon next to the port to verify you are using the correct port. To remove the keyboard, turn off the power before removing the connector end of the keyboard cable from the keyboard connector.

To install a USB keyboard, enable USB Legacy mode in the system BIOS (see Chapter 4, "BIOS," for details); then plug the keyboard into a USB port built into the computer, or into a USB hub plugged into a USB port built into the computer. With Windows 98 Second Edition and newer versions of Windows, the keyboard can be plugged and unplugged as desired without shutting down the system. Note that some USB keyboards include an adapter that enables them to connect to PS/2 keyboard ports (refer to Figure 7-25). USB keyboards are part of the *HID (human interface device)* device category, and Windows installs HID drivers after the keyboard is connected.

Installing a Mouse or Other Pointing Device

The physical installation of a serial or PS/2 mouse or other point devices such as a touchpad is extremely simple. Turn off the computer and plug the mouse into the appropriate connector. Then, restart the computer. That's it!

To install a USB mouse or other pointing device (such as a touchpad), plug it into any USB port on a system running Windows 98 or newer versions. Install any software drivers required.

Unlike keyboards, mouse devices require software drivers. Windows includes support for standard mice from Microsoft and other vendors. However, if you are installing a mouse that includes zooming, tilt-wheel, or additional buttons, you might need to install the drivers provided with the mouse or updated versions provided by the vendor to assure full support for additional features.

Installing a Bar Code Reader

Wired bar code readers typically interface through the USB port, PS/2 keyboard port, or the serial (COM, RS-232) port. Bar code readers that plug into the PS/2 keyboard port use a device known as a keyboard wedge to enable a keyboard and bar code reader to be plugged into the keyboard port at the same time. Serial interface bar code readers use a software program to convert serial data into keystrokes or to perform dynamic data exchange (DDE) to applications. USB-based bar code readers emulate either the PS/2 or Serial interface, depending upon the software used to interface the reader.

See the documentation for the reader to determine if you install the driver before or after connecting the reader. If the reader plugs into a PS/2 keyboard or serial port, you must shut down the computer before connecting the reader. If the reader plugs into a USB port, you can connect the reader while the system is running.

NOTE   Some bar code readers use Bluetooth to make a wireless connection between the reader and the computer or other data-acquisition device.

Installing a Webcam

Webcams connect to the PC's USB port, and can thus be connected while the computer is running. However, before connecting the webcam, check the documentation to determine if you need to install drivers and application software before or after connecting the webcam.

Most webcams work with modern instant messaging (IM) software to provide live video chat capabilities, but some might also include proprietary software. Check the documentation to determine compatible software.

Installing a Digital Camera

To connect a digital camera to your PC, follow these steps:

Step 1.   Connect the USB cable provided with the camera to the camera's USB port and the computer's USB port.

Step 2.   Turn on the camera.

Step 3.   If the camera is not recognized after a few seconds, select the picture playback option on the camera. If the camera is still not recognized, install drivers for the camera.

Some digital cameras are assigned a drive letter, while others show up as an imaging device in My Computer. If the camera is assigned a drive letter, you can drag and drop photos from the camera to other storage locations just as you would with any other disk drive. If the camera is detected as an imaging device, you should install the software drivers and utilities included with your camera to provide the necessary support for transferring and converting photos.

Installing a MIDI Port

Many sound cards include MIDI interfacing as part of the card's standard features. However, it is usually necessary to connect MIDI ports to the card. If the card's MIDI ports are not connected, follow this procedure:

Step 1.   Shut down the computer and disconnect it from AC power.

Step 2.   Connect the MIDI ports to the sound card. If the game port is also used for MIDI interfacing and the game port is already connected to the sound card, connect the MIDI adapter cable to the game port. However, if the game port is not connected, or if the MIDI ports are built into a separate adapter, connect the game port or adapter to the sound card.

Step 3.   Restore AC power and restart the system.

Step 4.   Provide drivers as prompted.

Installing a Microphone

To install a microphone on a PC with a sound card or integrated audio, follow this procedure:

Step 1.   Plug the microphone into the microphone jack, which is marked with a pink ring or a microphone icon.

Step 2.   Systems that support AC'97 version 2.3 audio might pop up a dialog that asks you to confirm the device you have plugged into the microphone jack. Select Microphone from the list of devices.

To verify that the microphone is working:

Step 1.   Open the Sounds and Audio Devices icon in Control Panel.

Step 2.   Click Test Hardware.

Step 3.   Click Next.

Step 4.   If prompted by Windows Firewall, unblock the test program (you might see more than one prompt).

Step 5.   Speak into the microphone when prompted to test your microphone and then click Next.

Step 6.   Speak into the microphone when prompted to test your speakers and then click Next.

Step 7.   Click Finish.

If you do not hear any output from the microphone, open the Audio tab, click the Volume button in the Sound Recording section of the dialog, and make sure the Mic volume control is not muted. Adjust the volume level as desired.

Installing a Biometric Device

The most common biometric device used with PCs is a fingerprint reader. Fingerprint readers plug into a computer's USB port, and the driver software should be installed before the reader is connected:

Step 1.   Install the software provided with the reader. This might include a driver program and a password-management program.

Step 2.   After the programs are installed, connect the reader to a USB port built into the PC.

Step 3.   Run the configuration program to set up the reader to recognize the user. This will require the user to press or wipe his or her finger against the reader and save the results for comparison during later attempts to start the system or access secure websites.

Installing a Touch Screen

To install a touch screen monitor, follow these steps:

Step 1.   Shut down the computer and disconnect it from AC power.

Step 2.   Connect the monitor to the appropriate VGA or DVI port on your computer.

Step 3.   Connect the serial or USB cable to the touch screen and to the appropriate port on the computer.

Step 4.   Restart the computer.

Step 5.   Install the serial or USB driver for the touch screen interface.

Installing a Sound Card

To install a sound card, follow these steps:

Step 1.   Shut down the computer and disconnect it from AC power.

Step 2.   Open the case to gain access to the PC's expansion slots.

Step 3.   Determine the type of slot needed for the sound card. Some use PCI slots, while others use PCI Express x1 slots.

Step 4.   Locate an empty PCI or PCI Express expansion slot as needed.

Step 5.   Remove the corresponding bracket from the back of the case.

Step 6.   Slide the card into the slot.

Step 7.   Fasten the card bracket into place, using the screw or locking mechanism you removed or released in Step 5.

Step 8.   Close the system.

Step 9.   Restore AC power and restart the system.

Step 10.   Install the drivers provided with the sound card, or updated versions provided by the vendor.

Step 11.   Connect speakers, microphone, line-in and line-out cables as needed to support your audio or home theater subsystem.

Step 12.   Open the Sound and Audio Devices icon in Control Panel and configure volume and speaker settings to match your configuration.

Installing a Video Capture Card

The process of installing a video capture card includes the following steps.

Step 1.   Shut down the computer and disconnect it from AC power.

Step 2.   Open the case to gain access to the PC's expansion slots.

Step 3.   Determine the type of slot needed for the sound card. Some use PCI slots, while others use PCI Express x1 slots.

Step 4.   Locate an empty PCI or PCI Express expansion slot as needed.

Step 5.   Remove the corresponding bracket from the back of the case.

Step 6.   Slide the card into the slot.

Step 7.   Fasten the card bracket into place, using the screw or locking mechanism you removed or released in Step 5.

Step 8.   Close the system.

Step 9.   Restore AC power and restart the system.

Step 10.   Install the drivers provided with the video capture card, or updated versions provided by the vendor.

Step 11.   Connect the cables needed for video sources, such as composite or S-video (to capture video from VCRs, TV-out ports, or analog camcorders) or RG-6 coaxial (to capture video from TV sources such as antennas or cable TV).

Step 12.   Set up the video capture software to work with the video source(s) you are using.

Troubleshooting Input and Multimedia Devices

The following sections tell you how to troubleshoot the most common input and multimedia devices. For more information about using Windows Device Manager, see the section "Device Manager," in Chapter 13 "Using and Managing Windows."

Troubleshooting Keyboards

Keyboard problems usually result from a few simple causes:

■   A damaged keyboard connector on the computer

■   A damaged keyboard cable

■   Dirt, dust, or gunk in the keyboard

To learn how to clean a keyboard, see the section "Maintaining Keyboards," later in this chapter.

The following are some ways to avoid these problems:

■   Don't plug a PS/2 keyboard into a system that's powered up. This is an excellent way to destroy the motherboard!

■   Don't plug a PS/2 keyboard into a system at an angle. This tends to break the solder joints that attach the keyboard connector to the motherboard.

To determine whether a keyboard has failed, plug it into another system. A defective keyboard will not work in any system. However, if every keyboard plugged into a keyboard port fails to work, the keyboard port is defective. Use a USB keyboard or replace the motherboard.

If the normal keys on the keyboard work but multimedia or other special keys do not work, reinstall the drivers made for that keyboard.

Troubleshooting Mice and Pointing Devices

Although Windows supports keyboard shortcuts for some operations, a mouse is required for maximum utility. Use this section to prepare for troubleshooting questions on the A+ Certification Exam and day-to-day mouse problems.

Table 7-12 shows you how to use the Mouse Properties sheet for Windows XP to solve common pointing device problems. Other versions of Windows offer similar features, although some advanced options might not be present. All Properties sheet tabs are shown in Figure 7-28.

Table 7-12   Using the Pointing Device Properties Sheet

Problem	Properties Sheet Tab to Use	Solution
I need to set up a mouse for a left-handed user.	Buttons	Select the Switch Primary and Secondary Buttons box.
Double-click doesn't work consistently.	Buttons	Use the Double-Click Speed slider and test box to adjust speed.
Items are dragged around the screen after I click on them, even if I don't hold down the primary mouse button.	Buttons	Clear the ClickLock option box; if the ClickLock option isn't selected, the primary mouse button is probably broken and you should replace the mouse.
I need different (larger, animated, high-contrast) mouse pointers.	Pointers	Select the desired mouse scheme from the menu; install the mouse software provided by the mouse vendor to provide additional schemes.
The pointer moves too fast or too slow.	Pointer Options	Adjust the Motion slider to the desired speed.
The pointer is hard to move over short distances or hard to stop.	Pointer Options	Enable the Enhance Pointer Precision option.
I'm tired of moving the pointer to the dialog box to click OK.	Pointer Options	Enable the Snap To option.
The pointer disappears when moved quickly (especially on LCD displays).	Pointer Options	Enable the Pointer Trails option and select the desired length of the trail.
The pointer covers up typed text.	Pointer Options	Enable the Hide Pointer While Typing option.
The pointer is hard to find on a cluttered screen.	Pointer Options	Enable the Show Location of Pointer When I Press the CTRL Key option.
The scroll wheel motion is too fast (or too slow).	Wheel	Select the number of lines to scroll with each click of the wheel, or select one screen at a time.
I'm not sure which pointing devices are active.	Hardware	Look at the listing of the current device(s) to determine which are active. Use the shortcuts to Troubleshooter and Properties if necessary.

Table 7-12   Using the Pointing Device Properties Sheet

Problem	Properties Sheet Tab to Use	Solution
The mouse pointer disappears or only appears on parts of the screen.	Pointer Options	Enable the Show Location of Pointer When I Press the CTRL Key option. *Note; You might also want to minimize and maximize the active application to force Windows to rewrite the screen.*

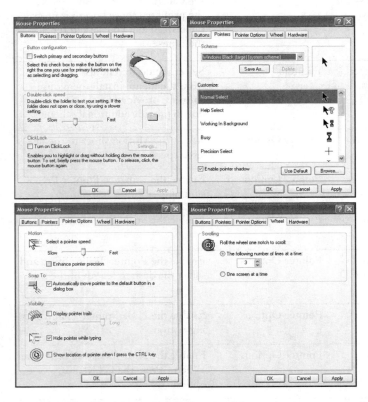

Figure 7-28   The Mouse Properties sheet for a wheel mouse used on a system running Windows XP.

Mouse Pointer Won't Move

If the mouse pointer won't move when the mouse is moved, check the following:

- **Check the mouse software driver**—Use the Mouse icon in the Control Panel to verify that the correct mouse driver has been selected under Windows. Using the wrong mouse driver can cause the mouse pointer to freeze.

- **Check the mouse connection to the system**—If a PS/2 mouse isn't plugged in tightly, the system must be shut down, the mouse reconnected to the PS/2 mouse port, and the system restarted to enable the mouse to work. USB mouse devices can be hot-swapped at any time with Windows 98 Second Edition and newer versions. If a serial mouse is used on the system and it is not detected during Windows startup, Windows normally will display a message instructing you to plug in the mouse.

- **Check for hardware conflicts**—Serial and PS/2 mouse devices must have exclusive access to the IRQ used by the port to which the mouse is connected. If you use another device that uses the same IRQ, the mouse pointer will freeze onscreen and the system can lock up. Use the Windows Device Manager to verify that there are no IRQ conflicts between the port used by the mouse and other devices. If necessary, use the PnP configuration in the system BIOS setup to select IRQ 12 (used for PS/2 mouse devices) as excluded or as an ISA IRQ.

- **Make sure the port used by the mouse is enabled in the system BIOS**—If the PS/2 mouse port is disabled, a PS/2 mouse won't work. If the USB ports are disabled, a USB mouse won't work. Recent systems with four or more USB ports sometimes provide an option for enabling only some of the USB ports. Check the system BIOS and make any changes needed. (See Chapter 4 for details.)

- **Make sure the mouse can work with a port adapter**—Many mouse devices sold at retail can be used with either a serial port or PS/2 port, or with either a USB port or PS/2 mouse port. The mouse has one port type built in and uses an adapter supplied with the mouse to attach to the other port type with which it is compatible. These mouse devices also contain special circuitry to enable them to work with either port type. Don't mix up the adapters used by different brands and models of mouse devices; mismatches might not work. Mouse devices bundled with systems typically don't have the extra circuitry needed to work with an adapter; they're built to attach to one port type only. Mouse devices that can work with adapters are sometimes referred to as *hybrid mouse devices*.

Jerky Mouse Pointer Movement

The most common causes of jerky mouse pointer movement include

- Dirt or dust on the mouse or trackball rollers which are used to transmit movement signals to the computer—Applies to mechanical mice.

- Low battery power—Applies to wireless mice.

- Unsuitable mousing surface—Applies to wired and wireless mice with optical sensors.

- Interference from other wireless devices—Applies to wireless mice.

- Obstructions between mouse and receiver—Applies to wireless mice.

Mice with optical (non-laser) sensors cannot use surfaces with no detail (such as a mirror) or repetitive detail. Mice with laser sensors can use these surfaces.

If a wireless mouse uses a manual frequency control, try alternative frequencies to avoid interference. If a wireless mouse relies upon IR signaling, make sure there are no obstacles between the IR transmitter in the mouse and the IR receiver plugged into the PC. For details on how to clean a mouse or other pointing device, see the section "Maintaining Mice and Pointing Devices," later in this chapter.

The speed of the mouse pointer can also be adjusted with the Mouse icon in the Windows Control Panel. Select the Movement tab and adjust the Cursor Speed and Acceleration tab to make the mouse pointer move faster or slower across the screen.

User Can't Double-Click Icons

Damaged mouse buttons can prevent a user from double-clicking on icons in Windows. Turn off the system if necessary, substitute an identical mouse, and restart the system to see if the mouse is the problem. If changing mouse devices doesn't solve the problem, use the Mouse icon in the Windows Control Panel to adjust the double-click speed to the user's preference.

Troubleshooting Touch Screen

Touch Screens can malfunction for several reasons, including

- Display problems common to any monitor (loss of signal, incorrect colors, and so on).

- Software problems such as corrupted or incorrectly configured drivers or applications.

- Video alignment problems (you touch the screen but the wrong menu item or action takes place or the cursor moves in the opposite direction of your finger or stylus).

- Hardware problems caused by the touchscreen itself, the controller, cabling, or power.

To troubleshoot hardware or software problems, use the diagnostic programs supplied with the touchscreen to verify that the hardware is working. If the hardware is working correctly, the driver software used to interface the operating system and the touchscreen must be checked. See the documentation for the touchscreen monitor for details.

To solve problems caused by misalignment, realign the video using the utilities provided with the touchscreen.

To troubleshoot hardware problems, use the diagnostic features provided with the touchscreen controller to determine if it is working correctly. The controller might use LEDs or onscreen messages to indicate problems. Next, use utilities provided by the touchscreen vendor to determine if the controller is transmitting touch data.

If constant touch data is being sent by the controller when you aren't touching the screen, the controller might be defective, the monitor bezel might be touching the screen, or the touchscreen or cable has a short. If no touch data is being sent by the controller when you touch the screen, check the controller, cable, power supply, or controller setup.

Troubleshooting Sound Card

Sound cards can be difficult to troubleshoot because of their complex hardware requirements, software driver requirements, need to use add-on speakers for output, and potential for conflicts. Use this section to prepare for sound card troubleshooting questions that might appear on the A+ Certification exams or in your day-to-day work.

Sound Card Plays Sounds But Can't Record CD-Quality Sound

Older sound cards that emulate the ISA Sound Blaster use two different DMA channels, typically DMA 1 for 8-bit sounds and DMA 5 for 16-bit sounds. If your sound card plays Windows startup and event sounds but you can't record sounds in CD quality (44KHz, stereo), check for conflicts between the sound card's DMA channels and another device that uses DMA. Verify that a 16-bit DMA (5, 6, or 7) is being used by the card's configuration by checking the sound card's configuration with the Windows Device Manager. Move any conflicting device to a different DMA channel.

Sound Card Works in Some Systems But Not in Others

Motherboards with onboard audio will conflict with add-on sound cards unless the motherboard-based sound is disabled before the sound card is installed.

Sound Playback Is Distorted or Choppy

Out-of-date drivers are the most common cause for distorted or choppy sound. Download and install the latest drivers for the sound card. Use a different expansion slot to help avoid resource sharing with other devices.

No Sound at All from Sound Card

A sound card that doesn't play sound might not be defective; instead, the cause could be volume controls or speaker problems. Check the following:

■ **On-card volume controls**—Some very old sound cards use an external rotary volume control; make sure this is set to at least the midway point.

- **Windows mixer controls**—When a sound card is installed on a Windows system, a volume control for playback and recording features is normally installed in the system tray. Double-click the speaker icon to view the volume controls. If the play control is muted or set to minimum volume, you will not hear anything from the sound card. If individual features are muted or set to minimum volume, the sound card will play some types of sounds but not others.

- **Incorrect jack used for speakers**—As seen in Figure 7-1, the 1/8 inch mini-jacks used for speaker, microphone, and line-in are identical in shape. They are not always color coded with the PC99 standard discussed in the section "1/8-inch Audio Mini-Jack" earlier in this chapter. If the speakers are plugged into the wrong jack, you will hear nothing from the sound card. Verify you are using the correct jack for the speakers.

- **No power to speakers**—Most speakers used for computers can be powered by an AC adapter (some speakers also use batteries). Many low-cost speakers can play sounds at a low volume without power, but the speakers' built-in amplification is turned off if the speaker is turned on but no power is present. Leave the speaker power off if no external power is present, and use the Windows volume control to control the speaker volume.

- **Windows Device Manager**—If the sound card is not visible in the Windows Device Manager, install it with the Add/Remove Hardware icon in Control Panel. If one or more components are listed with the yellow ! symbol indicating a problem, view the component properties and make sure that the proper drivers are installed and that there are no conflicts with other devices. Install new drivers or correct conflicts as needed, and restart the system if prompted to restore proper sound card operation.

Sound Card Can't Play MIDI Files

MIDI files are special types of sound files that store an instrumental music score that is played by the sound card using either FM-based simulation of different musical instruments or stored samples of different musical instruments. If the sound card can't play MIDI files, check the following:

- **MIDI port (also called the MPU-401 port) might be disabled in the sound card configuration or have a conflict with another device**—Use the Windows Device Manager to choose a configuration that enables the MIDI port or prevents a conflict with another device.

- **MIDI samples might not be loaded into RAM or have been corrupted**—MIDI instrumentation is built into some sound cards, but most use a so-called *soft wavetable* feature that stores the samples on the hard disk and loads them into RAM. Reload the samples from the original sound card driver disks or CD-ROM and verify that they are being loaded into RAM.

TIP Many sound cards come with a diagnostic routine that will

- Play digitized sounds through each speaker (left and right) and both (stereo)
- Play MIDI tracks

Use the sound card's diagnostics to check proper operation.

Troubleshooting SCSI Devices

SCSI problems can usually be traced to incorrect device ID, termination, or cabling.

External SCSI Device Isn't Available

External SCSI devices might not be available for any of the following reasons:

- Device not powered on when the system was turned on
- Incorrect termination
- Excess cable length or excessive daisy-chain length

If an external SCSI device isn't turned on a few seconds before the system is turned on, it might not initialize properly. If an external SCSI device is not turned on and the system has booted, it might be possible to use the Device Manager to activate the device by following this procedure:

Step 1. Turn on the device.

Step 2. Open Windows Device Manager.

Step 3. Click Refresh and wait for the system to recheck all connected devices.

Step 4. If the SCSI device now appears in Device Manager, you should be able to use it normally.

Step 5. If the device doesn't appear, restart the system.

SCSI is a daisy-chained interface; both ends of the daisy-chain must be terminated. Make sure that the terminator switch or external terminator is located at the end of the external daisy-chain (the external terminator is plugged into the SCSI port not used by the SCSI cable attached to the device). If a new device has been added to the end of the daisy-chain, you must disable termination of the old device and add termination to the new device.

Faster SCSI standards support shorter maximum cable lengths than slower standards. Check the overall length of the daisy-chain if some external devices are unavailable and use the shortest cable lengths possible to avoid exceeding standards.

External or Internal SCSI Device Isn't Available

If a new external or internal SCSI device is not available, two common reasons include

- Duplicate device ID numbers
- Failure to install drivers for device

If multiple SCSI devices have the same device ID number, the devices will interfere with each other. To solve this problem, power down all SCSI devices and the system and make sure each device has a unique device ID number before restarting.

Both the SCSI host adapter card and the SCSI devices attached to the card need operating system–compatible drivers to operate. With Windows 9x and newer Windows versions, SCSI devices are typically PnP, prompting you to install the driver the first time the device is found in the system. If the drivers are not loaded, use the Device Manager's Properties sheet for each device to install a new driver.

If you need to install multiple SCSI devices, you should install one device and its device drivers before installing another device.

Troubleshooting I/O Ports

A multimedia or input device might appear to fail because of problems with the port the device is connected to. Use the following sections to diagnose port-specific problems.

Troubleshooting USB Ports and Devices

USB ports are the most common type of I/O port used on current systems. Use the following sections to solve problems with USB ports.

USB Devices Not Recognized

The following are several reasons why a USB device won't be recognized when it is installed:

- **USB port not enabled in system BIOS—** USB ports can be disabled in the system BIOS. To re-enable USB ports, follow these steps:

  Step 1. Restart the system.

  Step 2. Start the BIOS setup program.

  Step 3. Locate the correct menu for the USB ports (might be Advanced Chipset, Peripherals, or others, depending on the system).

  Step 4. Enable USB function.

  Step 5. Save the changes.

  Step 6. Exit the system and reboot.

  Step 7. Windows will install drivers for USB ports if they are not already installed.

- **USB port not properly designed on older systems**—Some of the early USB ports do not conform to current USB 1.1 or 2.0 standards and will not work with some or all USB peripherals, even using a supported version of Windows. Disable these ports and replace them with an add-on card containing USB ports.

- **Drivers for device not properly installed**—Windows 2000, Windows XP, Windows Vista, and Windows 7 contain drivers for USB mass storage and input devices, but other types of USB devices, such as printers, scanners, digital cameras, and network adapters, require manufacturer-specific drivers that must be installed first. See the documentation for the device for details.

USB Port Problems

Problems with the USB port after operating system and driver issues have been resolved might be caused by the following issues:

- **Not enough power for the device**—If a device that uses more power than a bus-powered generic hub can provide is connected to a bus-powered generic hub, the device will fail. In some cases, you might see a warning displayed in the Windows system tray (see Figure 7-29). However, in all cases, the Power tab in the Generic USB Hub Properties sheet in Device Manager indicates the power usage per connected device and the per-port power available.

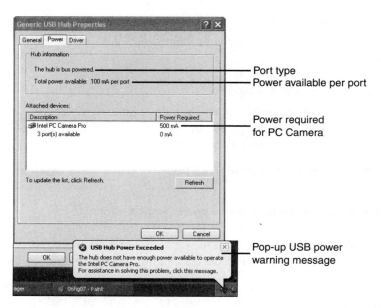

Figure 7-29 The Power tab in the Generic USB Hub Properties sheet in Windows XP indicates the Intel PC Camera Pro requires more power than the (bus-powered) hub can provide. In some cases, a pop-up warning appears to indicate this problem.

- **USB controller displays yellow exclamation point (!) sign in Windows Device Manager**—The USB PCI to USB controller (which runs the USB ports in the computer) might require a unique IRQ and I/O port address range on some older systems, unless IRQ sharing has been enabled in the system BIOS. Select nonconflicting IRQ and I/O port address ranges in the Properties sheet (Resources tab) for the USB controller, and restart the system if necessary.

- **Too many full-speed (12Mbps) USB devices attached to a single USB 1.1 port**—If the speed of existing devices drops after attaching a new device to the same USB hub, connect the new device to another USB port. If your system has USB 1.1 ports only, use a new hub connected to a separate USB port if needed to separate full-speed from low-speed USB devices. If your system has both USB 1.1 and USB 2.0 ports, attach a USB 2.0–compatible hub to a USB 2.0 port and attach all low-speed USB 1.1 devices to it.

- **USB 2.0 devices do not operate at full (480Mbps) speed**—Some systems can be configured to run USB ports in USB 1.1 or USB 2.0 modes. If USB ports are configured to run in USB 1.1 mode only, USB 2.0 devices will run very slowly, and a few might not work at all. Make sure USB ports are configured to run in USB 2.0 mode. Upgrade Windows XP to Service Pack 1 or greater to obtain USB 2.0 support. Upgrade Windows 2000 to Service Pack 4 to obtain USB 2.0 support.

Troubleshooting IEEE 1394 Ports and Devices

The following sections discuss the most common problems and solutions that apply to IEEE 1394 ports.

System Can't Detect the IEEE 1394 Card or Port

So, you put the card in the system, turned it on, and Windows ignored it? If an IEEE 1394 card can't be detected after it is physically installed in the system, check the following (be sure to turn off the system if you need to open it up again!):

- **The card's position in the slot**—If the card is not properly seated in the expansion slot, reseat it.

- **Power lead on cards that require an external power source**—Some IEEE 1394 cards require additional power from a 4-pin power connector. If the power connector isn't connected to the card, the card will not work when the system is turned on. Connect the power to the card and restart the system.

CAUTION If you need to use a power splitter or extender to reach the card, make sure it's connected to the power supply.

- **IRQ conflict**—Systems that use the advanced peripheral interrupt controller (APIC) can assign IRQs above 15 to PCI devices, and these devices can share IRQs. However, on older systems that do not support APIC or have APIC disabled in the system BIOS, IRQ conflicts can take place. If the IEEE 1394 card listing in Windows Device Manager indicates a problem, use one of the following solutions: Restart the system and use the system BIOS setup program to select an unused IRQ for a particular PCI expansion slot; use the Windows Device Manager to reset either the IEEE 1394 card or the conflicting device to a different IRQ; move the card to a different slot.

- **Port not enabled in system BIOS**—If the 1394 ports built into the system don't work, chances are they're not enabled in the system BIOS. Restart the computer, enter the BIOS setup program, and enable them. Save the changes and exit.

Incorrect Driver for IEEE 1394 Card or Device

Several different chipsets are used on IEEE 1394 cards and devices. If drivers for the wrong chipset are installed, the card or device will not function. If an IEEE 1394 card or device displays the yellow ! sign in Windows Device Manager, check the properties for the card or device. If an IRQ or memory address conflict is not present, use the Driver tab to manually update to the correct driver. Download an updated driver from the vendor's website.

Troubleshooting Parallel (LPT) Ports and Devices

If you are unable to use devices connected to parallel ports (such as printers), check the following:

- Parallel port mode not compatible with devices attached to the parallel port

- Incorrect order of devices when daisy-chaining multiple devices

- Cabling problems, including inadequate cabling for the parallel port mode selected, cabling too long for reliable printing, damage to port or cable, and incorrect cabling of parallel port header cable on multi-I/O cards

- Inadequate printer sharing device for mode selected

Parallel Port Mode Problems

If a parallel device designed to use an IEEE-1284 mode, such as EPP, ECP, or EPP/ECP, is attached to a parallel port that has the wrong mode selected or is set to slower modes, such as PS/2 bidirectional or standard/compatible, the device will work very slowly, or it might not work at all. Use the correct parallel port mode for the devices you need to attach to the port, and use an IEEE-1284–compatible cable to provide support for all parallel port modes.

Problems with Daisy-Chained Devices

Some systems daisy-chain devices such as Zip or other types of removable media drives or scanners to the same port as their printer. In many cases, the printer and any other single device can share the printer port. However, trying to use two or more devices along with the printer can cause slow performance or device failure.

To achieve success in using multiple parallel devices

Step 1.   Check the device documentation for suggestions on which devices can be installed and in what order—in many cases, a printer and scanner or printer and removable-media drive will work, but other combinations might not work. Note that the printer is always at the end of the daisy-chain.

Step 2.   Use the correct parallel port mode for the devices.

Step 3.   Consider adding a second parallel port for some devices, switch to USB devices that can be connected to a USB hub, or connect the printer to a USB port with a USB-to-parallel-port adapter.

Cabling and Port Problems

Cables are always the weak point in any computer peripheral. Printers and other parallel devices are no exception. Parallel cables can cause several problems with printers and other devices. Low-quality cables that are longer than 10 feet can cause garbled printing, and cables that don't support the port mode will prevent the port from reaching its maximum speed.

To avoid cabling problems, use a high-quality printer cable. Cables that meet the IEEE-1284 standard are recommended and will work well with any parallel port mode. IEEE-1284 cables provide the shielding necessary to ensure reliable printing beyond the 10-foot distance limitation of low-quality cables.

If you need to print at very long distances away from your computer, consider attaching the printer to a network or use a line converter (which changes parallel to serial signals).

Damaged cables will cause printing problems. If the printer will not print at all or prints garbage output, replace the cable with a known-working cable and retry the print job. Damaged ports will cause problems with any cable.

If a device connected to a parallel port that uses a header cable from a motherboard or add-on card doesn't work, make sure the header cable is properly attached to the motherboard or add-on card. If the header cable is not connected properly, devices connected to the header cable will not work.

Testing Parallel Ports

To determine whether a parallel port is damaged, first make sure there are no IRQ conflicts and that the header cable (if any) is properly attached to the motherboard. Then, use a diagnostic program such as AMIDIAG, CheckIt, or others and attach the appropriate loopback plug to the port. If the port is unable to pass a loopback test, the port is damaged and you should replace it. Figure 7-30 illustrates the use of loopback plugs to test parallel and serial ports.

TIP   Parallel and serial port loopback plugs resemble the connectors at the ends of parallel or serial cables, but they don't have cables, and internally they're very different. Each loopback plug routes the transmit pins to the receive pins in the connector. The testing software used with the loopback plug sends data and compares the sent data to the data received. If the data doesn't match, the port is defective. Different programs used for loopback testing use different pin combinations for testing, so make sure you get the loopback plugs that are made especially for the testing software you use. You can purchase them in a bundle with the software, or you can purchase them separately.

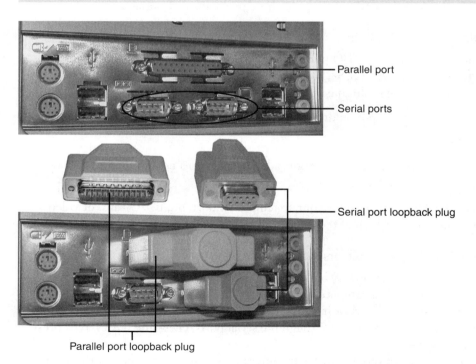

Figure 7-30   An ATX motherboard's serial and parallel ports before and after loopback plugs (middle) are installed for testing.

Switchbox Problems

A switchbox is a popular way to help two or more printers or other parallel devices share a single port. However, inexpensive switchboxes that use a rotary switch can damage the sensitive parallel ports on laser printers. Also, non-IEEE-1284–compliant switchboxes will prevent bidirectional operation of printers. Without a bidirectional connection to the printer, some printers can't be configured or send status reports back to the computer. To determine whether the switchbox is the problem, connect the printer or other device directly to the computer. If the device functions properly when connected directly but has problems when connected through a switchbox, the switchbox is not properly transmitting all the signals.

NOTE   With any combination of parallel devices (printers, drives, scanners, and so on), use IEEE-1284–compatible switchboxes that can be switched electronically and IEEE-1284–compatible switchboxes.

Troubleshooting Serial Ports and Devices

Use the following sections to help diagnose problems with serial ports.

COM 4 I/O Port Conflicts

Some video cards use an I/O port range that conflicts with the default I/O port range used by COM 4 (2E8-2EF). To prevent conflicts, you will need to choose one of the following solutions:

- Change the I/O port address used by COM 4.

- Disable COM 4.

- Change the video card's I/O port address range to a nonconflicting option with Windows Device Manager.

Check the documentation for your system, serial port, multi-I/O card, or video card to determine which of these methods to use.

Serial Port Drops Characters When Multitasking

The first-in/first-out (FIFO) buffers used in the 16550AF and higher series of UART chips enable a computer to reliably multitask while receiving or sending data through a serial port or internal modem. If characters are being dropped when data is sent or received through the serial ports, check the UART type present in the system. If the UART is an 8250 series or 16450 series device (which lack FIFO buffers), you should replace the internal modem or serial port with a device containing a 16550AF or better UART.

If characters are being dropped on a system with the correct UART, you can use the Control Panel options in Windows to adjust the connection.

To adjust the connection in Windows 2000/XP/Vista for an external modem connected to a serial port or for a modem with a hardware UART, follow these steps:

Step 1.   Click Start and alternate-click My Computer. This will open the System Properties window.

Step 2.   Access Device Manager. In Windows 2000/XP click the hardware tab and then the Device Manager button. In Windows Vista, simply click the link for Device Manager on the left-side under Tasks.

Step 3.   Click the plus (+) sign next to the Ports.

Step 4.   Double-click the serial (communications) port used by the modem.

Step 5.   Click Port Settings, Advanced.

Step 6.   To solve problems with receiving data, adjust the Receive buffer toward Low. To solve problems with sending data, adjust the Transmit buffer toward High.

Step 7.   Make sure that Use FIFO Buffers is checked if your modem or serial port has a 16550AF or faster UART.

Step 8.   Click OK until all dialog boxes are closed; then close the Device Manager.

Step 9.   Click OK to close the System Properties sheet.

Can't Connect Serial Devices to Port Because of Mismatched Connectors

Some older systems might use a 25-pin serial port (the original design used by the IBM PC) instead of the now-standard 9-pin connector. Occasionally, some serial devices using one type of connector must be connected to serial ports that use the other type of connector. Use the appropriate 9-pin to 25-pin adapter to allow a 9-pin port to use a 25-pin device, or vice versa.

Serial Cabling and Port Problems

Damaged or incorrectly wired serial cables can cause several problems with any serial device. To avoid cabling problems, verify that you are using the correct serial cable with any given device. For serial port external modems, purchase a modem cable; for serial printers, buy a cable made especially for that printer, and so forth.

Damaged cables will cause device problems. If an external serial device will not work at all or produces garbage input or output, first check the communications parameters for the port and the devices. If these are correct, replace the cable with a cable that you know to be working and retry the device. Damaged ports will cause problems with any cable.

If the serial port is connected to the motherboard or add-on card with a header cable, make sure the header cable is properly connected to the motherboard or add-on card.

Serial Configuration Problems

The serial port or modem connected to a serial port must be configured correctly to communicate properly with devices such as serial printers or remote computers. If gibberish output from a printer or gibberish screen display during a remote communications session occurs, make sure the baud rate, parity, and word length are set correctly. For more information about these settings, refer to the section "Serial Port Software Configuration," earlier in this chapter.

Testing Serial Ports

To determine whether a serial port is damaged, first make sure there are no IRQ conflicts (use the Windows Device Manager as described in Chapter 13) and that the header cable (if any) is properly attached to the motherboard. Then, use a diagnostic program, such as AMIDIAG, CheckIt, or others, and attach the appropriate loopback plug to the port. If the port is unable to pass a loopback test, the port is damaged and you should replace it. For more information about using loopback plugs, see the section "Testing Parallel Ports," earlier in this chapter.

Maintaining Input Devices

Input devices such as mice, pointing devices, and keyboards can become dirty over time, and can fail to operate properly if not cleaned periodically. The following sections discuss how to maintain these devices.

Maintaining Mice and Pointing Devices

There are three types of motion sensors that have been used in mouse devices: mechanical, optical, and laser, as seen in Figure 7-31.

Most mice with mechanical sensors use a ball and roller design. The motion of the mouse ball against a mouse pad, desk, or tabletop can pick up dust and dirt that can cause erratic mouse-pointer movement. The ball and the rollers should be cleaned periodically. Clean the mouse with a specially designed mouse cleaning kit or use a nonabrasive damp cloth to remove gunk from the rollers and the ball.

To remove the mouse ball as shown in Figure 7-1 for access to the rollers, follow these steps

Step 1.   Turn over the mouse; an access cover on the bottom of the mouse holds the ball in place.

Step 2.   Follow the arrows on the access cover to turn or slide the cover to one side; lift the plate out of the way to release the ball.

1. Motion-detecting rollers
2. Ball
3. Retaining ring for ball
4. Sensor camera lens
5. LED light
6. Laser motion sensor

Figure 7-31   A mechanical mouse (left) with the retaining ring and ball removed for cleaning compared to an optical mouse (center) and a laser mouse (right).

Step 3.   Turn the rollers until you see dirt or grit; wipe them clean and clean the ball.

Step 4.   Shake loose dust and gunk out of the mouse.

Step 5.   When you've finished the cleaning process, replace the ball and access panel.

Optical mice and laser mice do not require disassembly. To keep an optical mouse in proper working order, wipe dust and dirt away from the LED light and sensor camera lens. To keep a laser mouse working properly, wipe dust and dirt away from the laser.

For wireless mice, be sure to check batteries periodically for leakage, and replace batteries when the cursor action becomes erratic. For mice that use rechargeable batteries, be sure to use approved types and charge the batteries as recommended by the battery vendor.

To maintain trackballs, remove the trackball and clean the rollers to keep the trackball working properly.

To maintain touchpads, periodically wipe the surface with a dampened cloth to remove skin oils that can prevent proper sensing of finger movements.

Maintaining Keyboards

Keyboards can become unresponsive or erratic due to dust, dirt, and debris under the keytops, and the keytops can become dirty and sticky. Here's how (and how not) to clean them:

Step 1.   **Don't** use sprays to clean a keyboard; use a cloth dampened with an antistatic surface cleaner to wipe off grime while the system is turned off.

Step 2.   **Use** compressed air or a data-grade vacuum cleaner to remove dirt and dust under the keys, or remove the keys if possible for cleaning with compressed air or a data-grade vacuum cleaner.

TIP   If you're not certain if the keytops can be removed, check with the keyboard vendor.

To remove the keytops from the keyboard, I recommend you use a chip puller, a U-shaped tool included with many computer toolkits. Grasp two sides of the keytop with the chip puller and lift it from the keyboard. If you don't have a chip puller, use a pair of flat-bladed screwdrivers to carefully lift the keytop from opposite sides at once.

Exam Preparation Tasks

Review All the Key Topics

Review the most important topics in the chapter, noted with the key topics icon in the outer margin of the page. Table 7-13 lists a reference of these key topics and the page numbers on which each is found.

Table 7-13   Key Topics for Chapter 7

Key Topic Element	Description	Page Number
Figure 7-1	A typical ATX motherboard's I/O ports.	225
Figure 7-2	USB plugs and sockets.	226
Figure 7-4	The USB section of the Windows XP Device Manager on a typical system.	228
Figure 7-5	A SCSI host adapter card with internal and external connectors.	230
Table 7-4	Popular SCSI Standards.	232
Figure 7-11	A 9-pin serial port and a 25-pin serial port.	238
Table 7-9	Standard Settings for COM Ports 1–4.	243
Figure 7-15	General (left) and Advanced (right) dialog boxes used in Windows XP to configure a serial port connected to an external modem.	245
Figure 7-16	Parallel and Centronics ports.	246
Table 7-11	Typical Parallel Port Hardware Configuration Settings.	251
Figure 7-19	A typical IEEE 1394a host adapter card with three external and one internal port.	253
Figure 7-31 and Table 7-12	Mouse Properties and Troubleshooting table.	271, 287

Complete the Tables and Lists from Memory

Print a copy of Appendix B, "Memory Tables," (found on the CD), or at least the section for this chapter, and complete the tables and lists from memory. Appendix C, "Memory Tables Answer Key," also on the CD, includes completed tables and lists to check your work.

Definitions of Key Terms

Define the following key terms from this chapter, and check your answers in the glossary.

USB, SCSI, Daisy-Chaining, Device ID, Serial Port, RS-232, Parallel port, LPT, IEEE 1394, IEEE 1284, Centronics, PS/2, FireWire, Loopback plug, Switchbox

Troubleshooting Scenario

You have been asked about a printing issue on a specific computer. You have looked in the Windows Control Panel Printers and Faxes folder and determined that the printer is installed correctly. What procedure would you use to try to fix the problem?

Refer to Appendix A for the answer.

This chapter covers the following subjects:

- **Video (Graphics) Cards Types**—In this section you learn about the different types of video cards including PCI, AGP, and PCIe, and the various methods of cooling video cards.

- **Installing a Video Card**—Learn the ins and outs of video card installation, from the BIOS, to physical installation and driver setup.

- **Display Types**—This section describes CRTs, LCDs, and data projectors.

- **Video Connector Types**—This section talks about VGA, DVI, HDMI, and all the other video connections you need to know for the exam.

- **Display Settings**—This section demonstrates how to configure resolution and the refresh settings.

- **Installing a Monitor**—This section briefly demonstrates how to install a video monitor.

- **Troubleshooting Displays and Video Cards**—Due to the many possible video issues you might encounter, this section demonstrates how to troubleshoot with OSD and the advanced display properties.

- **Preventative Maintenance for Displays**—This section describes how to keep the display clean and maintain good airflow.

This chapter covers a portion of the CompTIA A+ 220-701 objectives 1.7 and 1.9, and CompTIA A+ 220-702 objectives 1.1 and 1.2.

CHAPTER 8

Video Displays and Graphics Cards

The monitor and video card work together as the display subsystem to provide real-time notification of the computer's activities to the user. Because you might spend all day (and sometimes all night) gazing into the display, keeping it working to full efficiency is important. This chapter helps you prepare for the A+ Certification Exams by enhancing your understanding of the major types of video cards and displays and showing you how to configure and troubleshoot them.

"Do I Know This Already?" Quiz

The "Do I Know This Already?" quiz allows you to assess whether you should read this entire chapter or simply jump to the "Exam Preparation Tasks" section for review. If you are in doubt, read the entire chapter. Table 8-1 outlines the major headings in this chapter and the corresponding "Do I Know This Already?" quiz questions. You can find the answers in Appendix A, "Answers to the 'Do I Know This Already?' Quizzes and Troubleshooting Scenarios."

Table 8-1 "Do I Know This Already?" Foundation Topics Section-to-Question Mapping

Foundations Topics Section	Questions Covered in This Section
Video (Graphics) Card Types	1, 2
Installing a Video Card	3, 4
Display Types	5
Video Connector Types	6, 7
Display Settings	8
Installing a Monitor	9
Troubleshooting Displays and Video Cards	10, 11
Preventative Maintenance for Displays	12

1. Which of the following bus types are used for video cards? (Choose all that apply.)

   a. PCI

   b. AGP

   c. DMI

   d. PCI Express

2. Which of the following are used to keep the video card cool? (Choose all that apply.)

   a. Passive heat sinks

   b. Thermal glue

   c. Cooling fans

   d. Shrouds

3. When installing a new video card, there are three phases. What are they? Select the best three answers.

   a. Configuring the BIOS for the video card being installed.

   b. Physically installing the video card.

   c. Making sure the video card is in the protective anti-static bag.

   d. Installing drivers for the video card.

4. You install a new video card in your system, but are not getting all the features. What would you need to do to correct the problem?

   a. Reboot the computer

   b. Install the device driver

   c. Take the card out and put it back in

   d. Call a technician

5. What are three major types of display devices that are in use in today's industry? (Choose all that apply.)

   a. CRT monitors

   b. LCD monitors

   c. Data projectors

   d. USB monitors

6. Identify three types of video connectors.

    a. VGA type

    b. DVI type

    c. HDMI type

    d. USB type

7. If you are installing a new LCD monitor, what current standard port will you need for digital signals?

    a. LCD monitor

    b. AGP slot

    c. A DVI port on the video card

    d. A VGA video port

8. Where would you go to set your display resolution in Windows XP?

    a. My Computer

    b. Display Properties

    c. Screen Saver tab

    d. Appearance tab

9. When installing a new monitor, what should you do first? (Choose the best answer.)

    a. Determine what type of cable is compatible with your video card

    b. Go to the advanced dialog screen and choose a resolution

    c. Connect the cable to the video card

    d. None of these options is correct

10. If the colors are flickering on your monitor, what could be the problem?

    a. Refresh rate too slow

    b. Refresh rate too fast

    c. Loose video cable

    d. The monitor is bad

11. If your monitor has low contrast and brightness, what might you do to correct the problem?

   a. Change the refresh rate

   b. Re-install the monitor

   c. Check the connection

   d. Use the OSD buttons on the front of the monitor

12. Which of the following steps should you take when maintaining monitors? (Choose all that apply.)

   a. Do not block ventilation holes in CRT and LCD displays.

   b. Use antistatic cleaners made for electronics to clean screens and other surfaces.

   c. Do not spray cleaners directly onto screens or enclosures.

   d. Use thumbscrews to hold VGA and DVI cables in place on displays, projectors, and video cards.

   e. When a system is opened for upgrades or service, check the condition of the cooling features of the video card. Remove hair, dust, or dirt in or on the heat sink, cooling fan, fan shroud, or heat pipe radiator. Make sure airflow around and behind the video card is not obstructed by cables, dirt, dust, or other components.

   f. Allow plenty of clearance around the video card slot. Don't use the slot next to the video card if the card would limit airflow to the video card's cooling features.

Foundation Topics

Video (Graphics) Card Types

The video card (also known as the graphics card or graphics accelerator card) is an add-on card (or circuit on the motherboard of portable computers and some desktop computers) that creates the image you see on the monitor. No video card means no picture.

Currently, video cards use the following bus types:

- PCI
- AGP
- PCI Express (PCIe)

Many low-cost desktop systems use integrated video instead of a video card, although many recent desktops also include a PCIe slot. For more information about these expansion slot standards, see the section "Expansion Slots," in Chapter 3, "Motherboards, Processors, and Adapter Cards."

In the mid 1990s, the most common type of expansion slot used for video cards was PCI. Although PCI is still the leading general-purpose expansion slot type, the advent of the Pentium II CPU led to the development of the Accelerated Graphics Port (AGP) expansion slot, which is dedicated solely to high-speed video.

AGP slots have largely been replaced in recent systems by PCI Express x16 slots. Many recent high-performance systems feature two PCI Express x16 slots that support either the NVIDIA-developed SLI or the ATI-developed CrossFire technologies for rendering 3D scenes on one video card with two (or more) graphics processing units (GPUs), or two video cards that work in unison; a GPU is the graphics processing chip on a video card. To see a typical motherboard that supports NVIDIA's SLI, refer to Figure 3-1 in Chapter 3.

Video Card Cooling

All video cards contain a component called the graphics processing unit (GPU). The GPU is used to render information on its way to the display, and especially when performing 3D rendering, it can become very hot. Memory chips on the video card can also become very hot. Consequently both the GPU and memory require cooling.

Cooling can be provided through passive heat sinks or through cooling fans and fan shrouds as shown in Figure 8-1. Passive heat sinks on older video cards typically cover only the GPU, but newer ones provide cooling for both the GPU and memory. Video cards with passive heat sinks are good choices for home theater PCs, such as those running Windows XP Media Center Edition or Windows Vista and Windows 7 editions running Windows Media Center, because these PCs need to run as quietly as possible.

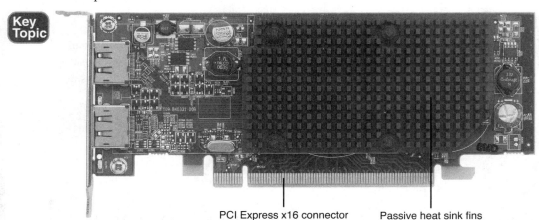

Figure 8-1   This AMD FireMV 2260 video card for technical workstations uses a passive heat sink to cool the GPU and memory. Photo courtesy of AMD.

NOTE   Some video cards use a variation of passive heat sinks known as cooling pipes. Cooling pipes use pipes to route heat from the GPU and memory to a radiator-type passive cooler on the card. A cooling pipe cooler provides better cooling than a standard passive heat sink, but requires extra space around the video card.

The video card shown in Figure 8-2 uses a fan and a fan shroud to cool the GPU and memory. Some low-performance video cards that use a fan for cooling the GPU don't use a fan shroud, relying on case fans to cool video card memory.

Installing a Video Card

The installation process for a video card includes three phases:

Step 1.   Configuring the BIOS for the video card being installed

Step 2.   Physically installing the video card

Step 3.   Installing drivers for the video card

BIOS Configuration

The BIOS settings involving the video card might include some or all of the following, depending upon the video card type:

■   **AGP speed settings**—Found in systems with an AGP slot. Most systems automatically detect the type of AGP card installed (2x, 4x, or 8x) and configure speed settings accordingly. However, you can override the settings if necessary.

1. Cooling fan over GPU
2. Power connector for cooling fan
3. PCI Express x16 connector
4. DVI-I ports
5. S-video/composite video port
6. Exhaust vents
7. Fan shroud

Figure 8-2   This AMD ATI HD3870 video card includes a high-performance fan cooler and shroud over the GPU and memory to dissipate heat. Photo courtesy of AMD.

For example, enable AGP Fast Write to improve graphics performance, but disable it if the system crashes.

- **Primary VGA BIOS (also known as Primary Graphics Adapter)**—Set this to AGP or AGP->PCI if you use an AGP video card; PCIE or PCIE->PCI if you use a PCI Express video card. Use PCI, PCI->PCIE, or PCI->AGP if you use a PCI video card. For onboard video, see the manufacturer's recommendation (onboard video can use PCI, AGP, or PCI Express buses built into the motherboard).

- **Graphics aperture *size***—Found in systems with an AGP slot. Use the default size, which is typically the same as the amount of memory on the AGP card.

Adjust these settings as needed.

Video Card Physical and Driver Installation

Although all video cards created since the beginning of the 1990s are based on VGA, virtually every one uses a unique chipset that requires special software drivers to control acceleration features (faster onscreen video), color depth, and resolution. So, whenever you change video cards, you must change video driver software as well. Otherwise, Windows will drop into a low-resolution, ugly 16-color mode and give you an error message because the driver doesn't match the video card.

Here's how to replace a video card (or upgrade from integrated video to a video card) and install the drivers in Windows 2000/XP/Vista/7:

Step 1.   Go into Device Manager and delete the listing for the current graphics card.

Step 2.   Shut down the system and unplug it.

Step 3.   Turn off the monitor.

Step 4.   Disconnect the data cable attached to the video card.

Step 5.   Open the case and remove the old video card. Remove the screw holding the card bracket in place and release the card-retention mechanism that holds an AGP or PCI Express video card in place (refer to Figure 8-3).

Card-retention mechanism is
open; card can be removed.

Figure 8-3   Releasing the card-retention mechanism before removing an AGP video card.

NOTE   Card-retention mechanisms vary widely from motherboard to motherboard. In addition to the design shown in Figure 8-3, some use a lever that can be pushed to one side to release the lock, while others use a knob that is pulled out to release the lock.

Step 6.   Insert the new video card. Lock the card into position with the card retention mechanism (if you are installing an AGP or PCI Express card) and with the screw for the card bracket.

Step 7.   Reattach the data cable from the monitor to the new video card. If you are connecting a monitor with a VGA cable to a video card that uses only DVI-I ports (refer to Figure 8-2), attach an adapter between the DVI-I port and the VGA connector (see Figure 8-4).

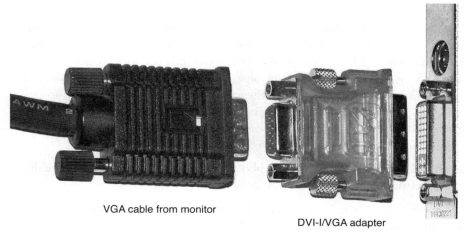

VGA cable from monitor

DVI-I/VGA adapter

DVI-I port on video card

Figure 8-4 Using a DVI-I/VGA adapter.

Step 8.   Turn on the monitor.

Step 9.   Turn on the computer and press F8 to display the startup menu.

Step 10.   Select Enable VGA Mode from the startup menu.

Step 11.   Provide video drivers as requested; you might need to run an installer program for the drivers.

Step 12.   If the monitor is not detected as a Plug and Play monitor but as a Default monitor, install a driver for the monitor. A driver disc might have been packed with the monitor, or you might need to download a driver from the monitor vendor's website. If you do not install a driver for a monitor identified as a Default monitor, you will not be able to choose from the full range of resolutions and refresh rates the monitor actually supports.

To learn more about connector types used by monitors and video cards, see the section "Video Connector Types," later in this chapter.

Display Types

There are three major types of displays you need to understand for the A+ Certification exams:

■ CRT monitors

■ LCD monitors

■ Data projectors

The following sections help you understand the common and unique features of each.

CRT Monitor

Cathode ray tube (CRT) displays are now fading in popularity but are still in widespread use on older systems. CRTs use a picture tube that is similar to the picture tube in a tube-based TV set. The narrow end of the tube contains an electron gun that projects three electron beams (red, blue, green) toward the wide end, which is coated with phosphors that glow when they are hit by the electron beams. Just before the phosphor coating, a metal plate called a shadow mask is used to divide the image created by the electron guns into red, green, and blue pixels or stripes that form the image. Shadow masks use one of three technologies:

- A phosphor triad (a group of three phosphors—red, green, and blue). The distance between each triad is called the *dot pitch*.

- An aperture grill, which uses vertical red, green, and blue phosphor strips. The distance between each group is called the *stripe pitch*.

- A slotted mask, which uses small blocks of red, green, and blue phosphor strips. The distance between each horizontal group is also called *stripe pitch*.

If you look closely at a CRT display, you can see the individual triads or strips. However, from normal viewing distances, they blend into a clear picture.

Figure 8-5 shows the design of a typical CRT monitor.

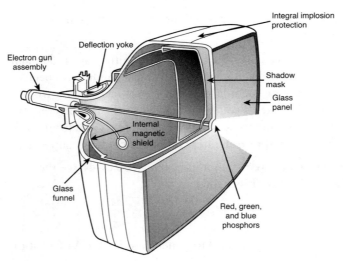

Figure 8-5   A cutaway of a typical CRT display.

Generally, the smaller the dot or stripe pitch, the clearer and sharper the onscreen image will be. Typical standards for CRT monitors call for a dot pitch of .28 millimeters (mm) or smaller. Generally, low-cost monitors have poorer picture quality than higher-cost monitors of the same size because of wider dot pitch, low refresh rates at their highest resolutions, and poor focus at their highest resolutions.

Typical CRT displays range in size from 15 inches (diagonal measure) to 19 inches, and feature support for a wide range of resolutions. CRTs are analog display devices that can display an unlimited range of colors, and use the 15-pin VGA connector. To learn more about VGA connectors, see the section "VGA," later in this chapter.

LCD Monitor

LCD displays use liquid crystal cells to polarize light passing through the display to create the image shown on the monitor. In color LCD displays, liquid crystal cells are grouped into three cells for each pixel: one each for red, green, and blue light.

All LCD displays use active matrix technology, which uses a transistor to control each cell, as the basic technology. Variations in how quickly a display can refresh, how wide the viewing angle, and how bright the display help distinguish different brands and models from each other.

An LCD monitor is a digital design, but many models, particularly low-end models and older designs, use the same VGA analog interface as CRTs. In such cases, the monitor must include an analog-digital converter to change the analog signal received by the VGA cable into a digital signal. High-end LCD displays and most recent midrange models also support digital signals and use DVI-D ports. To learn more about active-matrix displays, see "LCD Screen Technologies," in Chapter 9, "Laptops and Portable Devices." To learn more about DVI-D connectors, see the section "DVI," later in this chapter.

Compared to CRT monitors, LCDs are much lighter, require much less power, emit less heat, and use much less desk space.

An LCD display has only one native resolution; it must scale lower resolutions to fit the panel, or, depending upon the options configured in the video card driver, might use only a portion of the display when a lower resolution is selected. When a lower resolution is scaled, the display is less sharp than when the native resolution is used.

LCD displays are found in both standard (4:3 or 1.33:1) and widescreen (16:9 or 16:10) aspect ratios, and range in size from 14 inches (diagonal measure) to 24 inches or larger.

Data Projector

Data projectors can be used in place of a primary display or can be used as a clone of the primary display to permit computer information and graphics to be displayed on a projection screen or a wall.

Data projectors use one of the following technologies:

- Liquid crystal display (LCD)

- Digital light processing (DLP)

LCD projectors use separate LCD panels for red, green, and blue light, and combine the separate images into a single RGB image for projection, using dichroic mirrors. A dichroic mirror reflects light in some wavelengths, while permitting light in other wavelengths to pass through. In Figure 8-6, red and blue dichroic mirrors are used to split the image into red, blue, and green wavelengths. After passing through the appropriate LCD, a dichroic combiner cube recombines the separate red, green, and blue images into a single RGB image for projection.

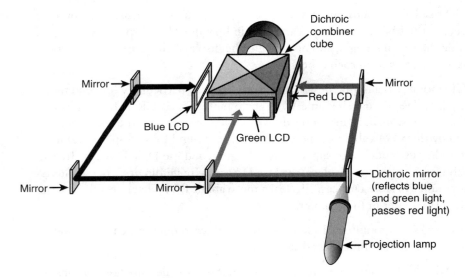

Figure 8-6   How a typical three-LCD data projector works.

LCD projectors use a relatively hot projection lamp, so LCD projectors include cooling fans that run both during projector operation and after the projector is turned off to cool down the lamp.

DLP projectors use a spinning wheel with red, green, and blue sections to add color data to light being reflected from an array of tiny mirrors known as a digital micromirror device (DMD). Each mirror corresponds to a pixel, and the mirrors reflect light toward or away from the projector optics. The spinning wheel might use only three segments (RGB), four segments (RGB+clear), or six segments (RGB+RGB). More segments help improve picture quality. Figure 8-7 illustrates how a DLP projector works.

Video Connector Types

When selecting a monitor or projector for use with a particular video card or integrated video port, it's helpful to understand the physical and feature differences be-

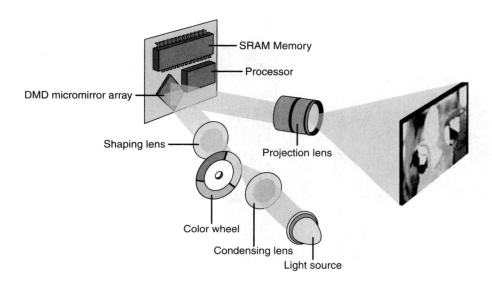

Figure 8-7   How a typical DLP projector works.

tween different video connector types, such as VGA, DVI, HDMI, Component/RGB, S-video, and composite.

VGA

VGA is an analog display standard. By varying the levels of red, green, or blue per dot (pixel) onscreen, a VGA port and monitor can display an unlimited number of colors. Practical color limits (if you call more than 16 million colors limiting) are based on the video card's memory and the desired screen resolution.

All VGA cards made for use with standard analog monitors use a DB-15F 15-pin female connector, which plugs into the DB-15M connector used by the VGA cable from the monitor. Figure 8-8 compares these connectors.

DVI

The DVI port is the current standard for digital LCD monitors. The DVI port comes in two forms: DVI-D supports only digital signals, and is found on digital LCD displays. Most of these displays also support analog video signals through separate VGA ports. However, video cards with DVI ports use the DVI-I version, which provides both digital and analog output and supports the use of a VGA/DVI-I adapter for use with analog displays (refer to Figure 8-4). Figure 8-9 illustrates a DVI-D cable and DVI-I port.

DB15M VGA cable   DB15F VGA port

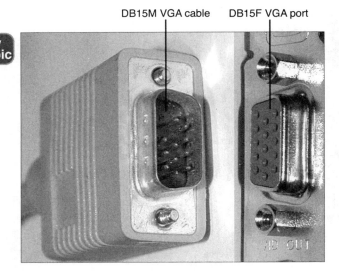

Figure 8-8   DB15M (cable) and DB15F (port) connectors used for VGA video signals.

DVI-D video cable supports digital signals only

DVI-I video port supports
analog and digital signals

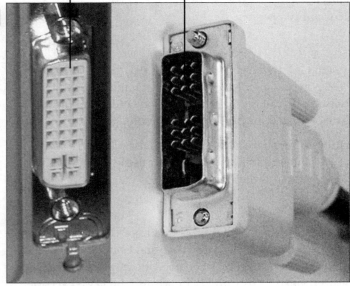

Figure 8-9   DVI-I video port and DVI-D video cable.

HDMI

Video cards and systems with integrated video that are designed for home theater use support a unique type of digital video standard known as High-Definition Multimedia Interface (HDMI). HDMI is unique in its ability to support digital audio as well as video through a single cable. HDMI ports are found on most late-model HDTVs as well as home theater hardware such as amplifiers and DVD players.

The most recent HDMI standard, version 1.3b, supports up to 1080p HDTV, 24-bit or greater color depths, and various types of uncompressed and compressed digital audio. However, all versions of HDMI use the cable shown in Figure 8-10 and the port shown in Figure 8-11.

DVI-D cable (for comparison)

HDMI cable

Figure 8-10   HDMI cable (right) compared to DVI-D cable (left).

Systems and video cards with integrated HDMI ports might also feature DVI-I or VGA ports, as in Figure 8-11.

A converter cable with a DVI connector on one end and an HDMI connector on the other end can be used to interface a PC with an HDTV if the PC doesn't have an HDMI port.

Component/RGB

Some data projectors and virtually all HDTVs support a high-resolution type of analog video known as component video. Component video uses separate RCA cables and ports to carry red, green, and blue signals, and can support up to 720p HDTV resolutions.

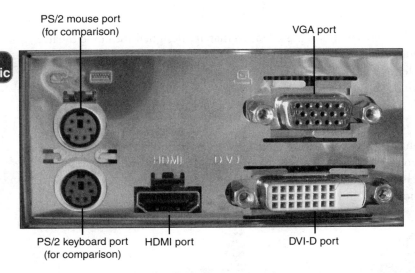

PS/2 mouse port
(for comparison)

VGA port

Key
Topic

PS/2 keyboard port   HDMI port
(for comparison)

DVI-D port

Figure 8-11   HDMI, DVI-D, and VGA ports on the rear of a typical PC built for use with Windows Media Center and home theater integration.

S-Video

S-video divides a video signal into separate luma and chroma signals, providing a better signal for use with standard TVs, projectors, DVD players, and VCRs than a composite signal. The so-called "TV-out" port on the back of many video cards is actually an S-video port (refer to Figure 8-1).

Composite

The lowest-quality video signal supported by PCs is composite video, which uses a single RCA cable and port to transmit a video signal. Video cards sold in Europe usually use a composite signal for their TV-out signal.

Composite video can be used by standard definition TVs (SDTVs) and VCRs. If you need to connect a PC with an S-video port to a TV or VCR that has a composite port, you can use an S-video to composite video adapter.

Figure 8-12 compares component, S-video, and composite video cables and ports to each other. Note that composite video cables are often bundled with stereo audio cables, but can also be purchased separately.

Display Settings

Once a display is connected to your computer, it might need to be properly configured. The following sections discuss display settings issues you might encounter in A+ Certification exams.

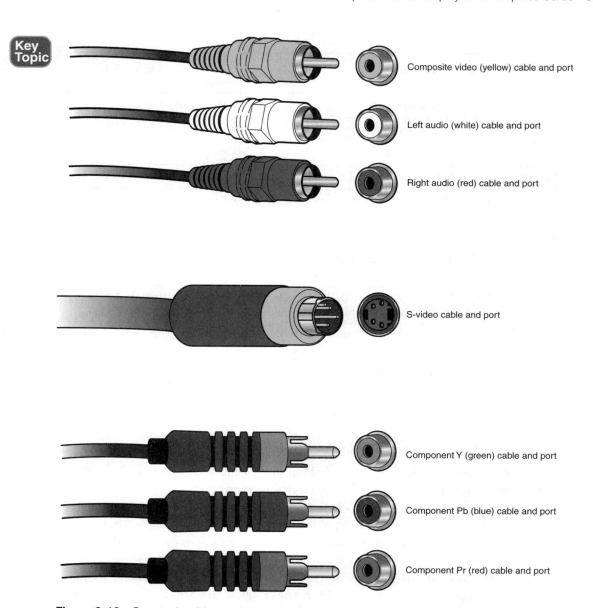

Figure 8-12   Composite video and stereo audio, S-video, and component video cables and ports compared.

Resolution

Display resolution is described as the amount of pixels (picture elements) on a screen. It is measured horizontally by vertically (HxV). The word *resolution* is somewhat of a misnomer, and will also be referred to as *pixel dimensions*. Table 8-2 shows some of the typical resolutions used in Windows. The more commonly used resolutions are in bold.

Table 8-2   List of Resolutions Used in Windows

Resolution Type	Full Name	Pixel Dimensions	Aspect Ratio
VGA*	Video Graphics Array	640×480	4:3 (1.333)
SVGA*	Super Video Graphics Array	800×600	4:3 (1.333)
XGA	eXtended Graphics Array	1024×768	4:3 (1.333)
WXGA	Widescreen eXtended Graphics Array	1280×800	16:10 (1.6:1)
WXGA (HD)	Widescreen eXtended Graphics Array (High Definition)	1366×768	16:9 (1.78:1)
SXGA	Super eXtended Graphics Array	1280×1024	5:4 (1.25)
WSXGA+	Widescreen Super Extended Graphics Array Plus	1680×1050	16:10 (1.6:1)
WSXGA+ (HD)	Widescreen Super Extended Graphics Array Plus (High-Definition)	1680×945	16:9 (1.78:1)
WUXGA	Widescreen Ultra eXtended Graphics Array	1920×1200	8:5 (1.6)
1080P and 1080i	Full High Definition	1920×1080	16:9 (1.778)

*VGA and SVGA modes are usually only seen if you attempt to boot the system into Safe Mode or another advanced boot mode, or if the driver has failed.

To modify screen resolution do the following:

- **In Windows 7**—Right-click the desktop and select Screen Resolution. Use the vertical slider to select the desired pixel dimensions.

- **In Windows Vista**—Right-click the desktop and select Personalize. Then click the Display Settings link. Toward the bottom left of the window is a box called "Resolution," which has a slider that enables you to configure the pixel dimensions.

- **In Windows XP**—Right-click the desktop and select Properties. Then click the Settings tab within the Display Properties window. Toward the bottom left of the window is a box called "Screen resolution," which has a slider that enables you to configure the pixel dimensions.

These dialogs are also used to select color quality and to enable multiple displays on a system that supports two or more monitors (see Figure 8-13).

Unless you need to select a lower resolution for specific purposes, you should select an LCD monitor's native resolution (see the instruction manual or specification sheet for this information). For a CRT, choose a resolution that is comfortable to view and enables the monitor to run in a flicker-free refresh rate, ideally 75Hz or higher.

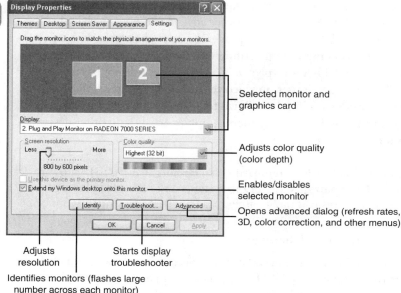

Selected monitor and graphics card

Adjusts color quality (color depth)

Enables/disables selected monitor

Opens advanced dialog (refresh rates, 3D, color correction, and other menus)

Adjusts resolution

Starts display troubleshooter

Identifies monitors (flashes large number across each monitor)

Figure 8-13 The Settings tab controls display resolution, multiple monitor support, color quality (color depth), and provides access to advanced settings.

Color Quality (Color Depth)

Color quality (also known as color depth or bit depth) is a term used to describe the number of bits that represent color. For example, 1-bit color is known as monochrome, those old screens with a black background and one color for the text, as in the classic movie *War Games*. But what is 1-bit? 1-bit in the binary numbering system means a binary number with one digit; this can be a zero or a one, a total of two values: usually black and white. This is defined in scientific notation as 2^1, (2 to the 1st power, which is 2). Another example would be 4-bit color, used by the ancient but awesome Commodore 64. In a 4-bit color system you can have 16 colors total. In this case $2^4 = 16$.

Now that you know the basics, take a look at Table 8-3 which shows the different color depths used in Windows.

Table 8-3 List of Color Depths Used in Windows

Color Depth	Number of Colors	Calculation
8-bit	256	2^8
16-bit	65,536	2^{16}
24-bit	16,777,216	2^{24}
32-bit	4,294,967,296	2^{32}

8-bit color is used in VGA mode, which is uncommon for normal use. But you might see it if you boot into Safe Mode, or other advanced modes that disable the video driver. 16-bit is usually enough for the average user who works with basic applications, however many computers are configured by default to 24-bit or 32-bit (also known as 3 bytes and 4 bytes respectively). Most users will not have a need for 32-bit color depth; in fact, it uses up video resources. If the user only works on basic applications, consider scaling them down to 24-bit or 16-bit in order to increase system performance. However, gamers, graphics artists, and other designers will probably want 32-bit color depth.

NOTE   Typically, only video cards or onboard video circuits that lack 3D support list 24-bit color as the best color quality option; systems and onboard video with 3D support list 32-bit color instead of 24-bit color as the best color quality option.

To modify color quality, do the following:

- **In Windows 7**—Right-click the desktop, select Screen Resolution, and click Advanced Settings. Click List All Modes (adapter tag) and select the pixel dimensions, color quality, and refresh rate desired.

- **In Windows Vista**—Right-click the desktop and select **Personalize**. Then click the **Display Settings** link. A drop-down menu for color quality is located on the bottom right.

- **In Windows XP**—Right-click the desktop and select **Properties**. Then click the **Settings** tab within the Display Properties window. A drop-down menu for color quality is located on the bottom right.

Refresh Rates

The vertical refresh rate refers to how quickly the monitor redraws the screen and is measured in hertz (Hz), or times per second. Typical vertical refresh rates for CRT monitors vary from 56Hz to 85Hz or higher, with refresh rates of 75Hz causing less flicker onscreen.

TIP   Flicker-free (75Hz or higher) refresh rates are better for users running CRTs, producing less eyestrain and more comfort during long computing sessions. Note that LCD monitors never flicker, so the Windows default refresh rate of 60Hz works well with any LCD display.

The vertical refresh in Windows XP and Vista can be adjusted through the Advanced portion of the Display Properties sheet. You can select a different vertical refresh rate in one of two ways:

Step 1.   Select the Monitor dialog and choose a refresh rate from the Screen Refresh Rate dialog (Figure 8-14a).

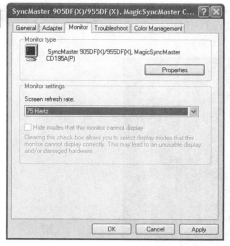

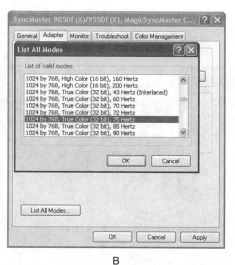

A   B

Figure 8-14   Selecting the vertical refresh rate from the Monitor dialog (a) and from the Adapter dialog (b).

Step 2.   Select the Adapter dialog, click List All Modes, and choose the combination of resolution, color depth, and refresh rate desired (Figure 8-14b).

NOTE   If your monitor is listed as Default monitor rather than Plug and Play monitor or as a specific monitor model, you will not be able to choose flicker-free refresh rates. Install a driver provided by the vendor.

CAUTION   Selecting a refresh rate that exceeds the monitor's specifications can damage the monitor or cause the monitor to display a blank screen or a "signal out of range" error. If you select a refresh rate that exceeds the monitor's specifications, press the ESC (Escape) key on the keyboard to return to the previous setting.

Installing a Monitor

To install a monitor in Windows, follow this procedure:

Step 1.   Determine if the monitor is using a cable that is compatible with your video card. If you can change the cable, do so if necessary. In the case of an LCD display, you will have better picture quality if you use DVI rather than VGA interfacing.

Step 2.   If the system is currently running, open the Advanced dialog and choose a resolution and refresh rate that are supported by both the current monitor and the new monitor, and then shut down the system.

Step 3.   Connect the cable between the monitor and the video card. Fasten the thumbscrews to hold the VGA or DVI cable in place (see Figure 8-15).

Figure 8-15   Fastening the video cable into place.

Step 4.   Plug the monitor into an AC outlet, turn it on, and restart the computer.

Step 5.   Open the Display properties sheet and select Settings (refer to Figure 8-13).

Step 6.   If your monitor is listed as Plug and Play or by brand and model, adjust the resolution. If not, install a new driver for the monitor before continuing. The monitor driver might be provided on a CD, or you might need to download it.

Step 7.   If you are installing a CRT display, open the Advanced dialog and choose an appropriate flicker-free refresh rate.

Troubleshooting Displays and Video Cards

Some problems with the display subsystem are caused by the video card, while others are caused by the monitor or projector, and still others might involve the Windows driver. Use the following sections to determine the causes and find solutions for common problems.

Troubleshooting Picture Quality Problems with OSD

Picture quality problems of all types, ranging from barrel or pincushion distortion and color fringing on CRT monitors to picture size and centering, contrast and brightness on both CRT and LCD monitors, can be fixed by using onscreen picture controls, also known as the OSD. The OSD is controlled with push buttons on the front of both CRT and LCD displays, and provide a greater number of adjustments than older types of digital display controls.

Typical picture adjustments available on virtually all monitors include

- Horizontal picture size

- Horizontal picture centering

- Vertical picture size

- Vertical picture centering

- Contrast

- Brightness

CRT displays also offer settings for removing picture distortion, color balance, color temperature, degaussing (removes color fringing in a CRT display caused by the magnetic fields in the monitor), and options for the language and position of the onscreen display (OSD).

Figure 8-16 shows typical examples of OSDs for CRT and LCD monitors.

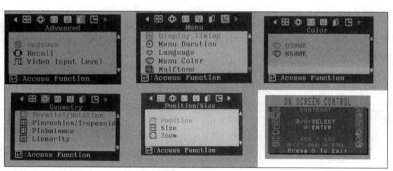

Figure 8-16 Typical OSD adjustments for CRT and LCD monitors. A portion of an LCD monitor's OSD is shown in the inset at lower right; the other images are from a typical CRT's OSD.

Figure 8-17 shows examples of barrel (outward curving image sides) and pincushion (inward curving image sides) distortion that can take place on CRT displays when different resolution settings or image-size adjustments are made. OSDs can adjust these picture geometry errors away as well.

NOTE   Typically, once you make an adjustment to picture size, centering, or geometry, a CRT display will "remember" the settings and use them again. However, if you change to a different refresh rate, you will need to reset these options so they can be stored for that refresh rate as well.

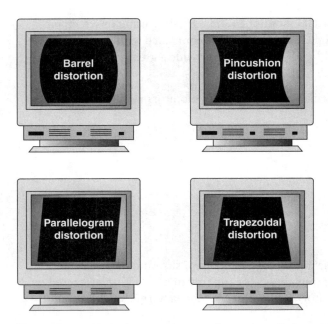

Figure 8-17 Typical geometry errors in monitors that can be corrected with digital or OSD controls available on most monitors.

Using Advanced Display Properties for Troubleshooting

The Advanced Display properties sheet offers a variety of ways to solve various types of display problems as shown in Table 8-4.

Table 8-4 Advanced Adjustments for Display Quality and Features

Adjustment Needed	Tab	Menu Item or Button	Notes
Icons and text too small	General	DPI setting	Custom lets you select the setting you want.
Need to update video card driver	Adapter	Properties	Click Driver tab to update driver.
Need to adjust vertical refresh rate to eliminate flicker	Adapter or Monitor (varies by Windows version)	(Screen) refresh rate	Use 75Hz or higher refresh rate (up to limits of monitor) to reduce or eliminate flicker.
Graphics or mouse pointer problems	Troubleshoot (Windows XP/Vista) or Performance (other Windows versions)	Hardware Acceleration	Drag to left to reduce acceleration; download and install new mouse and display drivers as soon as possible. See Figure 15-8 and Table 15-5, Chapter 15.

Table 8-4   Advanced Adjustments for Display Quality and Features

Adjustment Needed	Tab	Menu Item or Button	Notes
Colors don't match between screen and printer	Color Management	Add (color profile)	Get color profiles from printer or graphics software vendors.
3D game performance too low	OpenGL or Direct3D	Adjust settings for performance	If not available on your system, download the latest driver from your 3D graphics card vendor.
3D game image quality too low	OpenGL or Direct3D	Adjust settings for quality	If not available on your system, download the latest driver from your 3D graphics card vendor.
Color balance, brightness, and contrast need adjusting	Color	Adjust options as needed	Many 3D games are very dark; use Full Screen 3D option (if available) to adjust display for 3D gaming only.

Troubleshooting Video Hardware

Table 8-5 lists suggestions for troubleshooting other video hardware issues.

Table 8-5   Troubleshooting Monitors, Projectors, and Video Cards

Symptom	Problem	Solution
Color fringes around text and graphics on monitor screen	Magnetic distortion is affecting image quality	Use degaussing option (use degauss button, turn monitor off and on, or check OSD menu on some monitors).
Colors flicker on-screen	Loose video cable	Turn off monitor and system; tighten cable and restart.
Picture changes size	Power supply not supplying consistent voltage	Repair or replace monitors.
Picture occasionally displays wavy lines	Interference caused by poorly shielded devices in the area	Look for source of interference (such a microwave oven); move interference away from computer.
Picture quality garbled while changing video mode in Windows	Wrong resolution or refresh rate selected	Press Esc key to cancel change; check video card and monitor documentation for resolutions and refresh rates supported by both; select from these.

Table 8-5   Troubleshooting Monitors, Projectors, and Video Cards

Symptom	Problem	Solution
Can't select desired color depth at a given resolution	Video card does not have enough memory onboard for desired color depth/resolution combination	Upgrade video card memory, reduce color depth or resolution, or replace video card.
Can't select desired color depth at a given resolution	Incorrect video card driver might be in use	Double-check video card driver selected; replace with correct video driver if necessary.
Can't select resolution or refresh rate desired	Wrong monitor might be selected	Double-check monitor type; replace with correct monitor driver if necessary.
No picture when replacing built-in video with a replacement video card	Old and new video circuits have a conflict	Move new video card to a different slot; check for a motherboard setting to disable onboard video; try a different video card model.
LCD or DLP projector won't display image	The projector has not been recognized by the system	Shut down the computer and projector. Wait 30 seconds, then turn on the projector first. After the projector is turned on, turn on the computer. In some cases, you might need to select the computer as the video source.
	The monitor is running at a different resolution than the projector	Use the Display properties sheet to set the primary display (computer display) to the same resolution as the projector. Enable the Clone Display or Mirror option (see the computer or video card documentation for details).
	The refresh rate for the projector is set too high	Adjust the refresh rate to 60Hz using the Adapter or Monitor setting in the Advanced Display properties.
LCD projector won't display some colors	One of the LCD panels might have failed or cable might be loose	Try the projector with a different system. If the problem persists, replace the video cable. If the problem persists, the projector needs to be repaired or replaced.
LCD or DLP projector projected image is dim	Projector might be set for bulb-saver (low power mode) or bulb might need replacing	If the projector has a bulb-saver (low-power) setting, turn off the setting. If not, replace the bulb.
LCD projector has colored dots on the image	Clean the LCD panels inside the projector	Contact the vendor for service.

Table 8-5 Troubleshooting Monitors, Projectors, and Video Cards

Symptom	Problem	Solution
LCD or DLP projector image is not square	The projector is tilted in relation to the screen	Adjust the screen position; use the keystone correction feature in the projector menu.

Preventative Maintenance for Displays

The display is one of the most expensive components used by a PC, and a video card can be the biggest single expense inside a computer, so keeping them in good working order makes sense. Here's how:

- Do not block ventilation holes in CRT and LCD displays. Blocked ventilation holes can lead to overheating and component failure.

- Use antistatic cleaners made for electronics to clean screens and other surfaces.

- Do not spray cleaners directly onto screens or enclosures; an electrical short could result if the cleaner drips inside the unit. Instead, spray the cleaner on a lint-free cloth, and use the cloth to clean the screen or enclosure.

- Use thumbscrews to hold VGA and DVI cables in place on displays, projectors, and video cards. Loose cables can cause poor-quality images and can lead to broken pins if the cable is snagged and pulled out of place. Broken pins could also cause poor-quality picture or loss of picture altogether.

- When a system is opened for upgrades or service, check the condition of the cooling features of the video card. Remove hair, dust, or dirt in or on the heat sink, cooling fan, fan shroud, or heat pipe radiator. Make sure airflow around and behind the video card is not obstructed by cables, dirt, dust, or other components.

- Allow plenty of clearance around the video card slot. Don't use the slot next to the video card if the card would limit airflow to the video card's cooling features.

Exam Preparation Tasks

Review All the Key Topics

Review the most important topics in the chapter, noted with the key topics icon in the outer margin of the page. Table 8-6 lists a reference of these key topics and the page numbers on which each is found.

Table 8-6 Key Topics for Chapter 8

Key Topic Element	Description	Page Number
Figure 8-1	Video card designed to cool the GPU and memory.	298
Figure 8-2	Video card designed to dissipate heat.	299
Figure 8-8	DB15M (cable) and DB15F (port) connectors used for VGA video signals.	306
Figure 8-9	DVI-I video port and DVI-D video cable on the rear of a typical PC built with Windows Media Center and home theater integration.	306
Figure 8-11	HDMI, DVI-D, and VGA ports.	308
Figure 8-12	Composite video and stereo audio, S-video, and component video cables and ports compared.	309
Figure 8-13	The Settings tab controls display resolution, multiple monitor support, color quality (color depth), and provides access to advanced settings.	311
Figure 8-14	Selecting the vertical refresh rate from the monitor dialog (a) and from the adapter dialog (b).	313
Figure 8-16	Typical OSD adjustments for CRT and LCD monitors.	315
Table 8-5	Troubleshooting Monitors, Projectors, and Video Cards.	317

Complete the Tables and Lists from Memory

Print a copy of Appendix B, "Memory Tables," (found on the CD), or at least the section for this chapter, and complete the tables and lists from memory. Appendix C, "Memory Tables Answer Key," also on the CD, includes completed tables and lists to check your work.

Definitions of Key Terms

Define the following key terms from this chapter, and check your answers in the glossary.

Video Card, CRT, LCD: Liquid Crystal Display, VGA, SVGA, DVI, HDMI, RGB, S-Video, Resolution, Refresh Rate, Degaussing

Troubleshooting Scenario

Your client is experiencing problems with the display on his monitor. He informs you that the screen is blurry and will not provide a display over 800 by 600. What would you tell the client to try?

Refer to Appendix A for the answer.

This chapter covers the following subjects:

■ **Fundamental Features of Laptops and Portable Devices**—In this section you will learn about the components of a laptop. This section also describes what makes a laptop different from a PC.

■ **Configuring Power Management**—This section describes ACPI, APM, and how to make the most out of your battery power.

■ **Applications for Portable and Laptop Hardware**—This section talks about WLAN, Bluetooth, Ethernet connections, and other applications specific to laptops.

■ **Safe Removal of Laptop-Specific Hardware**—This section demonstrates how to remove hard drives, memory, batteries, and more!

■ **Portable and Laptop Diagnostics**—This section demonstrates how to troubleshoot power, displays, and peripherals.

■ **Preventative Maintenance for Laptops and Portable Devices**—This section describes how to keep the laptop cool and clean, where to store it, and how to prevent catastrophes.

This chapter covers portions of the CompTIA A+ 220-701 objectives 1.10 and 2.4, and CompTIA A+ 220-702 objective 1.3.

CHAPTER 9

Laptops and Portable Devices

Laptops were originally designed for niche markets, but today they are used in businesses almost as much as regular PCs are. Laptops (also known as notebooks or portable computers) have integrated displays, keyboards, and pointing devices, which makes them easy to transport and easy to use in confined spaces. There are plenty of other portable devices on the market today, including PDAs, Ultra-Mobile PCs, and more, but the bulk of the portable devices that you will troubleshoot are laptops. For the A+ exams it is important to know the components of a laptop, how to safely remove hardware, the ports that are built into a typical laptop, and care and preventative maintenance of the laptop.

"Do I Know This Already?" Quiz

The "Do I Know This Already?" quiz allows you to assess whether you should read this entire chapter or simply jump to the "Exam Preparation Tasks" section for review. If you are in doubt, read the entire chapter. Table 9-1 outlines the major headings in this chapter and the corresponding "Do I Know This Already?" quiz questions. You can find the answers in Appendix A, "Answers to the 'Do I Know This Already?' Quizzes and Troubleshooting Scenarios."

Table 9-1 "Do I Know This Already?" Foundation Topics Section-to-Question Mapping

Foundations Topics Section	Questions Covered in This Section
Fundamental Features of Laptops and Portable Devices	1–9
Configuring Power Management	10
Applications for Portable and Laptop Hardware	11
Safe Removal of Laptop-Specific Hardware	12
Portable and Laptop Diagnostics	13
Preventative Maintenance for Laptops and Portable Devices	14

1. To save space on most laptops, the computer keyboards have fewer keys than desktop computers have. Which of the following is an example of a key that saves space?

   a. The F keys
   b. Fn key
   c. Num Lock key
   d. Delete key

2. What type of laptop memory is installed in all newer model laptops?

   a. DIMMs
   b. SIMMs
   c. SDRAM
   d. SODIMMs

3. What is the size of a typical laptop hard drive?

   a. 3.5 in
   b. 2.5 in
   c. 5.5 in
   d. 4.5 in

4. Which technology can be used to expand the capability of a portable computer?

   a. A docking station
   b. A laptop case
   c. A smart card
   d. None of these options is correct

5. Which of the following is referred to as an expansion slot for laptops?

   a. PCI card
   b. AGP card
   c. PCI Express card
   d. PCMCIA

6. Which of the following are considered input devices? (Choose all that apply.)

   a. A mouse
   b. A keyboard
   c. A stylus
   d. A printer

7. What technique is used for the processor to run at lower clock speed when processor loads are light and to run at higher clock speeds when processor loads increase?

   a. Memory optimizing

   b. CPU filtering

   c. Processor throttling

   d. Load balancing

8. Which of the following technologies can you find on newer laptops today? (Choose all that apply.)

   a. Bluetooth

   b. Infrared

   c. Wireless cards

   d. Ethernet

9. Which type of built-in mouse equivalent do laptops commonly use? (Choose the best answer.)

   a. Roller ball

   b. Touch pad

   c. Stylus

   d. Pointing stick

10. Which tab would you use to configure user alerts and automatic actions to take when the system reaches low or critical battery power levels?

    a. Advanced tab

    b. Suspend tab

    c. Power Schemes tab

    d. Alarms tab

11. Which of the following can automatically locate wireless networks in Windows?

    a. Ethernet

    b. Bluetooth Devices applet

    c. Wireless Zero Configuration

    d. WPA2

12. When working with laptops, what is the safe removal standard for a PC card? (Choose two.)

   a. Look for the ejector button

   b. Update the drivers

   c. Turn off laptop

   d. Disconnect any cables from the card

13. Which of the following are ways to troubleshoot power problems on a laptop?

   a. Use a multimeter

   b. Turn off the computer

   c. Make sure the laptop is unplugged

   d. None of these options is correct

14. Which of the following can cause a laptop to have stop errors that are sometimes called the blue screen of death?

   a. Blocked cooling fan

   b. Cooling fan failure

   c. Damage to the heat sink

   d. All these options are correct

Foundation Topics

Fundamental Features of Laptops and Portable Devices

What makes portable computers different than desktop computers? They perform the same types of tasks, but their hardware differs. See Table 9-2 for a comparison of desktop computers and portable computers.

Table 9-2   Portable and Desktop Computers Comparison by Features

Feature	Desktop Computer	Portable Computer
Display	Separate LCD or CRT VGA, DVI, or HDMI port	Integrated LCD plus external VGA, DVI, or HDMI port
Keyboard	Standard 104-key keyboard with separate numerical keypad; full-size keys	Compact integrated keyboard with embedded numerical keypad; non-standard layout of directional keys
Mouse or pointing device	Separate unit; wide choice of types	Integrated into keyboard; can be replaced with external units
Battery use	Battery used for CMOS maintenance only	Battery used to power computer and many peripherals attached to computer; separate battery used for CMOS maintenance
Expansion bus	PCI, PCI Express, AGP slots enable interchange of many different components	Connector for docking station and/or port replicator is proprietary; present primarily on business-oriented laptops
Hard disk form factor	3.5-inch SATA or PATA	1.8- or 2.5-inch SATA or PATA (connectors on PATA vary from desktop PCs)
PC Card slot	Optional card reader	Standard on many older systems
ExpressCard slot	Not used	Standard on most recent systems
Floppy drive location	Internal on older machines; optional external USB on newer systems	Might be internal or external, using hot-swappable proprietary or USB interface
Optical drive	Internal or external	Might be internal or external location
Memory expansion	Uses standard-sized DIMM or other modules	Uses Small Outline (SO) or proprietary modules

Table 9-2 Portable and Desktop Computers Comparison by Features

Feature	Desktop Computer	Portable Computer
CPU upgrades	Common on virtually any model	Not supported by vendor; can be performed
Video	PCI Express, AGP, or PCI slot or integrated into chipset	Integrated into motherboard chipset or separate chip soldered to motherboard; some systems include modular video

A typical portable computer has the following components:

- Integrated LCD display with output for external display using a VGA, DVI, HDMI, and/or S-video port

- Integrated keyboard with pointing device

- Standard I/O ports (USB, PS/2 mouse and keyboard; some might also include serial and parallel)

- ExpressCard or PC Card (CardBus) expansion slot

- Integrated drives

- Battery

- Proprietary motherboard with integrated video or 3D graphics and mobile-optimized processor; some memory might be built into the motherboard

- Integrated speakers

- Integrated wired (10/100 or Gigabit Ethernet) or wireless (Wi-Fi) network adapters

- Integrated analog (dial-up) modem

Some late-model portable computers also feature

- IEEE-1394a ports

- eSATA port

- Flash memory card reader

- Connector for docking station or port replicator

Tablet PCs are similar to traditional portable computers, but support handwriting recognition, and sometimes have detachable keyboards. Tablet PCs running Windows XP use a modified version called Windows XP Tablet Edition. Windows Vista and Windows 7 include support for handwriting recognition in their standard editions.

Although portable and desktop computers have many differences, systems that use the same version of Microsoft Windows and have similar CPU types, CPU speeds, and memory sizes are capable of performing work in similar ways.

Memory

Generally, portable systems have only one or two connectors for additional memory. Older portable systems might use proprietary memory modules, whereas recent systems use SODIMMs (a reduced-size version of a DIMM module).

> **TIP** The best memory upgrade for a portable system is to add the largest memory module (in MB) that can be installed in the system. Because a future memory upgrade would require the removal of the original memory module on systems with a single memory upgrade socket, it's best to add all the memory a system can take from the beginning.

Figure 9-1 compares a typical DDR2 SODIMM with a DDR2 DIMM.

Figure 9-1 Comparison of a DIMM (above) and SODIMM (below).

Storage Devices

Laptop and portable computers use storage devices that vary in several ways from those found in desktop computers:

- **Smaller form factors**—Laptop and portable systems use 2.5-inch or 1.8-inch hard disks, instead of the 3.5-inch hard disks found in desktop computers. Also, laptop and portable systems use slimline optical drives rather than the half-height drives that are used in desktop computers.

- **Different implementations of common interfaces**—Although laptop and portables with SATA drive support use the same power and data connectors as desktop systems with SATA drives, PATA (ATA/IDE) drives found in laptops and portable systems use a single 44-pin connector for both power and data. Figure 9-2 shows a typical notebook PATA hard drive and interface.

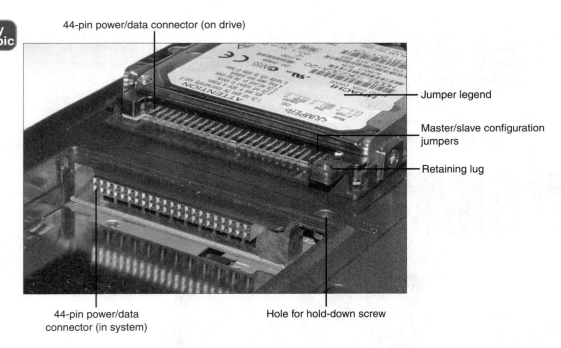

Figure 9-2   A typical 2.5-inch EIDE/PATA hard drive for notebook computers and its 44-pin interface.

NOTE   You can purchase bare 2.5-inch notebook ATA/IDE or SATA drives to use as replacements for failed or outdated drives, but many vendors sell special kits that include data-transfer software and a data-transfer cable to "clone" the old hard drive's contents to the new hard drive.

If you plan to reuse the hard disk you replaced, you can also install the old hard disk into an external disk enclosure that connects to your system with USB, IEEE-1394a, or eSATA cables.

Systems that have no internal provision for the type of drive desired can attach an external drive to any of the following ports if available on the computer:

- USB 2.0 port

- IEEE-1394a port

- eSATA port

- PC Card or ExpressCard with USB, IEEE-1394a, or eSATA port

Peripherals

Low-end laptop and portable computers usually feature limited expandability; if the device can't connect to one of the ports built into the computer (or to a hub connected to the computer), you can't use it. However, many mid-range and high-end laptop and portable computers feature various methods for connecting additional devices.

Docking Stations and Port Replicators

A docking station expands the capability of a portable computer by adding features such as

- One or more expansion slots

- Additional I/O ports, such as serial, parallel, ExpressCard or PC Card, display output (VGA, DVI, HDMI, component video), SPDIF digital audio, or USB 2.0

- Additional drive bays

- Connectors for a standard keyboard and mouse

Most docking stations are produced by the vendor of the portable computer and connect to the computer through a proprietary expansion bus on the rear or bottom of the computer. The user can leave desktop-type peripherals connected to the docking station and can access them by connecting the portable computer to the docking station.

NOTE   Some thin and light portable computers are designed to use a modular *media slice* for optical and removable-media drives. This unit connects to the bottom of the computer and can be left in place at all times, or it can be removed when it's not needed.

Figure 9-3 shows a typical docking station for an HP or Compaq laptop computer.

To see the expansion port used by the docking station shown in Figure 9-3, refer to Figure 9-12 in this chapter.

A port replicator usually connects to the same proprietary expansion bus that can be used by a docking station; however, many portable computers that do not have docking stations support optional port replicators.

Port replicators don't have expansion slots or drive bays but replicate the same ports that are found on the host PC. These ports might include VGA, Ethernet network, USB 2.0, and legacy ports (PS/2 mouse, keyboard; serial; parallel).

Port replicators enable a portable computer user fast, easy connection to a full-sized keyboard, regular mouse or pointing device, desktop monitor, modem, and printer without needing to attach or remove multiple cables. Because portable cable connectors can wear out, using a port replicator extends the life of the system and makes desktop use faster and easier.

The difference between a port replicator and a docking station is that the port replicator has the same ports as those found on the laptop computer itself, while a docking station offers additional ports and sometimes other features. For example, the docking station shown in Figure 9-3 adds additional USB 2.0 ports as well as SPDIF coaxial digital audio and component video ports.

Port replicators normally are built by the same company that makes the portable computer, but some third-party vendors produce both *dedicated* models (designed to attach to the proprietary expansion bus of a given model) and *universal* versions, which attach through the ExpressCard or PC Card slot or USB port and can be freely moved among different brands and models of portable computers.

NOTE   Software drivers are required for universal port replicators but not for standard port replicators.

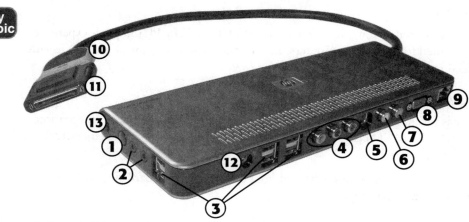

1. Power switch
2. Audio minijacks
3. USB ports (6)
4. Component video ports for HDTV
5. S-video port
6. Composite video port
7. SPDIF coaxial digital audio port

8. VGA port
9. 10/100 Ethernet port
10. Connector to laptop
11. Connector adapter
12. Power connector
13. Security lock port

Figure 9-3   The HP QuickDock docking station supports several series of HP and Compaq laptop computers.

Media and Accessory Bays

Some portable computers have interchangeable drives built into a special media or accessory bay. These drive bays are often able to accommodate the user's choice of

- Hard disk drive

- Optical drives, such as rewritable DVD or combo DVD-ROM/CD-RW

- Extra batteries

Some older systems might also have support for removable-media drives such as floppy, Zip, or LS-120/240 SuperDisk drives, all of which are now obsolete.

Some models with interchangeable drives allow you to hot-swap, which enables the user to exchange drives without shutting down the computer, whereas others require the user to shut down the system, change drives, and then restart the computer. Portable computers with interchangeable media or accessory bays are more expensive but are also more versatile than portable computers that lack these features.

Expansion Slots

Laptop and portable computers don't use the PCI, AGP, or PCI Express expansion slots designed for desktop computers. Instead they feature expansion slots especially designed for portable use.

PCMCIA (PC Card, CardBus)

PC Cards (originally referred to as Personal Computer Memory Card International Association [PCMCIA] cards) provide a range of options for portable computers with PC Card slots.

Most older portable computers have at least one Type II PC Card slot, as shown in Figure 9-4. Many have two.

Eject button   Type II PC Card partly inserted

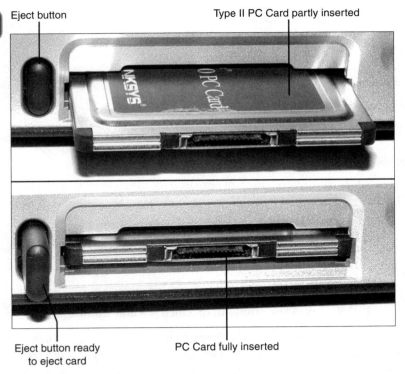

Eject button ready   PC Card fully inserted
   to eject card

Figure 9-4   A typical notebook with a Type II PC Card partly installed (top) and completely installed (bottom). Note the positions of the ejection button.

PC Cards can be hot-swapped; the card can be shut down, removed, and replaced with another without shutting down the system. Cards must be "stopped" before being removed or the system can become unstable and the cards or system can be damaged. For details, see the section "Safe Removal of PC Cards," later in this chapter.

The Personal Computer Memory Card International Association gave PC Cards their original name of PCMCIA cards and is responsible for developing standards for these cards. There are three types of PC Card slots, each designed for particular types of devices (see Table 9-3).

Table 9-3   PC Card Type Comparison

PC Card Type	Thickness	Typical Uses	Notes
Type I	3.3mm	Memory	Obsolete
Type II	5.5mm	I/O ports, wired or wireless networking, modems, external drive interfaces, hard disks	—
Type III	10.5mm	Hard disks, combo I/O ports	Type III slot also supports two Type II devices

All three types use a two-row connector with 68-pins total.

Most systems with PC Card slots feature two stacked Type II slots that can handle all types of cards: a single Type III card, two Type II cards, or two Type I cards at a time. Figure 9-5 compares the thicknesses of these cards.

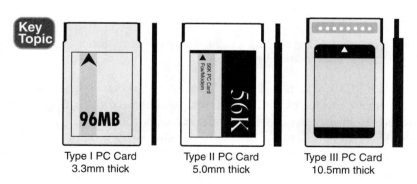

Type I PC Card
3.3mm thick

Type II PC Card
5.0mm thick

Type III PC Card
10.5mm thick

Figure 9-5   Typical Type I, Type II, and Type III PC cards and cross-sections.

Most portable systems with PC Card slots support *CardBus*. CardBus slots are compatible with both ordinary (16-bit) PC Cards and 32-bit CardBus cards, but CardBus cards *can't* be used in ordinary PC Card slots.

To verify if a portable system has CardBus support, open Windows Device Manager and the category marked PCMCIA Adapters. If a CardBus controller is listed, the portable supports CardBus. If it's not listed, you can use only 16-bit PC Cards in that system.

NOTE   CardBus cards have a gold edge on the connector, but ordinary PC Cards do not. Figure 9-6 illustrates a standard PC Card, and Figure 9-7 illustrates a CardBus card.

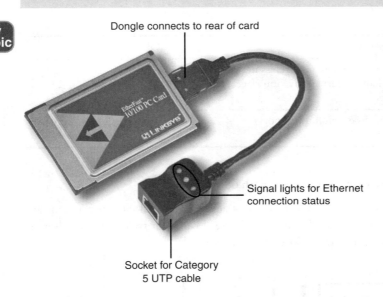

Dongle connects to rear of card

Signal lights for Ethernet connection status

Socket for Category 5 UTP cable

Figure 9-6   A typical Type II PC Card 10/100 Ethernet card with the dongle used to attach the card to standard Category 5 UTP cable. Photo courtesy Linksys.

Another variation on standard PC Card slots is Zoomed Video (ZV) support. Portable systems that support ZV can use PCMCIA cards with a high-speed video connector for processes such as teleconferencing or dual-display support. As with CardBus, use ZV-compatible cards only in compatible systems. However, ZV is not supported by all CardBus slots. To determine if a system with CardBus slots also supports ZV, check with the vendor. *Combo* PC Cards contain multiple functions and connections on a single card. The most common combination includes a modem plus Ethernet network interfacing or USB 2.0 plus IEEE-1394a interfacing.

Type I and Type II PC Card cards aren't thick enough to use standard RJ-11 telephone (for modem), SCSI, RJ-45 UTP network cables, or video cables. Some Type II PC Cards use a pop-out connector for telephone or network cables; others require the use of a device called a *dongle*—a proprietary extension to the PCMCIA card that enables standard cables to be connected to the card. Type III PC Cards are thick enough to provide standard connections but don't fit into some systems.

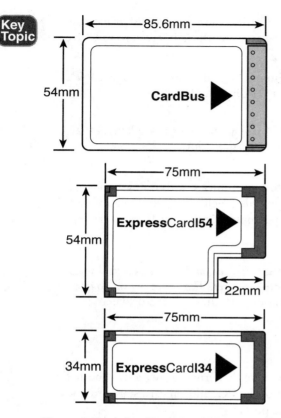

Figure 9-7   A CardBus 32-bit PC Card compared to ExpressCard/34 and ExpressCard/54 cards.

Figure 9-6 shows a typical PC Card network adapter with its dongle.

NOTE   If you lose or damage the dongle, your PC Card is useless until you replace it. For this reason, most vendors no longer use dongles for modem or network cards.

ExpressCard

Most recent laptops and portable computers have replaced PC Card slots with ExpressCard slots. The ExpressCard standard was developed by the same organization that developed the PCMCIA (PC Card) standard, but ExpressCard provides a much faster interface than PC Card or CardBus and is compatible with PCI Express and USB 2.0 standards. ExpressCard is up to 2.5 times faster than Card-Bus cards, and uses a 26-contact connector.

ExpressCard slots and devices support one of two variations:

■   ExpressCard/34 is 34mm wide.

- ExpressCard/54 is 54mm wide; ExpressCard/54 slots can use either Express-Card/54 or ExpressCard/34 devices, and are sometimes referred to as Universal slots.

Both types of ExpressCard modules are 75mm long and 5mm high. Figure 9-7 compares typical ExpressCard modules to a CardBus module.

NOTE   Some vendors supply ExpressCard/34 cards with removable adapters that permit cards to be inserted securely into ExpressCard/54 slots.

ExpressCard can use one of two methods to communicate with the system chipset: PCI Express or USB 2.0. These methods provide much faster performance than with CardBus, which connects to the system chipset via the CardBus controller and the PCI bus.

NOTE   For more information about PCMCIA, CardBus, and ExpressCard slots and devices, see the official website of the USB Implementers Forum at www.usb.org. USB Implementers Forum took over responsibility for these standards when PCMCIA was dissolved in March 2009.

Mini-PCI and Mini-PCIe

Many notebook computers with built-in modem, Ethernet, or wireless Ethernet (Wi-Fi) support use a reduced-size version of the PCI add-on card standard known as mini-PCI to support some or all of these ports.

There are three major types of mini-PCI cards:

- Type I
- Type II
- Type III

Type I and Type II cards use a 100-pin stacking connector that plugs directly into the system board. Type II cards, unlike Type I cards, have network or modem connectors built into the card. Type III, which uses an edge connector, has become the most popular of the three formats. Like Type I, Type III mini-PCI cards do not incorporate RJ-11 (modem) or RJ-45 (Ethernet network) connectors; Type I and Type III mini-PCI cards use modem and network connectors built into the system.

Although mini-PCI cards can sometimes be replaced in the field, they are not available at retail stores; they must be purchased from the portable computer supplier because they are customized to the characteristics of a particular product family. Mini-PCI cards are used to configure different models of a particular portable computer with different features. Because mini-PCI cards can be replaced, this enables you to replace a failed or outdated network/modem component without replacing the entire motherboard.

NOTE   Some wireless routers also use radios in the mini-PCI form factor.

Figure 9-8 shows a typical Type III mini-PCI modem card and connector compared to a typical Type II PC Card.

Protective plastic covering over components

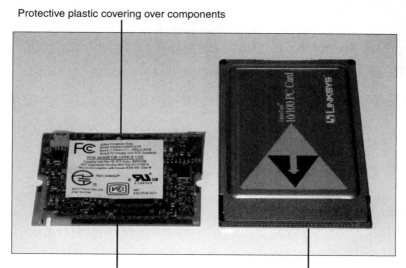

Edge connector (Type III mini-PCI card)   68-pin connector (Type II PC card)

Figure 9-8   A typical mini-PCI Type III modem (left) compared to a typical PC Card Type II network adapter (right).

NOTE   Some mini-PCI cards that include wireless Ethernet (Wi-Fi) radios have the antenna leads soldered to the card. If these cards become damaged, a factory-trained technician should replace them.

In many recent laptop models, mini-PCI has been replaced by mini-PCI Express (also known as Mini-PCIe). Mini-PCIe cards are much smaller than mini-PCI cards, and use a two-part, double-sided 52-pin edge connector. Mini-PCIe supports PCIe, USB 2.0, SMBus, GPS, SIM card and Wi-Fi connections and runs on 1.5V and 3.3V DC power. As with mini-PCI, mini-PCIe cards are not sold at retail and are customized to the requirements of specific OEMs.

Figure 9-9 compares a mini-PCI Type III card similar to the one shown in Figure 9-8 with a mini-PCIe card.

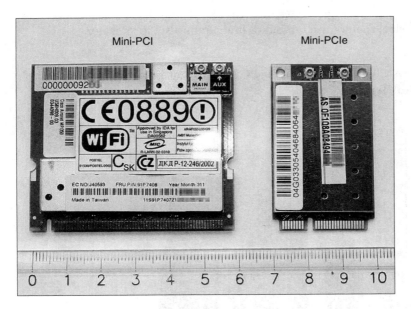

Figure 9-9   A typical mini-PCI Type III modem (left) compared to a typical Mini-PCIe card (right). Image source: Wikimedia Commons.

Communications Connections

Laptop and portable computers usually include some or all of the communications capabilities discussed in the following sections.

Bluetooth

The Bluetooth personal area network (PAN) standard is used for connections with Bluetooth-enabled printers, mice, and keyboards, and for data transfer between computers or PDAs that also include Bluetooth support.

To determine if a computer includes a Bluetooth adapter, you can check its documentation, or examine Device Manager. A computer with a Bluetooth adapter will display a category called Bluetooth Radios and list two Bluetooth entries in the Network Adapters section, as shown in Figure 9-10. You can also add a Bluetooth adapter to an available USB port.

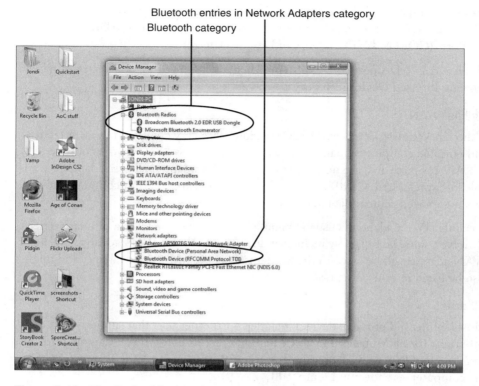

Figure 9-10   The Device Manager for a system offering Bluetooth support has a separate Bluetooth category as well as Bluetooth entries in the Network Adapters category (Windows Vista shown, but Windows 7 and Windows XP list Bluetooth devices the same way).

Infrared (IrDA)

Some portable computers feature an infrared (IR) port. This port usually follows the IrDA standard and can be used for the following tasks if the other device also follows the same standard:

- Networking to connect to computers with compatible IR ports

- Printing to laser and other printers equipped with a compatible IR port

NOTE   IrDA ports emulate serial ports and provide very slow data transfer compared to USB, Ethernet, Wi-Fi, or other interfaces. IrDA is a suitable choice only if other connection types are not available or not convenient.

Portable computers with integrated IrDA ports have a red window covering the IrDA transceiver on the side or rear of the system and will list an IrDA or IR port in the Ports (COM & LPT) category of Device Manager.

If you add an IrDA port with a USB or other adapter, the IrDA port shows up in a separate Infrared Devices category.

Cellular WAN

Although Wireless Ethernet (WLAN) adapters are very common in recent laptops and portable computers, many users who need to access data networks outside of WLAN coverage area are now using cellular WAN adapters. These adapters, available in ExpressCard, CardBus, and USB 2.0 form factors, permit computers to access high-speed cellular data networks.

A cellular WAN adapter is usually bundled with a data plan from a cellular carrier. However, some laptops now include an integrated cellular WAN adapter. A cellular WAN adapter will be listed in the Modems category of Device Manager and might also be listed in other categories.

Ethernet

Most laptops and portable devices include an Ethernet port that supports Fast Ethernet (10/100Mbps) or Gigabit Ethernet (10/100/1000Mbps). Laptops with an integrated Ethernet adapter have an RJ-45 port located on the side or rear of the computer, as shown in Figure 9-11.

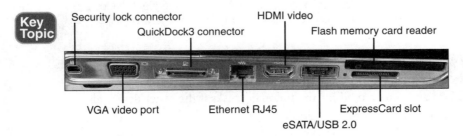

Figure 9-11   The Ethernet (RJ-45 port) and other ports on a typical laptop computer.

You can add Ethernet support to a laptop that doesn't have an integrated Ethernet port by plugging in a PC Card, CardBus card, or USB adapter with Ethernet support. To see a PC Card with Ethernet support, refer to Figure 9-6.

To determine what level of Ethernet support a particular system includes, open Device Manager's Network Adapters category and look up information on the network adapter chip model number at the chip vendor's website.

Wireless Ethernet (WLAN or Wi-Fi)

Most late-model laptops include wireless Ethernet (WLAN) support, typically implemented through a mini-PCI adapter that incorporates a wireless Ethernet radio that is connected to an antenna built around the LCD display screen.

To determine what type of wireless Ethernet a laptop supports, check the documentation, open Device Manager's Network Adapters category (see Figure 9-12), or examine the markings on the mini-PCI card providing wireless Ethernet support.

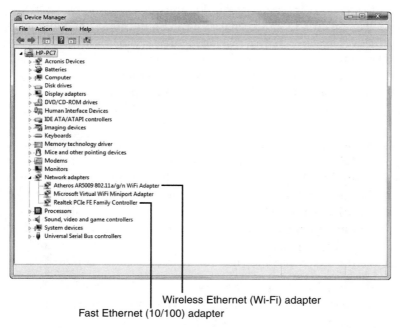

Wireless Ethernet (Wi-Fi) adapter
Fast Ethernet (10/100) adapter

Figure 9-12   Typical wireless and wired Ethernet network adapters as listed in Device Manager.

LCD Screen Technologies

One of the biggest differences between portable and desktop computers is the display. Desktop computers enable both the screen and the graphics card to be changed; in portable computers, both the screen and graphics card are normally built into the system (although a few high-end laptops now support removable graphics modules). Although most portables feature an external VGA or DVI port, which enables a separate monitor or video expansion device such as the Matrox Graphics DualHead2Go or TripleHead2Go to be plugged into the computer, that is the extent of the video expandability of most portable systems. Almost all recent systems support DualView, a Windows XP, Vista, and 7 feature that enables supported graphics chipsets to use an external monitor as a true secondary monitor as well as a mirror of or replacement for the built-in display.

Two major types of LCD display screens have been used on portables: active-matrix and passive matrix.

Active Matrix

Active-matrix refers to screens that use a transistor for every dot seen onscreen: for example, a 1,024×768 active-matrix LCD screen has 786,432 transistors. The additional transistors put the "active" in active-matrix, making them nearly as bright as CRT displays. They also offer wide viewing angles for easier use by groups of people and tend to display rapid movement and full-motion video with less blur than dual-scan displays. Active-matrix displays are used in all levels of laptop and portable computers.

Passive Matrix

Until the early 21st century, only high-end laptops and portable computers used active-matrix screens. Mid-range and low-end laptops and portable computers used passive-matrix or dual-scan (DSTN) displays instead. Both are controlled by an array of transistors along the horizontal and vertical edges of the display. For example, a 1,024×768 resolution display features 1,024 transistors along the horizontal edge of the display and 768 transistors along the vertical. The transistors send out a pulse of energy, and the individual LCDs polarize at varying angles to produce the picture. Dual-scan screens split the screen into a top half and a bottom half for faster response.

Both types of Passive-matrix LCD displays are dimmer, have slower response times, and feature a narrower viewing angle than active-matrix screens; they are now obsolete.

Screen Resolutions

Screen resolutions are identified in one of two ways: either by the number of horizontal and vertical pixels, or by the display standard. Common display standards and pixel resolutions used by recent laptop and portable computers are listed in Table 9-4.

Table 9-4   Common Laptop Screen Resolution Standards

Standard	Also Known As	Horizontal Resolution	Vertical Resolution	Aspect Ratio
XGA	Extended Graphics Array	1024	768	1.33:1
WXGA*	Wide XGA	1280	800	1.6:1
SXGA+	Super Extended Graphics Array Plus	1400	1050	1.33:1
UXGA	Ultra Extended Graphics Array	1600	1200	1.33:1
WUXGA	Wide Ultra Extended Graphics Array	1920	1200	1.6:1

*Resolutions such as 1360×768 or 1366×768 are also identified as WXGA. Aspect ratios larger than 1.33:1 are widescreen.

Screen Quality Considerations

When comparing laptops and portable computers, consider the following factors that affect screen quality:

- **Contrast Ratio**—The difference in brightness between the lightest and darkest portions of the display. When looking at two otherwise-similar displays, the one with the higher contrast ratio is preferred.

- **Viewing Angles**—The angle at which an LCD display provides acceptable viewing quality. For example, if a display provides acceptable viewing quality at an angle of 80° from either side of a straight on (0°) view, it has a viewing angle of 160° (80°×2). A narrower viewing angle is preferred for privacy (because it's more difficult for onlookers to view the screen), but a wider viewing angle is preferred when multiple users need to see the display.

- **Recommended (native) and Scaled Resolutions**—LCD displays have only one native resolution (also known as recommended resolution), and might scale (zoom) the display to achieve lower resolutions or use only the actual pixels needed for the lower resolution. This might be necessary when running the display in a cloned mode when an external display or projector is used, or if a particular resolution is required for creating screen shots or for other technical reasons. Non-native resolutions are selected through the Screen Resolution dialog in Windows 7 (see Figure 9-13), which is also used to detect additional displays and change orientation. Windows XP uses the Display properties Settings tab (refer to Figure 9-33); Windows Vista's Display Settings section of the Personalize menu is almost identical to Windows 7's Screen Resolution dialog.

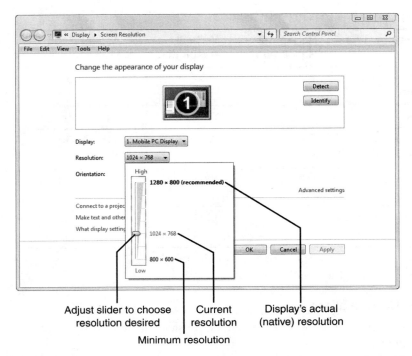

Figure 9-13   Recommended and currently set resolutions on a typical widescreen laptop running Windows 7.

When a scaled resolution is selected, the screen will usually appear slightly less sharp than when the native resolution is selected.

NOTE   When only the actual pixels needed for the lower resolution are used instead of scaling the resolution, a black border around the display results. This effect is called windowboxing.

Input Devices

Laptop and portable computers include a variety of specialized input devices, as discussed in the following sections.

Stylus and Digitizer

Portable computers in the tablet form factor use a stylus to enable data entry without using a keyboard. The stylus acts as a digital pen and the touch-sensitive screen digitizes the input from the stylus. Operating systems such as Windows XP Tablet Edition and all versions of Windows Vista and Windows 7 support tablets. These operating systems include utilities that support digital ink, conversion of printed text into editable documents, and conversion of drawings made by the stylus into bitmapped graphics. Windows 7 also supports multitouch tablets and touch screens when connected.

Convertible systems include a movable screen and a keyboard, enabling the computer to be used either as a tablet or as a traditional portable system.

Fn Keys

To save space, laptops and portable computers use keyboards with fewer keys than desktop computers have. However, laptop and portable computers also need to control screen displays and other options not needed on desktop computers.

To enable reduced-size keyboards to perform all of the functions needed, laptop and portable keyboards use Fn keys. While the Fn key is held down, pressing any key with an additional Fn function performs the Fn function; when the Fn key is released, the key reverts to its normal operation. Fn functions are usually printed below the normal key legend in blue. Figure 9-14 shows a typical portable keyboard with the Fn key and Fn functions highlighted.

Touch Pad

This mouse alternative uses a square or rectangular touch-sensitive surface located beneath the spacebar (see Figure 9-15). To move the mouse pointer, the user slides his or her finger on the surface. Clicking and double-clicking can be done by tapping on the touch pad surface with the finger or with the touch pad buttons.

The mouse buttons for the touchpad are also located beneath the spacebar; if the buttons are arranged vertically, the top button corresponds to the left mouse button and the bottom button corresponds to the right mouse button. Some systems might feature an additional button or side-mounted slider for scrolling the screen.

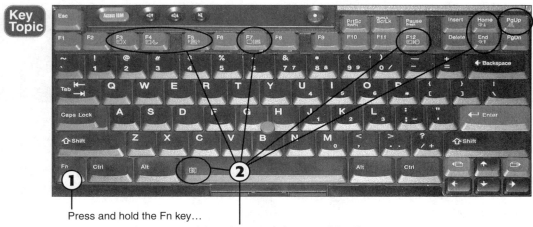

Press and hold the Fn key…

…and press any of these keys to perform special tasks, such as adjusting screen brightness or audio volume.

Figure 9-14   A typical laptop keyboard's Fn keys.

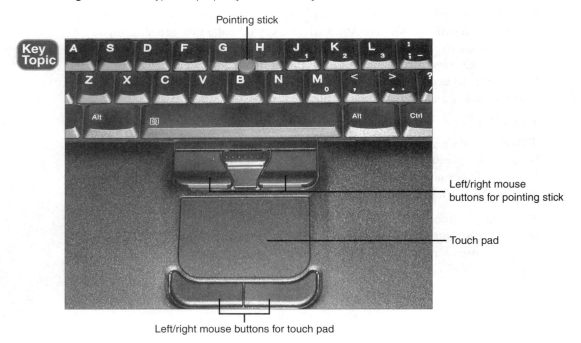

Pointing stick

Left/right mouse buttons for pointing stick

Touch pad

Left/right mouse buttons for touch pad

Figure 9-15   A laptop that includes both a touch pad and a pointing stick.

Select the touchpad in the Mouse properties sheet in Windows to configure clicking or other touchpad options (see Figure 9-16).

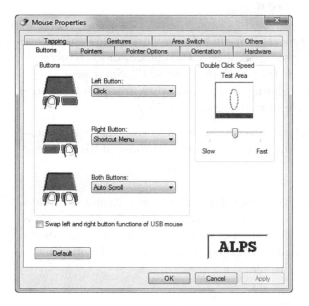

Figure 9-16   The Buttons tab of the properties sheet for a typical touch pad.

Pointing Stick / TrackPoint

This mouse alternative (originally called the TrackPoint II by IBM) enables the user to keep his or her hands on the keyboard at all times. The user moves the mouse pointer by pushing a small button shaped like a pencil eraser that's located in the middle of the keyboard to move the mouse pointer. Although this technology was developed by IBM for its portable computers, it has been licensed by several other vendors, including Toshiba and HP, and it is now found on some laptop computers produced by Lenovo, which purchased IBM's personal computer division in 2005. Refer to Figure 9-15 to see an example of a pointing stick on a laptop that also includes a touch pad.

The mouse buttons for a computer equipped with a pointing stick are located beneath the spacebar. Some systems use the conventional left and right buttons, but others use buttons arranged vertically, in which the top button corresponds to the left mouse button and the bottom button corresponds to the right mouse button. Newer systems might feature an additional button used to scroll the screen.

Power Management Issues

Most laptops and portable computers use processors that are designed to draw less power than their desktop counterparts and support power management technologies such as processor throttling, peripheral power management, and others.

Processor Throttling

Processor throttling enables the processor to run at lower clock speeds when processor loads are light and to run at higher clock speeds when processor loads increase. This is a feature of recent processors from both Intel and AMD. Some processors also reduce the front side bus speed during time periods when processor loads are light, a feature Intel calls Front Side Bus Frequency Switching.

Processor throttling might be enabled through the use of a driver that works automatically, such as the AMD Processor Driver or through customized BIOS code.

Peripheral Power Management

Peripherals connected to USB ports or plugged into CardBus or ExpressCard slots can also be configured to go into low-power sleep modes when idle. These options can be configured through the device properties sheet's Power tab or by adjusting the Power Management settings used in Windows. For details, see "Configuring Power Management," later in this chapter.

Power Sources

Laptops and portable computers can use battery power or external DC power sources, such as AC adapters, 12V cigarette lighter adapters, or airline power connectors. Battery power is a vital feature for portable computers, which are frequently used when away from an AC power source. Battery life depends on several factors, including

- Battery type
- Recharging practices
- Power-management options
- Memory size
- CPU speed and type
- PC Card or ExpressCard type and use

Battery Types

The rechargeable battery type used by a portable computer has a great deal to do with the amount of time you can use a computer between recharges (the *run time*).

The most common battery types include

- Lithium-ion (Li-ion)
- Nickel-metal hydride (NiMH)
- Nickel-cadmium (NiCd)

The original rechargeable standard, NiCd, has fallen out of favor for use as a notebook computer's main power source because of a problem called the memory effect. If NiCd batteries are not fully discharged before being recharged, the memory effect enables the battery to be recharged only to the level it was used. In other words, if you use a NiCd battery and recharge it when it's only 50% exhausted, the memory effect will enable you to use only 50% of the battery's actual capacity. You might be able to correct the memory effect if you'll allow your battery to fully discharge before recharging it; however, the memory effect can permanently affect your battery's condition.

Low-cost notebook computers use NiMH batteries instead of NiCd. NiMH batteries have fewer problems with the memory effect and can be used in place of NiCd in most cases.

The most efficient battery technology in widespread use is Li-ion, which has little problem with memory effect, puts out the same power as NiMH, but is about 35% lighter.

TIP   Battery power is measured in milliampere hours (mAh) or by the number of cells in the battery pack. The larger the mAh value or the larger the number of cells in the battery, the longer the battery will last. If you need to replace the battery in a portable computer, find out if you can get a high-capacity battery instead of the standard capacity battery originally supplied with the computer.

NiCd batteries are sometimes used today as CMOS batteries or as "RAM" or "bridge" batteries, which store a system's configuration when the suspend mode is used. However, in most recent systems, a lithium watch battery is used to store CMOS settings (see Figure 9-17).

To determine the type of battery installed in a system, open the Power Options properties sheet in Device Manager, click the Power Meter tab shown in Figure 9-18a, and click each battery icon listed. The Detailed Information listing displays the battery type (chemistry) as shown in Figure 9-18b.

AC Adapters

Most systems use an external AC adapter and battery-charging unit, sometimes referred to as a *brick*. To make portable use easier, some systems build the AC adapter/battery charger into the portable computer and use a special polarized power cord for recharging.

Just as with desktop power supplies, notebook battery recharging systems must be compatible with the local electrical power source. Most portable computers use an automatically switching recharger, capable of handling either European and Asian 50-cycle, 230V power or North American 60-cycle, 115V power (see Figure 9-19). However, a few systems are shipped with a single voltage recharger, requiring that you use a power converter or recharger with a different voltage if you travel internationally.

CR2032 battery

Mini-PCI card including a
wireless Ethernet radio

Figure 9-17 A lithium watch battery (CR2032) used to maintain CMOS settings in a typical laptop.

Click to display battery details

Key Topic

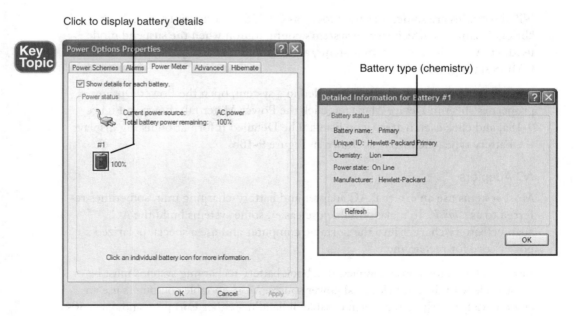

Battery type (chemistry)

Figure 9-18 The Power Meter tab (a) displays battery type and power state for a laptop computer's primary battery (b) when the battery icon is clicked.

Supported voltage/frequency
input and output levels

Figure 9-19 A typical laptop AC adapter that can be used with 115V/60-cycle or 230V/50-cycle AC power sources.

Configuring Power Management

Understanding how power management works and how to configure it are essential skills, especially given the increasing number of laptops and portable computers in use today.

ACPI

For several years, all portable and laptop computers have supported the advanced configuration and power interface (ACPI) standard for power management. ACPI power management provides power management for all plug-and-play devices installed in a system, and it permits Windows to perform all power-management configurations rather than force the user to modify the BIOS setup to make some of the needed changes as with the older advanced power management (APM) standard.

To determine which power management mode the computer is using, open Windows Device Manager and open the System Devices category. On a portable system that uses ACPI power management (Figure 9-20), you will see a number of ACPI system devices.

Portable systems running Windows XP (and Windows 2000) use the Power Options properties sheet in Control Panel to configure power management. The Power Options properties sheet has five tabs on a system that uses ACPI power management (a sixth tab, for APM power management, is seen only on systems that use APM power management rather than ACPI).

The Power Schemes tab shown in Figure 9-21a is used to control how long the system is idle before the monitor and hard disks are turned off or the system goes into standby or hibernation modes. Note that portable systems have two groups of settings: one for AC power (plugged in) and one for battery power.

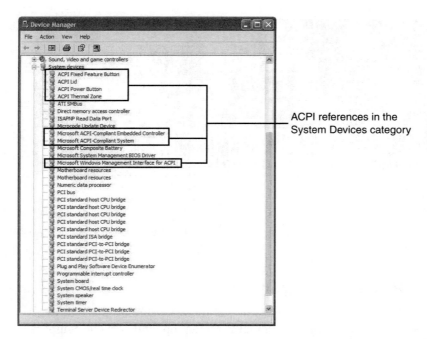

Figure 9-20   A portable computer with ACPI power management support installed.

The Alarms tab shown in Figure 9-21b is used to configure user alerts and automatic actions to take when the system reaches low or critical battery power levels.

For details on the Power Meter tab, refer to the section "Battery Types," earlier in this chapter.

The Advanced tab (Figure 9-22a) configures actions the computer will perform when the lid is closed or the power or sleep buttons are pressed. The Hibernate tab (Figure 9-22b) enables or disables hibernation and displays the amount of disk space the hibernation file (hiberfil.sys) will occupy.

Power options on portable systems running Windows 7 or Vista can be modified by going to the Control Panel, selecting a view that displays all icons, and double-clicking the Power Options applet. (You can also display this applet by clicking the AC/battery icon in the notification area.) By default in Windows 7 and Vista, there are three preferred plans: Balanced, power saver, and high performance; however, users can create their own power plans as well. Each of these plans can be modified by clicking the **Change Plan Settings** link. There are a lot of settings in this window; let's show one example.

In Balanced, click **Change Plan Settings**. The display is set to turn off in 20 minutes by default; it can be set from 1 minute to 5 hours, or set to never. If you click the **Change Advanced Power Settings** link, the Power Options button will appear. Click it to open the Advanced Settings dialog shown in Figure 9-23.

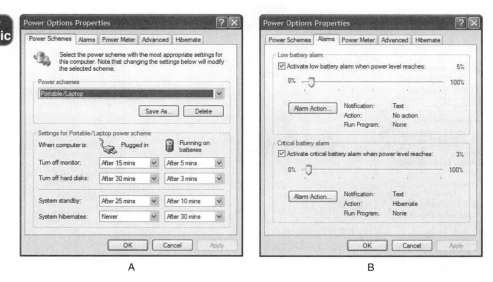

Figure 9-21   The Power Schemes tab (a) and Alarms tab (b) of the Power Options properties sheet.

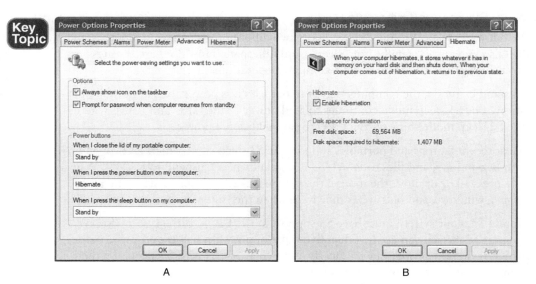

Figure 9-22   The Advanced tab (a) and Hibernate tab (b) of the Power Options properties sheet.

In this dialog, you can specify how long before the hard disk turns off, and set power savings for devices such as the processor, wireless, USB, and PCI Express. To configure alarms in Windows 7 or Vista go to the Battery area, and find the Low Battery notification. Take a few minutes to look through these options and the options for the other power plans.

Figure 9-23   The Advanced tab in Windows Vista's Power Options dialog.

Suspend, Standby, and Hibernate Modes

Windows 7, Vista, XP, and 2000 support two different power-saving modes, stand by (also known as "standby" or "sleep") and hibernate. How do these settings vary from each other, and from normal computer operation?

In stand by mode, the computer stays on, but uses less power than in normal operation. The S1 sleep mode continues to feed power to the CPU and RAM, whereas the S2 sleep mode shuts off the CPU to save additional power.

Most recent laptops and portables support the S3 sleep state, which saves open programs, windows, and files to RAM (S3 is also known as "suspend to RAM"). When you press a key or move the mouse, the system wakes up from S3 sleep and all programs, windows, and files are as they were when the system went into sleep mode.

To use S3, your system must have S3 support in the BIOS. If the system doesn't support S3, which can use less than five watts of power, it will use S1 or S2 modes, which save some power, but not nearly as much as S3. As with S3 sleep, use the mouse or keyboard to wake up a system from S1 or S2 sleep.

In hibernate mode (also known as S4 sleep state), the computer creates a file called hiberfil.sys and then shuts down. Hiberfil.sys stores the system's current state, so when you wake up the system, the same programs and files are open as when you shut down the system. To wake up a system that is in hibernate mode, press the power button. By default, hibernation is disabled. To turn it on in Windows XP click the **Hibernate** tab in Power Options and then check **Enable Hibernation**. To turn it on in Windows 7 or Vista, open the Command Prompt as an administrator.

Then type **powercfg.exe/hibernate on**; it will then show up in the shut down area of the Start menu. To turn it off, type **powercfg.exe/hibernate off**.

> **NOTE** To determine which sleep modes a portable or desktop system supports, download the free (for personal use) Sleeper program from PassMark (www. passmark.com/products/sleeper.htm; licensed versions are available for organizations). Sleeper can be used in a GUI or command-line mode to test your system to determine supported sleep modes, and can also be used to put a system into a specified sleep mode for either a specified amount of time or until the user decides to wake the system.

Stand by or hibernate are two of the options available when configuring the Power Buttons section of the Advanced tab in Power Options, and the system can go into these modes automatically after being idle for a specified period.

To select stand by or hibernate from the Shut Down menu in Windows XP, follow these steps:

Step 1.   Click **Start**.

Step 2.   Click **Shut Down Computer**.

Step 3.   To send the system into standby mode, click Stand By. To send the system into hibernate mode, press the shift key to toggle Hibernate in place of **Stand By**, and click **Hibernate**.

To select stand by or hibernate from the Shut Down menu in Windows Vista or 7, follow these steps:

Step 1.   Click **Start**.

Step 2.   Click the right-pointing arrow to the right of the padlock (Vista) or Shut Down button (7).

Step 3.   To send the system into standby mode, click **Sleep**. To send the system into hibernate mode, click **Hibernate**. Remember, you must enable hibernation before the Hibernate option will be listed.

Applications for Portable and Laptop Hardware

While portable and laptop systems can perform the same tasks as desktop computers, their ability to work away from the office, on AC or battery power, and to be used for presentations distinguish them from their desktop counterparts, as discussed in the following sections.

Using Communications Connections

Portables and laptops can use a variety of communications and network connections, as described in the following sections.

Using Bluetooth

Windows XP SP2 and SP3 as well as Windows 7 and Windows Vista include Bluetooth support. The Bluetooth Devices applet in Control Panel is used to add or remove Bluetooth devices, view device properties, change Bluetooth options, or add a COM port.

The properties for a Bluetooth device include the device type, the hardware address of the Bluetooth adapter, the date and time of the last connection, and whether a passkey is used to pair the device to your system.

To control whether Bluetooth devices can connect to your computer, or to be alerted when a new Bluetooth device wants to connect to your computer, use the Options tab.

When Bluetooth computers connect to each other in a personal area network (PAN), at least one of the computers must have discovery turned on. You can join a PAN from the Bluetooth taskbar icon menu, the Bluetooth Network Connection in Network Tasks, or by using View Bluetooth Network Devices from the Network Tasks pane. Each Bluetooth item in a PAN is assigned a unique IP address using automatic private IP addressing (APIPA), which assigns IP addresses in the 169.254.x.x range.

If you use programs that require the Bluetooth device to be assigned a COM port number, use the port configuration option to select a COM port. Bluetooth printers are automatically assigned a virtual printer port after being configured with the Add a Printer option in the Control Panel Printers and Faxes area.

To add a device, run the Add Bluetooth Device Wizard after starting the bthprops.cpl application from the Start menu's Run command. You can also use this wizard to generate a passkey, which creates a more secure connection between devices.

The fsquirt.exe program is used to perform file transfers (send or receive) between computers or computers and other devices using Bluetooth. The telephon.cpl program is used to configure Bluetooth devices that support dial-up networking as modems.

For more information on using Bluetooth with Windows XP SP2 and newer versions of Windows, see http://support.microsoft.com/kb/883259.

Using Infrared (IrDA)

To assure that IrDA devices such as printers can be recognized by PnP detection, make sure the IrDA port built into (or connected to) your system is properly configured before installing a printer. Note that IrDA relies on line-of-sight connections between computers and devices.

If Windows detects an IrDA printer during printer installation, it automatically sets up the correct port type. To print to the printer, just start the print job and Windows will send the print job via the IrDA port.

IrDA ports are assigned COM port numbers, so if you want to use an IrDA port for file transfer, you must configure your file transfer program to use the appropriate COM port. Use Windows Device Manager to determine this information.

Using Cellular WAN

A cellular WAN card typically contains a SIM card, just as a digital cell phone does. Before you can connect to a mobile network with a cellular WAN card, you must activate the SIM card it contains. Use the utility provided by the mobile network provider.

Use the mobile network provider's utility to make the connection to the cellular network. Once a connection is made to the network, users can browse the Web, send or receive email, perform file transfers, or other activities just as with a wired or wireless Ethernet connection.

Using Ethernet

To use an Ethernet connection in a laptop or portable computer, connect a network cable on a working network to the RJ-45 port on the laptop.

If the laptop is configured to receive an IP address and DNS servers automatically and a server on the network provides this information, the network can be used immediately. If the laptop is connected to a network that requires that this information be entered manually, enter the correct values into the configuration for the network port. For details, see "Networking Configuration," in Chapter 16, "Networking."

Using Wireless Ethernet (WLAN)

The methods used for connecting to a wireless network with Windows vary with the version of Windows used and with the configuration of the network. Windows 2000 does not include a built-in wireless Ethernet client; you must use a client provided by the wireless adapter vendor.

To connect to a wireless network using a vendor-provided client and Windows, you need to know the wireless network's SSID, the type of encryption used (WPA, WPA2, WEP, or open), the channel number, the type of connection (ad-hoc or infrastructure), and the encryption key. If the network uses WEP encryption, you must also know the length of the encryption key used: 64-bit, 128-bit, or 256-bit. Enter this information as prompted by the vendor-supplied client. Figure 9-24 illustrates a Linksys wireless client.

If the system uses Windows XP and the network is an open (unencrypted) network, Windows can automatically detect the network and start a connection, using Windows's Wireless Zero Configuration (WZC) service (see Figure 9-25). Windows

Vista and Windows 7 replace WZC with the WLAN AutoConfig service for auto-matic connection. Figure 9-26 illustrates the connection process with Windows 7.

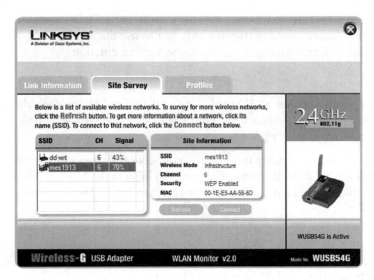

Figure 9-24   Connecting to a wireless network using a Linksys wireless client.

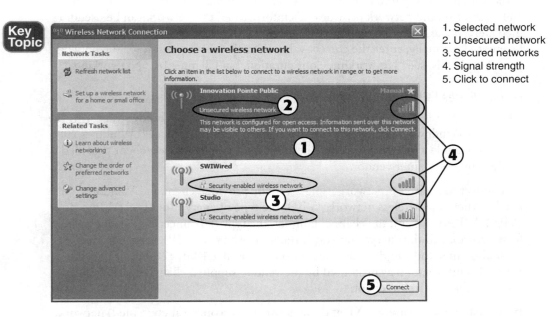

Figure 9-25   Connecting to a wireless network with Windows XP.

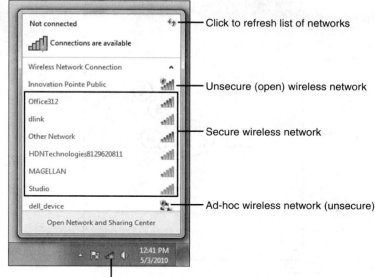

Click to refresh list of networks

Unsecure (open) wireless network

Secure wireless network

Ad-hoc wireless network (unsecure)

Click to open the Wireless Connection dialog

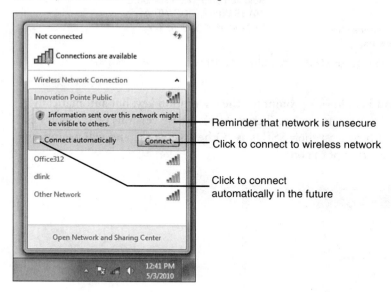

Reminder that network is unsecure

Click to connect to wireless network

Click to connect
automatically in the future

Figure 9-26 Connecting to an unsecured wireless network with Windows 7.

If the network uses WPA, WPA2, or WEP encryption, Windows prompts the user to provide the correct encryption type and encryption key. If the wireless network does not broadcast its SSID, you must manually enter the SSID and other information, either when prompted, or by using the properties sheet for the connection in the Wireless Networks Connection dialog shown in Figure 9-27.

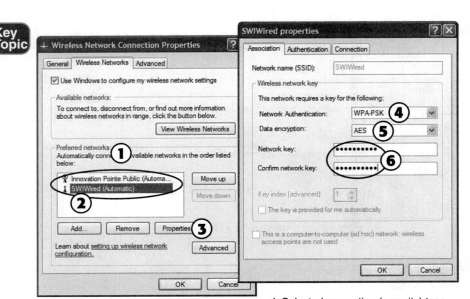

1. Preferred networks
2. Selected network
3. Click to open properties sheet
   for selected network

4. Selected encryption (security) type
5. Selected encryption standard
   (AES WPA2, TKIP WPA)
6. Network (encryption) key

Figure 9-27   Configuring a secured wireless network connection in Windows XP.

Windows Vista and Windows 7 prompt for the encryption key, but automatically detect the encryption type in use (see Figure 9-28). These versions of Windows list networks that don't broadcast their SSIDs as "Other Network" and will prompt for the SSID when you attempt to connect.

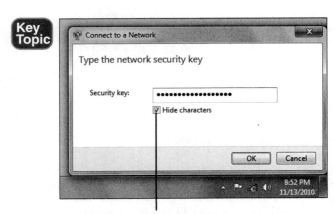

This box unchecked by default

Figure 9-28   Connecting to a secured wireless network connection in Windows 7.

For more information about wireless security and other configuration settings, see "Wireless Ethernet (WLAN) Configuration," in Chapter 16.

Working with Power Sources

Laptops and portables use AC power when it's available, and they automatically switch to battery power when AC power is not available. To determine the type of power in use and to determine battery state or charge level, hover the mouse over the power icon in the notification area. Figure 9-29 shows typical messages for Windows XP. Windows 7's messages are shown in Figure 9-30.

> **TIP**   If the AC or battery status icons or other icons you need to see in the notification area are not visible in Windows 7, click the Show Hidden Icons left arrow. To hide some icons, click the right arrow. Refer to Figure 9-29.

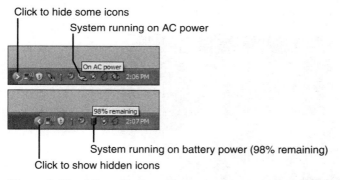

Figure 9-29   AC and battery status messages as displayed by Windows XP's notification area.

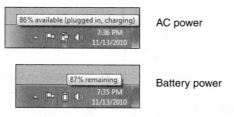   AC power

Battery power

Figure 9-30   AC and battery status messages as displayed by Windows 7's notification area.

Working with Display Subsystem Components

Although very few laptops offer upgradeable graphics, there are several ways to adjust how the display subsystem works, including adjusting the amount of system RAM set aside for use by integrated graphics, adjusting brightness and contrast on the internal display, and configuring a secondary monitor to act as either an extended desktop or a clone of the internal display.

Adjusting the Amount of Shared Video Memory

Some systems with integrated graphics (graphics built into the system chipset) can adjust the amount of system RAM used for graphics through the BIOS setup program. Increasing the amount of RAM used for graphics can improve 3D rendering and gaming performance, while decreasing the amount of RAM used for graphics provides more memory for Windows when 3D rendering or gaming is not important. To make this adjustment on a typical laptop follow these steps:

Step 1.   Save all open files.

Step 2.   Restart the computer.

Step 3.   When the system restarts, press the appropriate key to run the setup program (see system documentation or an onscreen prompt for details).

Step 4.   Locate the Shared Video Memory dialog in the BIOS setup program and select the amount of memory (see Figure 9-31).

Step 5.   Save the changes and exit the BIOS setup program. The new amount of video memory will take effect immediately.

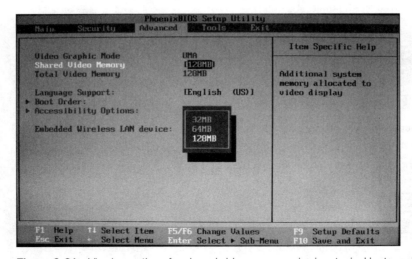

Figure 9-31   Viewing options for shared video memory size in a typical laptop with integrated graphics.

Adjusting Brightness and Contrast on a Laptop Computer's Display

Depending upon the specific graphics solution installed in a laptop computer, there might be more than one way to adjust brightness and contrast. Virtually all laptop computers provide Fn key adjustments for display brightness, and some might also offer contrast adjustments as well. Refer to the keyboard shown in Figure 9-14.

Some systems also provide a proprietary brightness, contrast, and gamma adjustment on the Advanced portion of the display properties sheet in Windows XP, or as a separate program that can be launched from the display's right-click menu or notification area (see Figure 9-32).

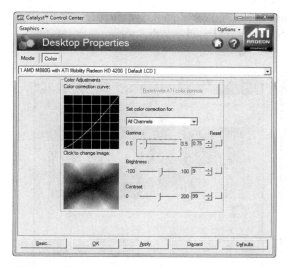

Figure 9-32   Adjusting brightness, contrast, and gamma with the Color tab provided as part of the ATI Mobility Radeon HD 4200 display driver's Catalyst Control Panel.

NOTE   Gamma is the way that brightness is distributed across the spectrum from lightest to darkest tones on a display, scanner, or printer. By adjusting the gamma, you can adjust how midtones are displayed.

Using DualView to Work with a Secondary Monitor or Projector

Windows XP, Windows Vista, and Windows 7 support DualView with virtually all recent laptop display hardware. DualView enables a secondary display that is plugged into a laptop's external video ports, such as TV-out, S-video, VGA, DVI, or HDMI, to be used to extend the desktop; it can also be used to mirror the desktop if desired.

To enable this feature in Windows XP or Vista, follow these steps:

Step 1.   Before turning on the computer, plug the appropriate video cable into the video port.

Step 2.   Turn on the external monitor, TV, or projector.

Step 3.   Turn on the computer.

Step 4.   If the computer does not automatically extend the desktop, right-click an empty area on the desktop and select Properties (XP) or Personalize (Vista), or open Control Panel and open the Display properties icon.

Step 5.   Click the Settings tab on the Display properties icon (see Figure 9-33a) in Windows XP; in Windows Vista, click Display Settings.

Step 6.   To enable the secondary display, click it, and select **Extend My Windows Desktop Onto This Monitor**.

Step 7.   Adjust the screen resolution as needed for the second display (see Figure 9-33b). To determine usable resolutions, check the documentation for the display.

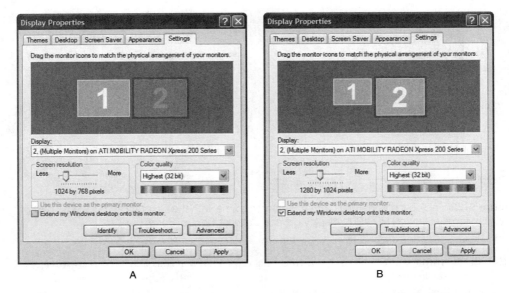

Figure 9-33 The settings dialog before (a) and after (b) enabling a secondary display as an extended desktop.

Step 8.   Click **Apply** and then **OK** to use the settings.

To enable this feature in Windows 7, follow these steps:

Step 1.   Before turning on the computer, plug the appropriate video cable into the video port.

Step 2.   Turn on the external monitor, TV, or projector.

Step 3.   Turn on the computer.

Step 4.   Right-click an empty area on the desktop and select **Screen Resolution**.

Step 5.   To enable the secondary display, click **Detect** (see Figure 9-34).

Step 6.   Open the Multiple Displays menu and select whether to Extend These Displays (Dual View) or Duplicate These Displays (display cloning).

Step 7.   Click **Apply**.

Step 8.   Select the second display and adjust the screen resolution as needed (refer to Figure 9-13). To determine usable resolutions, check the documentation for the display.

Step 9.   Click **Apply** and then **OK** to use the settings.

Detects additional displays

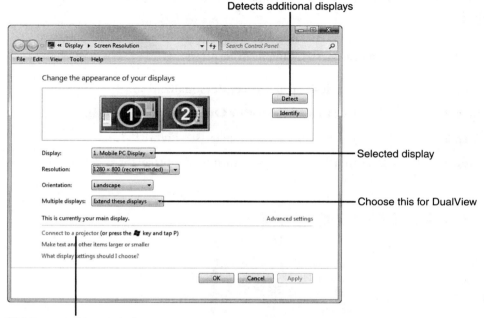

Selected display

Choose this for DualView

Click to connect to a projector

Figure 9-34 The Windows 7 Screen Resolution dialog after enabling a secondary display as an extended desktop.

Cloning the Laptop Display to a Secondary Display or Projector

If you need to display the same information on an external display or projector, such as for a presentation, follow this procedure for Windows XP:

Step 1.   Determine the resolution of the secondary display or projector. Most projectors offer resolutions such as 800×600 or 1024×768.

Step 2.   Use the Settings tab on the Display properties sheet to adjust the resolution of the laptop's internal display to match the secondary display or projector's resolution.

Step 3.   Do *not* extend the desktop to the secondary display. Instead, locate the Fn key combination on the keyboard that toggles the display into clone mode. Typically, you must press this key combination several times to move through different display combinations until the displays are cloned. Wait a few moments after you press the key combination to allow the display mode to change before continuing.

NOTE   Some laptops use a proprietary display-management program to clone the displays. Access it by right-clicking an empty portion of the desktop and selecting it from the menu.

With Windows Vista Business/Ultimate/Enterprise:

Step 1.   Right-click the desktop and select **Personalization**.

Step 2.   Click **Connect to a Projector or Other External Device**.

Step 3.   The Windows Mobility Center opens (see Figure 9-35).

Step 4.   Click **Presentation Settings** to turn on the projector and clone your desktop to the projector.

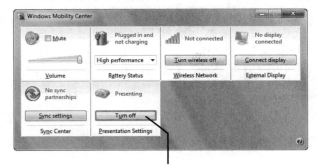

Toggles presentation settings On/Off

Figure 9-35 Using Windows Mobility Center.

NOTE   To adjust Presentation Settings (which also turns off notifications), click the Projector icon and make changes as desired.

Mobility Center also provides options for turning off wireless connections, and Presentation Settings also turns off notifications and prevents the computer from going to sleep or turning off the display. Some vendors offer additional Windows Mobility Center options customized to their hardware.

With Windows 7 Professional/Ultimate/Enterprise, you can run Windows Mobility Center by searching for Mobility Center with Instant Desktop Search or by running it from Control Panel. However, you can also connect to a projector and choose from a variety of display options by using this method:

Step 1.   Right-click the desktop and select **Screen Resolution**.

Step 2.   Click **Connect to a Projector**.

Step 3.   Select the settings you want from the popup menu (see Figure 9-36).

Step 4.   When you are finished, repeat Steps 1–3 to reset the display to your normal configuration.

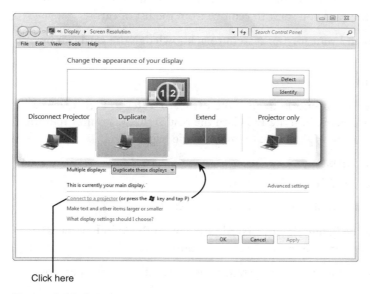

Click here

Figure 9-36 Selecting a projector with Windows 7.

Safe Removal of Laptop-Specific Hardware

Understanding how to safely remove (and install) laptop-specific hardware is an important part of the A+ Certification exams. Although some types of hardware, such as PC Cards and ExpressCard cards, might be removed and installed on a daily basis, other types of hardware are removed and installed only when an upgrade or equipment failure takes place.

NOTE The following sections provide basic instructions for removing hardware. For specific information for a particular model, see the service manual or guide provided by the laptop vendor.

The Laptop Repair 101 website (www.laptoprepair101.com) provides many useful resources, including links to major vendors' laptop service manuals (www.laptoprepair101.com/laptop/category/laptop-service-manual/) and illustrated step-by-step procedures for the removal of many components.

Safe Removal of PC Cards

To remove a PC Card, follow these steps:

Step 1.   Look for an ejector button next to the PC Card slot; on some systems, the button is folded into the unit for storage. Unfold the button.

Step 2.   Disconnect any cables or dongles from the card.

Step 3.   Right-click the Safely Remove Hardware icon in the Windows taskbar and select the card you want to remove from the list of cards.

Step 4.   Click **Stop** and wait for the system to acknowledge the card can be removed.

Step 5.   Click **OK** to close the message.

Step 6.   Push in the ejector button to eject the PC Card (refer to Figure 9-4 earlier in this chapter). Pull the PC Card the rest of the way out of the slot and store it in its original case or an antistatic bag.

Safe Removal of ExpressCards

To remove an ExpressCard, follow these steps:

Step 1.   Disconnect any cables or dongles from the card.

Step 2.   Right-click the Safely Remove Hardware icon in the Windows taskbar and select the card you want to remove from the list of cards.

Step 3.   Click **Stop** and wait for the system to acknowledge the card can be removed.

Step 4.   Click **OK** to close the message.

Step 5.   Push in the card to release it. Pull the ExpressCard the rest of the way out of the slot and store it in its original case or an antistatic bag.

NOTE   Some systems with ExpressCard slots use the slot to store a media remote control. If a remote control is stored in the ExpressCard slot, go directly to Step 5 to remove it.

Safe Removal of Batteries

Follow this procedure to replace computer batteries:

Step 1.   Turn off the computer.

Step 2.   Unplug the AC adapter or line cord from the computer.

Step 3.   Locate the battery compartment in the unit; it might be secured by a sliding lock or by screws.

Step 4.   If the battery is under a removable cover, remove the battery compartment cover.

Step 5.   Release the lock that holds the battery in place.

Step 6.   Slide or lift out the battery (see Figure 9-37). If the battery is a flat assembly, it might be held in place by a clip; push the clip to one side to release the battery.

Step 7.   Check the battery contacts inside the computer for dirt or corrosion, and clean dirty contacts with a soft cloth.

Step 8.   Insert the replacement battery. Make sure you insert the battery so the positive and negative terminals are in the right directions.

Step 9.   Close the cover and secure it.

Step 10.   If the battery must be charged before use, plug in the line cord or AC adapter into both the computer and wall outlet. Check the computer's manual for the proper charge time for a new battery.

Step 11.   Unplug the system or AC adapter when the battery has been charged for the recommended time period.

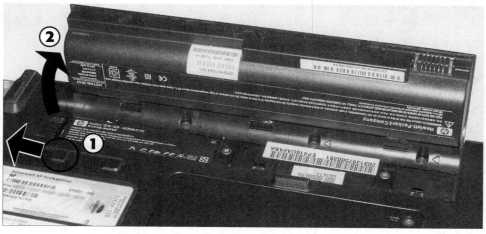

1. Releasing the battery catch
2. Rotating the battery up and out of the battery compartment

Figure 9-37   Removing a battery from a typical laptop computer.

CAUTION   Take precautions against ESD when you change the battery. Discharge any static electricity in your body by touching a metal object before you open the battery compartment, and don't touch the contacts on the battery or the contacts in the battery compartment with your hands.

Safe Removal and Installation of Mini-PCI Cards

To remove a Type III mini-PCI card, follow this procedure:

Step 1.   Turn off the computer.

Step 2.   Unplug the computer and remove the battery pack.

Step 3.   Locate the mini-PCI card in the unit. It might be accessible from the bottom of the system (see Figure 9-38 for an example), or you might need to remove the keyboard or other components.

Step 4.   Remove the cover or other components over the card.

Step 5.   Release the spring latches that hold the card in place.

Step 6.   Lift the top of the card up until the card is released from the socket.

To install a mini-PCI card, follow these steps

Step 1.   Push the mini-PCI card edge connector into place.

Step 2.   Push the top of the card down into the socket until the spring clips lock into place.

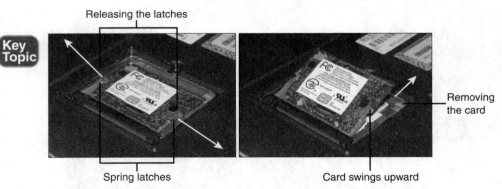

Figure 9-38   Removing a mini-PCI card from a typical notebook computer.

Step 3.   Replace the cover or other components you removed to gain access to the card socket.

Step 4.   Reinstall the battery.

Step 5.   Plug the computer in.

Step 6.   Start the computer. Install any additional drivers required.

> **NOTE**   If the mini-PCI card is used for wireless Ethernet, it might be necessary to remove antenna cables from the card before removing it. See the laptop vendor's service manual for details.

Safe Removal and Installation of Hard Disk Drives

Although a few laptop computers require you to remove the keyboard to access the hard disk, most laptops feature hard disks that can be accessed from the bottom of the system. Follow this procedure to remove and replace a hard disk:

Step 1.   Turn off the laptop and unplug it from AC power.

Step 2.   Remove the battery (refer to Figure 9.37).

Step 3.   Loosen or remove the screw or screws used to hold the drive cover in place.

Step 4.   Push the cover away from the retaining lug or clips and remove it. On some systems, the drive might be mounted to the cover (Figure 9-39a), while on other systems, the drive is mounted to the chassis (Figure 9-39b).

Step 5.   If the drive is fastened to the chassis, as in Figure 9-39b, remove the screws holding the drive to the chassis.

Step 6.   Push the drive away from the retaining screw holes and lift it out of the chassis.

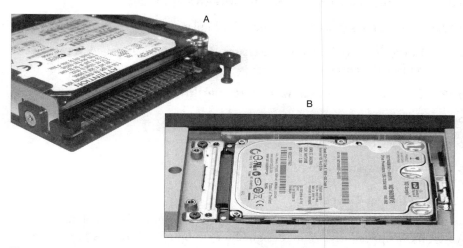

A

B

Figure 9-39   A laptop hard disk that fastens to the cover (a) compared to one that fastens to a separate frame inside the chassis (b).

Step 7.   Remove the screws fastening the drive to the drive cover or frame (see Figure 9-40.

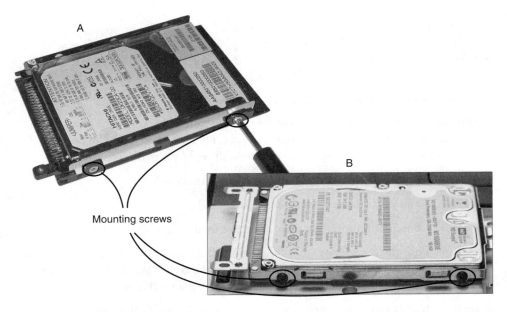

A

B

Mounting screws

Figure 9-40   Removing the hard disk mounting screws from the cover (a) or the frame (b).

Step 8.   Remove the drive from the drive cover or frame.

Step 9.   Place the new hard disk into the drive cover or frame.

Step 10.   Replace the screws to hold the drive in place.

Step 11.   Insert the drive back into the chassis. If the drive is fastened to the cover, replace the cover screw.

Step 12.   Replace the chassis screws to fasten the drive back into place.

Step 13.   Replace the cover.

Step 14.   Replace the battery.

Step 15.   Plug the system into AC power.

Safe Removal of Optical Drives

Some laptops feature modular optical drives that are designed for swapping. However, if the optical drive is not designed for swapping, follow this procedure to remove it:

Step 1. Release the latch that holds the drive in place, or locate the mounting screw that holds the drive in place and unscrew it. It might be located inside the access panel for another component, such as the mini-PCI board or memory modules.

Step 2. Pull the drive out of the system. See Figure 9-41 for a typical example.

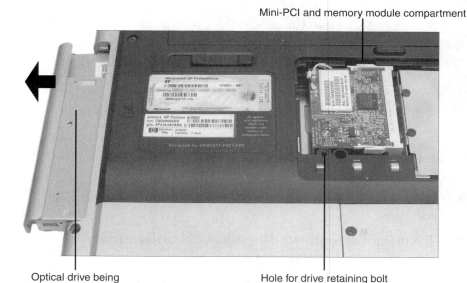

Mini-PCI and memory module compartment

Optical drive being removed from system

Hole for drive retaining bolt

Figure 9-41   Removing an optical drive from a typical laptop.

Safe Removal and Installation of Memory

Memory upgrades often can be performed without removing the keyboard, which covers most other internal components. Follow these steps to perform a typical memory upgrade:

Step 1. Remove the cover over the memory upgrade socket on the bottom of the system.

Step 2. Remove any screws or hold-down devices.

Step 3. Remove the old memory upgrade if necessary.

Step 4. Insert the new memory upgrade, making sure the contacts (on the back side or edge of the module) make a firm connection with the connector.

Step 5. If you are installing an SODIMM or small-outline Rambus module, push the top of the module down until the latches lock into place (see Figure 9-42).

Push SODIMM
module into slot

Push rear of module until
latches lock into place

Locking latches

Figure 9-42   Installing an SODIMM module on a typical portable computer.

Step 6. If the memory socket uses screws to secure the memory in place, install them.

Step 7. Test the module by starting the system and observing the memory counter; use third-party diagnostics if possible.

Step 8. Close the cover and secure it to complete the upgrade.

Safe Removal of LCD Panels

LCD display panels built into portable computers are customized for each model of portable computer and require the disassembly of the computer for removal and replacement. You can get replacements from either the vendor or an authorized repair parts depot. Many vendors require that you be an authorized technician before you remove or replace LCD display panels in portable computers. However, the process of replacing the entire LCD display assembly is simpler and *might* be possible for you to perform in the field.

CAUTION   Should you do your own LCD display panel replacement? Vendors are of two minds about this. Some vendors provide online documentation that guides you through the entire process of reducing an intact portable into a pile of parts and rebuilding it. However, this information is primarily intended for professional computer service staff. Portables require specialized tools to deal with their tiny screws and snap-together cases and they contain proprietary parts. If you break an internal drive or an integrated keyboard, you can't run to your favorite electronics superstore for a replacement. You have been warned.

The details of the process for removing an LCD display assembly from a portable computer vary by model, but you can follow these basic steps:

Step 1. If the system has an integrated wireless Ethernet adapter, disconnect the antenna leads coming from the display from the adapter (usually a mini-PCI card).

Step 2. Remove the keyboard frame and keyboard.

Step 3. Disconnect the FPC cable from the system board (also known as the display cable); this cable transmits power and data to the LCD display assembly.

Step 4. If the system has an integrated wireless Ethernet adapter, remove the antenna leads from the clips in the top cover.

Step 5. Rotate the display assembly to a 90-degree angle to the base unit.

Step 6. Remove the screws that secure the display assembly.

Step 7. Lift the display assembly free from the base unit.

Step 8. Be sure to save all screws, ground springs, and other hardware that you removed during the disassembly process.

Depending on the vendor, you might be able to purchase a replacement LCD display assembly that can be installed by following the previous steps in reverse order, or you might need to disassemble the display assembly to remove and install the LCD display panel itself. Replacing the LCD display panel (which requires the disassembly of the display assembly) should be performed at a repair depot.

Because of differences in chipsets, BIOSs, and display circuitry between systems with passive matrix (including dual-scan) and active-matrix LCD panels, dual-scan and active-matrix LCD panels are generally not interchangeable. However, you might be able to swap a reduced-glare display assembly or panel for a brighter panel with more glare, or vice-versa.

Safe Removal and Replacement of Pointing Devices

There are two main types of integrated pointing devices used in laptops and portable computers: touchpads and pointing sticks. Touchpads are generally located in the palm rest (which extends below the keyboard), while pointing sticks such as the IBM/Lenovo TrackPoint and Toshiba AccuPoint are located in the middle of the keyboard (the buttons are located in the palm rest).

If you need to replace the pointing device built into the palm rest (including buttons used by pointing sticks), you need to partially disassemble the portable computer. Details vary from unit to unit (check with your vendor for details), but the basic procedure is described here.

To remove the palm rest, follow these steps:

Step 1.   Remove the display panel assembly (if necessary) and keyboard.

Step 2.   Turn over the system.

Step 3.   Release the clips or screws holding the palm rest in place.

Step 4.   Turn the system right side up.

Step 5.   Remove the palm rest from the system.

To remove a pointing device, such as a touchpad or others, from the palm rest

Step 1.   Disconnect or unscrew the pointing device from the touchpad.

Step 2.   Remove the pointing device from the touchpad.

Step 3.   You might need to remove the pointing device cable from the pointing device or from the system board; check the specific instructions for the device.

To replace the pointing device, follow these steps in reverse order to install a new pointing device into the palm rest and to reinstall the palm rest into the portable computer.

To replace the pointing stick, it is necessary to remove and replace the keyboard that contains the pointing stick. Details vary from unit to unit (check with your vendor for the details of the particular model you are repairing), but the following is the basic procedure:

Step 1.   Remove the display assembly if the vendor recommends it; some portable systems don't require this step.

Step 2.   Remove screws or bezels that hold the keyboard in place.

Step 3.   Lift up the keyboard to expose the keyboard cable.

Step 4.   Remove any hold-down devices used to hold the keyboard cable in place.

Step 5.   Disconnect the keyboard cable from the system board.

Step 6.   Remove the keyboard.

TIP   If you have purchased a replacement integrated keyboard, it might include detailed disassembly/reassembly instructions. Contact the parts or system vendor to get this information if your replacement keyboard didn't include this information.

Portable and Laptop Diagnostics

With more portables and laptops being sold these days than desktops, it's more important than ever to understand how to diagnose them. The following sections help prepare you for questions you might encounter on the A+ Certification exams as well as in your day-to-day work.

Power Troubleshooting

Portables and laptops can get power from two sources: AC power (wall outlet) and DC power (internal battery).

AC Power Troubleshooting

To verify that the laptop is receiving AC power, check the following:

- Make sure the laptop is plugged into a working AC outlet. Check the outlet with an outlet tester. Use a voltmeter or a multimeter set to AC voltage to determine if the output is within acceptable limits.

- Make sure the AC power cord running from the AC outlet to the external AC adapter "power brick" shown in Figure 9-43 is plugged completely into the outlet and the adapter. If the power cord or plug is damaged, replace the cord.

AC power cord

Figure 9-43   A typical laptop "power brick" AC adapter.

- To determine if the adapter is outputting the correct DC voltage, use a voltmeter or multimeter set to DC voltage to test the voltage coming from the adapter and compare it to the nominal output values marked on the adapter. As Figure 9-44 illustrates, it might be necessary to use a bent paperclip to enable an accurate voltage reading. A value of +/- 5% is acceptable.

1. Nominal output voltage
2. AC adapter tip polarity
3. Positive (red) lead from multimeter
4. Negative (black) lead from multimeter
5. Measured DC voltage output
6. Bent paperclip inserted into adapter tip
7. Multimeter mode selector

Figure 9-44 Checking the output voltage from a laptop's AC adapter.

DC Power Troubleshooting

If the system works when plugged into AC power, but not on battery power, check the following:

■ Make sure that the battery is installed properly.

■ Determine whether the battery can hold a charge. Make sure the battery is properly installed and the AC adapter has proper DC voltage output levels. Leave the system plugged in for the recommended amount of time needed to charge the battery, then try to run the system on battery power. If the battery cannot run the system at all, or the system runs out of battery power in less than an hour, replace the battery.

■ If the battery is hot after being charged or has a warped exterior, it might have an internal short. Replace it.

Display Troubleshooting

When a laptop or portable computer's built-in display stops working, there are a variety of possible causes. Use the material in this section to troubleshoot the display subsystem.

Using an External Monitor to Check the Display Subsystem

To determine whether the problem with the display subsystem is limited to the LCD display or affects the video circuit itself, connect an external monitor to the system and see if you can perform the following:

- Extend the desktop

- Toggle between internal and external displays using Fn keys

If the external display works, then you know that the problem is limited to the integrated LCD display. However, if neither the integrated nor the external display works, the problem is with the discrete graphics chip or the motherboard.

Solving Internal Display Problems

If the internal display fails displaying a white picture, but the external monitor works properly, the connector between the display and the motherboard might be loose. Follow the instructions for removing the LCD display subsystem to access the connector and reattach it. For more details, see "Safe Removal of LCD Panels," in this chapter. If part of the display is white at all times, the LCD is cracked and you should replace it.

LCD Cutoff Switch

The LCD cutoff switch is used to turn off the bulb that lights an LCD. This is normally enabled on a laptop when the lid is closed. The switch is usually found inside the display; if it fails, the display needs to be opened to repair or replace it. Some laptops have an LCD cutoff button that enables a user to turn off the LCD (bulb) manually.

NOTE   If you are servicing an old laptop with a monochrome screen, note that damaged areas of the screen might be black rather than white.

Checking for Backlight Problems

If the backlight fails or the inverter fails, the screen might appear to have failed entirely. Before you assume the screen has failed, look closely at the screen to see if you can make out items on the display, such as the boot dialog or the Windows desktop. If you can see items on the screen, but the screen is very dark, the backlight or the inverter has probably failed. Shine a flashlight on the screen to help determine if there are items visible on the screen.

TIP   To help you determine what should be on-screen, connect an external display and press the appropriate Fn keys to switch the display into cloned mode.

If the inverter fails, it's easier to replace yourself than the backlight, but partial disassembly of the display is necessary. Although it's possible to replace the backlight yourself if you are very careful, this type of repair requires that the display assembly be completely disassembled.

CAUTION   Backlights typically are fluorescent tubes and contain mercury. Because mercury is a hazardous chemical that should not be put into a landfill, some laptop service manuals discuss the removal of the backlight in the recycling section.

Dead Pixels

LCD displays can suffer from dead pixels; a dead pixel won't light up or displays only red, green, or blue light at all times. Laptop manufacturers have varying policies on the number and location of dead pixels a display must have before the laptop can be returned for service during the limited warranty period. If you notice one or more dead pixels, consult the laptop manufacturer for your options.

TIP   In some cases, gently tapping your finger on the screen over the dead pixel can correct the problem.

Other Components

To solve problems with other peripherals, such as the stylus and digitizer, keypad, and wireless Ethernet antenna wires, you need to know the following:

■   Where the components are located

■   How to disassemble your laptop, troubleshoot it, and reassemble it

Removing Peripherals

The following items can usually be removed by accessing them through the bottom of the laptop or portable computer:

■   Memory

■   Mini-PCI or Mini-PCIe card (network, wireless network)

■   Hard disk

■   Optical drive

If any of these components stop working, follow this general procedure:

Step 1.   Open Device Manager and delete the item from the listing.

Step 2.   Reinstall the item's driver by clicking Action, Scan for Hardware Changes.

Step 3.   After Device Manager reinstalls the device and its drivers, try the device again. If Device Manager is unable to detect the hardware, download new drivers from the vendor, install them, and restart Windows to detect the drivers.

Step 4.   If the device continues to fail, shut down Windows, physically remove the device and check it for obvious problems (physical damage, burnt chips, cut wires, warping, and so on).

Step 5.   If you don't see any physical damage to the device, reinstall it and restart Windows.

Step 6.   Use the device again. If it continues to fail, replace the item.

For details, see the section "Safe Removal of Laptop-Specific Hardware," earlier in this chapter.

Stylus and Digitizer Problems

To solve stylus and digitizer problems, you must determine where the stylus is used and disassemble that area as needed to locate loose connections or to replace defective components:

- If the digitizer pad is located on the keyboard, you must disassemble the keyboard and chassis.

- If the digitizer is a touch-sensitive display, you must disassemble the chassis to locate the connection between the display and the motherboard, or you might need to replace the display assembly.

For details, see the section "Safe Removal of Laptop-Specific Hardware," earlier in this chapter.

Keypad Problems

To solve keypad and keyboard problems, follow this procedure:

Step 1.   Connect a desktop keyboard to the computer. If you connect a PS/2 keyboard, you must shut down the laptop or portable computer first. If you connect a USB keyboard, you can do so while the laptop or portable computer is running.

Step 2.   Open a program such as Notepad or WordPad and type characters.

Step 3.   If you are unable to enter characters using the keyboard, the motherboard has failed and must be replaced. However, if you are able to enter characters using the keyboard, the problem is limited to the keyboard or keypad.

Step 4.   Shut down the computer, disconnect it from AC power, and remove the battery.

Step 5.   Unplug the keyboard.

Step 6.   Disassemble the keyboard and keypad assembly and check the connection.

Step 7.   Disconnect the keyboard wire from the motherboard, and then reconnect it.

Step 8.   Reassemble the laptop and restart it.

Step 9.   Use the laptop's own keyboard. If it continues to fail, replace the keyboard/keypad subassembly.

> **NOTE**   See your laptop or portable computer's service manual for disassembly/reassembly details.
>
> You can order replacement keyboards from your computer's manufacturer, or you might be available to get them from third-party firms.

Antenna Wires

If Device Manager shows that the wireless Ethernet network adapter in a notebook computer is working properly and other computers can connect to the wireless access point or router, it's possible that the antenna wires connected to the mini-PCI wireless Ethernet radio card are loose or damaged.

To check the connection between the mini-PCI card and the antenna wires, open the access panel covering the mini-PCI card and verify that the wires are connected to the card—and that the wires are connected to the correct locations on the card. If the card was removed and the wires detached from the card, the wires might be reversed. For details, see the section "Safe Removal of Laptop-Specific Hardware," earlier in this chapter. If the wires are properly connected, the wireless transceivers built into the display assembly might be damaged. To replace them, you must disassemble the display assembly. See the service manual for your laptop or portable computer for details.

Preventative Maintenance for Laptops and Portable Devices

Preventative maintenance can help prevent failure of laptop and portable computer components. Use the procedures in the following sections to help assure long-term reliable operation.

Cooling Devices

An overheated system might quit, display STOP errors (also known as Blue Screen of Death, or BSOD), or throttle down the processor to very low clock speeds. Overheating can be caused by a blocked cooling fan outlet, cooling fan failure, or damage to the heat sink.

Laptops and portable computers use cooling fans that might be located in the side or bottom of the system. To avoid overheating, make sure the fan outlet is not blocked.

CAUTION   Resting a laptop or portable computer with a bottom-mounted fan on a bed, pillow, or blanket is not recommended because the surface tends to block the fan outlet and can cause the system to overheat.

If the fan outlet or blades are dirty, clean them with compressed air or a brush.

If the fan fails, the fan assembly can be removed and replaced. See the service manual for your system for details.

If the fan is working, but the system is overheating, the heat sink assembly might be damaged, or might not be properly secured to the processor. To determine if either of these problems has occurred, you must disassemble the computer to gain access to the heat sink. A heat sink dissipates heat from the processor to a passive fin assembly that is cooled by the system's cooling fan.

If the heat sink is loose, the thermal paste or thermal transfer material between the heat sink and the processor needs to be removed and replaced before the heat sink is reattached to the processor. Isopropyl alcohol and a lint-free cotton cloth can be used to remove old thermal paste from the heat sink and processor.

Before reinstalling the heat sink as shown in Figure 9-45, reapply a small amount of thermal paste to the center of the processor's integrated heat shield and push the heat sink down over the processor to distribute the thermal paste. Then, secure the heat sink.

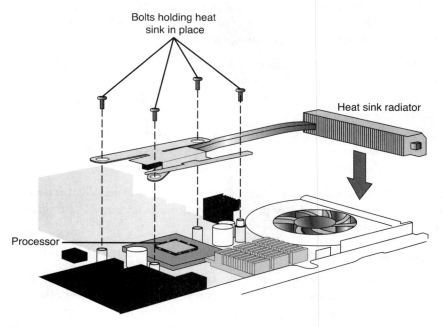

Figure 9-45   Reattaching the heat sink on a typical laptop or portable computer.

Display Screens

You should clean display screens with anti-static cleaners meant for display use. If you use a spray cleaner, spray the cloth or paper towel and use the towel to apply the cleaner.

Suitable Operating Environments

Laptops and portable computers can be operated in a wide range of environments. However, exceeding the recommendations can damage the screen or other components.

Air Temperature

Typical operating range for a laptop is from 50–95°F (10–35°C). Typical non-operating range (for storage and other situations in which the laptop is not in use) is from -4–140°F (-20–60°C). You can find exact values for a particular model in its specifications sheet. Note that batteries discharge more quickly at higher temperatures.

TIP   If a laptop must be operated at temperatures above its operating temperature, use an external fan to help keep the laptop cool. An auxiliary cooling pad that contains its own fans can also help cool the laptop.

Air Quality

Air quality issues are a concern primarily if a laptop or portable computer will be used in an environment that contains a lot of particulates, such as an office that permits smoking, coal mines, grain elevators, and so forth.

To protect the internal parts of the laptop, consider using an air filter over the air intake on the laptop and clean or replace the filter frequently.

Storage Methods

If a laptop or portable computer will be stored for a long period (more than six months), you should remove the rechargeable main battery and the CMOS battery from the computer to prevent leakage and subsequent damage.

The computer should be stored in a water-resistant container, especially if it is located in a flood-prone area or an area protected by sprinkler systems. The original shipping box and plastic protection bag can be used.

Transportation and Shipping

If the original shipping box and protection blocks are not used for transporting the computer, the computer should be placed in a protective bag or sleeve that offers shock protection. You might be able to get a suitable replacement box from the vendor.

Exam Preparation Tasks

Review All the Key Topics

Review the most important topics in the chapter, noted with the key topics icon in the outer margin of the page. Table 9-4 lists a reference of these key topics and the page numbers on which each is found.

Table 9-4   Key Topics for Chapter 9

Key Topic Element	Description	Page Number
Table 9-2	Portable and Desktop Computers Comparison by Features.	327
Figure 9-1	Comparison of a DIMM and SODIMM.	329
Figure 9-2	A typical 2.5-inch ATA/IDE hard drive for notebook computers.	330
Figure 9-3	HP QuickDock docking station.	333
Figure 9-4	A typical notebook with a Type II PC Card.	334
Figure 9-5	Typical Type I, Type II, and Type III PC cards and cross-sections.	335
Figure 9-6	A typical Type II PC Card 10/100 Ethernet card with the dongle used to attach the card to standard Category 5 UTP cable.	336
Figure 9-7	A CardBus 32-bit PC Card compared to ExpressCard/34 and ExpressCard/54 cards.	337
Figure 9-11	The Ethernet (RJ-45 port) and other ports on a typical laptop computer.	342
Figure 9-14	A typical laptop keyboard's Fn keys.	348
Figure 9-15	A laptop that includes both a touch pad and a pointing stick.	348
Figure 9-18	The Power Meter tab.	352
Figures 9-21 through 9-22	The Power Schemes tab, Alarms tab, Advanced tab, and Hibernate tab in thePower Options properties sheet.	355
Figures 9-25 through 9-26	Connecting to a wireless network with Windows XP	360-361

Table 9-4   Key Topics for Chapter 9   *continued*

Key Topic Element	Description	Page Number
Figures 9-27 through 9-28	Connecting to a wireless network with Windows 7	362
Figure 9-37	Removing a battery from a typical laptop computer.	371
Figure 9-38	A laptop hard disk that fastens to the cover (a) compared to one that fastens to a separate frame inside the chassis (b).	372
Figure 9-42	Installing an SODIMM module on a typical portable computer.	376

Complete the Tables and Lists from Memory

Print a copy of Appendix B, "Memory Tables," (found on the CD), or at least the section for this chapter, and complete the tables and lists from memory. Appendix C, "Memory Tables Answer Key," also on the CD, includes completed tables and lists to check your work.

Definitions of Key Terms

Define the following key terms from this chapter, and check your answers in the glossary.

SODIMM, Docking Station, Port Replicator, Zoomed Video, PC Card, ExpressCard, Bluetooth, IrDA, WLAN, Active-Matrix, Passive-Matrix, Lithium-ion, NiMH Battery, NiCd, ACPI, APM

Troubleshooting Scenario

You have been asked to change out the hard drive in a laptop computer. The laptop is a small compact model. How would you change the hard drive without removing the keyboard?

Refer to Appendix A for the answer.

This chapter covers the following subjects:

- **Security Fundamentals**—This section covers the mindset you should have when securing a computer. File systems, authentication, and how to protect against malware are all dealt with in this section.

- **Securing Wireless Networks**—This section talks about wireless encryption and maximizing security on wireless devices.

- **Data and Physical Security**—This section describes encryption types, the Local Security Policy, backups, password management, and much more.

- **Access Control Purposes and Principles**—Windows uses an Access Control Model to set what users have rights to what resources. User Access Control (UAC), NTFS permissions, and auditing are also described.

- **Installing, Configuring, and Troubleshooting Security Features**—This section demonstrates how to secure the BIOS, configure a firewall, and set up a secure wireless connection.

This chapter covers a portion of the CompTIA A+ 220-701 objectives 5.1 and 5.2 and CompTIA A+ 220-702 objectives 4.1 and 4.2.

CHAPTER 10

Security

Some of the more significant changes to the 2011 A+ Certification exams include the additional security objectives. It's not surprising, however. With widespread reports of security breaches, identity theft, and lost hardware, understanding how to secure individual's computers and networks is an important skill.

The A+ Certification exams include objectives measuring your understanding of security as it relates to both individual computer and network environments. Mastering these objectives will help you pass the exams, and will also help you handle the increasing challenges of computer security in the real world.

"Do I Know This Already?" Quiz

The "Do I Know This Already?" quiz allows you to assess whether you should read this entire chapter or simply jump to the "Exam Preparation Tasks" section for review. If you are in doubt, read the entire chapter. Table 10-1 outlines the major headings in this chapter and the corresponding "Do I Know This Already?" quiz questions. You can find the answers in Appendix A, "Answers to the 'Do I Know This Already?' Quizzes and Troubleshooting Scenarios."

Table 10-1 "Do I Know This Already?" Foundation Topics Section-to-Question Mapping

Foundations Topics Section	Questions Covered in This Section
Security Fundamentals	1–4
Securing Wireless Networks	5, 6
Data and Physical Security	7–9
Access Control Purposes and Principles	10
Installing, Configuring, and Troubleshooting Security Features	11, 12

1. Which type of authentication technology uses a credit card–sized device that stores information about the user?

   a. Smart card

   b. Credit card

   c. Keyless entry

   d. Biometrics

2. What technology uses human body characteristics as a way of allowing users into a secured area?

   a. Smart card

   b. Biometrics

   c. PIN number

   d. Keyless entry

3. What are special products that can protect you from viruses and malware?

   a. Antivirus software

   b. Malware protection

   c. Phishing protection

   d. All of these options are correct

4. Which of the following can help protect your computer from inbound and outbound attacks?

   a. Gateway

   b. Router

   c. Software firewall

   d. Hub

5. What are the three standards for encryption of wireless networks?

   a. WEP

   b. WPA

   c. WAP

   d. WPA2

6. To prevent a hacker from obtaining useful information about a wireless network, what should you change from the manufacturer's defaults? (Choose all that apply.)

    a. Reset the default password

    b. Change the SSID name

    c. Hide the SSID name

    d. All of these options are correct

7. Windows 2000, Windows XP, Windows Vista, and Windows 7 come with which type of encryption technology?

    a. NAT

    b. EFS

    c. User account

    d. WEP

8. You are using a computer with Windows 7 Enterprise installed. You need to encrypt the entire disk for security purposes. What technology will allow you to do this?

    a. IPSEC

    b. EFS

    c. BitLocker

    d. L2TP

9. When attackers ask questions to obtain information, what is this type of attack called?

    a. Social engineering

    b. System hacking

    c. Spam

    d. Spyware

10. You are working on a Windows 7 computer. You keep getting messages from the operating system asking you for permissions. What is the name of this feature?

    a. User State Migration

    b. User Account Control

    c. User State Control

    d. User Account Information

11. Your company has a desktop that has a BIOS password assigned. The user who was in charge of the computer has left the company. What would you need to do to resolve this issue?

    a. Use a password reset CD.

    b. Reset the BIOS to the defaults.

    c. You cannot do this.

    d. Remove the jumper from the motherboard.

12. You receive a call from a customer for whom you have just installed a wireless router. They tell you that they cannot connect to the router for Internet access. Which of the following solutions would you have them try?

    a. Reset the device to default.

    b. Turn the router off and back on.

    c. Make sure they are using the same passphrase to connect to the router.

    d. Tell them to re-run the wireless network setup wizard.

Foundation Topics

Security Fundamentals

Security is more than a set of techniques, it is a mindset. The information your clients or company stores on computers can be highly damaging to those organizations or to society at large if it falls into the wrong hands. When you understand that fact, you understand why the gamut of security techniques discussed in the following sections are necessary to protect that information.

Secure and Insecure File Systems

The decisions made about the file system used to set up a computer have a big impact on how secure that computer will be against intruders. Windows 2000, XP, Vista, and 7 are all designed to use the New Technology File System (NTFS) as the default file system. NTFS was designed from the start as a much more secure file system than the FAT file systems used on MS-DOS, Windows 3.x, and Windows 9x/Me.

NTFS supports the creation of user and group accounts with different levels of access to folders and files (to use this feature in Windows XP Professional, disable Simple File Sharing) and the use of the Encrypted File System (EFS) for user-specific encryption of individual files and folders (EFS support varies by Windows version). FAT file systems, such as FAT12 (floppy disks), FAT16 (small hard disks), and FAT32 (large hard disks), do not support user and group accounts, nor do they include file/folder encryption. Consequently, NTFS should be used whenever possible. Note that Windows Vista and Windows 7 cannot be installed on a drive that uses a FAT file system. However, Windows 2000 and Windows XP can be installed on drives that use FAT.

NOTE Windows includes the command line Convert.exe utility for converting the file system from FAT to NTFS, and drives can be converted from FAT to NTFS during an upgrade installation of Windows. Once converted, drives cannot be changed back to FAT unless a third-party utility is used.

Authentication Technologies

Authentication is a general term for any method used to verify a person's identity and protect systems against unauthorized access. It is a preventative measure that can be broken down into three categories:

- Something the user knows, for example a password or PIN
- Something the user has, for example a smart card or other security token
- Something the user is, for example the biometric reading of a fingerprint or retina scan
- Something the user does, for example a signature

The devices that are used to authenticate a user, such as smart cards, biometrics, key fobs, and other products, are often referred to as *authentication technologies*.

Username/Password/PIN

Username/password or personal identification number (PIN) authentication technologies can take many forms. Some examples include:

- **An authentication server on a network maintains a list of authorized users and passwords**—Only users with a recognized username and password (credentials) are allowed to access the network's resources.

- **A keypad lock on an entrance into a secure area can store a list of authorized PINs**—Only users with a recognized PIN can enter the secure area.

These technologies can be used in conjunction with other methods for additional security, such as a smart card or biometric reading.

Smart Cards

A smart card is a credit-card–sized card that contains stored information and might also contain a simple microprocessor or a radio-frequency identification (RFID) chip. Smart cards can be used to store identification information for use in security applications, stored values for use in prepaid telephone or debit card services, hotel guest room access, and many other functions. Smart cards are available in contact, contactless, or proximity form factors. Key fobs containing RFID chips work in a similar fashion to proximity-based smart cards.

A smart card–based security system includes smart cards, card readers that are designed to work with smart cards, and a back-end system that contains a database that stores a list of approved smart cards for each secured location. Smart card-based security systems can also be used to secure individual personal computers.

To further enhance security, smart card security systems can also require the user to input a PIN number or security password as well as provide the smart card at secured checkpoints, such as the entrance to a computer room.

Biometrics

Biometrics refers to the use of biological information, such as human body characteristics, to authenticate a potential user of a secure area. The most common type of biometric security system for PCs is fingerprint-based, but other methods include voice measurements and eye retina and iris scans.

A biometric security system uses a reader or scanner to analyze the characteristic being used for access control and digitizes it into a series of match points, a database that stores the match points of approved users, and software that determines if the information coming from the reader or scanner matches a user in the database. To prevent identity theft, biometric information is usually encrypted.

Biometrics are increasingly being used to prevent unauthorized access to desktop and laptop PCs. Many laptop and portable PCs now include fingerprint readers and biometric software, and USB-based fingerprint readers can be added to desktop and laptop PCs. Some fingerprint readers require the users to swipe the finger across the reader, while others use a pad that the user pushes, similar to the way a fingerprint is placed on an ink pad.

Protection Against Viruses and Malware

Protection against viruses and malware is a necessary protection for every type of computing device, from portable PC to server. Computer protection suites that include antivirus, anti-malware, anti-adware, and anti-phishing protection are available from many vendors, but some users prefer a "best of breed" approach that uses the best available products in each category.

These programs can use some or all of the following techniques to protect users and systems:

- Real-time protection to block infection
- Periodic scans for known and suspected threats
- Automatic updating on a frequent (usually daily) basis
- Renewable subscriptions to obtain updated threat signatures
- Links to virus and threat encyclopedias
- Inoculation of system files
- Permissions-based access to the Internet
- Scanning of downloaded files and sent/received emails

When attempting to protect against viruses and malware, the most important thing to remember is to keep your anti-malware application up to date. The second most important item is to watch out for unknown data, whether it comes via email, USB flash drive, or elsewhere.

Software Firewalls

A software firewall is a program that examines data packets on a network to determine whether to forward them to their destination or block them. Firewalls can be used to protect against inbound threats only (one-way firewall) or against both unauthorized inbound and outbound traffic; this type of firewall is often referred to as a two-way firewall. The standard firewall in Windows XP, Windows Vista, and Windows 7 is a one-way firewall. However, many third-party firewall programs, such as Zone Alarm, are two-way firewalls.

NOTE   Firewalls for Windows Vista and Windows 7 can also be used in two-way mode by modifying their configuration through the Windows Firewall with Advanced Security Microsoft Management Console (MMC) snap-in. For details, see http://technet.microsoft.com/en-us/library/cc732283(WS.10).aspx.

A software firewall can be configured to permit traffic between specified IP addresses and to block traffic to and from the Internet except when permitted on a per-program basis.

Corporate networks sometimes use a proxy server with a firewall as the sole direct connection between the Internet and the corporate network and use the firewall in the proxy server to protect the corporate network against threats.

Hardware Recycling and Deconstruction

Even after a computer has reached the end of its useful life, the hard disk it contains represents a potential security risk. To prevent confidential company or client information from being accessed from a computer that is being disposed of for resale, recycling, or deconstruction for parts, you can use one of the following methods:

- Remove the hard disk(s) and destroy their platters with a hammer or other device, then recycle the scrap. Use this method when preserving the hard disk as a working device is not necessary.

- Overwrite the hard disk(s) with a program that meets or exceeds recognized data-destruction standards such as the U.S. Department of Defense 5220.22-M (7 passes) or Peter Guttman's 35-pass maximum security method. These programs destroy existing data and partition information in such a way as to prevent data recovery or drive forensics analysis. Use this method when maintaining the hard disk as a working device is important (such as for donation or resale). A variety of commercial and freeware programs can be used for this task, which is variously known as disk scrubbing or disk wiping.

External hard disks should also be handled in one of these ways when being disposed of. Floppy disks that contain sensitive information can be physically destroyed or can be bulk-erased to prevent information from being recovered. To protect information on CD or DVD media, shredding is recommended.

Securing Wireless Networks

Wireless networks have become important to businesses of all sizes as well as individual users. However, they also represent a significant potential vulnerability if they are not properly secured. The following sections help you understand how the different encryption methods work and the additional steps that must be taken to completely secure a wireless network.

WEP and WPA Encryption

An encrypted wireless network relies on the exchange of a passphrase between the client and the wireless access point (WAP) or router before the client can connect to the network. There are three standards for encryption: WEP, WPA, and WPA2.

Wireless equivalent privacy (WEP) was the original encryption standard for wireless Ethernet (Wi-Fi) networks. It is the only encryption standard supported by most IEEE 802.11b-compliant hardware. Unfortunately, WEP encryption is not strong enough to resist attacks from a determined hacker. There are several reasons this is true, including key length (64-bit WEP uses a ten-character hex key, and 128-bit WEP uses a 26-character hex key) and the use of unencrypted transmissions for some parts of the handshaking process. Because WEP encryption is not secure, it should not be used to "secure" a wireless network.

As a replacement to WEP, Wi-Fi Protected Access (WPA) was developed a few years ago. It is available in two strengths: WPA (which uses TKIP encryption) and the newer, stronger WPA2 (which uses AES encryption). WPA and WPA2's encryption is much stronger than WEP, supports a key length from 8 up to 63 alphanumeric characters (enabling the use of punctuation marks and other characters not permitted with WEP) or 64 hex characters, and supports the use of a RADIUS authentication server in corporate environments.

NOTE   In some environments, WPA and WPA2 are both referred to as WPA, so the encryption method selected during wireless security configuration determines whether WPA or WPA2 has been chosen.

Because all clients and WAPs or wireless routers on a wireless network must use the same encryption standard, use the strongest standard supported by all hardware.

Ideally, all wireless networks should be secured with WPA2 (WPA has been cracked, although cracking WPA is much harder than cracking WEP). However, the use of WPA2 encryption might require upgraded drivers for older network adapters and upgraded firmware for older WAPs or wireless routers. Wi-Fi Certified adapters and WAPs or wireless routers must support WPA2 as of March 13, 2006.

TIP   There are various ways to create a strong passphrase for use with a WPA or WPA2 network. Some vendors of WAPs and wireless routers include a feature sold under various brand names that is compliant with the Wi-Fi Protected Setup standard (also known as Easy Config). If this cannot be used on some hardware, you can obtain a dynamically generated strong passphrase at Gibson Research Corporation's Perfect Passwords website: https://www.grc.com/passwords.htm.

Copy and paste the passphrase provided into Notepad or another plain-text editor and then copy or paste it into the configuration dialog for a WAP, wireless router, and wireless client as needed.

Access Point Configuration for Maximum Security

Configuring your wireless network with the strongest possible encryption (and using a strong WPA or WPA2 passphrase) is just the beginning of true wireless network security. The following sections discuss other changes to the default configuration of a WAP or wireless router to help improve security.

DHCP Versus Static IP Addresses

By default, almost all WAPs and wireless routers are configured to act as DHCP servers; that is, they hand out IP addresses to all computers they're connected to. This is a convenience, but if you want to limit access to the Internet for certain computers or log activity for computers by IP address, this setting should be disabled and static IP addresses should be assigned instead, using each client's IP configuration dialog. Make sure you assign an IP address range supported by the router. For details, see "TCP/IPv4 Configuration" in Chapter 16, "Networking."

Even if you don't want to disable DHCP, you will probably want to adjust the number of IP addresses that the WAP or wireless router will assign. A good rule of thumb is to configure the router to assign the number of addresses equal to the number of clients that will connect to the router at any one time. If additional portable clients connect from time to time, add those to the number. In many cases, the result is that you will need to greatly reduce the default number of DHCP addresses the router is configured to provide.

Figure 10-1 illustrates a typical wireless router's DHCP configuration dialog.

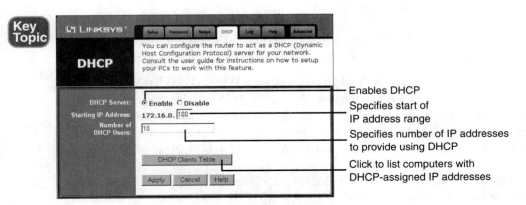

Figure 10-1 Specifying a range of IP addresses for DHCP on a Linksys router.

Changing the SSID

The Service Set Identifier (SSID) can provide a great deal of useful information to a potential hacker of a wireless network. All wireless networks must have an SSID, and by default, WAPs and wireless routers typically use the manufacturer's name or the device's model number as the default SSID. If a default SSID is broadcast by a wireless network, a hacker can look up the documentation for a specific router or the most common models of a particular brand and determine the default IP address range, the default administrator user name and password, and other information that would make it easy to attack the network.

To help "hide" the details of your network and location, a replacement SSID for a secure wireless network should *not* include any of the following:

- Your name

- Your company name

- Your location

- Any other easily identifiable information

An SSID that includes a sports team popular in the area or obscure information (such as the name of your first pet) would be a suitable replacement.

Figure 10-2 shows a typical WAP or wireless router Basic Setup dialog that includes this and other configuration options discussed later in this chapter.

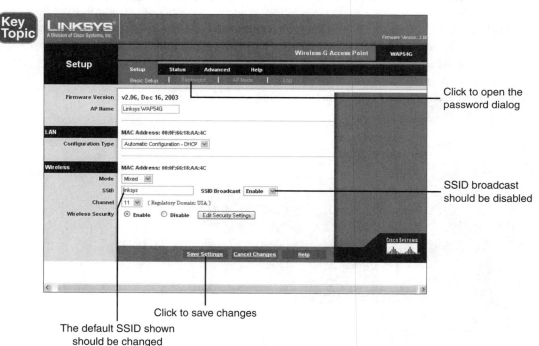

Figure 10-2   Preparing to change the default wireless settings on a Linksys router.

Disabling SSID Broadcast

In addition to changing the default SSID for a WAP or wireless router, you can disable SSID broadcast. This is widely believed to be an effective way to prevent your wireless network from being detected, and is so regarded by the A+ Certification exams (see Figure 10-2 for a typical dialog).

CAUTION   Although disabling SSID broadcast will prevent casual bandwidth snoopers from finding your wireless network, Microsoft does *not* recommend disabling SSID broadcasting as a security measure. According to a TechNet white paper, "Non-broadcast Wireless Networks with Microsoft Windows," available at http://technet.microsoft.com, wireless client systems running Windows XP transmit ("advertise") the names of non-broadcast (also known as hidden) wireless networks they are configured to connect to. This information can be used by wireless network hacking programs to help launch an attack against the network.

MAC Address Filtering

Every network adapter—whether it's built in to a PC, an add-on card, or built in to a specialized device such as a media adapter or a networked printer—has a unique identification known as the media access control address or MAC address. The MAC address (sometimes known as the physical address) is a list of six two-digit hexadecimal numbers (0–9, A–F). The MAC address is usually found on a label on the side of the network adapter, as shown in Figure 10-3. Depending on the device, the MAC address might be labeled MAC, MAC address, or ID No. Many devices that have integrated network adapters also list their MAC address on a label. Note that MAC addresses are sometimes listed as 12 digits rather than in six groups of 2 digits.

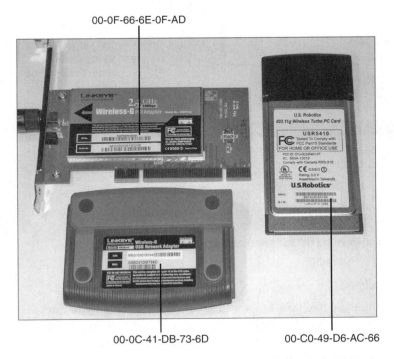

Figure 10-3   Typical locations for MAC addresses on wireless adapters.

To determine the MAC address for an adapter that is already installed in a PC, or the MAC address for an integrated adapter for a system running Windows 2000, Windows XP, Windows Vista, or Windows 7, run the Ipconfig.exe command with the /all switch: **ipconfig /all**. The physical address (MAC address) is listed for each adapter in the computer (see Figure 10-4).

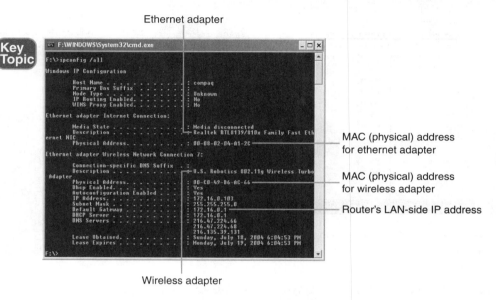

Figure 10-4   Using **ipconfig /all** to determine MAC addresses for installed network adapters.

With most wireless routers and WAPs, you can specify the MAC addresses of devices on your network (see Figure 10-5). Only these devices can access your network; some routers can also be configured to block a list of specified MAC addresses from accessing the network.

MAC address filtering can be a useful way to block casual hackers from gaining access to a wireless (or wired) network. However, keep in mind that it is possible to use software to change the MAC address of a network device (a feature sometimes referred to as MAC address cloning), and that MAC addresses are not encrypted and can be detected by software used to hack networks. Thus, MAC address filtering alone should not be relied upon to stop serious attacks.

Changing Default Administrator User Password

As mentioned previously, the documentation for almost all WAPs and wireless routers lists the default administrator password, and the documentation can be readily downloaded in PDF or HTML form from the vendors' websites. Because an attacker could use this information to "take over" the device, it's a very good idea to change the default.

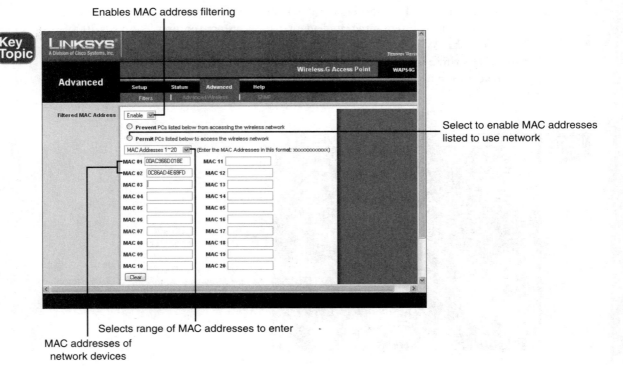

Figure 10-5   Configuring a Linksys WAP54G WAP to use MAC address filtering.

Most routers use the Administration or Management dialog for the password and other security settings.

TIP   To further secure the router or WAP, configure the device so it can be managed only with a wired Ethernet connection.

Updating Access Point Firmware

Most vendors issue firmware updates for each model of WAP and wireless router. These updates solve operational problems and might add features that enhance Wi-Fi interoperability, security, and ease of use. To determine whether a WAP or wireless router has a firmware update available, follow these steps:

Step 1.   View the device's configuration dialogs to see the current firmware version (see Figure 10-4).

Step 2.   Visit the device vendor's website to see if a newer version of the firmware is available. Note that you must know the model number and revision of the device. To find this information, look on the rear or bottom of the device.

Step 3.   Download the firmware update to a PC that can be connected to the device with an Ethernet cable.

Step 4.   Connect the PC to the device with an Ethernet cable.

Step 5.   Navigate to the device's firmware update dialog.

Step 6.   Follow instructions to update the firmware.

Firewall Features

By default, most WAPs and wireless routers use a feature called Network Address Translation (NAT) to act as a simple firewall. NAT prevents traffic from the Internet from determining the private IP addresses used by computers on the network. However, many WAPs and wireless routers offer additional firewall features that can be enabled, including

- Access logs

- Filtering of specific types of traffic

- Enhanced support for VPNs

See the router documentation for more information about advanced security features.

Data and Physical Security

Even if the computer network is secure, a PC and its information is not completely secure if data and physical security issues are overlooked. The following sections help you understand how to ensure that these potential security risks are dealt with properly.

Data Access Local Security Policy

The Local Security Policy window provides access to a variety of policies that can be used to protect data residing on the system. In Windows 7/Vista/XP/2000 this can be accessed by navigating to the **Start** menu and then choosing **Control Panel**. Verify that you are in Classic view (known in Windows 7 as Large Icons or Small Icons), double-click **Administrative Tools**, and then double-click **Local Security Policy**. Alternatively, you can press **Windows+R** to open the **Run** prompt, and type **secpol.msc**.

These policies include:

- **Enable auditing**—Open the Local Policies section of the Security Settings dialog, click Audit Policy, and change the policies listed from No Auditing (default) to auditing success and failure. To audit user access to files, folders, and printers, make sure Audit Object Access is configured to audit Success and Failure to access; to specify a file, folder, or printer to audit, use the object's Auditing tab (located in the Advanced dialog of the object's Security tab). For details, see Microsoft Help and Support article 310399 at http://support.microsoft.com/.

This function is available on Windows XP only if Simple File Sharing is disabled. Success and Failure information is stored in the Event Viewer's Security logfile.

■ **Shutdown: Clear Virtual Memory Pagefile**—The pagefile might store passwords and user information. By enabling this option, you can prevent this information from being used to compromise the system.

■ **Take ownership of files or other objects**—This setting is located in Security Settings, Local Policies, User Rights Assignments. By default, this is set to the Administrators group, but to reduce the chance of ownership changes by unauthorized persons, modify this to just one account, for example the primary account on the computer.

■ **Turn on Ctrl+Alt+Del**—The actual name of this policy is "Interactive logon: Do not require Ctrl+Alt+Del." By disabling this policy, the actual Ctrl+Alt+Del screen will appear before logging in, a valuable security feature that can deter would-be hackers from getting into the system and accessing its data.

TIP   For other security settings, see the Windows XP security checklists at LabMice.net (http://labmice.techtarget.com/articles/winxpsecuritychecklist.htm) and the Computer Protection Program at the Berkeley Lab (http://www.lbl.gov/cyber/systems/wxp-security-checklist.html).

Encryption Technologies

Microsoft includes two types of built-in encryption with some of their versions of Windows. The Encrypting File System (dependent on an NTFS-formatted volume) is used to encrypt individual files and folders. BitLocker is used to encrypt an entire disk.

Encrypting File System

Windows 2000, Windows XP Professional, and certain Windows Vista and Windows 7 editions (Windows Vista Business, Enterprise, and Ultimate; Windows 7 Professional, Enterprise, and Ultimate) all include support for EFS (Encrypting File System). EFS can be used to protect sensitive data files and temporary files, and can be applied to individual files or folders (when applied to folders, all files in an encrypted folder are also encrypted).

EFS files can be opened only by the user who encrypted them, by an administrator, or by EFS keyholders (users who have been provided with the EFS certificate key for another user's account). Thus, they are protected against access by hackers.

Files encrypted with EFS are listed with green filenames when viewed in Windows Explorer or My Computer (Windows XP) or Computer (Windows 7/Vista). Only files stored on a drive that used the NTFS file system can be encrypted.

To encrypt a file, follow this process:

Step 1.   Right-click the file in Windows Explorer or My Computer or Computer and select **Properties**.

Step 2.   Click the **Advanced** button on the General tab.

Step 3.   Click the empty Encrypt contents to secure data checkbox.

Step 4.   Click **OK**.

Step 5.   Click **Apply**. When prompted, select the option to encrypt the file and parent folder or only the file as desired and click **OK**.

Step 6.   Click **OK** to close the properties sheet.

To decrypt the file, follow the same procedure, but clear the Encrypt contents to secure data checkbox in Step 3.

NOTE   To enable the recovery of EFS encrypted files in the event that Windows cannot start, you should export the user's EFS certificate key. For details, see the Microsoft TechNet article Data Recovery and Encrypting File System (EFS) at http://technet.microsoft.com/en-us/library/cc512680.aspx.

BitLocker Encryption

To encrypt an entire disk, you will need some kind of full disk encryption software. There are several currently available on the market; one developed by Microsoft for Windows Vista and Windows 7 is called *BitLocker*—available only on the Ultimate and Enterprise editions. This software can encrypt the entire disk which, after complete, is transparent to the user. However, there are some requirements for this including:

■   A Trusted Platform Module (TPM): a chip residing on the motherboard that actually stores the encrypted keys.

or

■   An external USB key to store the encrypted keys. Using BitLocker without a TPM requires changes to Group Policy settings.

and

■   A hard drive with two volumes, preferably created during the installation of Windows. One volume is for the operating system (most likely C:) which will be encrypted, the other is the active volume that remains unencrypted so that the computer can boot. If a second volume needs to be created, the BitLocker Drive Preparation Tool can be of assistance and can be downloaded from Windows Update.

BitLocker software is based on the Advanced Encryption Standard (AES) and uses a 128-bit encryption key.

Starting with Windows Vista SP1, BitLocker can be used to encrypt internal hard disk volumes other than the system drive. For example, if a hard disk is partitioned as C: and D: drives, BitLocker could encrypt both drives.

In Windows 7, BitLocker functionality is extended to external USB drives (including flash drives) with BitLocker To Go. Windows 7 also simplifies BitLocker and BitLocker To Go configuration: simply right-click a drive and select Enable Bit-Locker to start the encryption process. During the process, you are prompted to specify a password or a SmartCard for credentials to access the drive's contents.

To enable access to the contents of BitLocker To Go USB drives on Windows Vista and Windows XP, Microsoft now offers the BitLocker To Go Reader. Download it from the Microsoft website.

Backups

Securing backups prevents them from being misused by unauthorized users. Some backup applications include an option to password-protect the backup files so they can be restored only if the user provides the correct password. If you use a backup program that does not support password protection (such as Windows 2000 and XP's integrated NTBackup.exe or Windows Vista's and Windows 7's Windows Backup), you must physically secure the backup media or drive to prevent it from access by unauthorized users.

Data Migration

The process of migrating data from one system to another, such as during the re-placement of an old system by a new system, provides another potential security risk if the data migration is not performed in a secure manner.

If possible, perform the data migration with a direct network or USB connection between the old and new computers. If this is not possible, make sure you use a mi-gration program that can password protect the migration file. The Files and Set-tings Transfer Wizard in Windows XP and the Windows Easy Transfer program in Windows Vista and Windows 7 automatically provides a password after collecting information from the old computer. This password must be used on the new com-puter before the migration file can be accessed.

If you use other migration programs, check their documentation to determine whether and how password protection is provided.

Data and Data Remnant Removal

After data is migrated to the new computer, the old computer should be cleared of data or data remnants. If the computer will no longer be used, you can use a full-disk scrubbing program to wipe out the entire contents of the hard disk, including the operating system. For details, see the section "Hardware Recycling and Deconstruction," earlier in this chapter.

However, if the computer will still be in use with its current operating system, you can use software that overwrites only data files and "empty" disk space (no-longer-allocated disk space that might still contain recoverable files). Programs such as Microsoft Sysinternals SDelete, Norton Wipe Info (included as part of Norton System Works and Norton Utilities), McAfee Shredder (included in various McAfee programs), and others offer options to wipe files and folders, "empty" disk space, or an entire disk drive.

Password Management

PC users should use passwords to secure their user accounts. Through the local security policy and group policy in Windows, you can set up password policies that require users to do the following:

- Change passwords periodically (Local Policies, Security Options)

- Be informed in advance that passwords are about to expire (Account Policies, Password Policy)

- Enforce a minimum password length (Account Policies, Password Policy)

- Require complex passwords (Account Policies, Password Policy)

- Prevent old passwords from being reused continually (Account Policies, Password Policy)

- Wait a certain number of minutes after a specified number of unsuccessful logins has taken place before they can log in again (Account Policies, Account Lockout Policy)

To make these settings in Local Security Settings, open the Security Settings node and navigate to the appropriate subnodes (shown in parentheses in the preceding list). In Group Policy (gpedit.msc), navigate to

- **Computer Configuration, Windows Settings, Security Settings, Account Policies, Password Policy**

- **Computer Configuration, Windows Settings, Security Settings, Account Policies, Account Lockout Policy**

- **Computer Configuration, Windows Settings, Security Settings, Local Policies, Security Options** as appropriate

Locking a Workstation

You should lock your computer whenever you are not at the keyboard. The ability to lock the computer depends upon each user being assigned a password. You can use the following methods to lock a computer:

- To lock the computer automatically after the screen saver is enabled do the following, depending on which Windows operating system you are running:
    - In Windows XP/2000, select the **On Resume, Password Protect** check box. This option is located on the Display properties sheet's Screen Saver tab.
    - In Windows Vista and Windows 7, select the **On Resume, Display Logon Screen** check box. This option is located in the Screen Saver Settings window, which can be accessed from Control Panel, Personalization.

- To lock the computer immediately, press **Windows key+L** on your keyboard, or press **Ctrl+Alt+Del** and select **Lock Computer**.

To log back on to the computer, provide your username and password or password (if your user name is already displayed) when prompted.

Incident Reporting

In addition to enabling auditing of local security policy settings and checking the audit logs periodically, organizations should also set up and follow procedures for reporting security-related incidents. These could include the following:

- Repeated attempts to log into password-protected accounts

- Unlocked doors to areas that should be secure, such as computer or server rooms, backup media storage, or network wiring closets

- Unknown clients detected on wireless networks

- Viruses and malware detected on clients or servers

- Unauthorized access in the form of denial-of-service (DoS) and other malicious attacks, remote access Trojans (RATs), and the detection of unrecognized network sniffers

Organizations will have varying procedures when it comes to incident reporting. One common process for incident reporting and response includes the identification and containment of problems, and then evidence gathering and further investigation. Afterward, the process will usually include procedures for the eradication of threats and the recovery from them. Finally, documentation and monitoring procedures are common to attempt to avoid the same issues in the future.

Social Engineering

Social engineering is a term popularized by the career of successful computer and network hacker Kevin Mitnick, who used a variety of methods to convince computer users to provide access to restricted systems. Some of these methods include

- **Pretexting**—Pretending to be from the company's help desk, telephone, or Internet provider, or an authorized service company and asking the user to provide login credentials to enable routine maintenance to be performed or to solve an urgent computer problem.

- **Phishing**—Setting up bogus websites or sending fraudulent emails that trick users into providing personal, bank, or credit card information. A variation, phone phishing, uses an interactive voice response (IVR) system that the user has been tricked into calling to trick the user into revealing information.

- **Trojan horse**—Malware programs disguised as popular videos or website links that trap keystrokes or transmit sensitive information.

- **Baiting**—Leaving physical media (such as a CD, DVD, or USB drive) that appears to be confidential information lying around. The media autoruns when inserted and can deliver various types of malware, including backdoor access to a company's computer network.

Although antivirus and antiphishing programs and features in the latest web browsers can stop computer-based social engineering exploits, pretexting can only be stopped by users who refuse to be gulled into letting down their guard. Teach users to do the following:

- Ask for ID when approached in person by somebody claiming to be from "the help desk," "the phone company," or "the service company."

- Ask for a name and supervisor name when contacted by phone by someone claiming to be from "the help desk," "the phone company," or "the service company."

- Provide contact information for the help desk, phone company, or authorized service companies and ask users to call the authorized contact person to verify that the service call or phone request for information is legitimate.

- Log into systems themselves and then provide the tech the computer, rather than giving the tech login information.

- Change passwords immediately after service calls.

- Report any potential social engineering calls or in-person contacts, even if no information was exchanged. Social engineering experts can gather innocuous-sounding information from several users and use it to create a convincing story to gain access to restricted systems.

Access Control Purposes and Principles

Controlling access to files, folders, printers, and physical locations is essential for system and network security. The following sections discuss the purposes and principles of access control.

Operating System Access Control

Operating system access control in Windows 2000, XP, Vista, and 7 requires the use of the NTFS file system. To use access control in Windows XP Professional, the default Simple File Sharing setting must also be disabled.

User, Administration, and Guest Accounts

There are three standard account levels in Windows:

■ Limited (known as Standard user accounts in Windows Vista and Windows 7 and Restricted users in Windows 2000)—Limited accounts have permission to perform routine tasks. However, these accounts are blocked from performing tasks that involve system-wide changes, such as installing hardware or software. (Windows Vista and Windows 7 permit Standard user accounts to perform some UAC-restricted tasks, such as adding hardware, if they can provide an administrator password.)

■ Administrator—Users with an administrator can perform any and all tasks.

■ Guest—The guest account level is the most limited. A guest account cannot install software or hardware or run already-existing applications and cannot access files in shared document folders or the Guest profile. The Guest account is disabled by default. If it is enabled for a user to gain access to the computer, that access should be temporary, and the account should be disabled again when the user no longer requires access.

When a user is created using the Users applet in Windows, the user must be assigned a limited (Standard) or Administrator account. Guest accounts are used for visitors.

User Account Control (UAC)

User Account Control (UAC) is a security component of Windows Vista and Windows 7 that keeps every user (besides the actual Administrator account) in standard user mode instead of as an administrator with full administrative rights—even if they are a member of the administrators group. It is meant to prevent unauthorized access, as well as avoid user error in the form of accidental changes. With UAC enabled users perform common tasks as non-administrators, and when necessary, as administrators, without having to switch users, log off, or use Run As.

Basically, UAC was created with two goals in mind:

- To eliminate unnecessary requests for excessive administrative-level access to Windows resources

- To reduce the risk of malicious software using the administrator's access control to infect operating system files

When a standard end-user requires administrator privileges to perform certain tasks such as installing an application, a small popup UAC window will appear notifying the user that an administrator credential is necessary. If the user has administrative rights and clicks Continue, the task will be carried out, but if the user does not have sufficient rights, the attempt will fail. Note that these popup UAC windows will not appear if the person is logged on with the actual Administrator account.

In Windows Vista, turning UAC on and off can be done by going to **Start**, **Control Panel**, **User Accounts and Family Safety**. Then select **User Accounts**, and **Turn User Account Control On or Off**. From there, UAC can be turned on and off by checking or unchecking the box. If a change is made to UAC, the system will need to be restarted. Note that if you are using the Classic View in the Control Panel, User Accounts and Family Safety is bypassed.

In Windows 7, UAC offers a range of settings. To adjust UAC settings, go to Start, Control Panel, System and Security, Action Center. Then select Change User Account Control settings. The default setting, **Notify me only when programs try to make changes to my computer**, enables UAC to protect your computer against unauthorized change by programs. The **Always notify** option works similarly to the default UAC setting in Windows Vista, as it displays notifications when either the user or a program attempts to makes changes to the computer. The **Never notify** option, which turns off UAC notifications, works similarly to turning off UAC in Windows Vista. **The Notify me only when programs try to make changes to my computer (do not dim my desktop)** option should be used only if the computer takes a long time to dim the desktop and bring up the UAC prompt.

Groups

Users in Windows 2000, XP, Vista, and 7 can be assigned to different groups, each with different permissions. The Local Policy (local PCs) and Group Policy (networked PCs connected to a domain controller) settings can restrict PC features by group or by PC. Aside from the Administrator, User, and Guest groups (whose corresponding accounts were explained previously) there is one additional group you should know for the exam: the Power Users group. Power users have more permissions than standard users, but fewer permissions than administrators. Power users can install drivers, run non-certified programs, and in general modify computer-wide settings. Because of this, members of the Power Users group might be able to expose the computer to security risks such as running a Trojan horse program or executing a virus. Be especially careful which users are added to the Power Users and Administrators groups. Because the Power Users group can be a security risk, Microsoft has decreased the amount of "power" these users have in Windows Vista. For example, power users can no longer customize file associations the way they did in Windows XP. Windows 7 maintains support for the Power Users group only for compatibility with legacy applications. Power users on Windows Vista or Windows 7 may need to run some applications with the Run as Admin option and provide administrator credentials when prompted by UAC.

Permissions Actions, Types, and Levels

Permissions for folders, files, and printers are assigned via the Security tab of the object's properties sheet. Folder and file permissions vary by user type or group, and can include the following:

- **Full control**—Complete access to contents of file or folder. When Full Control is selected, all of the following are selected automatically.

- **Modify**—Change file or folder contents.

- **Read & Execute**—Access file or folder contents and run programs.

- **List Folder Contents**—Display folder contents.

- **Read**—Access a file or folder.

- **Write**—Add a new file or folder.

Each permission has two settings: Allow or Deny. Generally, if you want a user to have access to a folder, you would add them to the list and select **Allow** for the appropriate permission. If you don't want to allow them access, normally you simply wouldn't add them. But in some cases, an explicit Deny is necessary. This could be because the user is part of a larger group that already has access to a parent folder, but you don't want the specific user to have access to this particular subfolder. This leads us to permission inheritance.

Permission Inheritance and Propagation

If you create a folder, the default action it takes is to inherit permissions from the parent folder. So any permissions that you set in the parent will be inherited by the subfolder. To view an example of this, locate any folder within an NTFS volume (besides the root folder), right-click it and select **Properties**, access the Security tab, and click the **Advanced** button. Here you will see an enabled checkbox named **Inherit from Parent the Permission Entries** that apply to Child Objects toward the bottom of the window. This means that any permissions added or removed in the parent folder will also be added or removed in the current folder. In addition, those permissions that are being inherited cannot be modified in the current folder. To make modifications to the permissions you would need to deselect the **Inherit from Parent the Permission Entries** that apply to Child Objects checkbox. When you do so, you have the option to copy the permissions from the parent to the current folder or remove them entirely. So by default, the parent is automatically propagating permissions to the subfolder, and the subfolder is inheriting its permissions from the parent.

You can also propagate permission changes to subfolders that are not inheriting from the current folder. To do so, select the **Replace Permission Entries on All Child Objects** with entries shown here that apply to Child Objects checkbox. This might all seem a bit confusing; just remember that folders automatically inherit from the parent unless you turn inheriting off—and you can propagate permission entries to subfolders at any time by selecting the **Replace** option.

Moving and Copying Folders and Files

Moving and copying folders will have different results when it comes to permissions. Basically, it breaks down like this:

■ If you *copy* a folder on the same, or to a different volume, the folder inherits the permissions of the parent folder it was copied to (target directory).

■ If you *move* a folder to a different location on the same volume, the folder retains its original permissions.

Components

Use the Security tab on a printer's properties sheet to restrict access to the printer. To restrict access to other components, such as CD or DVD drives, use Local Policy or Group Policy settings.

Restricted Spaces

To this may simply be referred to as prevent users from accessing restricted spaces, such as computer or server rooms or LAN wiring closets, use physical access restriction devices, such as smart cards or key fobs.

Auditing and Event Logging

Windows 2000, XP, Vista, and 7 all support auditing and event logging, both of which enable you to find out what issues affecting security might be taking place on a particular computer.

Event logs are enabled by default, while auditing of files, folders, and printers must be enabled by the system administrator. When auditing is enabled, success and failure entries for audited devices are stored in the Security log.

To view event logs in these versions of Windows, follow these steps:

Step 1.   Right-click **My Computer** (2000, XP) or **Computer** (Vista, 7) and select **Manage**. The Computer Management console opens.

Step 2.   Expand the Event Viewer node. In Windows 2000, Windows XP, and Windows Vista, it contains four subnodes: Application, Internet Explorer, Security, System. In Windows Vista and Windows 7, click the Windows Logs subnode to see these subnodes; these versions of Windows also include a Forwarded Events subnode.

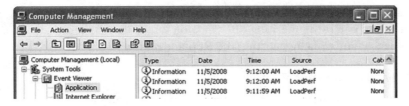

Figure 10-6   Viewing the Application Event Log.

Step 3.   Select the desired node to see events (see Figure 10-6).

Step 4.   To view details of a particular event, double-click the event (see Figure 10-7).

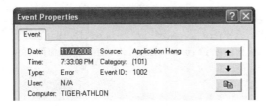

Figure 10-7   Viewing the details of an application hang in the Application Event log.

To enable auditing, see the section "Data Access Local Security Policy," earlier in this chapter.

Periodically, event logs should be cleared. Before clearing these logs, you might want to archive their contents. For details, see Microsoft Help and Support article 308427 at http://support.microsoft.com. To learn how to archive event logs in Windows XP, see Microsoft Help and Support article 308427 at http://support.microsoft.com. To archive event logs in Windows Vista or 7, click **Save All Events As** and select the appropriate format for your needs (Event files, XML files, tab delimited text, or CSV text).

Installing, Configuring, and Troubleshooting Security Features

The following sections help you understand how to set up and configure major security features.

BIOS Security Features

Several common BIOS features can be used to help prevent unauthorized access to the computer. These include

- **Boot sector virus protection**—Enable this feature to prevent boot sector viruses and malware from infecting the system hard disk.

- **Boot sequence**—Place the system hard disk first in the boot order to prevent unauthorized users from booting from a floppy disk, CD, DVD, or USB device.

- **BIOS setup password**—Enable this feature to prevent unauthorized users from altering BIOS setup information.

NOTE   In the event that the setup password is mislaid, the CMOS chip used to store BIOS settings can be reset with a jumper on the motherboard, or by removing the battery for several minutes.

- **BIOS HDD Password**—On a semi-related note, many laptops come equipped with *drive lock* technology; an HDD password. If enabled, it prompts the user to enter a password for the hard drive when the computer is first booted. If the user of the computer doesn't know the password for the hard drive, the drive will lock and the OS will not boot. An eight digit or similar hard drive ID usually associates the laptop with the hard drive that is installed. On most systems this password is clear by default, but if the password is set and forgotten, it can usually be reset within the BIOS. Some laptops come with documentation clearly stating the BIOS and drive lock passwords.

If you are unable to boot from CD, DVD, USB device, or floppy disk to perform PC maintenance or troubleshooting, change the boot sequence to place removable media earlier in the boot order than the system hard disk.

If the BIOS setup program is protected by a password and the password is lost, you can clear the password on most desktop systems by using the BIOS clear jumper on the motherboard or by removing the battery for several seconds.

> **CAUTION** Some laptops use the password to permanently restrict access to only the password holder. In such cases, the password cannot be bypassed. See the documentation for your laptop or portable system before applying a BIOS password to determine whether this is the case.

For details, see Chapter 4, "BIOS."

Software Firewalls

Software firewalls, such as the firewalls incorporated in Windows XP SP2 and SP3, Windows Vista, and Windows 7, can be configured to permit specified applications to pass through the firewall, to open specific ports needed by applications, or to block all traffic. Whenever possible, it's easier to permit traffic by application rather than by UDP or TCP port numbers.

To enable the Windows Firewall in Windows XP SP2/SP3 while permitting exceptions, click **On** (recommended) and leave the Don't Allow Exceptions checkbox cleared (see Figure 10-8). To block all incoming traffic (recommended when the computer is used in a public location, such as a hotel or restaurant), click the **Don't Allow Exceptions** checkbox.

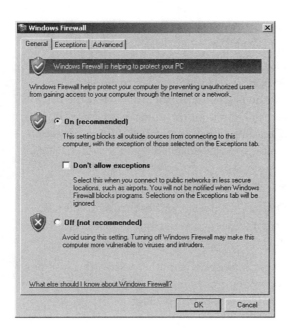

Figure 10-8 The Windows Firewall's General tab (Windows XP).

To enable the Windows Firewall in Windows Vista or Windows 7 while permitting exceptions, select **Home** (Vista, 7), **Work** (7), or **Office** (Vista) network locations when prompted after setting up a new network connection. The location setting also can be changed with the Network and Sharing Center. To configure the Windows Firewall for **Don't Allow Exceptions**, select the network location as **Public Network**. Figure 10-9 shows the Set Network Location dialog used by Windows 7 (Windows Vista's is similar).

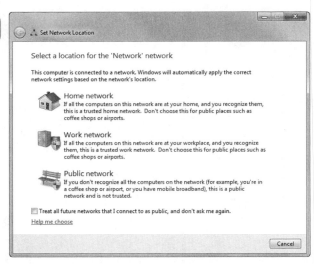

Figure 10-9   Setting a network location in Windows 7 (shown) or Windows Vista configures the Windows Firewall.

Turn off the Windows Firewall only if directed by an installer program, or if you prefer to use a third-party firewall.

Configuring Exceptions

In Windows XP SP2/SP3, click the **Exceptions** tab to view programs that are permitted to access your computer (checked programs). To access the tabbed Windows Firewall interface in Windows Vista, click the **Change Settings** link. You can then click the **Exceptions** tab to see checked programs.

With either version of Windows, click **Add Program** to add a program, or **Add Port** to add a TCP or UDP port number to the list of Exceptions.

To revoke an exception temporarily, clear the checkbox. To remove the program or port from the list of Exceptions, select the program or port and click **Delete**. Use **Edit** (Windows XP only) to change the program, port number or scope (list of IP addresses) for the selected item. In Windows 7, click **Allow a program or feature through Windows Firewall** to view checked programs. Windows 7's version of Windows Firewall provides separate settings for Home/Work and Public networks (see Figure 10-10).

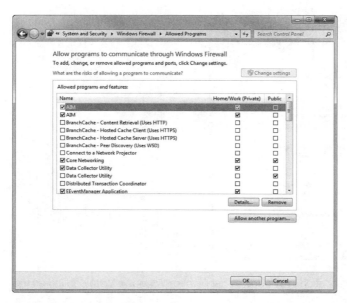

Figure 10-10   Windows 7 provides separate settings for allowed programs based on the network location.

In Windows XP SP2/SP3 and Windows Vista, use the Advanced tab (see Figure 10-11) to specify which connections are protected by Windows Firewall, to set up a security log, to set up ICMP for messaging between networked computers, and to reset Windows Firewall's defaults.

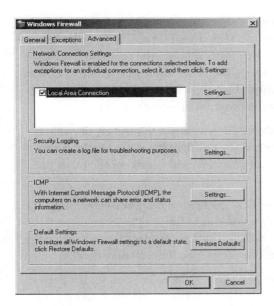

Figure 10-11   The Windows Firewall's Advanced tab (Windows XP).

In Windows 7, the **Advanced settings** link opens a dialog that enables Windows Firewall to be configured to block unauthorized outbound as well as inbound traffic and to use user-defined firewall rules.

Troubleshooting Software Firewalls

If users are unable to connect to shared folders on your system, or if you are unable to use programs that require inbound connections, you might have one of the following situations:

- **Your firewall is configured to block all connections (No exceptions setting)—** In Windows XP, turn the Windows Firewall on but clear the **No exceptions** checkbox. In Windows Vista and Windows 7, select the **Home, Work**, or **Office** network location as appropriate.

- **A Windows Firewall is blocking x program dialog has appeared—**Click **Unblock** to permit the program access to your system.

- **Your firewall does not have an exception set up for the program—**With the Windows Firewall in Windows XP and Windows Vista, open the **Exceptions** dialog and make sure the program that is being blocked is listed and is checked. Click an empty checkbox to reenable an exception. Use **Add Program** to add the program. To enable Windows Firewall to permit access to your computer's shared files and printers, File and Printer Sharing must be on the Exceptions list and the exception must be enabled. In Windows 7, click the **Allow a Program or Feature Through Windows Firewall** task, click **Change Settings**, and click **Allow Another Program**. Choose the program from the list of programs, or use **Browse** to locate the program manually, and click **Add**. Use the **Allow a Program or Feature Through Windows Firewall** to specify which network locations will allow the program or feature to run.

■ **You might have two firewalls (Windows Firewall and a third-party firewall, or two third-party firewalls) running and one or both of them are blocking connections**—Turn off one of the firewall programs and configure the other one properly.

■ **You did not open the correct TCP or UDP ports for a program**—Generally, it's easier to set up exceptions by adding a program. However, in some cases, you might need to use Add Port to set up the exceptions needed. Be sure to specify each of the port numbers and the correct port type for each port number.

Ports are usually the culprit when it comes to firewall troubleshooting. If a person cannot ping your computer, yet you can access the network and the Internet, and people need to access your system remotely, consider checking the ports of your firewall.

Wireless Network Configuration

After configuring a WAP or wireless router to provide WEP, WPA, or (preferably) WPA2 encryption, you must configure wireless clients with the same encryption information. You can set up clients manually or automatically. Note that each wireless client connecting to a WAP or wireless router must use the same encryption standard and passphrase and specify the SSID used by the WAP or wireless router.

You can configure a client in the following ways:

■ Use Microsoft Connect Now. This technology, supported by most recent WAPs and wireless routers, enables Windows to set up clients automatically.

■ Create a USB flash drive that includes configuration information on one computer, and use it to set up other clients.

■ Configure each client manually.

The following sections describe in more detail the steps to configure a wireless client in Windows XP, Windows Vista, and Windows 7.

Configuring a Wireless Client with Windows XP SP2/SP3

Windows XP SP2 and SP3 include a Wireless Network Setup wizard. This wizard can be used to set up a brand new wireless network or to add a client to an existing wireless network. To run the wizard, in Windows XP SP2/SP3 follow this procedure:

Step 1.   Click **Start**, **All Programs**, **Accessories**, **Communications**, **Wireless Networking** wizard. At the introductory screen, click **Next** to continue.

Step 2.   In the Create a Name for Your Wireless Network dialog (see Figure 10-12), enter the service set identifier (SSID) you want to use for your network. You can create an SSID up to 32 characters.

Step 3.   Select whether you want to automatically assign a network key (default) or manually assign a network key. Use the manual option if you are adding your system to an existing network. If you use the manual option, you will be prompted to enter your wireless network's existing WEP or WPA key later (see Step 6).

Step 4.   By default, the wizard uses WEP encryption; to use WPA encryption, click the **Use WPA Encryption** check box. Click Next to continue. Note that you will see an error dialog onscreen if your network hardware is already connected to your system and it does not support WPA. Click **OK** to continue.

Step 5.   If you select the default "automatic" option shown in Figure 10-12, you can select from two options to save your settings: a USB flash (keychain) drive or manual network setup. The USB flash memory drive option can be used by any devices that support Microsoft Connect Now. Such devices automatically read the XML-format network setup files from the USB flash memory drive when the drive is connected to the device.

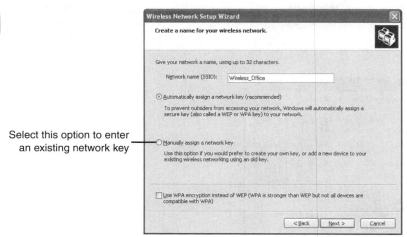

Select this option to enter an existing network key

Figure 10-12   Creating an SSID and selecting network encryption with the Windows XP SP2 Wireless Network Setup Wizard.

Step 6.   If you select the option to enter a network key yourself, you will see the dialog shown in Figure 10-13. Enter the network key and then reenter it. Click **Next** to continue.

Figure 10-13   Entering a WEP key manually with the Windows XP Wireless Network Setup Wizard.

Step 7.   On the following screen, select the option to store the network settings to a USB flash drive or to configure the network manually.

Step 8.   If you selected the option to store the network settings on a USB flash drive, insert the drive when prompted. Click **Next**. A dialog displays the setup files as they are transferred to the flash drive.

Step 9.   Follow the instructions shown in Figure 10-14 to transfer the settings from the USB flash drive to your wireless access point (or router) and other network client PCs and devices. Click **Next** to continue.

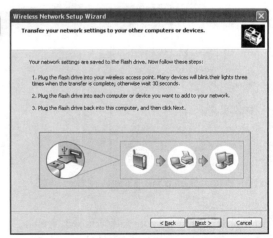

Figure 10-14   How to transfer settings to other computers and devices.

Step 10. At the end of the process, the wizard displays a "completed successfully" dialog. If you transferred settings to other devices using the USB flash memory drive (Step 9), the devices are listed by name.

Step 11. Click the **Print Network Settings** button to open the settings in Notepad (see Figure 10-15).

Step 12. Click **File**, **Save As** and name the file to create a backup of your settings, or click **File**, **Print** to make a printout that you can use to manually enter the settings on your wireless access point, router, or other network clients.

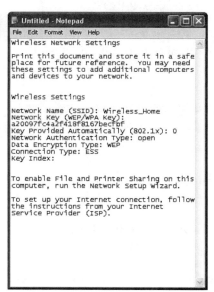

Figure 10-15   Using Notepad to view, save, or print your settings.

Configuring a Wireless Client with Windows Vista

The wireless client configuration process in Windows Vista is performed when you connect to a wireless network. Follow these steps:

Step 1. Click Start, Control Panel, Connect to the Internet.

Step 2. Select the network you want to connect to.

Step 3. Click Connect.

Step 4.   If you selected a secured network in Step 2, enter the security key (passphrase) when prompted. If you selected an unnamed network (a network that does not broadcast its SSID), enter the SSID when prompted.

Step 5.   To save the network for reuse, make sure the Save This Network checkbox is checked. To connect automatically when the network is in range, make sure the Start This Connection Automatically checkbox is checked. To disable either feature, clear the checkbox.

Step 6.   Click Next to start the connection.

Step 7.   Click Browse the Internet Now to open your web browser.

Step 8.   Click Close to close the wizard.

Step 9.   When prompted, select the network location (Home, Office, Public) to set up the Windows Firewall.

> **NOTE**   Connections marked with the Windows security shield are unsecured.

Configuring a Wireless Client with Windows 7

The wireless client configuration process in Windows 7 is performed when you connect to a wireless network. Follow these steps:

Step 1.   Click **Start, Control Panel, View Network Status and Tasks.**

Step 2.   Click **Connect to a Network**.

Step 3.   A list of wireless networks appears. Select the network you want to connect to.

Step 4.   To save the network for reuse, make sure the Connect Automatically box is checked.

Step 5.   Click **Connect** (see Figure 10-16).

Step 6.   If you selected a secured network in Step 3, enter the security key (passphrase) when prompted. If you selected Other Network (a network that does not broadcast its SSID), enter the SSID when prompted.

Step 7.   If prompted, click **Additional Log On Information May Be Required**. When your browser opens, provide the authorization needed.

Step 8.   When prompted, select the network location (Home, Work, Public) to set up the Windows Firewall.

> **NOTE**   If you need to set up a wireless router with Windows 7, open the Network and Sharing Center and select Set Up a New Connection or Network. With Windows Vista, open the Network and Sharing Center and select Set Up a Connection or Network.

Figure 10-16   Connecting to an unsecured wireless network in Windows 7.

Troubleshooting Wireless Clients

If you are unable to connect to a wireless network, check the following settings:

- **You might have selected the wrong SSID from the list of available wireless networks**—If you did not change the default SSID for your WAP or wireless router to a custom name, you might be trying to connect to the wrong wireless network. If you are entering the SSID for a non-broadcast network, double-check your spelling, punctuation, and capitalization.

- **If the network is encrypted, you might have selected the wrong encryption type or entered the wrong passphrase**—Be sure to select the same encryption type and enter the same passphrase as those used on the WAP or wireless router. This step is not necessary when using WCN-based routers in Windows Vista SP2 or Windows 7.

- **If you are connecting directly to another wireless device using an ad-hoc connection with Windows XP, you might have specified the wrong channel**—Both devices in an ad-hoc connection must use the same channel. Windows Vista and Windows 7 automatically determine the correct channel for ad-hoc connections.

- **If you have not connected to the network before and you are not using a dual-channel (2.4GHz and 5GHz) wireless adapter, you might not have the correct adapter for the network**—This is much more likely if you have an 802.11a (5GHz) wireless adapter, as there are relatively few wireless networks using this standard.

- **If you have not connected to an 802.11g network before and you are using an 802.11b wireless adapter, the network might be configured to permit only 802.11g clients**—To permit both 802.11b and 802.11g clients to connect to an 802.11g network, configure the network security to use WEP and make sure the network is set as mixed rather than G-only. See the router or WAP documentation for details.

Unused Wireless Connections

As you make connections to wireless networks, Windows XP, Windows Vista, and Windows 7 can store the connections for reuse. Periodically, you should review this list of connections and delete connections you no longer need. By removing unused connections, you prevent your system from connecting to wireless networks that might not be secure.

To view the list of stored connections in Windows XP, follow these steps:

Step 1.   Open **My Network Places**.

Step 2.   Click **View Network Connections** in the Network Tasks pane.

Step 3.   Right-click your wireless network connection and select **Properties**.

Step 4.   Click the **Wireless Networks** tab. Your connections are listed.

Step 5.   To delete an unused connection, select it and click **Remove** (see Figure 10-17).

Step 6.   Repeat Step 5 until you have deleted all of the unused connections you no longer need.

Step 7.   Click **OK** to close the dialog.

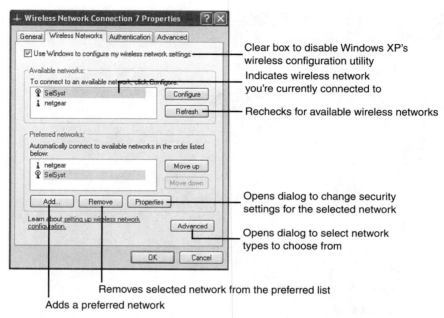

Figure 10-17 Windows XP's Wireless Networks dialog lists the connections you have made to various networks.

To view the list of stored connections in Windows Vista or Windows 7, follow these steps:

Step 1. Open **Control Panel**.

Step 2. Click **Network and Internet**.

Step 3. Open **Network and Sharing Center**.

Step 4. Click **Manage Wireless Networks** in the Tasks pane. Your connections are listed.

Step 5. To delete an unused connection, select it and click **Remove** (see Figure 10-18).

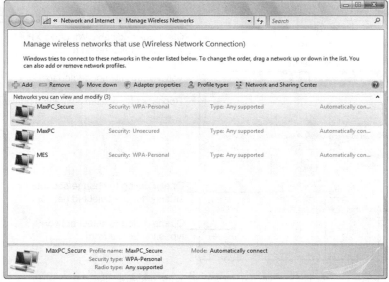

Figure 10-18   Windows Vista's Wireless Networks dialog lists the connections you have made to various networks.

Step 6.   Repeat Step 5 until you have deleted all of the unused connections you no longer need.

Step 7.   Click the Close button (red X) to close the dialog.

File Systems (Converting From FAT32 To NTFS)

Windows 2000 and Windows XP can be installed on either FAT32 or NTFS file systems. However, the FAT32 file system lacks the security and user/group permissions features of NTFS. Windows Vista and Windows 7 can only be installed on NTFS file systems. In addition, the scheduled backup feature in these operating systems requires the use of a backup location formatted as NTFS.

To convert a FAT32 drive to NTFS so you can use NTFS's security and user/group permissions features, use the command-line Convert.exe program:

Step 1.   Click **Start, Run**.

Step 2.   Enter **cmd.exe** and click **OK** to open a Windows command prompt session.

Step 3.   To convert drive C:, enter **convert c: /fs:ntfs.**

Malicious Software Protection

Windows XP, Windows Vista, and Windows 7 include Windows Defender, which provides real-time and scan-based protection against malware types such as Trojan horses and worms. However, for complete protection, you also need to install an antivirus program.

To determine whether antivirus, anti-malware, and firewall programs are running properly and are up to date with Windows XP or Windows Vista, open the Security Center in Control Panel (see Figure 10-19). It reports the status of both Microsoft and third-party security programs.

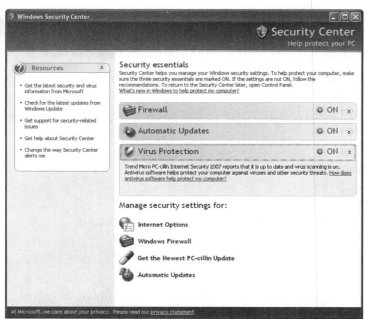

Figure 10-19   The Windows XP Security Center.

TIP   When you install third-party security programs that support Security Center, you will be asked if you want Security Center or the third-party security program to report potentially dangerous conditions. To avoid duplicate warnings, select the option to use Security Center to provide warnings.

Windows 7 replaces Security Center with Action Center, which also monitors maintenance activities such as Defrag. Open Action Center to determine the status of antivirus, anti-malware, and firewall programs.

Types of Malware and Infection Methods

Malware types and infection methods you should understand for the A+ Certification exams include

- **Trojan horse**—Programs that purport to be useful utilities or file converters, but actually install various types of harmful programs on your computer, including spyware, remote access, and rootkits.

- **Rootkits**—A concealment method used by many types of malware to prevent detection by normal antivirus and anti-malware programs.

- **Spyware**—Software that spies on system activities and transmits details of Web searches or other activities to remote computers.

- **Remote access**—Programs that enable unauthorized control of your system; can be used to set up networks of compromised computers known as botnets.

- **Adware**—Software that displays popup ads and banners related to your Web searches and activities.

- **Grayware**—General term for dialers, joke programs, adware, and spyware programs.

Training Users in Malware Protection

Users should be educated in how to do the following:

- Keep antivirus, antispyware, and anti-malware programs updated

- Scan systems for viruses, spyware, and malware

- Understand major malware types and techniques

- Scan removable-media drives (CDs, DVDs, USB drives, and floppy disks) for viruses and malware

- Configure scanning programs for scheduled operation

- Respond to notifications when viruses, spyware, or malware have been detected

- Quarantine suspect files

- Report suspect files to the help desk and to the software vendor

- Removal of malware

- Disable antivirus when needed (such as during software installations) and to know when to reenable antivirus

- Use antiphishing features in web browsers and email clients

Exam Preparation Tasks

Review All the Key Topics

Review the most important topics in the chapter, noted with the key topics icon in the outer margin of the page. Table 10-2 lists a reference of these key topics and the page numbers on which each is found.

Table 10-2   Key Topics for Chapter 10

Key Topic Element	Description	Page Number
Figure 10-1	Specifying a range of IP addresses for DHCP on a Linksys router.	400
Figure 10-2	Preparing to change the default wireless settings on a Linksys router.	401
Figure 10-4	Using `ipconfig /all` to determine MAC addresses for installed network adapters.	403
Figure 10-5	Configuring a Linksys WAP54G WAP to use MAC address filtering.	404
Figure 10-9	The Windows Firewall's Exceptions tab (Windows XP).	419
Figures 10-12–10-15	Wireless networking wizard step-by-step explanation including four figures.	423-425
Figure 10-18	The Windows XP Security Center.	430

Definitions of Key Terms

Define the following key terms from this chapter, and check your answers in the glossary.

Biometrics, Virus, Malware, Firewall, WAP, WEP, WPA, SSID, EFS, UAC

Troubleshooting Scenario

You are called to a customer's computer. They are complaining of pop-up messages and they are being redirected to websites that they do not want to go to. You must fix this problem as soon as possible. What would you need to do to get the computer back up and running?

Refer to Appendix A, "Answers to the 'Do I Know This Already?' Quizzes and Troubleshooting Scenarios," for the answer.

This chapter covers the following subjects:

- **Printing Fundamentals**—This section describes the basics of laser, inkjet, impact, and thermal printers.

- **Printer and Scanner Control**—This section briefly describes how drivers and firmware affect the behavior of printers and scanners.

- **Print Processes**—This section explains the steps involved when printers actually print, including the six-step laser printing process.

- **Interface Types**—This section describes the different ways of connecting a printer to a computer or to the network using such options as USB, parallel port, wired to the network, wireless networking, and Bluetooth.

- **Printer Installation**—This section demonstrates how to install printers properly with step-by-step instructions.

- **Optimizing Printer Performance**—This section demonstrates how to set up tray switching and work with the print spooler. It also describes the different ways to orient paper.

- **Installing and Configuring Printer Upgrades**—This section explains how to install RAM into a printer and how to update the printer's firmware.

- **Printer Troubleshooting Tools and Techniques**—This last section describes how to gather information when troubleshooting printers, how to print test pages, how to use diagnostic tools, and how to define and isolate any problems such as print quality issues. It also covers how to employ preventative maintenance by using maintenance kits and how to clean the devices. Finally, this section shows the proper tools to use when working on printers.

This chapter covers a portion of the CompTIA A+ 220-701 objectives 1.11, 2.1, and 2.3, and CompTIA A+ 220-702 objective 1.5.

CHAPTER 11

Printers

Printers are important output devices, second only to video displays. They output hard copy versions of files stored on the computer, such as documents, spreadsheets, and web pages. Printers can connect to a computer's USB or parallel port, or they can connect directly to the network. Newer printers can interface with USB memory sticks, memory cards, and digital cameras. Some printers are known as multifunction devices because of their ability to print, fax, copy, and scan documents. This chapter focuses on laser, inkjet, thermal, and impact printers.

Generally, Windows Vista and Windows 7 behave the same as Windows XP when it comes to printers and scanners. So whenever Windows is mentioned in this chapter, the information will apply to Windows XP, Vista, and 7 unless otherwise stated.

"Do I Know This Already?" Quiz

The "Do I Know This Already?" quiz allows you to assess whether you should read this entire chapter or simply jump to the "Exam Preparation Tasks" section for review. If you are in doubt, read the entire chapter. Table 11-1 outlines the major headings in this chapter and the corresponding "Do I Know This Already?" quiz questions. You can find the answers in Appendix A, "Answers to the 'Do I Know This Already?' Quizzes and Troubleshooting Scenarios."

Table 11-1   "Do I Know This Already?" Foundation Topics Section-to-Question Mapping

Foundations Topics Section	Questions Covered in This Section
Printing Fundamentals	1, 2
Printer and Scanner Control	3, 4
Print Processes	5, 12
Interface Types	6, 7, 13
Printer Installation	8, 14
Optimizing Printer Performance	9
Installing and Configuring Printer Upgrades	10
Printer Troubleshooting Tools and Techniques	11

1. What is the major difference between a laser printer and an LED printer? (Choose all that apply.)

    a. LED printers use an LED array to perform the transfer of images.

    b. LED printers use an LED drum.

    c. Laser printers are of better print quality.

    d. Laser printers use a laser to transfer the image to the drum.

2. What happens if a page you print on a laser printer requires more memory than the printer has installed?

    a. It will use hard drive space to print.

    b. The printer will try to print the page but will stop before the job is finished.

    c. The printer will continue to work but at a slower than normal pace.

    d. The printer will notify you that you need to free some resources.

3. Which of the following will provide you with the most configuration options and utilities when installing a new printer?

    a. A driver from Microsoft

    b. A plug-and-play driver

    c. A driver from the printer vendor

    d. A driver from Automatic Updates

4. Which of the following must you do to determine what firmware version the printer is using?

    a. Print a test page

    b. Look on the back of the printer

    c. Review the printer properties page

    d. Review the firmware update page

5. Which of the following are true about the laser printing process? (Choose all that apply.)

    a. A page does not start printing until the entire page is received.

    b. The print is transferred to the paper.

    c. The page is transferred to the print mechanism.

    d. The page will start printing immediately after the print button is pushed.

6. Most inkjet, laser, and thermal printers use this interface to connect a printer to a computer. (Choose two.)

    a. RJ-45

    b. USB

    c. Parallel

    d. LED

7. You must provide which of the following in order to add a printer to a network?

    a. A printer device

    b. A print server

    c. A printer NIC card

    d. A Bluetooth adapter

8. When installing a printer, what is the easiest way to ensure compatibility to make sure that Windows recognizes the new hardware?

    a. Windows Update

    b. A search engine

    c. Vendor's website

    d. Hardware compatibility list

9. Where would you find the setting for the print spooler on a Windows operating system?

    a. Computer Management

    b. The Printers folder

    c. In Server Properties

    d. User Manager

10. When upgrading a printer's memory, you notice that the printer is using a DIMM memory module. Can you use the same type of memory as a laptop or desktop?

    a. Yes, they use the same memory.

    b. Yes, you can also use printer memory in a desktop.

    c. No, they do not use the same type of memory.

    d. Yes, but the printer will run more slowly.

11. Which of the following are considered troubleshooting tools and techniques for printers? (Choose all that apply.)

    a. Increase memory

    b. Print a test page

    c. Identify symptoms

    d. Review device error codes

12. What is the first process you must follow to print a page out of your printer?

    a. Send it to the print queue.

    b. An application must send a request that is relayed to the printer.

    c. Insert the paper in the print feeder.

    d. An application prints it out for you.

13. What will you need to connect a printer if you wish to use Bluetooth technology?

    a. A USB key

    b. A dongle key

    c. A network interface card

    d. A Bluetooth print adapter

14. When connecting a printer or scanner, which of the following should you use to install the correct driver for the device? (Choose all that apply.)

    a. Vendor's website

    b. Windows Update

    c. HCL

    d. The CD

Foundation Topics

Printing Fundamentals

There are four types of printers covered by A+ Certification exams:

- Laser
- Inkjet
- Thermal
- Impact

The following sections introduce you to the basic features of each printer type:

- How printers create a page (note in particular the steps used by a laser printer to create a page)
- Major components of each printer type covered (thermal printers as well as impact, inkjet, and laser/LED)
- Typical printer operation and output problems and their solutions
- How printers are interfaced to the computer

To master the printer objectives on the A+ Certification exams, pay careful attention to these details.

Laser Printers

Laser printers are similar in many ways to photocopiers:

- Both use an electrostatically charged drum to receive the image to be transferred to paper.
- Both use a fine-grained powdered toner that is heated to adhere to the paper.
- Both must feed the paper through elaborate paper paths for printing.

However, significant differences exist between the photocopier and its computer-savvy sibling:

- Laser printers produce images digitally, turning individual dots on and off; some copiers, however, are still analog devices.
- Laser printers work under the control of a computer; copiers have a dedicated scanner as an image source.

■   Laser printers use much higher temperatures than copiers to bond printing to the paper; using copier labels or transparency media in a laser printer can result in damage to the printer due to melted label adhesive, labels coming off in the printer, or melted transparency media.

One type of laser printer is the LED printer. LED stands for light-emitting diode, which the LED printer uses as its light source. The essential difference between a laser and an LED printer is in the imaging device. The laser printer uses a laser to transfer the image to the drum, whereas an LED printer uses an LED array to perform the same task. Otherwise, these technologies are practically identical. The laser printing process described in the following sections also applies to LED printers.

How Laser Printers Use Memory

Because a laser printer is a page printer and the graphics, text, and fonts on the page all use memory, the amount of memory in the laser printer determines the types of pages it can print successfully—and on some models, how quickly the pages are printed.

All laser printers are shipped with enough memory to print with built-in typefaces or with a typical mix of scalable OpenType or TrueType typefaces. However, graphics, especially photographs, require a great deal of printer memory.

If you send a page to a laser printer that requires more memory than the laser printer contains, the laser printer tries to print the page but stops after the printer's memory is full. The printer displays an error message or blinks error status lights, at which point you must manually eject the page. Only a portion of the page is printed.

If the page requires an amount of memory close to the maximum in the laser printer, most laser printers have techniques for compressing the data going to the printer. Although this technique means that more pages can be printed successfully, compressing the data can slow down the print process.

Three options can be used if the pages you need to print require too much memory:

■   Reduce the resolution of the print job. Most laser printers today have a standard resolution of 600dpi or 1,200dpi. Reducing the graphics resolution to the next lower figure (from 1,200 to 600dpi or from 600 to 300dpi) will reduce the memory requirement for printing the page by a factor of four. The laser printer's Graphics or Advanced – Printing Defaults – Paper/Quality Properties sheet (see Figure 11-1) enables this factor to be adjusted as needed.

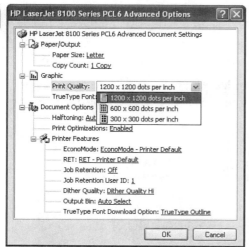

Figure 11-1   The Advanced – Printing Defaults – Paper/Quality Properties sheet in Windows XP for a typical laser printer enables you to adjust the graphics resolution from the default of 1200dpi to 600dpi or less; text quality is not affected by this option.

NOTE   If you reduce the graphics resolution, text resolution stays the same, so a document that is not designed for reproduction or mass distribution will still have acceptable quality.

However, graphics resolutions of 600 dots per inch (dpi) or less produce poor-quality photo output.

- Eliminate or reduce the size of graphics on the page.

- Convert color photos to black-and-white photos before placing in a desktop publishing document or printing them directly from the file. This can actually enhance the output quality from a monochrome laser printer as well as reduce the memory requirement for pages with photos.

These options are temporary workarounds that might be unsatisfactory for permanent use. The best solution to "out-of-memory" problems with a printer, as with the computer, is to add more RAM. To learn more about memory upgrades for laser and LED printers, see the section "Memory," later in this chapter.

Toner Cartridges

Most monochrome laser printers use toner cartridges that combine the imaging drum and the developer with black toner. This provides you with an efficient and easy way to replace the laser printer items with the greatest potential to wear out.

Depending on the model, a new toner cartridge might also require that you change a wiper used to remove excess toner during the fusing cycle. This is normally packaged with the toner cartridge.

NOTE   Recycled toner cartridges are controversial in some circles, but I've used a mixture of new and rebuilt toner cartridges for several years without a problem. Major manufacturers, such as Apple, HP, and Canon, place a postage-paid return label in cartridge boxes to encourage you to recycle your toner cartridges.

Reputable toner cartridge rebuilders can save you as much as 30% off the price of a new toner cartridge.

When you install the toner cartridge, be sure to follow the directions for cleaning areas near the toner cartridge. Depending on the make and model of the laser printer, this can involve cleaning the mirror that reflects the laser beam, cleaning up stray toner, or cleaning the charging corona wire or conditioning rollers inside the printer. If you need to clean the charging corona wire (also called the *primary corona wire* on some models), the laser printer will contain a special tool for this purpose. The printer instruction manual will show you how to clean the item.

Keep the cartridge closed; it is sensitive to light, and leaving it out of the printer in room light can damage the enclosed imaging drum's surface. Figure 11-2 shows a typical laser printer toner cartridge and mirror cleaning tool. The tool above the toner cartridge is used to clean the printer's mirror.

CAUTION   When you change a toner cartridge, take care to avoid getting toner on your face, hands, or clothing. It can leave a messy residue that's hard to clean.

Color laser printers differ from monochrome laser printers in two important ways: They include four different colors of toner (cyan, magenta, yellow, and black); and the imaging drum is separate from the toner. Thus, instead of waste toner being reused as in a monochrome laser printer that has a toner cartridge with an integrated imaging drum, waste toner in a color printer is sent to a separate waste toner container.

Depending upon the toner transfer technology used, a color laser printer might require four passes to print a color page (one pass per color), or only one pass to print all four colors. For details, see the section "Color Laser Printing Differences," in this chapter.

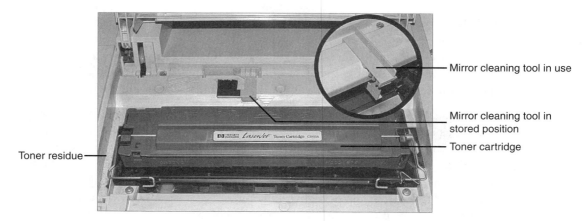

Mirror cleaning tool in use

Mirror cleaning tool in
stored position

Toner cartridge

Toner residue

Figure 11-2   A typical laser printer toner cartridge. The inset shows the mirror cleaning tool in use after the old toner cartridge has been removed and before the new cartridge is put into position.

Laser Printer Paper and Media

For best results with laser printing, use these guidelines when selecting paper and media:

- Use paper made for laser or photocopier use. Extremely rough-surfaced specialty papers might not enable the toner to fuse correctly to the paper.

- Use envelopes made for laser printing, especially if the printer doesn't offer a straight-through paper path option. Standard envelopes can lose some of their flap adhesive or have the flap stick to the back of the envelope when used in a laser printer.

- Use only labels made for laser printers; these labels have no exposed backing, requiring you to separate the labels from the backing after printing.

CAUTION   Labels made for copiers have exposed backing, and the labels can come off inside the printer, leading to expensive repairs.

- Use only laser-compatible transparency stock; it can resist the high heat of the fuser rollers better than other types, which can melt and damage the printer.

- Avoid using paper with damaged edges or damp paper; this can cause paper jams and lead to poor-quality printing.

- Load paper carefully into the paper tray; fan the paper and make sure the edges are aligned before inserting it.

Inkjet Printers

Inkjet printers (also known as ink dispersion printers) represent the most popular type of printer in small-office/home-office (SOHO) use today and are also popular in large offices. Their print quality can rival laser printers and virtually all inkjet printers in use today are able to print both color and black text and photographs.

From a tightly spaced group of nozzles, inkjet printers spray controlled dots of ink onto the paper to form characters and graphics. On a typical 5,760×1,440 dots per inch (dpi) printer, the number of nozzles can be as high as 180 for black ink and more than 50 per color (cyan, magenta, yellow). The tiny ink droplet size and high nozzle density enables inkjet printers to perform the seemingly impossible at resolutions as high as 1,200dpi or higher: fully formed characters from what is actually a high-resolution, non-impact, dot-matrix technology.

Inkjet printers are character/line printers. They print one line at a time of single characters or graphics up to the limit of the printhead matrix. Inkjet printers are functionally fully formed character printers because their inkjet matrix of small droplets forming the image is so carefully controlled that individual dots are not visible.

Larger characters are created by printing a portion of the characters across the page, advancing the page to allow the printhead to print another portion of the characters, and so on until the entire line of characters is printed. Thus, an inkjet printer is both a character and a line printer because it must connect lines of printing to build large characters. Some inkjet printers require realignment after each ink cartridge/printhead change to make sure that vertical lines formed by multiple printhead passes stay straight (this may be automatic or require the user to start the process); with other models, alignment can be performed through a utility provided as part of the printer driver when print quality declines due to misalignment.

Ink Cartridges

Some inkjet printers, especially low-cost models, use a large tank of liquid ink for black and a separate tank with separate compartments for each color (typically cyan, magenta, and yellow; some models feature light versions of some of these colors for better photo-printing quality). However, the trend in most recent models has been to use a separate cartridge for each color. This improves print economy for the user because only one color at a time needs to be replaced. With a multicolor cartridge, the entire cartridge needs to be replaced, even when only one of the colors runs out.

NOTE   Inkjet printers are sometimes referred to as CMYK devices because of the four ink colors used on most models: *c*yan, *m*agenta, *y*ellow, and blac*k*.

Figure 11-3 shows some of the typical components of an inkjet printer.

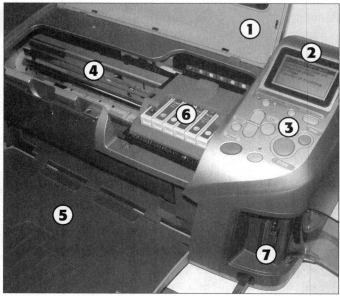

1. Dust cover
2. LCD instruction panel
3. Control panel
4. Printhead drive belt
5. Output tray
6. Ink cartridges
7. Flash memory card reader

Figure 11-3   A typical inkjet printer with its cover open.

Depending on the printer, the printhead might be incorporated into the ink tank; be a separate, user-replaceable item; or be built into the printer.

Some inkjet printers feature an extra-wide (more nozzles) printhead or a dual printhead for very speedy black printing. Some models enable the user to replace either the ink cartridge only or an assembly comprising the printhead and a re-placeable ink cartridge.

An inkjet printer is only as good as its printhead and ink cartridges. Clogged or damaged printheads or ink cartridges render the printer useless. If an inkjet printer fails after its warranty expires, you should check service costs carefully before re-pairing the unit. Failed inkjet printers are often "throwaway" models and can be replaced, rather than repaired, even during the warranty period.

CAUTION   Inkjet printers should *never* be turned off with the power switch on a surge protector; doing so prevents the printer from self-capping its ink cartridges, which is a major cause of service calls and printer failures. Cleaning the printhead, either with the printer's own cleaning feature, a cleaning utility built into the print-er driver, or with a moistened cleaning sheet, will restore most printers to service.

Always use the printer's own power switch, which enables the printer to protect the ink cartridges and perform other periodic tasks (such as self-cleaning) properly.

Inkjet Printer Paper and Media

Although papers made for copiers and laser printers provide adequate results, you must use inkjet-specific media of the following types to achieve best print quality:

- Glossy photos
- Transparencies
- Business cards
- Labels (especially clear labels)

It is also critical to use the correct print setting for the media type to avoid smudging, lines, and other print defects. For details, see "Configuring Options and Device Settings," later in this chapter.

Thermal Printers

Thermal printers use heat transfer to create text and graphics on the paper. Thermal printers are used in point-of-sale and retail environments as well as for some types of portable printing.

Thermal printers are available using three different technologies:

- Thermal transfer
- Direct thermal
- Dye sublimation

Thermal printers can use a dot-matrix print mechanism or a dye-sublimation technology to transfer images. Some thermal printers use heat-sensitive paper, while others use an ink ribbon to create the image. Let's start by discussing the thermal printer ribbon.

Thermal Printer Ribbons

Thermal transfer printers use wax or resin-based ribbons, which are often bundled with paper made especially for the printer. The most common type of thermal transfer printer uses dye-sublimation (dye-sub) technology to print 4×6 continuous-tone photographs. Examples of dye-sublimation printers include Kodak printer docks and Canon's Selphy CP series.

Figure 11-4 illustrates a typical dye-sublimation ribbon for a Canon Selphy CP printer.

Thermal transfer printers used in point-of-sale or retail environments typically use non-impact dot-matrix printheads.

Figure 11-4 A dye-sublimation ribbon for a 4×6-inch photo printer (Canon Selphy CP).

Thermal Printer Paper

Direct thermal printers use heat-sensitized paper, while thermal transfer printers might use either standard copy paper or glossy photo paper, depending upon their intended use.

If the printer uses direct thermal printing, heat-sensitive paper with characteristics matching the printer's design specifications must be used. For portable printers using direct thermal printing such as the Brother (formerly Pentax) PocketJet series, the usual source for such paper is the printer vendor or its authorized resellers. If the direct thermal printer is used for bar codes or point-of-sale transactions, you can get suitable paper or label stock from bar code or POS equipment suppliers and resellers.

If the printer uses thermal transfer and is not designed for photo printing, most smooth paper and label stocks are satisfactory, including both natural and synthetic materials. However, dye-sublimation photo printers must use special media kits that include both a ribbon and suitable photo paper stocks.

Impact Printers

Impact printers are so named because they use a mechanical printhead that presses against an inked ribbon to print characters and graphics. Impact printers are the oldest printer technology, and are primarily used today in industrial and point-of-sale applications.

Dot-matrix printers, the most common form of impact printers, are so named because they create the appearance of fully formed characters from dots placed on the page.

NOTE   Years ago, many impact printers used a daisy-wheel printhead similar to those used in electronic typewriters. This type of printhead created typewriter-style fully formed characters. However, virtually all recent impact printers use a dot-matrix printhead.

The print mechanism of the dot-matrix printer is almost always an impact mechanism: A printhead containing various numbers of fine wires (called *pins*) arranged in one or more columns is used along with a fabric ribbon, similar to typewriter technology. The wires are moved by an electromagnet at high speed against the ribbon to form dot patterns that form words, special characters, or graphics. Figure 11-5 shows actual print samples from a typical 9-pin printer's draft mode, a typical 24-pin printer's draft mode, and the Near Letter Quality (NLQ) mode of the same 24-pin printer.

```
RN_clients.html.Z ──────────9-pin printer draft mode
RN_loc_cal.html.Z
RN_loc_doc.html.Z
RN_loc_uucp.html.Z

This is a test of switching──24-pin printer draft mode
Congratulations!──────────24-pin printer NLQ mode

If you can read this inform
Panasonic KX-P1624.

The information below descr
```

Figure 11-5   Actual print samples illustrating the differences in 24-pin and 9-pin impact dot-matrix printers.

NOTE   The print samples shown in Figure 11-5 are taken from printers that use 8.5″×11″-inch or wider paper sizes. The printhead design and print quality vary greatly on printers that use smaller paper sizes in point-of-sale applications.

Figure 11-6 illustrates a typical impact dot-matrix printer.

Impact Printer Ribbons

Printer ribbons for impact printers use various types of cartridge designs. Some span the entire width of the paper, and others snap over the printhead. Figure 11-7 compares various types of ribbons for impact printers.

Impact Printer Paper and Media

Impact printers use plain uncoated paper or labels in various widths and sizes. Impact printers designed for point-of-sale receipt printing might use roll paper or larger sizes of paper. When larger sizes of paper are used, these printers typically use a tractor-feed mechanism to pull or push the paper past the printhead. Paper used with tractor-fed printers has fixed or removable sprocket holes on both sides of the paper.

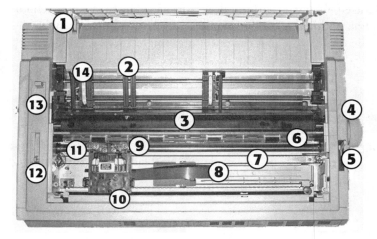

1. Rear cover (top cover removed, not shown)
2. Paper supports for tractor-feed paper path
3. Platen for using single sheets of paper
4. Manual paper advance knob
5. Paper bail lifter
6. Paper bail
7. Timing/drive belt
8. Printhead signal control cable
9. Printhead with heat sink
10. Ribbon holder
11. Printhead support rod
12. Head gap adjustment
13. Tractor/friction-feed selector lever
14. Tractor feed

Figure 11-6   Components of a typical impact dot-matrix printer. The model pictured is a wide-carriage version, but its features are typical of models using either standard or wide-carriage paper.

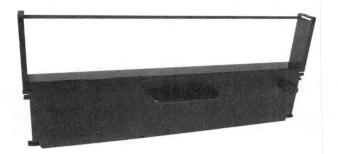

Figure 11-7   Some typical ribbons for impact dot-matrix printers.

Printer and Scanner Control

The behavior of a printer is controlled in large degree by two factors:

- Drivers

- Firmware

The following sections help you understand these features.

Drivers

Printer drivers are used to control and configure printers and the print features of multifunction devices.

Printer drivers might be supplied by Microsoft on the Windows distribution media or by the printer vendor itself. Generally, printer drivers provided by the printer vendor offer more configuration options and utilities for cleaning and maintenance than the drivers provided by Microsoft. Note that driver features might vary by Windows version, even if a single driver file supports more than one Windows version.

NOTE   It's a good idea to check for updated versions of printer or multifunction device drivers before installing the device and periodically thereafter. Updated drivers might include bug fixes or enhanced features. Also, if a system is upgraded to a newer version of Windows or another operating system, you will need new drivers. You can use Windows Update to locate drivers or download them directly from the printer vendor.

Firmware

Some printers, most often laser printers, might offer upgradeable firmware. Firmware, which is software on a chip, controls the basic operation of a printer.

To determine the firmware revision installed in a printer, use its self-test function to make a test printout. Firmware can be implemented in a flash-upgradeable chip built into the printer, or in a special memory module sometimes called a "personality" module.

Print Processes

Although all printers are designed to turn electronic documents into hard copy, the specifics of the printing process vary a great deal among printer types. In this section, you first learn the overall printing process, followed by specifics for each type of printer.

The printing process has the following steps:

Step 1.   An application program in the computer sends a print request to the Windows operating system.

Step 2.   Windows uses a print queue to manage print jobs, storing one or more print jobs in the default temporary directory until the printer is ready.

Step 3.   After the printer is ready, it receives a stream of data from the computer through its interface. The data stream contains commands that begin the printing process, select a page orientation and margins, and select built-in fonts and typefaces, or it contains instructions to create fonts and typefaces especially for this print job, depending on the printer and the typefaces and fonts in the document.

If the data stream is appropriate for the printer, printing works correctly; if the data stream contains commands the printer doesn't recognize, unrecognized characters (often referred to as "garbage printing") will be printed, with much paper wasted. That's why it's important to use the correct printer driver for your printer.

Step 4.   The printer feeds a page and prepares to print the document from the top of the page.

Step 5.   When the page is complete, the paper is ejected and the process starts again with the next page of a multipage document or a new document.

Laser Print Process

A laser printer (and its close relative, an LED printer) is an example of a page printer. A page printer does not start printing until the entire page is received. At that point, the page is transferred to the print mechanism, which pulls the paper through the printer as the page is transferred from the printer to the paper.

TIP   To master this section, make sure you

- Memorize the six steps involved in laser printer imaging
- Master the details of each step and their sequence
- Be prepared to answer troubleshooting questions based on these steps

The laser printing process often is referred to as the *electrophotographic (EP) process*.

Before the six-step laser printing process can take place, the following events must occur:

- Laser printers are page based; they must receive the entire page before they can start printing.
- After the page has been received, the printer pulls a sheet of paper into the printer with its feed rollers.

After the paper has been fed into the print mechanism, a series of six steps takes place, which results in a printed page:

1. The excess toner is cleaned from the drum and the electrical charge discharged to prepare for the next page.
2. The image drum is conditioned.
3. The page is written to the drum.

4. The image is developed on the drum with the toner.

5. The toner image of the page is transferred to the paper.

6. The toner image of the page is fused permanently to the paper.

See Figure 11-8 to learn where each of these steps takes place in the printer. The following sections explain each step of the process in greater detail.

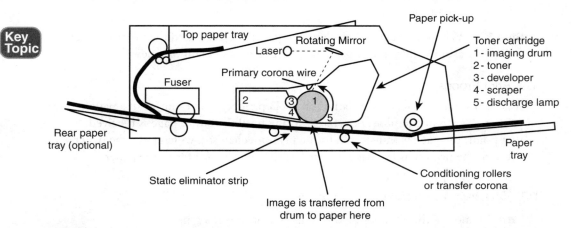

Figure 11-8   A typical monochrome laser printer's components. The heavy line indicates the paper path; paper enters the printer at the right and is pulled through the printer to either the left output tray or the top output tray.

Step 1: Cleaning

To prepare the drum for a new page, the image of the preceding page placed on the drum by the laser or LED array (see Step 3) is removed by a discharge lamp. Toner that is not adhering to the surface of the drum is scraped from the drum's surface for reuse.

Step 1 prepares the drum for the conditioning step (Step 2).

Step 2: Conditioning

The cylinder-shaped imaging drum receives an electrostatic charge of –600Vdc (DC voltage) from a primary corona wire or conditioning roller. The smooth surface of the drum retains this charge uniformly over its entire surface. The drum is photosensitive and will retain this charge only while kept in darkness.

Step 3: Writing

A moving mirror moves the laser beam across the surface of the drum. As it moves, the laser beam temporarily records the image of the page to be printed on the surface of the drum by reducing the voltage of the charge applied by the charger corona to -100Vdc. Instead of using a laser beam, an LED printer activates its LED array to record the image on the page.

Step 4: Developing

The drum has toner applied to it from the developer; because the toner is electro-static and is also at -600Vdc, the toner stays on only the portions of the drum that have been reduced in voltage to create the image. It is not attracted to the rest of the drum because both the toner and the drum are at the same voltage, and like charges repel each other. This "like charges repel" phenomenon is the similar to two like poles of magnets that repel each other.

Step 5: Transferring

While the sheet is being fed into the printer, it receives an electrostatic charge of +600Vdc from a corona wire or roller; this enables it to attract toner from the drum, which is negatively charged (see Step 3). As the drum's surface moves close to the charged paper, the toner adhering to the drum is attracted to the electrostatically charged paper to create the printed page.

As the paper continues to move through the printer, its charge is canceled by a static eliminator strip, so the paper itself isn't attracted to the drum.

Step 6: Fusing

The printed sheet of paper is pulled through fuser rollers, using high temperatures (about 350F degrees) to heat the toner and press it into the paper. The printed image is slightly raised above the surface of the paper.

The paper is ejected into the paper tray, and the drum must be prepared for another page.

Color Laser Printing Differences

Color laser printers use the same basic process as monochrome lasers, but some use a transfer belt instead of an imaging drum. The use of a transfer belt enables all four colors (cyan, magenta, yellow, and black) to be placed on the paper at the same time, enabling color print speeds comparable to monochrome print speeds. When a transfer belt is used, the conditioning and transferring processes are performed on the transfer belt.

Inkjet Print Process

Two major methods are used by inkjet printers to create the ink dots that make up the page. Most inkjet printers heat the ink to boiling, creating a tiny bubble of ink that is allowed to escape through the printhead onto the paper. This is the origin of the name BubbleJet for the Canon line of inkjet printers.

Another popular method uses a piezo-electric crystal to distribute the ink through the printhead. This method makes achieving high resolutions easier; the Epson printers using this method were the first to achieve 5,760×1,440dpi resolutions. This method also provides a longer printhead life because the ink is not heated and cooled. Both types of inkjet printers are sometimes referred to as drop-on-demand printers.

During the print process:

1. The paper or media is pulled into position by a roller mechanism.

2. The printhead moves across the paper, placing black and color ink droplets as directed by the printer driver.

3. At the end of the line, the paper or media is advanced, and the printhead either reverses direction and continues to print (often referred to as Hi-Speed mode) or returns to the left margin before printing continues.

4. After the page is completed, the media is ejected.

Thermal Print Processes

Although thermal transfer, direct thermal printing, and dye-sublimation all involve heating the elements in a printhead to a particular temperature to transfer the image, there are some differences in operation. The basic process of thermal printing works like this:

1. The printhead has a matrix of dots that can be heated in various combinations to create text and graphics.

2. The printhead transfers text and graphics directly to heat-sensitive thermal paper in direct thermal printing, or to a ribbon that melts onto the paper in thermal transfer printing.

3. If a multicolor ribbon is used on a thermal transfer or dye-sublimation printer, each ribbon is moved past the printhead to print the appropriate color.

Figure 11-9 compares direct thermal and thermal transfer printing technologies.

Dye-sublimation, like thermal transfer and direct thermal printing, also relies on heat to transfer the image to the media, but the process is very different than with traditional thermal printers:

1. During printing, the printhead heats up to transfer yellow, magenta, and cyan dyes from special dye-sublimation ribbons to the paper under computer control (some can print directly from flash or CD media). One pass is used for each color. Black is created by mixing yellow, magenta, and cyan dyes.

2. Unlike thermal transfer, which melts the wax or resin material to the surface of the paper, dye-sublimation dyes turn into a gas when heated and penetrate the surface of the paper. This creates a continuous-tone image. Thus, the relatively modest-sounding typical dye-sub resolutions of around 300–400dpi provide better real-world image quality than higher-resolution inkjet printers. Figure 11-10 illustrates this process.

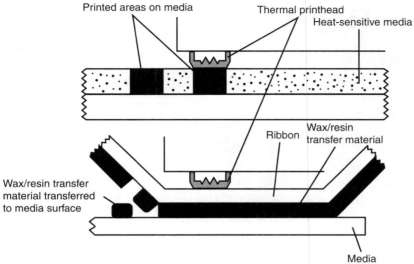

Figure 11-9   Direct thermal (top) and thermal transfer (bottom) printing technologies.

3. Many recent dye-sub printers apply a protective coating (overcoat) to the surface of the print before ejecting it .

Impact Print Process

Impact dot-matrix printers have the following parts moving in coordination with each other during the printing process:

Step 1.   The paper is moved past the printhead vertically by pull or push tractors or by a platen.

Step 2.   The printhead moves across the paper horizontally, propelled along the printhead carriage by a drive belt, printing as it moves from left to right. Bidirectional printing prints in both directions but is often disabled for high-quality printing because it can be difficult to align the printing precisely.

Step 3.   As the printhead moves, the pins in the printhead are moving in and out against an inked ribbon as the printhead travels across the paper to form the text or create graphics.

Step 4.   The ribbon is also moving to reduce wear during the printing process.

Steps 1–4 are repeated for each line until the page is printed.

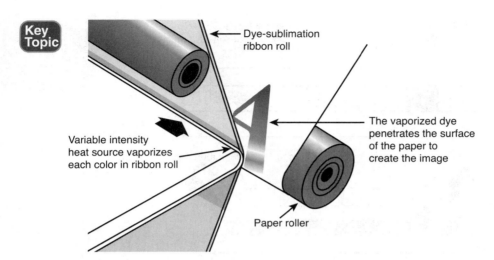

Figure 11-10   Illustration of dye-sublimation printing process.

> **NOTE**   Impact dot-matrix printers have a lot of moving parts and traditionally high noise levels. This, along with their incapability to create truly high-quality, letter-quality text except at low speeds, has moved them out of most homes and offices. They are largely used for utility tasks (bank receipts, point-of-sale receipts, and warehouse reports) where their capability to print multipart forms is more important than print quality or noise level. Because impact dot-matrix printers use inexpensive ribbons designed to print millions of characters and can use fan-fold or single-sheet papers of all types, they have the lowest cost per page of all printers.

Interface Types

Interface types used by printers and scanners include the following:

- **USB 2.0**—Used by most inkjet, solid ink, dye-sublimation, thermal, and laser printers, either when connected directly to a PC or connected to a network via a print server. Also used by most multifunction (all-in-one) units.

- **Parallel**—Used by legacy impact printers as well as older inkjet and laser printers. Also used by some legacy all-in-one units.

- **RS-232 (serial)**—Used by legacy impact and laser printers.

- **SCSI**—Used by high-end Postscript laser printers.

- **Bluetooth**—Used by some recent inkjet and laser printers.

- **Infrared**—Used by some legacy inkjet, impact, and laser printers.

- **Ethernet**—Used by inkjet and laser printers that are network-ready.

- **IEEE 802.11 (wireless Ethernet)**—Used by some recent inkjet and other types of printers.

- **FireWire (IEEE 1394)**—Used by some recent high-end inkjet printers used by graphic designers.

Many printers include more than one interface.

If you need to connect a printer using a different interface than its normal interface, you can sometimes use an adapter or print server device.

Adding Bluetooth Support

To add support for the Bluetooth short-range wireless network to a printer or scanner with a USB 2.0 port, connect a Bluetooth printer adapter. Note that the best results are usually obtained when the adapter is made especially for your printer.

Adding Ethernet Support

To add support for Ethernet local area networking to a printer that does not have a built-in Ethernet port, connect it to an Ethernet print server. Print servers are available in versions that support USB or parallel printers, and they enable the printer to be accessed via the print server's IP address. Figure 11-11 illustrates a typical Ethernet print server for USB printers.

Figure 11-11   Front and rear views of an Ethernet print server that supports USB printers.

NOTE   Some laser printers can be upgraded with an internal Ethernet print server card.

When a printer includes its own Ethernet port, it is assigned an IP address on a TCP/IP network; similarly, a print server is also assigned an IP address on a TCP/IP network. To configure a printer for network use, you might need to install a network printer driver instead of the normal printer driver; you will also need to specify whether the printer has a manually-assigned IP address or receives an IP address from a DHCP server on the network. To learn more about TCP/IP, see Chapter 16, "Networking."

Adding 802.11 Wireless Ethernet (WLAN) Support

To add support for 802.11 Wireless Ethernet (WLAN) local area networking to a printer, connect it to a Wireless Ethernet (Wi-Fi) print server. Print servers are available in versions that support USB or parallel printers, and enable the printer to be accessed via the print server's IP address.

NOTE Most Wireless Ethernet print servers also include Ethernet support.

Adding Infrared Support

To add support for infrared (IrDA) printing to a printer, connect it to an IrDA adapter. These are available for either USB printers or parallel printers. To learn more about Infrared (IrDA) ports for computers and other devices, see the section "Infrared," in Chapter 16.

Printer Installation

There's more to installing a printer than just plugging it in and hoping it works. The A+ Certification exams expect you to know the right way to "Git-R-Done," so here's how to do it.

Verifying Device Compatibility with Operating System and Applications

With Windows occupying the middle ground between printers on the one hand, and your PC on the other hand, the main concern is to make sure that Windows recognizes your printer or multifunction device. The easiest way to assure compatibility for a device is to visit the vendor's website and look for the drivers for that device. Get the driver you need for your device and your operating system, and you're ready to continue.

If you are unable to locate a driver made especially for a particular printer, you might be able to use a driver made for a similar printer. If the printer has an emulation mode, you can use it to make it emulate (act like) a different model so you can use a different driver.

TIP In a pinch, you might be able to use printer drivers made for Windows 2000 with Windows XP, or printer drivers made for Windows XP with Windows Vista or Windows 7. However, you're better off to use drivers made especially for your operating system.

You must use 64-bit drivers with a 64-bit version of Windows XP, Vista, or 7. If a 64-bit driver is not available for your printer for Windows Vista or Windows 7, but a driver is available for Windows XP Professional x64 (a 64-bit version of Windows XP), try it.

Connecting the Device

When should you connect the printer? It's a common myth that you can plug in USB-based devices without installing drivers. This is true if, and only if, the computer already has a suitable driver installed. Although Windows includes drivers for many printers, it might not include drivers for your printer, especially if you are using a late-model printer with Windows XP. Therefore, you should normally install the drivers provided by the vendor (either on the CD packaged with the device or by downloading updated versions) first.

NOTE   Many recent devices are now labeled to remind you to install the driver first; the labeling might be on the device itself or on the driver CD package. However, if you are reinstalling a device or moving an already-installed device to another system, this labeling has usually been removed and discarded. Check the documentation for the device to determine when to connect it during the installation process.

Devices using USB and FireWire (IEEE-1394) are hot-swappable; you can connect them without shutting down the computer. Devices using SCSI, parallel, and serial ports require that the device and the computer be shut down before the device is connected.

Installing Device Drivers

Device drivers for printers can be installed in one of the following ways:

- Using the Add Printer option in the Printers and Faxes folder in Control Panel

- Using the Add Printer option in the Devices and Printers folder in Control Panel (Windows 7)

- Installing from a vendor-supplied driver disc

- Installing from a vendor-supplied downloadable file

Device drivers for all-in-one units are not supplied with Windows; you must use a vendor-supplied driver disc or downloadable file.

Using the Add Printer Wizard (Windows Vista and XP)

The Add Printer option is suitable if Windows includes a suitable driver and the enhanced features that might be provided by a vendor-supplied driver are not necessary. To install a printer using the Add Printer Wizard, follow these steps:

Step 1.   Open the **Printers** (Vista) or **Printer and Faxes** (XP) folder. You can use the Control Panel or a shortcut located on the Start button such as Settings, Printer, or Printer and Faxes.

Step 2.   Click the **Add a Printer** link in the Printer Tasks pane to open the **Add Printer** wizard.

Step 3.   Specify whether the new printer is connected through a local port or through a network—Windows XP/Vista will automatically detect a Plug-and-Play (PnP) printer by default (assuming the printer is turned on and connected to your computer).

Step 4.   Choose the port (for local printers) or network share, wireless or Bluetooth network (for network, wireless, or Bluetooth printers). If the printer is a network printer, specify whether you want to send MS-DOS print jobs to the printer.

Step 5.   Select the brand and model of your printer.

If you have an installation disk or CD-ROM provided by the vendor, click **Have Disk** and browse to the installation disk or CD-ROM for the printer (see Figure 11-12). Windows Vista also offers Windows Update for a driver source.

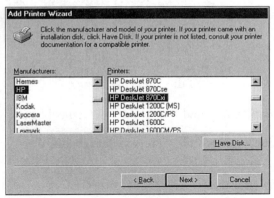

Figure 11-12   Selecting a printer by brand and model; if the printer isn't listed, or if you have a driver disk, click Have Disk.

Step 6.   Specify whether the printer will be the default printer (if you are installing an additional printer).

Step 7.   Specify whether you want to share the printer if prompted.

Step 8.   Specify whether you want to print a test page. You should do this to make sure your new printer is working properly. This is the default.

Step 9.   Windows Vista and XP display the printer selections. With Windows XP only, you can click the **Back** button to make changes. Windows Vista does not let you go back at this point.

Step 10.   Click Finish to install the driver.

After you click Finish, the printer will be installed into the Printers folder, and it will be available to all Windows applications.

Using the Add Printer Wizard (Windows 7)

The Add Printer option can be used if Windows includes a suitable driver and the enhanced features that might be provided by a vendor-supplied driver are not necessary. To install a printer using the Add Printer Wizard in Windows 7, follow these steps:

Step 1.   Open the Devices and Printers folder. You can use the Control Panel or a shortcut located on the Start button.

Step 2.   Click the **Add a Printer** link in the menu.

Continue with Step 3–Step 10 from the instructions for Windows XP and Vista described in the preceding section.

Installing a Printer or Multifunction Unit with a Vendor-Supplied Driver

Whether you use a vendor-supplied install disc or a downloaded file, the installation process is quite different from the Add Printer method:

Step 1.   Insert the install disc into the computer's CD or DVD drive. After a few moments, the install program might start automatically. If it doesn't, open **My Computer** or **Computer**, navigate to the CD or DVD drive and double-click the setup program's icon. If the driver file was downloaded, navigate to the folder containing the downloaded install program. Double-click the .exe file to start the installation program.

Step 2.   Connect your device to the USB or FireWire port, but do not turn it on (if the device uses a non-PnP port, you must connect it while the system is turned off).

Step 3.   The install program starts. If prompted, select your device.

Step 4.   When prompted, turn on your device. When the install program detects your device, it will complete the installation process.

Step 5.   You might be prompted to restart your computer after the installation process is over. If that happens, remove the install disc and restart your system.

Calibrating the Device

Inkjet printers and multifunction units might require or recommend some type of calibration, most typically printhead alignment. This process involves printing one or more sheets of paper and selecting the print setting that produces straight lines. Some printers perform this step automatically, while others might require user intervention to determine the best setting.

> **NOTE** With some printers and multifunction units, it might be necessary to realign the printhead each time after changing ink cartridges. However, with others, it might be an optional utility that you can run on an as-needed basis.

Configuring Options and Device Settings

Printer options can be changed by the user before printing a document. However, if the printer will be used in the same way most of the time, it can be useful to configure the device with the most commonly-used settings.

Printer Options

Printer options are configured through the printer's properties sheet. You can access printer properties sheets by doing one of the following:

- Right-clicking the printer's icon in the Printers, Printers and Faxes, or Devices and Printers folder in Control Panel and selecting **Properties**. Use this method to set defaults that will be used for all print jobs.

- Opening the **Print** dialog in an application and clicking the **Properties** button. Use this method to change settings for the current print job.

If the printer uses a Microsoft-supplied printer driver, the properties sheet will have some or all of the following tabs:

- **General**—Features the Print Test Page button, which prints a test page of graphics and text, listing the driver files, and the Printing Preferences button, which opens the Printer Preferences menu.

- **Sharing**—Enables or disables printer sharing over the network. In Windows 2000/XP this is available only if File and Print Sharing is enabled on the system. To enable Printer Sharing in Windows 7/Vista go to **Start**, **Control Panel**, **Network and Sharing Center**, click on the down arrow for Printer Sharing, and select the radio button labeled **Turn on Printer Sharing**.

- The Sharing tab also features the Additional Drivers button. Once configured by the local user, this permits remote users to connect to the printer with other versions of Windows. If this feature is not configured, users running other versions of Windows must download and install the appropriate driver for their version of Windows before they can connect to a remote printer.

- **Ports**—Lists and configures printer ports and paths to network printers.

- **Advanced**—Schedules availability of printer, selects spooling methods, printer priority, print defaults (quality, paper type, orientation, and so forth), printer driver, print processor, and separator page.

- **Security**—Enables you to select which users can print and manage print jobs and documents; available only if user-level sharing is enabled, such as if the printer is connected to a computer that is part of a network being managed by a Windows server or if Windows XP's Simple File Sharing feature is disabled.

- **Device Settings**—Selects default paper tray, font substitutions, page protection, font cartridges, and printer memory.

- **Color Management**—Selects default color profile.

- **About/Version Information**—Lists driver version and/or driver files used by printer.

TIP Some laser printers report the amount of memory installed to the operating system so that the properties sheet reflects this information. However, you should not assume that all laser printers do so. Be sure to verify that the memory size shown in the printer properties sheet is accurate. If not, change it to match the installed memory size.

To determine the installed memory size, use the printer's own print test option.

The selections made on these tabs are automatically saved as the defaults when you click OK and close the dialog.

The Printer Preferences button on the General tab opens the preferences menu for the printer. The preferences menu can vary a great deal from printer to printer, but typically includes options such as these:

- **Inkjet printers**—Paper type, paper size, paper layout, print mode, utilities (head cleaning, alignment, ink levels), and watermarking.

- **Laser printers**—Layout, page order, resolution, font substitutions, printer features, pages per sheet, and watermarking.

As you can see from Figures 11-13 and 11-14, these options can appear in various menus, depending upon the printer. Figure 11-13 shows General, Device Settings, and Advanced Print Properties for a laser printer, and Figure 11-14 shows the Main, Advanced, Page Layout, and Maintenance preference sheets menu for an inkjet photo printer in Windows 7.

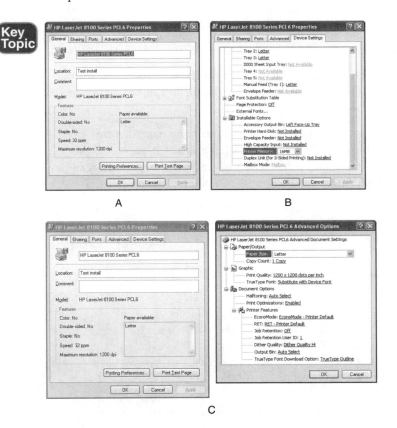

Figure 11-13   Windows XP General (a), Device Settings (b), and Advanced Print Properties (c) properties sheets for a typical departmental laser printer.

> **NOTE**   In Windows 7, select Printing Preferences from the right-click menu to go directly to the multi-tabbed printing preferences menu, such as the one in Figure 11-14. To go to more general settings such as the ones shown in Figure 11-13, select Printer Properties. If you select Properties (not Printer Properties or Printing Preferences) from the right-click menu in Devices and Printers for a printer or multifunction device, you will see a two-tabbed interface: General lists basic device information and Hardware lists the device functions.

To save changes to default settings, click **Apply** and then **OK**. Some printers offer the option to save settings under different names, so you can retrieve a particular setting before printing a particular type of document, such as a photo on glossy paper or a web page on plain paper.

> **TIP** Before configuring options and settings on a printer, consult with the user to find out how the printer will be used.

Figure 11-14 Windows 7 Main (a), Advanced (b), Page Layout (c), and Maintenance (d) preference sheets for a typical ink jet multifunction device using a vendor-supplied driver.

Printing a Test Page

If you use the Add Printer wizard to install a printer, you are prompted to print a test page at the end of the installation process. You can also print a test page by clicking the **Print Test Page** button from the General tab of Printer properties. A typical Windows XP test page resembles the one in Figure 11-15.

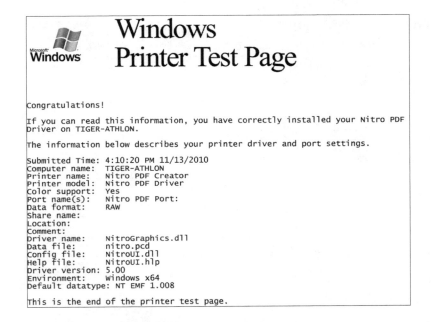

Figure 11-15   A Windows 7 test print page.

Note in particular whether the Windows logo looks correct: the upper-left quadrant is red; the upper-right quadrant is green; the lower-left quadrant is blue, and the lower-right quadrant is yellow. All quadrants feature shading. If you see streaks, lines or other print quality problems in either the logo or text printing, or if the printer doesn't print, you need to troubleshoot your printer to solve the problem. See "Printer Troubleshooting Tools and Techniques," in this chapter.

With most laser printers, you can also print a self-test page by pressing a button or combination of buttons on the printer. The self-test page lists the firmware revision used by the printer, the number of pages printed, and the amount of installed memory.

Educating the User About Basic Functionality

If possible, take a few minutes to acquaint the user(s) of the computer with the basic functionality of the new printer or multifunction unit. The demonstration should include

- How to use online or PDF-based documentation (if a printed manual is not provided)

- How to access the device's properties sheet

- How to change settings for printing documents and photos

- How to print multiple-page documents

- How to use advanced features (printing multiple pages on a single sheet of paper, changing paper sizes, page orientation, and so on)

- How to open the print spooler to manage or delete print jobs

- How to perform routine maintenance (cleaning printheads, checking ink levels, and so on)

Optimizing Printer Performance

After a printer is installed, you can make it work even better by optimizing aspects of its performance, as discussed in the following sections.

Tray Switching

Most laser printers include two or more paper sources, such as internal paper trays, fold-down feeders for envelopes or card stock, and more. If a particular paper source is the primary or sole location for media, save time when printing by selecting the preferred source. On most printers, you'll find the setting on the Paper/Quality tab in the Printing Preferences menu (see Figure 11-16).

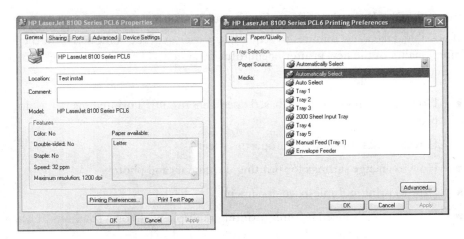

Figure 11-16   Selecting the default tray on a laser printer.

If the user needs to switch sources, this menu is also used to specify alternatives.

Print Spooler Settings

The print spooler service should be configured to start automatically (as of Windows XP Service Pack 2, this is the default setting). To verify that the spooler is properly configured, follow this procedure:

Step 1.   Right-click **Computer/My Computer** and select **Manage** (this opens the Computer Management Console).

Step 2.   Click **Services and Applications** in the right-hand pane.

Step 3.   Click **Services** in the right-hand pane.

Step 4.   Scroll down to Print Spooler and make sure the spooler status is listed as "Started" and the startup type is listed as "Automatic." See Figure 11-17.

Step 5.   To make changes in the Print Spooler settings, double-click the **Print Spooler** listing. This opens the Print Spooler properties sheet. Make the changes desired, click **Apply**, and then **OK**.

NOTE   Some inkjet printers use their own print spooler or other printer utility service. These services should also be configured to start automatically. Check the printer's documentation to determine the name of the service.

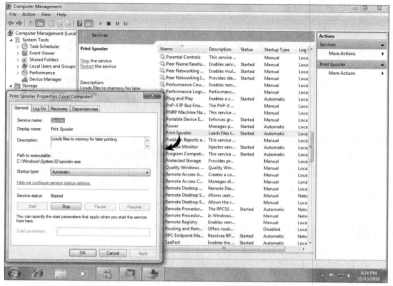

Figure 11-17   Viewing print spooler settings in Windows XP's Microsoft Management Console.

XPS Features in Windows 7 and Vista

Windows Vista and Windows 7 incorporates the XML Paper Specification (XPS) print path. The XPS spooler is meant to replace the standard Enhanced Metafile print spooler that Windows has used for years. With XPS (part of the Windows Presentation Foundation) Vista provides improved color and graphics support, as well as support for the CMYK colorspace, and reduces the need for colorspace conversion.

This is implemented as the Microsoft XPS Document Writer that can be found in **Start**, **Control Panel**, **Printers** (Vista) or **Start**, **Devices and Printers** (7). A document created within any application in Windows can be saved as an .XPS file, to be viewed later on any computer that supports XPS. It can also be printed from any computer that supports XPS, but it will only print with proper fidelity if the computer has an XPS-compliant printer.

> **NOTE**   To create and view XPS documents with Windows XP, download and install the appropriate version of the XPS Essentials Pack from the Microsoft Downloads website at www.microsoft.com/downloads/.

Device Calibration

Some inkjet printers can use two printing methods: unidirectional, in which the printer prints only when the print head is moving from left to right, and bidirectional, in which the printer prints when the print head is moving in either direction (left to right or right to left). If the printhead is misaligned, bidirectional printing (sometimes referred to as high speed printing) will have much poorer print quality than unidirectional printing.

Be sure to align the print head as needed, using the alignment utility provided in the printer driver (Figure 11-18a), to permit successful use of bidirectional printing. To enable bidirectional printing, select this option (when it's offered) in the Print Preferences menu (Figure 11-18b).

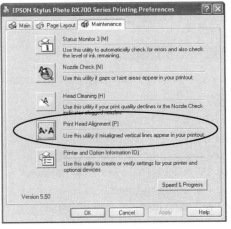
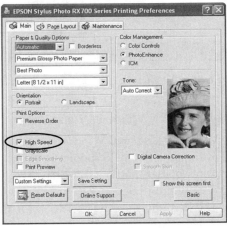

A   B

Figure 11-18   Aligning the printhead (a) helps produce better-quality high-speed (bidirectional) printing (b).

Media Types

As discussed elsewhere in this chapter, printer performance is heavily dependent upon using the right paper and media for the printer. In the case of inkjet printers, it is equally important to match the media type with the printer setting. Plain paper, glossy photo paper, matte photo paper, transparencies, and other types of media can be selected in the Printing Preferences menu (see Figure 11-19), and each selection configures the printer to place appropriate amounts of ink and adjusts the placement of ink droplets for best results.

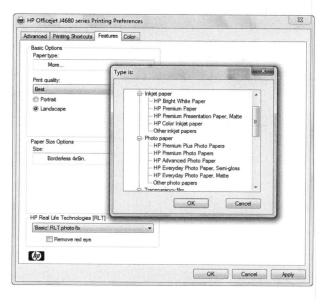

Figure 11-19   Inkjet printers support a variety of media types.

NOTE   Some inkjet printer drivers offer brand-specific settings in the paper and media selection menu. For best results, use the recommended brands and types of paper.

Paper Orientation

Most printers (with the exception of a few large-format inkjet printers made for graphic arts) are designed to use paper in the portrait mode (long side to left and right; short side to top and bottom).

Some printers provide significantly better-quality and faster results when printing in portrait mode than in landscape mode, while other printers provide the same results in either portrait or landscape mode.

Some applications automatically switch the printer driver to the appropriate mode to match the layout of the document being printed, while others do not. If the document does not match the printer's current mode, the printout might be cut off on one side, or it might be scaled to fit the dimensions of the paper.

If users will be printing in both portrait and landscape modes, they should be shown how to adjust the mode the printer uses. Users can change the layout through the Layout or Paper tab of the printer's Printing Preferences menu (see Figure 11-20).

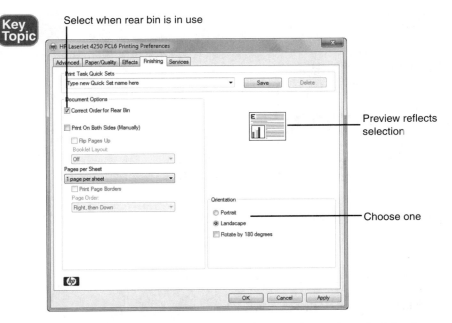

Figure 11-20   Selecting portrait or landscape print mode and print order.

Print Order

In printers that deliver pages in face-down mode, as is typically the case with laser and solid-ink printers that use a curved paper path, multiple-page documents will be in the correct order when removed from the output tray.

However, if the printer uses a straight-through paper path, as is the case with inkjet and thermal printers (or with laser and solid-ink printers if the fold-down auxiliary paper tray is used), multi-page documents should be reordered, as the first page is on the bottom of the stack and the last page is on the top of the stack. To solve this problem, use an option such as Print Reverse Order or Correct Order for Rear Bin in the Printing Preferences menu or Page Order: Back to Front in the Layout menu to print the document back to front (refer to Figure 11-20).

Installing and Configuring Printer Upgrades

Installing memory (RAM) and firmware upgrades can help printers provide better performance, handle more complex documents, support new types of memory cards and interfaces, and enhance other printer functions. The following sections help you understand these processes.

Memory

Laser and solid ink printers use memory modules to hold more page information, to reduce or eliminate the need to compress page information when printing, or to enable higher-resolution printing with complex pages.

Most recent printers with upgradeable memory use the DIMM memory module form factor, but printers do not use the same types of DIMMs as desktop or laptop computers. To order additional memory, you can

- Contact the printer vendor
- Contact a third-party memory vendor that offers compatible memory

To install a DIMM or SODIMM-based memory module, follow this basic procedure:

Step 1.   Check the printer's service manual to determine how to upgrade printer memory properly.

Step 2.   Shut down the printer and disconnect it from AC power.

Step 3.   Disconnect interface cables (USB, parallel, and so on) from the printer.

Step 4.   Open the door covering the upgrade socket.

Step 5.   Remove the DIMM from its antistatic packaging. Don't touch the memory chips or connectors on the DIMM.

Step 6.   Line up the module with the socket and make sure the label and contact side of the DIMM faces toward you.

Step 7.   Insert the DIMM into the socket at a slight angle and lower it into place until the retaining clips on each side of the socket click (see Figure 11-21).

Step 8.   Close the door over the upgrade socket.

Step 9.   Reconnect power and data cables, and restart the printer.

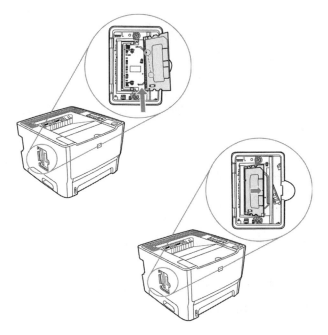

Figure 11-21   Inserting a DIMM into a printer and locking it into place.

TIP   After installing memory, make sure the printer properties sheet accurately reflects the installed amount of RAM.

For details, refer to the section "Printer Options," earlier in this chapter.

Some printers might use other types of memory modules. For information on installation of other types of modules, see the documentation for the printer.

Firmware

Firmware (software on a chip) is used to change the personality of a printer or to add features. You can use firmware updates to add Postscript compatibility to a printer that supports PCL, add support for Bluetooth or other interface types, or to fix various bugs and problems.

You can perform firmware updates for printers in a variety of ways, including

- Update via the USB cable

- Update via connection of a flash memory card or USB flash memory drive

- Install a personality DIMM

- Update flash memory via sending the upgrade file via FTP to a networked printer (this method also works if a directly attached printer is connected via the USB port and is shared on the network)

- Update flash memory via sending the file via the parallel port to a directly attached printer

The exact method you should use depends upon the printer. Consult the support website for the printer to determine if a firmware update is available, what its benefits are, and how to install it.

Printer Troubleshooting Tools and Techniques

When printers and all-in-one units fail, many businesses are unable to function until the problem is solved. Use the techniques and tools discussed in the following sections to get these devices working properly again, applying the A+ Certification six-step troubleshooting process:

Step 1. Identify the problem

Step 2. Establish a theory of probable cause

Step 3. Test the theory to determine cause

Step 4. Establish a plan of action to solve the problem

Step 5. Verify full functionality and implement protective measures

Step 6. Document the problem, the actions you took to solve the problem, and the results

Identify the Problem

The first step in troubleshooting problems with these devices is to identify the problem.

Identifying Symptoms

Symptoms of print problems include

- An inability to print anything

- Slow print performance

- Poor print quality

To help determine more accurately why these events might be taking place, use the following methods.

Review Device Error Codes

Laser and solid ink printers can often display numeric or text error codes, sometimes with an LCD display or sometimes with specific patterns of flashing lights. Write down the message or code and check the documentation and vendor knowledge base to determine the problem.

Other types of printers might display a simple error indicator or simply not print. Consult printer documentation to determine the meaning of the signal and status displays on the printer.

Review Computer Error Messages and Logs

Virtually all printers in use today use bidirectional interfaces that can send messages back to the computer, such as

- Ink out
- Toner out
- Paper jam
- Printer offline

To view status messages like these, check the print spooler. Most printers use Windows's own built-in print spooler, although some inkjet printers use their own spooler software instead. Normally, the print spooler is transparent to the user, sending print jobs to the printer as they are received and as the printer is available. However, special circumstances, such as a network printer going offline or the need to discard a print job, might require the user to open the print spooler.

To view the print spooler, you can

- Double-click the Printer icon shown in the Windows toolbar; this icon appears whenever one or more print jobs are waiting to print.
- Double-click the icon for your printer in the Printers or Printers and Faxes folder.

The spooler displays the following information:

- The name of the printer

Document Name	Status	Owner	Pages	Size	Submitted	Port
19fig02_callout.pcx	Offline - Printing	Mark	1	3.98 MB/3.98 MB	5:02:58 PM 7/21/2003	LPT1:
1	2	3	4	5	6	7

HP LaserJet 5P — Printer Document View Help

1 document(s) in queue

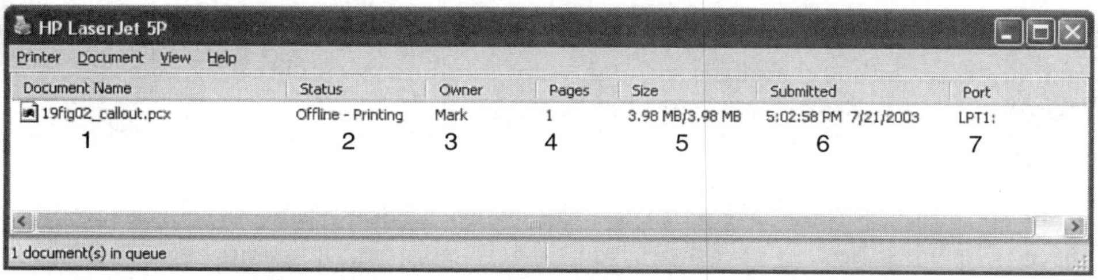

Figure 11-22   Windows XP print spooler in offline mode.

- The print jobs waiting to print in order (newest at the top), with the following information, as shown in Figure 11-22:
  - **1.**   Document name
  - **2.**   Status
  - **3.**   Owner (user who sent the job)
  - **4-5.**   Progress (number of pages or size of document)
  - **6.**   Time and date the job began printing
  - **7.**   The number of print jobs waiting to print

Using the Self-Test Feature

Printing a test page is a useful method for determining if the printer can print at all. If the printer has a built-in self test, use this function to determine if the printer is capable of printing. To print a test page from Windows, see "Printing a Test Page," earlier in this chapter for details.

Impact Printers   Most impact dot-matrix printers have a self-test feature onboard. Use this to determine

- Which firmware the printer is using

- Which fonts and typefaces the printer includes

Normally, the self test is activated by holding down a button, usually the LF (line feed) button, while the printer is turned on. If the printer is wide-carriage, make sure the paper in place is also wide-carriage; if you don't use wide-carriage paper, the printer will try to print on the platen, which could damage the printhead.

Inkjet Printers   Use the printer's self test (activated by pressing a button or button combination on most printers when you turn it on; it varies by printer; see documentation or the printer vendor's website for details) to see if the printer can print.

NOTE   Some recent printers don't include a built-in self-test function, but the vendors might offer online diagnosis through your computer's web browser. See the support website for your printer for details.

If the self test fails (you hear noise, but the printhead doesn't move), check the drive belt; if it is broken or if the drive gears are jammed, the printer must be repaired or replaced. (Low-cost printers usually are not worth repairing.) Try using the paper advance button; if the paper won't advance, check for obstructions, such as stuck labels or torn sheets, in the paper path.

If the self test works correctly, make sure the printer cable is attached correctly to the printer and computer, and retry the print job. If you get no results, make sure the proper port and driver are selected in Windows. If Windows sends print jobs to the wrong port, the printer won't receive the data and can't print. USB printers require a printer-specific driver as well as working USB ports.

Using Diagnostic Tools

The Utility menu included in many inkjet printers provides a variety of diagnostic tools you can use to solve printing problems. These might include the following:

- **Status or ink monitor**—Use this to determine the ink level in each cartridge
- **Nozzle check**—Use to determine if any printheads are clogged
- **Head cleaning**—Use to clean heads (this option uses ink, so use only if you have clogged nozzles)
- **Print head alignment**—Use to correct misaligned vertical straight lines or large characters

Many laser printers include a special Diagnostics mode that you can use to test the printer's cartridge check, paper path sensors, and components. To run built-in diagnostics, select this option from the printer's control panel.

Establishing a Theory of Probable Cause

Depending upon the type of problem you encounter with a printer, the probable cause might be obvious (toner out, head clog, and so on) or it might be more difficult to determine. To help determine the most likely causes, perform the steps in the following sections.

Reviewing Service Documentation

Some simple service documentation (such as how to replace a toner or ink cartridge) is usually included with most printers. However, for more complex operations, such as removal or replacement of motors or other components, you will probably need to consult the service documentation for the printer.

Some vendors offer detailed service documentation on their websites at no charge, while others might require you to purchase a service manual for the printer to get detailed service information.

TIP If you have a close relationship with a printer service shop, contact your representative to see if they can provide you with detailed information. Some companies that sell replacement and service parts for printers provide detailed procedure guides on their websites.

Reviewing Knowledge Base

If you are having a printer problem, be sure to consult the following knowledge bases for solutions:

- **The device vendor's knowledge base**—Typically, you need to specify the name and model number of the printer or device to see a range of articles. Some provide a free-text search to help you find solutions.

- **The knowledge base provided by the operating system vendor (Microsoft)**—Searching the Microsoft Help and Support (http://support.microsoft.com) is helpful if the problem appears to be related to the operating system.

- **The application vendor's website**—Although applications communicate with Windows via the printer or scanner driver to work with the hardware, you might find recommendations here as well.

Defining and Isolating the Problem

After reviewing the information provided by your own or customer tests, service information, and knowledge base searches, you are in a good position to define and isolate the problem. However, if you need more help in this process, determine the following:

- **What other hardware or software was in use at the time the problem occurred?**—The user probably will answer these types of questions in terms of open applications, but you will also want to look at the taskbar and system tray in Windows for other programs or routines that are running. Pressing Ctrl+Alt+Del will bring up a task list in Windows that has the most complete information about programs and subroutines in memory. To determine the exact version of a Windows-based program in use, click **Help**, **About**. View the System properties sheet to determine the version of Windows in use.

- **What task was the user trying to perform at the time the problem occurred?**—Ask the questions needed to find out the specific issues involved. For example, "Printing" isn't a sufficient answer. "Printing a five-page brochure from InDesign to a laser printer" is better, but you'll probably want the user to re-create the situation in an attempt to get all the information you need. Don't forget to check the Event Viewer in Windows XP, Vista, or 7 for details about the software running at the time of the error.

- **Is the hardware or software on the user's machine or is it accessed over the network?**—If the network is involved, check with the network administrator to see if the network is currently working properly, and check with other users to see if they can print to the network printer. If the hardware and software are not networked, your scope for troubleshooting is simpler.

- **What were the specific symptoms of the problem?**—Some users are very observant, but others might not be able to give you much help. Ask about the approximate time of the failure and about error messages, beeps, and unusual noises.

- **Can the problem be reproduced?**—Reproducible problems are easier to find than those that mysteriously "heal" themselves when you show up. Because power and environmental issues at the customer's site can cause printer or scanner problems, try to reproduce the problem at the customer's site before you move the device to your test bench, where conditions are different.

- **Does the problem repeat itself with a different combination of hardware and software, or does the problem go away when another combination of hardware and software is used?**—For example, if the user can print from Microsoft Word but not from Adobe Photoshop, this means that the printer is working, but there might be a problem with configuration or data types used by different applications. If the user can't print anything, there might be a general problem with the printer hardware or drivers.

Use the information you have gathered to develop a theory of probable cause. Start with the most likely cause first.

Testing the Theory to Determine Cause

To test your theory, try to confirm it. Here are a couple of examples:

Problem: A complex document (one with many fonts or graphics) does not print

Research findings: The greater the number of fonts or graphics in a document, the larger the amount of printer memory needed to print the document.

Theory: Not enough memory in printer.

Test: Print a simple document (one or two fonts, no graphics).

Desired Result: If the simple document prints but the complex document does not, a printer memory upgrade is probably needed.

Dealing with Other Results: If neither document prints, check for other possible causes (driver problems, cabling, port problems, and so on) and construct a new theory.

Problem: Repetitive marks on laser-printed document

Research findings: The distance between the marks is consistent with a dirty fusing roller or damage to the toner cartridge.

Theory: The fusing roller needs to be cleaned.

Test: Clean the fusing roller and print a test page.

Desired Result: If test pages no longer show repetitive marks, the problem is solved.

Dealing with Other Results: If test prints continue to show repetitive marks, replace the toner cartridge and reprint the test page.

Establishing a Plan of Action to Resolve the Problem and Implement the Solution

The plan of action to resolve the problem and implement the solution needs at least three elements, in the following order:

Step 1. **Determining the problem resolution**—Examples include installing more memory, cleaning the fusing roller, changing the toner cartridge, changing inkjet cartridges, and so on.

Step 2. **Developing a plan to implement the solution**—Specifying where to obtain upgrades or replacement parts, how to install them, what schedule to follow, and so on.

Step 3. **Implementing the solution**—Applying the solution to all affected printers and multifunction devices using the procedure in Step 2.

Verifying Full System Functionality and Implementing Preventative Measures (if Applicable)

After implementing the solution, be sure to test the printer or device to determine that the device has full functionality. In some cases, you might need to update settings in the printer properties sheet (such as memory size or paper tray settings). In addition to performing self-tests and test prints, be sure to print the same documents that were being printed when the problem was first reported.

Documenting Findings, Actions, and Results

The final step recommended in CompTIA's A+ Certification troubleshooting theory is the documentation of your findings, actions, and results. You can make notes of your process in any form, but if you want to research similar problems and possible solutions more quickly, consider developing a spreadsheet or database that can store this information in an easily searchable format.

If the problem and solution involve Windows error messages or dialogs, use screen capture or a digital camera (useful for recording STOP blue-screen errors) to save this information for future review.

Troubleshooting Print Failures

Print failures can be caused by a variety of issues, as described in the following sections. Use this information to prepare for troubleshooting questions on the A+ Certification exams and in real-world circumstances.

Paper Out

A paper-out error is one of the easiest problems to solve. Depending upon the printer and printer driver, you might see an on-screen error or a numeric error or error code on the printer's control panel or signal lights.

To solve a paper out error, load additional paper and press the printer's online button (or click the **Continue** or **Retry** button in an error dialog in Windows) to continue printing.

If a paper-out error is displayed when the printer has paper installed, remove the paper stack and reinstall it into the paper tray. If the problem persists, shut down the printer, wait a few seconds, and restart it. If the problem persists, have the printer serviced.

Clearing Print Queue

You might need to clear a print queue for a variety of reasons:

- The wrong options selected for the installed paper
- Gibberish printing because of a problem with the printer driver, cable, or port
- You decide not to print the queued documents

You can clear selected print jobs or all print jobs in a queue.

To access the print queue (also known as the print spooler), open the printer icon in the notification area, or open the Printers and Faxes folder in Control Panel and double-click the appropriate printer icon.

To discard a print job in the print queue, follow these steps:

Step 1.   Open the print queue.

Step 2.   Right-click the print job you want to discard.

Step 3.   Select **Cancel Print** and the print job will be discarded.

To discard all print jobs in the queue, follow these steps:

Step 1.   Open the print queue.

Step 2.   Click **Printer**.

Step 3.   Click **Cancel All Documents** (varies by Windows version) to discard all print jobs.

Restarting Print Queue

To release print jobs stored in the queue in offline mode after the network printer is available, use one of these methods:

Step 1.   Open the print queue.

Step 2.   Click **Printer**.

Step 3.   Uncheck **Use Printer Offline** and the print jobs will go to the printer.

Alternatively:

Step 1.   Right-click the printer icon in the Printers and Faxes folder.

Step 2.   Click **Use Printer Online**.

Power Off, Power On Printer

Turning off and turning on the printer can sometimes solve print problems, but if the printer is accepting a large print job from a Windows print queue, it might also be necessary to clear the print queue to prevent continued printing of garbage pages.

The memory in laser printers is used to store multiple pages. Check the printer documentation to see how to clear out the printer's page memory.

Paper Jams

Paper jams have a variety of causes, depending upon the printer type. Use the following sections to solve paper jams.

NOTE   Some printers require special tools to remove the plastic shell; contact the printer's manufacturer for detailed disassembly instructions and recommended tools.

Paper Path Issues   The more turns the paper must pass through during the printing process, the greater the chances of paper jams. Curved paper paths are typical of some inkjet and many laser printers as well as dot-matrix printers using push tractors: The paper is pulled from the front of the printer, pulled through and around a series of rollers inside the printer during the print process, and then ejected through the front or top of the printer onto a paper tray. Because the cross-section of this paper path resembles a *C*, this is sometimes referred to as a *C-shaped paper path*.

Some printers, especially those with bottom-mounted paper trays, have more complex paper paths that resemble an *S*.

A straight-through paper path is a typical option on laser printers with a curved paper path. Printers with this feature have a rear paper output tray that can be lowered for use, which overrides the normal top paper output tray. Some also have a front paper tray. Use both front and rear trays for a true straight-through path; this is recommended for printing on envelopes, labels, or card stock. Inkjet printers with input paper trays at the rear of the printer and an output tray at the front also use this method or a variation in which the paper path resembles a flattened V.

Paper Loading, Paper Type, and Media Thickness Issues   Paper jams can be caused by incorrect paper-loading procedures, overloading the input tray, or using paper or card stock that is thicker than the recommended types for the printer. If the printer jams, open the exit cover or front cover or remove the paper tray(s) as needed to clear the jam.

TIP   When you insert paper into any type of printer, be sure to fan the pages before you insert the paper into the tray to prevent sticking.

Print Quality Problems

Print quality problems have many causes, but the following sections will help you understand the leading causes and their solutions for each printer type covered by the A+ Certification exams.

Laser/LED Printers   Black marks on a page are usually caused by debris stuck to or surface damage to the imaging drum or dirty components in the printer (fuser, paper rollers, charging rollers, and so on). To determine which component is the cause, compare the distance between marks on the paper with the circumference of each component. The printer's manual will provide this information. Replace the imaging drum (part of the toner cartridge on many printer models) if the drum is at fault. Clean other components if they're at fault, and retest.
If printing is uneven or there are blank spots on the page, the toner is running low. Remove the toner cartridge and gently shake it to redistribute the toner. Install a new toner cartridge as quickly as possible. If the printing is even, the printer might be set for Economode or a similar mode that uses less toner. Adjust the printer properties to use normal print modes for final drafts.

If the printer produces a blank page immediately after the toner cartridge has been changed, remove the toner cartridge and make sure the tape that holds the toner in place has been removed; without toner, the printer can't print.

If the printer produces a blank page after printing thousands of pages, the toner probably is exhausted. Replace the toner cartridge.

If the printed output can be wiped or blown off the paper after the printout emerges from the laser printer, the fuser needs to be repaired or replaced. The fuser is supposed to heat the paper to fuse the toner to the paper; if it fails, the toner won't stick to the paper.

Inkjet Printers   Smudged print output from an inkjet printer can be caused by dirty printheads, incorrect head gap settings, or paper rollers and by incorrect resolution and media settings. First, check the head gap setting; use the default setting for paper up to 24 lb. rating; the wider gap for labels, card stock, and envelopes. Clean the printhead by using the printer's built-in nozzle cleaning routine. Typically, the cleaning routine can print a test sheet before and after cleaning. Repeat the cleaning process until all colors and black print properly. If the cleaning process doesn't result in acceptable results, remove the printhead and clean it. If the printhead is built into the printer or if the paper-feed rollers or platen have ink smudges, use a cleaning sheet to clean the paper-feed rollers, platen, and printhead.

Check the Printer Properties setting in the operating system to ensure that the correct resolution and paper options are set for the paper in use. Incorrect settings can lead to excessive ink being used for a particular print job, leading to smudged output.

Unlike laser output—which can be handled as soon as the page is ejected—inkjet output, particularly from older printers or output on transparencies or glossy photo paper, often requires time to dry. For best results, use paper specially designed for inkjet printers. Paper should be stored in a cool, dry environment; damp paper also will result in smudged printing.

If uneven characters occur after the ink cartridge has been replaced, you might need to realign the printhead with the printer's utility program or Printer Properties sheet. This process prints out a series of long bars, after which the user selects which bar is properly aligned.

Gaps in printed output usually indicate a partially clogged printhead. See "Inkjet Printers" (in the preceding section) for instructions. Replacing the ink cartridge replaces the printhead on some printers, but on other printers the printhead is a separate, removable device or is fixed in position.

TIP   Third-party and poorly refilled OEM inkjet cartridges are among the major causes for poor-quality prints, printhead clogs, and ink leakage in inkjet printers. For maximum print quality, you should use same-brand consumables when replacing ink in inkjet printers.

Impact Printers   If the print is evenly faded, the ribbon is dried out. Replace the ribbon to achieve better print quality and protect the printhead. If the print appears more faded on the top of each line than on the bottom, the head gap is set too wide for the paper type in use. Adjust the head gap to the correct width to improve printing and protect the printhead from damage.

If the printhead won't move, check the drive belt and the gear mechanism. Jammed gears in the printer or a broken drive belt will prevent the drive belt from moving the printhead. Check the drive belt first to see if it is broken, and then check the gears that move the printhead. You might need to disassemble the printer to check the gears.

Thermal and Dye-Sublimation Printers   Poor print quality in thermal and dye-sublimation printers can have several causes, including

- Incorrect printhead temperature

- Wrong paper or media type for printer or print mode

- Dirty printer parts, paper, or media

- Incorrect printhead pressure or head-gap settings

- Defective ribbons

- Distorted colors

- Incorrect print density settings

If the printhead is too hot or too cold for the media in use, the printing will be of poor quality. Check the following:

- **Environmental temperature**—Move the printer to a warmer room if the area is much colder than normal room temperature, or to a cooler room if the room is much warmer than normal room temperature.

- **Print mode setting**—If the printer can be used in both direct thermal (ribbonless) or thermal transfer (uses ribbons) modes, make sure the correct mode is selected and that the printer is using a ribbon only when used in thermal transfer mode.

Thermal transfer printing can be performed on a wider range of media than direct thermal printing, but you should still use only recommended types of paper, labels, and other media. Because thermal transfer printing melts wax or resin to the paper, smooth paper and label stock works better than textured paper or label stock.

Direct thermal printing uses heat-sensitive paper, so don't try using plain paper in a direct thermal printer. If the printer can be switched between direct thermal and thermal transfer modes, make sure to switch to the correct type of paper stock for the mode and insert or remove the ribbon as needed (the ribbon is used for thermal transfer, but not for direct thermal).

Printheads used for thermal transfer printing can become contaminated with wax or resin residue from the ribbon. Follow the printer vendor's recommendations for cleaning the printhead.

On a direct thermal printer, check the rollers used to transport paper for dust and dirt. If they are dirty, clean them with a cleaning sheet, soft wipe, or compressed air according to the vendor's recommendations.

Dust or dirt on any type of paper stock, especially that used for direct thermal printing, can cause dropouts in printed text or graphics. Store paper or media in a clean, dust-free location.

Thermal transfer printers rely on heat transfer from the printhead to the ribbon and from the ribbon to the paper or media to produce a printed image. If the head-gap or printhead pressure settings are incorrect, the print quality will be faded or uneven.

Use the color-matching features provided in the photo editor and with the printer to assure accurate colors. You might need to use a calibration sheet with your scanner and photo editor.

Be sure to replace ribbons on a thermal transfer printer when print quality declines. Although some thermal transfer printers work with multiuse ribbons, eventually these ribbons don't have enough useful wax or resin left to produce a high-quality image.

Both types of thermal printing can use adjustments in print density. It might be done with an adjustment on the printer or through the Printer Properties sheet in Windows. Increase the density to achieve dark, well-formed letters, but reduce the density if closed letters such as *a*, *e*, or *o* start to fill in.

Error Messages and Codes

Printers use many different methods to provide error messages and codes, including

- **On-printer error codes and messages**—These can be provided by the printer's LCD display or by signal lights flashing in different patterns.

- **Windows printer driver error messages**—These can be displayed within the print spooler window or by the print progress dialog used by many inkjet printers.

HP LaserJet printers use the following error codes to describe printing problems:

- **13 or 13.xx**—Paper Jam (replace .xx with specific numeric values that indicate exactly where the paper jam has occurred)

- **20**—Insufficient memory; press Go to print partial page

- **40**—Bad transmission to EIO interface card

- **41.xx**—Various printer errors involving media or other problems (replace .xx with value indicating specific error)

- **49.xx**—Firmware error

- **50.4**—Line voltage

- **50.x**—Fuser error

- **51.x**—Beam detect (.1) or laser error (.2)

- **52.x**—Scanner speed errors; startup error (.1); rotation error (.2)

- **53.xy.zz**—DIMM memory error in specified module (x= DIMM type; y=location; zz=error number)

- **54.1**—Sealing tape not removed from toner cartridge

- **54.4**—Line voltage error

- **55.xx**—Internal communications error; can be caused by formatter, firmware DIMM, engine controller board, or fuser problems

- **56.x**—Error in paper input or accessory (.1) or output bin (.2) connection

- **57.x**—Printer fan (.4), duplex fan (.7), or main motor (older printer models in LaserJet 4, 5 series) failure

- **58.2**—Environmental thermistor (TH3) failure

- **59.x**—Main motor error (.0), startup error (.1), or rotation error (.2)

- **62.x**—Printer memory error in internal memory (.0) or DIMM slots (.1–.4)

- **64**—Scan buffer error

- **66.xx.yy**—External paper-handling device error

- **68**—NVRAM or permanent storage error

- **69.x**—Temporary printing error

- **79**—Printer detected error (can be caused by memory, firmware, EIO, formatter)

- **8x.yyyy**—EIO device or slot error

A good resource for both numerical and text-based error codes for HP LaserJet printers is the HP Laserjet Error Codes page at PrinterTechs.com: http://www.printertechs.com/tech/error-codes/error-codes-index.php.

Performing Preventative Maintenance

A properly-maintained printer is capable of producing hundreds of thousands of pages—*if* it is properly maintained. The recommendations in this section are based on years of real-world experience as well as the A+ Certification exam objectives.

Installing Maintenance Kits

Many HP and other laser printers feature components that should be replaced at periodic intervals. These components often include fuser assemblies, air filters, transfer rollers, pickup rollers, other types of rollers, and separation pads. These components wear out over time, and can usually be purchased as a maintenance kit as well as separately.

A printer that uses a maintenance kit will display a message or an error code with a meaning such as "Perform printer maintenance" or "Perform user maintenance" when the printer reaches the recommended page count for maintenance kit replacement. Depending upon the printer model and whether it is used for color or monochrome printing, the recommended page count could be at as few as 50,000 pages or as much as 300,000 pages or more.

NOTE   See PrinterTechs.com, Inc. (http://www.printertechs.com/maintenance-kits.php) or DepotAmerica (http://www.depot-america.com) to purchase maintenance kits for HP and Lexmark laser printers and for useful installation instructions.

Resetting Paper Counts

After a fuser assembly or full maintenance kit is installed in a laser printer, the page count must be reset; otherwise, you will not know when to perform recommended maintenance again. Typically, the page count is reset by pressing a specified combination of buttons on the printer's control panel.

NOTE   If the printer is under service contract or being charged on a per page (or click) basis, it is not recommended to reset the paper count after servicing. However, most laser printers print the page count when you perform a self-test.

Cleaning Rollers, Printheads, and Other Components

Most types of printers need periodic cleaning of various components, including rollers, printheads, wiper and cleaning blades, and others. The following sections help you determine the components in each printer type that need to be cleaned, and how to clean them.

Laser Printers   Because laser printers use fine-grain powdered toner, keeping the inside of a laser printer clean is important in periodic maintenance. Turn off the laser printer before using a damp cloth to clean up any toner spills. To keep the paper path and rollers clean, use cleaning sheets made for laser printers, as follows:

Step 1.   Insert the sheet into the manual feed tray on the laser printer.

Step 2.   Create a short document with Notepad, WordPad, or some other text editor and print it on the sheet.

As the sheet passes through the printer, it cleans the rollers. If a specialized cleaning sheet is not available, you can also use transparency film designed for laser printers.

CAUTION   *Never* use transparency media not designed for laser printers in a laser printer. Copier or inkjet media isn't designed to handle the high heat of a laser printer and can melt or warp and possibly damage the printer.

Inkjet Printers   Cleaning an inkjet printer's printhead—either with the printer's own cleaning feature, a cleaning utility built into the printer driver, or with a moistened cleaning sheet—will restore most printers to service. Most inkjet printers have built-in or software-controlled routines for cleaning the ink cartridges and checking the alignment of two-pass characters. Use these options when you notice poor-quality printouts.

CAUTION   Because both cleaning liquids and plain water can be used to clean up excess ink (unplug the printer first!), inkjet printers should *not* be used when water resistance is of paramount concern. Inkjet inks are more water resistant today than previously, but a careless spill can still destroy a digital masterpiece printed on an inkjet printer.

To learn more about inkjet printer cleaning kits, see "Cleaning Solutions," later in this chapter.

Thermal Transfer and Direct Thermal Printers   Printheads used for thermal transfer printing can become contaminated with wax or resin residue from the ribbon. Follow the printer vendor's recommendations for cleaning the printhead. On a direct thermal printer, check the rollers used to transport paper for dust and dirt. If they are dirty, clean them with a cleaning sheet, soft wipe, or compressed air according to the vendor's recommendations.

Checking for a Suitable Environment

Check the printer documentation to determine the vendor's recommendation for a suitable environment for the printer. If the printer is located in a room with too high a relative humidity level (85% or higher), paper might swell or stick together, toner might not transfer or set up properly, and inkjet output might not stick to the paper. Too low a humidity level (15% or lower) can cause static electricity to build up.

Using Recommended Supplies

Printer manufacturers have two reasons for encouraging users to use same-brand ink, toner, and paper, and only one of them involves profitability. Yes, printer makers often make more money from inkjet printer cartridges than from the sale of the printer itself (so much so that I actually overheard a shopper at a discount store call home and say that he was buying a new printer rather than buying ink for the family's old printer). However, the other reason to buy same-brand supplies is print quality, particularly with inkjet printers.

While third-party ink for inkjet printers is much less expensive per page than OEM ink, it also fades much more quickly in most cases but also produces poorer-quality output.

NOTE   The *PC World* June 2008 study, "Cheap Ink: Will It Cost You?" by Jeff Bertolucci (available at www.pcworld.com/article/147267/cheap_ink_will_it_cost_you.html), provides a recent demonstration of the poorer print quality and shorter image lifespan produced by third-party inks. The story also features side-by-side comparisons of photos printed with OEM and third-party inks.

Wilhelm Imaging Research (HYPERLINK "http://www.wilhelm-research.com" www.wilhelm-research.com) provides links to many recent professional studies of inkjet print permanence ratings.

Recommended Tools

The following sections discuss tools you can use to solve printer problems.

Multimeter

The multimeter can be used to check AC and DC voltage and to check cable continuity. If a printer is not receiving power, you can use the multimeter to determine if it is plugged into a working AC power source, or to verify that the DC power levels coming from an AC/DC converter are correct.

Be sure to select the appropriate AC or DC voltage range on manual-ranging meters, and if you use the meter to test voltages inside the printer, make sure the meter is designed to handle the voltage range(s) it will encounter.

Screwdrivers

At a minimum, you should have narrow and wide-blade screwdrivers and jewelers' screwdrivers. Some printers might require specialty drivers such as hex or Torx drivers.

Cleaning Solutions

Cleaning sheets and solutions are available for most types of printers. Moistened cleaning sheets can be used to help clean clogged inkjet and solid-ink printheads or print rollers in a variety of printers.

Inkjet printer cleaning kits come in two forms:

- A special sheet and cleaning spray
- A cleaning pad and liquid cleaner

The sheet and spray is used to clean the paper paths in the printer and to remove ink buildup on the printheads. Spray the cleaner onto the sheet, insert it into the printer as directed, and print a few lines of text to clean the printer.

The cleaning pad is designed for models with removable printheads (which are part of the ink cartridge on thermal-inkjet printer models). Soak the pad with the supplied fluid and rub the printhead over it to remove built-up ink.

Be sure to use cleaning sheets or solutions designed for the particular printer or device you need to clean, and follow the vendor's recommendations.

If you need to remove fingerprints and other markings from scanner cover glass, printer or scanner enclosures, or other computer components, Endust for Electronics is a good choice. Available in aerosol or pump spray or premoistened wipes, Endust for Electronics does not cause static buildup.

Extension Magnet

An extension magnet can help you retrieve dropped screws or other components from inside a printer, scanner, or all-in-one unit.

Exam Preparation Tasks

Review All the Key Topics

Review the most important topics in the chapter, noted with the key topics icon in the outer margin of the page. Table 11-2 lists a reference of these key topics and the page numbers on which each is found.

Table 11-2   Key Topics for Chapter 11

Key Topic Element	Description	Page Number
Figure 11-1	The Advanced – Printing Defaults – Paper/Quality Properties sheet in Windows XP.	441
Figure 11-3	A typical inkjet printer with its cover open.	445
Figure 11-5	Actual print samples illustrating the differences in 24-pin and 9-pin printers.	448
Figure 11-8	A typical monochrome laser printer's components.	452
Figure 11-9	Direct thermal, and thermal transfer, printing technologies.	455
Figure 11-10	Illustration of dye-sublimation printing process.	456
Figure 11-11	Front and rear views of an Ethernet print server that supports USB printers.	457
Figure 11-12	Selecting a printer by brand and model.	460
Figures 11-13 and 11-14	Windows XP and Windows 7 Print screens.	464-465
Figure 11-17	Viewing print spooler settings in Windows 7's Microsoft Management Console.	469
Figure 11-20	Selecting portrait or landscape print mode.	472
Figure 11-22	Windows XP print spooler in offline mode.	477

Definitions of Key Terms

Define the following key terms from this chapter, and check your answers in the glossary.

Laser printer, Inkjet printer, Thermal printer, Impact printer, Solid ink printer, Toner cartridge, CMYK, Near Letter Quality, Electrophotographic process, Piezo-electric, Print spooler

Troubleshooting Scenario

You have just purchased a new printer. You have set up the printer where it needs to be. Once you have completed the setup and try to print a test page, you notice that the page is unreadable. What process should you complete to correct the problem?

Refer to Appendix A for the answer.

This chapter covers the following subjects:

- **Floppy Disk Drives**—Standard end-users might not use these anymore, but technicians do, for several reasons. We'll cover what a PC technician needs to know about floppy drives, including types, hardware configuration, installation, BIOS configuration, and care of floppy drives.

- **Hard Disk Drives**—Hard drives are the most common and most important storage device. You'll learn about SATA, PATA (IDE), jumpering, installation, creating arrays of redundant disks, and optimizing performance.

- **CD, DVD, and Blu-ray Optical Drives**—This section describes the various types of CD, DVD, and Blu-ray drives and media; how to install optical drives; optical drive interfaces; how to record to CD, DVD, and Blu-ray; any possible installation issues you may encounter.

- **Removable Storage**—This section talks about various Iomega storage products including REV and Zip.

- **Tape Drives**—This section covers the major types of tape drives, interfaces, and native and compressed capacity.

- **Flash Memory and Card Readers**—This section describes flash media such as Compact Flash, SD cards, memory sticks, flash card readers, and how to install and hot-swap flash memory.

- **USB Flash Memory Drives**—This section describes how USB flash drives are formatted and how to hot-swap them using the "Safely Remove Hardware" icon.

- **External Hard Disks**—This section defines the various external disks that are available, demonstrates how to hot-swap them, and describes the connections that are normally used.

- **Troubleshooting Storage**—In this last section you will learn how to identify and fix problems related to floppy drives; SATA, eSATA, and PATA drives; optical drives; removable and external media.

This chapter covers a portion of the CompTIA A+ 220-701 objectives 1.1, 1.2, and 2.5 and CompTIA A+ 220-702 objective 1.1 and 1.2.

CHAPTER 12

Storage Devices

Modern desktop computers feature a variety of storage devices, from the venerable floppy disk drive to its replacement, USB flash memory drives. Other typical storage devices include hard drives; Blu-ray, CD, and DVD optical drives and media; removable storage using tape cartridges or flash memory cards; and external storage devices of various types. The following sections teach you what you need to know about each item.

"Do I Know This Already?" Quiz

The "Do I Know This Already?" quiz allows you to assess whether you should read this entire chapter or simply jump to the "Exam Preparation Tasks" section for review. If you are in doubt, read the entire chapter. Table 12-1 outlines the major headings in this chapter and the corresponding "Do I Know This Already?" quiz questions. You can find the answers in Appendix A, "Answers to the 'Do I Know This Already?' Quizzes and Troubleshooting Scenarios."

Table 12-1 "Do I Know This Already?" Foundation Topics Section-to-Question Mapping

Foundations Topics Section	Questions Covered in This Section
Floppy Disk Drives	1
Hard Disk Drives	2, 3
Blu-Ray, CD, and DVD Optical Drives	4, 5
Removable Storage	6
Tape Drives	7
Flash Memory and Card Readers	8
USB Flash Memory Drives	9, 10
External Hard Disks	11
Troubleshooting Storage	12

1. Which of the following drives uses a 1.44MB disk to store data and can also be used for bootable diagnostics?

   a.   CD-ROM

   b.   Floppy disk

   c.   USB drive

   d.   External hard drive

2. Which of the following is installed in all computers and is used for storing the operating system?

   a.   USB drive

   b.   CD drive

   c.   Hard drive

   d.   Firewire drive

3. What is the sector size on the platter on a hard drive?

   a.   1024 bytes

   b.   750 bytes

   c.   512 bytes

   d.   128 bytes

4. What are the two listed interfaces that are used to connect internal Blu-ray, DVD, and CD drives to the computer? (Choose two.)

   a.   SATA

   b.   IrDA

   c.   PATA

   d.   USB

5. You have just installed a CD-ROM drive to your computer. You want to listen to music so you insert a music CD into the drive. Windows Media Player starts up and you can see a song title and the elapsed time of the song within the player. Everything *looks* correct; however, for some reason you cannot hear the music. What could be the problem?

   a.   The power cable is not connected to the CD-ROM drive.

   b.   You need to connect the CD audio cable to the sound card.

   c.   You need to go the manufacturer's website for an updated CD-ROM driver.

   d.   The CD is faulty.

6. What are the sizes available for the Iomega Zip removable storage drives? (Choose all that apply.)

   a. 100MB

   b. 250MB

   c. 300GB

   d. 750MB

7. Which of the following storage devices uses magnetic tape to store large amounts of data?

   a. External hard drive

   b. USB drive

   c. ATA drive

   d. Tape drive

8. You are in need of a device that will read the different types of memory cards. You purchase a flash card reader. How would you install this device on your computer?

   a. Connect it to the motherboard

   b. Connect it to an available USB port

   c. Connect it to the serial port

   d. Connect it to the removable disk drive slot

9. Which of the following devices is the best solution for quickly transferring data between systems and running utility programs?

   a. USB drive

   b. 3.5-inch floppy

   c. 100 MB Zip drive

   d. CD-ROM drive

10. You purchase a new USB flash memory drive. Which of the following file systems has this drive been pre-formatted with? (Select two.)

   a. NTFS

   b. NFS

   c. FAT16

   d. FAT32

11. Which of the following connections are used for external hard disks? (Choose all that apply.)

    a.   eSATA

    b.   USB

    c.   IEEE 1394

    d.   PCIe

12. You have just installed a new floppy drive on a computer. You notice that when you turn the computer on, the drive light stays on. What could be causing this problem?

    a.   The cable has been installed incorrectly.

    b.   The drive is faulty.

    c.   The drive has been installed improperly.

    d.   The BIOS has not been configured properly.

Floppy Disk Drives

Floppy drives are used primarily for backups of small amounts of data, for bootable diagnostic disks, and for the creation of bootable emergency disks with some versions of Windows. The 1.44MB floppy drive shown in Figure 12-1 and Figure 12-2 is found in some recent and virtually all older desktop and laptop computers, although many recent computers no longer use floppy drives. The 1.44MB drive uses 3.5-inch double-sided high-density (DSHD) media, and also supports the 720KB 3.5-inch double-sided double-density (DSDD) media used by 3.5-inch drives produced in the 1980s. Some older IBM systems used a 2.88MB DSED floppy drive, but were also compatible with 1.44MB and 720KB floppy disks.

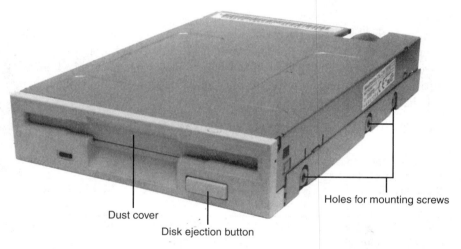

Holes for mounting screws

Dust cover

Disk ejection button

Figure 12-1 A typical 3.5-inch floppy disk drive.

Figure 12-1 shows the front and sides of a typical 3.5-inch floppy drive, and Figure 12-2 shows the data and power connectors used by 3.5-inch floppy drives.

NOTE Most desktop systems that use 3.5-inch drives use internal drives (refer to Figure 12-1), but floppy drives can also be connected to the USB port.

In the following sections, you will learn about the different types of floppy disk drives and media, and how drives are installed, configured in the BIOS, and maintained.

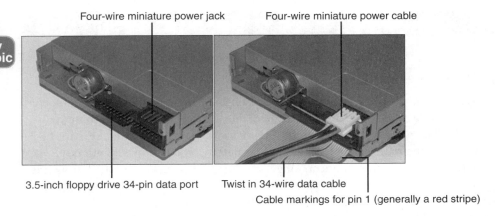

Figure 12-2   The rear of a typical 3.5-inch drive before (left) and after (right) data and power cables are attached.

Floppy Disk Types

Floppy drives use flexible magnetic media protected by a rigid plastic case and a retractable shutter. There have been three different types of 3.5-inch floppy disk media used over time, although only the 1.44MB floppy disk is used currently. Figure 12-3 compares the capacities and distinguishing marks of each disk type. Note that all 3.5-inch disks use the write-enable slider shown in Figure 12-3.

Table 12-2 helps you distinguish between the different disk types.

Table 12-2   Physical Characteristics of 3.5-inch Floppy Media

Disk Type	Capacity	Jacket	Reinforced Hub	Write-Protect	Media Sensor
3.5-inch DSDD	720KB	Rigid with metal shutter	N/A	Open write-protect slider	N/A
3.5-inch DSHD	1.44MB	Rigid with metal shutter	N/A	Open write-protect slider	Opposite write-protect slider
3.5-inch DSED	2.88MB	Rigid with metal shutter	N/A	Open write-protect slider	Offset from write-protect slider

Of the disks pictured in Figure 12-3, only the 3.5-inch DSHD disk is commonly used today. 1.44MB disks are often marked *HD* on their front and always have a media-sensing hole in the opposite corner from the write-enable/protect slider.

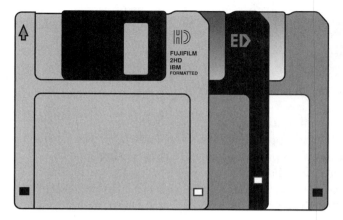

Figure 12-3   A 3.5-inch 1.44MB floppy disk (left) compared to a 720KB floppy disk (right) and a 2.88MB floppy disk (center).

NOTE   Some older desktop and portable systems might use an LS-120 or LS-240 SuperDisk drive in place of a standard 1.44MB floppy drive. These drives can read and write 1.44MB and 720KB 3.5-inch floppy media, but can also use high-capacity 3.5-inch media. The LS-120 SuperDisk uses 120MB media, and the LS-240 SuperDisk can use 120MB or 240MB media. These drives usually plug into the ATA/IDE (PATA) interface if internal, or the parallel or USB port if external.

5.25-inch floppy drives were used before 3.5-inch drives became commonplace, but they have been obsolete for some years and are seldom used.

Floppy Disk Drive Hardware Configuration

Floppy disk drive hardware configuration depends on several factors, including

- **Correct CMOS configuration**—The system's BIOS configuration screen must have the correct drive selected for A: and B:.

- **Correct cable positioning and attachment**—The position of the drive(s) on the cable determine which is A: and which is B:. If the cable is not oriented properly, the drive will spin continuously and the LED on the front of the drive will stay on.

CAUTION   If you insert disks into a floppy drive while the cable is reversed, the contents of the media can be damaged or the media can be rendered unusable.

The standard floppy disk drive interface uses a single IRQ and single I/O port address range, whether the interface is built in or on an expansion card:

■   Floppy Drive IRQ: 6

■   Floppy Drive I/O Port Address: 3F0–3F7h

The standard floppy disk drive interface can support two drives: drive A: and drive B:. However, some recent systems support only one floppy drive (A:). The 34-pin floppy disk drive data cable has wires numbered 10 to 16 twisted in reverse between the connectors for drive A: and drive B:. The drive beyond the twist is automatically designated as drive A:; the drive connected between the twisted and the untwisted end of the cable (which connects to the floppy controller) is automatically designated as drive B:.

Figure 12-4 compares five-connector universal (3.5-inch/5.25-inch) and three-connector 3.5-inch floppy cables. (The cable connector to the floppy controller is not visible in this photo.)

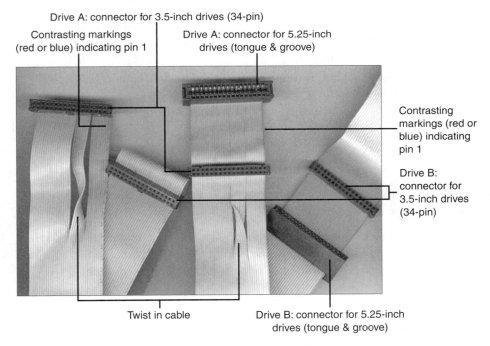

Figure 12-4   Two types of floppy drive cables compared. On the left, a cable designed for 3.5-inch drives only; on the right, a cable designed for 3.5-inch and 5.25-inch drives.

Floppy Disk Drive Physical Installation and Removal

To install a 3.5-inch 1.44MB floppy disk drive as drive A:, follow these steps:

Step 1. Select an empty 3.5-inch external drive bay; an external drive bay is a drive bay with a corresponding opening in the case.

Step 2. Remove the dummy face plate from the case front.

Step 3. For an ATX tower system, remove the left side panel (as seen from the front). For a BTX tower system, remove the right side panel (as seen from the front). For a desktop system, remove the top.

Step 4. If the 3.5-inch drive bay is a removable "cage," remove it from the system. This might involve pushing on a spring-loaded tab or removing a screw. Some drive bays pull straight out (as here), whereas others swing to one side.

Step 5. Remove the floppy disk drive from its protective packaging. Test the screws you intend to use to secure the drive and ensure they're properly threaded and the correct length.

Step 6. Check the bottom or rear panel of the drive for markings indicating pin 1; if no markings are found, assume pin 1 is the pin closest to the power supply connector.

Step 7. Secure the drive to the drive bay with the screws supplied with the drive or with the computer (see Figure 12-5).

Step 8. Replace the drive bay into the computer.

Step 9. Attach the 34-pin connector at the end of the floppy disk drive data cable with the twist to the data connector on the drive.

Step 10. Run the other end of the floppy disk drive data cable through the drive bay into the interior of the computer. Then, connect it to the floppy disk drive interface on the motherboard or add-on card.

Step 11. Attach the correct type of four-wire power cable to the drive. You might need to slide the drive part way into the drive bay to make the connection.

Step 12. Double check power and data cable keying before starting the computer.

Step 13. Follow these steps in reverse to remove the drive from the system.

Floppy Drive BIOS Configuration

Floppy disk drives cannot be detected by the system; you must manually configure the floppy disk drive or floppy disk drives you add to the system.

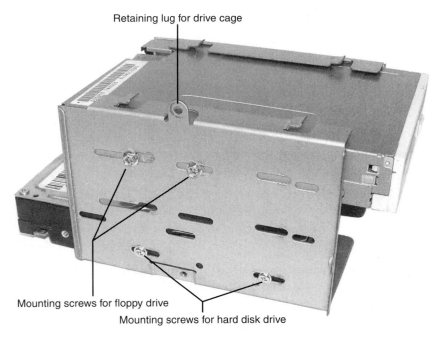

Figure 12-5   A removable drive cage with the attachment screws for the floppy disk drive and hard drive. The opposite side of each drive is also secured with screws (not shown).

To configure the floppy disk drive in the ROM BIOS, follow these steps:

Step 1.   Verify the correct physical installation as listed previously.

Step 2.   Turn on the monitor and the computer.

Step 3.   Press the appropriate key(s) to start the BIOS configuration program.

Step 4.   Open the standard configuration menu.

Step 5.   Select Drive A: or the first floppy disk drive.

Step 6.   Use the appropriate keys to scroll through the choices; 3.5-inch 1.44MB is the correct choice for virtually all systems with an onboard floppy drive (see Figure 12-6).

Step 7.   No other changes are necessary, so save your changes and exit to reboot the system.

If you only need a floppy drive for occasional use, you can connect an external floppy drive to the USB port. If you need to boot from an external floppy drive or need to load drivers from it during the installation of Windows, check the system BIOS setup program to verify that the drive is listed as a bootable device.

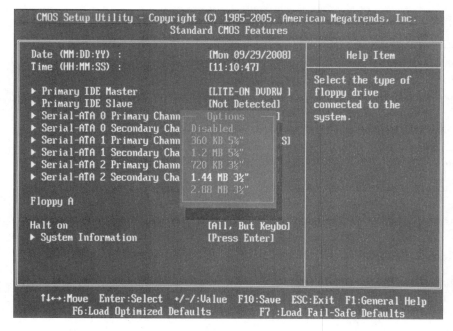

Figure 12-6 Viewing floppy drive type options in the BIOS setup program of a typical system.

Maintaining Floppy Disks, Data, and Drives

You can protect the data on your floppy disks by following these recommendations; most of these suggestions also apply to higher-capacity magnetic removable media such as Zip, REV, and tape backups:

- Do not open the protective metal shutter on 3.5-inch disks or tape backups.

- Do not touch the magnetic media itself.

- Store disks away from sources of magnetism (CRT monitors, magnetized tools, unshielded speakers, and unshielded cables) or heat.

- Open the sliding write-protect hole on 3.5-inch disks to prevent the contents of the disk from being changed.

Floppy disk drives are a type of magnetic storage in which the read/write heads make direct contact with the media. This is similar to the way that tape drives work, and just like tape backup, music cassette, or VCR heads, a floppy disk drive's read/write heads can become contaminated by dust, dirt, smoke, or magnetic particles flaking off the disk's media surfaces. For this reason, periodic maintenance of floppy disk drives will help to avoid the need to troubleshoot drives that cannot reliably read or write data.

The following are some guidelines for cleaning a floppy disk drive:

■   Approximately every six months, or more often in dirty or smoke-filled conditions, use a wet-type head-cleaning disk on the drive.

These cleaning kits use a special cleaning floppy disk that contains cleaning media in place of magnetic media, along with an alcohol-based cleaner. Add a few drops to the media inside the cleaning disk, slide it into the drive, and activate the drive with a command such as DIR or by using Windows Explorer; as the read/write heads move across the cleaning media, they are cleaned. Allow the heads to dry for about an hour before using the drive.

■   Whenever you open a system for any type of maintenance or checkup, review the condition of the floppy disk drive(s). Use compressed air to remove fuzz or hair from the drive heads and check the mechanism for smooth operation.

Hard Disk Drives

Hard disk drives are the most important storage device used by a personal computer. Hard disk drives store the operating system (Windows, Linux, or others) and load it into the computer's memory (RAM) at startup. Hard disk drives also store applications, system configuration files used by applications and the operating system, and data files created by the user.

Traditional hard disk drives use one or more double-sided platters formed from rigid materials such as aluminum or glass. These platters are coated with a durable magnetic surface that is divided into sectors. Each sector contains 512 bytes of storage along with information about where the sector is located on the disk medium. Sectors are organized in concentric circles from the edge of the media inward toward the middle of the platter. These concentric circles are called tracks.

Hard disk drives, unlike floppy drives, are found in every PC. Internal hard disk drives for desktop computers use the same 3.5-inch form factor as floppy drives, but are installed into internal drive bays. Their capacities range up to 2TB, but most desktop drives in recent systems have capacities ranging from 320GB to 1TB.

The most common types of hard disk interfaces in current PCs are Serial ATA (SATA) and Parallel ATA (PATA). PATA is also known as ATA/IDE. Both SATA and PATA interfaces can also be used by optical drives (Blu-ray, DVD, and CD), removable-media drives such as Zip and REV, and tape backup drives.

Figure 12-7 compares typical SATA and PATA hard disks to each other.

In the following sections, you will learn about the data and power cables used by SATA and PATA drives, how PATA drives are configured by jumper blocks, the various ATA specifications, how PATA and SATA drives are installed, how to configure PATA and SATA drives in the system BIOS, and how to improve PATA drive performance.

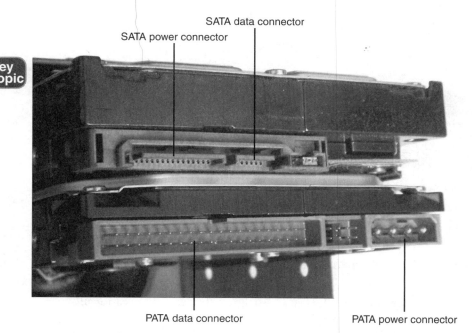

SATA data connector

SATA power connector

PATA data connector

PATA power connector

Figure 12-7   The power and data cable connectors on SATA and PATA (ATA/IDE) hard disks.

PATA and SATA Data and Power Cables

PATA drives use a 40-pin data cable, while SATA drives use an L-shaped seven-wire data cable. PATA drives use a five-pin Molex power cable, while SATA drives use an L-shaped power cable. Figure 12-8 compares PATA and SATA power and data cables.

SATA data
cable

SATA power cable

PATA power cable

PATA data cable

Figure 12-8   The power and data cables used by SATA and PATA (ATA/IDE) hard disks.

One or two PATA hard disks or other types of ATA/IDE drives can be connected to a single data cable. Current hard disk designs use an 80-wire cable, while most optical and removable-media drives can use either the 80-wire cable or the older 40-wire design. Figure 12-9 compares these cables to each other.

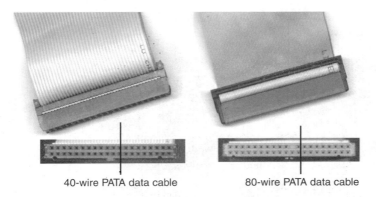

40-wire PATA data cable   80-wire PATA data cable

Figure 12-9   40-wire and 80-wire PATA data cables. 80-wire cables are required by modern PATA hard disks and recommended for other types of PATA devices.

PATA Drive Jumpering and Cable Select

PATA drives are identified as primary/secondary or master/slave. To make this determination, jumper blocks on the drive (usually on the rear, but occasionally on the bottom) are used (See Figure 12-10).

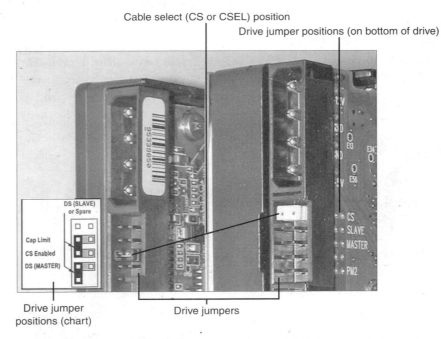

Cable select (CS or CSEL) position

Drive jumper positions (on bottom of drive)

DS (SLAVE) or Spare

Cap Limit

CS Enabled

DS (MASTER)

CS
SLAVE
MASTER
PM2

Drive jumper positions (chart)

Drive jumpers

Figure 12-10   Two typical PATA (ATA/IDE) drives configured for cable select. Some drives, such as the one on the left, require the user to consult a chart on the drive's top plate or in the system documentation for correct settings, whereas others silk-screen the jumper settings on the drive's circuit board.

With an 80-wire cable, jumper blocks on both drives are set to Cable Select (CS), and the drive's position on the cable determines primary/secondary:

- The blue connector on the cable plugs into the PATA host adapter on the motherboard or add-on card.

- The gray connector in the middle of the cable is used for the secondary (slave) drive.

- The black connector on the far end of the cable is used for the primary (master) drive.

The older 40-wire cable uses only jumper blocks to determine drive configuration. When a single drive is installed on a cable, the drive is configured as master or single. When two drives are installed on a cable, one is configured as master (primary) and the other as slave (secondary).

Only one SATA drive can be connected to an SATA host adapter port, so jumper blocks are unnecessary.

ATA Specifications

A series of standards for ATA/IDE and SATA drives are referred to as the *ATA specifications* (AT Attachment). Table 12-3 provides an overview of the differences in the various ATA specifications.

Key Topic

Table 12-3 ATA Specifications and Features

ATA Specification	Major Features
ATA-1 (original)	Standardized master/slave jumpers
	IDE Identify command for automatic configuration and detection of parameters
	PIO modes 0–2
	CHS (standard cylinder head sector) and LBA (logical block addressing, sector-translated) parameters
ATA-2	PIO modes 3–4
	Power management
	CHS/LBA translation for drives up to 8.4GB
	Primary and secondary IDE channels
	IDE block mode
ATA-3	S.M.A.R.T. self-diagnostics feature for use with monitoring software

Table 12-3   ATA Specifications and Features

ATA Specification	Major Features
	Password protection
	Improved reliability of PIO mode 4
ATA-4	UDMA 33 (33MBps)
	ATAPI support
	80-wire/40-pin cable
	BIOS support for LBA increased to 136.9GB
ATA-5	UDMA 66 (66MBps)
	Required use of 80-wire/40-pin cable with UDMA 66
ATA-6	UDMA 100 (100MBps)
	Increased capacity of LBA to 144 petabytes (PB; 1PB = 1 quadrillion bytes)
ATA-7	UDMA 133 (133MBps)
	Serial ATA (SATA)
ATA-8	Hybrid solid-state/mechanical and solid-state drives; SATA 3Gbps (SATA Revision 2.0); SATA 6Gbps (SATA Revision 3.0)

ATA/IDE Drive Physical Installation

The following steps apply to typical ATA/IDE drive installations of hard disks, optical (Blu-ray/DVD/CD) drives, removable-media drives, or tape drives:

Step 1. Open the system and check for an unused 3.5-in drive bay or an unused 5.25-inch drive bay. The 3.5-inch drive bay is used for hard disks and some tape and removable-media drives. The 5.25-inch drive bay is used for optical drives and can be used for other types of drives as well.

Step 2. For 3.5-inch drives: If a 3.5-inch drive bay is not available but a 5.25-inch drive bay is, attach the appropriate adapter kit and rails as needed, as shown in Figure 12-11.

For 5.25-inch drives: If the 5.25-inch drive bays on the system use rails to hold drives in position, attach the appropriate rails.

Step 3. Jumper the drive according to the cable type used: 40-wire cables use master and slave; 80-wire cables use cable select or master and slave.

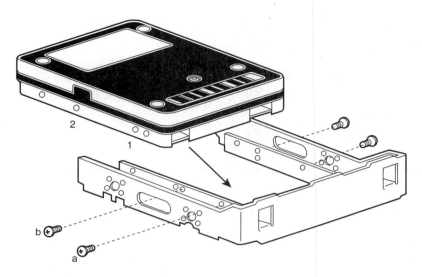

Figure 12-11   A typical adapter kit for a 3.5-inch drive. Screw a attaches the frame at hole #1; screw b attaches the frame at hole #2, with corresponding attachments on the opposite side of the drive and frame. Drive rails used by some cases can be attached to the adapter kit.

Use only 80-wire cables for hard disks. Other types of drives can use 40-wire or 80-wire cables, but 80-wire cables are preferred.

Step 4.   Attach the appropriate connector to the drive, making sure to match the colored marking on the edge of the cable to the end of the drive connector with pin 1. Pin 1 might be marked with a square solder hole on the bottom of the drive or silk-screening. If no markings are visible, pin 1 is usually nearest the drive's power connector. Disconnect the cable from the host adapter or other ATA/IDE drive if necessary to create sufficient slack.

Step 5.   Slide the drive into the appropriate bay and attach as needed with screws or by snapping the ends of the rails into place.

Step 6.   Attach the power connector; most PATA drives use the larger four-wire (Molex) power connector originally used on 5.25-inch floppy disk drives. Use a Y-splitter to create two power connectors from one if necessary.

Step 7.   Reattach the data cable to the other ATA or ATAPI drive and host adapter if necessary.

Step 8.   Change the jumper on the other ATA or ATAPI drive on the same cable if necessary. With 80-wire cables, both drives can be jumpered as Cable Select, with the drive at the far end of the cable being treated as master, and the middle drive as slave. With 40-wire cables, only Master and

Slave jumper positions are used with most brands. See the drive markings or documentation for details.

> **NOTE** Move the jumper simply by grasping it with a pair of tweezers or small needle-nose pliers and gently pulling straight backward. It's always best to change jumper settings before inserting the drive into the PC because they can be especially difficult to reach after the drive is installed.

Step 9. Verify correct data and power connections to all installed drives and host adapters.

Step 10. Turn on the system and start the BIOS configuration program.

Figure 12-12 shows a typical PATA drive before and after power and data cables are attached.

ATA/IDE data connector on drive

ATA/IDE data cable (80-wire)   Drive jumper (set to Cable Select)
Molex power cable

Figure 12-12 Attaching power and data cables to a typical PATA drive.

SATA Hard Drive Physical Installation

The process of installing an SATA drive differs from that used for installing an ATA/IDE drive because there are no master or slave jumpers and the SATA data cable goes directly from host adapter to drive. The following instructions assume the system has an onboard or add-on card SATA host adapter already installed. If you need to install an SATA host adapter, see the next section for details.

Step 1. Open the system and check for an unused 3.5-in drive bay or an unused 5.25-inch drive bay. The 3.5-inch drive bay is used for hard disks and some tape and removable-media drives. The 5.25-inch drive bay is used for optical drives and can be used for other types of drives as well.

Step 2.   For 3.5-inch drives: If a 3.5-inch drive bay is not available but a 5.25-inch drive bay is, attach the appropriate adapter kit and rails as needed (refer to Figure 12-11).

For 5.25-inch drives: If the 5.25-inch drive bays on the system use rails to hold drives in position, attach the appropriate rails.

Step 3.   Attach the SATA cable to the drive; it is keyed so it can only be connected in one direction.

Step 4.   Slide the drive into the appropriate bay and attach as needed with screws or by snapping the ends of the rails into place.

Step 5.   Attach the power connector; if the computer's power supply doesn't have an SATA edge connector, use the adapter provided with the drive or purchased separately to convert a standard Molex connector to the edge connector type used by SATA.

Step 6.   Attach the data cable to the host adapter.

Step 7.   Verify correct data and power connections to SATA drives and host adapters.

Step 8.   Turn on the system and start the BIOS configuration program if the SATA host adapter is built into the motherboard. Enable the SATA host adapter, save changes, and restart your system.

Step 9.   If the SATA drive is connected to an add-on card, watch for messages at startup indicating the host adapter BIOS has located the drive. See the section "SATA BIOS Configuration," later in this chapter, for details.

Step 10.   Install drivers for your operating system to enable the SATA drive and host adapter to function when prompted. See Chapter 14, "Installing and Upgrading Windows Operating Systems," for details.

Figure 12-13 shows a typical SATA drive before and after attaching power and data cables. Figure 12-14 shows typical PATA and SATA host adapter connections on a recent motherboard.

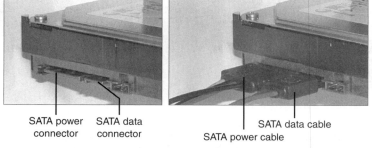

SATA power   SATA data
connector   connector

SATA data cable

SATA power cable

Figure 12-13   Attaching power and data cables to a typical SATA drive.

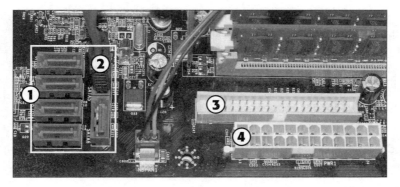

1. SATA host adapters
2. SATA data cable
3. PATA host adapter
4. ATX 24-pin power connector (for size comparison)

Figure 12-14   PATA and SATA host adapters on a recent motherboard.

Installing an SATA Host Adapter

Some older systems don't include an SATA host adapter on the motherboard. Thus, to add an SATA drive to these systems, you will also need to install an SATA host adapter card such as the one pictured in Figure 12-15. Follow this procedure:

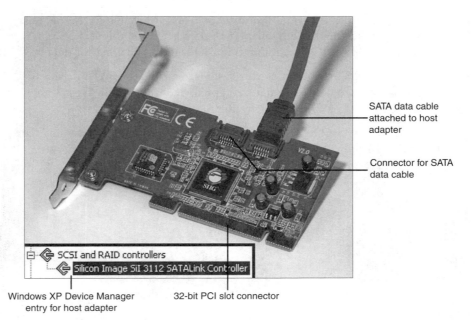

SATA data cable attached to host adapter

Connector for SATA data cable

Windows XP Device Manager entry for host adapter

32-bit PCI slot connector

Figure 12-15   A typical SATA host adapter card that supports two SATA drives. The inset shows how this host adapter appears in the Windows XP Device Manager after installation.

Step 1. Shut down the system and disconnect the power cable from the outlet to cut all power to the system.

Step 2. Use ESD protection equipment, such as a wrist strap and work mat, if available. (See Chapter 17, "Safety and Environmental Issues," for details.)

Step 3. Open the computer and locate an unused PCI slot.

Step 4. After removing the slot cover, insert the SATA card into the slot. See Chapter 3, "Motherboards, Processors, and Adapter Cards," for basic instructions on adding expansion cards, such as the SATA host adapter described here.

Step 5. Secure the card into place with the screw removed from the slot cover.

Step 6. Connect the card to the SATA drive with an SATA data cable. The cable might be provided with the card or with the drive.

Step 7. Reconnect the power cord and restart the computer.

Step 8. Install drivers when prompted.

Step 9. Restart your computer if prompted.

Step 10. Open Windows Device Manager to verify that the SATA host adapter is working. It should be listed under the category SCSI Controllers, SCSI Adapters, or SCSI and RAID Controllers (see Figure 12-15).

PATA BIOS Configuration

For PATA drives controlled by the motherboard BIOS, the following information must be provided to the BIOS:

- Hard drive geometry
- Data transfer rate
- LBA translation

Hard drive geometry refers to several factors used to calculate the capacity of a hard drive. These factors include the following:

- The number of sectors per track
- The number of read/write heads
- The number of cylinders

The surface of any disk-based magnetic media is divided into concentric circles called tracks. Each track contains multiple sectors. A sector contains 512 bytes of data and is the smallest data storage area used by disk drives.

NOTE   Although floppy disks also have tracks and sectors, modern operating systems do not require you to specify the track layout of the disk when formatting the media.

Each side of a hard disk platter used for data storage has a read-write head which moves across the media. There are many tracks on each hard disk platter, and all the tracks on all the platters are added together to obtain the cylinder count.

Figure 12-16 helps you visualize sectors, tracks, and cylinders.

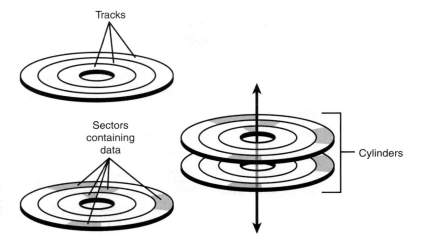

Figure 12-16   Tracks, sectors, and cylinders compared.

Before the drive can be prepared by the operating system, it must be properly identified by the system BIOS.

Most system BIOS programs are designed to perform auto-detection, reading the appropriate configuration from the drive itself. When installing a drive, make sure the system detects the hard disk (see Figure 12-17). After the drive is detected, the changes to the CMOS setup should be saved, the system rebooted, and the drive prepared for use.

Auto-detection is the best way to install a new PATA drive because other settings such as LBA translation, block mode (multisector transfers), and UDMA transfer rates will also be configured properly.

NOTE   If LBA translation is turned off in the system BIOS, only 8.4GB of the hard disk's capacity will be recognized by the system BIOS. If disk writes take place while a drive prepared with LBA translation is being accessed without LBA translation, data could be corrupted or overwritten.

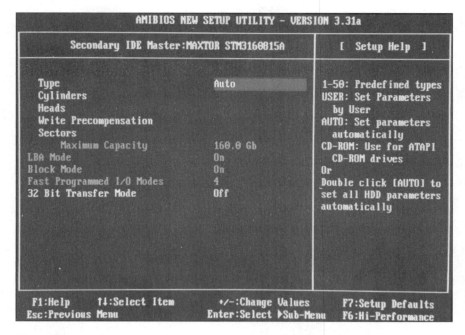

Figure 12-17   Configuring a 160GB Maxtor PATA drive with the auto-detection feature in a typical system BIOS.

Some BIOS programs perform the automatic detection of the drive type every time you start the system by default. Although this enables you to skip configuring the hard drive setting, it also takes longer to start the system and prevents the use of nonstandard configurations for compatibility reasons.

Depending on the system, removable-media ATAPI (ARMD) drives such as Zip and LS-120 should be configured as Not Present or Auto in the system BIOS setup or as ARMD drives depending upon the BIOS options listed. These drives do not have geometry values to enter in the system. The CD-ROM setting should be used for ATAPI CD-ROM and similar optical drives, such as CD-R, CD-RW, DVD, and Blu-ray. Using the correct BIOS configuration for ATAPI drives will enable them to be used to boot the system on drives and systems that support booting from ATAPI devices.

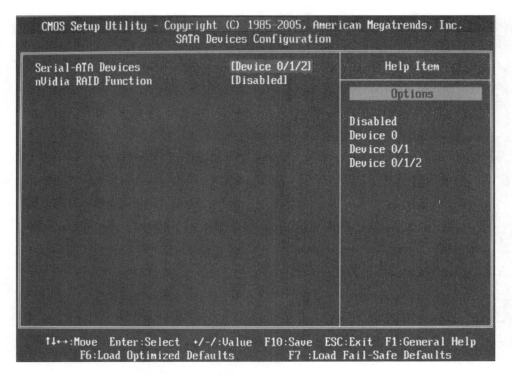

Figure 12-18   Enabling an onboard SATA host adapter.

SATA BIOS Configuration

Before you can install an SATA hard disk to an SATA host adapter on the motherboard, you must make sure the host adapter is enabled in the system BIOS (see Figure 12-18).

After the SATA host adapter is enabled, save changes to the BIOS and shut down the system. After connecting the SATA drive to one of the onboard SATA host adapters, restart the system and reenter the BIOS setup program. Verify that the system has detected the SATA drive (see Figure 12-19). Save changes to the BIOS, restart, and prepare the hard disk for use.

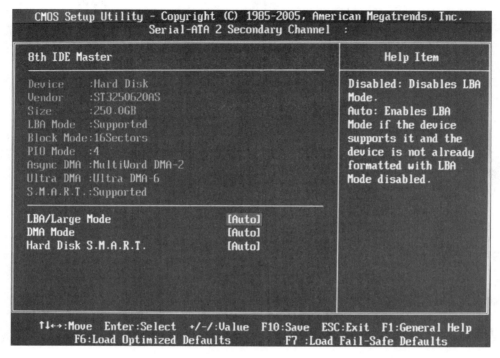

```
    CMOS Setup Utility - Copyright (C) 1985-2005, American Megatrends, Inc.
                      Serial-ATA 2 Secondary Channel  :

   8th IDE Master                                       Help Item

   Device     :Hard Disk                            Disabled: Disables LBA
   Vendor     :ST3250620AS                           Mode.
   Size       :250.0GB                               Auto: Enables LBA
   LBA Mode   :Supported                             Mode if the device
   Block Mode :16Sectors                             supports it and the
   PIO Mode   :4                                     device is not already
   Async DMA  :MultiWord DMA-2                        formatted with LBA
   Ultra DMA  :Ultra DMA-6                            Mode disabled.
   S.M.A.R.T. :Supported

   LBA/Large Mode                      [Auto]
   DMA Mode                            [Auto]
   Hard Disk S.M.A.R.T.                [Auto]

   ↑↓←→:Move  Enter:Select  +/-/:Value  F10:Save  ESC:Exit  F1:General Help
           F6:Load Optimized Defaults          F7 :Load Fail-Safe Defaults
```

Figure 12-19   Auto-detecting an SATA hard disk.

NOTE   On many recent systems, you can configure a SATA drive as running in AHCI, RAID, or IDE (also known as Legacy) mode. Choose AHCI if you want to use the SATA interface's advanced features such as Native Command Queuing (NCQ) or hot-swapping. Choose IDE mode if you are installing the drive in a Windows XP or Windows Server 2003 computer and don't want to provide a driver on floppy disk during installation or if you are installing Windows Vista or Windows 7 as a dual-boot configuration with Windows XP. Choose RAID if you are setting up a RAID array.

If you have already installed Windows or another operating system, do not change the current BIOS setting, as the system will not be able to boot.

eSATA

eSATA is an extension of SATA standards, enabling SATA-based external drives to be connected to desktop and laptop PCs via modified SATA ports.

eSATA host adapters plug into PCI Express (PCIe) x1 or x4 slots. An SATA port can be converted to an eSATA port by connecting a header cable that mounts in an empty expansion slot. Single-port and dual-port cables are available. Figure 12-20 illustrates a dual eSATA header cable.

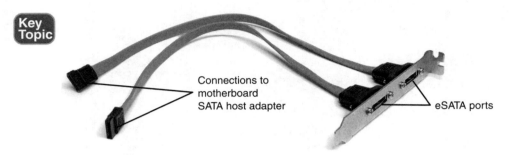

Connections to motherboard SATA host adapter

eSATA ports

Figure 12-20   A dual-port eSATA header cable.

NOTE   If you want to adapt SATA ports on the motherboard to use eSATA ports with a header cable, you must configure the computer's SATA ports to run in AHCI mode.

Figure 12-21 illustrates an eSATA cable, and Figure 12-22 illustrates an external hard disk with USB 2.0, eSATA, and dual IEEE-1394a (FireWire 400) ports.

Figure 12-21   An eSATA data cable.

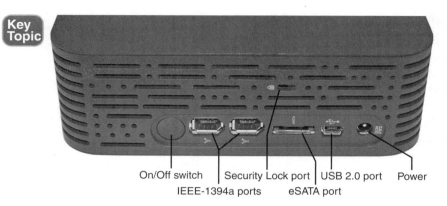

On/Off switch   Security Lock port   USB 2.0 port   Power
    IEEE-1394a ports   eSATA port

Figure 12-22   A multi-interface external hard disk with IEEE-1394a, eSATA, and USB 2.0 ports.

Creating an ATA or SATA RAID Array

RAID (redundant array of inexpensive drives) is a method for creating a faster or safer single logical hard disk drive from two or more physical drives. RAID arrays have been common for years on servers using SCSI-interface drives. However, a number of recent systems feature ATA RAID or SATA RAID host adapters on the motherboard. ATA and SATA RAID host adapter cards can also be retrofitted to systems lacking onboard RAID support. These types of RAID arrays are also re-ferred to as hardware RAID arrays. RAID arrays can also be created through operat-ing system settings, and are sometimes called software RAID arrays. However, software RAID arrays are not as fast as hardware RAID arrays.

ATA and SATA RAID types include the following:

- **RAID Level 0 (RAID 0)**—Two drives are treated as a single drive, with both drives used to simultaneously store different portions of the same file. This method of data storage is called striping. Striping boosts performance, but if either drive fails, all data is lost. Don't use striping for data drives.

- **RAID Level 1 (RAID 1)**—Two drives are treated as mirrors of each other; changes to the contents of one drive are immediately reflected on the other drive. This method of data storage is called mirroring. Mirroring provides a built-in backup method and provides faster read performance than a single drive. Suitable for use with program and data drives.

- **RAID Level 0+1 (RAID 10)**—Four drives combine striping plus mirroring for extra speed plus better reliability. Suitable for use with program and data drives.

- **RAID Level 5 (RAID 5)**—Three or more drives are treated as a logical array, and parity information (used to recover data in the event of a drive failure) is spread across all drives in the array. Suitable for use with program and data drives.

Table 12-4 provides a quick comparison of these types of RAID arrays.

Table 12-4   Comparisons of RAID Levels

RAID Level	Minimum Number of Drives Required	Data Protection Features	Total Capacity of Array	Major Benefit over Single Drive	Notes
0	2	None	2×capacity of both drives (if same size) OR 2× capacity of smaller drive	Improved read/write performance	Also called "striping"
1	2	Changes to contents of one drive immediately performed on other drive	Capacity of one drive (if same size); OR capacity of smaller drive	Automatic backup; faster read performance	Also called "mirroring"
10	4	Changes on one two-drive array are immediately performed on other two-drive array	Capacity of smallest drive × Number of drives/2	Improved read/write performance and automatic backup	Also called "striped and mirrored"
5	3	Parity information is saved across all drives	(x-1) ×Capacity of smallest drive (x equals the number of drives in the array)	Full data redundancy in all drives; hot swap of damaged drive supported in most implementations	

Motherboards that support only two drives in a RAID array support only RAID 0 and RAID 1. Motherboards that support more than two drives can also support RAID Level 0+1 (also known as RAID 10), and some support RAID 5 as well. RAID-enabled host adapters support varying levels of RAID.

NOTE   ATA or SATA RAID host adapters can sometimes be configured to work as normal ATA or SATA host adapters. Check the system BIOS setup or add-on card host adapter setup for details.

An ATA or SATA RAID array requires

- **Two or more identical drives**—If some drives are larger than others, the additional capacity will be ignored. See Table 12-4 above.

- **A RAID-compatible motherboard or add-on host adapter card**—Both feature a special BIOS, which identifies and configures the drives in the array.

Because RAID arrays use off-the-shelf drives, the only difference in the physical installation of drives in a RAID array is where they are connected. They must be connected to a motherboard or add-on card that has RAID support.

> **NOTE**   Sometimes ATA RAID connectors are made from a contrasting color of plastic than other drive connectors. However, the best way to determine if your system or motherboard supports ATA or SATA RAID arrays is to read the manual for the system or motherboard.

After the drive(s) used to create the array is connected to the RAID array's host adapter, restart the computer. Start the system BIOS setup program and enable the RAID host adapter if necessary. Save changes and exit the BIOS setup program.

After enabling the RAID array host adapter, follow the vendor instructions to create the array. Generally, this requires you to activate the RAID array setup program when you start the computer (Figure 12-23 shows a typical RAID setup program) and follow the prompts to select the type of array desired. After the RAID array is configured, the drives are handled as a single physical drive by the system.

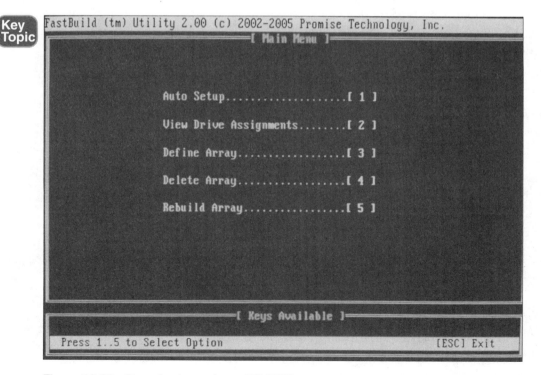

Figure 12-23   Preparing to create an ATA RAID array.

CAUTION If one or more of the drives to be used in the array already contains data, *back up the drives before starting the configuration process*! Most RAID array host adapters delete the data on all drives in the array when creating an array, sometimes with little warning.

NOTE If you want to create a striped volume (equivalent to RAID 0) in Windows XP, Windows Vista, or Windows 7 but your system does not include PATA RAID or SATA RAID host adapters, you can use Computer Management Console's Disk Management node (`diskmgmt.msc`).

To create a striped volume, use the New Volume wizard from the right-click menu, and select Striped as the volume type. After selecting one or more additional drives and adding them to the volume, you are prompted to assign the volume a new drive letter, mount the volume to an empty NTFS folder on another drive, or do nothing. After the array is formatted, it can then be used. Note that Windows cannot create a mirrored volume.

ATA/IDE Performance Optimization

If your hard drive is stuck in first gear, so is your system. Fortunately, most systems that support LBA mode also offer several different ways to optimize the performance of IDE drives and devices. These include

- Selecting the correct PIO or DMA transfer mode in the BIOS
- Selecting the correct block mode in the BIOS
- Installing busmastering Windows drivers
- Enabling DMA mode in Windows
- Adjusting disk cache software settings

PIO and DMA Transfer Modes

PATA (ATA/IDE) storage devices are capable of operating at a wide variety of transfer speeds. Virtually all recent hard disk and other drives support one of various Ultra DMA (UDMA) modes (also known as Ultra ATA modes).

The correct speed is determined when the drive is detected by the computer during CMOS setup. However, if you use a 40-wire PATA cable, the fastest Ultra DMA speed available is Ultra DMA 33. For this reason, you should use 80-wire cables for hard disks and other PATA storage devices.

To achieve a given transfer rate, the hard disk, the host adapter (card or built-in), and the data cable must be capable of that rate. In addition, the host adapter must be configured to run at that rate.

Table 12-5 lists the most common transfer rates. Check the drive documentation or with the drive vendor for the correct rating for a given drive.

Table 12-5   UDMA (Ultra ATA) Peak Transfer Rates

Mode	Peak Transfer Rate	PATA Cable Requirement
UDMA 2 (UDMA-33)	33.33MBps	40- or 80-wire cable
UDMA 4 (UDMA-66)	66.66MBps	80-wire cable
UDMA 5 (UDMA-100)	100MBps	80-wire cable
UDMA 6 (UDMA-133)	133MBps	80-wire cable

These modes are backward compatible, enabling you to select the fastest available mode if your system lacks the correct mode for your drive. ATA/IDE drives are backward compatible; you can select a slower UDMA mode than the drive supports if your system doesn't support the correct UDMA mode. Performance will be slower, but the drive will still work.

TIP   Some older UDMA drives are shipped with their firmware configuration set to a lower transfer rate than the maximum supported by the drive. This helps avoid data loss that could happen if the drive were connected to a system that doesn't support the drive's maximum transfer rate. Fortunately, these drives usually include a software utility that can ratchet up the speed to the maximum allowed. If you can't find the driver disk or CD, check out the vendor's website for the utility and download it.

If a particular drive and host adapter combination is not capable of running at any UDMA speed, the system will revert to the slower PIO drive access method. PIO transfer rates are shown in Table 12-6.

Table 12-6   PIO Peak Transfer Rates

Mode	Peak Transfer Rate	Interface Type Required
PIO 0	3.33MBps	16-bit
PIO 1	5.22MBps	16-bit
PIO 2	8.33MBps	16-bit
PIO 3	11.11MBps	32-bit
PIO 4	16.67MBps	32-bit

As you can see from Table 12-6, even the fastest PIO mode is only half the speed of the slowest UDMA mode.

IDE Block Mode

IDE block mode refers to multi-sector data transfers. Originally, a PATA hard drive was allowed to read only a single 512-byte sector before the drive sent an IRQ to the CPU. Early in their history, some PATA hard drives began to use a different method called block mode, which enabled the drive to read multiple sectors, or blocks, of data before an IRQ was sent. All recent drives support block mode, and the correct value is configured when the drive is detected. If block mode is disabled, a drive that supports block mode transfers data more slowly.

NOTE   Some very old ATA/IDE drives do not support block mode and run more slowly when it is enabled.

IDE Busmastering Drivers

A third way to improve PATA (ATA/IDE) hard disk performance is to install busmastering drivers for the IDE ATA/ATAPI host interface. A busmaster bypasses the CPU for data transfers between memory and the hard disk interface. This option is both operating system–specific and motherboard/host adapter–specific.

If you have installed a new motherboard, busmastering drivers are provided on a driver CD or floppy disk. They are preinstalled on complete systems. You might find more up-to-date versions at the vendor's website or by running Windows Update. Because busmastering bypasses the CPU, be sure you are installing the correct drivers. Carefully read the motherboard or system vendor's instructions.

Enabling DMA Transfers for PATA Devices in Windows

All versions of Windows from Windows NT 4.0 (Service Pack 3 and greater) and Windows 95 through Windows 7 enable the user to allow DMA transfers between PATA devices and the system. DMA transfers bypass the CPU for faster performance and are particularly useful for optimizing the performance of both hard drives and optical drives, such as high-speed CD-ROM drives and DVD drives.

NOTE   The correct busmastering drivers for your system and Windows version must be installed before you can enable DMA transfers.

Follow this procedure to enable DMA transfers for a particular IDE host adapter in Windows 2000/XP/Vista/7:

Step 1.   Open the System Properties sheet. Right-click **My Computer** and select **Properties**, or open the **Control Panel** and select **System**.

Step 2.   Click **Hardware**, **Device Manager**. (In Windows Vista/7, just click **Device Manager** under Tasks.)

Step 3.   To determine which drives are connected to which host adapter, open the category containing the drives (Disk Drives for hard or removable-media drives or DVD/CD-ROM Drives for optical drives) and double-click the drive to open its Properties sheet. The location value visible on the General tab shows to which host adapter and device number the drive is connected. For example, location 0 (1) indicates the drive is connected to the primary host adapter (0) as the secondary device (1).

Step 4.   Click the plus sign next to the IDE ATA/ATAPI Controllers category.

Step 5.   Double-click the host adapter for which you want to adjust properties (primary or secondary IDE channel) to open its Properties sheet.

Step 6.   Click **Advanced Settings**.

Step 7.   To enable DMA for a particular drive, select DMA if available for the Transfer mode. To disable DMA in Windows XP, select PIO only (see Figure 12-24). (In Windows Vista and Windows 7 you would just clear the checkbox labeled Enable DMA.)

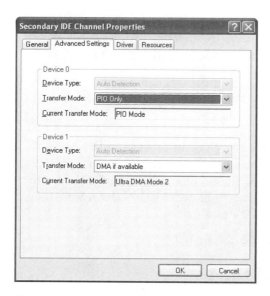

Figure 12-24   The secondary IDE channel on this system is configured to run one drive in PIO mode and one drive in UDMA mode.

Step 8.   Click **OK**.

Step 9.   Restart the computer as prompted.

If DMA is not available, you might need to install the correct busmastering driver for your system.

CAUTION   Before enabling DMA or UDMA mode, check the documentation for the drive to see if it supports this mode. Enabling DMA or UDMA on a drive that does not support it can have disastrous effects.

If the drive can't go faster than UDMA 2 even though it's rated for higher speeds (see Figure 12-21), you might want to change the cable. You must use the 80-wire cable shown earlier in Figure 12-9 to run at UDMA 4 (66MBps) or faster transfer rates. It's also okay to use the 80-wire cable for slower transfer rates. If the cable in use is an 80-wire cable, you might need to enable the drive to run at faster UDMA rates. Depending upon the drive, this might require you to change a jumper on the drive or use a utility program from the drive manufacturer. See your drive's documentation for details.

Adjusting Disk Caching Settings in Windows

Disk caches use a portion of memory to hold information flowing to and from disk drives. The system accesses the cache memory before accessing the main memory. If the information on disk is already in the cache memory, it is accessed far more quickly than if it were read from disk.

To adjust disk-cache settings for Windows 2000/XP/Vista/7, follow this procedure:

Step 1.   Open the **System Properties** sheet and click **Advanced (Advanced System Settings** in Vista/7).

Step 2.   Click the **Settings** button in the Performance section.

Step 3.   Click **Advanced**.

Step 4.   Click **System Cache** (Windows 2000/XP) or **Background Services** (Vista/7) to use more memory on a computer that provides server features to other computers or to improve overall disk-caching performance. To avoid reducing system performance, you should enable this feature only on systems with 512MB of RAM or more.

Step 5.   Click **OK** and restart the system as prompted.

CD, DVD, and Blu-ray Optical Drives

Optical drives fall into three major categories:

■   Those based on CD technology, including CD-ROM, CD-R (recordable CD), and CD-RW (rewritable CD)

■   Those based on DVD technology, including DVD-ROM, DVD-ROM/CD-RW combo, DVD-RAM, DVD-R/RW, DVD+R/RW, and DVD±R/RW

■   Those based on Blu-ray technology, including BD-ROM, BD-R, and BD-RE

CD, DVD, and Blu-ray drives store data in a continuous spiral of indentations called *pits* and *lands* on the nonlabel side of the media from the middle of the media outward to the edge. All drives use a laser to read data; the difference between the storage capacities of Blu-ray, DVD, and CD is due to the difference in laser wavelength: Blu-ray, which has the highest capacity, uses a blue laser with a shorter wavelength than DVD or CD; DVD uses a red laser with a longer wavelength than Blu-ray but shorter than CD; CD, which has the lowest capacity, uses a near-infrared laser with the longest wavelength. The shorter the wavelength, the smaller the pits and lands, enabling more data to be stored in the same space.

Most CD, DVD, and Blu-ray drives are tray-loading, but a few use a slot-loading design. Slot-loading designs are more common in home and automotive electronics products.

CD-R and CD-RW drives use special media types and a more powerful laser than that used on CD-ROM drives to write data to the media. CD-R media is a write-once media—the media can be written to during multiple sessions, but older data cannot be deleted. CD-RW media can be rewritten up to 1,000 times. 80-minute CD-R media has a capacity of 700MB, while the older 74-minute CD-R media has a capacity of 650MB. CD-RW media capacity is up to 700MB, but is often less, depending upon how the media is formatted.

Similarly, DVD-R and DVD+R media is recordable, but not erasable, whereas DVD-RW and DVD+RW media uses a phase-change medium similar to CD-RW and can be rewritten up to 1,000 times. DVD-RAM can be rewritten up to 100,000 times, but DVD-RAM drives and media are less compatible with other types of DVD drives and media than the other rewritable DVD types, making DVD-RAM the least popular DVD format.

- **DVD-RAM**—A rewriteable/erasable media similar to CD-RW but more durable; it can be single sided (4.7GB) or double sided (9.4GB).

- **DVD-R**—A writeable/nonerasable media similar to CD-R; capacity of 4.7GB; some DVD-RAM and all DVD-RW drives can use DVD-R media. DL media includes a second recording layer (capacity of 8.4GB).

- **DVD-RW**—A single-sided rewriteable/erasable media similar to CD-RW; capacity of 4.7GB. DVD-RW drives can also write to DVD-R media.

- **DVD+RW**—A rewritable/erasable media. Also similar to CD-RW, but not interchangeable with DVD-RW or DVD-RAM; capacity of 4.7GB.

- **DVD+R**—A writeable/nonerasable media. Also similar to CD-R, but not interchangeable with DVD-R; capacity of 4.7GB. DL media includes a second recording layer (capacity of 8.4GB).

So-called SuperMulti DVD drives can read and write all types of DVD media as well as CD media.

All Blu-ray drives are compatible with BD-ROM (read-only Blu-ray media), such as the media used for Blu-ray movies. BD-R media is writeable/nonerasable. Thus, BD-R media is the Blu-ray equivalent of CD-R, DVD-R, or DVD+R. BD-RE media is rewriteable and eraseable, making it the Blu-ray equivalent of CD-RW, DVD-RW, or DVD+RW.

All single-layer standard size Blu-ray media has a capacity of 25GB; dual-layer Blu-ray media has a capacity of 50GB.

Drive speeds are measured by an X-rating:

- When working with CD media, 1X equals 150KBps, the data transfer rate used for reading music CDs. Multiply the X-rating by 150 to determine the drive's data rate for reading, writing, or rewriting CD media.

- When working with DVD media, 1X equals 1.385MBps; this is the data transfer rate used for playing DVD-Video (DVD movies) content. Multiply the X-rating by 1.385 to determine the drive's data rate for reading, writing, or rewriting DVD media.

- When working with Blu-ray media, 1X equals 4.5MBps; this is the data transfer rate for playing Blu-ray movies. Multiply the X-rating by 4.5 to determine the drive's data rate for reading, writing, or rewriting Blu-ray media.

Note that Blu-ray drives are also compatible with CD and DVD media. Check the specifications for a particular drive to determine the specific types of media a drive supports and the maximum read/write/rewrite speeds for each media type.

CD, DVD, and Blu-ray Drive Interfaces

Most older internal CD and DVD drives use the same ATA/IDE interface used by PATA hard disks. When this interface is used by drives other than hard disks, it is often referred to as the ATAPI interface. Most recent rewritable DVD drives and Blu-ray rewriteable drives use the SATA interface. External CD and DVD drives typically use the USB 2.0 interface. Some internal and external CD drives used the SCSI or Parallel (LPT) interfaces, but these drives are obsolete.

Physical Installation of Optical Drives

The installation of these drives follows the standard procedure used for each interface type:

- Internal optical drives must be installed into 5.25-inch drive bays.

- ATAPI/IDE optical drives must be configured as master, slave, or cable select (depending upon the cable type and other drives on the same cable).

- SCSI optical drives must be set to a unique device ID.

- SATA optical drives do not require special configuration.

- USB and IEEE-1394a optical drives must be connected to ports with adequate hub power, or they must provide their own power.

If you want to play music CDs through your sound card's speakers, especially with older versions of Windows, you might need to connect a CD audio patch cable (it may be supplied with the drive or sold separately) to the CD audio jack on the sound card or motherboard audio support. Older drives support a four-wire analog cable, whereas newer drives support both the four-wire analog and newer two-wire digital cable. The digital cable provides for faster speed when ripping music CDs (*ripping* is the process of converting music CD tracks into compressed digital music files such as MP3 and WMA). Figure 12-25 shows a typical internal PATA (ATAPI) optical drive before and after connecting power, data, and music cables.

> **NOTE**   Although internal optical drives support four-wire analog audio and two-wire digital audio cables, you do not need to install these cables to permit CD audio playback unless you use versions of Windows or music playback applications that do not support ripping or playback from the ATA/IDE or SATA interface.

Recording CDs and DVDs in Windows XP

DVD-RAM drives are recognized as rewritable drives by all versions of Windows. However, recordable and rewriteable CD and DVD drives were treated as CD-ROM or DVD-ROM drives prior to Windows XP.

Windows XP provides rudimentary CD-R/RW recording capabilities with both CD-R/RW and rewritable DVD drives. However, commercial CD/DVD rewriting and mastering software such as Nero, Roxio Easy Media Creator, and others is highly recommended with Windows XP (and is required if you want to write to DVDs), and is required with older versions of Windows in order to use the rewritable/recordable features of CD and DVD drives. Most rewritable drives sold at stores are equipped with some version of one or more of these programs. However, some computer vendors relied on the Windows XP recording feature to support their bundled CD-RW drives.

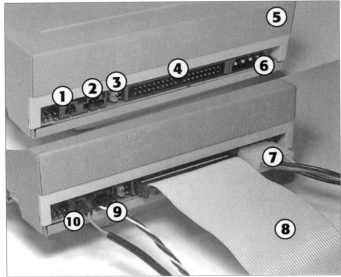

1. CD-digital audio port
2. CD-analog audio port
3. Drive jumper set to slave
4. ATA/IDE port
5. Connector legend
6. Molex power connector
7. Molex power cable
8. 40-wire ATA/IDE cable
9. CD-analog audio cable
10. CD-digital audio cable

Figure 12-25 A typical ATAPI (PATA) internal optical drive before (top) and after (bottom) data, power, and CD music cables have been attached.

Windows XP's CD writing capability is automatically activated for any CD or DVD rewritable drive (although only CD-R/RW media is supported). To write files to the drive, insert a blank disc, drag files to the CD/DVD drive icon using Windows Explorer/My Computer, and click the CD/DVD drive icon. When the drive icon opens, files waiting to be written are listed. Click the task menu option **Write These files to CD** (see Figure 12-26).

The files are written, albeit much more slowly than if you use a commercial CD-mastering or packet-writing program. When the files are written to disc, you will be prompted to insert another disc or to close the wizard.

To erase files from a CD-RW disc, place the disc in the drive, open its icon in Windows Explorer/My Computer, select the file(s) to erase, and press the **Del** key to erase them.

NOTE Because Windows XP doesn't format a CD-RW disc the same way a packet-writing (UDF disk format) program such as Drag to Disc, InCD, DLA, or the built-in DVD writing feature in Windows Vista and Windows 7 does, you cannot use a third-party program or Windows 7/Vista to erase files from a CD-RW disc written by Windows XP. You must use Windows XP to erase unwanted files. You can then reformat the media as desired with a different program.

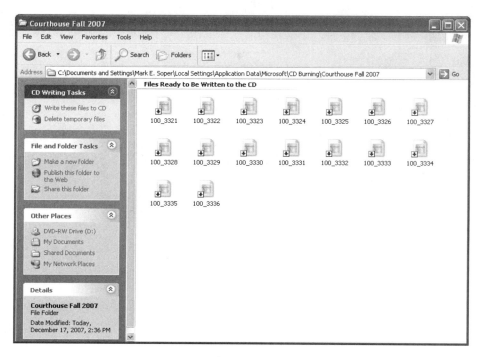

Figure 12-26   Preparing to write files to a CD using the Windows XP CD-writing wizard.

Recording CDs and DVDs in Windows Vista and 7

Windows Vista adds support for recordable and rewritable DVDs, and also adds additional functionality to the CD- or DVD-writing process. When you copy files to a recordable/rewritable CD or DVD drive using Windows Explorer, Send To, or other commands, Windows prompts you to insert a blank disc, and prompts you for a disc title. However, if you click on the Show Formatting Options button, you can also choose how to format the disc (see Figure 12-27).

WHICH FILE SYSTEM IS BEST—AND WHEN

The default choice, Live File System, enables drag-and-drop file copying with both recordable and rewritable media, the ability to erase files when used with rewritable media, and supports individual file sizes over 2GB. (2GB is the limit of the ISO 9660 file system used by the Mastered option.) However, Live File System discs (which use Universal Disc Format version 2.01 file system) might not be compatible with older operating systems and aren't suitable for use with CD or DVD drives in consumer and auto electronics systems.

Use the Mastered option if you want to create a disc that can be read by virtually any drive on a PC, consumer electronics, or auto electronics device.

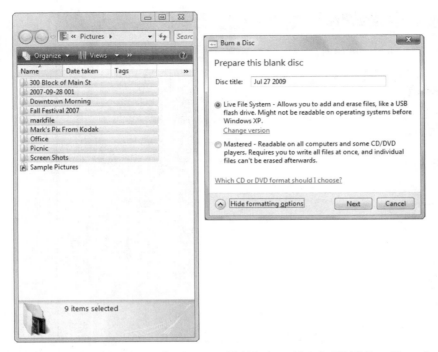

Figure 12-27   Selecting a disc format with Windows Vista's CD/DVD-writing wizard.

After selecting a format, click **Next** to continue. After the disc is formatted, Windows copies the files to the drive and displays a progress bar. At the end of the process, Windows displays the contents of the newly written CD or DVD.

If you use the Live File System, open Windows Explorer, right-click the disc, and select **Eject** so that the media will be prepared for use on other computers.

NOTE   When you use Windows XP, Windows Vista, or Windows 7 to create CDs (or DVDs), you might have an AutoPlay dialog appear during the process. If you don't want to use any of the options on the AutoPlay menu, or you have already begun a process, close it.

Windows 7 includes all the CD and DVD writing features of Windows Vista, and adds the ability to write a CD or DVD from an ISO image file (these files usually have the extension .iso).

IDE/ATAPI Optical Drive Installation Issues

On systems using PATA hard disks and ATAPI optical or removable-media drives, PATA hard disks should be connected to the primary IDE interface and other types of drives should be connected to the secondary IDE interface.

Be sure to select the specific type of drive (CD-ROM, Zip, or other; use CD-ROM for CD or DVD drives) as the drive type, when offered, in the BIOS drive setup menu. If you want to boot from an optical drive, be sure that the optical drive is specified as the first device in the boot order.

Removable Storage

Removable storage is a blanket term for any type of drive that uses removable media, including both tape and disk-based technologies.

Although removable-storage devices are no longer common on most systems, the following removable-storage devices are still used by some systems:

- **Iomega Zip (100, 250, 750MB)**—Zip drives use flexible media inside a rigid cartridge.

- **Iomega REV (35GB, 70GB, 120GB)**—REV drives use hard disk-type media inside a rigid cartridge.

Both Iomega Zip and REV drives (now discontinued) were available in both internal and external versions. See Table 12-7 (Zip) and Table 12-8 (REV).

Table 12-7   Iomega Zip Drive Interfaces and Capacities

Drive Capacity	External			Internal			Supported Media[2]
	USB 1.1	USB 2.0 (Hi-Speed USB)	Parallel Port	SCSI[1]	ATAPI	IEEE-1394a	
100MB	Yes	No	Yes	Yes	Yes	No	100MB R/W
250MB	Yes	No	Yes	Yes	Yes	No	250/100MB R/W[3]
750MB	Yes	Yes	No	No	Yes	Yes	750/250MB R/W[3] 100MB R/O[4]

[1]Uses DB-25F connectors
[2]R/W—read/write; R/O—read-only
[3]750MB and 250MB versions can read and write the next-lower capacity of media, although performance drops drastically with smaller media.
[4]750MB drives can read, but not write, to 100MB media.

Table 12-8 Iomega REV Drive Interfaces and Capacities

| | External | | Internal | | | |
Drive Capacity	USB 2.0 (Hi-Speed USB)	FireWire (IEEE-1394a)	SCSI	PATA (ATAPI)	SATA	Supported Media
35GB	Yes	Yes	Yes	Yes	Yes	35GB REV
70GB	Yes	No	No	Yes	Yes	35GB REV[1], 70GB REV
120GB	Yes	No	No	Yes	Yes	70GB REV[2], 120GB REV

[1]Write speeds to 35GB REV media are significantly slower than to 70GB REV media on 70GB REV drives
[2]70GB REV media is read-only when used in a 120GB REV drive.

REV drives were discontinued in late 2009 and early 2010, but Iomega continues to provide cartridges and accessories, and some vendors still sell autoloader versions designed for server backup. Other types of removable storage have been discontinued for some years and are seldom encountered today. These include

- Imation LS-120 (120MB) and LS-240 (240MB) SuperDisk

- Iomega Jaz (1GB, 2GB)

- Iomega Peerless (10GB, 20GB)

- Castlewood Orb (2.2.GB, 5.7GB)

NOTE SuperDisk drives are also compatible with standard 1.44MB floppy disk media.

Tape Drives

Although tape drives are primarily used by servers, rather than desktops, they are also considered to be removable storage devices. Unlike disk-based removable storage, tape drives are used only for backup.

Tape drives use various types of magnetic tape. Some tape drive mechanisms can be incorporated into autoloaders or tape libraries for large network backup and data retrieval.

Their capacities are typically listed in two ways:

- Native (uncompressed) capacity

- Compressed capacity, assuming 2:1 compression

For example, a tape drive with a 70GB native capacity would also be described as having a 140GB compressed capacity. However, keep in mind that, depending upon the data being backed up, you may be able to store more or (more typically) less than the listed capacity when using data compression.

NOTE Windows Vista and Windows 7 do not include Removable Storage Manager (RSM). Removable Storage Manager supports tape backup drives that do not include drivers for Windows. To determine if a particular tape drive is supported by drivers to be used with Windows Vista or Windows 7, check with the tape drive vendor. For workarounds and third-party tape backup programs that work with Windows 7, see http://pariswells.com/blog/research/windows-7-tape-drive-support.

Major types of tape drives include

- Travan (up to 40GB at 2:1 compression)
- DDS (up to 72GB at 2:1 compression)
- SLR (up to 140GB at 2:1 compression)
- VXA (up to 320GB at 2:1 compression)
- AIT (up to 800GB at 2:1 compression)
- DLT (up to 1.6TB at 2:1 compression)
- LTO Ultrium (up to 3TB [Generation 5] at 2:1 compression)

Most tape drives connect via SCSI interfaces, but some internal drives also connect via PATA or SATA interfaces, and some external tape drives use USB or FireWire interfaces. Most tape drives are also available in autoloader or tape library forms to permit backup automation, enabling unattended backup of drives that require multiple tapes.

Flash Memory and Card Readers

Flash memory, unlike standard RAM, does not require electrical power to maintain its contents. Thus, flash memory can be used for long-term storage. And, unlike disk-based storage, flash memory contains no moving parts, making it very durable.

Flash memory is used in a variety of products, including digital media players with capacities up to 64GB as this book went to press, USB thumbdrives, and various types of storage cards used by digital cameras and other digital devices.

Figure 12-28 compares the most common types of flash memory cards to each other.

Table 12-9 lists the capacities and typical uses of the most common flash memory card types.

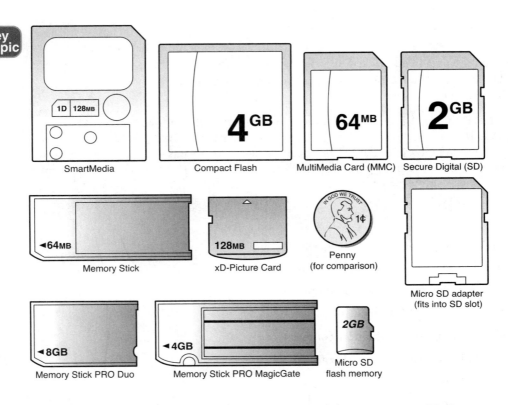

Figure 12-28 A U.S. penny compared in size to the most common types of flash memory cards.

Table 12-9 Flash Memory Card Capacities and Uses

Media Type	Common Capacity	Common Uses	Notes
SmartMedia (SM)	Up to 128 MB	Digital cameras	Now obsolete.
CompactFlash (CF)	Up to 32 GB	Digital SLR cameras; high-end point-and-shoot digital cameras	Check manufacturer's speed rating for best performance in burst mode.
MultiMedia Card (MMC)	Up to 4 GB	Various devices	Largely replaced by SD, SDHC.
Memory Stick	Up to 128 MB	Sony digital cameras and digital media devices	Older Sony digital cameras and digital media devices; also PlayStation 3 (PS3).

Table 12-9 Flash Memory Card Capacities and Uses

Media Type	Common Capacity	Common Uses	Notes
Memory Stick PRO Magic-Gate	Up to 4 GB	Sony digital cameras and digital media devices, including PlayStation Portable	Recent Sony digital cameras and digital media devices, including PlayStation Portable (PSP) and PS3.
Memory Stick PRO Duo	Up to 32 GB	Sony digital cameras and digital media devices, including PlayStation Portable	Recent Sony digital cameras and digital media devices, including PSP and PS3.
Secure Digital (SD)	Up to 2 GB	Most models of point-and-shoot digital cameras; some digital SLR cameras; many flash memory-based media players	Can also be used in place of SDHC memory.
Secure Digital High Capacity (SDHC)	Up to 32 GB	Many recent models of point-and-shoot digital cameras, digital SLR cameras, flash memory-based media players	SDHC media has the same physical form factor as SD. However, many devices that support SD cannot use SDHC. Check with device vendor for details.
xD-Picture Card	Up to 512 MB (standard) Up to 2 GB (Type M, Type M+, Type H)	FujiFilm and Olympus digital point-and-shoot cameras	Most recent models of these cameras also support SD and SDHC memory or exclusively use SD/SDHC memory.
microSD	2 GB	Various portable devices: mobile phones; video games; expandable USB flash memory drives	Can also be used in place of microSDHC; can be used in SD or SDHC slots with an optional adapter.
microSDHC	64 GB	Various portable devices: mobile phones; video games; expandable USB flash memory drives	Device must support microSDHC; can be used in SDHC slots with an optional adapter.

Flash Card Reader

To enable flash memory cards like those shown in Figure 12-28 and Table 12-9 to be used with a computer, use a card reader. Figure 12-29 shows a typical external multislot card reader.

Figure 12-29   A multislot card reader supports a wide variety of flash memory cards.

> **NOTE**   Many recent computers incorporate a multislot card reader. Some printers and multifunction devices also include card readers. Some card readers built into printers and multifunction devices are used only for printing, while others can be used to transfer files to and from the host computer.

Most card readers assign a separate drive letter to each slot.

Installing and Using a Flash Card Reader

To install a flash card reader on Windows 2000, XP, Vista, or 7, connect it to an available USB port. The system will automatically detect the reader, assign drive letters as required, and display a notification at the end of the installation process. With older versions of Windows or other operating systems, it might be necessary to install a driver first before connecting the reader.

When you insert a flash memory card containing files, Windows XP/Vista/7 might display an AutoPlay dialog providing various programs that can be used to view or use the files on the card (see Figure 12-30). If AutoPlay does not appear, open Computer/My Computer or Windows Explorer and navigate to the appropriate drive letter to use the files on the card.

Figure 12-30 A typical AutoPlay menu displayed when a flash memory card containing photos is inserted into a card reader.

Hot-Swapping Flash Memory Cards

Windows optimizes flash memory cards for quick removal. To safely remove a flash memory card from a card reader, close any Explorer window displaying the card's contents or navigate to a different folder. Check the status light to make sure the card is not being accessed and then remove the card.

USB Flash Memory Drives

USB flash memory drives have largely replaced floppy drives for transfers of data between systems or for running utility programs. USB flash memory drives, like flash memory cards, use flash memory, a type of memory that retains information without a continuous flow of electricity. However, USB flash memory drives do not require a card reader.

USB flash memory drives are preformatted with the FAT16, FAT32, or exFAT (FAT64) file system and are ready to use. Simply plug one into a USB port, and it is immediately assigned a drive letter. You can copy, modify, and delete information on a USB flash memory drive, just as with a hard disk or floppy drive. A typical USB flash memory drive is shown in Figure 12-31.

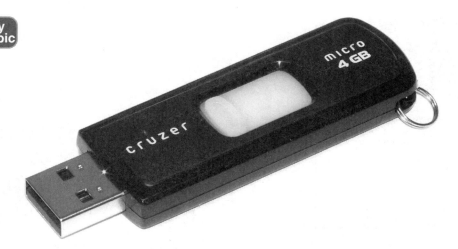

Figure 12-31   A typical USB flash memory drive with a retractable connector.

Hot-Swapping USB Flash Memory Drives

Windows optimizes USB flash memory drives for quick removal; devices optimized for quick removal do not use disk caching. To safely disconnect a USB flash drive from your system, you should make sure no data is being read from or written to the device. To do this, use the Safely Remove Hardware icon in the notification area (systray). Click **Safely Remove Hardware** to bring up the dialog shown in Figure 12-32. Click the device and click **Yes** to confirm the selection to remove the device. After Windows displays a dialog indicating that you can remove the device, you can unplug it from your system.

NOTE   Some USB flash memory drives include their own management software. In such cases, use the Eject feature provided with the drive instead of Safely Remove Hardware.

List of devices to remove   The Safely Remove Hardware icon

Figure 12-32   Preparing to remove a USB flash memory drive with Safely Remove Hardware.

You can also right-click the **Safely Remove Hardware** icon and click select **Safely Remove Hardware** to bring up a list of removable devices. From this list, you can see the properties of each device before you stop it.

CAUTION If internal SATA hard disks in the list of removable drives support hot-swapping, they will also show up in the Safely Remove Hardware list. Do not select these drives for removal.

External Hard Disks

Most external hard disks connect via the USB or IEEE-1394 ports, but some external SCSI and eSATA hard disks are also available. External USB, IEEE-1394, and eSATA–based hard disks are preformatted (typically with the FAT32 file system) and are ready to work. Plug in the drive, and it appears in Computer/My Computer or Windows Explorer. If you want to use an external hard disk with the scheduled backup features in Windows Vista or Windows 7, you can use the Convert.exe program to convert the file system to NTFS.

NOTE If you connect an external drive to a system that does not have appropriate drivers installed, the device cannot be used until drivers are installed. However, Windows XP, Vista, and 7 include drivers for most external storage devices.

SCSI-based external hard disks must be prepared using a format utility provided with the SCSI host adapter or built into the SCSI host adapter's BIOS.

External USB hard disks are available in three form factors: 3.5-inch, 2.5-inch, and 1.8-inch. Most USB drives use the larger 3.5-inch or 2.5-inch form factors.

Hard disks using 3.5-inch drive mechanisms require an AC adapter, but offer higher capacities and greater performance than those based on 2.5-inch hard disks.

Hard disks based on 2.5-inch or 1.8-inch drive mechanisms can be powered by the USB port itself, and usually do not need external AC power.

Figure 12-33 compares typical 3.5-inch and 2.5-inch USB hard disks.

Hot-Swapping USB or IEEE-1394–Based External Hard Disks

Windows optimizes USB and IEEE-1394a external hard disks for performance; that is, disk caching is used to improve system responsiveness. Windows uses a feature sometimes called "lazy writing" to delay writing to the disk. As a consequence, you should never disconnect a USB or IEEE-1394–based hard disk from a system unless you use Safely Remove Hardware to stop the drive.

Figure 12-33   Typical 3.5-inch (left) and 2.5-inch (right) external USB hard disk drives.

Solid State Drives (SSDs)

Solid state drives (better known as SSDs) combine the permanent storage characteristics of flash memory drives with SATA hard disk interfaces. SSDs provide faster read and write performance than conventional hard disks thanks, in part, to faster access times across the entire capacity of the drive, but are much more expensive per GB than conventional hard disks. Because of the higher cost and limited capacity of SSDs versus conventional hard disks, SSDs are best used as system drives instead of data drives.

There are two types of flash memory used in SSDs: multi-level cell (MLC) and single-level cell (SLC). MLC flash memory is slower and less reliable than SLC, and is rated to last for about 10,000 program/erase (P/E) cycles, compared to about 100,000 P/E cycles for SLC. The vast majority of SSDs currently on the market use MLC designs.

Windows 7 is the first Windows version designed specifically for use with SSDs. Windows 7 automatically disables defragmentation for SSDs and disables other features that are not necessary for SSDs. To prevent excessive wear, the page file should not be placed on an SSD.

NOTE   To learn more about SSDs, see the Intel SSD Frequently Asked Questions page at http://www.intel.com/support/ssdc/hpssd/sb/CS-029623.htm.

Troubleshooting Storage

Use the following sections to learn the most common problems affecting storage devices and how to solve them.

Troubleshooting Floppy Disk Drives

Floppy drives are relatively complex devices despite their small storage capacity. Problems can result from incorrect cabling, mechanical drive or media failures, incorrect BIOS configuration, dirt or dust, and interface failures. Use this section to prepare for troubleshooting questions on the A+ Certification Exams as well as your day-to-day work with floppy drives.

Internal Floppy Drive Cabling Problems

Floppy drive data cables that are reversed (pin 1 to pin 33) at either the floppy drive interface on the motherboard/floppy controller card or at the drive itself will cause the drive light to come on and stay on. To correct this, turn off the system, remove and reattach the data cable, and restart the system. Although some floppy drives and cables are keyed to prevent improper insertion of the data cable, others are not.

Floppy drive data or power cables that are not attached to the drive will cause the system to display a floppy drive error when the drive is checked at system startup. Turn off the system, attach the missing cables, and restart the system to correct this problem.

BIOS Configuration Problems

Users must properly configure floppy drives in the BIOS setup program—floppy drives do not support an auto-detect feature. If the system produces a floppy drive error at startup or is unable to format, read, or write disks at the proper capacities, the drive type set in the system BIOS setup program might be inaccurate. Restart the system, start the BIOS setup program, and verify that the correct drive types are set for drive A: and drive B:.

If you can use a USB floppy drive within the Windows GUI, but it is not accessible during boot or Windows installation, the drive might not be configured properly in the system BIOS, or the system might not support USB floppy disk drives.

Drive Reliability and Compatibility Problems

Problems with drives reading and writing media can stem from the following issues:

- **Dirty read/write heads**—Dirty read/write heads can result from the constant pressure of the drive's read/write heads on the relatively fragile magnetic surface of the disk and from the constant flow of air being pulled through the system by cooling fans located in the power supply and elsewhere. Dirty heads can cause read and write errors. To clean the drive heads, use a wet-technology head cleaner, which uses a blank disk containing a fabric cleaning disk instead of media and an alcohol-based head cleaner. Place a few drops of head cleaner solution on the cleaning disk surface, insert the cleaning disk into the floppy drive and spin the drive with a program such as Explorer or Scandisk to clean the heads. Allow the heads to dry for a few minutes, and try the operation again.

- **Defective drive mechanisms**—Several parts of the floppy drive are subject to failures, including the drive motor, the read/write heads, the head-positioning mechanism, and the shutter-retraction mechanism (3.5-inch drives only).

A floppy drive with a motor that runs too fast or too slow or has misaligned read/write heads will cause a drive to write data that can be read only by that drive. Media from other drives can't be read on a drive with these defects, and drives with these defects can't write data that can be read by other drives. Floppy drives with misaligned heads or off-spec drive motors can't be fixed and must be replaced.

If the head-positioning mechanism fails, data can't be read or written and the drive will not perform a seek at system startup. The head-positioning mechanism frequently uses a worm-drive mechanism that can be replaced or freed up if stuck.

If the shutter-retraction mechanism is jammed, you cannot insert a disk into a 3.5-inch drive. Remove the drive's top cover so that the drive mechanism is visible, as shown in Figure 12-34, and you should be able to insert the disk. The usual cause is a bent top cover; adjust the cover and replace it.

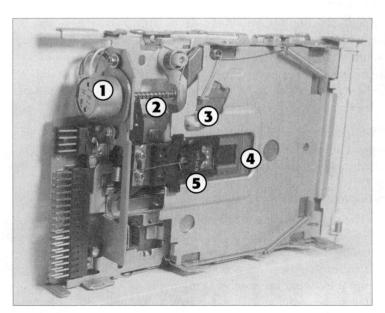

1. Drive motor
2. Worm-gear mechanism
3. Shutter-retraction mechanism
4. 3.5-inch disk with exposed media
5. Read/write heads (moved back and forth by worm-gear mechanism)

Figure 12-34 A typical 3.5-inch 1.44MB internal floppy disk drive with its top cover removed.

NOTE   These repair tips should be used only in emergencies. In most cases, the best solution for a broken floppy drive is a brand new replacement, especially because these drives usually cost about $15.

Figure 12-34 shows the major components of a typical 3.5-inch disk drive. Components include a drive motor; a worm-gear mechanism, which moves read/write heads; and a shutter-retraction mechanism. The drive shown in Figure 12-34 has a 3.5-inch disk inserted; the shutter-retraction mechanism has pushed the shutter to one side so that the media is visible.

Changeline Problems

On 3.5-inch internal floppy drives, pin 34 of the floppy interface senses disk changes and forces the system to reread the disk's file allocation table and display the content of the new disk when the disk is changed and viewed from a command prompt. This feature is referred to as *changeline support*.

If the DIR (directory) command displays the same contents for a different disk as for the first disk, changeline support has failed; this problem is also called the *phantom directory*.

CAUTION   If this problem isn't corrected, the computer could trash the contents of the floppy disk because it uses the original disk's file allocation table to determine where to place files on the new disk.

Because pin 34 uses the last connector on the floppy cable, check to see whether the cable is loose or damaged. If an adapter is being used to convert a tongue and groove floppy cable made for 5.25-inch drives to connect to the pin connector on 3.5-inch drives, remove the adapter and cable and replace the cable with one which has the correct pin connector. (See the next section for further troubleshooting steps.) Note that Windows file/disk management programs such as Windows Explorer and My Computer don't always automatically detect disk changes; you can press the F5 key to reread the contents of a floppy disk.

To force the system to reread the contents of a floppy disk from a command prompt, press Control+C keys after inserting a new floppy disk but before you use the DIR command.

Isolating Floppy Subsystem Problems

The floppy disk drive subsystem consists of three parts: the drive, the interface cable and the host adapter (built into the motherboard on most recent systems), along with the BIOS configuration for the drive. The troubleshooting options listed earlier dealt with the most likely causes of particular floppy disk drive problems. However, any part of the subsystem could cause a floppy disk drive problem. If you suspect a hardware failure, follow this procedure:

Step 1.   With most floppy disk drive problems, you should exchange the floppy disk drive cable first for a spare that is known to be working. This solves many problems because the cable is inexpensive and easily damaged.

Step 2.   Disconnect any tape drive sharing the floppy cable (either on the drive B: connector or with an adapter cable). If the floppy drive works correctly without the tape drive connected to the system, replace the adapter cable for the tape drive if you still need to use the drive. If the tape drive is no longer needed (floppy-interface models are very outdated), remove the tape drive from the system.

Step 3.   Replace the drive. Floppy disk drives are also inexpensive and easily damaged; their design no longer permits major repairs.

Step 4.   If the problem persists, check the cable and drive on another system. If they check out okay, the floppy disk controller on the motherboard or host adapter card is probably defective. Replace the motherboard or host adapter with a new one.

Troubleshooting PATA (ATA/IDE) Drives

Problems with PATA drives can result from cabling, detection, geometry, physical damage, and jumpering issues. Use this section to prepare for IDE troubleshooting questions on the A+ Certification Exam and in your day-to-day work.

Incompatible PATA Cables

PATA cables that use one keying method (plugged pin 20 or raised projection) cannot be plugged into drives or motherboards that use the other keying method. To correct the problem, replace the cable with a cable that either is not keyed or supports the same keying method as the motherboard and drive.

UDMA-66 or Faster Drive Limited to UDMA-33 Speeds

This error is caused by using a 40-wire cable instead of the 80-wire cable required for UDMA-66, UDMA-100, and UDMA-133 transfer rates. In most cases, changing the cable is all that's required. With some older drives, you might also need to run the drive vendor's speed-change utility after you install the 80-wire cable to enable UDMA-66 or faster modes.

No Power to Drive

If the power cable is not plugged into a PATA drive during installation, it will not spin up when the system is turned on—you will not be able to hear the drive running and the system will not detect it. To correct the problem, turn off the system and reattach the power cable.

Cables Attached Incorrectly to ATA/IDE Interface or Drive

User errors in attaching cabling to ATA/IDE interfaces can cause detection problems. Some old 40-wire PATA cables do not use either keying method that is supported by PATA drives, making it easy to reverse either end of the cable or to install the cable over only one row of connectors. If a PATA cable is reversed when it is attached to either the drive or the PATA host adapter, one of two symptoms are typical:

- Many systems will not display any information onscreen when restarted. These systems send a query to the drive and wait to complete the boot process until the drive responds. The drive never gets the message because the cable is attached incorrectly.

- Other systems will display a drive error because the drive cannot be detected during startup.

In both cases, if the power cable is attached to the drive, you will be able to hear the drive spinning as soon as the system is turned on.

The solution in either case is to make sure that the PATA cable's pin 1 (normally marked by a colored stripe) is attached to pin 1 on both the IDE host adapter (card or motherboard) and the PATA drive and that the cable attaches to both rows of pins on the drive and interface.

Physical or Electronic Damage to Drive

PATA drives can be damaged by shock and impact; don't drop your drive and expect it not to notice. If the BIOS cannot detect a drive and you already have checked BIOS configuration and cabling, the drive itself might be damaged. PATA drives should operate very quietly. A drive that makes scraping or banging noises when the system is turned on has sustained head or actuator damage and must be repaired or replaced.

If the system fails to start when a drive is attached to a power lead from the power supply, but starts normally when the drive is disconnected from power, the drive's power connector has a short. You should repair or replace the drive. If the drive is connected to the power supply via an extender or Y-splitter, remove the extender or splitter and connect the drive directly to the power supply; if the system starts, the extender or Y-splitter is defective.

Jumpering Issues

If two PATA drives are attached to a single 40-wire ATA/IDE cable, one drive must be jumpered as master and the other as slave. If both drives are jumpered as master or both as slave, neither drive can be auto-detected by the BIOS or accessed by the system. If the original drive on the cable was working properly until a new drive was installed, check the jumpering on both the original (it should be set to master) and new drive (it should be set to slave).

If an 80-wire cable is being used, both drives can be set to cable select; the cable sets master and slave according to the drives' positions on the cables.

Some combinations of different brands of drives cannot be used on a single cable even if the jumpering is correct. If you are unable to detect one or both drives when two drives are connected to a single ATA/IDE cable and you have verified the jumpering is correct, the drives might not be fully compatible with ATA standards. Change the master to slave and the slave to master, move the slave drive to the other IDE cable, and rejumper both drives, or use a UDMA-66 cable with cable select settings to enable both drives to work.

Drive Not Ready Error

Some PATA hard drives report "not ready" errors during initial system power-on, but if the system is restarted with a warm boot, the drive runs normally and starts the system. This is caused by a hard drive that has not spun up when the system tries to boot from the drive. To solve this problem, allow the system more time during the boot process to make sure the drive is ready before attempting to boot from it. Use the following methods:

- Adjust the Delay Timer option available in some BIOS programs; this pauses the boot process a few seconds to allow the drive to start.

- Disable the Quick Boot option available in some BIOS programs.

- Allow the system to perform a full memory count and test before booting.

Troubleshooting SATA and eSATA Drives

Problems with SATA drives can result from cabling, detection, BIOS settings, and physical damage. Use this section to prepare for SATA and eSATA troubleshooting questions on the A+ Certification Exam and in your day-to-day work.

Loose Data and Power Cables

Most SATA power and data cables simply push into place, and can easily be accidentally disconnected from the host adapter or drive when other upgrades are taking place. While some SATA data cables now use locking clips to help secure the cable to the drive, this is not yet common. Be sure to check power and data cable connections after installing an SATA drive or after installing other internal upgrades.

eSATA Drive Cannot Be Accessed

If an eSATA drive cannot be accessed, check the following:

- Make sure the eSATA cable is securely connected to the eSATA port and the drive. Some eSATA cables don't have long enough connectors to make a secure connection with some eSATA drives: replace these cables with cables that have longer connectors.

- If the eSATA drive is connected to the computer with an eSATA header cable, check the header cable connection with the motherboard.

- If the eSATA drive is connected to the computer with an eSATA header cable, also verify that the SATA port configuration in the BIOS has not changed since the drive was first connected (eSATA drives must run in AHCI mode). If you are already running other SATA drives in other modes, use an eSATA host adapter card instead of changing BIOS options .

SATA 3Gbps Drive Runs in Reduced Performance Mode (1.5Gbps)

Some 3Gbps SATA drives are jumpered to run at 1.5Gbps transfer rates to enable compatibility with the original 1.5Gbps SATA standard. If the drive is connected to a 3Gbps or 6Gbps SATA port, remove the drive jumper to enable full performance.

Physical or Electronic Damage to Drive

SATA drives can be damaged by shock and impact; don't drop your drive and expect it not to notice. If the BIOS cannot detect a drive and you already have checked BIOS configuration and cabling, the drive itself might be damaged. SATA drives should operate very quietly. A drive that makes scraping or banging noises when the system is turned on has sustained head or actuator damage and must be repaired or replaced.

If the system fails to start when a drive is attached to a power lead from the power supply, but starts normally when the drive is disconnected from power, the drive's power connector has a short. You should repair or replace the drive. If the drive is connected to the power supply via an extender or Y-splitter, remove the extender or splitter and connect the drive directly to the power supply; if the system starts, the extender or Y-splitter is defective .

Using Hard Disk Diagnostics

Most hard disk vendors provide diagnostic programs that can be used to test drives for errors. The latest versions of these programs can be obtained from the drive vendors' websites.

Typically, these programs offer a quick and a long test option. To determine if a hard disk is functioning, run the quick test first (see Figure 12-35). If the drive passes, use the long test to determine if the drive is working within specifications.

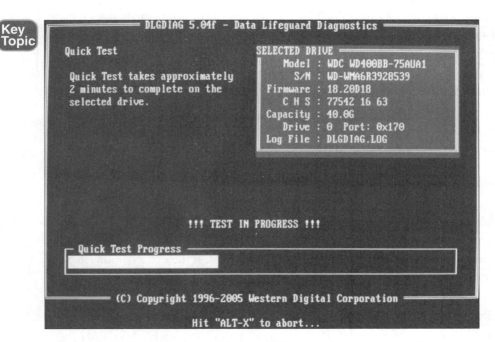

Figure 12-35   Performing a quick test on a Western Digital hard disk with vendor-supplied diagnostic software.

During the long test, defective areas on the drive can be replaced by spare capacity built into the drive. Because defective areas on the disk might not be able to be moved to another location, drive vendors often recommend you perform a full backup before testing a hard disk.

Troubleshooting CD-ROM and DVD Drives

The same problems can occur with CD-ROM and DVD drives as with other drives or devices that use the same interface, but additional problems can occur because these drives use removable optical media. The following are some typical problems:

- Read delays after new media is inserted
- Can't use a particular drive with a CD/DVD mastering program
- Can't write to media
- Buffer underrun failures
- Can't read some media types in CD-ROM or DVD drives
- Damage to media prevents drive from reading media
- Can't play music through sound card's speakers

The following sections describe details related to each problem.

Read Delays After New Media Is Inserted

Read delays of several seconds are normal when you insert media into an optical drive; the drive must spin up the media to read it, and delays are sometimes longer with faster drives. The AutoPlay feature in Windows XP, Vista, and 7 reads the contents of the media and by default brings up a list of programs that can be used to access the drive, adding further delays. A delay of more than about 20 seconds can indicate drive or media problems; clean the drive with a cleaning CD, which uses small brushes to wipe debris and dust away from the laser, and try the CD again.

TIP   If the media is not marked, it might have been inserted upside down into the drive. Most blank CDs have a light green reflective surface (some have a gold or blue reflective surface). Blank CD-RW media has a mirror-like reflective surface. Blank DVD media has a blue reflective surface: make sure the reflective surface (not the label side) is facing toward the media tray.

Drive Not Supported by CD/DVD Mastering Program

Originally, the only way to write to CD-R media was with a mastering program such as Roxio Media Creator or Nero. These and similar programs typically feature a Windows Explorer–style interface, which you use to create a list of files and folders you want to write to a CD or DVD (see Figure 12-36).

After the layout is created, an additional dialog is used to configure the burn process (see Figure 12.37).

Although recent CD and DVD mastering programs support any connected drive, some older CD and DVD programs do not. If your particular brand and model of writeable drive isn't supported by the mastering program you want to use, you can't use the program to write to your media.

Here are some indications your mastering program doesn't work with your drive:

- The program doesn't detect your drive at all.

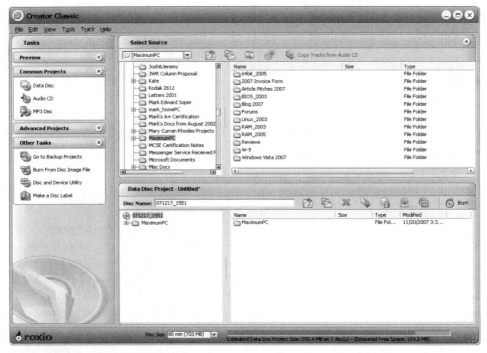

Figure 12-36   Creating a layout for a mastered CD with Roxio Easy Media Creator's Creator Classic module.

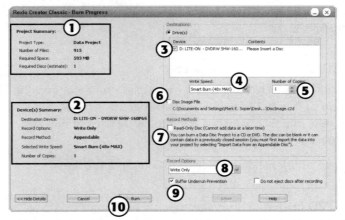

1. Information about the project
2. Drive and drive settings used for recording
3. Selects drive to use
4. Selects write speed
5. Selects number of copies
6. Select to create disk image instead of burning disc
7. Closes (finalizes) disc when checked
8. Selects from test and record, test only, record only
9. Enables buffer underrun protection when checked
10. Starts burn process

Figure 12-37   The Burn Progress dialog box in Roxio Easy Media Creator's Creator Classic module.

- The program doesn't list your drive as a target drive for writing files.

- When you install the program, it informs you that no compatible CD or DVD drives were found.

■ The program detects your drive, but displays an error message when you try to write files to the drive.

To solve problems like these, try

■ **Downloading the latest CD or DVD recorder support files from the vendor's website**—Some vendors provide a database of supported recorders and software versions you can query. If your recorder appears on the list of supported recorders, but the version of software listed is more recent than the one you use, download the recommended update. Keep checking the software vendor's website for further updates if your recorder isn't listed yet.

■ **Upgrading to the latest version of your preferred software**—If you use a no-longer-current version of CD-mastering software and your recorder isn't listed as supported, see if the latest version will support it and purchase the upgrade if a free update isn't available.

■ **Using the recording software provided with the drive instead of a third-party product**—Although many writeable drives come with bare-bones software that might lack the features of a commercial product, the program packaged with the drive will work.

■ **Changing to a different CD/DVD mastering program**—If the latest version of your preferred program does not support your drive, switch to a different program.

Can't Write to Media

Problems writing to media can be caused by

■ Incompatible media

■ Closed media

■ Packet-writing problems

■ Media problems

■ Incorrect insertion of media

Although current Super Multi DVD drives support all recordable and rewritable CD and DVD media, older drives might not support some media types. For example, drives that support only DVD-R/RW media will not work with DVD+R/RW media; drives designed for single-layer DVD media cannot write to dual-layer (DL) media.

All but the earliest CD-ROM drives are designed to read media that can be added to (multiple session) or media that has been closed (write-protected).

If your CD or DVD-mastering program displays an error message indicating that you need to insert media that has enough room for the files you want to write, and the media has more than enough space, the media was closed when it was created, and no more files can be placed on the media. You can determine how much space is used on a writeable CD or DVD with Windows Explorer/Computer/My Computer. Right-click on the drive and select **Properties** to see the amount of space used. 74-minute media can hold about 650MB, whereas 80-minute media can hold about 700MB of information; single-layer DVDs can hold about 4.7GB of information, whereas dual-layer DVD can store about 8.5GB of information. The Properties sheet will also say the media has 0 bytes free, but this is misleading. Most mastering programs will also list the amount of space used by the files you want to transfer to CD or DVD.

TIP   If you want to write files to the media more than once, be sure that you select the option that doesn't close (finalize) the media when you create the disc. Some programs choose this option for you by default, whereas others might close (finalize) the disc unless you choose otherwise. If you are writing to a DVD-RW disc, you might need to unfinalize (open) the media before you can add additional files.

CD/DVD mastering is an excellent way to copy a large number of files to a CD or DVD all at once, but it's not designed to enable files to be dragged from their original location and dropped (copied) to a disc. Hence, most CD- and DVD-mastering programs include separate packet-writing programs to enable drag-and-drop file copying. For example, Easy Media Creator includes Drag and Drop, and Nero includes InCD (or you can download a copy if your version of Nero doesn't include it). Packet-writing software writes files that correspond to a standard called Universal Disk Format (UDF); UDF is also used by the Windows Live File System format used by Windows Vista and Windows 7's built-in DVD recorder support.

Floppy disks, Zip disks, SuperDisks (LS-120/LS-240), and other types of magnetic removable-media storage are preformatted; you can copy files to them as soon as you insert them into the drive. However, optical media must be formatted before you can use it for drag-and-drop copying.

The packet-writing software supplied with your drive (or as part of a CD/DVD-creation program you purchased) is used to perform this task. After you start the program, insert your media and click the **Format** button (see Figure 12-38).

You should provide a label (descriptive name) for your media to make it easy to distinguish between different discs. (The label is displayed in Windows Explorer/Computer/My Computer.) Use compression to save space.

If you are unable to start the formatting process, check the following:

■   If you have another writeable drive installed, close any resident software used by the other drive (check the system tray).

■   Use the correct type of media for your recorder and packet-writing program.

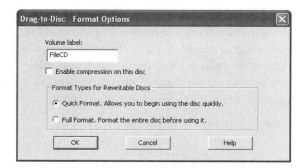

Figure 12-38   The Roxio Drag-to-Disc formatting program preparing a blank CD-RW disc for use.

No matter what type of media you use, make sure you insert it correctly. The unlabeled side faces towards the tray.

Can't Read Some Media Types in CD-ROM or DVD Drives

Older CD-ROM drives (generally those under 24X speed) and first-generation DVD drives are unable to read CD-RW media, which has a lower reflectivity than CD-ROM or CD-R media. Newer DVD drives and virtually all CD-ROM drives at 24X or faster speeds use a modified laser to enable them to read CD-RW media.

CD-ROM drives that can read CD-RW media are sometimes called MultiRead drives. DVD drives that can read CD-RW and different types of DVD media are called MultiRead2 drives. To determine if a drive can read a specified type of media, check its specification sheet. Older drives that lack CD-RW compatibility cannot be upgraded—they must be replaced.

If the drive is MultiRead- or MultiRead2-compliant but you can't read the media, install the UDF reader provided by the vendor whose software was used to create the disc. Some UDF reader software is copied to the rewritable CD or DVD for installation on the target PC, whereas others require you to download the reader and install it manually.

Because rewritable CD/DVD support can be spotty, it's best to use recordable media (CD-R, DVD-R, or DVD+R) recorded with a mastering program to distribute files to other users.

Buffer Underrun Failures

Ever since the first recordable CD drive was introduced, users have created untold numbers of useless coasters because of buffer underruns. A buffer underrun takes place when the writeable CD or DVD drive transfers data to the disc faster than the computer can provide it to the drive. Because the flow of data is interrupted, the recording stops and the media is useless.

All current writeable CD and DVD drives include some type of buffer underrun–prevention technologies such as BURN-Proof, SmartBurn, and others. These technologies work by suspending the CD creation process whenever the buffer memory in the CD runs out of information and continuing the process when more data is available. Upgrading from a drive that lacks this feature to a drive that supports this feature is the easiest way to avoid buffer underruns and enjoy much faster disc creation times.

Here are some other ways to avoid creating a coaster with your drive (refer to Figure 12-37 for examples):

■ If your drive supports buffer-underrun prevention, make sure your CD-mastering software also supports this feature and make sure you leave it enabled.

■ If your CD-mastering software offers a Test option, use it to simulate CD recording at various speeds. If the program reports an error at the highest recording speed, reduce the speed and try the test again.

■ Upgrade the firmware in the drive to the latest version.

Damage to Media Prevents Drive from Reading Media

Because all types of optical drives read data recorded in a single spiral track, fingerprints or surface damage to the clear protective layer over the media surface will prevent data beneath the dirty or damaged surface from being read. A cracked or severely scratched optical disc cannot be read at all.

Dirty optical discs can be cleaned with the same cleaners used for music CDs. Some surface scratches can be polished away with special repair kits available from computer and music stores, and special protective shields can be attached to the nonlabel (data) side of frequently used optical discs to protect the media. Media should be stored in a protective sleeve or jewel case when not in use.

Can't Play Music Through Sound Card's Speakers

Many users like to use their computers as stereo systems, taking advantage of their optical drives and sound card hardware to play music in their homes or offices. If the user is unable to hear CDs being played through the CD player software supplied on most systems, check the following:

■ **CD audio cable**—If your digital media software cannot play music via the PATA or SATA interface, connect a two-wire (digital) or four-wire (analog) music cable between your optical drive and the correct jack on the sound card or motherboard audio.

■ **Windows sound mixer controls**—In most cases, a speaker icon will be visible in the Windows system tray when sound hardware is installed. Click the speaker icon to display the mixer control. If the volume for CD audio is turned down to minimum or is muted, or if all audio is muted, no sound will be audible. Enable the sound and adjust the volume to hear music.

- **Volume control in CD player application**—The volume control in the player program might be set too low if the sound is not audible after checking the first two items. Adjust it as required.

Troubleshooting Removable-Media, External, and Tape Drives

Typical problems with removable-media, external, and tape drives include

- Drive not recognized

- Read/write problems

Use the following sections to learn how to troubleshoot these drives.

Drive Not Recognized Problems

Removable-media drives plugged into PnP interfaces such as IEEE-1394 and USB should be recognized by the system as soon as they are connected to the appropriate port. If they are not recognized, check the following:

- Make sure the interface has been enabled and its drivers loaded. If the interface is not enabled, any devices using it can't be detected. See Chapter 7, "I/O and Multimedia Ports and Devices," for details.

- Install drivers and utility software before connecting the drive. This helps the system to better recognize the drive.

- If the tape drive isn't recognized by tape backup software, verify the drive is supported by the software. If not, update the software or use compatible software. You might also need to install drivers provided by the backup vendor for your drives in place of the normal Windows drivers; check with the backup software vendor for details. Note that Windows Vista and Windows 7's backup program does not support tape drives; you must use third-party backup software to enable tape backups with Windows Vista and Windows 7, and the tape drive must not rely on Windows' RSM (which is not included in Windows Vista/7).

- Check cable connections between the port and the drive. If the cables are loose, reattach the cables. If the cables are bad, use approved replacements. Note that some vendors recommend that only the cables shipped with the drive be used.

- If the drive is bus powered, verify that the USB or IEEE-1394 port has enough power to run the drive. Bus-powered USB hubs or daisy-chain connections on IEEE-1394 devices might not provide enough power to run the drive. Connect the drive directly to a port on the PC and try again, or connect an AC adapter to the drive if available.

- Verify that other devices plugged into USB or IEEE-1394 ports are working. If no other devices are working, the port might have failed. Check the Windows Device Manager for the port status and power level available for each USB port.

NOTE   Some vendors of portable (2.5-inch based) USB hard disk drives provide, or sell as an option, a Y-shaped USB cable that draws power from two USB ports. Use this cable if you are unable to run the drive from the power available from a single USB port.

If the removable-media drive is plugged into a SCSI host adapter, check the following:

- Inspect terminator settings. A drive or device at the end of the SCSI daisy-chain should be terminated; other drives/devices should *not* be terminated.

- Verify the drive has a unique device ID.

- Make sure an external SCSI drive is turned on *before* the system is turned on.

- Make sure the drive is properly connected to the data cable; an internal drive also needs to be connected to a power lead from the power supply.

If the removable-media drive is plugged into a PATA host adapter, check the following:

- Drive jumpers should be set to a unique setting (master or slave) if a 40-wire cable is used. If the existing drive is master, the removable-media drive must be jumpered to slave. If an 80-wire cable is used, both the existing drive and new removable-media drive can be jumpered as cable select.

- Make sure the drive is properly connected to the data and power cables.

Read/Write Problems

Read/write problems with removable-media drives can involve problems with the media or with the drives themselves. Check the following:

- Try the media in another drive. If the media can be read or written to in another drive, the first drive you tried is defective.

- Make sure the media isn't write protected. SuperDisk, 3.5-inch floppy disks, SD, and SDHD media use mechanical sliders to write-protect the media's contents, but most other types use write protection configured by the drive's utility software. Tape drives might use mechanical or software write protection.

- Use an approved cleaning disk or cartridge made especially for the drive. Check with the drive vendor for recommended models, and don't use other types.

- Double check power and data cable connections to the drive.

- Download and install the latest drivers and utilities for the drive; run diagnostic software provided by the vendor to pinpoint problems.

- If the drive makes unusual noises, it could indicate damage to the drive heads or media. Contact the vendor immediately for help, and don't use media containing valuable data until you determine if the disk cartridge or drive itself has failed.

- Re-tension tapes before reading or writing.

Exam Preparation Tasks

Review All the Key Topics

Review the most important topics in the chapter, noted with the key topics icon in the outer margin of the page. Table 12-9 lists a reference of these key topics and the page numbers on which each is found.

Table 12-10   Key Topics for Chapter 12

Key Topic Element	Description	Page Number
Figure 12-2	The rear of a typical 3.5-inch drive before (left) and after (right) data and power cables are attached.	502
Figure 12-7	The power and data cable connectors on SATA and PATA (ATA/IDE) hard disks.	509
Figure 12-8	The power and data cables used by SATA and PATA (ATA/IDE) hard disks.	509
Table 12-3	ATA Specifications and Features.	511
Figure 12-12	Attaching power and data cables to a typical ATA/IDE drive.	514
Figure 12-13	Attaching power and data cables to a typical SATA drive.	515
Figure 12-20	Dual-port eSATA header cable.	522
Figure 12-21	eSATA data cable.	522
Figure 12-22	External hard disk with eSATA, IEEE-1394a, and USB ports.	523
Figure 12-23	Preparing to create an ATA RAID array.	525
Table 12-5	UDMA (Ultra ATA) Peak Transfer Rates.	527
Figure 12-25	A typical ATAPI (PATA) internal optical drive before (top) and after (bottom) data, power, and CD music cables have been attached.	534
Figure 12-28	A U.S. penny compared in size to the most common types of flash memory cards.	540
Figure 12-29	A multislot card reader supports a wide variety of flash memory cards.	542
Figure 12-31	A typical USB flash memory drive with a retractable connector.	544
Figure 12-32	Preparing to remove a USB flash memory drive with Safely Remove Hardware.	544
Figure 12-35	Performing a quick test on a Western Digital hard disk with vendor-supplied diagnostic software.	554

Complete the Tables and Lists from Memory

Print a copy of Appendix B, "Memory Tables," (found on the CD), or at least the section for this chapter, and complete the tables and lists from memory. Appendix C, "Memory Tables Answer Key," also on the CD, includes completed tables and lists to check your work.

Definitions of Key Terms

Define the following key terms from this chapter, and check your answers in the glossary.

FDD, HDD, PATA, IDE, SATA, Serial ATA, Block mode, PIO, UDMA, CD-ROM, DVD-ROM, Flash memory, Phantom directory

Troubleshooting Scenario

You are working on a computer. You plug up your external hard drive and for some reason it does not show up in the Explorer window. You then happen to notice that this computer is actually running a server-based operating system. What would be the steps you need to take to fix this problem?

Refer to Appendix A for the answer.

This chapter covers the following subjects:

■ **Differences in Windows Versions**—This section teaches you how to differentiate between Windows 7, Windows Vista, and XP. The graphical user interfaces (GUI) are different as well as the hardware requirements necessary to run each operating system. This section also covers how to make older programs run properly in newer versions of Windows.

■ **Primary Windows Components**—This section describes the registry, virtual memory, and file systems like NTFS and FAT32.

■ **Windows Interfaces**—This section talks about the tools you will use to interface with Windows such as Windows Explorer, Computer/My Computer, Control Panel, Command Prompt, Network/My Network Places, as well as the Start menu, taskbar, and System Tray.

■ **Essential Operating System Files**—Windows 7, Windows Vista, and Windows XP need several files to boot and run the system; this section describes those files in detail.

■ **Disk Partition, File, and Folder Management**—In this section, you learn about the different types of partitions (primary, extended, and so on) and how to work with and back up files and folders effectively.

■ **Command-Line Functions**—Every technician needs to know how to use the command-line, especially the Windows Command Prompt. This section shows how to open and use the Command Prompt and how to work with commands.

■ **System Management Tools**—Keeping the system well managed is important. This section covers tools such as Device Manager, Task Manager, Registry Editor (Regedit), and System Restore, which help to administer a sparkling Windows operating system.

■ **Optimizing Windows**—Making Windows be all it can be is no small task; this section delves into virtual memory, services, applications, temporary files, and how to optimize Windows at startup.

This chapter covers a portion of the CompTIA A+ 220-701 objectives 3.2 and 3.3 and CompTIA A+ 220-702 objectives 2.2 and 2.3.

CHAPTER 13

Using and Managing Windows

Until now, we have focused on hardware and sprinkled in little bits of software here and there. That's about to change. This chapter goes into depth concerning the fundamentals of Windows 7, Windows Vista, and Windows XP. When you are done with this chapter, you might even want to read it again because there is so much information packed in it. And if you can pass the "Do I Know This Already?" quiz, then our hats are off to you.

There is a slight amount of Windows 2000 Professional (hereafter referred to as 2000 or Windows 2000) coverage in this chapter as well (because it is covered on the CompTIA objectives); however most of the concepts and techniques used in Windows 2000 work the same way in Windows XP. Unless Windows 2000 is specifically mentioned, you can safely assume that any time XP is described, the concept is the same for Windows 2000.

You might ask why there is so much Windows XP content within this chapter, as well as on the CompTIA A+ objectives. Well, even though XP is currently nine years old, there are still a slew of companies using it. Consequently, it is very important to know Windows XP for the exam. Windows 7 is now the newest operating system that CompTIA includes on the A+ exam.

Note that you will sometimes see references to Windows 7 and Windows Vista's "Computer" and Windows XP's equivalent "My Computer" within the same sentence. Sometimes this will be written as Computer/My Computer or My Computer/Computer. The same holds true for other Windows interfaces that have undergone name changes with the advent of Windows Vista and Windows 7.

There is a lot of content to cover in this chapter; so, without further ado, let's demonstrate how to use and manage Windows!

"Do I Know This Already?" Quiz

The "Do I Know This Already?" quiz allows you to assess whether you should read this entire chapter or simply jump to the "Exam Preparation Tasks" section for review. If you are in doubt, read the entire chapter. Table 13-1 outlines the major headings in this chapter and the corresponding "Do I Know This Already?" quiz questions. You can find the answers in Appendix A, "Answers to the 'Do I Know This Already?' Quizzes and Troubleshooting Scenarios."

Table 13-1   "Do I Know This Already?" Foundation Topics Section-to-Question Mapping

Foundations Topics Section	Questions Covered in This Section
Differences in Windows Versions	1, 2, 14, 15
Primary Windows Components	3, 4
Windows Interfaces	5, 6, 16
Essential Operating System Files	7, 8
Disk Partition, File, and Folder Management	9
Command-Line Functions	10, 11
System Management Tools	12
Optimizing Windows	13

1. Which of the following technologies is the graphical user interface used by default in Windows Vista and Windows 7?

    a. Windows PowerGUI

    b. Windows Aero

    c. Windows GUI version II

    d. Windows Powershell

2. You are the PC technician for your company. You are upgrading your computers to Windows 7. There are certain users who have older applications. What tool can you use to make the application run under the newer operating system?

    a. XP Mode

    b. You cannot do this

    c. Program Compatibility Wizard

    d. Install the application in a virtual machine

3. Which of the following is a central database for Windows, applications, and user settings that should be backed up on a regular basis?

   a. The Hardware Layer

   b. The Registry

   c. Windows Machine Database

   d. The Windows Hives

4. You are working on a computer. You receive a message about virtual memory being low on resources. What is virtual memory?

   a. Physical memory sticks on the motherboard

   b. Memory that only runs in a virtual environment

   c. Your system memory and virtual memory are the same

   d. Your system memory has borrowed some hard disk space

5. Which of the following is a file management utility that is used on Windows-based operating systems?

   a. Windows Explorer

   b. File Manager

   c. Server Manager

   d. Internet Explorer

6. You are working on your Windows XP desktop computer. You need to modify your network settings. Which of the following will you use to modify this?

   a. My Computer

   b. Network Spot

   c. My Network Places

   d. My Network Manager

7. Which of the following files are required to boot the Windows 7 operating system? (Choose all that apply.)

   a. Bootmgr

   b. BCD

   c. hal.dll

   d. Ntoskrnl.exe

   e. Boot.ini

8. Which of the following files is a specially formatted text file that configures the startup process for the Windows XP operating system?

   a. NTDETECT.com

   b. BOOT.ini

   c. NTLDR

   d. Ntoskrnl.exe

9. You have just been given a new hard drive to install in a client's computer to be installed with a new Windows operating system. What processes must you go through while you install the operating system on the drive? (Choose two.)

   a. Create a new partition

   b. Nothing; the drive is ready to go

   c. Format the drive

   d. Install the drive utility

10. You are doing some phone support for your company. A user calls up and says he is not able to get out to network resources. You need him to run the ipconfig utility to check for a valid IP address. How would you tell the user to pull up the command prompt in Windows 7? (Choose all that apply.)

   a. Start, Run, and type command

   b. Start, Run, and type cmd

   c. Start, right-click Computer, and click Open

   d. Start > Programs > Accessories > Command Prompt icon

11. Which of the following parameters (switches) will copy all files, folders, and subfolders, including empty subfolders, to the TEST folder?

   a. xcopy *.* c:\test /T

   b. xcopy *.* c:\test /S

   c. xcopy *.* c:\test /E

   d. xcopy *.* c:\test \T

12. You are providing some phone support for your clients. They are telling you that the video seems to be showing poorly. You need to see if there is a problem with the video card. Where would you instruct them to go to view this information?

   a. Display Properties

   b. The screensaver tab

   c. Device Manager

   d. MSCONFIG

13. You are contacted by a client that is having problems because her computer is running very slowly. You need to run a utility to see if the system needs to have more memory installed. Which of the following utilities should you use?

    a. Performance Monitor

    b. System Performance wizard

    c. Memory Tasks wizard

    d. System Configuration Utility

14. What is the minimum processor requirement for Windows 7?

    a. 133MHz

    b. 233MHz

    c. 800MHz

    d. 1GHz

15. What is the minimum RAM requirement for Windows 7 32-bit version?

    a. 256MB

    b. 512MB

    c. 1024MB

    d. 2048MB

16. A user wants to modify his network connection from the Windows Vista Network window. Which of the following options will allow the user to do this?

    a. Task Manager

    b. Command Prompt

    c. My Network Places

    d. Network and Sharing Center

Differences in Windows Versions

The 2011 A+ Certification exams cover Windows 7, Vista, XP, and 2000. It is important to know the differences between these operating systems, and the minimum hardware requirements necessary to install each of the operating systems. We'll start with Windows 7, Vista, and XP's graphical user interface (GUI), which is what Windows employs to interact with the user. Normally, a keyboard and pointing device, such as a mouse, are used to input information to the operating system's GUI, and whatever is input will be shown on the screen. Basically, everything you see on the display, including windows, icons, menus, and other visual indicators, is part of the GUI. Following the GUI section, we'll discuss system requirements for the different versions of Windows.

GUI

The Windows 7 GUI, shown in Figure 13-1, is different in several ways from Windows XP and also differs from Windows Vista:

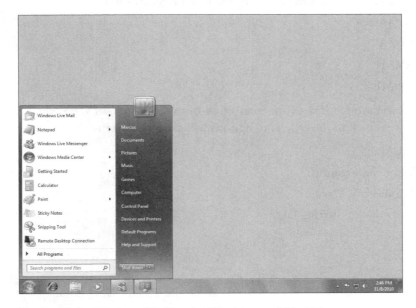

Figure 13-1   Windows 7's Standard Desktop and Start Menu

- **Windows Aero**—Introduced with Windows Vista, Aero features translucent windows, window animations, three-dimensional viewing of windows, and a modified taskbar. You can make modifications to the look of Aero by right-clicking the desktop and selecting **Personalization**. From here, you can modify things such as the window color and transparency of windows. To disable Windows Aero, select **Windows 7 Basic from the Themes** menu.

- **Welcome Center—**Welcome Center, available from the Start menu or from Control Panel, is a good starting point for running initial tasks such as connecting to the Internet, transferring files from another computer, adding users, installing Windows Live Essentials 2011 (which provides an email client, photo organizer, and other features), and learning more about Windows 7.

- **Windows Gadgets—**Windows 7 enables you to place gadgets anywhere on the desktop. Gadgets are mini applications that provide a variety of services, such as the time in a different time zone, weather updates via the Web, and news feed headlines. They can also interact with other applications to streamline the Windows experience. Additional gadgets can be downloaded from Microsoft.

- **Modified Start menu—**The new Start menu has a number of changes compared to Windows XP. For example, there is a useful search field directly above the Start button. However, the Run prompt has been removed by default, but can be added by accessing the Taskbar and Start Menu Properties window. As with Windows Vista and Windows Windows XP, when you run a program, it is automatically added to the left pane of the Start menu. To keep a program you run on the left pane, right-click the program name and select **Pin to Start** menu. You can also disable this option or adjust the number of programs to display on the Start menu.

The Windows Vista GUI, as shown in Figure 13-2, represents a transition from Windows XP to Windows 7. Many features of the Windows Vista GUI are similar to those of Windows 7. Some differences include

| A | B |

Figure 13-2 Windows Vista's standard desktop and start menu (A) and classic desktop and start menu (B).

- **Changing from Windows Aero**—In Windows Vista, you can make modifications to the look of Aero by right-clicking the desktop and selecting **Personalize**, and then clicking **Windows Color and Appearance**. From here, you can modify things such as the transparency of windows. To disable Windows Aero, click the **Theme** link from within the **Personalize** window. Then, from the Theme drop down menu, select **Windows Classic**.

- **Starting Welcome Center**—Welcome Center automatically opens when you first start Windows Vista. After installing the operating system, it's a good starting point for running initial tasks such as connecting to the Internet, transferring files from another computer, adding users, and learning more about Windows Vista. The Welcome Center will continue to show up every time you start Windows unless you deselect the checkbox to the bottom left of the window. To open Welcome Center later, go to **Control Panel**, **System and Maintenance**.

- **Using Windows Sidebar and gadgets**—While Windows 7 and Windows Vista offer the same gadgets, in Windows Vista gadgets must be run from within the Windows Sidebar, which defaults to the right side of the desktop. You can modify the Sidebar by right-clicking on it and selecting **Properties**. From here, you can select whether the Sidebar starts when Windows does, place it above other Windows, change its orientation, and remove gadgets. To add gadgets, click the + directly over the topmost gadget.

- **Displaying the Start menu**—The major difference between the Windows Vista and Windows 7 Start menu is the option to run Windows Vista in "Classic mode" similar to the one used by Windows 2000 and by XP, if it was configured that way. In Classic mode, the Start menu displays the name of the operating system along the left side in the same way that earlier versions of Windows display the name. This is usually done to optimize Windows performance.

The Windows XP GUI has several differences compared to its predecessor Windows 2000:

- **Personalized start menu**—Windows XP offers a personalized start menu for each user.

- **Two-column start menu**—As shown in Figure 13-3A, the left column displays the most recently or frequently used programs and access to default applications for Internet and email, while the right column provides access to the user's documents folders and Control Panel. To see all programs, hover your mouse over **All Programs**.

- **Taskbar**—The taskbar adjusts in size according to the number of programs that are running and the number of quick launch icons in use.

■ **Classic mode**—You can configure the Start menu and desktop to run in a Classic mode similar to the one used by Windows 2000 (Figure 13-3B). In Classic mode, the Start menu displays the name of the operating system along the left side in the same way that earlier versions of Windows display the name.

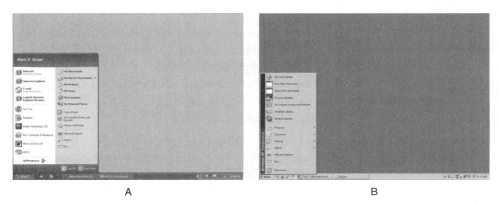

A   B

Figure 13-3   Windows XP's standard desktop and start menu (A) and classic desktop and start menu (B).

NOTE   To change only the start menu to the Classic mode, right-click the **Start** button, select **Properties**, and choose **Classic Start** menu. To change the start menu and the desktop to the Classic mode as in Figure 13-3B, open the **Display** properties sheet, select **Themes**, and select **Windows Classic**. You can open the Display properties sheet from Control Panel or by right-clicking an empty area of the desktop and selecting **Properties**.

System Requirements

System requirements for different versions of Windows vary widely. Table 13-2 compares the hardware requirements for Windows 7, Vista, XP, and 2000.

Table 13-2   Minimum Hardware Requirements for Windows 7, Vista, XP, and 2000

Component	7	Vista	XP	2000
Processor	1GHz	800MHz	233MHz	133MHz
RAM	1GB (32-bit) 2GB (64-bit)	512MB	64MB	64MB
Free disk space	20GB	15GB (20GB partition)	1.5GB (2GB partition)	650MB (2GB partition)
Other	DVD-ROM drive	DVD-ROM or CD-ROM drive	CD-ROM or DVD-ROM	CD-ROM/Floppy drive

NOTE   The specs in Table 13-2 are the *minimum* requirements. Microsoft recommends a 1GHz processor for all versions of Vista and 1GB of RAM plus a 40GB HDD for Vista Home Premium/Business/Ultimate. The Windows 7 hardware requirements vary according to whether a 32-bit or 64-bit version is being installed.

You may hear the terms x86 and x64. x86 refers to older CPU names that ended in an "86"—for example, the 80386 (shortened to just 386), 486, or 586 CPU and so on. Generally, when people use the term x86 they are referring to 32-bit CPUs that allow for 4GB of address space. x64 (or x86-64) refers to newer 64-bit CPUs that are a superset of the x86 architecture. This technology can run 64-bit software as well as 32-bit software and can address a maximum of 1 TB.

Windows 7, Vista, and XP come in 64- and 32-bit versions, so that users from both generations of computers can run the software efficiently. Windows 2000 Professional was designed for 32-bit CPUs only.

Application Compatibility

Most commercial business applications should run properly on Windows 7/Vista/XP as well as on older versions of Windows. However, some commercial and custom applications designed for older versions of Windows might not run properly on Windows 7/Vista/XP.

To enable applications written for older versions of Windows to run properly on Windows 7/Vista/XP, you can use the Program Compatibility Wizard built into Windows or the Compatibility tab located on the executable file's properties sheet to run the program in a selected compatibility mode.

Program Compatibility Wizard in Windows 7

To start the program in Windows 7, click **Start, Control Panel, Programs, Run Programs Made for Previous Versions of Windows**.

After the wizard is started, click **Next** on the opening screen and select the program that doesn't work properly. To try recommended compatibility settings, click **Try Recommended Settings**, and click **Start the Program**. If the program runs properly, click **Next** and then **Yes**.

If the program doesn't run properly, click **No, Try Again** and answer questions about the problems you noticed (see Figure 13-4). From the answers you select, Windows selects settings to try (see Figure 13-5) and prompts you to run the program. After you find settings that work, Windows uses them every time you run the program.

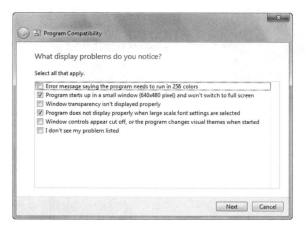

Figure 13-4   Answering questions about problems with an older program with Windows 7's Program Compatibility Wizard.

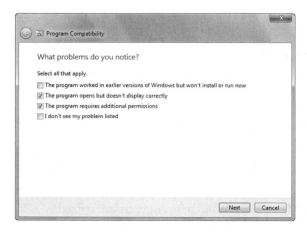

Figure 13-5   Based on your answers, Windows 7's Program Compatibility Wizard selects settings to help your older program run properly.

Program Compatibility Wizard in Windows XP and Vista

To start the wizard in Windows XP, click **Start, All Programs, Accessories, Program Compatibility Wizard**. To start the wizard in Windows Vista, click **Start, Control Panel, Programs, Use an Older Program with This Version of Windows**.

After the wizard is started, you can select from programs already installed on your computer, select the current program in the CD-ROM drive, or browse to the program manually. After you select a program, you can select the version of Windows the program worked best under (see Figure 13-6).

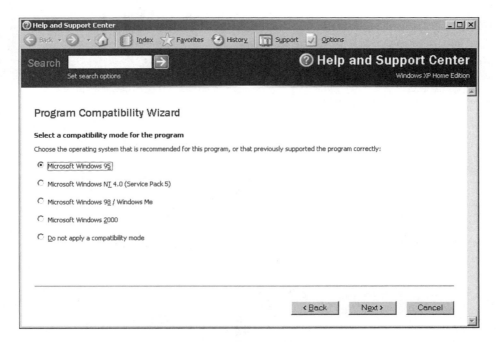

Figure 13-6   Using the Program Compatibility Wizard to run an older Windows program under Windows XP as Windows 95 would run it.

On the next screen, you can select one or more of the following options to aid compatibility:

- **256 Colors**—Many older Windows programs can't run under 16-bit or higher color depths.

- **640×480 Screen Resolution**—Many older Windows programs use a fixed screen size and can't run properly on a high-resolution screen.

- **Disable Visual Themes**—Many older Windows programs were created before visual themes were common.

After selecting the options, test the program (which applies the settings you selected and runs the program). After you close the program, Windows switches back to its normal screen settings if necessary, and you can decide whether to use these settings for your software or try others. You can choose whether to inform Microsoft of your settings, and the settings you chose for the program are used automatically every time you run the program.

Keep in mind that the Program Compatibility Wizard won't work with all old Windows programs; in particular, the wizard should not be used with antivirus, disk, or system utilities that are not compatible with the Windows version in use.

Instead, replace outdated applications with updated versions made for the version of Windows in use.

Additional Application Compatibility Features

Microsoft periodically offers Application Compatibility Updates through Windows Update. These updates improve Windows's compatibility with older applications. If you can't get an older program to work with Windows now, it might be able to work in the future. To see which programs are affected by a particular Application Compatibility Update, click the Details button on the listing in Windows Update.

As an alternative to the Program Compatibility Wizard, you can apply the same settings by using the Compatibility tab on an executable file's properties sheet (see Figure 13-7). Use this method if you already know the appropriate settings to use.

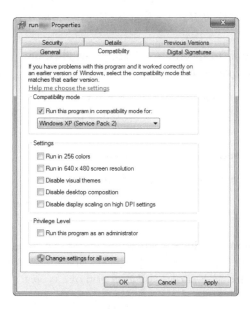

Figure 13-7   Using the Compatibility tab to specify compatibility settings in Windows 7.

Primary Windows Components

You don't need to know everything about Windows to master the A+ Certification exams, but you do need to understand the following essential Windows components:

- Registry

- Virtual Memory

- File Systems

Registry

The Windows Registry acts as a central database for Windows, applications, and user settings. When you install a program, update Windows, or even change the color of the desktop, a part of the Windows Registry changes. There are five different sections (known as hives) to the Windows Registry, whether it's the Registry in Windows 7, Vista, XP, or 2000:

- **HKEY_CLASSES_ROOT**—Links file extensions to specific applications installed on the computer (also stored in HKEY_LOCAL_MACHINE)

- HKEY_CURRENT_USER—Stores configurations specific to the current user, such as screensaver, desktop theme, and Microsoft Office user information (also stored in HKEY_USERS)

- HKEY_LOCAL_MACHINE—Stores hardware and software setup information

- HKEY_USERS—Stores user-specific information for all users of this computer

- HKEY_CURRENT_CONFIG—Stores the settings for the current hardware profile (also stored in HKEY_LOCAL_MACHINE)

As you can see from this listing, any setting in Windows is stored in one of two top-level keys (HKEY_LOCAL_MACHINE and HKEY_USERS). The other three keys provide shortcuts to sections of these two keys. Figure 13-8 shows you a section of a typical Registry listing for Windows XP.

To learn more about the data files used to store the Registry and to learn how to edit the Registry, see "Registry Data Files," later in this chapter.

Figure 13-8 Viewing some of the Registry settings for Windows XP; Windows 7 and Windows Vista's registries are similar in appearance and function.

Windows Interfaces

Windows features a variety of user interfaces, from Windows Explorer to the Start menu. The following sections discuss the major features of each.

Windows Explorer

Windows Explorer is the file-management utility used by Windows (see Figure 13-9 and Figure 13-10). Windows can use Explorer to view both local drive/ network and Internet content. In Windows XP, it integrates tightly with My Computer and Internet Explorer. However, in Windows 7 and Windows Vista (and in Windows XP systems using Internet Explorer 7 or higher), Windows Explorer will launch a new process when connecting to Internet sites.

Path to current location

Click to change view

Click to enable preview pane

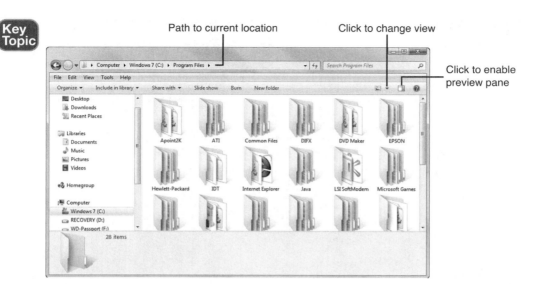

Figure 13-9   The Windows Explorer in Windows 7; the Explorer bar uses a "breadcrumb" motif to indicate the current location and the path to that location.

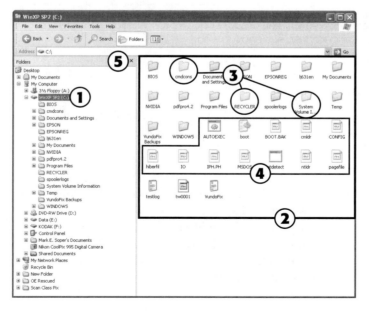

1. Selected object (C: drive)
2. Contents of C: drive (default large icons view)
3. Hidden and system folders
4. Hidden and system files
5. Click to switch to Common Tasks View

Figure 13-10   The Windows Explorer in Windows XP; the current object's name appears in the Address bar.

By default, Windows Explorer doesn't display hidden and system files unless the View options are changed; see the section "Changing Viewing Options in Windows Explorer," later in this chapter for details.

Windows Explorer can be started in any of the following ways in Windows:

- From the Start menu, click **Start**, All **Programs**, **Accessories**, **Windows Explorer**.

- Open the Run prompt (Windows XP) or click the Search box (Windows 7, Vista), type **Explorer** and press **Enter**.

- Open My Computer (XP) or Computer (7, Vista) to start Explorer automatically.

Common Tasks View in Windows XP

When you start My Computer in Windows XP, the Common Tasks view shown in Figure 13-11 is displayed by default. The Common Tasks view displays the properties of the selected object and displays a preview when available. However, the most significant feature is the changeable task pane in the upper-left of the display. In Windows Vista, this has been replaced by "Favorite Links."

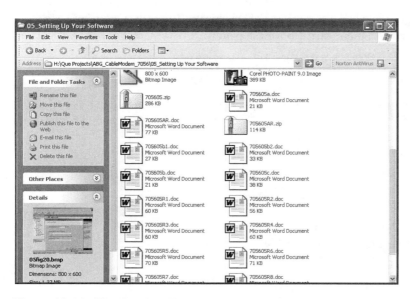

Figure 13-11   The Common Tasks view of a folder in Windows XP.

As shown in Figure 13-11, the Details pane at lower left displays a preview of the selected file as well as its properties. The File and Folder Tasks task pane at upper left changes its name and contents to provide task options suitable for the folder or selected object.

The contents and name of the task pane change according to the characteristics of the selected or displayed object. For example, click My Computer, and the task pane is titled System Tasks, with a choice of options such as View System Information, Add or Remove Programs, or Change a Setting. The contents of Other Places also changes to display related objects.

TIP   To switch between Common Tasks and Classic view, click the Folders icon on the toolbar.

Windows Vista Favorite Links View

Windows Vista uses the Favorite Links view shown in Figure 13-12 in place of Windows XP's Common Tasks view. Favorite Links provides shortcuts to the current user's Documents, Pictures, and Music folders, searches for recently changed files, saved searches, and the system's Public folder (replaces Windows XP's Shared Folders). Click the up or down pointer below Favorite Links to toggle Folders on/off. The right pane lists the contents of the current location. Common tasks have been moved to a menu strip above the panes.

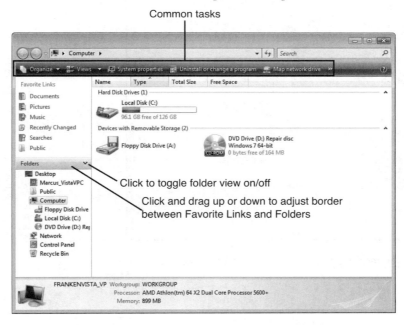

Figure 13-12   The Favorite Links view in Windows Vista provides shortcuts to the most common locations.

Windows 7 Explorer View

Windows 7 groups shortcuts to a wide variety of locations in its left pane (see Figure 13-13). The Favorites section includes shortcuts to the current user's desktop, downloads folder, and recently visited objects (folders and libraries). The Libraries section includes shortcuts to the current user's Documents, Music, Pictures, and Videos libraries. If the computer is part of a homegroup network (a new type of network for Windows 7 computers only), the Homegroup section lists other computers in the homegroup. The Computer section lists all connected drives. The Network section lists all computers on the network. The right pane lists the contents of the current location. As in Windows Vista, common tasks have been moved to a menu strip above the panes.

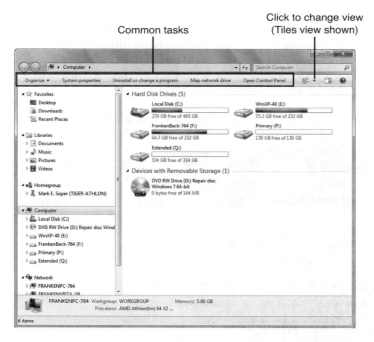

Figure 13-13   Windows 7's Explorer view provides a scrolling pane with access to libraries, local and network locations, and homegroup computers.

Changing Viewing Options in Windows Explorer

By default, Windows Explorer prevents users from seeing information such as

■ File extensions for registered file types; for example, a file called LETTER.DOC will be displayed as LETTER because WordPad (or Microsoft Word) is associated with .DOC files.

■ The full path to the current folder in Windows XP.

■ Files with hidden or system attributes, such as Bootlog.txt and Msdos.sys.

■ Folders with hidden or system attributes, such as INF (used for hardware installation).

■ The Windows folder.

Concealing this information is intended to make it harder for users to "break" Windows, but it makes management and troubleshooting more difficult.

To change these and other viewing options, follow this procedure:

Step 1.   Start Windows Explorer.

Step 2.   Click **Tools** on the menu bar, **Folder Options**, and select the **View** tab.

NOTE   In Windows Vista and Windows 7, the Menu Bar is hidden by default. To show it temporarily, press **Alt+T** (which in this case will bring up the Tools menu). To show it permanently, click on the **Organize** button, then **Layout**, then **Menu Bar**.

Step 3.   Select the options you want (see Figure 13-14). I recommend the following changes for experienced end users:

■ Enable the **Display the Full Path in the Title Bar** option. (In Vista, this only works if you are using the Classic theme.)

■ Disable the **Hide Extensions for Known File Types** option.

  If you are maintaining or troubleshooting a system, I also recommend you change the following:

■ Enable the **Show Hidden Files and Folders** setting.

■ Disable the **Hide Protected Operating System Files** setting. You should probably change these settings back to their defaults before you return the system to normal use.

Step 4.   Click **OK** to close the Folder Options window.

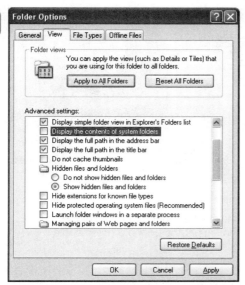

Figure 13-14 The Windows Explorer Folder Options, View tab in Windows XP after selecting recommended options for use by technicians and experienced end users.

Displaying Objects in Files and Folders

Objects such as files and folders can be displayed in several ways within Windows Explorer:

- **Tiles**—The default (refer to Figure 13-11) in Windows XP; similar to Large Icons view in earlier Windows versions.

- **Icons**—Displays more objects onscreen without scrolling vertically; might require the user to scroll horizontally to view multiple columns; similar to Small Icons view in earlier Windows versions. Vista and 7 also have options for small, medium, large, and extra large icons. (Medium, large, and extra large icons are actually thumbnails when photos are being viewed.)

- **List**—Displays more objects onscreen than large icons in a single column.

- **Details**—The same size of icons used by Small or List, plus size and last-modified date details (see Figure 13-15A).

- **Content**—Lists items along with their creation date (Windows 7 only).

Figure 13-15   Comparing the Details and Filmstrip views of a folder containing digital photos. Note that the task pane lists Picture Tasks such as printing photos or copying items to a recordable/rewritable CD.

- **Thumbnails**—Displays a thumbnail (small-sized graphic) sample of previewable files and folders (.BMP, .JPG, and some other graphics file formats and folders containing these files) in the selected folder and uses large-tiled icons for non-previewable files. Thumbnail view can be used in any folder.

- **Filmstrip**—Displays a larger preview of the selected graphic file at the top of the right window and smaller thumbnails below it. Buttons below the large preview can be used to rotate the graphic or to move to another graphic. This view is available in the My Pictures folder or other folders that contain digital photos in formats recognized by Windows Preview, such as .TIF or .JPG (see Figure 13-15B). Filmstrip view is found in Windows XP only.

To change the view for the current folder, use the Views button or the View pull-down menu.

Windows Vista Additions to Windows Explorer

The version of Windows Explorer in Windows Vista incorporates the "Stacks" view, which groups files according to what is specified by the user. You can click the stacks to filter the files shown in Windows Explorer. You also have the ability to save searches as virtual folders or Search Folders. Another new addition to Windows Explorer in Vista is the Details pane, which displays information relating to the currently selected file or folder.

Windows 7 Additions to Windows Explorer

When you open Windows Explorer in Windows 7, the default view shows your libraries (see Figure 13-16). A library includes the contents of the current user's documents, music, pictures, or videos folder, but also includes the contents of the corresponding public folder and can also display the contents of any other local or network folder the user adds to the library. In any Windows Explorer view in Windows 7, click **Organize** to display file, folder, and layout options and to view properties for the currently selected object.

Libraries not only help users to view all files of a particular type in a single view, but also are used by the Windows 7 backup program to determine what folders to back up.

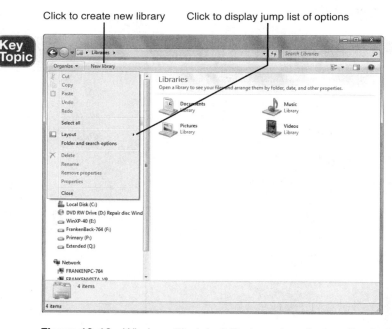

Figure 13-16 Windows 7's default Explorer view displays libraries. In this example, the Organize menu has been opened.

My Computer

My Computer (known as Computer in Windows 7/Vista) is integrated tightly with Windows Explorer. My Computer is still available on all versions of Windows but many users prefer to use Windows Explorer due to its two-pane style and additional functionality. My Computer provides access to the following features and utilities:

■   Open My Computer to view the local drives on your system, available network drives, the Control Panel folder, and imaging devices (see Figure 13-17). In Windows XP, use the System Tasks left pane menu to open the System proper-ties sheet (View system information), Add or remove programs (runs Add or Remove Programs applet from Control Panel), or Change a setting (opens Control Panel). In Windows 7/Vista, similar options are listed just below the navigation bar (see Figure 13-18).

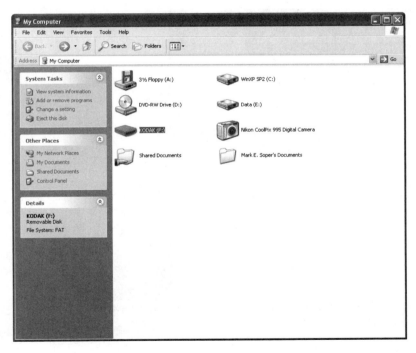

Figure 13-17   My Computer window and available System Tasks in Windows XP.

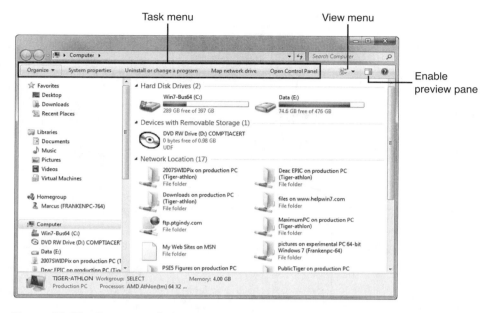

Figure 13-18 Computer window and available tasks in Windows 7.

- Right-click the My Computer icon or the My Computer option in the Start Menu to choose options such as Properties (which opens the System properties sheet), Manage (which opens the Computer Management Console), Windows Explorer, Search/Find, drive mapping, and creating shortcuts.

Control Panel

The Control Panel is the major starting point for adjusting the hardware and user interface settings in Windows. The Control Panel's default view is known as Category view. When you click on an icon, it displays various available tasks. Figures 13-19, 13-20, and 13-21 show the Windows 7, Vista, and XP versions of the Control Panel configured for the default view.

If you're a Windows newcomer, you might prefer the Category view's task-oriented design. However, if you're already familiar with Control Panel, you'll probably prefer to see each individual applet. This option is known as the Classic View in Windows XP and Vista, and the All Control Panel Items view (available in Large or Small Icons variations) in Windows 7. Figures 13-22, 13-23, and 13-24 show Windows 7, Vista, and XP versions of the Control Panel configured to display individual applets.

May trigger UAC prompt   Click to change view

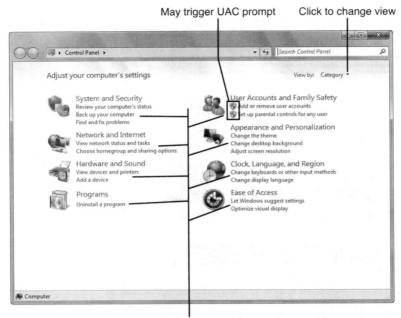

Figure 13-19   The Windows 7 Control Panel in its default Category view.

Figure 13-20   The Windows Vista Control Panel in its default Category view.

Switches Control Panel to Classic view

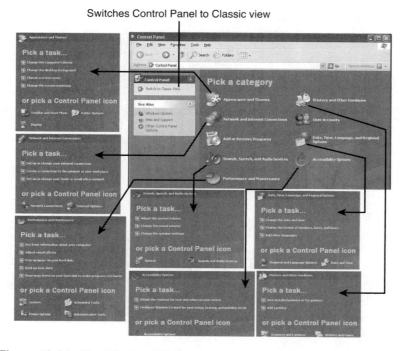

Figure 13-21   The Windows XP Control Panel in its default Category view, and the submenus triggered by each icon.

NOTE   Switching to a view that displays all applets is sometimes necessary to locate applets not part of a category. You can also use the Search tool to locate an applet by name.

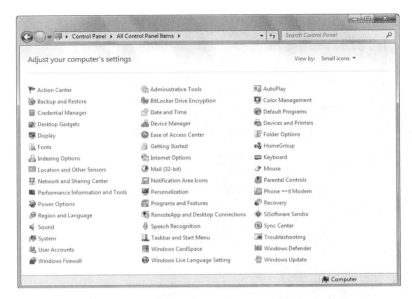

Figure 13-22 The Windows 7 Control Panel in its alternative All Control Panel Icons (small icons) view.

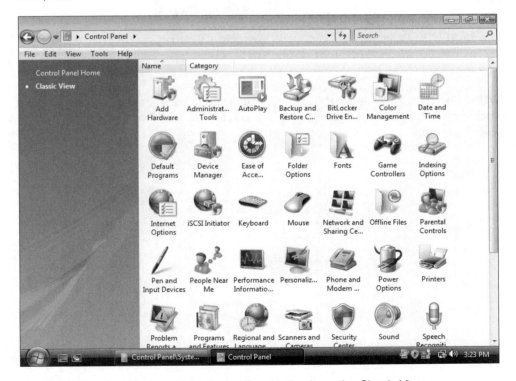

Figure 13-23 The Windows Vista Control Panel in its alternative Classic View.

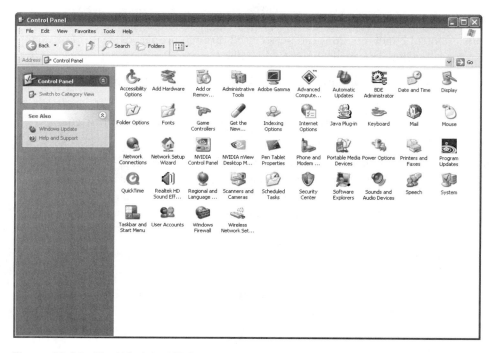

Figure 13-24   The Windows XP Control Panel in its alternative Classic View.

For the exam, it is important to know how to open the Control Panel and how to access some of the Control Panel functions by way of Properties sheets, which are located in various areas of Windows.

Starting Control Panel

You can open the Control Panel from the Start button, Computer/My Computer, or the left window pane of Windows Explorer. (Note: If you're using the Classic Start menu in Windows XP, you will have to click **Start**, **Settings**, **Control Panel**.)

Open any Control Panel icon or link to see current settings and make adjustments for the devices it controls. If the Classic view is used for the Control Panel folder in Windows XP, double-click an icon to open it. If Web view is used in Windows XP, a single click will open an icon. Single click is the default for Windows Vista and 7.

Shortcuts to Control Panel Functions

Some Control Panel functions can be accessed through properties sheets. For example, the following list explains how to access the Control Panel by right-clicking:

- **Computer/My Computer** and select **Properties**; it will open the System Window.

- **Taskbar** and select **Properties**; it will open the Taskbar and Start Menu Properties window.

- **Desktop** in Windows XP and select **Properties**; it will open the Display window. (In Windows Vista, there is no Properties option; it is known as Personalize, which opens the Personalization window. In Windows 7, you can use the Personalize, Screen Resolution, and Gadgets options on the right-click menu to configure various display properties).

- **Network** in Windows Vista and Windows 7 and select **Properties**; it will open the Network and Sharing Center window.

- **My Network Places** in Windows XP and select **Properties**; it will open the Network Connections window.

Command Prompt

Although most computer users won't use the command prompt often, technicians use it frequently, as it enables you to:

- Recover data from systems that can't boot normally.

- Reinstall lost or corrupted system files.

- Print file listings (believe it or not, you can't do this in Windows Explorer or My Computer!).

- Copy, move, or delete data.

- Display or configure certain operating system settings.

For more information on starting a command-prompt session and running command-prompt commands and functions, see the section "Command-Line Functions," later in this chapter. For more information about running Windows Explorer from the command prompt, see "Windows Explorer Command-Line Options," in this chapter. For more information on the command-line Attrib.exe command, see "Setting and Displaying File and Folder Attributes in Windows Explorer," in this chapter.

Network

Windows Vista and 7 use the Network window to view connections to other computers and their shares. This is the successor to My Network Places. The Network window can be accessed from the Start Menu or from within the left window pane of the Computer window. To manage network connections while in the Network window, click the **Network and Sharing Center** button. After that window is displayed, click **Manage Network Connections**. From here, you can make whatever changes you want to the network connection. You will notice that by default a connection delivered by a wired network adapter is known as "Local Area Connection," but you can change that name at any time. Similarly, a connection delivered by a wireless Ethernet network adapter is known as *Wireless Network Connection*. Many of the settings can be accessed by right-clicking the network connection and selecting **Properties**.

The properties sheet for a network connection displays the protocols (for example TCP/IP), services (such as File and Printer Sharing), and network clients installed (such as Client for Microsoft Networks), as shown in Figure 13-25.

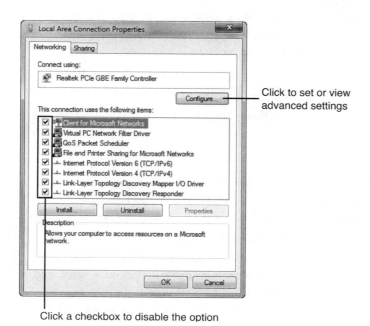

Figure 13-25 Windows 7 Local Area Connection Properties window.

NOTE   If you cannot connect to other computers on the network, keep in mind that your computer must

- Use the same protocol

- Use the same client

- Have a unique name and unique IP address on the network

- Use the same workgroup (when connecting to a Windows XP network) or be part of the same homegroup (Windows 7 only)

My Network Places

Windows XP uses My Network Places to manage dial-up and local area network connections. When you open My Network Places, you see a list of network locations, including those located on the local computer and on remote computers (see Figure 13-26).

To view connection types (dial-up, wired network, wireless network), click **View Network Connections** in the Network Tasks pane. To configure a connection, right-click the connection and click **Properties**. To repair a connection, select it and click **Repair This Connection** from the Network Tasks pane.

The properties sheet for a network connection displays the protocol (TCP/IP), services (File and Printer Sharing), and network clients installed (see Figure 13-27).

To learn more about configuring TCP/IP and other network settings, see Chapter 16, "Networking."

Devices and Printers

Windows 7 includes the new Devices and Printers folder to make access to managing the most common devices in (or connected to) your computer easier to perform. You can launch Devices and Printers from the Hardware and Sound category of Control Panel or add it to your Start menu.

Devices and Printers is divided into two sections. The upper section contains icons for connected devices, and the lower section contains icons for printers, faxes, and all-in-one units. To manage a device, right-click it and choose from the options listed. The options available for each device vary with the device selected.

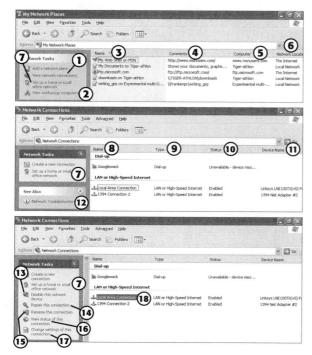

1. Click to view network connections (LAN and dial-up)
2. Displays computers in workgroup
3. Lists available network places (shared resources and connections)
4. UNC path to resource or other comments
5. Computer name and comments
6. Type of connection
7. Starts network setup wizard
8. Lists network connections by name and type
9. Lists network connection types
10. Status
11. Device providing connection (NIC, modem, and so on)
12. Starts network troubleshooter
13. Disables selected device
14. Repairs selected connection
15. Renames selected connection
16. View connection status (duration, speed, throughput)
17. Changes settings for selected connection
18. Selected connection

Figure 13-26 Windows XP's My Network Places shows all types of shared resources, including LAN and Internet. Clicking View Network Connections displays connection details. Select a connection for more details.

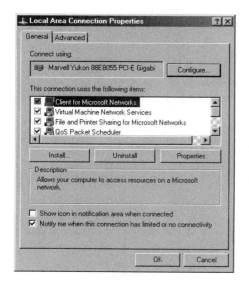

Figure 13-27 The General tab for a local area connection in Windows XP.

For example, if you right-click the computer icon, you can AutoPlay removable-media drives; browse files; eject drives; configure network, sound, mouse, keyboard, and region and language settings; and view and configure system properties, power options, device installation settings, and Windows Update (see Figure 13-28). Right-click a display, and you can access the Display settings dialog. Right-click a mouse, and you can access the Mouse properties dialog.

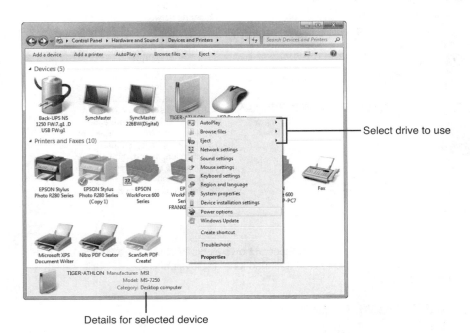

Figure 13-28   Using Devices and Printers to manage a computer's components.

To learn more about managing printers, faxes, and multifunction devices with Devices and Printers, see Chapter 11, "Printers."

Taskbar/Notification Area

It's obvious that any open applications show up on the taskbar. However, some users don't make use of another component of the taskbar: the Quick Launch. The Quick Launch is located directly to the right of the Start button. You can enable it by right-clicking on the **Taskbar** and selecting **Properties**, and then clicking the **Show Quick Launch** checkbox. This is disabled in Windows XP by default, but is enabled in Windows Vista. It's a nice tool because the shortcuts within the Quick Launch are the same size as shortcuts on the desktop; however you always have easy access to them.

Windows 7 enables you to add programs to the taskbar as a replacement for the Quick Launch feature. To add a program to the taskbar, right-click the **Start** menu or desktop shortcut or executable file for the program and select **Pin to Taskbar**. To remove the program, right-click the icon in the taskbar and select **Unpin This Program from Taskbar**.

Even before you click on the Start menu, most Windows installations already have several programs running in the Notification area (sometimes referred to as the system tray), which is located in the lower-right corner of the screen, next to the clock.

Although programs you launch manually can wind up in the Notification area, most programs you find there are started automatically from one of these locations:

- The Startup group in the Start menu

- Load= or Run= statements in Win.ini

- Shell=explorer.exe filename in System.ini

- Various Registry keys, such as

        -HKEY_LOCAL_MACHINE\Software\Microsoft\Windows\CurrentVersion\Run
        -HKEY_LOCAL_MACHINE\Software\Microsoft\Windows\CurrentVersion\RunServices

TIP These and other methods for autolaunching programs, including methods used by spyware, are discussed at http://antivirus.about.com/od/windowsbasics/tp/autostartkeys.htm.

Figure 13-29 shows the Run key in the Registry of a Windows XP system with more than 20 entries. Running so many programs can slow down the Windows startup process and use memory.

Most Notification area programs wait for an event (such as a disc insertion or a mouse click) after they are started. To see what each icon in the Notification Area does, right-click the icon.

NOTE You can disable startup programs in the Notification area by using the Microsoft System Configuration utility (Msconfig); see Chapter 15, "Troubleshooting and Maintaining Windows," for details.

The Notification area is part of the Taskbar, which displays running programs that do not insert themselves into the Notification area. By default, the Taskbar displays one row of program icons, reducing the amount of space given to each program as more and more programs are run. Figure 13-30 shows a typical Windows 7 system's

Notification area and Taskbar and their properties sheet. To display the Taskbar's properties sheet, right-click on an empty section of the Taskbar and select Properties.

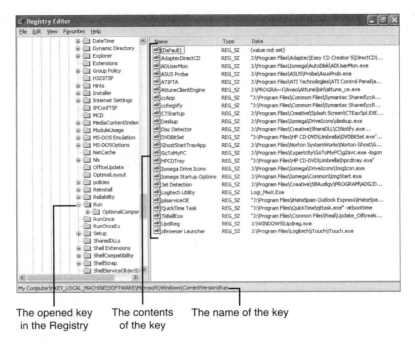

The opened key   The contents   The name of the key
in the Registry   of the key

Figure 13-29   The contents of HKEY_LOCAL_MACHINE\Software\Microsoft\Windows\ CurrentVersion\Run indicates this computer starts more than 20 processes at startup. Other autostart methods such as the Startup group can start additional programs and processes.

To make the Taskbar more useful if you have many programs running, you can resize it by dragging; drag its top edge up to create additional rows or drag the top edge down to the edge of the screen to make it vanish. You can also drag the Taskbar to any side of the screen.

> **TIP**   To prevent the Taskbar from being accidentally resized or dragged, enable the Lock the Taskbar option in the Taskbar properties sheet. You can also auto-hide the Taskbar to provide more display area with the Taskbar properties sheet. When the Taskbar is set to auto-hide, it is displayed only when you move the mouse to the edge of the screen where the Taskbar is hiding or if you press Ctrl+Esc to bring up the Start menu.

Start Menu

Although the Start Menu has a default configuration and most programs add one or more shortcuts to it when they are installed, you can add items to the Start menu, remove items from it, create or remove folders, move an item from one folder to another, and switch between large icons (default) and small icons. You can also right-click on the menu and select Sort by Name. The default Start menu in Windows XP, Vista, and 7 automatically adds the most frequently used programs to a special section of the Start menu.

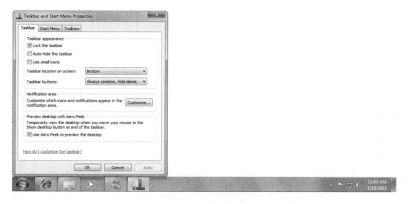

Figure 13-30   The Taskbar and Notification area, and their properties sheet, on a typical Windows 7 system.

Adding, Removing, and Sorting Start Menu Items and Folders with Windows Vista/XP

The Start menu is comprised of shortcuts to programs and other objects on your system. To add items to the default Windows Start menu with Windows XP and Windows Vista, follow these steps:

Step 1.   Right-click the **Start** button.

Step 2.   To add a shortcut for the current user only, select **Explore**. To add a shortcut for all users, select **Explore All Users**.

Step 3.   The Start menu folder opens in the left window (see Figure 13-31); shortcuts on the Start menu are shown in the right window. To see additional Start menu folders, click the plus sign (+) next to Programs in the left window.

Step 4.   To create a new folder for the shortcut, click the folder in the left window where you want to create the shortcut to open it in the right window. Right-click an empty area in the right window and select **New**, **Folder**. Name the folder as desired.

Figure 13-31   Preparing to add items to the default Windows XP Start menu.

Step 5.   To select a folder for the shortcut, click the folder in the left window. The folder's contents appear in the right window.

Step 6.   Click **File**, **New**, **Shortcut** to start the Shortcut Wizard. (This will only function if you have chosen Explore in Windows Vista. Explore All Users will not allow a new shortcut.)

Step 7.   You can enter the path to the program (such as `C:\Windows\System32\cmd.exe`) or click the **Browse** button to locate the program for which you are making a shortcut. Click **Next**.

Step 8.   The shortcut name created by Windows is displayed. To keep the name created by Windows, click **Finish**. You can also change the name as desired and click **Finish**.

Step 9.   Click **OK**. The new shortcut (and new folder, if any) appear on your Start button menu.

Windows Vista/XP can also be configured to use the Classic Start menu (see the next section "Adjusting Start Menu Properties," for details).

If you are using the Classic Start menu, follow these steps:

Step 1.   Right-click an empty portion of the Taskbar and select **Properties**.

Step 2.   Select the **Start Menu** tab and click the **Customize** button.

Step 3.   Click Add.

Step 4.   You can enter the path to the program (such as
`C:\Windows\System32\cmd.exe`) or click the **Browse** button to locate the
program for which you are making a shortcut. Click **Next**.

Step 5.   Select the folder to place the shortcut in, or click **New Folder** to create
a new folder for the shortcut. Enter a name for the new folder if desired.
Click **Next**.

Step 6.   The shortcut name created by Windows is displayed. To keep the name
created by Windows, click **Finish**. You can also change the name as desired and click **Finish**.

Step 7.   Click **OK**. The new shortcut (and new folder, if any) appears on your
Start button menu.

TIP   It's much easier to add shortcuts to the Windows Vista/XP Start menu if you
switch to the Classic Start menu. Even if you prefer the normal Windows Vista/XP
menu, I recommend you switch to the Classic Start menu, add the shortcuts you
need to make, and switch back to the default menu.

To remove an item from the Start menu, follow the steps to add an item, but instead
of adding a new item, click the **Remove** button and select the shortcut to remove. If
you use the Windows Explorer view of the Start menu, press **Del** to send the shortcut to the Recycle Bin or **Shift+Del** to discard the shortcut. To sort shortcuts, click
Start, **All Programs**, right-click a folder or shortcut, and select **Sort by Name**.

Adding and Removing Start Menu Items and Folders with Windows 7

Windows 7's new Pin to Start Menu feature enables you to add a program to the
Start menu from many different locations. To add a program to the Start menu,
follow these steps:

Step 1.   Right-click the program's shortcut or executable file.

Step 2.   Select **Pin to Start Menu** (see Figure 13-32). The program is placed on
the top of the Start menu's left pane.

To remove a pinned item from the Start menu, right-click it and <$IUnpin
from Start Menu commandselect **Unpin
from Start Menu**. Windows 7 automatically sorts menu items in the All Programs
display. You can also pin a program to the taskbar from the right-click menu.

Adjusting Start Menu Properties

You can adjust the appearance of the Start menu in various ways. To modify the
Start menu, right-click the taskbar and select **Properties**. This opens the Taskbar
and Start Menu Properties window. Click on **Start Menu** tab and select the
Customize button. Windows offers the following options and customizations, as

listed in Table 13-3. To perform some of these customizations in Windows XP, click the **Advanced** tab.

Figure 13-32   Pinning an item to the Windows 7 Start menu.

Table 13-3   Customizing the Start Menu

Item	Windows 7	Vista	Vista (Classic)	XP	XP (Classic)
Select objects to appear on Start menu and Taskbar	Yes	Yes	Yes	Yes	Yes
Specify whether to list Start menu items as links or menus (expanded)	Yes	Yes	Yes	Yes	Yes
Number of recent programs to display	Yes	Yes	N/A	Yes	No
Select icon size	Yes	Yes	Yes	Yes	Yes
Power button action	Yes	No	N/A	No	No
Clear shortcuts to recently opened documents	No	No	Yes	Yes	Yes

Table 13-3 Customizing the Start Menu

Item	Windows 7	Vista	Vista (Classic)	XP	XP (Classic)
Clear IE browser history	No	No	Yes	No	Yes
Automatically expand sub-menus	Yes	Yes	Yes	Yes	Yes
Automatically list recently opened documents	Yes˙	Yes	Yes	Yes	No

˙As jump list entries for programs on the Start menu or Taskbar

Jump ListsWindows

7's Start menu lacks an option for recent documents. Instead, Windows 7 enables most programs to store a list of recently-opened files, web pages, or typical tasks. This list is known as a *jump list*. To see the jump list for a program in the Start menu, click the right pointer next to the program listing. Figure 13-33 shows the jump list for Windows Live Photo Gallery.

Figure 13-33 Start menu jump list for Windows Live Photo Gallery.

To see the jump list for a program currently running or pinned to the Taskbar, right-click the program icon in the Taskbar. To pin an item from either a Start menu or Taskbar jump list so it will stay on the jump list, hover your mouse over the item and click the pushpin icon that appears. Figure 13-34 shows the jump list for Windows Media Player after pinning a file. To unpin the item from a jump list, click the pushpin icon.

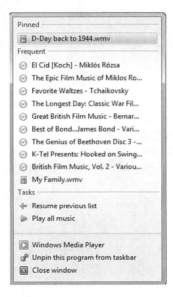

Figure 13-34   Taskbar jump list for Windows Media Player shows recently opened items and tasks.

Indexing

Windows 7, Vista, and XP offer indexing services in an attempt to help you find files faster. However, indexing too much content can lead to poorer operating system performance.

To adjust the indexing settings in Windows Vista, go to **Start, Control Panel, System and Maintenance**, and click **Indexing Options**. In Windows 7, go to **Start**, type index into the Search box and click on **Indexing Options**.

From here, you can modify whether folders are indexed by clicking on the **Modify** button and selecting or deselecting the folders you wish. It is not recommended to select an entire volume (such as C:) because it will cause poor performance. Use indexing for specific folders where you store important data that you search for on a regular basis. If you don't want indexing at all, you can either deselect all folders that are checked or disable the indexing in general. To disable indexing altogether, follow these steps:

Step 1.   Click **Start**, then right-click **Computer** and select **Manage**. This brings up the Computer Management window.

Step 2.   From here, expand Services and Applications in the left window pane and click **Services**.

Step 3.   In the right window pane, scroll down to **Windows Search**, right-click it and select **Stop**. You can restart the service at any time by right-clicking and selecting **Start**. Check the startup type by right-clicking the service and selecting **Properties**. If the startup type is set to Automatic, you should change it to manual or disabled; otherwise, the service will start back up again when you restart the computer.

You can also turn off indexing for individual drives, as follows:

Step 1.   Open **Windows Explorer**.

Step 2.   Right-click the volume you wish to stop indexing on; for example C:, and select **Properties**.

Step 3.   At the bottom of the window, deselect **Index This Drive for Faster Searching**.

To turn off indexing in Windows XP, follow these steps:

Step 1.   Click **Start**, right-click **My Computer**, and select **Manage**. This brings up the Computer Management window.

Step 2.   From here expand **Services and Applications** in the left window pane and click **Services**.

Step 3.   In the right window pane, scroll to **Indexing Service**, right-click it and select **Stop**. You can restart the service at any time by right-clicking and selecting **Start**. Check the startup type by right-clicking the service and selecting **Properties**. If the startup type is set to Automatic, you should change it to manual or disabled; otherwise the service will start back up again when you restart the computer.

You can also turn off indexing on any volume by right-clicking the volume, selecting **Properties** and deselecting **Allow Indexing Service to Index This Disk for Fast File Searching**.

Essential Operating System Files

The following sections cover essential operating system files, such as those used to boot Windows 7, Vista, and XP Registry data files and the hibernation file used to store system configuration settings on a system in hibernation.

Windows 7 and Vista Boot Sequence

After the BIOS starts up and the MBR and boot sector of the hard drive have been located and accessed, the Windows Boot Manager is started. This and the following files are required to start Windows Vista and 7:

- **Bootmgr (Windows Boot Manager)**—This is the Windows loader program. It takes the place of NTLDR in earlier versions of Windows, and determines which operating system to start.

- BCD **(Boot Configuration Data)**—Located in \boot\bcd. It furnishes the Windows Boot Manager with information about the operating system(s) to be booted. It is the successor to boot.ini and can be modified with MSCONFIG or with the bcdedit.exe program. BCD was developed to provide an improved mechanism for describing boot configuration data and to work better with newer firmware models such as the Extensible Firmware Interface (EFI).

- **Ntoskrnl.exe**—The Windows kernel, which completes the boot process after being initialized by the Windows Boot Manager.

- **Hal.dll**—The Hardware Abstraction Layer, a software translator between Windows and system hardware.

- **SYSTEM key in the Registry**—This is read to determine the system configuration.

- **Device drivers**—These are loaded according to the information stored in the Registry.

Windows XP Boot Sequence

The following files are required to start Windows XP:

- **NTLDR**—The Windows loader program.

- **Boot.ini**—Options in this file affect how Windows starts up.

- **Ntdetect.com**—This detects the hardware installed on your system.

- **Ntoskrnl.exe**—The Windows kernel, which completes the boot process after being initialized by NTLDR.

- **Hal.dll**—The Hardware Abstraction Layer, a software translator between Windows and system hardware.

- **SYSTEM key in the Registry**—This is read to determine the system configuration.

- **Device drivers**—These are loaded according to the information stored in the Registry.

The following files are optional:

- **Bootsect.dos**—This contains the boot sectors for another operating system if you are multibooting.

- **Ntbootdd.sys**—This device driver is used only if Windows is being started from a SCSI drive whose host adapter does not have an onboard SCSI BIOS enabled.

The following sections discuss some of these files in more detail.

BOOT.INI

The Boot.ini file is a specially formatted text file that configures the startup process for Windows XP. It resides in the default boot drive, even if Windows is installed on another drive.

NOTE   Windows XP also provides a command-line tool called Bootcfg, which can be used to insert the proper syntax for common commands. Bootcfg can also be used in the Windows XP Recovery Console.

Boot.ini indicates where the different versions of Windows are located. Here's the Boot.ini from a system that boots Windows XP Professional:

```
[boot loader]
timeout=30
default=multi(0)disk(0)rdisk(0)partition(1)\WINDOWS
[operating systems]
multi(0)disk(0)rdisk(0)partition(1)\WINDOWS="Microsoft Windows XP Professional"
/fastdetect
```

The `[boot loader]` section is configured to start Windows XP by default. It also provides a maximum time of 30 seconds to pause a dual-boot menu (if one exists) and to enable the user to choose a different version of Windows if she was running a dual-boot configuration; for example, Windows XP and Windows 2000.

The `[operating systems]` section identifies the locations of any Windows versions on the computer. The next line states that Windows XP Professional is located in partition 1 of the first hard disk (disk 0).

Many additional options can be added to Boot.ini if necessary for troubleshooting. `Boot.ini` can be viewed with Notepad. However, if you need to configure Boot.ini to run your system in a troubleshooting mode, you should use MSConfig to view Boot.ini and configure it.

CAUTION   Boot.ini should *not* be modified unless you cannot start your computer. You should consult the Microsoft Knowledge Base for help in such cases. Fiddling with Boot.ini is *not* a good idea on a working system because unnecessary changes could stop your system from booting.

NTLDR and NTDETECT.COM

After the computer completes the POST and the system BIOS's bootstrap loader locates the NTLDR file, NTLDR does the following:

- Enables the user to select an operating system to start (if more than one is installed). NTLDR examines the contents of Boot.ini to find out which operating systems are installed.

- Loads the Windows startup files.

- Uses the Ntdetect.com program to determine what hardware is installed and places a list of the detected hardware into the Windows Registry.

- Loads Ntoskrnl.exe (the Windows kernel) and the Hardware Abstraction Layer (`Hal.dll`) into memory and hands over control to Ntoskrnl.exe after loading device drivers appropriate for the system configuration.

The NTLDR and Boot.ini files are located in the root directory (folder) of the default Windows drive.

NTBOOTDD.SYS

This device driver is used only if Windows is being started from a SCSI drive whose host adapter does not have an onboard SCSI BIOS enabled. Most desktop computers no longer use SCSI hard disk drives, so the odds of encountering this on a Windows XP installation are slim to none.

Registry Data Files

The Windows Registry is stored in different files, roughly corresponding to different sections of the Registry. The following files are stored in the `SYSTEM32\CONFIG` folder beneath the default Windows folder (typically `\Windows`); the backup file for each is listed in parentheses:

- **default** (**default.LOG**)—Stores `.DEFAULT` settings from the `HKEY_USERS` section of the Registry.

- **SAM** (**SAM.LOG**)—Stores part of the Security Account Manager database from the `HKEY_LOCAL_MACHINE\SAM` section of the Registry.

- **SECURITY** (**SECURITY.LOG**)—Stores part of the Security Account Manager database from the `HKEY_LOCAL_MACHINE\SECURITY` section of the Registry.

- **software** (**SOFTWARE.LOG**)—Stores software settings from the `HKEY_LOCAL_MACHINE\SOFTWARE` section of the Registry.

- **system** (**system.LOG**)—Stores settings from the HKEY_LOCAL_MACHINE\SYSTEM section of the Registry.

Windows also has two additional files for each user:

- **ntuser.dat** (**NTUSER.DAT.LOG**)—Stores most user-preference settings in the \Documents and Settings\username folder for each user.

- UsrClass.dat (UsrClass.dat.LOG)—Stores user-preference settings for file associations and applications in the \Documents and Settings\username\Local Settings\Application Data\Microsoft\Windows folder for each user.

> **CAUTION**   SAM and SECURITY sections of the Registry don't contain user-editable keys, so they *appear* to be empty. Don't be fooled—and don't erase the matching Registry files either!

To view or edit the Registry, use the Windows application Regedit.exe.

For details, see the section "Regedit.exe," later in this chapter.

Backing Up Registry Data Files

To back up the Windows 2000 Registry, use the Windows 2000 backup program. Click **Start, Accessories, System Tools, Backup** to start it. From the opening menu, select Emergency Repair Disk and select the option to back up the Registry on the next screen; insert a blank, formatted disk when prompted to complete the process. Because the Windows 2000 Registry can occupy as much as 20MB of disk space on some systems, the Emergency Repair Disk (ERD) does not contain a copy of the Registry itself but includes other information necessary to help restore the system in case of a crash. The Registry is stored in a folder called RegBack, which is contained in the \WinNT\Repair folder. In the event of a serious system problem, both the Windows 2000 Emergency Repair Disk and the Registry backup in the RegBack folder would be used to restore the system. You should re-create the ERD and Registry backup whenever you install new hardware or software to keep a record of the latest system configuration.

Windows XP also uses the Windows Backup program to back up the Registry as part of backing up the System State (see Figure 13-35). In Windows XP Professional, the System State also includes boot files, COM+ Class Registration database, and files protected by Windows File Protection. This backup can be stored on tape, an external hard disk, or removable media.

For more information about NTBackup, see the "NTBackup" section later in this chapter.

In Windows Vista, there are a few ways to backup Registry data files. First of all, Vista does not use NTBackup; instead, it has a program called Backup and Restore Center. (It is listed as Backup Status and Configuration until you configure it.)

From here you would have to do a Complete PC Backup (on versions that include this option) because the Automatic file backup option doesn't backup the registry files. A simpler solution is to create a new restore point with the System Restore wizard. Or, you could simply export the entire registry from the Registry Editor. Keep in mind that this could be a big file—upwards of 200MB.

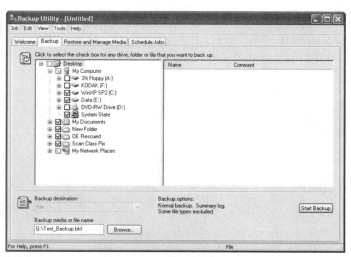

Figure 13-35   Preparing to back up the Windows XP Registry as part of the System State backup using the Windows XP backup program, NTBackup.

With Windows 7, you can make a Registry backup with the System Restore wizard by creating a new restore point or exporting the entire Registry from the Registry Editor; if you create a system image backup, this also backs up the Registry as it was at the time of the backup.

hiberfil.sys

When you select the option to hibernate your system from the Shut Down menu, Windows creates a file called `hiberfil.sys` to store information about open programs, program windows and data files. `hiberfil.sys` can range in size from 250MB to more than 1GB and can be safely removed after the system comes out of hibernation.

You should delete `hiberfil.sys` before using any defragmenting program, as the file is a system file that cannot be defragmented. To delete the file, follow this procedure to temporarily disable hibernation in Windows XP/2000:

Step 1.   Open the **Power Options** dialog in Control Panel.

Step 2.   Click the **Hibernate** tab.

Step 3.   Clear the **Enable Hibernation** checkbox and click **OK**.

`hiberfil.sys` is removed automatically. To re-enable hibernation, follow Steps 1–3, but in Step 3, click the empty **Enable Hibernation** checkbox to re-enable this feature.

To disable hibernation in Windows Vista or Windows 7, enter **CMD** into the Search box on the Start menu. Right-click **CMD** and select **Run as Administrator**. When the command-line interface appears, type **powercfg.exe/hibernate off**. To turn it back on, follow the same steps but instead type **powercfg.exe/hibernate on**. Type **Exit** and press **Enter** to close the command-line interface and return to the Windows desktop.

Disk Partition, File, and Folder Management

Understanding how to manage hard disks, files on all types of disks, and folders is an essential part of the A+ Certification exams. The following sections explain these concepts and the command-line and GUI-based tools and methods needed to work with disk partitions, files, and folders.

Disk Partitions

An internal hard disk (PATA, SATA, or SCSI) cannot be used until it is prepared for use. There are two steps involved in preparing a hard disk:

- Creating partitions and logical drives

- Formatting partitions and logical drives (which assigns drive letters)

A disk partition is a logical structure on a hard disk drive which specifies the following:

- Whether the drive can be bootable

- How many drive letters (one, two, or more) the hard disk will contain

- Whether any of the hard disk's capacity will be reserved for a future operating system or other use

Although the name "disk partition" suggests the drive will be divided into two or more logical sections, every PATA, SATA, and SCSI hard disk must go through a partitioning process, even if you want to use the entire hard disk as a single drive letter. All versions of Windows support two major types of disk partitions:

- **Primary**—A primary partition can contain only a single drive letter and can be made active (bootable). Only one primary partition can be active. Although a single physical drive can hold up to four primary partitions, you need only one primary partition on a drive that contains a single operating system. If you install a new operating system in a dual-boot configuration with your current operating system, a new version of Windows can be installed in a different folder in the same drive or can be installed in an additional primary partition.

If you want to use a non-Windows operating system along with your current operating system, it should be installed into its own primary partition.

Depending upon the layout and contents of your current disk partitions, you might be able to shrink the size of existing partitions with Windows Disk Management (Windows Vista and 7 only) to make room for a new primary partition, or you might need to use third-party software such as Acronis Disk Director 11 or EASEUS Partition Master.

- Extended—An extended partition differs from a primary partition in two important ways:
    - An extended partition doesn't become a drive letter itself but can contain one or more logical drives, each of which is assigned a drive letter.
    - Neither an extended partition nor any drive it contains can be bootable.

Only one extended partition can be stored on each physical drive.

If the drive will be used by a single operating system, one of these three ways of partitioning the drive will be used:

- **Primary partition occupies 100% of the physical drive's capacity**—This is typically the way the hard disk on a system sold at retail is used and is also the default for disk preparation with Windows. This is suitable for the only drive in a system or an additional drive that can be used to boot a system, but should *not* be used for additional drives in a system that will be used for data storage.

- **Primary partition occupies a portion of the physical drive's capacity, and the remainder of the drive is occupied by an extended partition**—This enables the operating system to be stored on the primary partition, and the applications and data to be stored on one or more separate logical drives (drive letters created inside the extended partition). This is a common setup for laptops, but requires the partitioning process be performed with different settings than the defaults. This configuration is suitable for the only drive or first drive in a multiple-drive system.

- **Extended partition occupies 100% of the physical drive's capacity**—The drive letters on the extended partition can be used to store applications or data, but not for the operating system. An extended partition cannot be made active (bootable). This configuration is suitable for additional hard disk drives in a system (not the first drive); an extended partition can contain only one logical drive or multiple logical drives.

You can also leave some unpartitioned space on the hard disk for use later, either for another operating system or another drive letter.

Partitioning creates drive letters; formatting creates file systems on the drive letters created during partitioning. Figure 13-36 helps you visualize how these different partitioning schemes could be used on a typical hard disk.

After a disk is partitioned, the drive letters must be formatted using a supported file system.

To learn more about preparing hard disks with Windows, see the following section "Using Disk Management."

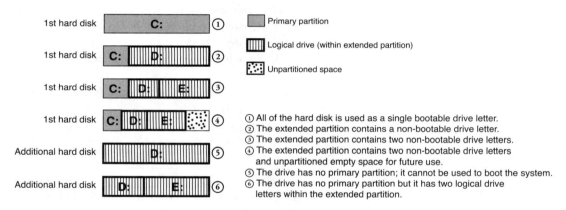

Figure 13-36   Typical disk partitioning schemes used for the first hard disk (first four examples) or an additional drive (last two examples).

Using Disk Management

The Disk Management snap-in of the Computer Management console is the GUI-based application for analyzing and configuring hard drives. You can do a lot from here, as shown in Table 13-4. Try some of the configurations listed on a test computer. All you need is a drive with unpartitioned space.

Table 13-4   Configurations in Disk Management

Configuration	Steps
Initialize a new disk	A secondary hard disk installed in a computer might not be seen by Windows Explorer immediately. To make it accessible, locate the disk (for example Disk 1), right-click Disk 1 or Disk 2, and so on and select Initialize Disk.
Create a primary partition (Windows XP)	1. Right-click on a disk's unallocated space (shown with a black header) and select New Partition, as shown in Figure 13-37. 2. Click **Next** for the wizard and then select **Primary Partition**. 3. Select the amount of unallocated space you want for the partition and click **Next**. 4. Select a drive letter. 5. Choose whether you want to format at this point. 6. Review the summary screen and if it is correct, click **Finish**. Note: For computers with limited resources, it is recommended that you hold off on formatting until after the partition is created.
Create an extended partition (Windows XP)	1. Right-click on a disk's unallocated space (shown with a black header) and select New Partition, as shown in Figure 13-38. 2. Click **Next** for the wizard, and then select **Extended Partition**. 3. Select the amount of unallocated space you want for the partition, and click **Next**. 4. Review the summary screen, and if it is correct, click **Finish**.

Table 13-4 Configurations in Disk Management

Configuration	Steps
Create a logical drive (Windows XP)	This can only be done within an extended partition that has already been created. 1. Right-click on the extended partition (shown with a green header) and select **New Logical Drive**, as shown in Figure 13-37. 2. Click **Next** for the wizard. You will notice that your only option is Logical drive. Click **Next**. 3. Select the amount of unallocated space you want for the partition and click **Next**. 4. Select a drive letter. 5. Choose whether you want to format at this point. 6. Review the summary screen, and if it is correct, click **Finish**.
Format a partition/logical drive (Windows XP)	1. Right-click the primary partition or logical drive and select **Format**. 2. In the Format x: window, select the file system and whether to do a quick format. If it is a new drive, you can select quick format. However, if the drive was used previously, you might want to leave this option unchecked. ALL DATA WILL BE ERASED during the format procedure.
Make a partition active	Right-click the primary partition and select **Mark Partition** as Active. You can have up to four primary partitions on a hard disk, but only one of them can be active.
Convert a basic disk to dynamic	To change the size of a partition in Windows XP, to create simple and spanned volumes, or to implement RAID, the hard disk(s) need to be converted to dynamic. It's highly recommended that you back up your data before attempting this configuration. 1. Right-click the hard disk where it says Disk 0 or Disk 1 and select **Convert to Dynamic Disk**. 2. In the ensuing window, you can select multiple disks to switch over to dynamic. This can also be done in Windows Vista and Windows 7; however, in Vista and 7 you now have the option to extend a partition, as shown later in this table.

Table 13-4   Configurations in Disk Management

Configuration	Steps
Create and Format a Partition (Vista and 7)	Windows Vista and 7 simplify the process of creating and formatting a partition. To create a partition on unallocated space: 1. Right-click unallocated space on a drive. (With a new drive. the entire drive will be listed as unallocated.) 2. Select **New Simple Volume**. 3. Click **Next**. 4. To use the entire space for a volume (drive letter), click **Next**. To use only part of the space, specify the amount of space to use (in MB), and then click **Next**. 5. Select the drive letter to install and click **Next**. (You can also select the option to not assign a drive letter or to mount the drive in an empty NTFS folder on an existing drive.) 6. Specify the file system (NTFS is default), the volume name, whether to use a quick format or prepare the drive as compressed. Click **Next**. 7. Review all options and click **Finish** (see Figure 13-39). Note: Windows Vista/7 can use extended partitions but cannot create create them with Disk Management. If you need to set up an extended partition with logical drives, use the command-line program Diskpart.exe. For details, see Microsoft Knowledge Base article 300415 at http://support.microsoft.com/

Table 13-4   Configurations in Disk Management

Configuration	Steps
Extend a partition (Vista and 7 only)	Windows Vista and 7 allow you to extend the size of a partition (volume) or shrink it within the Disk Management utility. It's highly recommended that you back up your data before attempting this configuration.

1. Right-click the volume to be extended.
2. Select **Extend Volume**. (Remember that a volume is any section of the hard drive with a drive letter.)
3. Click **Next** for the wizard and select how much space you'd like to add to the partition.
4. Select any other disks (with unpartitioned space) to combine with the first disk to create a spanned partition and click **Next**.
5. Click **Finish** at the summary screen.

A reboot is not required, and this process should finish fairly quickly. This process can also be done in the Command Prompt using the Diskpart command.

Note: Extended partitions are not fault tolerant. Make sure you have a backup plan in place.

Note: Extended partitions are also known as extended volumes, and when covering multiple disks, they are also known as spanned volumes. An extended volume (which can be a bootable volume) is not the same as an extended partition that can be subdivided into one or more logical, but non-bootable, drives.

In Figure 13-37, we also can see the disks at the top of the window and their status. For example, the C: partition is healthy. It also shows us the percent of the disk used, and other information such as whether the disk is currently formatting, if it's dynamic, or if it has failed. In some cases, you might see "foreign" status. This means that a dynamic disk has been moved from another computer (with another Windows operating system) to the local computer, and it cannot be accessed properly. To fix this and be able to access the disk, add the disk to your computer's system configuration. To add a disk to your computer's system configuration, import the foreign disk (right-click the disk, and then click **Import Foreign Disks**). Any existing volumes on the foreign disk become visible and accessible when you import the disk. For more information on the plethora of disk statuses, see the Microsoft TechNet article, "Disk Status Descriptions," at http://technet.microsoft.com/en-us/library/cc738101(WS.10).aspx.

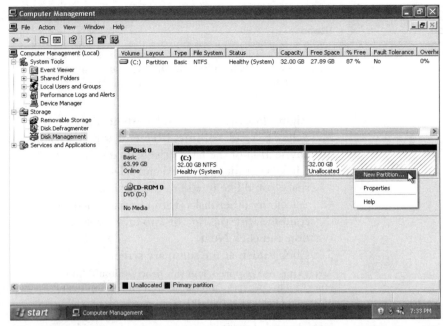

Figure 13-37   Creating a partition from Unallocated Disk Space with Windows XP.

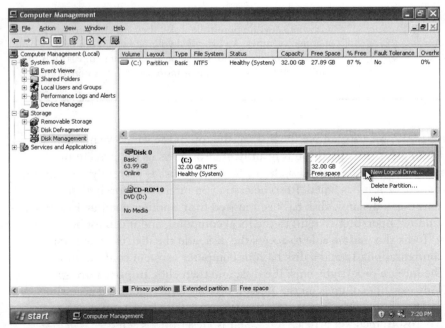

Figure 13-38   Creating a logical drive from within an extended partition with Windows XP.

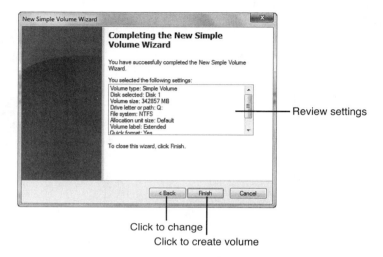

Figure 13-39 Preparing to create a new simple volume with Windows 7.

Mount Points and Mounting a Drive

You can also "mount" drives in Disk Management. A mounted drive is a drive that is mapped to an empty folder within a volume that has been formatted as NTFS. Instead of using drive letters, mounted drives use drive paths. This is a good solution for when you need more than 26 drives in your computer because you are not limited to the letters in the alphabet. Mounted drives can also provide more space for temporary files and can allow you to move folders to different drives if space runs low on the current drive. To mount a drive, follow these steps:

Step 1. Right-click the partition or volume you want to mount and select **Change Drive Letters and Paths**.

Step 2. In the displayed window, click **Add**.

Step 3. Then, browse to the empty folder you want to mount the volume to and click **OK** for both windows.

As shown in Figure 13-40, the DVD-ROM drive has been mounted within a folder on the hard drive called Test. The figure is showing the Properties window for the folder Test. It shows that it is a mounted volume, shows the location of the folder (which is the mount point), and the target of the mount point, which is the DVD drive containing a Windows Vista DVD. To remove the mount point, just go back to Disk Management, right-click the mounted volume and select **Change Drive Letters and Paths**, and then select **Remove**. Remember that the folder you want to use as a mount point must be empty, and it must be within an NTFS volume.

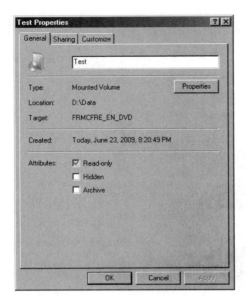

Figure 13-40   Empty NTFS folder acting as a mount point.

Windows File Systems

What exactly is a file system, anyway? A *file system* describes how data and drives are organized. In Windows, the file system you choose for a hard disk affects the following:

- The rules for how large a logical drive (drive letter) can be and whether the hard disk can be used as one big drive letter, several smaller drive letters, or must be multiple drive letters.

- How efficiently a system stores data; the less wasted space, the better.

- How secure a system is against tampering.

- Whether a drive can be accessed by more than one operating system.

The term *file system* is a general term for how an operating system stores various types of files. Windows supports two different file systems for hard disks, FAT32 and NTFS, and supports FAT for floppy disks.

FAT32

FAT32 was introduced in 1995 and is supported by Windows 7, Vista, XP, and 2000, although NTFS is preferred. FAT32 has the following characteristics:

- The 32-bit file allocation table, which allows for 268,435,456 entries (2^{32}) per drive. Remember, an entry can be a folder or an allocation unit used by a file.

- The root directory can be located anywhere on the drive and can have an *unlimited* number of entries, which is a big improvement over FAT.

- FAT32 uses an 8KB allocation unit size for drives as large as 16GB.

- The maximum logical partition size allowed is 2TB (more than 2 trillion bytes).

You can use FAT32 to format hard disks, flash memory, and removable media drives. However, FAT32 is recommended for hard disks *only* if the hard disk must also be accessed by dual-booting with an older version of Windows—for example Windows 95, 98, or Me, which do not support NTFS.

NOTE   If you want to store scheduled backups on a hard disk with Windows Vista or 7, you must use a backup hard disk that uses the NTFS file system.

exFAT (FAT64)

exFAT (also known as FAT64) is a new file system that is designed to enable mobile personal storage media to be used seamlessly on mobile and desktop computers. exFAT enables Windows 7, Vista, XP, and CE to have file system support parity. It is designed to be as simple as FAT32, but with many improvements in capacity and scalability.

exFAT is also called FAT64 because it supports 64-bit addressing. exFAT's main features include

- Support for volumes (drive letters) larger than 32GB (theoretical maximum for FAT32 in Windows XP). 512TB is the recommended maximum volume size, but the theoretical volume size is 64ZB.

- Recommended and maximum file sizes also increase to 512TB and 64ZB, respectively.

- Improvements in file system structure for better performance with flash media and for movie recording.

- Support for Universal Time Coordinate (UTC) date stamps.

exFAT support is included in Windows 7, Windows Server 2008, and Windows Vista SP1 and above. To add exFAT support to Windows XP SP2 and SP3, Windows XP x64 edition, Windows Server 2003 SP2 and SP1, download the appropriate driver from the links at http://support.microsoft.com/kb/955704. To find information about non-Microsoft operating systems that support exFAT, see http://en.wikipedia.org/wiki/ExFAT.

NTFS

The New Technology File System (NTFS) is the native file system of Windows 7, Vista, XP, and 2000. As implemented in Windows 7, Vista, and XP, NTFS has many differences from FAT32, including

- **Access Control**—Different levels of access control by group or user can be configured for both folders and individual files.

- **Built-in compression**—Individual files, folders, or an entire drive can be compressed without the use of third-party software.

- **A practical limit for partition sizes of 2TB**—The same as with FAT32, although partitions theoretically can reach a maximum size of 16 exabytes (16 billion billion bytes).

- **Individual Recycle Bins**—Unlike FAT32, NTFS includes a separate recycle bin for each user.

- **Support for the Encrypting File System (EFS)**—EFS enables data to be stored in an encrypted form. No password and no access to files!

- **Support for mounting a drive**—Drive mounting enables you to address a removable-media drive's contents, for example, as if its contents are stored on your hard disk. The hard disk's drive letter is used to access data on both the hard disk and the removable media drive.

- **Disk quota support**—The administrator of a system can enforce rules about how much disk space each user is allowed to use for storage.

- **Hot-swapping**—Removable-media drives that have been formatted with NTFS (such as Jaz, Orb, and others) can be connected or removed while the operating system is running..

- **Indexing**—The Indexing service helps users locate information more quickly when the Search tool is used.

NOTE   Windows 7, Vista, XP, and 2000 can't create a FAT32 partition larger than 32GB. However, if the partition already exists, they can use it.

Follow these steps to determine what file system was used to prepare a Windows hard drive:

Step 1.   Open Windows Explorer.

Step 2.   Right-click the drive letter in the Explorer Window and select **Properties**.

Step 3.   The Properties sheet for the drive will list FAT32 for a drive prepared with FAT32 and NTFS for a drive prepared with NTFS (see Figure 13-41).

Convert.exe

Windows includes the command-line Convert.exe program to enable users to change the current FAT32 file system on a drive to NTFS without reformatting the drive (which would wipe out all the information on the drive).

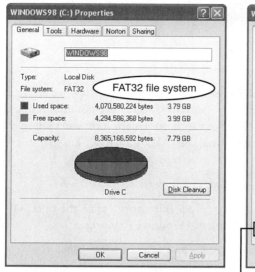

Disk compression and indexing
features available with NTFS 5

Figure 13-41   A hard disk formatted with FAT32 (left) and a hard disk formatted with NTFS version 5 (right).

To convert a drive's file system using Convert.exe, follow these steps:

Step 1.   Open a command-prompt window. (For Windows Vista, refer to the options that follow this list.)

Step 2.   Type **Convert x: /fs:ntfs** and press **Enter**.

NOTE   The x: is a variable. Replace it with the drive you want to convert, for example c:, d:, f:, and so on.

To see advanced options for Convert, type `convert /?`.

In Windows 7 and Vista, you will need to run this command in elevated mode. There are several ways to open a command-line in elevated mode. Here are two options:

- Click **Start, All Programs, Accessories, Command Prompt**. Right-click **Command Prompt** and select **Run as Administrator**. Click **Continue** at the permission window.

- Click **Start** and type **cmd**. Then, press **Ctrl+Shift+Enter** to execute cmd.exe in elevated mode. Click **Continue** at the permission window.

To learn more about preparing hard disks with Windows, see the section "Using Disk Management," earlier in this chapter.

NOTE   Windows XP/2000 also support the older FAT16 file system, but FAT16 is not covered on the exams.

Working with Folders/Directories

Windows provides two ways to work with folders (also called directories): visually, through Windows Explorer or Computer/My Computer, and at the command line (MKDIR/MD, CHDIR/CD, RMDIR/RD). For more information on working with folders and directories on the command line, see "MD/CD/RD," later in this chapter.

To navigate between folders in Windows Explorer, follow these procedures:

- To view the subfolders (subdirectories) in a folder (directory), click the plus (+) sign next to the folder name in the left pane of Windows Explorer.

- To view the contents of a folder (including files and other folders), click the folder in the left pane of Windows Explorer. The contents of the folder appear in the right pane.

- To navigate to the previous view, click the left arrow above the address bar.

- To move to the next view, click the right arrow.

- To navigate to the next higher folder in the folder hierarchy, click the up arrow/folder button.

Figure 13-42 illustrates these concepts.

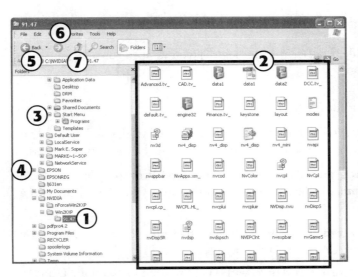

1. Selected folder
2. Contents of selected folder
3. Click to close subfolder view
4. Click to open subfolder view
5. Return to previous view
6. Advance to next view
7. Go up one level in the folder hierarchy

Figure 13-42   Working with folders (directories) in Windows Explorer.

To create a new folder in Windows Explorer, follow these steps:

Step 1.   Open the folder in which you want to create a new folder. The folder's contents are displayed in the right pane.

Step 2.   Right-click an empty space in the right pane and select **New**, **Folder** (see Figure 13-43).

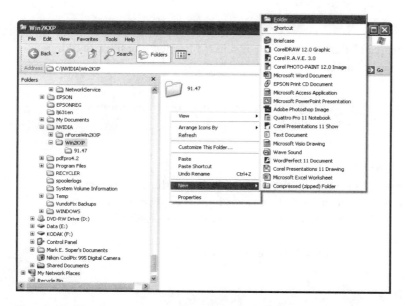

Figure 13-43   Creating a new folder in Windows Explorer.

Step 3.   Enter the new folder name and press **Enter**.

To remove a folder from either Windows Explorer or My Computer views, follow these steps:

Step 1.   Right-click the folder and select **Delete**.

Step 2.   Click **Yes** on the Confirm Folder Delete dialog.

The folder and its contents are moved to the Recycle Bin. To bypass the Recycle Bin, hold down either **Shift** key, select **Delete**, and then click **Yes**.

Working with Libraries in Windows 7

A library contains multiple folders, enabling you to see the contents of these folders at the same time. For example, the default contents of the Documents library include the current user's My Documents folder and the Public Documents folder. Likewise for music, pictures, and videos, each user's library contains the public folders and the user's individual folders for each content type. You can add any folder on a local or network hard disk to a library, so you can see the contents of external hard disks that contain pictures or other contents just by opening the appropriate library.

NOTE   Folders on USB flash drives, CD or DVD drives, or other removable-media drives cannot be added to a library.

Windows 7's Backup and Restore function also uses libraries; any file stored in a local folder that's part of a library will be backed up.

NOTE   Files that are part of a library but are stored in network locations are not backed up by Windows 7's Backup and Restore function.

Managing Folders in a Library

To see the folders in a library, open the library and hover the mouse over the Includes *x* location link. Figure 13-44 illustrates a typical Pictures library that includes the user's My Pictures folder and the Public Pictures folder.

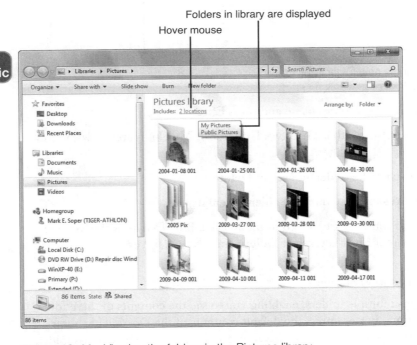

Figure 13-44   Viewing the folders in the Pictures library.

To add a folder to a library, click the locations link highlighted in Figure 13-44 to display the library locations dialog shown in Figure 13-45. Click **Add**, navigate to the folder you want to add, and click **Include Folder**. The new folder is added to the list of folders in the library.

Figure 13-45   The Pictures Library Locations dialog after adding a folder.

To remove a folder from the library, open the locations dialog for the library, select the folder, and click **Remove**. Removing a folder from a library does not delete the folder or the files, but means that you will need to navigate directly to the folder to see its contents.

Click **OK** to close the dialog and return to the library.

Changing Viewing Options

To change how a library displays its contents, open the **Arrange By** menu. The default setting is Folder, but you can also select other options based on the library type. Figure 13-46, for example, lists picture library contents by the date each photo was created or scanned.

File Management

File management skills such as file creation, filenaming, file attributes, compression, encryption, file permissions, and file types are necessary for the A+ Certification exams. The following sections discuss these skills.

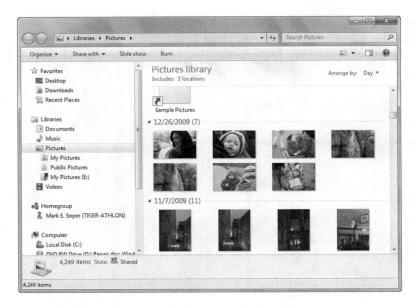

Figure 13-46   Viewing the contents of the Pictures Library arranged by day.

Creating Files

Data files that can be accessed by registered applications can be created within the Windows Explorer/My Computer/Computer interface. To create a new file, follow these steps:

Step 1.   Open the folder where you want to create the file.

Step 2.   Right-click empty space in the right window pane and select **New** to display a list of registered file types (see Figure 13-47).

Step 3.   Move the mouse pointer to the file type desired and click it. The new (empty) file is created in the open folder.

Step 4.   Enter a new name if desired.

Step 5.   To edit the file, double-click it.

File Types

Broadly speaking, there are two types of files used by Windows and other operating systems:

■   Text

■   Binary

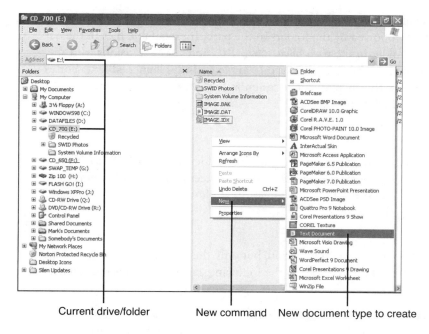

Current drive/folder   New command   New document type to create

Figure 13-47   Creating a new text document on drive E:.

Text files can be read with an ordinary text editor such as Notepad, WordPad, or Edit. However, most word processing and other types of document files, although they contain text, also contain formatting characters that a text editor cannot properly interpret.

Binary files look like gibberish when viewed in a text editor. Only the operating system (in the case of application binary files) or a compatible application (in the case of binary data files) can interpret their contents.

The following types of files can be started (executed) from a command prompt or from Windows Explorer/Computer/My Computer:

■ .COM

■ .EXE

■ .BAT

Both .EXE and .COM files are binary executable files, whereas a .BAT file (also called a batch file) is a series of commands that are processed in sequence. Simple batch files contain the same commands that could be entered manually at a command prompt. However, it is also possible to create batch files that have conditional logic and display progress messages.

When an executable filename is entered at a command prompt, the current folder is searched first, followed by the folders in the path. If executable files in the current folder or a folder in the path have .COM, .EXE, and .BAT extensions with the same name preceding the extension, the .COM file is always launched first. For example, assume that the current folder contains DOIT.COM, DOIT.EXE, and DOIT.BAT. DOIT.COM is launched if you enter DOIT.

Naming Files

Windows XP, Vista, and 7 support long file and folder names (LFN). LFNs can have as many as 255 characters and can contain spaces and most other alphanumeric characters, but cannot contain any of the following characters (which are used by the operating system):

\ / : * ? " < > |

A file can contain more than one period, but only the characters after the last period are considered the extension. In the following example, .doc is the extension:

mydocument.ltr.doc

By default, Windows Explorer doesn't show file extensions for registered file types. You can adjust the settings in Windows Explorer to show all file extensions by clicking **Tools**, **Folder Options**, **View**, and then deselecting the **Hide Extensions for Known File Types** checkbox. To view an individual file's extension, right-click the file and select **Properties** in Windows Explorer. File extensions can be seen normally within the Command Prompt when using the DIR command.

Long Filenames and DOS Alias Names

To enable files to be accessed by operating systems that don't support LFN, Windows stores a DOS alias (also known as the MS-DOS name) as well as the LFN when a file or folder is created.

The DOS alias name is created from the first six letters of the LFN, replacing illegal characters with an underscore, removing spaces, and ignoring additional periods in the LFN. To distinguish between different files with the same DOS alias names, the first DOS alias name in a folder is indicated with a tilde and the number 1 (~1); the second as ~2, and so on. If more than nine files with the same initial letters are saved to a given folder, the first five letters are used for files numbered ~10 and up, and so forth. The three-letter file extension is reused for the DOS alias. Table 13-5 shows the results of creating three files with the same initial files in the same folder. The underlined characters in the original LFN in Table 13-5 are used to create the DOS alias name.

Table 13-5   Examples of Creating DOS Aliases from LFNs

File Creation Order	Original LFN	DOS Alias
First	Budget Process.xls	BUDGET~1.XLS
Second	Budget Proposal.2003.xls	BUDGET~2.XLS
Third	Budget History+2002.xls	BUDGET~3.XLS

CAUTION   DOS alias names for existing files can change if the file is renamed or deleted and then re-created.

There is a limit of 255 characters for LFNs. However, the path to the file counts against this limit.

Windows 7/Vista/XP/2000 use LFNs by default; DOS alias names are used only for backward compatibility with other operating systems. The command-prompt mode uses LFNs with no special options. For example, to change to My Documents from a normal command prompt, the command would be

```
cd\My Documents
```

The Recovery Console used by Windows for troubleshooting and system recovery supports LFNs. However, you must use double quote marks around the LFN: CHDIR \"My Documents".

File Extensions

By default, Windows hides file extensions such as `.BAT`, `.DOC`, and `.EXE` for registered file types. However, you can change this default in Windows Explorer/Computer/My Computer.

See "Changing Viewing Options in Windows Explorer," earlier in this chapter.

NOTE   For a comprehensive list of file extensions and their meanings, I recommend the WhatIs? website's "Every File Format in the World" section, which lists more than 3,100 file formats at http://whatis.techtarget.com.

CAUTION   Don't remove or alter the file extension if you rename a file. If you do, Windows can't determine which program it should use to open the file.

Symbolic Links

A symbolic link is an alias that refers to another location. For example, instead of going to C:\Users*username*\My Virtual PCs\, you could create a symbolic link called C:\VPC that takes you to the C:\Users*username*\My Virtual PCs\ folder.

To make a symbolic link, start the command prompt program (CMD.exe) with Administrator privileges and run the MKLINK program from the command prompt. As an alternative, you can use the Junction program available from the Windows SysInternals website at http://technet.microsoft.com. Junction works with Windows XP, Vista, and 7.

Setting and Displaying File and Folder Attributes in Windows Explorer

You've probably heard of file attributes, but what are they used for? File and folder attributes are used to indicate which files/folders have been backed up, which files/folders need to be backed up, which files/folders should be hidden from normal display, and which files/folders are used by the system. Windows also supports additional attributes such as when a file/folder was created and last modified. When the NTFS file system is used on a drive and additional advanced attributes (encryption or compression) are also available, depending upon the version of Windows in use. Windows XP Home, Windows Vista Starter, Home Basic, and Home Premium, and Windows 7 Starter, Home Basic, and Home Premium do not support encryption (EFS).

The ATTRIB command can be used to set or display basic attributes for a file/folder from the Windows command line. However, to set or display advanced file attributes, you must use the Windows Explorer GUI interface.

Basic file attributes include

- **Archive**—Files with the archive attribute have not yet been backed up. When you back up a file with XCOPY or any backup program, the archive bit is turned off. Change a file's attribute to archive to force a backup program to back it up if "changed files only" are being backed up.

- **Read-only**—Files with the read-only attribute cannot be deleted or overwritten at an MS-DOS prompt and cannot be overwritten within a 32-bit or 64-bit Windows application. A read-only file can be deleted within Windows Explorer, but only after the user elects to override the read-only attribute. Change a file's attributes to read-only to provide protection against accidental deletion or changes.

- **System**—Files with the system attribute are used by the operating system; these files often have the hidden attribute as well. Windows Explorer will caution users when they attempt to delete system files.

- Hidden—Files with the hidden attribute cannot be copied with COPY or with XCOPY using default settings (use the /h switch with XCOPY to copy files with system and hidden attributes) and cannot be viewed with the normal Windows Explorer settings. Some log files created by Windows (such as Bootlog.txt) are stored with the hidden attribute.

A file or folder can have multiple attributes; for example, the NTLDR file used by Windows XP/2000 has the archive, system, hidden, and read-only attributes. If you wanted to edit NTLDR, you would use ATTRIB to remove these attributes before changing the file and reapply these attributes after changing the file.

Options for ATTRIB in Windows include

+	Sets an attribute.
-	Clears an attribute.
R	Read-only file attribute.
A	Archive file attribute.
S	System file attribute.
H	Hidden file attribute.
/S	Processes files in all directories in the specified path.
/D	Processes folders as well.
/L	Works on the attributes of the Symbolic Link versus the target of the Symbolic link (7, Vista only).
I	Not content indexed file attribute (7, Vista only).

When the ATTRIB command is run from the Windows XP/2000 Recovery Console, the /S and /D options are not available, but +C can be used to compress a file and -C can be used to uncompress a file.

Here are some examples:

- **ATTRIB**—Displays all files in the current folder with attributes (A for archive; R for read-only; S for system; H for hidden).

- **ATTRIB +R Command.com**—Sets the file Command.com to have the read-only attribute.

- **ATTRIB -H -R -S C:\MSDOS.SYS**—Removes the hidden, read-only, and system attributes from the Msdos.sys file in the root folder of drive C:.

- **`ATTRIB +H +R +S C:\MSDOS.SYS`**—Restores the hidden, read-only, and system attributes to the Msdos.sys file in the root folder of drive C:.

- **`ATTRIB +C *.doc`**—Compresses all .doc files in the current folder (valid for Windows 2000/XP Recovery Console only).

The Windows file properties sheet's General tab displays only two or three of the basic file attributes. On a drive formatted with NTFS, files display only the read-only and hidden attributes. On a drive formatted with FAT32 file system, the read-only, hidden, and archive attributes are displayed.

To view these attributes in Windows:

Step 1.   Start Windows Explorer or My Computer/Computer.

Step 2.   Right-click a file or folder and select **Properties**.

Step 3.   The General tab indicates read-only or hidden attributes for the file or folder. In addition to the basic attributes listed previously, Windows can also display the creation date of the file, the date the file was last accessed, and the date the file was last changed.

To select or deselect the archive attribute or to set encryption or compression options on a drive using the NTFS file system, click the **Advanced** button. Figure 13-48 shows the General and Advanced dialogs on a Windows XP system.

Encryption and compression are available only on Windows 7, Vista, XP, and 2000 drives formatted with the NTFS file system.

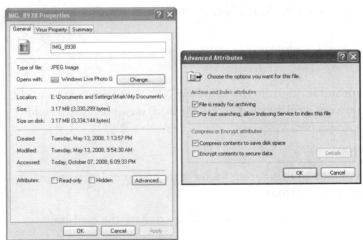

Figure 13-48   Compressing a file with Windows XP. You can select compression or encryption, but not both.

To set these options for a file or folder in Windows, you can use Windows Explorer or the command-line programs Compact (to compress a file) or Cipher (to encrypt a file). To encrypt or compress a file within the Windows GUI, follow these steps:

Step 1.   Start Windows Explorer/My Computer/Computer.

Step 2.   Right-click a file or folder and click **Properties**.

Step 3.   Click the **Advanced** button.

Step 4.   Select **Compression** to reduce the disk space used by the file, or **Encryption** to restrict access to only the system's administrator or the user who encrypted the file.

Step 5.   Click **OK** to apply either option (refer to Figure 13-48). Files can be compressed or encrypted, but not both.

Step 6.   If you are encrypting the file, Windows recommends that you encrypt the folder containing the file (which will also encrypt the file).

CAUTION   Only the user who originally encrypted the file (or the system's Administrator) can open an encrypted file and view its contents. Only the Administrator can apply compression to a file or folder.

NOTE   File folders' properties sheets have additional tabs:

- The Sharing tab configures how a folder is shared (if file/print sharing is installed).
- The Customize tab configures how a folder is displayed in Windows Explorer/My Computer/Computer.

File Permissions

Windows 7/Vista/XP/2000 systems that use the NTFS file system sometimes feature an additional tab on the file/folder properties sheet called the Security tab. It is used to control file permissions.

NOTE   If Windows XP is configured to use simple file sharing, the Security tab will not be visible. Simple file sharing is recommended for home and small-business networks, but reduces system security. Simple file sharing is enabled by default if the system is not connected to a domain, but is disabled automatically when the system is connected to a domain. (The domain controller is used to control network security.)

To disable simple file sharing on a system not connected to a domain, go to either Windows Explorer, My Computer/Computer, or Control Panel. Click **Tools** on the menu bar, select **Folder Options**, click the **View** tab, scroll to the bottom, and clear the check mark next to **Use Simple File Sharing (Recommended)**.

The Security tab permits you to control access to the selected file or folder by granting or denying permissions shown to selected users or groups:

- **Full Control**—Enables any and all changes to a file, including deletion.

- **Modify**—File can be modified.

- **Read & Execute**—File can be read and executed.

- **Read**—File can be read.

- **Write**—File can be overwritten.

- **List Folder Contents**—When viewing the permissions of a folder, this additional permission is listed. It allows the user to **view** what is inside the folder.

The Security tab has two sections. The top section shows the users and groups that have access to the selected file or folder. You can add or remove groups or users. The bottom section lets you specify the permissions available for the selected user or group.

DEFRAG

Over time, a hard disk becomes fragmented as temporary and data files are created and deleted. When a file can no longer be stored in a contiguous group of allocation units, Windows stores the files in as many groups of allocation units as necessary and reassembles the file when it is next accessed. The extra time needed to save and read the file reduces system performance. Windows includes a disk defragmentation tool to help regain lost read/write performance.

Defragment can be run in the following ways:

- From the Accessories menu's System Tools submenu (Disk Defragmenter)

- From a drive's properties sheet's Tools tab (Defragment Now)

- From the command line (a feature introduced in Windows XP): defrag (type **defrag /?** for options)

The Windows 7/XP/2000 defragmenter features an Analyze button that determines whether defragmentation is necessary (see Figure 13-49). There is no Analyze button in Vista; however, Defrag will analyze the disk automatically before defragmenting. If you want more control over Vista's defragment feature, use Vista's command-line defrag.exe utility. For details, see Knowledge Base article 942092 at http://support.microsoft.com

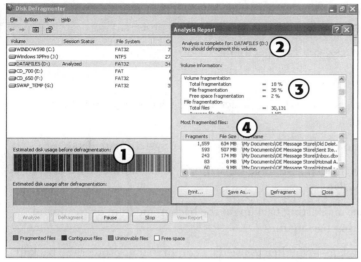

1. Visual display of drive fragmentation
2. Indicates whether defragmentation is necessary
3. Fragmentation of tested drive
4. The most fragmented files on the tested drive

Figure 13-49   Disk Defragmenter's analysis indicates this drive needs to be defragmented.

TIP   The narrower the colored stripes visible in the Estimated Disk Usage Before Defragmentation display, the more fragmented the drive is.

NTBackup

Windows XP/2000 includes a backup program that can be run from the Windows GUI or from the command line, NTBackup.

NOTE   The Microsoft Backup utility (NTBACKUP) for Windows XP Home Edition must be installed manually from the \ValueAdd\MSFT\NTBACKUP folder on the Windows XP Home Edition CD.

You can start NTBackup in the following ways:

■ From the System Tools submenu of the Start menu's Accessories submenu

■ From the command line (ntbackup.exe; for command-line options, open **Help and Support Center** and type **ntbackup** into the Search box)

■ From the Tools menu of the drive properties sheet; choose **Backup Now**

NTBackup supports backups to a wide variety of drive types, including tape drives, floppy disk drives, removable-media drives such as Zip, Jaz, and Rev drives, and external hard disks. A backup can be saved to a rewritable CD or DVD drive as long as the backup fits on a single disc; however, the backup file must be created first, it cannot be burned directly to the disc during the backup process.

During the backup process, you can specify the following:

■ Which drive(s) to back up

■ Which files to back up—whether to select all data files or new and changed files only

■ Whether to back up the Windows Registry (part of system state data)

■ Where to create the backup—to tape drive, floppy disk, another hard disk, or a removable-media drive

■ Whether to replace an existing backup on the backup medium or to append the backup to existing backup files

■ How to run the backup—whether to use data compression, protect the backup with a password, verify the backup, and use volume shadow copy (which enables open files to be backed up)

NTBackup can be run in interactive mode as shown in Figure 13-50 or in wizard mode as shown in Figure 13-51.

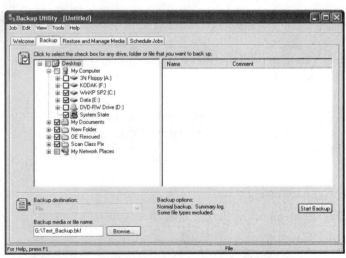

Figure 13-50   Preparing to create a backup to an external hard disk with NTBackup in interactive mode.

NTBackup in Windows XP adds the ability to perform an Automated System Recovery (ASR) backup/restore to rebuild a Windows installation after a system failure, but does not support the Emergency Repair Disk (ERD) function found in Windows 2000.

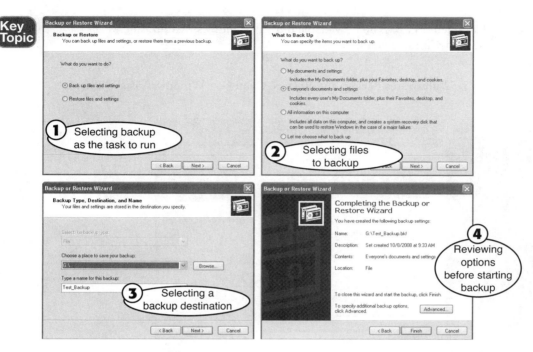

Figure 13-51   Running NTBackup in wizard mode.

To learn more about ASR, see "Using Automated System Recovery (ASR)," in Chapter 15. To learn more about ERD, see "Using the Emergency Repair Disk (Windows 2000)," in Chapter 15.

NOTE   If you need to restore backup files created with NTBackup to a system running Windows Vista, download and install Windows NT Backup-Restore Utility from the Microsoft website. This utility also requires that you enable Removable Storage Management.

Using Windows Vista's Backup and Restore Center

Backup and Restore Center is the successor to Windows XP's NTBackup. It can back up individual files to writeable CD or DVD, high-capacity removable media such as Iomega REV, external hard disk, or a network location (in Business, Ultimate, and Enterprise only). It can also back up an entire image of your system (using Complete PC Backup) to a writeable DVD, an external hard disk, or a network location. However, Windows Vista backup programs do not support tape drives.

NOTE   Complete PC Backup is available only in Windows Vista Business, Enterprise, and Ultimate editions.

Figure 13-52 illustrates Backup and Restore Center on Windows Vista Ultimate.

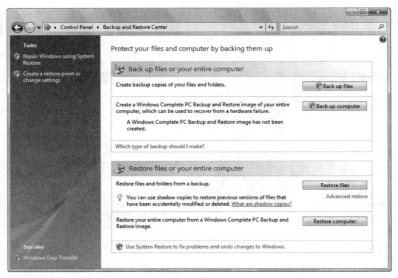

Figure 13-52   Windows Vista Ultimate's Backup and Restore Center.

NOTE   Before Backup and Restore Center is configured for the first time, it is listed as Backup Status and Configuration.

During the file backup process, you specify the types of files to back up as shown in Figure 13-53 and when to perform scheduled backups after the first backup is completed. The file backup process backs up data files and program settings, but not Windows files, program files, or a system image. Use Complete PC Backup (if available) or a third-party image backup program to create a system image backup.

Windows Vista stores its file backups as .zip files that can be opened by Windows Explorer as well as by Backup and Restore Center.

For more information about performing image backups with Windows Vista, see Chapter 15.

Using Windows 7's Backup and Restore

All editions of Windows 7 include Backup and Restore (see Figure 13-54). The backup function can create both an image and a file backup in a single operation.

By default, a backup includes a system image, files in libraries, and personal folders for all users.

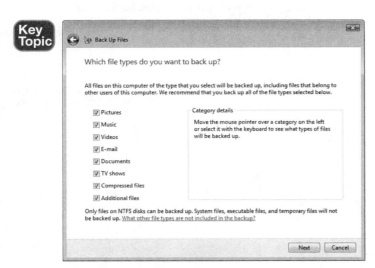

Figure 13-53   Specifying the file types to back up with Windows Vista's Back Up Files.

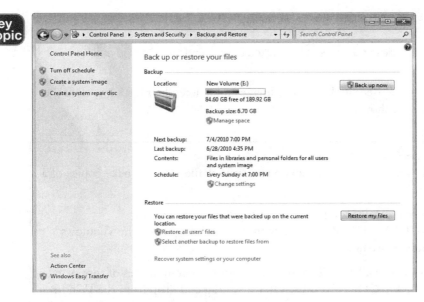

Figure 13-54   Windows 7's Backup and Restore after performing the initial file and image backup.

During the configuration process before the initial backup, you can specify the drives to include in the system image, the files to be backed up (see Figure 13-55), and when to perform scheduled backups. To perform scheduled backups, you must use a drive formatted with the NTFS file system (or a network location with Professional, Ultimate, and Enterprise editions). When you run scheduled backups after the initial backup, the backup image is updated and changed and new files are also backed up.

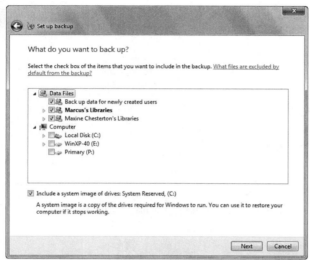

Figure 13-55   Selecting files and drives to be backed up by Window 7 Backup and Restore.

To manage the space used by the backup image and delete older backups, click the **Manage Space** link shown in Figure 13-54.

Backup versus File Copy Utilities

When considering whether to use a backup program or file copy to make copies of a file, consider the following:

- Backups are typically compressed; file copies performed with COPY/XCOPY/ROBOCOPY or with drag and drop from the Windows GUI generally are not.

- Backups can span a large file onto two or more separate pieces of supported media; COPY/XCOPY/ROBOCOPY and drag and drop from the Windows GUI cannot subdivide a large file.

- Backups must be restored by the same or compatible program; files copied by COPY/XCOPY/ROBOCOPY or drag and drop can be retrieved by Windows Explorer and standard Windows programs.

- Backups created by NTBackup can be stored to tape, floppy disk, or other types of removable storage such as Zip drives (but not rewritable CD or DVD) as well as external hard disks; backups created by Windows Vista and 7's Backup can be stored on recordable or rewritable CD or DVD or external hard disks; COPY/XCOPY/ROBOCOPY can work only with drives that can be accessed through a drive letter or a UNC (Universal Naming Convention) network path. However, COPY/XCOPY/ROBOCOPY and drag and drop from the Windows GUI can be used with CD-RW and CD-R media that have been formatted for UDF (drag-and-drop) file copying. Note that third-party backup utilities can use rewriteable CD and DVD media as well as other types of media.

  Essentially, if you want to retrieve the information at any time, use drag and drop from the Windows GUI or copy, xcopy.exe, or robocopy.exe (Windows 7 and Vista only) from the command prompt. However, if you need to back up very large files, an entire system image, want to save space, and don't mind restoring the files with a specific program, use NTBackup (XP and 2000), Backup and Restore Center (Vista), Backup and Restore (7), or a third-party backup program.

CHKDSK.EXE

Windows includes the chkdsk.exe program to check disk drives for errors. It can be run from the Windows GUI, as shown in Figure 13-56, or from the command-line.

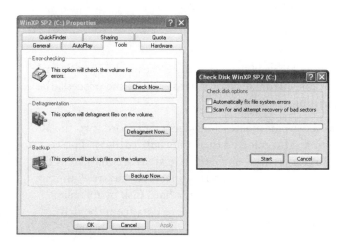

Figure 13-56   Windows C: Properties Sheet and Check Disk Window after the Check Now button has been clicked.

TIP It's no coincidence that Check Now is listed before Defragmentation and Backup in the Windows disk Tools menu. You should check the drive for errors *first* before you perform a defrag or backup operation.

As Figure 13-56 shows, you can also select whether to automatically fix file system errors and attempt the recovery of bad sectors with Chkdsk. If you select the option to automatically fix file system errors on the system drive, Chkdsk will be scheduled to run at the next restart. This is necessary because Chkdsk requires exclusive access to the drive. Chkdsk performs a three-phase test of the drive after the system is rebooted but before the Windows desktop appears.

You can also run Chkdsk from the command prompt. For options, type **Chkdsk /?** from the command prompt.

In Windows Vista and 7, you will need to run this command in elevated mode using either of these methods:

■ Click **Start, All Programs, Accessories, Command Prompt**. Right-click **Command Prompt** and select **Run as Administrator**. Click **Continue** at the permission window.

■ Click **Start** and type **cmd.** Then press **Ctrl+Shift+Enter** to execute cmd.exe in elevated mode. Click **Continue** at the permission window.

NOTE By default, **Chkdsk** runs automatically at boot time if a drive is dirty (has errors); to adjust this behavior, run Chkdsk with appropriate options from the command prompt. Use **chkdsk /?** to see the options you can use.

Format/Format.exe

In Windows, the Format command is used primarily to re-create the specified file system on a floppy disk, removable-media disk, or a hard disk. In the process, the contents of the disk are overwritten.

When Format is used on a hard drive, it creates a master boot record, two file allocation tables, and a root directory (also referred to as the root folder). The rest of the drive is checked for disk surface errors—any defective areas are marked as bad to prevent their use by the operating system. Format appears to "destroy" the previous contents of a hard disk, but if you use Format on a hard disk by mistake, third-party data recovery programs can be used to retrieve data from the drive. This is possible because most of the disk surface is not changed by Format.

If a floppy disk, USB flash memory drive, removable-media disk is prepared with Format and the unconditional /U option is used from the command line, or the Windows Explorer Full Format option is used, sector markings (a sector equals

512 bytes) are created across the surface of the floppy disk before other disk structures are created, destroying any previous data on the disk. If the Quick Format or Safe Format option is used, the contents of the disk are marked for deletion but can be retrieved with third-party data recovery software.

NOTE The hard disk format process performed by the Format command (which creates the file system) is sometimes referred to as a high-level format to distinguish it from the low-level format used by hard drive manufacturers to set up magnetic structures on the hard drive. When floppy disks are formatted with the Full or Unconditional options, Format performs both a low-level and high-level format on the floppy disk surface.

Using Format with Floppy, USB Flash, and Removable-Media Drives

Although floppy disks, USB flash memory drives, and removable-media drives are preformatted at the factory, Format is still useful as a means to

- Erase the contents of a disk quickly, especially if it contains many files or folders.

- Place new sector markings across the disk.

- Create a bootable disk that can be used to run MS-DOS programs.

Formatting Floppy and Hard Disks with Windows Explorer

You can use Windows Explorer to format both hard drives and floppy disks. Right-click the drive you want to format, select **Format**, and the Format options for Windows are displayed, as shown in Figure 13-57. (Windows 2000's options are almost identical, except for the lack of the MS-DOS startup disk option.) Windows Vista and 7 also offer the exFAT (FAT64) file system for hard disks and high-capacity flash drives.

Windows 2000 doesn't offer the Make an MS-DOS Startup Disk option, but is otherwise similar. To learn how to use Format.exe command-line options, see "FORMAT.EXE," later in this chapter.

NOTE Writeable CD and DVD media must also be formatted before it can be used. To learn more about the options used with these types of media, see Chapter 12, "Storage Devices."

The FORMAT.EXE command deletes all existing files and folders from a system. It overwrites the current contents of the target drive unless the /Q (Quick Format) option is used. When /Q is used, only the file allocation table and root folder are overwritten. To retrieve data from a drive that has been formatted, you must use third-party data-recovery software.

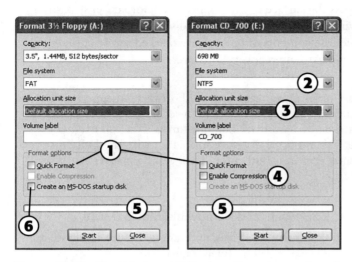

1. Reduces format time, but doesn't check for disk errors
2. Select FAT (FAT16), FAT32, or NTFS
3. Unless you have a specific requirement for a non-standard allocation unit size, use the Default Allocation Size setting
4. Compression available with NTFS file system only
5. Status bar indicates progress of format
6. Option available in Windows XP only; creates a bare-bones MS-DOS boot disk without optical drive or memory management software

Figure 13-57   The Windows XP Explorer Format menu for a floppy disk (left) and hard disk (right).

In Windows 7/Vista/XP, FORMAT.EXE includes a variety of options for use with floppy disks, hard disks, removable-media and optical drives, and USB flash memory drives. These include the following:

volume	Specifies the drive letter (followed by a colon), mount point, or volume name.
/FS:filesystem	Specifies the type of the file system (FAT, FAT32, or NTFS).
/V:label	Specifies the volume label.
/Q:	Performs a quick format.
/C	NTFS only: Files created on the new volume will be compressed by default.
/X:	Forces the volume to dismount first if necessary. All opened handles to the volume would no longer be valid.
/R:revision	(7/Vista only) UDF only: Forces the format to a specific UDF version (1.20, 1.50, 2.00, 2.01, 2.50). The default revision is 2.01.
/D	(7/Vista only) UDF 2.50 only: Metadata will be duplicated.

/A:size   Overrides the default allocation unit size. Default settings are strongly
                     recommended for general use. NTFS supports 512, 1024, 2048, 4096,
                     8192, 16K, 32K, 64K. FAT supports 512, 1024, 2048, 4096, 8192, 16K,
                     32K, 64K, (128K, 256K for sector size > 512 bytes). FAT32 supports 512,
                     1024, 2048, 4096, 8192, 16K, 32K, 64K, (128K, 256K for sector size >
                     512 bytes). Note that the FAT and FAT32 files systems impose the fol-
                     lowing restrictions on the number of clusters on a volume:

                     FAT: Number of clusters <= 65526
                     FAT32: 65526 < Number of clusters < 4177918

                     FORMAT will immediately stop processing if it decides that the preced-
                     ing requirements cannot be met using the specified cluster size. NTFS
                     compression is not supported for allocation unit sizes above 4096.

The following options apply to floppy disks only:

/F:size   Specifies the size of the floppy disk to format (1.44).
/T:tracks   Specifies the number of tracks per disk side.
/N:sectors   Specifies the number of sectors per track.

Windows Explorer Command-Line Options

To adjust how Windows Explorer displays windows, run Explorer.exe from the
command prompt with your choice of these options: /n, /e, /root (plus an object),
and /select (plus an object). Table 13-6 describes each option.

Table 13-6   Windows Explorer Command-Line Options

Option	Function
/n	Opens a new single-pane window for the default selection. This is usually the root of the drive that Windows is installed on. If the window is already open, a duplicate opens (will not function in Vista/7).
/e	Opens Windows Explorer in its default view (will not function in Vista/7).
/root,<object>	Opens a window view of the specified object.
/select,<object>	Opens a window view with the specified folder, file, or program selected.

As the following examples demonstrate, the command line options can be used
with local or network files and folders:

■ **Example 1: Explorer /select,C:\TestDir\TestProg.exe**—Opens a window
   view with TestProg selected.

■ **Example 2: Explorer /e,/root,C:\TestDir\TestProg.exe**—Opens Explorer
   with drive C: expanded and TestProg selected.

- **Example 3: Explorer /root,\\TestSvr\TestShare**—Opens a window view of the specified share.

- **Example 4: Explorer /root,\\TestSvr\TestShare,select,TestProg.exe**—Opens a window view of the specified share with TestProg selected.

Command-Line Functions

Command-line functions are run from the command prompt and are used primarily for diagnosis, repair, and troubleshooting. The following sections discuss the major command-line functions and utilities in more detail.

Starting a Command-Prompt Session with CMD.EXE

You can start a command-prompt session in Windows by clicking on the Command prompt option in the Start menu; it's usually located in the Accessories menu on most versions of Windows. However, it's faster to use the Run command or Search box:

- **In Windows XP/2000**—Click **Start > Run**. Then, type **cmd** and click **OK**.

- **In Windows 7/Vista**—Click **Start**, type **cmd** in the Search box, and then press **Enter** or press **Ctrl+Shift+Enter** to run in elevated mode (might be necessary for some commands). You can also right-click **cmd** and select **Run as Administrator**.

Figure 13-58 shows a typical command prompt session in Windows 7.

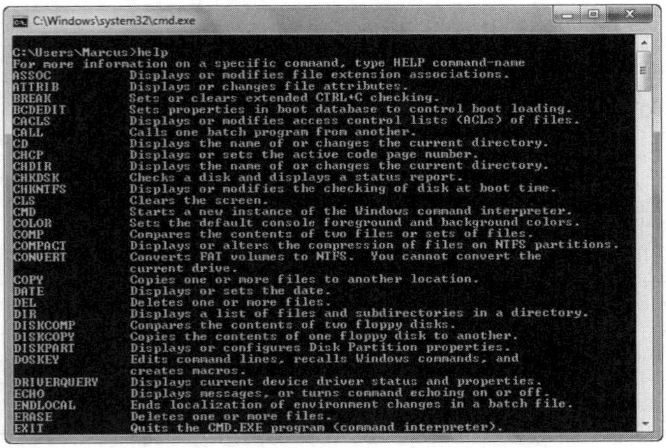

Figure 13-58 Using the Help command to view a list of command prompt commands in Windows 7.

The following sections discuss the command-line functions that are covered on the A+ Certification exams. These functions fall into two categories:

- Those that are included in CMD.EXE (the command interpreter used to start a command-prompt session). These are known as internal commands.

- Those that are separate programs on disk. These are known as external commands.

> **NOTE**   Ipconfig, ping, and tracert are discussed in Chapter 16.

Internal Commands Overview

`Cmd.exe` (Windows 7/Vista/XP/2000) contains the internal commands listed in Table 13-7. Commands marked (RC) can also be used by the Windows XP/2000 Recovery Console.

Table 13-7   Major Internal Commands

Internal Command	Category	Use	Example
DATE	System management	Views system current date and allows it to be changed	DATE
TIME	System management	Views system current time and allows it to be changed	TIME
COPY (RC)	Disk management	Copies one or more files to another folder or drive	COPY *.* A:\
DEL (RC)	Disk management	Deletes one or more files on current or specified folder or drive	DEL *.TMP
ERASE (RC)	Disk management	Same as DEL	ERASE *.TMP
DIR (RC)	Disk management	Lists files on current or specified folder or drive	DIR *.EXE
MD (MKDIR) (RC)	Disk management	Makes a new folder (subdirectory)	MD TEMP
CD (CHDIR) (RC)	Disk management	Changes your current location to the specified folder (subdirectory)	CD TEMP
RD (RMDIR) (RC)	Disk management	Removes an empty folder	RD TEMP
RENAME (REN)	Disk management	Renames a file	REN joe.txt jerry.txt

Table 13-7   Major Internal Commands

Internal Command	Category	Use	Example
VER	System management	Lists the version of operating system in use	VER
VOL	Disk management	Lists the current volume label and serial number for the default drive	VOL
SET	System management	Used to set options for a device or program; SET without options displays all current SET variables	SET TEMP=C:\TEMP
PROMPT	System management	Sets display options for the command prompt	PROMPT=$P $G (displays drive letter followed by greater-than sign)
PATH	System management	Sets folders or drives that can be searched for programs to be run	PATH=C:\DOS;C:\WINDOWS
ECHO	Batch files	Turns on or off the echo (display) of commands to the screen	ECHO OFF
CLS (RC)	Batch files, system management	Clears the screen of old commands and program output	CLS
TYPE (RC)	System management	Views text files onscreen	TYPE AUTOEXEC.BAT

TIP: To get help for any internal or external command-prompt function or program, type the program name followed by /?. For example, DIR /? displays help for the DIR command.

Using Wildcards to Specify a Range of Files

Command-prompt functions and utilities can be used to operate on a group of files with similar names by using one of the following wildcard symbols:

- ? replaces a single character.

- * replaces a group of characters.

For example, DIR *.EXE displays files with the .EXE extension in the current folder (directory). DEL MYNOVEL??.BAK removes the following files: MYNOVEL00.BAK, MYNOVEL01.BAK, but not MYNOVEL.BAK.

HELP

To see a list of valid commands you can run from the command prompt and to see a brief description of each command, type **HELP** from the command prompt (refer to Figure 13-58).

To get help with a specific command, type **HELP commandname**. For example, to get help with XCOPY.EXE, type HELP XCOPY. You can also type the command followed by /? (for example, dir /?).

DIR

The DIR command, which lists files and folders in either the current or any other specified drive or folder, has many options. For example, Windows DIR options include the following:

[drive:][path] [filename]	Specifies drive, directory, or files to list (could be enhanced file specification or multiple filespecs).
/P	Pauses after each screenful of information.
/W	Uses wide list format.
/A	Displays files with specified attributes:

	D	Directories
	R	Read-only files
	H	Hidden files
	A	Files ready for archiving
	S	System files
	-	Prefix meaning not
/O		List by files in sorted order:
	N	By name (alphabetic)
	S	By size (smallest first)
	E	By extension (alphabetic)

	D	By date & time (earliest first)
	G	Group directories first
	-	Prefix to reverse order
	A	By Last Access Date (earliest first)
/S		Displays files in specified directory and all subdirectories.
/B		Uses bare format (no heading information or summary).
/L		Uses lowercase.
/4		Displays year with four digits (ignored if /V also given).
/C		Display the thousand separator in file sizes. This is the default. Use /-C to disable display of separator.
/D		Same as wide but files are list sorted by column.
/N		New long list format where filenames are on the far right.
/Q		Displays the owner of the file.
/T		Controls which time field displayed or used for sorting:
	C	Creation
	A	Last Access
	W	Last Written
/X		This displays the short names generated for non-8dot3 filenames. The format is that of /N with the short name inserted before the long name. If no short name is present, blanks are displayed in its place.
/V		Verbose mode.

The options listed for DIR can be combined with each other, enabling you to use DIR to learn many different types of information about files and folders. The following are some examples:

- **DIR/AH**—Displays files with the hidden attribute (see the discussion of ATTRIB later in this chapter) in the current folder.

- **DIR/S command.com**—Displays all instances of Command.com in the current folder and all folders beneath the current folder.

- **DIR/O-S C:\WINDOWS**—Displays all files in the folder C:\Windows in order by size, largest first.

EDIT

EDIT is a plain-text text editor that can be used to read and edit batch (.BAT), .INI, CONFIG.SYS, and other types of text files. (EDIT is not available in Windows 7; you can use Notepad as a replacement.) To open a file with EDIT, type **EDIT filename**. Keep in mind that when you run EDIT, it is designed to work with 8+3 MS-DOS-style filenames and temporarily sets the command prompt environment to display only DOS aliases for file and folder names. The options shown here apply to all versions of EDIT:

Here are some examples:

/B	Forces monochrome mode.
/H	Displays the maximum number of lines possible for your hardware.
/R	Load file(s) in read-only mode.
/S	Forces the use of short filenames.
/<nnn>	Load binary file(s), wrapping lines to <nnn> characters wide.
/?	Displays this help screen.
[file]	Specifies initial files(s) to load. Wildcards and multiple filespecs can be given.

- **EDIT C:\MSDOS.SYS**—Opens the Msdos.sys file in the root folder of drive C: for editing; user must change file attributes of Msdos.sys with ATTRIB first to allow changes to file.

- EDIT—Opens editor; user must open File menu within Edit to select file(s) to open.

EDIT has pull-down windows you can activate with a mouse or with the keyboard. If you are using EDIT after booting from an EBD and no mouse driver is loaded, hold down the Alt key and press the first letter of each menu to display that menu:

- **File**—Opens, saves, prints, and closes a file; exits the program

- **Edit**—Cuts, copies, pastes, and clears selected text

- **Search**—Finds and replaces specified text

- **View**—Adjusts options for dual-screen editing (two documents at once)

- **Options**—Adjust tab stops, printer port (COM or LPT), and screen colors

- **Help**—Displays EDIT help screen

> **TIP**   `EDIT` uses the same keyboard cut, copy, and paste shortcuts as Windows:
>
> - Ctrl+X cuts text
> - Ctrl+C copies text
> - Ctrl+V pastes text
> - Del clears text

COPY

The `COPY` command copies files from one drive and folder to another folder and drive. The folder specified by `COPY` must already exist on the target drive. `COPY` will not work with files that have the system or hidden file attributes; to copy these files, use `XCOPY32` or `ROBOCOPY` instead.

/B (Vista/7 only) Copies the symbolic link itself versus the target of the link.

The options for `COPY` in Windows 7/Vista/XP include the following:

Here are some examples:

- **COPY *.* A:**—Copies all files in the current folder to the current folder on the A: drive.
- **COPY *.TXT C:\Mydocu~1**—Copies all .txt files in the current folder to the `Mydocu~1` folder on the C: drive.
- **COPY C:\WINDOWS\TEMP*.BAK**—Copies all *.bak files in the `\Windows\Temp` folder on drive C: to the current folder.
- **COPY C:\WINDOWS*.BMP D:**—Copies all .bmp files in the `\Windows` folder on drive C: to the current folder on drive D:.

XCOPY

The `XCOPY` command can be used in place of `COPY` in most cases and has the following advantages:

- **Faster operation on a group of files**—`XCOPY` reads the specified files into conventional RAM before copying them to their destination.
- **Creates folders as needed**—Specify the destination folder name in the `XCOPY` command line, and the destination folder will be created if needed.

- **Operates as backup utility**—Can be used to change the archive bit from on to off on files if desired to allow XCOPY to be used in place of commercial backup programs.

- **Copies files changed or created on or after a specified date**—Also useful when using XCOPY as a substitute for commercial backup programs.

The options for XCOPY.EXE in Windows 7/Vista/XP include the following:

source	Specifies the file(s) to copy.
destination	Specifies the location or name of new files.
/A	Copies only files with the archive attribute set; doesn't change the attribute.
/M	Copies only files with the archive attribute set; turns off the archive attribute.
/D:m-d-y	Copies files changed on or after the specified date. If no date is given, copies only those files whose source time is newer than the destination time.
/EXCLUDE:file1[+file2][+file3] ...	Specifies a list of files containing strings. Each string should be in a separate line in the files. When any of the strings match any part of the absolute path of the file to be copied, that file will be excluded from being copied. For example, specifying a string like \obj\ or .obj will exclude all files underneath the directory obj or all files with the .obj extension, respectively.
/P	Prompts you before creating each destination file.
/S	Copies directories and subdirectories except empty ones.
/E	Copies directories and subdirectories, including empty ones. Same as /S /E. May be used to modify /T.
/V	Verifies each new file.
/W	Prompts you to press a key before copying.
/C	Continues copying even if errors occur.

/I	If destination does not exist and copying more than one file, assumes that destination must be a directory.
/Q	Does not display file names while copying.
/F	Displays full source and destination file names while copying.
/L	Displays files that would be copied.
/G	Allows the copying of encrypted files to destination that does not support encryption.
/H	Copies hidden and system files.
/R	Overwrites read-only files.
/T	Creates directory structure, but does not copy files. Does not include empty directories or subdirectories. /T /E includes empty directories and subdirectories.
/U	Copies only files that already exist in destination.
/K	Copies attributes. Normal Xcopy will reset read-only attributes.
/N	Copies using the generated short names.
/O	Copies file ownership and ACL information.
/X	Copies file audit settings (implies /O).
/Y	Suppresses prompting to confirm you want to overwrite an existing destination file.
/-Y	Causes prompting to confirm you want to overwrite an existing destination file.
/Z	Copies networked files in restartable mode.
/B	(Vista/7 only) Copies the symbolic link itself versus the target of the link.
/J	(Vista/7 only) Copies using unbuffered I/O. Recommended for very large files.

XCOPY can be used to "clone" an entire drive's contents to another drive. For example, the following copies the entire contents of D: drive to H: drive:

XCOPY D:\. H:\ /H /S /E /K /C /R—Copies all files from drive D:'s root folder (root directory) and subfolders to drive H:'s root folder and subfolder, including system and hidden files, empty folders and subfolders, file attributes; this will continue even if errors are detected and will overwrite read-only files.

NOTE Note ROBOCOPY.EXE is a robust file-copying utility included in Windows Vista and 7 that can be used in place of XCOPY.EXE. ROBOCOPY.EXE has several advantages over XCOPY.EXE, including the ability to tolerate pauses in network connections and the ability to mirror the contents of the sources and destination folders by removing files as well as copying files.

ROBOCOPY.EXE uses much different syntax than XCOPY.EXE, and for that reason you might prefer to run it by means of a GUI such as the Robocopy GUI available at http://technet.microsoft.com/en-us/magazine/2006.11.utilityspotlight.aspx.

MD/CD/RD

You can make, change to, or remove folders (directories) with the following commands as shown in Table 13-8.

Table 13-8 Folder Management Commands

Command	Abbreviation*	Use	Example
MKDIR	MD	Creates a folder (directory)	MKDIR \Backups Makes the folder Backups one level below the root folder of the current drive
CHDIR	CD	Changes to a new folder	CHDIR \Backups Changes to the \Backups folder
RMDIR	RD	Removes a folder (if empty)	RMDIR \Backups Removes the \Backups folder (if empty)

Abbreviations are not supported in Windows XP Recovery Console

Folders (directories) can be referred to in two ways:

- Absolute
- Relative

An absolute path provides the full path to the folder. For example, to change to the folder \Backups\Word from the folder \My Documents on the same drive, you would use the command CHDIR\Backups\.

> **NOTE**   You can't use the CHDIR command to change to a different drive and folder. It only works on the current drive.

A relative path can be used to change to a folder one level below your location. For example, to change to the folder \Backups\Word from the folder \Backups, you would use the command CHDIR Word (or just CD Word). No backslash is necessary.

To change to the root folder from any folder, use CHDIR \ (or just CD \). To change to the folder one level higher than your current location, use CHDIR .. (or just CD..).

System Management Tools

The following sections discuss the major system management tools included in Windows, such as Device Manager, Task Manager, MSCONFIG.EXE, REGEDIT.EXE, Event Viewer, System Restore, and Remote Desktop.

Device Manager

Windows Device Manager is used to display installed device categories, specific installed devices, and to troubleshoot problems with devices.

To use Device Manager in Windows 7/Vista, follow these steps:

Step 1.   Click **Start**, right-click on **Computer**, and select **Properties**. This will display the System window.

Step 2.   From there, click the **Device Manager** link on the left side under Tasks.

To use the Device Manager in Windows XP/2000:

Step 1.   Open the System Properties window in the Control Panel, or right-click **My Computer** and select **Properties**.

Step 2.   Click the **Hardware** tab and select **Device Manager**.

NOTE   There are two other options for opening Device Manager. The first is by using the Search box within the Start menu. Just type **device manager**, and then click the link for Device Manager that appears in the results box. The second is from the Computer Management console window. It opens the same way in Windows 7, Vista, and XP. To open this, right-click on **Computer** (My Computer in XP), and select **Manage**. This displays the Computer Management window; from there, click **Device Manager** in the left window pane. Get in the habit of using Computer Management. It has lots of common settings in one location. Another way to open Computer Management is by going to the Run prompt and typing **compmgmt.msc**.

To view the devices in a specific category, click the plus (+) sign next to the category name, as in Figure 13-59.

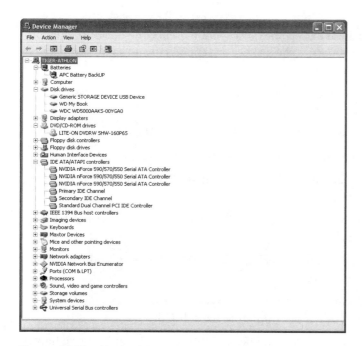

Figure 13-59   Device Manager with selected categories expanded.

NOTE   Different systems will have different categories listed in Device Manager, as Device Manager only lists categories for installed hardware. For example, the system shown in Figure 13-60 has a battery backup, so it has a Batteries category. Note also that the IDE ATA/ATAPI Controllers category also lists SATA controllers.

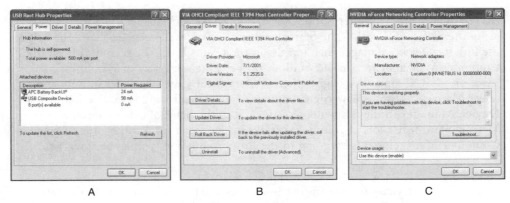

Figure 13-60   Selected Device Manager tabs: the Power tab for a USB hub (A); the Driver tab for an IEEE-1394 port (B); the General tab for an network controller (C).

To see more information about a specific device, double-click the device to open its properties sheet. Device properties sheets have a General tab and some combination of other tabs:

- **General**—Displays device type, manufacturer, location, status, troubleshoot button, and usage. All devices.

- **Properties**—Device-specific settings. Applies to multimedia devices.

- **Driver**—Driver details and version information. All devices.

- **Details**—Technical details about the device (added in Windows XP SP2 and newer versions). All devices.

- **Policies**—Optimizes external drives for quick removal or performance. USB, FireWire, and eSATA drives.

- **Resources**—Hardware resources such as IRQ, DMA, Memory, and I/O port address. Applies to I/O devices.

- **Volumes**—Drive information such as status, type, capacity, and so on. Click Populate to retrieve information. Applies to hard disk drives.

- **Power**—Power available per port. Applies to USB root hubs and generic hubs.

- **Power Management**—Specifies device-specific power management settings. Applies to USB, network, keyboard, and mouse devices.

Figure 13-60 illustrates some of these tabs.

Virtually all recent systems support Plug and Play (PnP) hardware with automatic resource allocation by a combination of the PnP BIOS and Windows. However, if you need to determine the hardware resources in use in a particular system, click **View** and select **Resources** by type (see Figure 13-61).

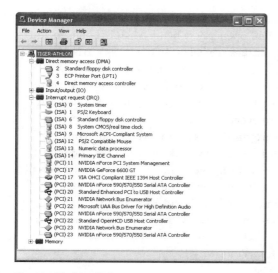

Figure 13-61   IRQ and DMA usage on a typical Windows XP system. ACPI power management enables IRQs above 15 and sharing of PCI IRQs 17, 20, 22, and 23 by multiple devices.

Troubleshooting problem devices with Device Manager is covered in Chapter 15.

Computer Management and the MMC

We've mentioned this component of Windows 7/Vista/XP a few times already, but it's worth mentioning again. Instead of hunting around for different utilities in different places in Windows, it's simpler to use the Computer Management console window because it has most of the tools you need in one organized two-pane (XP) or three pane (7/Vista) window system. Here are the ways to open Computer Management:

- Click **Start,** then right-click **Computer/My Computer** and select **Manage**.

- Navigate to **Start**, **All Programs**, **Administrative Tools, Computer Management**.

- Open the **Run** prompt (Windows+R) and type **compmgmt.msc** (a personal favorite).

In Computer Management, you find the Event Viewer, the Device Manager, Local Users and Groups, Services, and disk tools such as Disk Management. Consider using them often.

Now, to make it better, Windows 7, Vista, and XP offer you the Microsoft Management Console (MMC). This is the "master" console so to speak, and you can snap-in as many other console windows as you want. Add to that the fact that it saves all the consoles you snapped in and remembers the last place you were working, and this becomes a valuable and time saving tool.

To open it, open the **Run** Run program (Windows XP) or click the Search box (Windows 7, Vista) and type **MMC**. This will open a new blank MMC. Then, to add console windows, go to **File** and then **Add/Remove Snap-in** (or press **Ctrl+M**). From there, click the **Add** button to select the consoles you want such as Computer Management, Performance Logs and Alerts, or ActiveX Controls. You can also change the "mode" that the user works in when accessing the MMC—for example Author mode, which has access to everything, and User mode, which has various levels of limitation. When you are finished, save the MMC and consider adding it as a shortcut within the desktop or in the Quick Launch area and maybe add a keyboard shortcut to open it. The next time you open it, it will remember all of the console windows you added and will start you at the location you were in when you closed the program. By default, Windows 7 and Vista include version 3.0 of the MMC, and Windows XP includes Version 2.0. However, you can download version 3.0 for Windows XP from http://technet.microsoft.com. Just search for "Microsoft Management Console 3.0 for Windows XP."

Task Manager

The Task Manager utility provides a useful real-time look into the inner workings of Windows and the programs that are running. There are several ways to display the Task Manager including

- Right-click the taskbar and select **Task Manager**.

- Press **Ctrl+Shift+Esc**.

- Open the **Run** prompt and type **taskmgr**.

- Press **Ctrl+Alt+Del** and select **Task Manager** from the Windows Security dialog box. (Note: This only works in Windows XP if you have turned off the Welcome Screen option.)

The Task Manager tabs include Applications (shows running applications); Processes (program components in memory); Performance (CPU, memory, pagefile, and caching stats). Windows XP adds a Networking tab (lists network utilization by adapter in use) and a Users tab (lists current users). Windows 7/Vista add a Services tab (displays the services on the computer and their status).

Use the Applications tab to determine if a program has stopped responding; you can shut down these programs by using the End Task button. Use the Processes tab to see which processes are consuming the most memory. Use this dialog along with the System Configuration Utility (MSConfig) to help determine if you are loading unnecessary startup applications; MSConfig can disable them to free up memory. If you are unable to shut down a program with the Applications tab, you can also shut down its processes with the Processes tab, but this is not recommended unless the program cannot be shut down in any other way.

Use the Performance tab to determine whether you need to install more RAM memory or need to increase your paging file size. Use the Networking tab to monitor the performance of your network.

The top-level menu can be used to adjust the properties of the currently selected tab and to shut down the system. Figure 13-62 illustrates these tabs. Figure 13-63 shows the Services tab in Windows Vista's Task Manager.

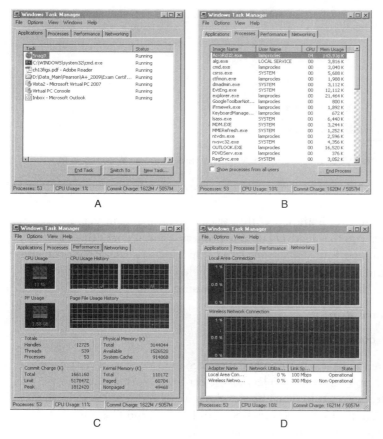

Figure 13-62 The Windows XP version of the Windows Task Manager's Applications (A), Processes (B), Performance (C), and Networking (D) tabs.

Figure 13-63   The Windows Vista version of the Windows Task Manager's Services Tab.

MSCONFIG.EXE

The Microsoft System Configuration Utility, `Msconfig` (available in Windows 7/Vista/XP), enables you to selectively disable programs and services that run at startup. If your computer is unstable, runs more slowly than usual, or has problems starting up or shutting down, using `Msconfig` can help you determine if a program or service run when the system starts is at fault. To start `Msconfig`:

Step 1.   Click **Start**, **Run**.

Step 2.   Type **msconfig** and click **OK**.

All versions of `Msconfig` have a multitabbed interface used to control startup options. The General tab (Figure 13-64) lets you select from Normal, Diagnostic (clean boot) or Selective Startup (you choose which items and services to load). Use the Tools tab (Figure 13-65) to launch System Restore, run Computer Management, or perform other system management tasks.

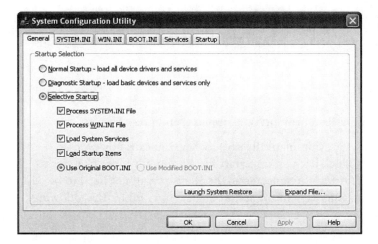

Figure 13-64 `Msconfig's` General tab (Windows XP).

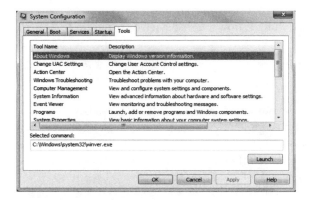

Figure 13-65 `Msconfig's` Tools tab (Windows 7).

Other tabs control settings in `Msconfig` include `System.ini` (legacy hardware), `Win.ini` (legacy software and configuration), `Boot.ini` (Windows XP), `Services` (Windows XP), `Boot` (Windows 7 and Vista), and `Startup` (startup programs. The Windows 7 and Vista versions of `Msconfig` do away with the System.ini and Win.ini tabs.

NOTE   Although Msconfig wasn't part of Windows 2000 by default, you can download it from the Internet or copy it from Windows XP, and it will function in the same manner.

REGEDIT.EXE

To start **Regedit**, open the **Run** prompt, type `regedit`, and press **Enter**.

Changes made in `Regedit` are automatically saved when you exit; however, you might have to log off and lock back on or restart the system, for those changes to take effect. Under most normal circumstances, the Registry will not need to be edited or viewed. However, Registry editing might be necessary under the following circumstances:

- To view a system setting that cannot be viewed through normal interfaces.

- To add, modify (by changing values or data), or remove a Registry key that cannot be changed through normal Windows menus or application settings. This might be necessary to remove traces of a program or hardware device that was not uninstalled properly or to allow a new device or program to be installed.

- To back up the Registry to a file.

CAUTION   The Registry should *never* be edited unless a backup copy has been made first because there is no Undo option for individual edits and no way to discard all changes when exiting Regedit.

Editing the Windows Registry is even more difficult because registry keys can be expressed in decimal, hexadecimal, or text. When editing the Registry, be sure to carefully follow the instructions provided by a vendor.

Figure 13-66 shows the Registry in Windows Vista with a modification being made to the MenuBar color, which isn't accessible within normal Windows display menus. Figure 13-67 shows the Registry in Windows XP, viewing the uninstall folder for Mozilla Firefox.

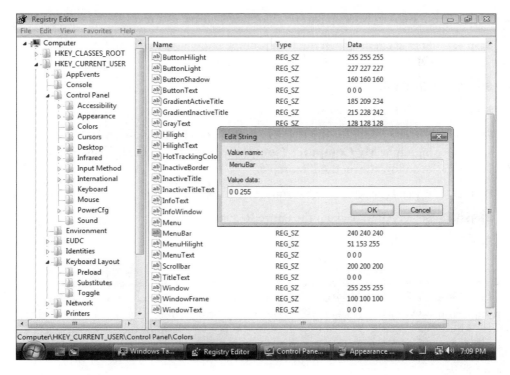

Figure 13-66   Using Regedit (Windows Vista).

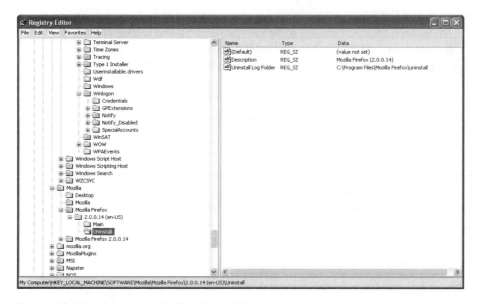

Figure 13-67   Using Regedit (Windows XP).

Follow these steps to back up part or all of the Registry to a text file:

Step 1.   Start **Regedit** (open the **Run** prompt and type **regedit**, and then click **OK**).

Step 2.   Click **File**.

Step 3.   Click **Export**.

Step 4.   Select a folder for the Registry backup. (To back up the entire Registry, highlight **My Computer/Computer** at the top of the left window pane or follow the method in Step 6.)

Step 5.   Enter a name for the backup.

Step 6.   Select **All** to back up the entire Registry.

Step 7.   Click **Save**.

NOTE   Windows 2000 included another registry editor known as regedt32, which had a different look then regedit. This command can still be used in the Run prompt within Windows 7/Vista/XP, but it simply brings up the standard registry editor known as regedit. It is not covered in the 2011 version of the A+ exams.

Event Viewer

If your customer is using Windows 7/Vista/XP/2000, these versions of Windows generate several log files during routine use that can be useful for determining what went wrong. Many of these can be viewed through the Event Viewer. To view the contents of the Event Viewer in Windows 7/Vista/XP/2000, right-click **Computer/My Computer**, click **Manage**, and click **Event Viewer**. The Event Viewer captures various types of information; the three most important logs to know for the exam are: Application, Security, and System. In Windows 7/Vista, they are inside Event Viewer\Windows Logs; however, in Windows XP, these are listed directly inside of the Event Viewer.

To view details about an entry in the Event Viewer for Windows XP, click on a log in the left window pane, and entries will appear in the right window pane. To open the event and view more information, double click the event or right-click it and select **Event Properties/Properties**. Windows Vista and 7 use a three-paned interface, which adds a new Actions pane (right) to the log (left) and entries (center) panes. Figure 13-68 shows the Application event viewer on a Windows 7 system being used to view the details of an application error.

System Restore

Ever wish you had a time machine so you could go back before you installed a bad driver or troublesome piece of software? Windows 7, Vista, and XP feature a "time machine" called System Restore.

System Restore enables you to fix problems caused by a defective hardware or software installation by resetting your computer's configuration to the way it was at a specified earlier time. The driver or software files installed stay on the system, and so does the data you created, but Registry changes made by the hardware or software are reversed so your system works the way it did before the installation. Restore points can be created by the user with System Restore and are also created automatically by the system before new hardware or software is installed.

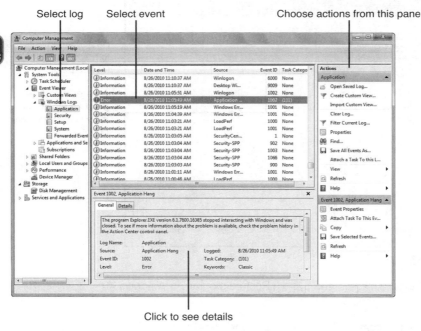

Figure 13-68   Viewing the details about an application error using the Application Event Viewer. The left window displays other major components of Windows 7's Computer Management Console.

To create a restore point in Windows 7 or Vista, follow these steps:

Step 1.   Right-click **Computer** and select **Properties**. This opens the System Properties window.

Step 2.   Click the **System Protection** task, which opens the System Protection tab on the System properties sheet.

Step 3.   Click the **Create** button. This opens the System Protection window.

Step 4.   Enter a name for the restore point and click **Create**.

To create a restore point in Windows XP, follow these steps:

Step 1.   Navigate to **Start**, **All Programs**, **Accessories**, **System Tools**, **System Restore**. This opens the System Restore window (see Figure 13-69).

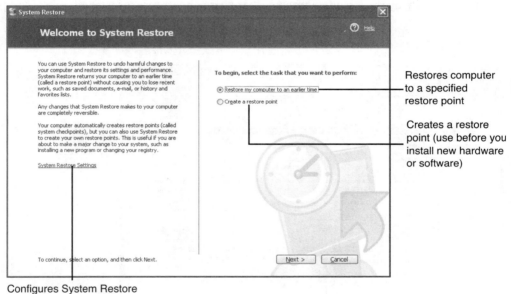

Figure 13-69   The main menu of the System Restore program in Windows XP.

Step 2.   Click **Create a Restore** Point and click **Next**.

Step 3.   Enter a descriptive name for the restore point, such as **Before I installed DuzItAll Version 1.0** and click **Create**.

Step 4.   The computer's current hardware and software configuration is stored as a new restore point.

Follow these steps to restore your system to an earlier condition in Windows 7 and Vista:

Step 1.   Access the System Protection tab again, and this time click the **System Restore** button. This opens the System Restore window.

Step 2.   Select either **Recommended Restore** or **Choose a Different Restore Point**.

Step 3.   The Recommended Restore point dialog will ask you to confirm. If you are choosing a different restore point, you will need to select the appropriate one and confirm.

Step 4.   The system will initiate the restore and will automatically restart.

Windows 7 and Vista also allow you to undo a system restore if it did not repair the problem.

To restore your system to an earlier condition in Windows XP, follow these steps:

Step 1.   Go to the same location you did when creating a restore point.

Step 2.   Click **Restore My Computer to an Earlier Time** and click **Next.**

Step 3.   Select a date from the calendar. (Dates that have restore points are in bold text.)

Step 4.   Select a restore point and click **Next** (see Figure 13-70).

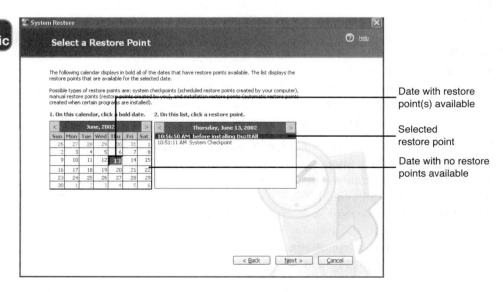

Figure 13-70   Choosing a restore point with Windows XP's System Restore.

Step 5. Close any open programs and save your work before you click **Next** to start the process; Windows will shut down and restart.

Step 6. The system will initiate the restore and will automatically restart.

If System Restore is not available, it might be turned off. Within Windows 7 and Vista, you can enable or disable System Restore on any volume from the System Properties window/System Protection tab. Simply check or uncheck any volume that you want to enable or disable. Within Windows XP, the state of System Restore affects all drives; you can only turn the utility on and off. This is done from the System Properties window/System Restore tab. You can also change the amount of disk space it uses here.

Be aware that System Restore is not necessarily the first step you should try when troubleshooting a computer. Simply restarting the computer has been known to "fix" all kinds of issues. It's also a good idea to try the Last Known Good Configuration. You can access this within the Windows Advanced Boot Options menu by pressing **F8** when the computer first boots. Also, if System Restore doesn't seem to work in normal mode, attempt to use it in Safe Mode. Safe Mode is another option in the Windows Advanced Boot Options menu. You can also run System Restore from the Windows Recovery Environment (Windows 7 and Vista only).

Be wary of using System Restore if you're fighting a computer virus or malware infection. If you (or the system) create a restore point while the system is infected, you could re-infect the system if you revert the system to that restore point. To prevent re-infection, most anti-virus vendors recommend that you disable System Restore (which eliminates stored restore points) before removing computer viruses.

Remote Desktop

Windows 7 Professional/Ultimate/Enterprise, Windows Vista Business/Ultimate/Enterprise, and XP Professional include Remote Desktop server (a subset of Terminal Services), a feature that enables a user on that system to access the system remotely and use its desktop, programs, drives, printers, and other resources.

You can also use other Windows versions as well for the Remote Desktop client. You can download the Remote Desktop client software from Microsoft's TechNet website (http://technet.microsoft.com); search for Remote Desktop Connection Software. It works with Windows 7, Vista, XP (Home and Professional), 2000, and older versions of Windows. The Microsoft Remote Desktop Connection Client for Mac 2.1 or greater, also available from the Microsoft TechNet website, enables MacOS-based systems to connect remotely to a Windows 7, Windows Vista, or Windows XP Professional system.

Windows 7, Vista, and XP Professional can handle only one remote connection at a time; if another user is currently logged on locally, he must log off to permit the remote connection.

Configuring Your Windows System to Accept Remote Client Connections

Windows Vista and XP Professional automatically run the Terminal Services service, which is required for Remote Desktop incoming connections. (Windows 7 starts the Terminal Services service only when you enable remote desktop connections.) To accept remote connections, you must also:

Step 1.   Make sure the remote user has been added as a user for this computer and has a password. Use the User Accounts applet in Control Panel (Classic mode) to check this information.

Step 2.   Configure your firewall to permit connections via TCP port 3389. If you use Windows Firewall, selecting Remote Desktop on the Exceptions menu automatically opens this port (see Figure 13-71). However, if you use a third-party firewall program or device, you might need to configure this setting manually. See your firewall documentation for details.

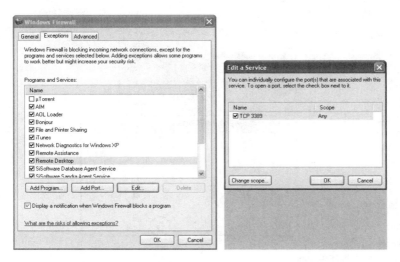

Figure 13-71   Configuring Windows Firewall to accept Remote Desktop connections.

Step 3.   Open the System properties sheet, click the **Remote** tab, and select the **Allow Users to Connect Remotely to This Computer** option in the Remote Desktop portion of the dialog (see Figure 13-72). With Windows 7 and Vista, you have two options: whether to allow connections from any version of Remote Desktop or only from Remote Desktop with Network Level Authentication (a more secure connection only available on Windows Vista and 7).

Step 4.   Click the **Select Remote Users** (**Select Users** on Windows 7 and Vista) button to view the list of Remote Desktop Users. If the user you want to grant remote access to isn't on the list, click **Add**. On the Select Users dialog, enter the name of the user, and click **Check Names**. If the name is on the list of users, the server name is added.

Step 5.   Repeat Step 4 until all remote user names are added. Click **OK** when finished.

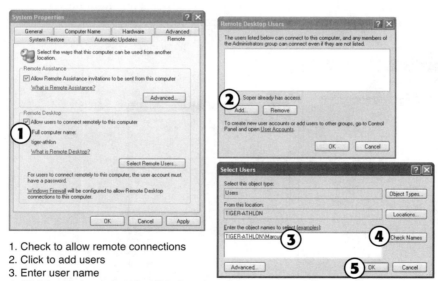

1. Check to allow remote connections
2. Click to add users
3. Enter user name
4. Click to check name against list of users
5. Click OK after remote user list is complete

Figure 13-72   Enabling the system to accept Remote Desktop connections from a specified user.

Connecting Remotely

To start the connection process, click **Start**, **All Programs**, **Accessories**, **Remote Desktop Connection**. The dialog shown in Figure 13-73 appears. Enter the name or IP address of the remote computer, and click **Connect**.

Provide a username and password from the list of authorized remote users and click **OK** when prompted. The remote desktop appears.

NOTE   If you need additional connection options, click the Options button shown in Figure 13-73. This opens a multi-tabbed connection dialog with options for saving connection settings (General); adjusting the size and color depth of the remote desktop (Display); configuring options for remote computer sound, keyboard, and devices (Local Resources); what program to start on connection (Programs); connection speed, screen handling, and reconnect options (Experience); security and advanced connection settings (Advanced).

Figure 13-73   Starting a Remote Desktop session.

A tab at the top of the remote dialog displays the name or IP address of the remote PC and provides options for minimizing, maximizing/windowing, and closing the session (see Figure 13-74).

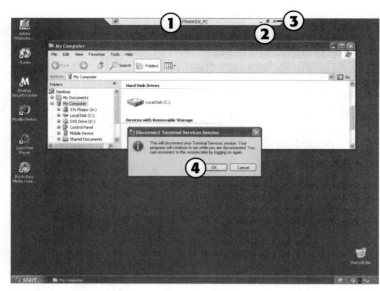

1. Name of remote PC hosting session
2. Window controls
3. Click to close session and stay logged in
4. Click to confirm end of session

Figure 13-74   Ending a Remote Desktop session.

Ending the Remote Session

You have three options for quitting the remote session:

■ To end the remote session but stay logged in, click the **X** in the remote dialog tab and click **OK** on the Disconnect Terminal Services Session dialog (refer to Figure 13-74).

■ To log out of the remote session, click **Start Log Off** and click **Log Off** when prompted.

■ To disconnect, click **Start**, **Disconnect** and click **Disconnect** when prompted.

Optimizing Windows

Understanding how to optimize Windows performance is also part of the A+ certification objectives. The following sections cover issues you might encounter on the exams and are likely to encounter in your work life.

Virtual Memory, Performance Monitor, and System Monitor

If you run short of money, you can borrow some from the bank (assuming your credit's in decent shape). However, there's a penalty: interest. Similarly, if your system runs short of memory, it can borrow hard disk space and use it as virtual memory. The penalty for this type of borrowing is performance: Virtual memory is much slower than real RAM memory. However, you can adjust how your system uses virtual memory to achieve better performance.

TIP   To minimize the need to use virtual memory, increase the physical memory (RAM) in a Windows system to at least 2GB (2.5GB on a system with integrated graphics). The largest amount of usable RAM on a 32-bit Windows system is 3.25GB; 64-bit Windows systems can use 4GB or more.

When additional RAM is added to a computer running Windows, it is automatically used first before the paging file.

The Windows 7/Vista Performance Monitor and Windows XP System Monitor can be used to determine whether more RAM should be added to a computer.

- To access the Windows 7/Vista Performance Monitor, open the **Run** prompt, type **perfmon.exe** and press **Enter**. Windows 7 opens the Performance Monitor window. In Windows Vista, the Reliability and Performance Monitor window opens. In either case, you must then click the **Performance Monitor** node.

- To access the Windows XP System monitor, open the **Run** prompt, type **perfmon.exe** and press **Enter**. This opens the Performance console window. Click on the **System Monitor** node.

Many different types of performance factors can be measured with these programs. This is done by measuring objects. Objects include physical devices, such as the processor and memory, and software, such as protocols and services. The objects are measured with counters. For example, a common counter for the processor is % Processor Time.

To see if additional RAM is needed in a system, select the object called **Paging File**, then select the counters **% Usage and Pages/Sec**, as shown in the following steps:

Step 1.   Click the **+** sign or right-click in the table beneath the graph and select **Add Counters**.

Step 2.   Choose **Paging File** as the Performance Object and then choose **% Usage**.. In Windows 7 and Vista, this is shown as a drop-down menu within the object.

Step 3.   Click **Add**.

Step 4.   Choose **Memory** as the Performance Object, and then choose **Pages/Sec**. In Windows 7 and Vista, this is shown as a drop-down menu within the object. In XP, it might be added already.

Step 5.   Click **Add**.

Step 6.   Click **Close** (XP) or **OK** (7, Vista), and then run normal applications for this computer.

If the Performance Monitor/System Monitor indicates that the Paging File % Usage is consistently near 100% or the Memory Pages/Sec counter is consistently higher than 5, add RAM to improve performance. Figure 13-75 shows an example of adequate memory within Windows XP's System monitor.

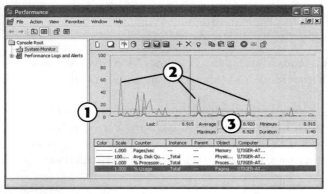

1. Paging file % usage
2. Memory page/second
3. Current average for selected counter

Figure 13-75   This Windows XP system has adequate memory at this time, as indicated by the low levels of usage of the Paging File % Usage and Memory Pages/Sec counters.

The performance of the paging file can be improved by

- Setting its minimum and maximum sizes to the same amount.

- Moving the paging file to a physical disk (or disk partition) that is not used as much as others.

- Using a striped volume for the paging file. A striped volume is identical areas of disk space stored on two or more dynamic disks that are referred to as a single drive letter. Create a striped volume with the Windows Disk Management tool. If a RAID 0 (striped) disk array is available, use it instead of a striped volume for even better paging file performance.

- Creating multiple paging files on multiple physical disks in the system.

- Moving the paging file away from the boot drive.

To adjust the location and size of the paging file in Windows, follow these steps:

Step 1.   Open the System Properties window.

- For XP: Click **Start**, right-click **My Computer**, and select **Properties**; or, open the **Control Panel** and click the **System** icon.

- For 7/Vista: Click **Start**, right-click **Computer**, and select **Properties**. Then, click **Advanced System Settings** under Tasks.

Step 2. Click the **Advanced** tab (not necessary in 7/Vista).

Step 3. Click the **Settings** button in the Performance Options (Performance in 7/Vista) box.

Step 4. Click the **Advanced** tab and then the **Change** button.

Step 5. Choose the initial and maximum sizes you want to use for the paging file and its location (see Figure 13-76). Click **Set** and then click **OK** to finish. (In 7/Vista, you will have to deselect the Automatically Manage Paging File Size checkbox first.)

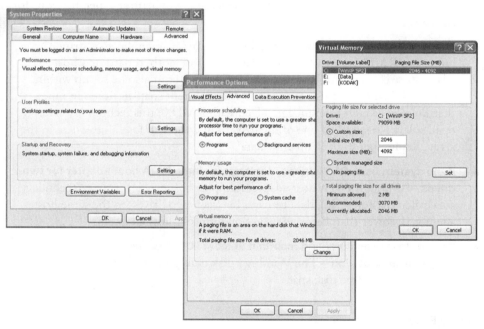

Figure 13-76 The Virtual Memory dialog in Windows XP enables you to set the size and location of virtual memory.

Step 6. If you make any changes to size or location, you must restart the computer for the changes to take effect.

NOTE For the longest, time the default settings for the paging file were Initial size = 1.5× RAM and Maximum size = 3× RAM. This was a good rule of thumb for a while. However, the rule might not work so well with the increasing need for fast memory and the resulting increase of RAM in today's computers. For example, a Windows XP computer with 4GB of RAM might be set this way: Initial size = 1/2

RAM and Maximum size = RAM. It will all depend on the system you are running and the applications being utilized.

Hard Disk

To optimize the performance of the hard disk, you can use the following methods:

- **Upgrade to a hard disk with a faster spin rate and larger cache buffer**—Typically, newer SATA hard disks have faster spin rates and larger cache buffer sizes than older SATA or most PATA hard disks. To determine the spin rate and cache size for an installed drive, check the manufacturer's specifications for the drive.

- **Set up a RAID 0 drive array**—A RAID 0 drive array is similar to a striped array, but uses a RAID-compatible host adapter on the motherboard or a host adapter card. A software-based version of RAID 0 can also be set up within Windows through the use of the Disk Management snap-in. Keep in mind that there is *no* fault tolerance involved with RAID 0; this technology is developed solely for speed. If one of the drives fails, you will lose all the data in the array. Remember to back up your data!

- **If the system uses PATA drives, don't use a single PATA host adapter for two drives**—Although PATA host adapters support two drives (primary/secondary; also called master/slave), data transfer between two drives on the same host adapter is slower than between drives on different host adapters.

- **Defrag drives regularly and maintain at least 20% free disk space to enable easy defragmentation**—The Windows disk defragmenter cannot run if there is less than 15% free disk space.

Temporary Files

The default location for temporary files in Windows versions prior to Windows 7/Vista/XP is the TEMP folder beneath the default Windows folder (\Windows or \WinNT). Windows 7, Vista, and XP use \Windows for system temporary files and XP uses \Documents and Settings*Username*\Local Settings\Temp for user-specific temporary files. 7/Vista uses\Users*Username*\AppData\Local\Temp for user-specific temporary files.

The location can be adjusted with a pair of SET statements.

NOTE Some applications use SET TEMP=location; others use SET TMP=location (replace location with the actual drive and folder path). Be sure to change both variables if you need to change the setting for temporary files.

Temporary File Settings in Windows 7/Vista/XP/2000

Use the Advanced tab on the System properties sheet to set environmental variables such as SET TEMP and many others. Here's how to make the change: You must be logged on as an administrator.)

Step 1.   Create a folder called TEMP in the root folder of the drive you want to use for your temporary files. You can use Windows Explorer/My Computer/Computer or the MKDIR (MD) command.

Step 2.   Open the System properties sheet. You can right-click on **My Computer** and select **Properties** or open the **System** icon in Control Panel.

Step 3.   Click the **Advanced** tab (Windows XP). In Windows 7/Vista, click **Advanced System Settings** in the tasks pane.

Step 4.   Click **Environmental Variables**. A new window opens.

Step 5.   Click **TEMP** in the System variables window and click **Edit**.

Step 6.   The Edit System Variable window opens (see Figure 13-77). Clear the variable value (%SystemRoot%\TEMP, typically shown as C:\WINDOWS\TEMP\) and enter the drive and folder you used in Step 1 (for example, E:\TEMP). Click **OK**.

Figure 13-77   Adjusting the location used for temporary files in Windows XP.

Step 7.   Repeat steps 5–6, selecting TMP instead of TEMP.

Step 8.   Click **OK** in the Environment Variables window.

Step 9.   Click **OK** on the System properties sheet.

NOTE   Use this same method to add, delete, or change other system variables. To change the location for individual users' temporary files, change the settings in the User variables window (top window).

Services

Many of Windows 7/Vista/XP/2000's core functions are implemented as services, including features such as the print spooler, wireless network zero configuration, DHCP client service, and many more. Services can be run automatically or manually and are controlled through the Services node of the Computer Management Console. To open the Computer Management Console, right-click **My Computer/ Computer** and select **Manage**. Then, expand the Services and Applications node and click **Services**. You can also access the Services dialog from the Services applet in Control Panel's Administrative Tools folder (Classic mode); opening Services this way displays the dialog shown in Figure 13-78. The Services dialog lists each service by name, provides a description, status message, startup type, and whether the service is for a local system or network service.

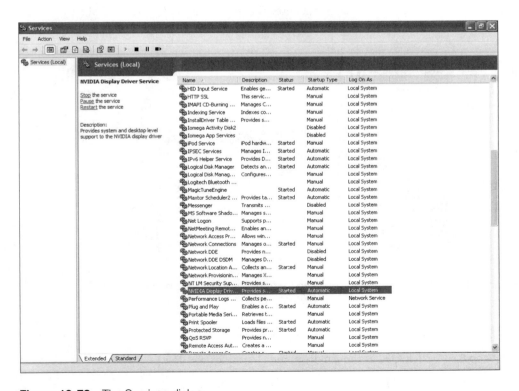

Figure 13-78   The Services dialog.

To view the properties for a particular service, double-click the service listing. The General tab of the properties sheet shown in Figure 13-79 displays the service name, description, path to executable file, startup type, and status. You can also stop, pause, or resume a service from this dialog, as well as from the Services dialog (refer to Figure 13-78).

Figure 13-79   Viewing the General tab for the Print Spooler service.

Use the Log On tab if you need to configure the service to run for a specific user, the Recovery tab to specify what to do if the service fails, and the Dependencies tab to see what other services work with the specified service.

If a system cannot perform a task that uses a service, go to the Services dialog and restart the service. If a service prevents another task from running (for example, a third-party wireless network client might not run if the Windows XP Wireless Zero Configuration service is running), go to the Services dialog and stop the service.

NOTE   For more information about specific Windows services, I recommend *The Elder Geek's Windows Services for Windows XP* guide at www.theeldergeek.com/services_guide.htm or the Answers that Work list of "Task List Programs" at www.answersthatwork.com/Tasklist_pages/tasklist.htm.

Startup

Most systems are configured to run programs at startup as well as services. In addition to starting some services at startup, Windows can also start programs automatically from these locations:

- **The Startup folder in the Start menu for all users**—To view the contents of this folder, open the **Run** prompt, type **%allusersprofile%\Start Menu\Programs\Startup**, and click **OK**.

- **The Startup folder in the Start menu for the current user**—To view the contents of this folder, click **Start**, **Run**, type **%userprofile%\Start Menu\Programs\Startup**, and click **OK**.

- Registry keys, such as

  - `HKEY_LOCAL_MACHINE\Software\Microsoft\Windows\CurrentVersion\Run`

  - `HKEY_CURRENT_USER\Software\Microsoft\Windows\CurrentVersion\Run`

  - `HKEY_LOCAL_MACHINE\Software\Microsoft\Windows\CurrentVersion\RunOnce`

  - `HKEY_CURRENT_USER\Software\Microsoft\Windows\CurrentVersion\RunOnce`

Startup programs might wind up in the Taskbar or the systray, or they might be displayed in a window or full-screen. If you don't want a program loading at startup, you might be able to configure the program not to run at startup. If the program lacks an option for this, however, you can use the Microsoft System Configuration Utility, MSConfig.exe, to block the program from running at startup. For details, see "MSCONFIG.EXE," earlier in this chapter.

Applications

Windows offers several ways to fine-tune application performance. These include

- Adjusting the balance between background services and application response

- Adjusting the priority of a process belonging to an application

- Stopping unresponsive applications

Adjusting the Balance Between Background Services and Application Response

Windows 7/Vista/XP/2000 can be configured to use more memory for background services (non-active windows, printing, and so on) instead of the default (Programs—improves performance for the foreground application). You might want to do this if your Windows computer was acting as a file or print server for a small network. To make this change, use the following steps:

Step 1. Open the **System Properties** window and click the **Advanced** tab (Windows XP); with Windows 7/Vista, click the **Advanced System Settings** task in the task pane.

Step 2. Click the **Settings** button in the Performance box. This opens the Performance Options window.

Step 3. Click the **Advanced** tab.

Step 4. From here, you can adjust for best performance of either: Programs or Background services by clicking the appropriate radio button.

Step 5. Click **OK** when done.

NOTE   A foreground application is the application you have clicked on and are actively using. For example, to write this text, I clicked on Microsoft Word; it becomes the foreground application. When I edit a screen capture, I click on Adobe Photoshop, making it the foreground application. Other running programs such as email, web browsers, and Microsoft Word become background applications.

Adjusting the Priority of a Process

The Windows Task Manager's Processes tab lists processes currently taking place by the name of the executable file. To adjust the priority for a particular process from the default (Normal) to a higher or lower priority, right-click the process, select **Set Priority,** and choose a priority from the listing (Figure 13-80).

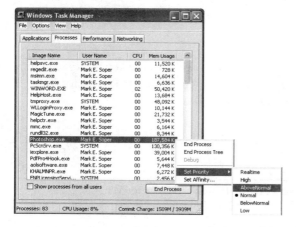

Figure 13-80   Adjusting the priority of a running application.

CAUTION   Be careful when setting custom priorities for processes. If you want to tweak application priority, make the change just one step at a time. Going to a high priority for one application could make other applications less responsive or could cause the operating system to freeze up. Also, changing the priority of SYSTEM processes isn't recommended. Doing so could make your system unresponsive.

If you don't like the changes, reboot the system. Priority changes last only for the current computing session.

Stopping Unresponsive Applications

You can also shut down an unresponsive application, preferably through the Applications tab of the Task Manager. A program listed as Not Responsive might start working again in a few moments. However, if it does not, select the program, click **End Task**, and Windows will (eventually) shut down the program.

If you are unable to shut down the program using the Applications tab, you can use the Processes tab's End Process button to stop the application's underlying process. For example Microsoft Word is an application, but its underlying process is winword.exe. However, you should use this method only as a last resort. Be careful when ending processes; make sure that you know the correct process name for the application you wish to terminate.

TIP   If you have a lot of problems with unresponsive applications, consider a memory upgrade and check for updates to the application, other applications that are running at the same time, and to Windows itself.

Review All the Key Topics

Review the most important topics in the chapter, noted with the key topics icon in the outer margin of the page. Table 13-9 lists a reference of these key topics and the page numbers on which each is found.

Table 13-9   Key Topics for Chapter 13

Key Topic Element	Description	Page Number
Table 13-2	Minimum Hardware Requirements for Windows 7, Vista, XP, and 2000.	575
Figure 13-8	Viewing some of the Registry settings for Windows XP.	581
Figure 13-9	The Windows Explorer in Windows 7; the Explorer bar uses a "breadcrumb" motif to indicate the current location and the path to that location.	582

Table 13-9 Key Topics for Chapter 13

Key Topic Element	Description	Page Number
Figure 13-14	The Windows Explorer Folder Options, View tab in Windows XP after selecting recommended options for use by technicians and experienced end users.	587
Figure 13-16	The default Windows Explorer view in Windows 7 displays libraries.	589
Figure 13-35	Preparing to back up the Windows XP Registry as part of the System State backup using the Windows XP backup program, NTBackup.	614
Table 13-4	Configurations in Disk Management.	618
Figure 13-44	Viewing the folders in the Pictures library.	630
Figure 13-48	Compressing a file with Windows XP. You can select compression or encryption, but not both.	638
Figure 13-49	Disk Defragmenter's analysis indicates this drive needs to be defragmented.	641
Figures 13-50, 13-51	Using NTBackup.	642-643
Figures 13-52, 13-53	Using Windows Vista's Backup and Restore Center.	644-645
Figures 13-54, 13-55	Using Windows 7's Backup and Restore.	645-646
Table 13-7	Major Internal Commands.	653
Figure 13-68	Viewing the details about an application error using the Application Event Viewer.	673
Figure 13-70	Choosing a restore point with Windows XP's System Restore.	675
Steps to accept remote connections including Figures 13-71 and 13-72	Configuring Windows Firewall to accept Remote Desktop connections. Enabling the system to accept Remote Desktop connections from a specified user.	677-679
Figure 13-75	This Windows XP system has adequate memory at this time, as indicated by the low levels of usage of the Paging File % Usage and Memory Pages/Sec counters.	682
Figure 13-76	The Virtual Memory dialog box of Windows XP enables you to set the size and location of virtual memory.	683

Table 13-9   Key Topics for Chapter 13

Key Topic Element	Description	Page Number
Figure 13-77	Adjusting the location used for temporary files in Windows XP.	685
Figure 13-79	Viewing the General tab for the Print Spooler service.	687

Complete the Tables and Lists from Memory

Print a copy of Appendix B, "Memory Tables," (found on the CD), or at least the section for this chapter, and complete the tables and lists from memory. Appendix C, "Memory Tables Answer Key," also on the CD, includes completed tables and lists to check your work.

Definitions of Key Terms

Define the following key terms from this chapter and check your answers in the glossary.

Virtual memory, Paging file, Registry, NTLDR, Partition, Primary Partition, Extended Partition, Logical drive, Control Panel, EFS, Executable, File system, FAT32, exFAT (FAT64), NTFS

Troubleshooting Scenario

You have a client that is having problems with network connectivity. She is complaining that things work fine for a while, and then there is no connectivity at all. What steps could you take to verify that there is a problem?

Refer to Appendix A for the answer.

This chapter covers the following subjects:

- **Installing Operating Systems**—This section describes how to install Windows Vista, Windows 7, and Windows XP and how to make sure your computer meets the minimum requirements for those operating systems. In it we also delve into the different methods of installation including using a DVD, CD, floppy, or USB drive, installing over the network, imaging a drive, and using recovery discs.

- **Upgrading Operating Systems**—Here you learn how to upgrade to Windows Vista, Windows 7, and Windows XP. This section describes the preparations you should make prior to upgrading, gives you step-by-step upgrade processes, and explains how to troubleshoot upgrades.

This chapter covers a portion of the CompTIA A+ 220-701 objectives 3.1 and 3.3.

CHAPTER 14

Installing and Upgrading Windows Operating Systems

It's hard to estimate how many operating system installations a PC technician will do over the course of a career, but you can be assured that it will be *a lot* of installations. Because there are so many different hardware configurations in PCs today, almost every computer will react differently to an installation or upgrade. In this chapter, you will gain a foundation of knowledge about the possible installations and upgrades of Windows. Later, after you have installed several operating systems yourself, this foundation will help you to build solid experience.

For the 2011 A+ 220-701 exam you need to know how to

- Install Windows 7

- Install Windows Vista

- Install Windows XP

- Upgrade to Windows 7 from Windows Vista or Windows XP

- Upgrade to Windows Vista from Windows XP or Windows 2000

- Upgrade to Windows XP from Windows 2000

- Troubleshoot Windows 7/Vista/XP installations and upgrades

For this chapter, it is highly recommended that you try to get your hands on full version copies of Windows Vista, Windows 7, and Windows XP. You should also have a test computer so that you can run clean installations of these operating systems, as well as running the upgrade scenarios in the preceding list.

"Do I Know This Already?" Quiz

The "Do I Know This Already?" quiz allows you to assess whether you should read this entire chapter or simply jump to the "Exam Preparation Tasks" section for review. If you are in doubt, read the entire chapter. Table 14-1 outlines the major headings in this chapter and the corresponding "Do I Know This Already?" quiz questions. You can find the answers in Appendix A, "Answers to the 'Do I Know This Already?' Quizzes and Troubleshooting Scenarios."

Table 14-1   "Do I Know This Already?" Foundation Topics Section-to-Question Mapping

Foundations Topics Section	Questions Covered in This Section
Installing Operating Systems	1–6
Upgrading Operating Systems	7–12

1. You need to install the Windows 7 operating system on a client's computer. Upon arrival you notice that the system is an older model. What should you do first before trying to install the operating system?

   a. Format the hard drive

   b. Verify the hard drive is large enough

   c. Check the Windows 7 Logo'd Products List

   d. Run Chkdsk

2. Which of the following are valid methods that can be used to install a Windows operating system? (Choose all that apply.)

   a. Distribution CD/DVD

   b. Network installation

   c. Drive imaging

   d. A recovery CD

3. You want to create an image for an unattended installation. Which of the following will you need to create this type of image for a Windows XP install? (Choose all that apply.)

   a. Unattend.txt

   b. Winnt.sif

   c. Backup.exe

   d. Sysprep.inf

4. Which of the following are the file systems supported by Windows XP, Windows Vista, and Windows 7? (Choose all that apply.)

   a. FAT16

   b. FAT32

   c. exFAT

   d. NTFS

5. You are installing the Windows Vista operating system. You have a SCSI hard drive installed. Where does Vista allow you to install the device drivers?

   a. By pressing F6 when the operating system starts loading

   b. By clicking on the Load Driver button where partitioning is done

   c. By pressing F8 during boot

   d. By clicking on the Load Vista Drivers Only button

6. You have just installed the Windows XP operating system. You need to verify the installation succeeded by viewing the setup log files. Where would you go to find this information?

   a. `C:\program files\logs`

   b. `C:\windows`

   c. `C:\windows\system32`

   d. `C:\system32`

7. You have been asked to install Windows 7 on a computer that is currently running Windows XP. You first need to verify if the system can run the new operating system. What is the minimum processor speed that will run Windows 7?

   a. 1000 MHz

   b. 1.5 GHz

   c. 800 MHz

   d. 850 MHz

8. You need to install Windows 7 on a computer that is currently running Windows XP. You need to verify that the upgrade will go smoothly. What should you do to determine if this computer can run the Windows 7 operating system?

   a. Run the Windows 7 Upgrade Advisor

   b. Check the HCL for computer specifications

   c. Run the checkupgradeonly program

   d. Run the 7 upgrade wizard

9. You are the technician for your company. You are about to replace Windows XP with Windows 7. You need to prepare the computer for the upgrade. What should you do before attempting this upgrade? (Choose all that apply.)

   a. Download any new device drivers

   b. Back up all important files

   c. Download any application updates

   d. Back up Internet Explorer favorites

   e. Download any new device drivers and download any application updates only

10. You have a computer running the Windows 2000 operating system. You are in charge of the upgrade and notice that the file system is FAT32. You need to convert the files system to NTFS. At what point can you do this?

   a. Once the install process is complete

   b. During the upgrade process

   c. You cannot convert FAT32 to NTFS

   d. During the text portion of the install

11. You are in the process of doing an upgrade to Windows 7. You start the process and then you cannot go any farther. Which of the following could be the problem?

   a. You are using a full version disc instead of the upgrade disc.

   b. Your installation key is incorrect.

   c. You don't have enough free disk space for the installation.

   d. The file system is FAT32.

12. Which of the following will prevent you from starting the upgrade process from Windows XP to Windows Vista? (Choose all that apply.)

   a. Not running the upgrade advisor

   b. Hardware conflicts

   c. Free disk space

   d. Processor speed

   e. Memory size

Foundation Topics

Installing Operating Systems

A computer without an operating system is useless. The process of preparing for an operating system installation includes

- Verifying that your system has sufficient resources and free disk space for the installation

- Verifying that you have drivers for the devices and peripherals you want to use with the operating system

- Preparing the appropriate startup disks (when required) to prepare the hard disk and start the installation

- Determining the location of the operating system if you are installing the new operating system as a dual-boot configuration that will enable you to run either the old or new operating systems

- Determining which edition of the operating system you wish to install

Verifying Hardware Compatibility and Minimum Requirements

Any system built in the last few years can easily achieve the hardware requirements needed for installing Windows Vista or Windows 7 and will far surpass the requirements of Windows XP. However, in the real world, digital dinosaurs that might not be fast enough or have enough free disk space to support some versions of Windows still roam the earth.

Table 14-2 lists the minimum requirements for Windows 7, Windows Vista, Windows XP, and Windows 2000 Professional.

Table 14-2 Minimum Hardware Requirements for Windows Vista/XP/2000

Component	7	Vista	XP	2000 Professional
Processor Speed	1GHz	800MHz	233MHz	133MHz
RAM	1GB (32-bit) 2GB (64-bit)	512MB	64MB	64MB
Free disk space	16GB (32-bit) 20GB (64-bit)	15GB (20GB Partition)	1.5GB (2GB partition)	650MB (2GB partition)
Other	DVD-ROM drive	CD-ROM or DVD-ROM drive	CD-ROM or DVD-ROM	CD-ROM/ Floppy drive

NOTE The specs in Table 14-2 are the *minimum* requirements. Microsoft *recommends* a 1 GHz processor for all versions of Vista, and 1GB of RAM plus a 40GB HDD for Vista Home Premium/Business/Ultimate. For additional information on Windows 7, see http://www.microsoft.com/windows/windows-7/get/system-requirements.aspx.

Note that Windows 7 has higher requirements than Vista, and has much higher requirements than XP, and XP has higher requirements than Windows 2000 Professional. As a consequence, a system that might run Windows XP acceptably well might be too slow to run Windows Vista or Windows 7.

TIP You might like to recycle old computer parts, but if the processor, hard disk size, and memory size of your PC barely meet the Microsoft requirements, prepare to be annoyed at how slowly your computer runs and how limited its capabilities are. You're much better off if your system greatly exceeds the minimums listed in Table 14-2.

You can use various types of system analysis programs and tools to verify that a system's hardware will be compatible with Windows 7, Windows Vista, or XP. If you are checking a computer that already has an operating system installed, use the following tools:

- For Windows 7:
    - Windows 7 Upgrade Advisor (runs on Windows XP SP2 or greater, Windows Vista, Windows 7): http://windows.microsoft.com/upgradeadvisor
    - Windows Logo'd Products List for Windows 7: http://winqual.microsoft.com/HCL/Default.aspx?m=7.
    - Windows 7 Compatibility Center: http://www.microsoft.com/windows/compatibility/.

- For Windows Vista:
    - Windows Vista Logo'd Products List: http://winqual.microsoft.com/HCL/Default.aspx?m=v.

- For Windows XP:
    - Windows XP Logo'd Products List (formerly the HCL): http://winqual.microsoft.com/HCL/Default.aspx?m=x.

- For Windows 7, Windows Vista, and Windows XP:
  - System Information—The Windows System Information tool can be accessed by opening the Run prompt and typing `msinfo32.exe.` In Vista, this takes the place of winmsd, but winmsd can still be run on Windows XP and 2000 in addition to msinfo32.exe.
  - Belarc Advisor—Currently a free download, this program can be found at http://www.belarc.com/free_download.html. It's extremely quick and painless; all you need to do is double-click it once the download is complete. It will automatically install, look for updates, and create a profile of your computer that runs in a browser window. Here you will find all of the hardware-related (and software-related) information on one screen. It also gives you system security status.
  - SiSoftware Sandra Lite (available from http://www.sisoftware.co.uk/).

For computers without an installed operating system, use self-booting diagnostic programs such as

- #1-TuffTEST (available from http://www.tufftest.com/)

- PC Check (available from http://www.eurosoft-uk.com)

- Ultimate Boot CD (available from http://www.ultimatebootcd.com/index.html)

NOTE   The Windows Vista DVD has a "Check compatibility online" option, but this is meant for upgrades as opposed to clean installations. More on this in the section titled "Upgrading Operating Systems" later in this chapter.

Comparing Windows 7 Editions

Windows 7 is an entire line of Microsoft operating systems designed for desktop PCs and laptops. Windows 7 was released in October 2009. Within the Windows 7 group are the versions Starter (32-bit only; bundled with netbooks), Home Premium, Professional, and Ultimate, available in 64-bit and 32-bit versions. Table 14-3 lists the components that are included in these various versions of 7.

Table 14-3 Comparison of Windows 7 Versions

Component	Starter	Home Premium	Professional	Ultimate
Create Homegroup	No	Yes	Yes	Yes
Join Homegroup	Yes	Yes	Yes	Yes
Domain support	No	No	Yes	Yes

Table 14-3 Comparison of Windows 7 Versions

Component	Starter	Home Premium	Professional	Ultimate
Multimedia*	No	Yes	Yes	Yes
64-bit support	No	Yes	Yes	Yes
Windows Aero**	No	Yes	Yes	Yes
Remote Desktop Connection	No	Client only	Client and server	Client and server
Windows XP Mode	No	No	Yes	Yes
Backup and Restore (file and system image)	Yes	Yes	Yes	Yes
Backup and Restore to network	No	No	Yes	Yes
BitLocker disk encryption	No	No	No	Yes
Encrypting File System (EFS)	No	No	Yes	Yes

*Create & play DVDs, Internet TV, Windows Media Center, more

**Requires onboard graphics or graphics card capable of running DirectX

For a fuller review of features, including features common to all Windows 7 versions, see http://windows.microsoft.com/en-US/windows7/products/compare.

NOTE There are two additional versions of Windows 7 not covered on the CompTIA A+ exam: Windows 7 Enterprise (not sold through retail or OEM channels) and Windows 7 Starter (shown in Table 14-3 for comparison). Starter is sold for use on netbooks and in world areas with less advanced technology.

Migrating User Data

If a user will be using a new operating system, either on the same computer or on a new computer, you might need to move his files and settings to the new system. When doing so, make sure that the destination computer has the latest service packs and updates and the same programs that are currently running on the original computer. There are a few options for migrating data:

■ **Windows Easy Transfer**—This program enables you to copy files, photos, music, email, and settings to a Windows 7 or Windows Vista computer; all this information is collectively referred to as user state. It is installed with Windows 7 and Vista and can be downloaded for Windows XP from **www.microsoft.com/ downloads**; just search for Windows Easy Transfer for Windows XP. Be sure to select the 32-bit version if you are transferring from 32-bit Windows XP to Windows 7 or the 64-bit version if you are transferring from 64-bit (x64) Windows XP to Windows 7. These versions are dated 9/15/2009 or later (older versions should be used for transferring to Windows Vista).

Either way, the program will be located in Start > All Programs > Accessories > System Tools after installation. Files and settings can be migrated over the network or by USB cable. The data can also be stored on media like a CD, DVD, or USB flash drive until the destination computer is ready. Normally you would start with the computer that has the files and settings that you want to transfer (the source computer). You can transfer the files and settings for one user account or all the accounts on the computer. All the files and settings will be saved as a single .MIG file (Migration Store). Then, you would move to the computer in which you want to transfer the files to (destination computer), and either load the .MIG file from CD, DVD, USB flash drive, or locate the file on the source computer through the use of a USB cable or network connection. For more information on how to migrate files with Windows Easy Transfer, see the following web page: http:// windows.microsoft.com/en-us/windows7/products/ features/windows-easy-transfer.

■ **User State Migration Tool (USMT)**—This is a command-line tool that can be used to migrate user files and settings for one or more computers. The program can be downloaded from www.microsoft.com/downloads. When installed, two different tools are used: Scanstate.exe saves all the files and settings of the user (or users) on a computer, known as the user state; and loadstate.exe transfers that data to the destination computer(s). There are many options when using the scanstate and loadstate commands, including the ability to select which users are migrated and whether the store of data is uncompressed, compressed, or compressed and encrypted. By utilizing scripting programs, the transfer of files to multiple computers can be automated over the network. For more information on how to transfer files and settings with USMT, see the following TechNet link: http://technet.microsoft.com/en-us/library/dd560801(WS.10).aspx.

■ **Files and Settings Transfer (FAST) Wizard**—This is the older version of Windows Easy Transfer and is installed by default on Windows XP. It is meant for transferring files and settings from a Windows XP, 2000, or 9x computer to a Windows XP computer but otherwise works in a similar fashion to Windows Easy Transfer. To transfer files from XP to Vista or from XP to 7, download the Windows Easy Transfer program for XP.

Installation Methods

A variety of installation methods can be used to install Windows, including the following:

- **Booting from the distribution DVD or CD**—This method can be used to install Windows to an individual PC and to create a master PC from which disk images can be created.

- **Installing from the network**—Use this method to install Windows to one or more systems that have working network connections. To use this method, network adapters need to be configured to boot to a network location.

- **Drive imaging**—An existing Windows installation (with or without additional software and drivers) is cloned for use with other identical systems.

- **Recovery CD or disk partition**—Some vendors provide a special recovery CD or partition that contains an image of Windows. This image is used to restore a system to its original as-shipped configuration.

- **Booting from downloaded floppy disk images**—Use this method when a system cannot boot from a CD. Floppy disk boot images for Windows XP can be downloaded from the Microsoft website and are used when a system cannot boot directly to the CD-ROM. Note: There is no Microsoft supported floppy boot disk for Windows Vista or Windows 7.

- **Booting from USB thumb drive**—Use this method when installing from a DVD isn't feasible, such as installing Windows 7 to a netbook or other portable computer which lacks a DVD drive.

In the following sections, you will learn how to perform clean installations of Windows 7, Windows Vista, and Windows XP.

Starting a Clean Installation of Windows 7 from the Distribution DVD

There are two ways to perform a clean install of Windows 7 from the distribution DVD:

- Install Windows 7 by running the Setup program from within the current version of Windows. Insert the Windows 7 DVD. If the disc does not start automatically, select the option to run the **Setup.exe** program from the AutoPlay menu. Otherwise, go to the DVD drive in Windows Explorer and double-click the **setup.exe** file to start the installation. The Windows 7 installation dialog shown in Figure 14-1 appears. If you start the installation this way, you will be prompted to download the latest updates for installation. Choose this option and continue as prompted.

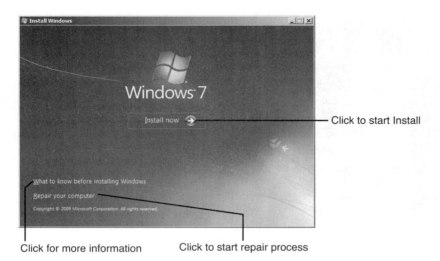

Click to start Install

Click for more information   Click to start repair process

Figure 14-1   Starting the Windows 7 installation from within an older version of Windows.

■   Boot the computer from the Windows 7 DVD. This is necessary if no operating system exists on the computer. If you choose this option, follow these steps:

Step 1.   Make sure the DVD drive is configured as the first boot device in the system BIOS.

Step 2.   Insert the Windows 7 DVD into the system's DVD drive. (If the drive won't open while in the BIOS, insert the disc immediately after saving settings to the BIOS and exiting, or just exiting the BIOS if no changes to settings are needed.). Save/Exit the BIOS and restart the system.

Step 3.   The DVD should boot automatically and start the installation. If you are prompted to boot from the DVD, press any key to continue.

The Windows 7 installation is much easier and more simplified than the Windows XP installation (it closely resembles the Vista installation). After the installation has begun, you should see a GUI-based window like the one in Figure 14-2.

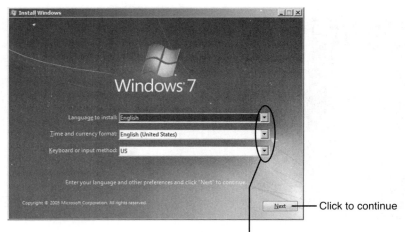

Click to continue

Open these menus to make changes if necessary

Figure 14-2   Windows 7 initial Install dialog when booting from the Windows 7 DVD.

When you run a default installation of Windows 7 from the distribution DVD, you are prompted to provide the following information during the process, in this order:

Step 1.   Select the correct settings for Language to Install, Time and Currency Format, and Keyboard or Input Method (refer to Figure 14-2). Once you have input your settings for Step 1, you must click **Next**, and then on the next screen click **Install Now**.

Step 2.   Accept the license terms.

Step 3.   Select whether you are doing an Upgrade or a Custom install, which includes a clean installation. If you are installing to a computer with no operating system, the Upgrade option will be disabled.

Step 4.   Select where to install Windows 7. From here you can select the drive, and administer partitions as you see fit. If necessary, you can also load third-party drivers for the media (hard drive) to be installed to.

The system automatically copies files from the DVD, expands those files, installs features and updates, and completes the installation. It displays a checklist on the left side of the installation window during the process, and then prompts you to continue as listed.

Step 5.   Select a user name and computer name.

Step 6.   Enter a password and password hint.

Step 7.   Enter the product key and specify whether to automatically activate Windows (can be delayed up to 30 days).

Step 8.   Configure Windows Update to **Use Recommended Settings**, **Install Important Updates Only**, or **Ask Me Later**. (Use Recommended Settings will automatically enable Windows Updates, Windows Defender, updated drivers, and the phishing filter for Internet Explorer.)

Step 9.   Set the time zone, time, and date.

Step 10.   Set the computer's location: either home, work, or public location. If you choose Home and you already have a homegroup running (a network only for Windows 7 computers), you will be prompted to select what you want to share and to enter the homegroup password. Enter the password and click **Next**, or click **Skip** to join the homegroup later.

Now it's time to start Windows. Your desktop appears. You can use Welcome Center (on the Start menu) to transfer files and settings or add users. To adjust screen resolution, right-click an empty portion of the desktop, select Screen Resolution, and choose the desired resolution.

Starting a Clean Installation of Windows Vista from the Distribution DVD

There are two ways to perform a clean install of Windows Vista from the distribution DVD:

■ Install Windows Vista by running the Setup program from within the current version of Windows. (This is the recommended method.) Insert the Windows Vista DVD. The disc will most likely autorun and you will see the setup screen shown in Figure 14-3. Otherwise, go to the DVD drive in Windows Explorer and double-click the **setup.exe** file to start the installation.

■ Boot the computer from the Windows Vista DVD. This is necessary if no operating system exists on the computer. If you choose this option, follow these steps:

Step 1.   Make sure the DVD drive is configured as the first boot device in the system BIOS.

Step 2.   Insert the Windows Vista DVD into the system's DVD drive. (If the drive won't open while in the BIOS, insert the disc immediately after saving the BIOS.)

Step 3.   Save the BIOS and restart the system.

Step 4.   The DVD should boot automatically and start the installation, but if you are prompted to boot from the DVD, press any key.

Figure 14-3   Windows Vista Installation Screen.

NOTE   Microsoft recommends that the DVD-ROM be used for installations of Windows Vista; however, it is possible to order a CD-ROM version, if you can provide proof of purchase. To do so, visit this site: http://www.microsoft.com/windowsvista/1033/ordermedia/default.mspx.

Keep in mind that unattended installations of Vista from CD-ROM are not possible due to the fact that the Vista files span multiple CDs. This link also enables you to order 64-bit installation media for versions of Windows Vista other than Ultimate (Ultimate ships with both 32-bit and 64-bit media).

The Windows Vista installation is much easier and more simplified than earlier versions of Windows. After the installation has begun, you should see a GUI-based window like the one in Figure 14-4.

When you run a default installation of Windows Vista from the distribution DVD, you are prompted to provide the following information during the process, in this order:

Step 1.   Specify Language to Install, Time and Currency Format, and Keyboard or Input Method. At this time there is also an option to learn more about the installation by clicking the **What to Know Before Installing Windows** link. Once you have input your settings for Step 1, you must click **Next**, and then on the next screen click **Install Now**.

Figure 14-4   Windows Vista initial Install Windows screen.

Step 2.   Enter the product key and whether to automatically activate Windows (can be delayed up to 30 days).

Step 3.   Accept the license terms.

Step 4.   Select whether you are doing an Upgrade or a Custom install, which includes a clean installation. If you are installing to a computer with no operating system, the Upgrade option will be disabled.

Step 5.   Specify where to install Windows Vista. From here you can select the drive, and administer partitions as you see fit. If necessary, you can also load third-party drivers for the media (hard drive) to be installed to.

The system automatically copies files from the DVD, expands those files, installs features and updates, and completes the installation. The system might have to restart several times during this installation process (for example, after it installs updates and after it completes the installation), but you can let the Vista installation work its magic until you get to the next step:

Step 6.   Select a user name, password, and picture.

Step 7.   Select a computer name and desktop background.

Step 8.   Configure Windows Update to **Use Recommended Settings**, **Install Important Updates Only**, or **Ask Me Later**. (Use Recommended Settings will automatically enable Windows Updates, Windows Defender, updated drivers, and the phishing filter for Internet Explorer.)

Step 9.   Set the time zone, time and date.

Step 10.   Set the computer's location: either home, work, or public location.

Now it's time to start Windows. Vista will check the computer's performance (which might take a while), and then ask you for your password (if you opted to use one), before you can access Vista. After you have logged on with the proper password, the Welcome Center window should appear and you can continue with initial tasks such as connecting to the Internet or transferring files and settings.

Installing Windows XP from the Distribution CD

To start the install process from the Windows XP distribution CD, follow these steps:

Step 1.   Make sure the CD or DVD drive is configured as the first boot device in the system BIOS.

Step 2.   Insert the Windows XP CD in the system's CD or DVD drive.

Step 3.   Restart the system.

Step 4.   When prompted to boot from CD press any key.

When you install Windows XP from the distribution CD, you are prompted to provide the following information during the process, in this order:

Step 1.   Specify the location of drivers for mass storage devices if needed.

Step 2.   Accept of the end-user license agreement.

Step 3.   If installing from an upgrade version, provide a CD from a previous version of Windows when prompted.

Step 4.   Specify the location for the installation.

Step 5.   Specify the file system (if installing to an unpartitioned location); NTFS is recommended.

   After the system reboots, the installer switches to graphics mode, and the process continues:

Step 6.   Specify the correct regional settings (languages, keyboard layout).

Step 7.   Enter the user and company name.

Step 8.   Enter the product key.

Step 9.   Enter the computer name.

Step 10.   Enter the Administrator password.

Step 11.   Provide dialing information (if the computer has a modem installed).

Step 12.   Specify the correct date, time, time zone, daylight savings adjustments.

Step 13.   Specify network settings (if the computer has a network adapter installed).

Step 14.   Specify the correct workgroup or domain name.

Step 15.   Specify whether to activate Windows (can be delayed up to 30 days).

At the end of the process, the Windows desktop appears. Remove the Windows XP CD.

For more information about attended and unattended installations, dialing information, and network settings, see "Installation Method Options," later in this chapter. For more information about drivers for mass storage devices, see "Providing Device Drivers During Installation," later in this chapter. For more information about preparing the hard disk for installation and the file system to select, see "Preparing the Hard Disk for Installation," in this chapter.

Network Drive Installation

You can install Windows from a network drive by starting the computer with a network client and logging on to the server to start the process. If you want to automate the process, Windows 7, Vista, XP, and 2000 can all be installed from a network drive automatically using either Windows Deployment Services (made specifically for deploying Windows Vista), which can be installed on Windows Server 2008/2003, or the Remote Installation Services (RIS) program, which can be installed on Windows Server 2003 and Windows 2000 Server.

These two server-based programs work along with the Windows System Image Manager program (for Vista/7), or the Setup Manager Wizard found on the Windows XP and 2000 CD-ROMs. These programs are used to create an answer file. The answer file provides the responses needed for the installation. In Windows Vista and Windows 7, there is a single answer file that is XML-based called **Unattend.xml**. In Windows XP/2000 the answer files are text-based—for example, **Unattend.txt**. For more information on how this works and the differences between Vista and XP, visit http://technet.microsoft.com/en-us/library/cc765993.aspx.

NOTE   The Windows System Image Manager (SIM) for Vista and Windows 7 is part of the Windows Automated Installation Kit (AIK), which can be downloaded from Microsoft's website—search for "Windows Automated Installation Kit (AIK)." For a free CBT tutorial on how to use WSIM, search the Microsoft TechNet for "Windows Vista Virtual Lab Express: Windows System Image Manager Overview."

Disk Image

Windows can be installed from a disk image of another installation created with a program such as Acronis True Image or Norton Ghost. This process is called *disk cloning*.

For disk cloning to work, the systems must be identical in every major feature, including

- Same motherboard

- Same SATA, ATA/IDE, or SCSI host adapter

- Same BIOS configuration

At a Windows software level, the systems must use the same Hardware Abstraction Layer (HAL) and the same `Ntoskrnl.exe` (NT kernel) file.

The hard disk of the target for a cloned installation must be at least as large as the original system, if not larger.

CAUTION Do *not* use disk cloning to make illegal copies of Windows. You can use disk-cloning software legally to make a backup copy of your installation, but if you want to duplicate the installation on another PC, make sure you are cloning a system created with a multiple-computer license for Windows and make sure that you do not exceed the number of systems covered by that license, or make sure you have the correct license number (Product key) for each duplicate system. You can clone standalone computers or those connected to a workgroup (but not those that are members of a domain).

A cloned system is identical in every way to the original, including having the same Security Identifier (SID). This can cause conflicts in a network. The SID and other differences in network configuration between the original and a cloned system can be automatically configured with the Sysprep utility from Microsoft. The Sysprep utility for Windows 7 and Vista is installed with the operating system and can be found by navigating to `C:\Windows\System32\Sysprep`. The Sysprep utility is available in separate versions for Windows XP and 2000. It is not provided on upgrade versions, but on full and OEM versions of the media, and is located on the CD-ROM at `\SUPPORT\TOOLS\` in a cabinet file called `DEPLOY.CAB`. The most recent version of Sysprep for Windows XP can also be downloaded from the Microsoft website as part of the Windows XP Service Pack 2 Deployment Tools. See the following link for more information: http://support.microsoft.com/kb/838080.

Sysprep is installed on a system that will be used for cloning before it is cloned. A special mini-Setup Wizard starts on the cloned computer the first time it is run after cloning. Sysprep uses an answer file created with either the System Image Manager

(SIM), or the Setup Manager (Setupmgr.exe) utility described earlier. When it runs on the cloned system, it creates a unique SID and makes other changes as needed to the network configuration of the system. If the answer file does not have the answer needed by the setup program, you will be prompted to provide this information, such as the Windows license number (Product key).

Installing Windows from a Recovery DVD/CD

Most vendors no longer provide a full installation DVD/CD of Windows for computers with preinstalled Windows installations. Instead, a recovery DVD/CD (or sometimes a hidden hard disk partition, or both) containing a special image of the Windows installation is provided. Systems that store the image on a hidden disk partition might offer the opportunity to create a restore image on a recordable DVD/CD.

NOTE A recovery disc is also known as a *system restoration disc*. These special versions of Windows aren't standalone copies of Windows, meaning you can't use them to install Windows on another PC (unless the PC is identical to the one for which the disc was made).

Typically, you have limited choices when you want to restore a damaged installation with a recovery disc or recovery files on a disk partition. Typical options include

- Reformatting your hard disk and restoring it to just-shipped condition (causing the loss of all data and programs installed after the system was first used)
- Reinstalling Windows only
- Reinstalling support files or additional software

After you run the recovery disc to restore your system to its original factory condition, you will need to activate your Windows installation again.

CAUTION You might need the Windows Product key or your system's serial number to run the recovery disc program. Keep this information handy. Note that most systems with preinstalled Windows have a sticker with the Windows license key (Product key) somewhere on the system case.

Using Boot Disks to Start the Installation (XP and 2000 only)

If you need to install Windows XP to a system that cannot be booted from the CD or DVD drive, you can download a file that can be used to make boot disks. Use these disks to start the installation process. The system will prompt you for each floppy disk, one by one, and after you have inserted the last one it should then be able to read off of the CD-ROM to complete the installation. Note that there are different sets of floppy disks for Windows XP Home, and XP Professional, and for the specific service pack that is packaged as part of the CD. Make sure to download the correct version. These disks are available from Microsoft at http://support.microsoft.com/kb/310994.

After downloading the appropriate file, you must provide six blank (or overwritable) floppy disks that will be used for the boot disk maker program. Start the program and provide each disk when prompted, followed by the Windows XP CD-ROM. At the end of the process, you will have six disks that are used to start the system.

To use the boot disks to start the install process:

Step 1.   Make sure the floppy drive is configured as the first boot device in the system BIOS.

Step 2.   Insert the Windows XP CD into the system's CD or DVD drive.

Step 3.   Insert the first boot disk into the floppy drive.

Step 4.   Restart the system.

Step 5.   Insert each additional boot disk as prompted.

The remainder of the process is as described in the section titled "Booting from the Windows XP Distribution CD" earlier in this chapter. Remove the last boot disk and Windows XP CD when finished.

Windows 2000 Professional comes with a CD and four boot disks in the case that the computer's CD-ROM is not bootable. These disks can also be created by accessing the CD and going to the folder called **bootdisk**. From here, simply double-click **makeboot.exe** and the program will guide you through the process of making the disks. To create disks from the CD on an older version of Windows, use **makebt32.exe**.

NOTE   If you can't find the boot disks that you need, you could search for them on the Internet. For example, www.bootdisk.com has an image file for just about every boot disk you can imagine!

Installing Windows 7 or Windows Vista from a USB Thumb Drive

To install Windows 7 or Windows Vista from a USB thumb drive, the drive must be partitioned with DiskPart as a bootable volume and have the contents of a Windows 7 or Windows Vista install DVD copied to it. The USB thumb drive should be 4GB or larger in capacity. Here are the steps needed to prepare the thumb drive on a Windows 7 or Windows Vista system after it has been booted to the Windows desktop:

Step 1.   Plug the USB flash memory drive into your computer. Make sure any files on the drive have been copied to another location, as the drive's contents will be deleted during this process.

Step 2.   Search for **cmd** using Desktop Search and run it.

Step 3.   Enter the command **diskpart** from the command prompt. The DISKPART> prompt appears.

Step 4.   Enter the command **list disk** to see the drives currently connected to the computer. Note the number of the USB flash memory drive (it will be disk number 1 or higher, and if you use a 4GB thumb drive, its capacity will be listed as over 3900MB).

Step 5.   Enter the command **select disk** x (use the number listed for the USB flash memory drive you noted in the previous step in place of x).

Step 6.   Enter the command **clean** to delete all files and other content from the USB flash memory drive.

Step 7.   Enter the command **create partition primary** to create a primary partition on the USB flash memory drive.

Step 8.   Enter the command **active** to make the primary partition on the USB flash memory drive active (bootable).

Step 9.   Enter the command **format fs=fat32** quick to format the partition as a FAT32 partition.

Step 10.   Enter the command **assign** to assign the next available drive letter to the USB thumb drive.

Step 11.   Enter the command **exit** to close diskpart.

Step 12.   Enter the command **exit** to close the command prompt and return to the Windows desktop.

Step 13.   Insert the Windows Vista or Windows 7 install DVD into the computer's DVD drive.

Step 14.   Open Windows Explorer.

Step 15.   Navigate to the DVD drive and view its contents.

Step 16.   Select all files and folders on the DVD drive and drag them to the thumb drive (identified as Removable Disk drive x: - with x: being replaced by the actual drive letter).

Step 17.   After all files and folders are copied to the thumb drive, eject the drive using the Safely Remove Hardware icon in the notification area.

Step 18. Remove the Windows DVD.

Step 19. With the computer where Windows will be installed shut off, plug the thumb drive into a USB port.

Step 20. Start the computer and open the BIOS setup program. In BIOS setup, change the boot order to place a USB device first in the boot sequence, followed by a CD/DVD drive and then the hard disk. Save changes and the system restarts.

Step 21. When the system boots from the thumb drive, it displays the same initial startup screen as if you had booted from the DVD. Follow the instructions to install Windows 7 or Windows Vista from DVD.

NOTE These instructions are adapted from a video made by Microsoft Singapore's Dennis Chung. See it at http://technet.microsoft.com/en-us/edge/installing-win7-using-a-usb-stick.aspx

Installation Method Options

There are several options to consider when installing Windows, including unattended versus attended installations, the type of file system to select, and the network configuration.

Attended Versus Unattended Installation

The processes outlined in the sections "Starting a Clean Installation of Windows 7 from the Distribution DVD," "Starting a Clean Installation of Windows Vista from the Distribution DVD,"and "Installing from the Windows XP from the Distribution CD" are the default attended installation processes. In an attended installation, you must provide information at various points during the process.

To create an unattended installation, you must create the appropriate type of answer file for the installation type. Windows 7 and Vista use the Windows System Image Manager, and both Windows XP Professional and Windows 2000 Professional include the `Setupmgr.exe` program to aid in the creation of an answer file.

In Windows 7 and Vista only the `Unattend.xml` file is created. This takes the place of all the previous files used by Windows XP/2000.

In Windows XP and Windows 2000 the following files are created:

- **Unattend.txt**—Provides answers when you start the installation from a network share or from a command line.

- **Sysprep.inf**—Provides answers when running the Sysprep mini-setup on a target machine after copying the image file prepared with Sysprep.

- **Winnt.sif**—Copy this to a floppy disk to use when booting the system from the Windows XP CD and starting the installation.

Network Configuration

Windows 7 and Vista will recognize and install most networking devices automatically. However, Windows XP recognizes dial-up modems, network adapters, and IEEE-1394 adapters as network devices, but during installation you might receive the following prompts:

- If you have a dial-up modem installed, Windows will ask you to provide dialing information, such as the area code for the telephone line used by the modem and whether you must dial 9 to get an outside line.

- If you have a network adapter installed, you are prompted to select either Typical or Custom as the network type (see Figure 14-5) and specify the network name and type (workgroup or domain name).

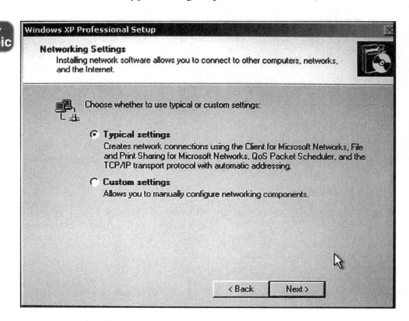

Figure 14-5   Use Typical network settings (default) if you don't have an IEEE-1394 host adapter and don't connect to older Windows systems. Otherwise, click Custom to fine-tune your network configuration.

You should select **Custom** to have the opportunity to fine-tune your network configuration:

- You can prevent your network from treating an IEEE-1394 adapter as a network device by clearing the network component checkboxes for the adapter.

■ You can improve network performance between Windows XP and older Windows or non-Windows systems by clearing the QoS Packet Scheduler checkbox (see Figure 14-6).

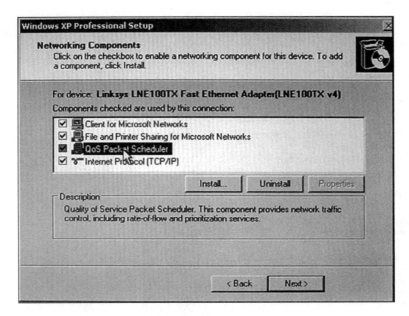

Figure 14-6   Adjusting the default settings for this computer's Fast Ethernet adapter.

■ You can install other network protocols, clients, or services with the Install button.

Preparing the Hard Disk for Installation

There are three different file systems supported by Windows 7/Vista/XP:

■ NTFS

■ FAT32

■ FAT16 (also known as FAT)

Which file system should you use for the operating system installation? With Windows XP, most of the time you will use NTFS, unless you want to install to a pre-existing FAT32 partition and do not want to lose data during the installation. The largest FAT32 partition that Windows can format during installation is 32GB; larger partitions must be formatted as NTFS. FAT16 is supported so that Windows can access other devices such as memory sticks or older hard drives, but chances are you won't come across it very often. FAT16 drives are limited to 2GB if you want older operating systems such as Windows 9x or Me to also access them, or to 4GB if used only with Windows 2000 or XP.

NOTE   Keep in mind that much of the data security of Windows comes from the use of NTFS. If NTFS is not used to prepare a drive, encryption and compression are not available, nor is user-level or group-level access control. Windows Vista and Windows 7 can be installed only on NTFS drives.

For more information about these file systems as well as exFAT (FAT64), see the section titled "File Systems" in Chapter 13, "Using and Managing Windows."

When prompted, you have the option to use all the unpartitioned space on an empty hard disk for Windows or to use only a part of the space.

In Windows Vista and Windows 7:

- To use all of the space in the disk, make sure that the disk and partition you want is highlighted and click **Next** (see Figure 14-7).

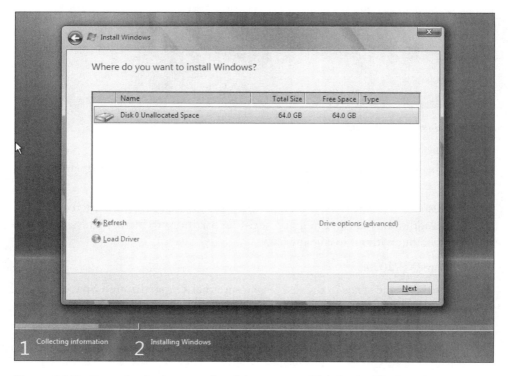

Figure 14-7   Example of using an entire disk as one partition for the Windows Vista Installation.

- To use only part of the space, click **Drive Options (Advanced)**, click **New**, specify the partition size, and click **Apply** (See Figure 14-8 and Figure 14-9).

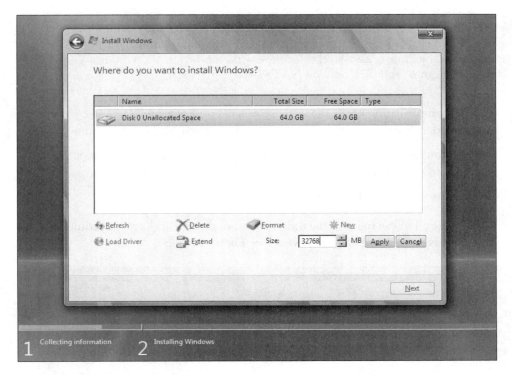

Figure 14-8   Specifying a partition size.

■ To use an existing partition, highlight the desired partition and click **Next**. Be careful; whatever partition you select for the installation will be formatted, and all data on that partition will be erased.

You can also format partitions from here; they are automatically formatted as NTFS. In addition, you can extend pre-existing partitions to increase the size of the partition but without losing any data.

In Windows XP/2000:

■ To use all of the space in the disk, make sure that **Unpartitioned Space** is highlighted and press **Enter** (see Figure 14-10).

■ To use only part of the space, press **C** to Create Partition, and specify the partition size on the next screen (See Figure 14-11). Press **Enter** after specifying the desired size.

■ To use an existing partition, arrow to that partition so that it becomes highlighted and press **Enter**. Be careful, whatever partition you select for the installation will be formatted.

■ To delete a pre-existing partition, press **D**, then press **Enter** at the next screen, and finally press **L** to confirm.

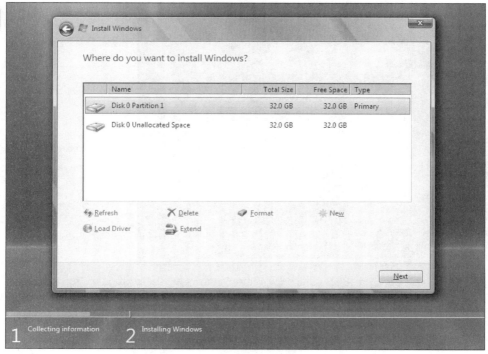

Figure 14-9   Partition table after creating a new partition.

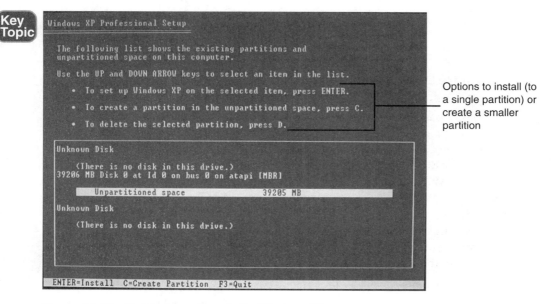

Figure 14-10   Partitioning options in the Windows XP program.

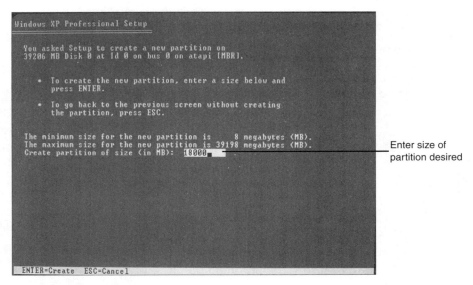

Figure 14-11   Creating an 18GB partition with the Windows XP setup program. You can create an extended partition and logical drives with the setup program, or leave the rest of the disk empty until a later time.

After partitioning is complete in Windows XP/2000, you need to format the partitions. Normally, you would select NTFS. Select FAT if the partition is under 32GB in size. If you specify FAT, the partition will be FAT16 if it is under 2GB in size and FAT32 if it is 2GB or larger. Windows XP offers the option to perform a quick format (saves time) or a regular format (takes longer but verifies the entire disk surface). Windows formats the partition with the file system you specify and continues the installation process.

Providing Device Drivers During Installation

In Windows 7 and Vista, device drivers are added within the same screen where partitioning was done by clicking **Load Driver**. These could be drivers for SATA or SCSI controllers, or other special hard disk controllers (such as RAID controllers). These drivers can come from floppy disk, CD, DVD, or USB flash drive. Microsoft recommends that before you install, you check if the devices you wish to use are listed at the Windows Vista Compatibility Center (http://www.microsoft.com/windows/compatibility/) or at the Windows Logo'd Products List (http://winqual.microsoft.com/HCL/Default.aspx?m=v [for Vista] or http://winqual.microsoft.com/HCL/Default.aspx?m=7 [for 7]). If you click **Load Driver** and cannot supply a proper driver for Windows Vista or Windows 7, or if the computer cannot read the media where the driver is stored, you will have to exit the installation program.

In Windows XP/2000, very early in the installation process, the status line at the bottom of the screen displays a prompt to press F6 if you need to provide drivers for the drive that will be used for the installation, such as an SATA or SCSI hard disk, a PATA hard disk connected to an adapter card, or a RAID array (see Figure 14-12).

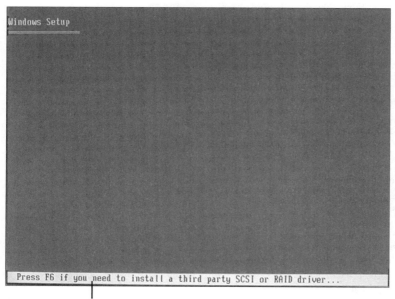

Prompt to install mass storage drivers

Figure 14-12 As soon as the Windows XP or 2000 setup program starts, you have only a few moments to press F6 if you need to install a third-party SCSI or RAID driver (or Serial ATA driver).

If you don't provide a driver when prompted and Windows cannot display your drive as an installation target, exit the installation program, restart it, and provide the driver when prompted. The driver must be provided on a floppy disk. Windows XP/2000 will not recognize a driver provided on a USB flash memory drive, CD, or DVD. Be sure to check for hardware compatibility with the Windows XP Logo'd list (formerly the HCL):
http://winqual.microsoft.com/HCL/Default.aspx?m=x.

NOTE If the SATA host adapter used by your hard disk is incorporated into the system chipset on the motherboard, you might not need to provide a driver.

Verifying Installation

At the end of the installation process, you should test the system by running Windows Explorer, running built-in programs such as Paint and WordPad, and connecting to the Internet. Make sure you don't see popup error messages or errors within the Event Viewer. If the installation process doesn't complete properly, you should check the log files to determine the problem.

Let's talk about Windows XP log files first. In Windows XP, most of these files are plain text, and are stored in the `%systemroot%` folder of the operating system. The `%systemroot%` folder is a variable that indicates the folder where the operating system was installed. In most cases this will be C:\Windows, which we will assume for Table 14-4. This table describes the most important log files you need to know for the exam, and their location within the operating system.

Table 14-4   Windows XP Installation Log Files

Log file	Description	Location
setuperr.log	Records errors (if any) during installation; check this one first if an installation fails. A file size of zero bytes indicates no errors during installation.	C:\Windows
setuplog.txt	Records events during the text-mode portion of installation.	C:\Windows
setupact.log	Logs all events created by the GUI-mode setup program (including updates to the system). This file doesn't use internal data/timestamps, so you might want to make a copy of it as soon as you install Windows. It grows with subsequent installations of hotfixes, updates, and so forth.	C:\Windows
setupapi.log	Records events triggered by an `.inf` file (typically used for hardware installation) from original installation (top of file) to present (bottom of file).	C:\Windows
setup.log	The Recovery Console utilizes this to acquire information about the Windows installation during repair.	C:\Windows \repair
comsetup.log	Installation information about Optional Component Manager and COM+ components.	C:\Windows
NetSetup.log	Information about membership to workgroups and domains.	C:\Windows \debug

For Windows 7 and Vista, matters become more complicated when it comes to log files. The Vista installation is broken down into four phases:

■ **Downlevel phase**—This is the phase that is run from within the previous operating system, meaning when you start the installation from the DVD, in Windows XP for example.

- **Windows Preinstallation Environment phase**—Also known as Windows PE, this phase occurs after the restart at the end of the downlevel phase. If installing to a new hard drive, this phase occurs when you first boot the computer to the Windows Vista or 7 DVD.

- **Online configuration phase**—The online configuration phase starts when a user receives the following message: "Please wait a moment while Windows prepares to start for the first time." Hardware support is installed during this phase.

- **Windows Welcome phase**—During this phase, a computer name is selected for the computer, and the Windows System Assessment Tool (`Winsat.exe`) checks the performance of the computer. This is the final phase before the user first logs on.

There are log files for each phase; they are pretty much the same log files but in different locations. However, we are most concerned with the last two phases. For the most part in these two phases, the log files are in the same location. Table 14-5 covers the important log files during these two phases.

Table 14-5   Windows 7 and Vista Installation Log Files

Log file	Description	Location
`setuperr.log`	Contains information about setup errors during the installation. Start with this log file when troubleshooting. A file size of 0 bytes indicates no errors during installation.	C:\Windows\Panther
`setupact.log`	Contains information about setup actions during the installation.	C:\Windows\Panther
`miglog.xml`	Contains information about the user directory structure. This information includes security identifiers (SIDs).	C:\Windows\Panther
`setupapi.dev.log`	Contains information about Plug and Play devices and driver installation.	C:\Windows\inf
`setupapi.app.log`	Contains information about application installation.	C:\Windows\inf

Table 14-5   Windows 7 and Vista Installation Log Files

Log file	Description	Location
`PostGatherPnPList.log`	Contains information about the capture of devices that are on the system after the online configuration phase.	C:\Windows\Panther
`PreGatherPnPList.log`	Contains information about the initial capture of devices that are on the system during the down-level phase.	C:\Windows\Panther
`Winsat.log` (Windows Welcome phase only)	Contains information about the Windows System Assessment Tool performance testing results.	C:\Windows\Performance\Winsat

NOTE   For a list of all log files within all phases of the Windows 7 and Vista installation, visit http://support.microsoft.com/kb/927521.

You'll notice that Vista and 7 don't have a `setuplog.txt` file like XP does. This is because there is no text portion to the installation of Windows Vista.

How can you view these files if your system will not start? If Windows XP/2000 is installed on an NTFS drive, you can use the Windows boot disks or CD to start the system, launch the Recovery Console, and view the files with the `More` command. For example, use the command **More setuplog.txt** to display the contents of the **Setuplog.txt** file. Windows Vista and 7 do not use the Recovery Console any longer; instead you can boot to the DVD to the System Recovery Options menu and open a command prompt session. For more information about the Recovery Console and System Recovery Options, see Chapter 15, "Troubleshooting and Maintaining Windows."

Upgrading Operating Systems

During the operational life of a computer, it might be necessary to upgrade the installed operating system to a newer version. Typical upgrade paths that might be on the 2011 A+ Certification exam include the following:

- Upgrading Windows Vista to Windows 7

- Upgrading Windows XP to Vista

- Upgrading Windows XP to Windows 7

- Upgrading Windows 2000 to Windows XP

TIP If you've installed Windows XP, Vista, or Windows 7 on a system that is marginal (slow processor, small hard disk, and so forth), you can remove it if you find it's not performing satisfactorily. Try it and see how you like it. If you want to install Windows XP, Vista, or Windows 7 on a system without hassles, don't activate it until you're sure you're happy. These versions of Windows don't need to be activated until 30 days have passed from the install date, so take your time and think it over.

The following sections cover the process of preparing for upgrading and performing the upgrade process for the different scenarios listed above.

Preparations to Make Before Upgrading to a Newer Version of Windows

To review, Windows 7, Vista, and XP raise the hardware ante compared to previous versions with these requirements. Each version requires more hard disk space and memory than the previous version. Refer to Table 14-2 for details.

Some older systems might require processor, memory, or hard disk upgrades to be qualified to run Windows 7 or Vista. You should make sure your computer meets or exceeds these standards before you start the upgrade process.

When you upgrade to Windows 7 from Vista, your existing application software and settings are retained. Thus, you should make sure that both your hardware and software are compatible with Windows 7.

Although we refer to "upgrading" from Windows XP to Windows 7, the fact is that Microsoft does not offer an "upgrade in place" installation for Windows 7 that would retain your Windows XP application software and settings. However, there's a way to enjoy the benefits of an upgrade in place installation: first, upgrade Windows XP to Windows Vista and then upgrade Windows Vista to Windows 7.

To determine the possible upgrade paths from Windows XP to Windows Vista, see http://windows.microsoft.com/en-US/windows-vista/Upgrading-from-Windows-XP-to-Windows-Vista. To determine the possible upgrade paths from Windows Vista to Windows 7, see http://windows.microsoft.com/en-US/windows7/help/upgrading-from-windows-vista-to-windows-7. Whether you are planning to move from Windows XP to Windows 7 (either directly or by upgrading to Windows Vista, and then to Windows 7) or from Windows Vista to Windows 7, you should run the Windows 7 Upgrade Advisor first. It will determine if your hardware or software has issues that would prevent it from running Windows 7, and provides specific guidance on what to do about it (see Figure 14-13).

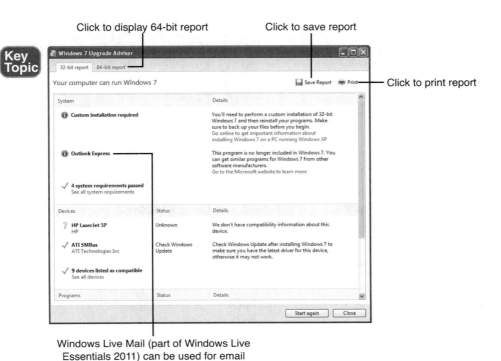

Figure 14-13 A typical report from the Windows 7 Upgrade Advisor.

You can download the Windows 7 Upgrade Advisor from http://windows. microsoft.com/en-US/windows/downloads/upgrade-advisor. In some cases, you might need to update drivers or make other changes to your system before upgrading to Windows 7.

Before you upgrade to Windows Vista or Windows 7, you should also download any new device drivers or new application updates that you need. Create a folder for your updates on your system and uncompress them if necessary so they can be used during the upgrade process. And of course, back up any important files, email, and settings: for example, Internet Explorer favorites, your email program's blocked sender list, or use the Files and Settings Transfer Wizard for the bulk of the files and settings on your computer.

Upgrading to Windows 7 from Windows Vista

Windows 7 is not only the newest desktop operating system from Microsoft, but Microsoft has decided to retire both Windows Vista and Windows XP. Windows Vista Anytime Upgrade (which enabled Windows Vista Home Basic, Home

Premium, and Business users to upgrade to a better version of Vista) has been discontinued; if you want to upgrade Vista, your only current upgrade path is to a comparable or better version of Windows 7. Follow this procedure to upgrade Windows Vista to Windows 7:

Step 1.   Insert your Windows 7 DVD into the DVD drive while Windows Vista is running.

Step 2.   If AutoPlay does not start the setup program automatically, click **Run Setup.exe**. If you do have AutoPlay disabled, go to your DVD-ROM drive and double-click **setup.exe.**

Step 3.   The Windows 7 installation dialog is shown in Figure 14-14. If you have not yet run Windows 7 Upgrade Advisor, choose **Check Compatibility Online.**

Click this if you have not already run the Windows 7 Upgrade Advisor

Click for more information   Starts information

Figure 14-14   The Windows 7 Install dialog.

Step 4.   After checking compatibility (if necessary), click **Install Now**.

Step 5.   Next is the updates screen. It is recommended that you select the first option **Go Online and Get the Latest Updates for Installation (see Figure 14-15)**. There is also an option to send anonymous information back to Microsoft during the install. If you do not want to do this, leave the **I Want to Help Make Windows Installation Better** checkbox blank.

Recommend for best results

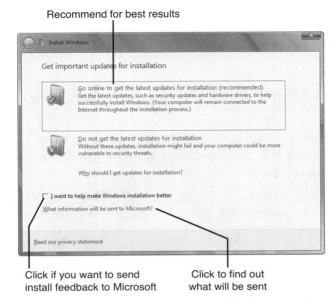

Click if you want to send
install feedback to Microsoft

Click to find out
what will be sent

Figure 14-15 Preparing to get the latest Windows 7 installation updates.

Step 6.   Review and agree to the terms of the license to continue. Click **Next**.

Step 7.   In the next window you have two options: upgrade or custom. Select **Upgrade** to upgrade Windows Vista to Windows 7.

Step 8.   Next, Windows 7 will copy files, gather files, expand files, install features and updates, and finally, complete the upgrade. This will take at least a half -hour to an hour or more, depending on the computer's resources.

Step 9.   Enter your product key. To activate Windows automatically when you're online, click the checkbox. Click **Next** to continue.

Step 10. Select the option desired on the Help Protect Windows Automatically screen.

Step 11. Review and configure the time zone, time, and date. Click **Next** to continue.

Step 12. Finally, select the location for the computer **(Home network**, **Work network**, or **Public network)**. Windows 7 configures its firewall based on the network selection you choose (see Figure 14-16).

Select if you want to create or
join a homegroup now or later

Select for
office networks

Select for cybercafes, hotels, airports;
sets firewall to block incoming traffic

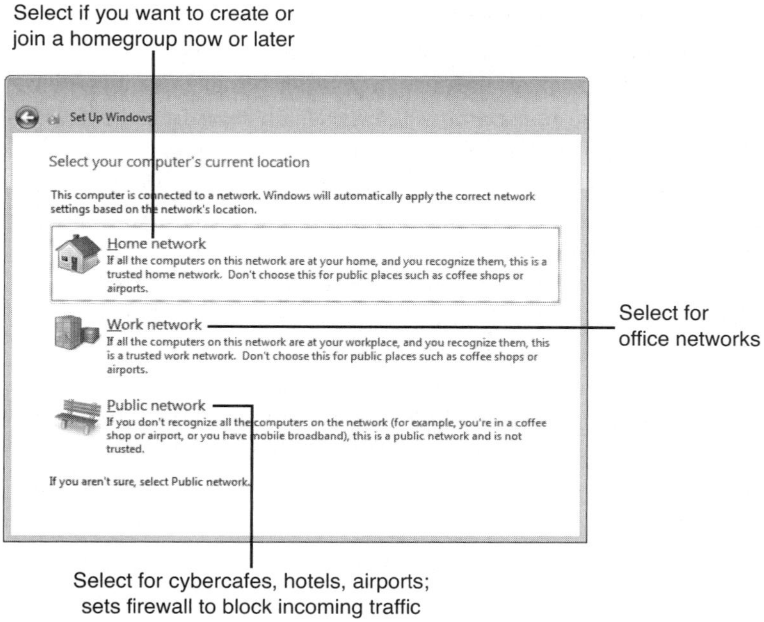

Figure 14-16 Selecting the correct location for the computer in Windows 7.

Step 13. If you already have a homegroup on the network (a secure network using only Windows 7 computers with the location set as Home network), you will be prompted to join the homegroup. Click **Skip**, then **Next** to bypass this step.

Step 14. Login to Windows 7 using the user name and credentials you used with Windows Vista.

NOTE If you elect to skip entering the product key and don't check the activation box, you will be prompted frequently to do so after Windows starts. You must enter your product key and activate Windows before you can obtain non-security updates for Windows.

TIP If you want to upgrade from one version of Windows 7 to a better version, you can obtain the appropriate Windows 7 Anytime Upgrade package from most retailers that sell Windows 7 or direct from Microsoft. To learn more, see http://windows.microsoft.com/en-US/windows7/help/videos/upgrade-to-another-edition-of-windows-7-by-using-windows-anytime-upgrade.

Upgrading to Windows Vista from Windows XP

There are two installation options when attempting to upgrade to Windows Vista. The first is an "upgrade in-place" which means that you can install Windows Vista and retain your applications, files, and settings. This is usually how an upgrade is accomplished from Windows XP. The second is a clean install. This means that you should use Windows Easy Transfer to copy files and settings to an external source before starting the "upgrade." This second option is necessary if you wish to upgrade from Windows 2000 Professional to Vista. Keep in mind that once a computer has been upgraded to Windows Vista, it cannot be "downgraded" back to XP or 2000, the way that older Microsoft operating systems could be; the only way to revert back to the older OS would be to reformat the hard drive and reinstall the older OS. For more information about the upgrade options, mapped to the various operating system editions, see the following link: http://windows.microsoft.com/en-US/windows-vista/Upgrading-from-Windows-XP-to-Windows-Vista. If you want to upgrade from Windows XP to Windows 7 and want to retain your existing files and settings, upgrade to Windows Vista first, then upgrade to Windows 7.

To start the Window Vista upgrade process from Windows XP or 2000, do the following:

Step 1.   Insert your Windows Vista DVD into the DVD-ROM drive while your old version of Windows is running.

Step 2.   Unless you've disabled Autorun, the Windows Vista splash screen is displayed. If you do have autorun disabled, go to your DVD-ROM drive and double-click **setup.exe.**

Step 3.   Click **Install Now**.

Step 4.   Next is the updates screen. It is recommended that you select the first option, **Go Online and Get the Latest Updates for Installation**. There is also an option to send anonymous information back to Microsoft during the install. If you do not want to do this, leave the **I Want to Help Make Windows Installation Better** checkbox blank.

Step 5.   Type in the product key. This was supplied with your upgrade disc.

Step 6.   Next, accept the terms of the license (otherwise the installation will end).

Step 7.   In the next window you have two options: upgrade or custom. Select the first option to upgrade the previous version of Windows to Windows Vista. If you receive any type of compatibility report window (like the one in Figure 14-17) that says you have potential issues, consider stopping the installation for now, and finding out what hardware or software needs to be replaced using the websites listed previously. Then start the upgrade again when you have fixed any issues. In some cases when you receive a compatibility report, the installation will not let you continue, and in other cases you can proceed at your own risk; but be warned, these devices or applications might not function when the upgrade completes.

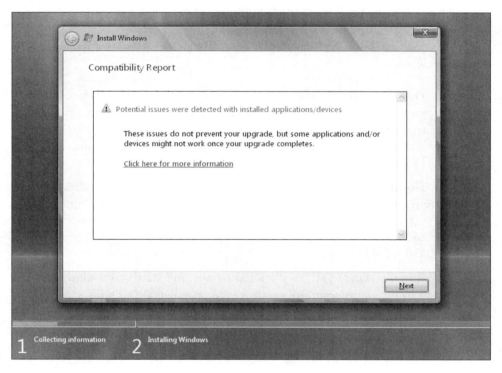

Figure 14-17 Compatibility Report Window.

Step 8. Next, Vista will copy files, gather files, expand files, install features and updates, and finally, complete the upgrade. This might require several restarts and will take at least several minutes to several hours to finish, depending on the computer's resources. Let the upgrade continue unhindered until you get to Step 9.

Step 9. After the final restart you should see the Help Protect Windows Automatically screen. Select the desired option.

Step 10. Then you will need to configure the time zone, time, and date.

Step 11. Finally, select the location for the computer, and click **Start** to begin using Windows Vista.

Upgrading to Windows 7 from Windows XP

As mentioned earlier in this chapter, Microsoft does provide upgrade pricing on Windows 7 for users who want to upgrade from Windows XP. However, an "upgrade in place" method to go directly from Windows XP to Windows 7 is not supported by Microsoft. Instead, you must perform a clean install of Windows 7. Here's a brief summary of the process. For more details, see http://windows.microsoft.com/en-US/windows7/help/upgrading-from-windows-xp-to-windows-7.

Step 1. Download and run Windows 7 Upgrade Advisor to determine whether your system has suitable characteristics to run Windows 7 (free hard disk space, processor speed, memory size, video card, and so on), to determine if your application software will work, and if you need to manually download updated drivers for your hardware.

Step 2. Download and run Windows Easy Transfer to back up your data files and application settings. Use an external hard disk to store your information until you can restore it. Remember, Windows Easy Transfer does not back up your applications. It's up to you to track down your install media and serial numbers.

Step 3. Run the Windows 7 installation program after starting Windows XP. The install program will create a location called WINDOWS.OLD for your current Windows XP installation.

Step 4. After Windows 7 is installed, reinstall the applications you want to use, including any compatible applications previously installed on Windows XP.

Step 5. Run Windows Easy Transfer to replace your data files and application settings, transferring them from the external hard disk where Windows Easy Transfer stored this information earlier.

To avoid reinstalling your applications when making the move from Windows XP to Windows 7, you have two choices. As already discussed, you can first upgrade to Windows Vista and then upgrade to Windows 7. If this is not possible, you can use a third-party program called Laplink PC Mover Upgrade Assistant to perform a direct "upgrade in place" from Windows XP to Windows 7. For more information, see http://laplink.com/pcmover/.

TIP If your existing hard disk doesn't have enough room for Windows 7, consider installing a larger hard disk before installing Windows 7. Use the disk cloning/copying option in the disk installation software provided by your hard disk vendor to copy the contents of your Windows XP drive to the new hard disk. Choose the option to make your Windows XP partition larger than it was previously to ensure there's room for Windows 7. If your current hard disk is used only for Windows XP as C: drive, you can choose the option to use the entire new hard disk for Windows 7.

TIP If you want to install Windows 7 as a dual-boot with Windows XP, you can clone your existing drive's contents to the new hard disk using the same size volume as before for Windows XP. Use the remaining portion of the drive for installing Windows 7. You would start the Windows 7 installation process by booting from the Windows 7 DVD. For more information about installing Windows 7 as a dual-boot with Windows XP, see http://technet.microsoft.com/en-us/edge/dual-boot-between-windows-xp-and-windows-7.aspx. As with an upgrade from Windows XP to Windows 7, you would need to install the programs you want to use with Windows 7.

Upgrading to Windows XP from 2000

To start the Window XP upgrade process do the following:

Step 1. Insert your Windows XP CD into the CD-ROM drive while your old version is running.

Step 2. Unless you've disabled Autorun, the Windows XP splash screen is displayed. Choose **Install Windows XP**, **Perform Additional Tasks**, or **Check System Compatibility**.

Step 3. If you haven't used the Windows Upgrade Advisor on this system, click **Check System Compatibility** as discussed earlier in this chapter.

Step 4. After completing the Upgrade Advisor check (if necessary), click **Install Windows XP**.

Step 5. Select Upgrade (the default setting) to change your installed version of Windows to Windows XP, which enables you to use your existing software and settings without reinstallation.

NOTE   During the upgrade process, you can convert the file system to NTFS. Do this to save space on your hard disk (NTFS is more efficient than FAT32) and if you want features such as encryption, file/folder compression, and better security. As an alternative to converting the file system during installation, use the command-line `convert.exe` program to perform this task after you verify that the Windows XP upgrade works properly.

Step 6.   Read the license agreement, click **I Accept**, and click **Next** to continue.

Step 7.   Enter the product key from the back of the CD package and click **Next** to continue.

Step 8.   The installation process begins; a display on the left side gives an estimate of how long the process will take until completion. The computer restarts several times during the process.

Step 9.   At the end of the process, the Welcome to Microsoft Windows dialog box is displayed. You can use it to activate your copy of Windows and set up users.

Step 10.   After you complete the steps listed in the Welcome dialog box, the Windows XP desktop is displayed.

Troubleshooting a Windows Upgrade

If any of the Windows upgrade scenarios discussed in this chapter go badly and you decide to revert to your old version of Windows, you will need to back up your data and re-install your previous version as a clean installation. For tips on reverting to Windows XP from Windows Vista, see http://support.microsoft.com/kb/925809. For tips on uninstalling Windows 7, see http://support.microsoft.com/kb/971762.

In general, try the following tips to make the upgrade go smoothly.

If you are unable to start the upgrade, check the following:

- **Free disk space**—Make sure your hard disk has more free space available than the minimum requirement listed by Microsoft.

- **Hardware conflicts or problems**—Use Windows Device Manager to ensure that all hardware is working correctly before you start the upgrade or dual-boot installation.

- **Processor speed and memory size**—If your system doesn't meet the minimums, upgrade it according to the minimum requirements listed earlier in Table 14-7. Remember that these are the bare minimums, again, more is better.

TIP   If you receive other types of errors during the upgrade, such as blue screen "STOP" errors, see http://support.microsoft.com and search for the specific error code.

For a list of specific errors concerning a Windows Vista upgrade, visit http://support.microsoft.com/kb/930743.

A useful resource for Windows XP installation/upgrade errors is http://labmice.techtarget.com/windowsxp/Install/installbugs.htm.

A list of Windows 2000 to Windows XP upgrade problems and solutions is available at http://labmice.techtarget.com/windowsxp/Install/win2kupgrade.htm.

Various problems can take place after you upgrade to Windows 7, Windows Vista, or XP from older versions, including

- Can't connect to network or Internet resources

- Can't remove programs with Uninstall

- Certain systems and hardware don't work properly

You should carefully study Microsoft Help and Support articles and any tips from your computer vendor to determine if your particular system might have problems with the upgrade to Windows 7, Vista, or XP.

Because some upgrade problems can prevent you from accessing the Internet for solutions, you should make sure you have performed the following before you start the upgrade process:

- Checked your hardware, applications, and utilities for compatibility using the proper compatibility tools mentioned earlier

- Downloaded updated drivers and application patches

- Removed or disabled applications and utilities that cannot be updated to Windows 7, Vista or XP–compatible versions

- Updated the system BIOS to handle the full capacity of your hard disk and removed nonstandard drivers such as EZ-BIOS or Disk Manager Drive Overlay

TIP   EZ-BIOS and Disk Manager Drive Overlay have been provided as part of older versions of vendor-supplied disk setup programs from most major drive vendors (Western Digital, Seagate, Maxtor, and so forth). Contact the maker of your drive for details of how to remove the driver (which is no longer necessary after you update your system BIOS or add a helper card to handle the full capacity of your hard disk). Keep in mind that you should make a *full* backup of your hard disk in case something goes wrong.

One final point: Many users agree that upgraded computers just don't seem to function as quickly as computers that had a fresh installation. If you can back up the data and settings and re-install applications, consider doing a fresh install whenever possible.

Review All the Key Topics

Review the most important topics in the chapter, noted with the key topics icon in the outer margin of the page. Table 14-8 lists a reference of these key topics and the page numbers on which each is found.

Table 14-7   Key Topics for Chapter 14

Key Topic Element	Description	Page Number
Table 14-2	Minimum Hardware Requirements for Windows 7/Vista/XP/2000.	699
Figure 14-5	Use Typical network settings (default) if you don't have an IEEE-1394 host adapter and don't connect to older Windows systems. Otherwise, click Custom to fine-tune your network configuration.	717
Figure 14-9	Partition table after creating a new partition.	721
Figure 14-10	Partitioning options in the Windows XP program.	721
Table 14-4	Windows XP Installation Log Files.	724
Table 14-5	Windows 7 and Vista Installation Log Files.	725
Figure 14-13	A typical report from the Windows 7 Upgrade Advisor.	728
Figure 14-16	Selecting the correct location for the computer in Windows 7.	731

Complete the Tables and Lists from Memory

Print a copy of Appendix B, "Memory Tables," (found on the CD), or at least the section for this chapter, and complete the tables and lists from memory. Appendix C, "Memory Tables Answer Key," also on the CD, includes completed tables and lists to check your work.

Definitions of Key Terms

Define the following key terms from this chapter, and check your answers in the glossary.

System Image Manager, Setup Manager Utility (`Setupmgr.exe`), Windows Deployment Services, Remote Installation Services (RIS), SID, Log files

Troubleshooting Scenario

You are a technician for a company that is in the process of upgrading the operating systems from Windows XP to Windows 7. You have a mixture of newer and older computers. To be more effective during this process you need to make sure that the Windows 7 operating system will install without any problems. What should you do to minimize the time to determine if the upgrade will work or not?

Refer to Appendix A for the answer.

This chapter covers the following subjects:

- **Troubleshooting Windows**—To troubleshoot Windows effectively, you need to know how to recover from errors and be able to identify and analyze the problem efficiently. This section covers common problems you might encounter in Windows, how to troubleshoot boot up errors, how to fix application issues, and how to decipher error codes and messages.

- **Maintaining Windows**—In this section you learn about image backups, how to configure and install operating system updates, and how to install service packs.

This chapter covers a portion of the CompTIA A+ 220-701 objectives 2.2, 2.5, and 3.4, and CompTIA A+ 220-702 objectives 2.1, 2.3, and 2.4.

CHAPTER 15

Troubleshooting and Maintaining Windows

Everyone has seen or heard of a Windows error. And it's not just Windows; every operating system will fail at some point—it's just a matter of time. Windows has lots of different kinds of errors, from boot errors, to non-critical application errors, to complete failures of Windows known as stop errors. A good troubleshooter will be able to discern whether the problem is software or hardware related and will analyze and repair all of these problems. In an effort to aid the PC technician, Windows offers tools such as the Windows Repair Environment, Recovery Console, Advanced Boot Options menu, and the Microsoft Help and Support website, formerly known as the Knowledge Base (MKSB), which we will refer to often in this chapter. The Help and Support website is chock full of articles about all kinds of problems you'll see in the field; it can be accessed at http://support.microsoft.com. We'll cover all these tools and much more throughout this chapter in an attempt to make you a well-rounded troubleshooter.

"Do I Know This Already?" Quiz

The "Do I Know This Already?" quiz allows you to assess whether you should read this entire chapter or simply jump to the "Exam Preparation Tasks" section for review. If you are in doubt, read the entire chapter. Table 15-1 outlines the major headings in this chapter and the corresponding "Do I Know This Already?" quiz questions. You can find the answers in Appendix A, "Answers to the 'Do I Know This Already?' Quizzes and Troubleshooting Scenarios."

Table 15-1 "Do I Know This Already?" Foundation Topics Section-to-Question Mapping

Foundations Topics Section	Questions Covered in This Section
Troubleshooting Windows	1–7
Maintaining Windows	8–12

1. You have just installed an updated driver for your video card. You reboot the system and, for some reason, Windows will not start. What could you do to fix this problem?

   a. Press F8 at boot and select the last known good configuration

   b. Select Ctrl+Alt+Del at the BIOS screen

   c. Create a boot disk on a floppy disk

   d. Reboot the computer and hope it comes back up

2. You are working on a computer running the Windows 7 operating system. You get a boot error. What is an option you can use to recover your system to normal?

   a. NTBACKUP

   b. System Restore

   c. ASR Disk

   d. WinRE

3. You are working on a computer running the Windows XP operating system. You receive a boot error that the NTLDR is missing or corrupt. Which of the following could you use to restore the file?

   a. Copy and paste from the CD

   b. The Recovery Console

   c. The NTBACKUP program

   d. Use the advanced boot options

4. You have just set up a new user's computer that is running the Windows XP operating system. This user wants to make sure that the computer's system state can be restored in the event of a failure. What system recovery option would you want to set up?

   a. Automated System Recovery

   b. Emergency Repair Disk

   c. There is not one

   d. Complete PC Backup

5. You are contacted by a customer who needs some help. He has a computer running the Windows 2000 operating system. He wants to be able to boot the system if the operating systems fails. You instruct him to create an emergency repair disk. Where would you tell him to look?

    a. MSCONFIG

    b. NTBackup

    c. System Properties

    d. By typing RDISK at the run line

6. Which of the following gives you the ability to recover an operating system if you have a system boot failure? (Choose all that apply.)

    a. WinRE

    b. Last Known Good Configuration

    c. Recovery Console

    d. All of these options are correct

7. You are the technician for your company. You are in charge of maintaining all desktop computers. You need to keep your systems updated. Which of the following would you need to install to maintain these computers? (Choose all that apply.)

    a. Install the latest service pack

    b. Defragment your computer

    c. Install all hotfixes

    d. Install anti-virus updates

8. You have a user who is having problems with her Windows XP-based PC. You inspect the computer and find that the computer is not running an up-to-date service pack. Where would you go to get the service pack?

    a. openoffice.org

    b. msn.com

    c. update.microsoft.com

    d. Your favorite search engine

9. Where would a user go in Windows XP to change settings regarding how up-dates are downloaded and installed?

   a. Control Panel\Automatic Updates

   b. Control Panel\Windows Update\Change Settings

   c. Microsoft Update site

   d. Control Panel\Updates

10. You are working as a desktop technician for your company. You have been asked to come up with a way to protect all users' documents in case they are deleted. Which of the following should you do?

   a. Create system restore points on all computers

   b. Schedule backups

   c. Save all data to a removable drive

   d. Send all documents to a remote location

11. You are the desktop technician for your company. You have been asked to come up with a plan to minimize the downtime of users' workstations in case of fail-ure during working hours. What should you do to make this happen?

   a. Create a NTBACKUP schedule

   b. Perform a system state backup

   c. Create an image backup of the system

   d. Setup a system restore point

12. Which of the following are programs that you as a technician can use to create an image backup on a computer running Windows XP?

   a. System Restore

   b. NTBACKUP

   c. Norton Ghost

   d. Acronis True Image

Foundation Topics

Troubleshooting Windows

A damaged Windows installation prevents the computer from getting any work done. It is important for a technician to know how to recover an operating system by using the Advanced Boot Options menu and recovery environments, such as Windows 7 and Windows Vista's WinRE and Windows XP's Recovery Console. A technician should also know how to restore a system using Windows Vista's Complete PC Backup, Windows 7's Backup, and Windows XP's Automated System Restore, as well as the System Restore utility. Understanding the tools provided in Windows for troubleshooting the operating system will help you pass the A+ Certification exams and solve plenty of real-world problems as well.

Recovering an Operating System

If Windows will not start properly, you have a variety of options you can use to get it working again:

- If the problem is caused by the most recent change to Windows, you can use the Last Known Good Configuration startup option to get things working again.

- If you are not sure of the problem, you can use Safe Mode or other advanced boot options to help diagnose the problem.

- If Windows will not boot, you can use the Windows Recovery Environment (WinRE) for Windows 7 or Windows Vista, or the Recovery Console for Windows XP/2000 to fix the problem.

- If Windows will not boot and needs to be restored, there are various tools that can be implemented including Windows Backup (7), Complete PC Backup (Vista), ASR System Restore (XP), and the Emergency Repair Disk (2000).

The following sections discuss these tools in detail.

Last Known Good Configuration, Safe Mode, and Other Advanced Boot Options

If you are unable to start Windows 7/Vista/XP/2000 but don't see an error message, the problem could be caused by a driver or startup program, video driver problems, or problems with the system kernel. Windows offers various advanced boot options to help you correct startup problems. To access these startup options, press the **F8** key immediately after the computer starts up; this will bring up the Windows Advanced Boot Options menu (which you may also see referred to as advanced startup options) as shown in Figure 15-1.

```
                         Advanced Boot Options

Choose Advanced Options for: Microsoft Windows Vista
(Use the arrow keys to highlight your choice.)

   Safe Mode
   Safe Mode with Networking
   Safe Mode with Command Prompt

   Enable Boot Logging
   Enable low-resolution video (640x480)
   Last Known Good Configuration (advanced)
   Directory Services Restore Mode
   Debugging Mode
   Disable automatic restart on system failure
   Disable Driver Signature Enforcement

   Start Windows Normally

Description: Start Windows with only the core drivers and services. Use
            when you cannot boot after installing a new device or driver.
```

Figure 15-1   Windows Vista Advanced Boot Options menu.

Windows 7/Vista/XP/2000 offers the following startup options as part of the Advanced Boot Options menu:

- **Repair Your Computer (7 only)**—Runs the Windows Recovery Environment (WinRE).

- **Safe Mode**—Starts system with a minimal set of drivers; can be used to start System Restore or to load Windows GUI for diagnostics.

- **Safe Mode with Networking**—Starts system with a minimal set of drivers and enables network support.

- **Safe Mode with Command Prompt**—Starts system with a minimal set of drivers but loads command prompt instead of Windows GUI.

- **Enable Boot Logging**—Creates an ntbtlog.txt file.

- **Enable low-resolution video (640×480)**—Uses a standard VGA driver in place of a GPU-specific display driver, but uses all other drivers as normal. (This is called *Enable VGA Mode* in Windows XP/2000.)

- **Last Known Good Configuration**—Starts the system with the last configuration known to work; useful for solving problems caused by newly installed hardware or software.

- **Directory Services Restore Mode**—This is used to restore a domain controller's active directory (Windows Server). Even though it is listed, it is not used in Windows 7/Vista/XP/2000.

- **Debugging Mode**—This is an advanced diagnostics tool that enables the use of a debug program to examine the system kernel for troubleshooting.

- **Disable automatic restart on system failure (Vista and 7 only)**—Prevents Windows from automatically restarting if an error causes Windows to fail. Choose this option only if Windows is stuck in a loop where Windows fails, attempts to restart, and fails again.

- **Disable driver signature enforcement (Vista and 7 only)**—Allows drivers containing improper signatures to be installed.

- **Start Windows Normally**—This can be used to boot to regular Windows. This option is listed in case a user inadvertently presses F8, but does not want to use any of the Advanced Boot Options.

If Windows 7 or Vista fails to start properly and then restarts automatically, it will normally display the Windows Error Recovery screen, and give you the following options: Safe Mode, Safe Mode with Networking, Safe Mode with Command Prompt, Last Known Good Configuration, and Start Windows Normally. This means that Windows has acknowledged some sort of error or improper shut down and offers a truncated version of the Advanced Options Boot menu.

Table 15-2 lists typical problems and helps you select the correct startup option to use to solve the problem.

Table 15-2   Using the Windows 7/Vista/XP/2000 Advanced Boot Options Menu

Problem	Windows Version	Startup Option to Select	Notes
Windows won't start after you install new hardware or software.	7/Vista, XP, 2000	Last Known Good Configuration	Resets Windows to its last-known working configuration; you will need to reinstall hardware or software installed after that time.
Windows won't start after you upgrade a device driver.	7/Vista, XP, 2000	Safe Mode	After starting the computer in Safe Mode, open the Device Manager, select the device, and use the Rollback feature to restore the previously used device driver. Restart your system. See "Device Manager" in Chapter 13, "Using and Managing Windows." Uses VGA resolution but retains the color settings normally used.

Table 15-2   Using the Windows 7/Vista/XP/2000 Advanced Boot Options Menu

Problem	Windows Version	Startup Option to Select	Notes
Windows won't start after you install a different video card or monitor.	7/Vista, XP, 2000	Enable low-resolution video (640×480)/ Enable VGA Mode	Most video cards should be installed when your system is running in VGA Mode. If a video error occurs, use this option, and then the Display Properties window to select a working video mode before you restart.
Windows can't start normally, but you need access to the Internet to research the problem or download updates.	7/Vista, XP, 2000	Safe Mode with Networking	You can use Windows Update and the Internet, but some devices won't work in this mode. This mode also uses 640×480 resolution, but retains the color settings normally used.
Windows doesn't finish starting normally, and you want to know what device driver or process is preventing it from working.	7/Vista, XP, 2000	Enable Boot Logging	This option starts the computer with all its normal drivers and settings and also creates a file called **ntbtlog.txt** in the default Windows folder (usually C:\Windows for Vista/XP or C:\WINNT for 2000). Restart the computer in Safe Mode and open this file with Notepad or Wordpad to determine the last driver file that loaded. You can update the driver or remove the hardware device using that driver to restore your system to working condition.
Windows is loading programs you don't need during its startup process.	7/Vista/ XP	Boot computer in Normal Mode (or Safe Mode if the computer won't start in Normal Mode); click **Start, Run**; then type MSConfig.	Use MSConfig to disable one or more startup programs, and then restart your computer. You can also use MSConfig to restore damaged files, or to start System Restore to reset your computer to an earlier condition.

There is only a small window of time available to press F8; it's right between the BIOS and when the normal operating system boots. Press F8 repeatedly right after the BIOS POST begins. It is important to note that the Last Known Good Configuration option will only be helpful before a successful logon occurs. After a user logs on, that becomes the last known good logon. It is recommended that you attempt to repair a computer with the Advanced Boot Options *before* using Windows 7 or Vista's System Recovery Options, or Windows XP/2000's Recovery Console.

Windows Recovery Environment (WinRE)

Windows Recovery Environment (WinRE) is a set of tools included in Windows 7, Windows Vista, Windows Server 2008, and other upcoming Windows operating systems. It takes the place of the Recovery Console used in Windows XP/2000. Also known as System Recovery Options, WinRE's purpose is to recover Windows from errors that prevent it from booting. These are three possible ways to access WinRE:

- Option 1—Booting to the Windows 7 or Vista DVD

- Option 2—Booting to the Windows 7 System Repair CD

- Option 3—Booting to a special partition on the hard drive that has WinRE installed

The first option is more common with an individual computer that has Windows 7 or Vista installed; for example, if you performed a clean installation with the standard Windows 7 or Vista DVD and made no modifications to it. To start WinRE, make sure that the DVD drive is first in the boot order of the BIOS, boot to the Windows 7 or Vista DVD (as if you were starting the installation), choose your language settings and click **Next**, and then select **Repair Your Computer**, which you will find at the lower-left corner of the screen.

CAUTION   Important! Do not select **Install Now**. That would begin the process of reinstalling Windows on your hard drive.

The second option uses a CD created by the Windows 7 user. To create a System Repair CD, open the Backup and Restore Center in Control Panel, click the Create a System Repair disc link, and follow the prompts to insert a blank writable CD and label it. You must use a disc made from a 32-bit Windows 7 repair disc to repair a 32-bit installation, and a 64-bit Windows 7 repair disc to repair a 64-bit system.

On Windows Vista, the third option is used by OEMs (original equipment manufacturers) so that users can access WinRE without having to search for, and boot off of, a Windows Vista DVD. These OEMs (computer builders and system integrators) will preinstall WinRE into a special partition on the hard drive, separate from the operating system, so that the user can boot into it at any time. Compare this to the older Recovery Console that was installed into the same partition as the operating system. On Windows 7, the Windows installation program automatically installs WinRE in a special partition.

To access WinRE that has been preinstalled, press **F8** to bring up the Advanced Boot Options menu, highlight **Repair Your Computer**, and press **Enter**. If you don't see "Repair your computer" in the Advanced Boot Options menu, then it wasn't installed to the hard drive, and you will have to use option 1 or 2 as appropriate. Note that you can still use option 1 even if WinRE was installed to the hard drive; for example, in a scenario where the hard drive installation of WinRE has failed.

> **NOTE**   The process to install WinRE to the hard drive is a rather complicated one and is not covered on the A+ exam. However, if you are interested, here is a link that gives the basics of installing WinRE on Windows Vista: http://blogs.msdn.com/winre/archive/2007/01/12/how-to-install-winre-on-the-hard-disk.aspx.

Regardless of which option you selected, at this point a window named "System Recovery Options" should appear, prompting you to select an operating system to repair. Most users will only have one listed. Highlight the appropriate operating system in need of repair and click **Next**. That will display the options at your disposal as shown in Figure 15-2. Table 15-3 describes these options in more depth.

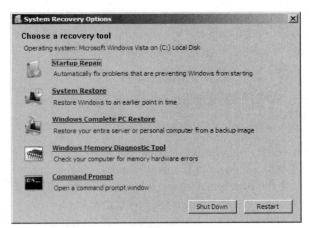

Figure 15-2   Windows Vista System Recovery Options window (most options are the same in Windows 7).

Table 15-3   Description of the Windows 7 and Vista System Recovery Options

System Recovery Option	Description
Startup Repair	When clicked, this automatically fixes certain problems, such as missing or damaged system files that might prevent Windows from starting correctly. When you run Startup Repair, it scans your computer for the problem and then tries to fix it so your computer can start correctly. If Startup Repair cannot fix all startup problems the first time you run it, you can run it up to four additional times.
System Restore	Restores the computer's system files to an earlier point in time. It's a way to undo system changes to your computer without affecting your personal files, such as email, documents, or photos. Note: If you use System Restore when the computer is in safe mode, you cannot undo the restore operation. However, you can run System Restore again and choose a different restore point if one exists.
System Image Recovery (Windows 7 only)	This restores the contents of a hard disk from an image backup performed with the Windows 7 backup program.
Windows Complete PC Restore (Windows Vista only)	This restores the contents of a hard disk from a backup performed with Windows Complete PC Backup (an image backup). Windows Complete PC Backup and Restore is only included with Vista Business and Vista Ultimate.
Windows Memory Diagnostic Tool	Scans the computer's memory for errors.
Command Prompt (Replaces the Recovery Console in XP/2000)	Advanced users can use the Command Prompt to perform recovery-related operations and also run other command-line tools for diagnosing and troubleshooting problems. Puts the user into a directory called X:\Sources. Offers many additional options compared to the Recovery Console in Windows XP/2000; the command prompt in Windows 7 and Vista enables you to copy or batch copy files in both directions between the computer and external USB drives with command-line programs such as Robocopy. Also, you can access any folder on the system, including users' data files.

Recovery Console

The Windows Recovery Console is a special command-line interface that is designed for copying files and performing disk repairs. It is used by Windows XP and 2000. In Windows 2000, you can use the Recovery Console as an alternative to the Emergency Repair process, such as if you need to restore only one system file. Windows XP lacks the Emergency Repair provision, so understanding how to use the Recovery Console is even more important.

Use Recovery Console when the system cannot start from the hard disk because of missing or corrupted boot files, or when other types of missing system files prevent the computer from starting in Safe Mode.

To start Windows XP's Recovery Console, you have two options:

■ Option 1—Boot your system with the Windows XP CD and run the Recovery Console as a repair option.

■ Option 2—While the system is working properly, install the Recovery Console from the Windows XP CD-ROM. It will appear automatically as a startup option when you restart your computer.

To start Recovery Console from the Windows XP CD, follow these steps:

Step 1. Boot the system from the Windows XP CD.

Step 2. When prompted, press **R** to start the Recovery Console. (In Windows 2000, you would press **R** for Repair, and then **C** for the Recovery Console.)

To log into Recovery Console:

Step 1. Select the installation to log into. (Do this by pressing the number that corresponds to the operating system.)

Step 2. Provide the administrator password for the system.

To copy Recovery Console from the Windows XP/2000 CD:

Step 1. While Windows is running, insert the Windows CD into the CD or DVD drive.

Step 2. Click **Start, Run**.

Step 3. In the Run prompt, type *x:\i386\winnt32.exe /cmdcons* where x is the drive letter for the CD or DVD drive.

Step 4. To confirm the installation, click **Yes** in the Windows Setup dialog box describing Recovery Console.

Step 5. Restart the computer. The next time that you start your computer, Microsoft Windows Recovery Console appears on the startup menu. Select it to start Recovery Console.

NOTE For Windows XP Professional x64 Edition, the path to use in Step 3 is *x:\amd64\winnt32.exe /cmdcons.*

NOTE If the C: partition or the boot sector of the hard drive is damaged, you will most likely not be able to boot to the Recovery Console on the hard drive. In this case, you will have to use Option 1 and boot off the CD-ROM.

The Recovery Console contains some of the same commands that are available in the normal command-line interface, along with additional commands that are necessary only for repairing the installation.

CAUTION The Recovery Console permits access to only the following locations:

- The root folder (root directory)
- The %SystemRoot% (Windows) folder and its subfolders
- The Cmdcons folder
- Removable media drives such as CD and DVD drives

In other words, you *cannot* use the Recovery Console to access files not stored in these folders, such as users' data files.

Table 15-4 lists Recovery Console commands and uses.

Table 15-4 Recovery Console Commands

Command	Uses
Attrib	Changes file/folder attributes.
Batch	Executes the commands specified in the text file.
Bootcfg	Boot file (`boot.ini`) configuration and recovery. Can also rebuild a lost `boot.ini`.
ChDir (Cd)	Displays the name of the current folder or changes the current folder. Requires quotes around folder names with spaces.
Chkdsk	Checks a disk and displays a status report. Use the /r option to repair bad sectors.
Cls	Clears the screen.
Copy	Copies a single file to another drive or folder. Automatically uncompresses files from the Windows CD during the copy process. Can't copy to removable media.
Delete (Del)	Deletes a single file.

Table 15-4   Recovery Console Commands

Command	Uses
Dir	Displays a list of files and subfolders in a folder. Lists file/folder attributes for each item listed.
Disable	Disables a system service or a device driver. Helpful if Ntbtlog.txt (the boot-log) indicates a service or device driver is preventing the system from starting.
Diskpart	Manages partitions on your hard drives. Can be used in interactive mode or with optional switches to add or remove partitions.
Enable	Starts or enables a system service or a device driver.
Exit	Exits the Recovery Console and restarts your computer.
Expand	Extracts a file from a compressed (.cab) file, or file with an underscore at the end of the extension (for example .DL_) from the CD to the hard disk.
Fixboot	Writes a new partition boot sector onto the specified partition. Often used with Fixmbr.
Fixmbr	Repairs the master boot record of the specified disk. Often used with Fixboot.
Format	Formats a disk with options for file system and quick format.
Help	Displays a list of the commands you can use in the Recovery Console.
Listsvc	Lists the services and drivers available on the computer.
Logon	Logs on to a Windows installation.
Map	Displays the drive letter mappings. Useful if run before using Fixboot or Fixmbr to make sure you work with the correct disk or drive letter.
Mkdir (Md)	Creates a directory.
More	Displays a text file.
Net Use	Connects a network share to a drive letter.
Rename (Ren)	Renames a single file.
Rmdir (Rd)	Deletes a directory.
Set	Displays and sets environment variables. Can be used to enable copying files to removable media, use of wildcards, and other options within the Recovery Console if the system security settings are adjusted.
Systemroot	Sets the current directory to the systemroot directory of the system you are currently logged on to.
Type	Displays a text file.

CAUTION

Use Help and the command-specific help (**/?**) to determine what options you can use in the Recovery Console, even if you're familiar with how the command works from a command prompt.

Commands in the Recovery Console often have different options and more limitations than the same commands used at a normal command prompt.

TIP If you need to recover users' files from a Windows XP system that cannot boot, even in Safe Mode, consider this alternative:

- Create a BartPE CD or DVD from the same version of Windows, and use its file manager to copy files or perform data recovery. Get more information on BartPE from http://www.nu2.nu/pebuilder/.

- Install the drive into another computer and use the other computer's operating system to access the drive.

Using System Restore with Advanced Boot Options

If you cannot boot into Windows XP, try starting your computer using the Safe Mode option and then click the **System Restore** link. Click **Restore My Computer to an Earlier Time**, select a previous restore point, and click **Next**. This will return your system to a previous state.

You can also start a System Restore with Safe Mode with the Command Prompt option. If you are prompted to select an operating system, use the arrow keys to select the appropriate operating system for your computer, and then press **Enter**. Log on as an administrator or with an account that has administrator credentials. At the command prompt, type `%systemroot%\system32\restore\rstrui.exe`, and then press **Enter**. Follow the instructions that appear on the screen to restore your computer to a functional state.

For more information about System Restore, see "System Restore," in Chapter 13.

Using Windows 7's Image Backup

By default, Windows 7 backup performs an image backup of your system as well as a file backup of files in the users' libraries. It backs up an entire image of your system to the removable media of your choice, for example DVD. You can also choose to create an image backup only. To create an image backup of your PC with Windows 7's Backup and Restore, follow these steps:

Step 1. Start the image backup process by going to **Start > Control Panel > Back Up Your Computer.**

Step 2. Click Create a System Image.

Step 3. Select a destination. Although you can use recordable or rewritable DVDs, I recommend using an external hard disk, especially if you have a system drive with more than 20GB in use.

Step 4. Click Next.

Step 5. Click Start Backup.

Step 6. At the end of the image backup, you are prompted to create a system repair disc (a single writable CD or DVD is required). Click Yes to create the disc, or No if you already have one. If you select No, skip to Step 8.

Step 7. If you answered Yes in Step 6, follow the prompts to make the disc and label it.

Step 8. Click **Close** to end the backup process.

To restore a system from the image backup, follow these steps:

Step 1. Connect the backup drive containing your image, insert the installation disc or system repair disc, and then restart the computer. (Make sure that the DVD drive is listed first in the BIOS boot order.)

Step 2. Press any key when prompted in order to boot off of the DVD or CD. If you are booting from the Windows 7 DVD, go to Step 3. If you are booting from the system repair disc, go to Step 5.

Step 3. Choose your language settings and click **Next.**

Step 4. Click **Repair Your Computer.** Go to Step 6.

Step 5. Click **Next.**

Step 6. Select **Restore Your Computer Using a System Image That You Created Earlier.**

Step 7. To restore the most recent system image, click **Next.**

Step 8. Click **Next** to continue.

Step 9. Click Finish.

Using Windows Vista's Complete PC Backup

Complete PC Backup is the successor to Windows XP's Automated System Recovery. It backs up an entire image of your system to the removable media of your choice, for example DVD. To create a backup of your PC with Vista's Complete PC Backup, follow these steps:

Step 1. Start the Complete PC Backup by going to **Start > All Programs > Accessories > System Tools > Backup Status and Configuration**.

Step 2. Click the **Complete PC Backup** button.

Step 3. Select Create a Backup Now and follow the directions. Have media ready that can hold an image of your operating system, such as writable DVD or an external hard disk. Be ready, this will be a sizeable image that might require multiple DVDs. If your system drive uses more than 20GB of space, I recommend using an external hard disk for backup.

To restore a system from the backup, follow these steps:

Step 1. Insert the installation disc, and then restart the computer. (Make sure that the DVD drive is listed first in the BIOS boot order.)

Step 2. Press any key when prompted in order to boot off of the DVD.

Step 3. Choose your language settings and then click **Next**.

Step 4. Click **Repair Your Computer**.

Step 5. Select the operating system you want to repair (usually there will be only one), and then click **Next**.

NOTE If you are restoring a 64-bit system using a 32-bit Complete PC backup or a 32-bit system using a 64-bit Complete PC backup and have more than one operating system installed, do not select an operating system. If an operating system is selected by default, clear the selection by clicking a blank area of the window, and then click **Next**.

Step 6. On the System Recovery Options menu, click **Windows Complete PC Restore**, and then follow the instructions. Insert the last DVD of the backup set when prompted to do so.

Using Automated System Recovery (ASR) (Windows XP)

Windows XP Professional does not include a true disaster-recovery backup program. However, the Automated System Recovery (ASR) option in NTBackup does enable you to restore the system state (user accounts, hard disk configuration, network configuration, video settings, hardware configuration, software settings, operating system boot files).

To create an ASR backup with NTBackup, follow these steps:

Step 1.   Switch to Advanced Mode (if NTBackup starts in Wizard mode) and click the **Automated System Recovery Wizard** button (see Figure 15-3).

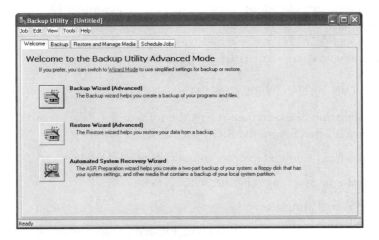

Figure 15-3   Preparing to start the ASR Wizard.

Step 2.   The Automated System Recovery Preparation Wizard's opening dialog appears. Click **Next** to continue.

Step 3.   Specify where to store the backup, and click **Next**.

Step 4.   Click **Finish** to complete the wizard. The backup starts. Provide a floppy disk when prompted to store configuration files.

The floppy disk created by the ASR Wizard contains three files that store information about storage devices (asr.sif), Plug and Play (PnP) information (asrpnp.sif), and a list of system state and critical files that were backed up (setup.log).

To restore a system with ASR, you need the following:

- The Windows XP Professional distribution CD
- The ASR backup

- The ASR floppy disk

- A supported floppy drive

If the computer does not have provision for a floppy drive connected to a floppy drive controller, there are a few USB floppy drives that are supported. The USB floppy drives that Microsoft supports for installing Windows XP (and for ASR) are listed in Microsoft Help and Support article 916196, available at http://support.microsoft.com.

Follow this procedure:

Step 1.   Start the system with the Windows XP Professional CD.

Step 2.   Press **F2** when prompted to start Automated System Recovery.

Step 3.   Insert the ASR floppy disk.

Step 4.   Provide backup files when prompted.

After completing the ASR restore, you will need to reinstall your applications and restore your most recent backup to return your system to service.

Using the Emergency Repair Disk (Windows 2000)

Windows 2000 has a feature called Emergency Repair that can fix some startup problems. The Windows 2000 Emergency Repair Disk (ERD) is created with the Windows 2000 Backup program.

To run the Emergency Repair feature with Windows 2000, follow these steps:

Step 1.   Start the system with the Windows CD; if the system can't boot from the CD, use the Windows setup floppy disks to start the system and insert the CD when prompted.

Step 2.   Select **Repair** when prompted, and then **Emergency Repair**.

Step 3.   Choose **Fast Repair** when prompted. Fast repair performs all three options provided with Manual repair: Inspect Startup Environment; Verify System Files; and Inspect Boot Sector. Manual repair lets you select which of these to run.

Step 4.   Insert the Emergency Repair Disk (ERD) (if available) when prompted. This disk contains a log file of the location and installed options for this copy of Windows.

Step 5.   After the process replaces damaged or missing files, follow the prompts to remove the ERD and restart the system.

Diagnosing and Troubleshooting Other Problems

The ability to diagnose and troubleshoot problems depends upon a combination of technical skills and the ability to interact with clients. Often, a combination of what clients tell you (or don't tell you) and your own detective skills are needed to solve a computer problem.

Identifying the Problem: User Interview

The client interview is the all-important first step in solving any computer trouble-shooting situation. During this interview, you need to determine the following facts:

■ The software in use at the time of the problem

■ The hardware in use at the time of the problem

■ The task the customer was trying to perform at the time of the problem

■ The environment in the office or work area at the time of the problem

■ If new software or hardware has been added to the computer or network

■ If any changes have been made to the system configuration

■ If other users are having the same or similar problems

The number-one question you're trying to answer is, "What changed since the last time it worked?" Sometimes the client can tell you what changed, and sometimes you must "ask" the computer what changed.

During the client interview, you need to ask questions to determine the following information:

■ **What hardware or software appears to have a problem?**—The user might have an opinion about this, but don't be unduly swayed by a statement such as "the printer's broken"; the device or software the user believes to be at fault might simply reflect a problem coming from another source.

■ **What other hardware or software was in use at the time of the problem?**—The user probably will answer these types of questions in terms of open applications, but you will also want to look at the taskbar and system tray in Windows for other programs or routines that are running. Pressing Ctrl+Alt+Del will bring up a task list in Windows that has the most complete information about programs and subroutines in memory. To determine the exact version of a Windows-based program in use, click **Help, About**. View the System properties sheet to determine the version of Windows in use.

■ **What task was the user trying to perform at the time of the problem?**—Ask the questions needed to find out the specific issues involved. For example, "Printing" isn't a sufficient answer. "Printing a five-page brochure from InDesign to a laser printer" is better, but you'll probably want the user to re-create the situation in an attempt to get all the information you need.

- **Is the hardware or software on the user's machine or accessed over the network?**—If the network was involved, check with the network administrator to see if the network is currently working properly. If the hardware and software are not networked, your scope for troubleshooting is simpler.

- **What were the specific symptoms of the problem?**—Some users are very observant, but others might not be able to give you much help. Ask about the approximate time of the failure and about error messages, beeps, and unusual noises.

- **Can the problem be reproduced?**—Reproducible problems are easier to find than those that mysteriously "heal" themselves when you show up. Because power and environmental issues at the customer's site can cause computer problems, try to reproduce the problem at the customer's site before you move the computer to your test bench, where conditions are different.

- **Does the problem repeat itself with a different combination of hardware and software, or does the problem go away when another combination of hardware and software is used?**—For example, if the user can print from Microsoft Word but not from InDesign, this means that the printer is working, but there might be a problem with configuration or data types used by different applications. If the user can't print anything, there might be a general problem with the printer hardware or drivers.

Sometimes, the client interview alone will reveal the answer. More often, however, you'll need to go to the client's work area and evaluate the hardware and software that are involved.

Analyzing the Problem

Depending on the clues you receive in the initial interview, you should go to the client's work area prepared to perform a variety of tests. You must look for four major issues when evaluating the customer's environment:

- Event logs and services

- Symptoms and error codes (might require you to try to reproduce the problem)

- Power issues

- Interference sources

You can select from the tests listed in Table 15-5 based on your evaluation of the most likely sources of problems. You might need to perform several tests to rule out certain problems.

Table 15-5   Troubleshooting Tests and Requirements

Test	Requires
Power	Multimeter, circuit tester
BIOS beep and error codes	List of BIOS codes, POST card
Printer self-test	Printer and paper
Windows bootlog	Start Windows with Bootlog option enabled
I/O Port tests	Connect Loopback plugs and run third-party diagnostics
Video tests	Run third-party diagnostics
Hardware resources	Windows Device Manager
Device drivers	Windows Device Manager

Identifying the Problem: Logs and Services

If the client interview alone doesn't point you in the right direction, check event logs and services.

Event Logs   You can view event logs by running the Computer Management Console (Press **Windows+R** to open the Run prompt and type `compmgmt.msc`). Event logs are stored in branches of the Event Viewer. Look for Error messages (marked with a white X on a red circle) first, then Warnings (yellow triangle). Frequent errors or warnings that point to the same program or device can indicate a serious problem (see Figure 15-4).

Services   Many Windows features, such as printing, wireless networking, and others, depend upon services. To see if a needed service is running, open the Services and Applications node of the Computer Management Console and click **Services**. Check the Status column for the service needed (see Figure 15-5). To start a stopped service, right-click it and select **Start**. Alternatively, you could click the **Start** button on the tool bar, or double-click the service and click the **Start** button from the Properties window.

The Properties window of the service also allows you to change the startup type as shown in Figure 15-5. There are three startup types. Sometimes you might need to set a service to Automatic, so that the service will start automatically every time the computer boots; many services are set this way by default. Or, you might want to set a service to Manual so that you have control over it. In other cases, you might want to set it to Disabled, for example, disabling the insecure Telnet service. This service is disabled by default in Windows Vista, 7, and XP, but you never know who or what may have enabled it.

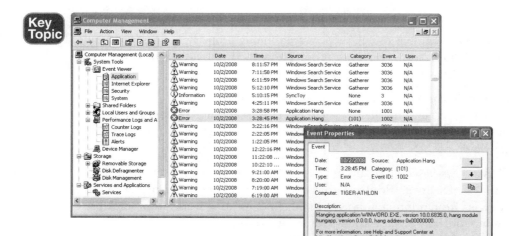

Figure 15-4   Viewing an error message in the Application event log.

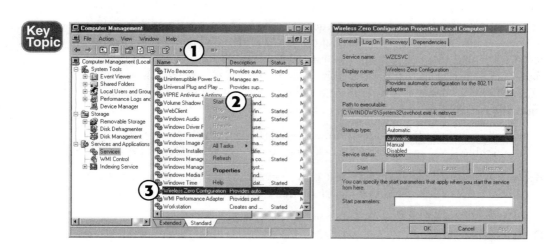

1. Start Service button
2. Right-click menu
3. Status of Service

Figure 15-5   A Common Service in the Computer Management Window and its Properties Window.

Recording Symptoms and Error Codes

If you don't find event logs useful, services are running properly, and your tests rule out power and interference, you must proceed to tests that focus on the hardware or software that appears to be the most likely cause of the problem.

Which test or diagnostic routine is the best one to start with? Before you perform any specific tests, review the clues you gathered from the client. Here's an example: a document in Microsoft Word would print to a laser printer, but a project in Adobe InDesign would not.

Since all Windows-based programs use the same Windows printer driver, we can rule out the printer driver. Printer hardware or driver failures would prevent all software programs from printing; however, in this case, printing works from some programs but not others when the same printer and printer drivers are in use. Before you can solve this problem, you need more information about the printer. It's time to use the printer's self-test (a technique listed earlier in Table 15-5) for more information about the printer.

A laser printer's self-test usually indicates the amount of RAM on board, the emulation (HP or PostScript), and firmware revisions. The amount of RAM on board is critical, because—as you learned in Chapter 11, "Printers"—laser printers are page printers: The whole page must fit into the laser printer's RAM to be printed.

Thus, there are two variables to this printing problem: the size of the RAM in the printer and the size of the documents the user is trying to print. The self-test reveals the printer has only the standard amount of RAM (2MB) on board. This amount of RAM is adequate for text, but an elaborate page can overload it. A look at the InDesign document reveals that it has a large amount of graphic content, whereas the Microsoft Word document is standard-sized text only with a minimal use of bold and italic formatting.

Your theory is to add RAM to the printer, and it can print the brochure. If you don't have a suitable RAM module, how can you prove it?

Because Microsoft Word printed a text-only document flawlessly, you might be able to convince your client from that fact alone that the printer isn't "broken" but needs a RAM upgrade—or a workaround.

Devising a workaround that will help the printer work is good for client satisfaction and will prove that your theory is correct. Have the client adjust the graphics resolution of the printer from its default setting to a lower amount, such as from 1,200 dpi to 600 dpi or from 600 dpi to 300 dpi, and print the brochure again. If a lack of printer memory is the cause of the problem, reducing the brochure's dots per inch for graphics objects will enable the brochure to print. The client will look at the lower print quality. If the client is not satisfied with the lower print quality caused by lower graphics resolution, you can recommend the RAM upgrade. Point out the provision for RAM upgrades in the printer manual if necessary. Remember, you're not selling anything, but solving problems.

If the printer will not print at all, other tests from Table 15-5 are appropriate, such as the I/O port loopback test or hardware resources check.

Checking Configurations and Device Manager

To check system configuration, use the following methods:

- To check integrated hardware, restart the system, start the BIOS configuration program, and examine the appropriate settings.

- To check Windows version, memory size, and processor speed, open the System properties sheet in Windows. The General tab lists this information.

- To check hardware resources, driver versions, and device status, open the Device Manager and open the properties sheet for any given device.

- To check program information, open the application program and use its Help, About option to view program version and service pack or update level.

For more information on using the BIOS setup program and device configurations in the BIOS, see Chapter 4, "BIOS."

Common Problems

The following sections discuss how to deal with common computer problems including

- STOP (blue screen) errors

- Auto restart errors

- System lockups

- I/O device problems

- Application install or start/load problems

- Stalled print spooler

- Incorrect or incompatible print driver

STOP (Blue Screen) Errors

STOP errors (also known as blue screen of death or BSOD errors) can occur either during start up or after the system is running. The BSOD nickname is used because the background is normally blue (or sometimes black) with the error message in white text. Figure 15-6 displays a typical BSOD.

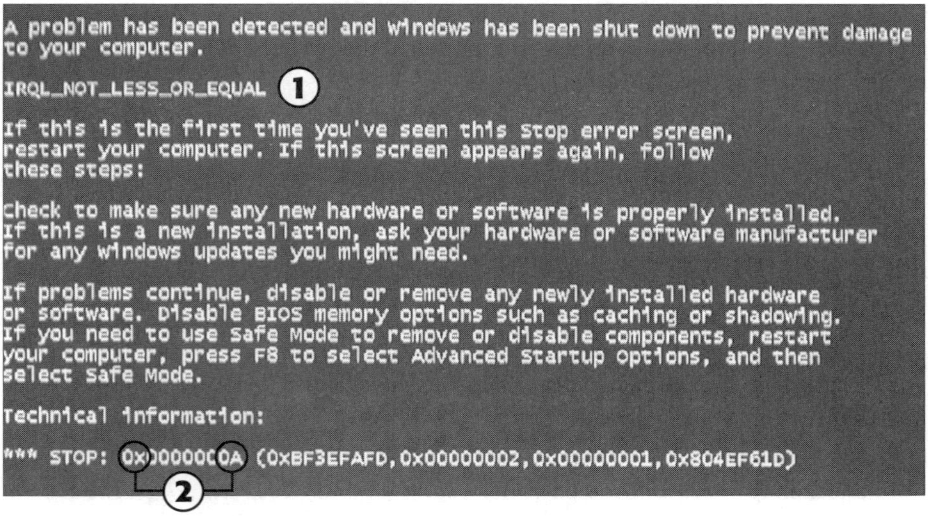

A problem has been detected and windows has been shut down to prevent damage
to your computer.

IRQL_NOT_LESS_OR_EQUAL (1)

If this is the first time you've seen this stop error screen,
restart your computer. If this screen appears again, follow
these steps:

check to make sure any new hardware or software is properly installed.
If this is a new installation, ask your hardware or software manufacturer
for any windows updates you might need.

If problems continue, disable or remove any newly installed hardware
or software. Disable BIOS memory options such as caching or shadowing.
If you need to use safe Mode to remove or disable components, restart
your computer, press F8 to select Advanced startup options, and then
select safe Mode.

Technical information:

*** STOP: 0x)0000C0A (0xBF3EFAFD, 0x00000002, 0x00000001, 0x804EF61D)
        (2)

1. Enter this text as shown to look up the error by name
   at http://support.microsoft.com or third-party websites.
2. STOP errors are often listed as 0x followed by the last
   two digits in the error code, such as 0x0A in this example.

Figure 15-6   A typical STOP (BSOD) error. You can look up the error by name or by number.

NOTE   Regardless of when a STOP/BSOD error occurs, your system is halted by default. To restart the computer, you must turn off the system and turn it back on. But, before you do that, record the error message text and other information so you can research the problem if it recurs. It is possible for the system to restart on its own. For more information on this, see the next section on "Auto Restart Errors."

BSOD errors can be caused by any of the following:

- **Incompatible or defective hardware or software**—Start the system in Safe Mode and uninstall the last hardware or software installed. Acquire updates before you reinstall the hardware or software. Exchange or test memory.

- **Registry problems**—Select Last Known Good Configuration as described earlier in this chapter and see if the system will start.

- **Viruses**—Scan for viruses and remove them if discovered.

- **Miscellaneous causes**—Check the Windows Event Viewer and check the System log. Research the BSOD with the Microsoft Help and Support website.

To determine the exact cause of the error, you must

Step 1.   Record the exact error message before restarting the computer.

Step 2.   Research the error at the Microsoft Help and Support website (http:/
/support.microsoft.com) if the BSOD keeps happening.

TIP   Unfortunately, you can't take a screen capture of a BSOD for printing
because a BSOD completely shuts down Windows. However, if you have a digital
camera handy, it makes a great tool for recording the exact error message. Just be
sure to use the correct range setting to get the sharpest picture possible (normal or
closeup, often symbolized with a flower icon). Turn off the flash on the camera and
use ISO 400 to enable handheld shooting in dim light.

Auto Restart Errors

An Auto Restart error is a STOP/BSOD error that immediately reboots the computer. There is no difference between an Auto Restart error and a STOP/BSOD
error itself. The difference is that a STOP/BSOD error triggers auto restart on
systems that are configured to restart the computer when a STOP error occurs.

If a system needs to be available at all times and STOP/BSOD errors are rare, it
might be preferable to configure the system to restart automatically (different versions of Windows enable or disable this option by default). To change this option,
follow these steps:

Step 1.   Open the **System Properties** window. With Windows 7 and Windows
Vista, click **Advanced System Settings**.

Step 2.   Click the **Advanced** tab.

Step 3.   Click **Settings** under the Startup and Recovery section.

Step 4.   To enable auto restart, click the empty checkbox for **Automatically
Restart** under the System Failure section (see Figure 15-7). To disable
auto restart if it is already enabled, clear this checkbox.

To enable diagnosis of a STOP/BSOD error when auto restart is enabled, make
sure the Write an Event to the System Log option is enabled (refer to Figure 15-
7). When a STOP error is saved to the System Log, it is listed with the type set as
Information (not as Error, as you might expect). To find the event, search for
events with the source listed as Save Dump. The STOP error will be listed thus:

The system has rebooted from a bugcheck. The bugcheck was (error number).

Look up the error number to find the solution.

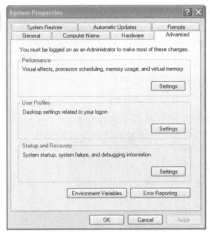 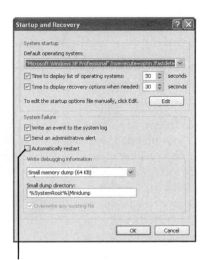

Click the empty checkbox to enable auto restart;
clear it (as shown here) to disable auto restart.

Figure 15-7 The Automatically Restart checkbox on the Startup and Recovery dialog deter-mines whether a STOP error halts or restarts the system.

When a stop error occurs, Windows will write debugging information to the hard drive for later analysis with programs like Dumpchk.exe; this debugging information is essentially the contents of RAM. The default setting in Windows XP is to only write a portion of the contents of RAM, known as a "Small memory dump"; this is written to `%systemroot%\Minidump` as shown in Figure 15-7. Or you could configure Windows to do a Kernel memory dump, which is the default in Windows Vista and 7. The Kernel memory dump is saved as the file `%systemroot\MEMORY.DMP` which is larger than the minidump file. This is where the phrase "My computer just took a dump..." comes from! For more information on how to analyze the debugging in-formation resulting from these stop errors, see the following link: http://support.microsoft.com/kb/315263.

System Lockups

System lockups can occur for a variety of reasons, including:

■ Corrupted or outdated display, mouse, or DirectX drivers

■ Overheating

■ Memory configuration problems in the BIOS

A computer that won't start except in VGA or Safe Mode or has frequent lockups or screen corruption when you move your mouse needs upgraded display, mouse, or DirectX drivers. However, as a workaround, you can reduce the video acceleration settings in Windows XP and Windows 2000. Although Windows Vista and Windows 7 include a Troubleshooting tab in their display drivers' Advanced Settings dialogs, the Change Settings button is disabled.

To access the Windows XP dialog shown in Figure 15-8 follow these steps:

Step 1.   Open the **Display Properties** window.

Step 2.   Click the **Settings** tab.

Step 3.   Click the **Advanced** button.

Step 4.   Click the **Troubleshoot** tab.

Use Table 15-6 to determine the best setting to use for the display problems you're having with XP and 2000.

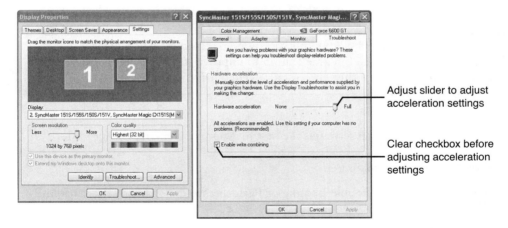

Figure 15-8   The Troubleshoot tab adjusts hardware acceleration settings and can be used to determine whether display, mouse, or DirectX drivers need to be updated.

Table 15-6 Using Graphics Acceleration Settings to Troubleshoot Windows XP and 2000

Acceleration Setting	Left	One Click from Left	Two Clicks from Left	Two Clicks from Right	One Click from Right	Right
Effects of Setting	No acceleration; use when system won't start except in Safe or VGA Mode	Disables all but basic acceleration	Disables DirectX, Direct-Draw, and Direct 3D acceleration (mainly used by 3D games)	Disables cursor and drawing accelerations	Disables mouse and pointer acceleration	Enables full acceleration
Long-Term Solution	Update display, DirectX, and mouse drivers	Update display, DirectX, and mouse drivers	Update DirectX drivers	Update display drivers	Update mouse drivers	N/A

*Disable write combining, a method for speeding up screen display, whenever you select any setting other than full acceleration to improve stability (see Figure 15-8). Re-enable write combining after you install updated drivers and retry.

If you're not sure which setting is the best for your problem, try this procedure:

Step 1. Start the computer.

Step 2. Open the Troubleshooting or Performance dialog box as described in the previous section.

Step 3. Slide the acceleration pointer one notch to the left from its current position.

Step 4. Click **Apply, OK**, and then **OK** again to close the Display Properties dialog box.

Step 5. Use your normal software and perform typical tasks.

Step 6. If the computer now performs acceptably (no more crashes), continue to use this setting until you can obtain and install updated drivers. If the computer continues to have problems, repeat Steps 2–5 and move the pointer one step to the left each time until the problems go away or until you can install updated drivers.

DxDiag

When it comes to making sure your devices are working properly, one of the most important is the video card, and a utility you can use to analyze and diagnose the video card is DxDiag. To run the DxDiag program, open the Run prompt and type dxdiag. First, the utility asks if you want it to check whether the corresponding drivers are digitally signed. A digitally signed driver means it is one that has been verified by Microsoft as compatible with the operating system. After the utility opens, you can find out what version of DirectX you are running. DirectX is a group of multimedia programs that enhance video and audio, including Direct3D, Direct-Draw, DirectSound, and so on. With the DxDiag tool, you can view all the DirectX files that have been loaded, check their date, and discern whether any problems were found with the files. You can also find out information about your video and sound card, what level of acceleration they are set to, and test DirectX components such as DirectDraw and Direct3D. Windows 7 includes DirectX version 11, Windows Vista ships with DirectX version 10 (Vista SP2 can be updated to DirectX 11), whereas Windows XP uses up to DirectX 9.0c. The latest DirectX features are important to video gamers and other multimedia professionals.

I/O Devices

Problems with I/O devices can be caused by Windows configuration issues, BIOS configuration issues (for ports built into the motherboard), cabling problems, and damage to the port itself.

Windows's primary method of displaying I/O device configurations and problems is Windows Device Manager. Device Manager displays information about disabled I/O devices, I/O devices that cannot start or run, and other information (such as USB device and hub power, hardware resource usage such as IRQ, DMA, I/O port address, and memory address, power management and technical information such as PnP identification and others).

Windows cannot display information for ports and devices that have been disabled in the system BIOS. If a port that is physically present in the system is not visible in Device Manager, or if the port has reduced functionality (for example, a system with USB 2.0 ports lists only the USB 1.1-compatible standard USB host controller instead of listing both the standard and enhanced USB host controllers), you must adjust the system's BIOS configuration. For details, see Chapter 4.

Driver Signing

Windows device driver files are digitally signed by Microsoft to ensure quality. The digital signature ensures that the file has met a certain level of testing, and that the file has not been altered. In Windows Vista and Windows 7, driver signing is configured automatically, and in Windows Vista and XP, only administrators can install unsigned drivers. By default, unsigned drivers cannot be installed on x64 editions of Windows XP, Vista, or 7. In Windows XP, driver signing can be configured to either ignore device drivers that are not digitally signed, display a warning when Windows detects device drivers that are not digitally signed (the default behavior), or prevent installing device drivers without digital signatures. To configure driver signing in Windows XP, open the System Properties window, click the Hardware tab, and select Driver Signing.

Application Troubleshooting

Application troubleshooting involves dealing with applications that cannot be installed or cannot start.

If you can't install an application, here are some reasons why—and some solutions:

- **Not enough disk space on C: drive**—Use the Custom Installation option, if available, to choose another drive, delete old files in the default Temp folder, or free up space by deleting .chk files created by ScanDisk or Chkdsk in the root folder.

- **Computer doesn't meet minimum requirements for RAM or CPU speed**—Check for installation program switches to turn off speed and RAM checks, or, better still, upgrade the system to meet or exceed minimums.

- **No more space available in root folder**—A FAT16 drive with 256 entries in the root folder cannot create any more folders or files in the root. Install to another folder, or convert the drive to FAT32, exFAT, (FAT64) or NTFS to eliminate this limitation. Keep in mind that a long file name (LFN) can use up multiple entries in the root folder.

- **Application incompatible with version of Windows in use**—Although most recent commercial applications are designed to be installed on several different Windows versions, some older commercial applications and some custom applications might not support a particular Windows version. If an update to a compatible version is available, update the application and try the installation again with an updated version. If no updated version is available, you can either use a different program or install a virtualization environment such as Microsoft's Windows Virtual PC (for Windows 7 Professional, Ultimate, and

Enterprise) or Virtual PC 2007 (for other Windows 7 editions, Windows Vista, and Windows XP), install an operating system supported by the application, and install the application itself into the virtualized environment. The virtualized operating system and application run in a window on the host PC.

NOTE To learn more about virtualization and Virtual PC, visit the Virtual PC website at http://www.microsoft.com/windows/virtual-pc/default.aspx.

CAUTION Even if you choose another drive rather than the default system drive (usually C:) for the application, a severe shortage of space on the system drive can still prevent a successful installation. That's because shared files are often installed on various areas of the default system drive.

Application Start or Load Failure

Applications might not start or load for several reasons, including

- Invalid working directory

- Missing or damaged shortcut

- System hardware, system configuration, or operating system version not compatible with program

- Program components not properly listed in system registry

If a program is configured to use a folder that isn't available, the Invalid Working Directory error might be displayed. Use the appropriate solution from this list:

- Adjust the program's operation to use a folder that is available using the program's properties sheet.

- If the working folder is on a network drive, make sure the user is logged on the network.

- If the working folder is a removable-media drive, the user must insert the correct disk or CD-ROM before starting the program. Or, if the drive is present but has been assigned a different drive letter than it was originally assigned by Windows, use Disk Management to assign the correct drive letter.

If a program isn't listed on the Start menu or the Windows desktop, it usually indicates that a shortcut was deleted or was never created. To add a desktop shortcut, follow these steps:

Step 1. Make sure desktop icons are visible. If they are not visible, right-click an empty part of the Windows desktop, select **Arrange Icons By**, and select **Show Desktop Icons**.

Step 2. Right-click an empty part of the Windows desktop and select **New, Shortcut**.

Step 3. You can enter the path to the program (such as C:\Windows\ System32\mspaint.exe) or click the **Browse** button to locate the program for which you are making a shortcut. Click **Next**.

Step 4. The shortcut name created by Windows is displayed. To keep the name created by Windows, click **Finish**. You can also change the name as desired and click **Finish**. To create a new Start menu shortcut, see "Start Menu," in Chapter 13.

You might be able to enable troublesome programs to run by using the Program Compatibility Wizard, located in the Accessories menu, to select an older version of Windows to emulate for a particular program or to customize display settings. For more information about the Program Compatibility Wizard see "Application Compatibility," in Chapter 13.

If the program is not listed as being compatible with your version of Windows, contact the vendor for patches, updates, or workarounds to make it work correctly.

If a program worked previously but has stopped working, its software components might be damaged or erased. Reload the program if possible. If the program stopped working after another program was installed or removed, some .dll program components might have been replaced or disabled. You can use the Microsoft command-line tool Regsvr32 to re-register .dll files used by applications.

NOTE To learn more about Regsvr32, see Microsoft Help and Support articles 249873 and 207132 (available at http://support.microsoft.com). TechRepublic has a very helpful article on using Regsvr32: http://articles.techrepublic.com.com/ 5100-6270-1054872.html.

Print Spooler Stalled

Windows 7/Vista/XP/2000 run the print spooler as a service. To restart it from the list of local services, use this procedure:

Step 1. Open **Computer Management**.

Step 2. Expand Services and Applications and click on **Services**.

Step 3. Scroll to the Print Spooler entry.

Step 4. Right click it and select **Restart** from the menu.

TIP Alternatively you can open the Command Prompt and type **net stop spooler** to stop the print spooler service, and then **net start spooler** to start it again. This is a common question in job interviews.

Incorrect/Incompatible Printer Driver

Gibberish printing can have several causes, but one of the most common is a corrupt or incompatible printer driver.

To install a new printer driver for an existing printer, you can use the New Printer Driver wizard (start it with the New Driver button on the printer properties sheet's Advanced tab). This wizard displays drivers for a wide variety of printers and all-in-one units, and includes the option to load a driver from a driver disk or folder.

> **NOTE**   The Device Manager cannot be used to install or update printer drivers; this must be done within the printer's Properties page.

This method might not work for printers that use a setup program to install the driver and all-in-one units, as is common with many inkjet printers and all-in-one units. To install a new driver in these cases, download an updated driver from the vendor's website, uncompress it as directed by the vendor, and run the setup program. You might need to turn off the printer before running setup, as most printers that use a setup program require that the driver be installed before turning on (or connecting) the printer.

If a printer continues to produce gibberish printing after updating the driver, check for cable or port damage.

Common Error Messages and Codes

The following sections discuss solutions for the most common error messages and codes that Windows might display.

Windows 7/Vista Boot Errors

As you learned in Chapter 13, Windows 7/Vista uses the bootmgr and BCD files during the startup process. If these files are corrupted or missing, you will see corresponding error messages.

- **BOOTMGR is missing**—This message is displayed if the bootmgr file is missing or corrupt. This black screen will probably also say "Press Ctrl+Alt+Del to restart," however doing so will probably have the same results.
  There are two ways to repair this error.
  1. Boot to the System Recovery Options and select the **Startup Repair** option. This should automatically repair the system and require you to reboot.
  2. Boot to the System Recovery Options and select the Command Prompt option. Type the command **bootrec /fixboot** as shown in Figure 15-9.

> **NOTE**   A hard drive's lifespan is not infinite. In more uncommon cases, it is not possible to repair this file, and unfortunately the hard drive will need to be replaced.

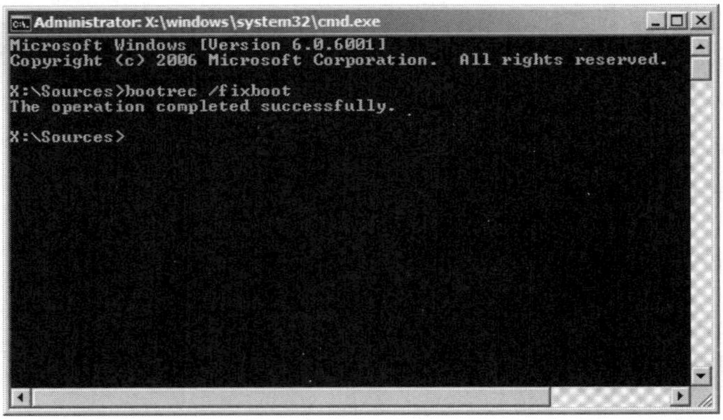

Figure 15-9   Repairing BOOTMGR.exe with Windows Vista's WinRE Command Prompt.

■ **The Windows Boot Configuration Data file is missing required information—**
This message means that either the Windows Boot Manager (Bootmgr) entry
is not present in the Boot Configuration Data (BCD) store or that the
Boot\BCD file on the active partition is damaged or missing. Additional information you might see on the screen includes: File: \Boot\BCD, and Status:
0xc0000034.

The BCD store needs to be repaired or rebuilt. Hold on to your hats, there
are three methods for repairing this error:

1. Boot to the System Recovery Options and select the **Startup Repair**
   option. This should automatically repair the system and require you to
   reboot. If not, move on to the second method.

2. Boot to the System Recovery Options and select the **Command Prompt**
   option. Type **bootrec /rebuildbcd**. At this point the bootrec.exe tool will
   either succeed or fail.

   ■ If the Bootrec.exe tool runs successfully, it presents you with an
     installation path of a Windows directory. To add the entry to the
     BCD store, type Yes. A confirmation message appears that indicates
     the entry was added successfully.

   ■ If the Bootrec.exe tool can't locate any missing Windows installa-
     tions, you'll have to remove the BCD store, and then re-create it. To
     do this, type the following commands in the order in which they are
     presented. Press **Enter** after each command.

     ```
     Bcdedit /export C:\BCD_Backup
     ren c:\boot\bcd bcd.old
     Bootrec /rebuildbcd
     ```

Methods one and two will usually work, but if they don't there is a third method that is more in depth and requires rebuilding the BCD store manually. More information on this step by step process can be found at the following link: http://support.microsoft.com/kb/927391.

> **NOTE**   Various issues can happen if you attempt to dual boot an older operating system with an existing Windows Vista or Windows 7 OS. For example, Vista or Windows 7 may cease to boot after the second operating system is installed. This could mean that the master boot record was overwritten, along with other issues. Several steps are involved to repair this problem. The initial command in this process, which will restore the MBR and the boot code that transfers control to the Windows Boot Manager program, is *X:\boot\Bootsect.exe /NT60 All*. *X* is the drive where the installation media exists. See the following Microsoft Help and Support link for more information on how to manually create an entry into the BCD store for the new operating system and how to troubleshoot this further: http://support.microsoft.com/kb/919529.

> **NOTE**   If you want to install two versions of Windows in a multi-boot configuration, install the older version first. For example, install Windows XP first, followed by Windows 7 or Windows Vista.

Windows XP/2000 Boot Errors

As you learned in Chapter 13, Windows XP and 2000 use the NTLDR, Boot.ini, NTDETECT.COM, and Ntoskrnl.exe files during the startup process. If these files are corrupted or missing, you will see corresponding error messages:

- **NTDETECT failed**—This message is displayed if the NTDETECT.COM file is missing or corrupted.

- **NTLDR is missing**—This message is displayed if the NTLDR file is missing or corrupted.

- **Invalid boot.ini**—This message is displayed if the boot.ini file is missing or corrupted. The system might boot anyway, particularly if there is only disk partition on the first hard disk. However, if the system is configured as a dual boot or if Windows is not installed on the first disk partition, you need to re-create or recopy the file to enable your system to boot.

> **NOTE**   An older message that you might still see once in a while is `Windows could not start because the following file is missing or corrupt: C:\Winnt\ntoskrnl.exe`. This message is typically displayed in Windows NT 4.0 only; the Windows XP and 2000 system file protection features should automatically restore deleted system files such as this one.

To fix these problems, you can

- Reboot with the Windows CD, select **Repair**, and run the Recovery Console (XP/2000) and recopy the file from the CD or a backup.

- Reboot with the Windows CD, select **Repair**, and run the Emergency Repair option (Windows 2000).

- Perform a Repair installation of Windows.

Device/Service Startup Errors

The Windows Registry, System.ini, and Win.ini files are used for hardware and software configuration information for Windows. These configuration files refer to programs and protected-mode drivers that must be accessed during the boot process. If you see an error message such as "Device x referred to in System.ini/Win.ini/Registry" not found, the most likely cause is that the file being referred to has been removed from the system incorrectly. To avoid this problem, use the appropriate option to uninstall or remove undesired programs and/or devices:

- For hardware, use the Remove button in the Device Manager before you physically remove the hardware from the system. Using Remove removes Registry and .ini file entries for the device so it will not be referred to when the system is restarted.

- Open Programs and Features (Vista/7), or Add/Remove Programs (XP) in the Windows Control Panel, select the program you want to remove. This starts the uninstall program for applications and utilities listed on the menu.

- Use the program's own uninstall option or a third-party uninstall program.

Any of these options should remove both the program and references to it in the Registry and other locations, such as System.ini or Win.ini.

If the program is removed by deleting its folder, leaving references in the Registry, System.ini, or Win.ini, use the error message to determine which file contains the reference.

In Windows the easiest way to remove a reference in System.ini, Win.ini, or any startup routine (including the Registry) is to use the MSConfig program (see "MSConfig.EXE," in Chapter 13, for more information).

You can also manually edit the Windows Registry to remove references to a missing device. See Chapter 13 for information on Registry editors.

CAUTION We can't stress this enough: If you are not fully versed in working with the Windows Registry, you are better off not tinkering with it! Although making changes to the Registry can dramatically enhance system performance, it can also result in dire consequences if you make but a single error while working with a Registry entry. Always, always, always be sure to make a backup of the Registry before you make any changes. Many experienced Windows users have rendered their PCs inoperable after fiddling with the Registry. You have been warned.

More Windows Errors and Error Reporting

Windows errors that are less serious than a STOP/BSOD error, such as a hung or crashed application, might display a pop-up dialog similar to the one shown in Figure 15-10 after the application has closed. Figure 15-11 shows a critical error (runaway loop) that caused an application to close. However, the operating system and other applications still function. Figure 15-12 displays a critical error known as a general protection fault (GPF), which also caused the application to fail.

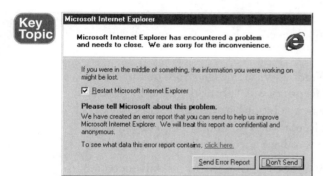

Figure 15-10 An Internet Explorer Error.

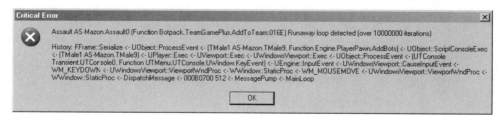

Figure 15-11 A Critical Error.

Figure 15-12   A General Protection Fault (GPF).

As you can see, Windows 7/Vista/XP/2000 can recover from these types of errors and continue to function. More information can be found about the error in the Event Viewer, and in the case of Figure 15-10, the error report information can be viewed just by clicking on the "click here" link within the error window. You also have the option of sending an error report to Microsoft, in the hopes of acquiring a solution or fix.

To enable/disable error reporting in Windows 7, navigate to **Control Panel**, **System and Security**, **Action Center**, **Change Action Center Settings**, **Problem Reporting Settings**. To find out if any new solutions are available, expand the Maintenance section of Action Center and click Check for Solutions. For a computer to successfully utilize this program, it needs to have a working Internet connection.

To enable/disable error reporting in Windows Vista, navigate to **Control Panel, System and Maintenance, Problem Reports and Solutions, Change Settings, Advanced Settings**. To find out if any new solutions are available, click the Check for new solutions link within Problem Reports and Solutions. For a computer to successfully utilize this program, it needs to have a working Internet connection.

To enable/disable error reporting in Windows XP, navigate to the **Advanced** tab in the System Properties window and click the **Error Reporting** button.

Solving Disk Problems

Table 15-7 lists common disk problems and their solutions.

Table 15-7 Common Disk Problems and Their Solutions

Problem	Causes	Solutions	Refer To
Disk access time gets longer over time	Files and empty space have become fragmented	Use Windows's Defrag utility to reorganize empty space	See "Defrag," in Chapter 13.
Data files have been deleted and need to be replaced	User error, defective software, malware	Back up data files with the backup utility supplied with Windows; check for program updates; check for malware	See "Windows Backup Programs," in Chapter 13.
Disk errors causing less reliable operation	System not being shut down properly; program error; disk failure	Test disk drive for errors with CHKDSK; check for program and Windows updates; test disk drive with vendor-supplied program and backup/replace drive if failing	See "CHKDSK.EXE," in Chapter 13.
Disk drives have developed disk errors; reformatting with Quick option does not solve problem	Errors in file system	Back up data from drive and then reformat using Full rather than Quick format option to rebuild sector markings and file system; note that all data on drive will be lost.	See "Format," in Chapter 13.
Hard disk is physically connected to system but cannot be used for storage	Drive is not partitioned	Use Disk Management to prepare hard disk for use.	See "Disk Management" in Chapter 13.

Using Diagnostic Utilities and Tools

The following sections discuss diagnostic utilities and tools and when to use them.

Can't Boot from Hard Disk

Boot sector viruses and magnetic errors can corrupt the master boot record (MBR), which is used by the BIOS's bootstrap program to locate a bootable drive. A damaged MBR will prevent your system from starting from a bootable hard disk. To repair a damaged or corrupted MBR, you can use one of the following options:

- Windows Vista and Windows 7 users can use the Command Prompt within WinRE (System Recovery Options) and type the command **bootrec /fixmbr** to repair the MBR. To repair the damaged Boot Manager program, the command would be **bootrec /fixboot**. For more information on this fix and other related fixes, see the following link: http://support.microsoft.com/kb/927392.

- Windows XP/2000 users can use the Recovery Console command Fixmbr on an NTFS-based drive. If the drive is FAT based, first use Fixboot, followed by Fixmbr. To rewrite the boot sector on a FAT-based drive, type **Fixboot** and press **Enter**. To repair the master boot record with an NTFS-based drive, type Fixmbr and press **Enter**. (If you boot from a different drive letter than the default Windows drive or a different hard disk than normal, you can specify the hard disk drive letter or drive number with these commands.)

Because damaged MBRs can be caused by a computer virus, you should test systems with an up-to-date antivirus program before using either of these commands. If a boot-sector virus is located by an antivirus program, the program's own disk-repair options should be used first. Don't forget that many BIOS programs come with the option to scan the boot sector for viruses. If you have this functionality in your motherboard's BIOS, consider using it!

If this is unsuccessful, you can use the appropriate repair tool to attempt to fix the MBR.

NOTE If you see a message at startup referring to **EZ-BIOS**, **Dynamic Drive Overlay**, or a similar message, it indicates the drive has been prepared using a third-party disk utility, such as old versions of DiscWizard, Disk Manager, MaxBlast, Data Lifeguard Tools, or other vendor-supplied hard disk setup programs. If a system has an outdated BIOS that cannot manage the full capacity of the drive, these programs will install a nonstandard MBR and drivers to manage the drive's full capacity. If systems running third-party hard disk management software can't boot, use the repair program provided by the software vendor, not Windows' own MBR repair programs.

Using Task Manager

Windows 7/Vista/XP/2000 can display the Windows Task Manager (see Figure 15-13) when you press Ctrl+Alt+Del (select Task Manager from the Windows Security dialog box).

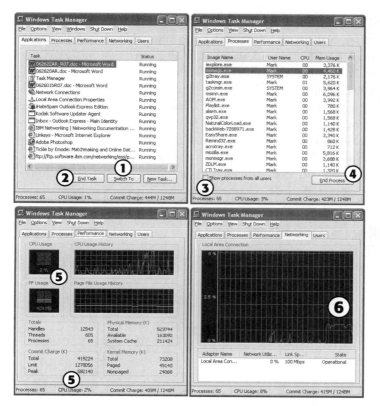

1. Click to switch tasks
2. Click to end selected task
3. Click to show processes for all users
4. Click to end selected process
5. Current CPU usage
6. Network usage history

Figure 15-13   The Windows XP version of the Windows Task Manager's Applications (top left), Processes (top right), Performance (bottom left), and Networking (bottom right) tabs.

Use the Applications tab to determine if a program has stopped responding; you can shut down these programs. Use the Processes tab to see which processes are consuming the most memory. Use this dialog along with the System Configuration Utility (MSConfig) to help determine if you are loading unnecessary startup applications; MSConfig can disable them to free up memory (see "MSConfig.exe," in Chapter 13, for details). If you are unable to shut down a program with the Applications tab, you can also shut down its processes with the Processes tab, but this is not recommended unless the program cannot be shut down in any other way.

Use the Performance tab to determine if you need to install more RAM memory or need to increase your paging file size. Use the Networking tab to monitor the performance of your network.

The top-level menu can be used to adjust the properties of the currently selected tab and to shut down the system.

Troubleshooting with Device Manager

If your computer has devices that are malfunctioning in a way that Device Manager can detect, or has devices that are disabled, they will be displayed as soon as you open Device Manager. For example, in Figure 15-14, the Ports (COM and LPT) category displays a malfunctioning port, COM 2, indicated by an exclamation mark (!) in a yellow circle. The parallel printer port, LPT1, has been disabled, as indicated by a red X. If the malfunctioning or disabled device is an I/O port, such as a serial, parallel, or USB port, any device attached to that port cannot work until the device is working properly. Windows Vista and Windows 7 use a down-arrow icon to indicate a disabled port or device, and an exclamation mark (!) in a yellow triangle to indicate a malfunctioning port or device.

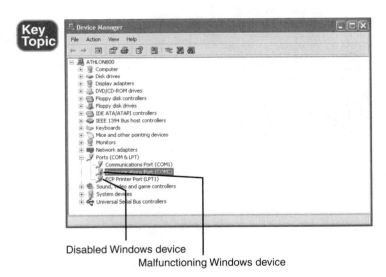

Disabled Windows device
Malfunctioning Windows device

Figure 15-14   Windows XP Device Manager displaying disabled and malfunctioning devices.

Not every problem with a device shows up in Device Manager, but most problems with resource conflicts or drivers will be displayed here.

To troubleshoot problems with a device in Device Manager, open its Properties sheet by double-clicking the device. Use the General tab shown in Figure 15-15 to display the device's status and to troubleshoot a disabled or malfunctioning device. For information about other tabs in Device Manager, see "Device Manager," in Chapter 13.

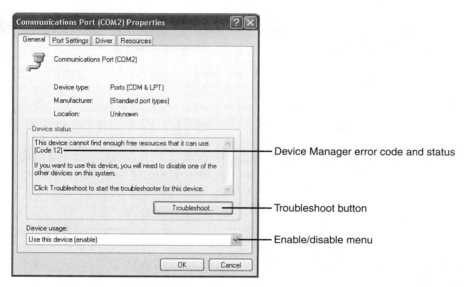

Figure 15-15 A problem device's General properties. If the device's General Properties sheet lacks a solution button, look up the Device Manager error code and take appropriate action manually.

When you have a malfunctioning device such as the one in Figure 15-15, you have several options for resolving the problem:

■   Look up the Device Manager code to determine the problem and its solution (see Table 15-8 for a few examples).

Table 15-8 Example of Some Device Manager Codes and Solutions

Device Manager Code Number	Problem	Recommended Solution
Code 1	This device is not config-ured correctly	Update the driver.
Code 3	The driver for this device might be corrupted, or your system might be running low on memory or other re-sources	Close some open applications. Uninstall and reinstall the driver. Install additional RAM.

Table 15-8   Example of Some Device Manager Codes and Solutions

Device Manager Code Number	Problem	Recommended Solution
Code 10	Device cannot start	Update the driver. View Microsoft Help and Support article 943104 for more information.
Code 12	This device cannot find enough free resources that it can use. If you want to use this device, you will need to disable one of the other devices on this system.	You can use the Troubleshooting Wizard in Device Manager to determine where the conflict is, and then disable the conflicting device. Disable the device.

- Click the **Troubleshoot** button (if any) shown on the device's General Properties tab; the button's name and usage depends upon the problem. Table 15-8 lists the codes, their meanings, and the solution button (if any).

- Manually change resources. If the nature of the problem is a resource conflict, you can click the Resources tab and change the settings and eliminate the conflict if possible. Most recent systems that use ACPI power management don't permit manual resource changes in Device Manager and also override any changes you might make in the system BIOS setup program. On these systems, if resource conflicts take place, you might need to disable ACPI power management before you can solve resource conflicts.

- Manually update drivers. If the problem is a driver issue but an Update Driver button isn't available, open the Driver tab and install a new driver for the device.

NOTE   These are just a few examples of the codes you might see in Device Manager. For a complete list, see the following link http://support.microsoft.com/kb/310123.

If the device has a conflict with another device, you might be able to change the settings in the device's Properties page/Resources tab (see Figure 15-16). If the device is a legacy (non-PnP) device, you might need to shut down the system and reconfigure the card manually before you can use Device Manager to reset its configuration in Windows.

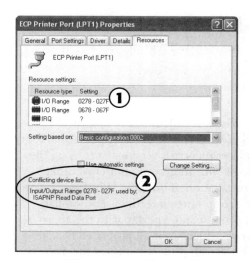 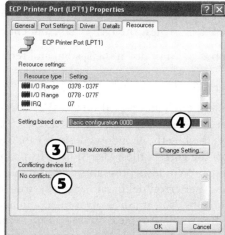

1. Conflicting resource (I/O port address)
2. Conflicting device
3. Can solve most configuration conflicts when selected
4. Selects from various preconfigured settings
5. Conflict resolved

Figure 15-16   The parallel port's current configuration (a) conflicts with another port. By selecting another configuration (b), the conflict is resolved.

You can also use the Device Manager to disable a device that is conflicting with another device. To disable a device, follow these steps:

Step 1.   Click the plus (+) sign next to the device category containing the device.

Step 2.   Right-click the device and select **Disable**.

or

Step 1.   Right-click the device and select **Properties**.

Step 2.   On the General tab, look for the Device Usage display at the bottom of the window. Click the menu and select **Do Not Use This Device** (disable). Refer to Figure 15-15. If you prefer to solve the problem with the device, click the **Troubleshoot** button.

Depending on the device, you might need to physically remove it from the system to resolve a conflict. To use the Device Manager to remove a device, follow these steps:

Step 1.   Click the plus (+) sign next to the device category containing the device.

Step 2.   Right-click the device and select **Uninstall**.

Step 3.   Shut down the system and remove the physical device.

or

Step 1.   Right-click the device and select Properties.

Step 2.   Access the Driver tab, and click the **Uninstall** button.

Step 3.   Shut down the system and remove the physical device.

Using System File Checker (SFC)

System File Checker (SFC) is a Windows 7/Vista/XP/2000 utility that checks protected system files (files such as .DLL, .SYS, .OCX, and .EXE, as well as some font files used by the Windows desktop) and replaces incorrect versions or missing files with the correct files. Use SFC to fix problems with Internet Explorer or other built-in Windows programs caused by the installation of obsolete Windows system files, user error, deliberate erasure, virus or Trojan horse infections, and similar problems. To run SFC, open the command prompt and type **SFC** with the appropriate switch. A typical option is **SFC /scannow**, which scans all protected files immediately. Another is **SFC /scanonce**, which scans all protected files at the next boot. If SFC finds that some files are missing, you are prompted to reinsert your Windows distribution disc so the files can be copied to the DLL cache. Other options include **/scanboot**, which scans all protected files every time the system starts; **/revert**, which returns the scan setting to the default; and **/purgecache** and **/cachesiz=x**, which allow a user to delete the file cache and modify its size.

Maintaining Windows

To keep a Windows installation healthy, it's important to maintain it by installing service packs, hotfixes, and creating image backups that can be used to restore the system to operation quickly. The following sections discuss these issues.

Installing Service Packs and Hotfixes

Currently, there are two service packs for Windows Vista. Service Pack 2 is the most recent as of the writing of this book. Service Pack 2 can be installed automatically via Windows Update, by downloading Service Pack 2 for manual installation, or by ordering a CD. Currently, there are three service packs for Windows XP. Service Pack 3 is the most recent. Hotfixes are updates that can be installed to a computer while the user is working on other things. They are usually installed one at a time, unlike Service Packs, which are groups of updates that should be installed while the user is not working on the computer.

> **NOTE**   For information on all three options, see Microsoft Help and Support article 322389, available at http://support.microsoft.com.
>
> If your organization is not using Service Pack 3 for Windows XP, Service Pack 2 is still available for download. Get it by going to http://www.microsoft.com/downloads and searching for "Windows XP Service Pack 2 Network Installation Package for IT Professionals and Developers."

To download and install a service pack for Windows manually, follow these steps:

Step 1.   Determine whether the system has any service packs installed. You should perform this check even if you have just installed Windows, because you can install Windows with service packs included, and newer Windows DVD/CDs will contain a service pack. Right-click **Computer/My Computer** and select **Properties** to find out the current service pack. The command `winver.exe` can also be used in the Command Prompt to discern this information. Figure 15-17 illustrates a Windows XP system with Service Pack 2 installed.

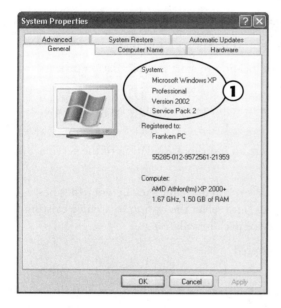

Figure 15-17   This Windows XP system has Service Pack 2 installed.

Step 2.   Go to the website containing the service pack needed.

Step 3.   Read the release notes for the service pack to see if it will cause any problems for your particular configuration, such as problems with networking, winmodems, CD/DVD mastering software, and so forth. Take the necessary actions as noted. (Some might require changes before you perform the service pack installation; others might take place afterward.)

TIP   To save the specific document referenced in the release notes so you can follow up on the problem, use the **Save as Web Archive** option in Internet Explorer. This saves the entire web page (including graphics) as a single file with an `.MHT` extension. You can then view the file offline with Internet Explorer if necessary.

Step 4.   Click the link to start the download; you might need to select the correct language for the service pack first.

Step 5.   Shut down real-time virus checkers such as Norton Anti-Virus's Auto-Protect.

Step 6.   Select **Express Installation** if you want to install the service pack on only one computer (this requires an Internet connection during the entire process); select **Network Installation** to download the entire service pack for use on multiple computers.

Follow steps 7a and 8a to perform a Network Installation.

Follow steps 7b and 8b to perform an Express Installation.

Step 7a.   Select a location to store the file with Network Installation.

Step 7b.   Open the file from its current location to start the installation process with Express Installation.

Step 8a.   Open the file you downloaded in step 7a to perform a Network Installation of the service pack.

Step 8b.   Follow the prompts to complete an Express Installation of the service pack.

Step 9.   You should update your system backup disk and back up your files before you install the service pack, and select the option to archive existing Windows files during the service pack installation.

Step 10.   Restart the system when prompted.

TIP   In some cases, you might need to reinstall third-party applications or utilities after you install a service pack.

Service packs are very large because they contain hundreds of updates and hotfixes. Hotfixes, which are solutions for specific problems experienced only by users with certain combinations of hardware and software, can also be downloaded individually. Once a hotfix is deemed safe for all users, it will usually be distributed via Windows Update or Microsoft Update. However, it can also be downloaded manually or requested by the user. Hotfixes are listed as part of Help and Support (formerly Knowledge Base) articles about specific problems. See http://support.microsoft.com for Help and Support articles.

At one time, it was necessary to call Microsoft to request hotfixes that were not available for automatic downloading. Now, Microsoft provides a link on the Help and Support pages where you can make the request. Enter the information desired and your email address, and a link to the requested hotfix will be emailed to you.

Using Windows Update and Microsoft Update

To install additional updates for Windows through Windows Update, follow these steps:

Step 1. Click **Start, All Programs, Windows Update**.

Step 2. Windows Vista and Windows 7 will open the Windows Update window where you can click the Install updates button. Windows XP will open a web page where you can select Express or Custom installation of updates. Follow the prompts to install the latest version of the Windows Update software if necessary.

NOTE Do not select Express or let Microsoft automatically install *all* updates if you do not wish to use newer applications, for example Internet Explorer 8.

Step 3. The system (or web page) will automatically scan for updates. Updates are divided into the following categories:

- **Critical Updates and Service Packs**—These include the latest service pack and other security and stability updates. Some updates must be installed individually; others can be installed as a group.

- **Windows Updates**—Recommended updates to fix noncritical problems certain users might encounter; also adds features and updates to features bundled into Windows.

- **Driver Updates**—Updated device drivers for installed hardware.

Step 4. Whether you have selected an Express install or if you selected updates desired, they are downloaded to your system and installed. You might need to restart your computer to complete the update process.

NOTE You can perform an Express Installation of the latest service pack only through Windows Update. If you prefer a Network Installation or need to install an earlier service pack, you must manually download it as discussed earlier in this section.

If you use Microsoft Office or other Microsoft applications as well as Microsoft Windows, Windows Update will offer to install Microsoft Update, which provides a common update mechanism for both Windows and other Microsoft products. Once you install Microsoft Update, it runs automatically whenever you run Windows Update. Keep in mind that Microsoft Office uses service packs as well. For example, currently the latest service pack for Office 2003 is SP3; Office 2007 is SP2.

Performing Scheduled Backup and Restore

To help ensure that documents are backed up on a timely basis, you might prefer to set up specific times to back up documents. In Windows 7 or Windows Vista, you specify when to run backups when you set up the backup programs included in these versions. In Windows XP, use the Scheduled Tasks wizard (Start, Control Panel, Scheduled Tasks) to enable NTBackup to run automatically. If you use a third-party backup program, it might use Scheduled Tasks, or it might use its own scheduler.

Image Backups

Windows 7's Backup and Restore and Windows Vista's Complete PC Backup has the ability to backup an image of your system, but Windows XP cannot do this. This is one reason to consider alternatives to Windows XP's NTBackup. An image backup backs up your entire system disk partition, including your Windows installation, programs, utilities, data files and settings, and can also be used to back up other disk partitions.

Early image backup programs could only be used to make image backups for complete restoration in case of a hard disk crash or failure. For this reason, image backups are sometimes referred to as disaster recovery backups, and the process of restoring an image is sometimes called a bare metal restore, because it can usually be done by booting the system with a restore floppy disk or CD set and using the image backup program's restore component to re-create disk partitions and restore the entire contents of the disk. After rebooting, the system is back to its as-imaged condition.

Modern image backup programs such as recent versions of Norton Ghost and Acronis True Image also make it possible to restore individual files and folders and to create incremental backups, enabling the image backup program to work as both an image and file/folder backup.

Image backups enable you to restore a system to operation without the need to perform separate reinstallations of Windows and applications, and can also be used to protect a test or experimental installation from being corrupted by beta or pre-release software. The time required to restore an image is a small fraction of what it would take to reinstall Windows and applications.

> **NOTE**   Seagate and Maxtor have licensed a recent version of Acronis True Image and offer it as Seagate DiscWizard for Windows and Maxtor MaxBlast 5. Western Digital has also licensed a recent version of Acronis True Image and offers it as Acronis True Image WD Edition. These programs can be run from bootable media as well as from within Windows for image backup and restore and new hard disk installation, and will work in any system that contains at least one drive from the same manufacturer (note that Seagate owns Maxtor, so you can use either Seagate Disc Wizard or Maxtor MaxBlast 5 on a system with either Maxtor or Seagate internal hard disks).

Exam Preparation Tasks

Review All the Key Topics

Review the most important topics in the chapter, noted with the key topics icon in the outer margin of the page. Table 15-9 lists a reference of these key topics and the page numbers on which each is found.

Table 15-9   Key Topics for Chapter 15

Key Topic Element	Description	Page Number
Figure 15-1	Windows Vista Advanced Boot Options menu.	745
Table 15-2	Using the Windows Vista/XP/2000 Advanced Boot Options Menu.	749
Table 15-3	Description of the Windows Vista System Recovery Options.	753
Table 15-4	Recovery Console Commands.	755
Figure 15-4	Viewing an error message in the Application event log.	765
Figure 15-5	A Common Service in the Computer Management Window and its Properties Window.	765
Figure 15-7	The Automatically Restart checkbox on the Startup and Recovery dialog determines whether a STOP error halts or restarts the system.	770
Figure 15-9	Repairing BOOTMGR.exe with Windows Vista's WinRE Command Prompt.	778
Figure 15-10	An Internet Explorer Error.	781
Table 15-7	Common Disk Problems and Their Solutions.	783
Figure 15-14	Windows XP Device Manager displaying disabled and malfunctioning devices.	786
Figure 15-15	A problem device's General properties. If the device's General Properties sheet lacks a solution button, look up the Device Manager error code and take appropriate action manually.	787

Complete the Tables and Lists from Memory

Print a copy of Appendix B, "Memory Tables," (found on the CD), or at least the section for this chapter, and complete the tables and lists from memory. Appendix C, "Memory Tables Answer Key," also on the CD, includes completed tables and lists to check your work.

Definitions of Key Terms

Define the following key terms from this chapter, and check your answers in the glossary.

Advanced Boot Options menu, Last Known Good Configuration, Windows Recovery Environment (WinRE), Recovery Console, Hotfix, Master Boot Record, Fragmentation

Troubleshooting Scenario

You are a technician for your company. You have been having problems with a user's computer hard drive. The user is losing her data. You need to come up with a solution that will keep the user's documents from being deleted. You do not have a network server to store the user's data. What should you do to prevent this from happening?

Refer to Appendix A for the answer.

This chapter covers the following subjects:

- **Network Models**—This section defines the client/server and peer-to-peer networking models and explains the differences between the two.

- **Internet Connectivity Technologies**—This section demonstrates how to install modems and make dial-up connections, and it defines services such as ISDN, DSL, Cable, and Satellite. It also talks about LAN connectivity to the Internet.

- **Network Protocols**—In this section, you will learn the basics about the Transmission Control Protocol/Internet Protocol (TCP/IP) suite.

- **TCP/IP Applications and Technologies**—This section covers the various protocols and services that run within the scope of TCP/IP, for example HTTP, e-mail, and FTP.

- **Network Topologies**—This portion briefly describes the four topologies you should know for the exam.

- **Network Types**—Here you will find out about wired and wireless network technologies.

- **Cable and Connector Types**—This section defines twisted pair cable, coaxial, fiber optic, and the different connectors each cable uses.

- **Installing Network Interface Cards**—This portion shows how to install network adapters into various busses such as PCI, USB, and PC Card bus.

- **Configuring Network Interface Cards**—Here you will learn how to configure the media type, duplex settings, and work with wireless protocols.

- **Switches and Hubs**—This section covers the differences between a hub and a switch.

- **Beyond LANs—Bridges, Repeaters, and Routers**—This section delves into the devices that allow data to flow past the LAN and out to the Internet.

- **Networking Configuration**—This section describes the different protocols supported by Windows, demonstrates how to configure TCP/IP, and covers IPv4 addressing concepts.

- **Setting Up Shared Resources**—This section demonstrates how to install File & Print Sharing and shows how to share folders, drives, and printers.

- **Setting Up the Network Client**—This section reveals how to install network client software and network printers.

- **Using Shared Resources**—Here you will find out how to utilize UNCs, FQDNs, and map drives to resources.

- **Browser Installation and Configuration**—This section lays bare the fundamentals of proxy server settings and security settings.

- **Using Network Command-Line Tools**—You have to know how to use ping, ipconfig, tracert, and more commands for the exam. Learn it here!

- **Network and Internet Troubleshooting**—This section describes what to do in the event of a network failure or loss of access to resources and printers.

This chapter covers a portion of the CompTIA A+ 220-701 objectives 4.1, 4.2, and 4.3 and CompTIA A+ 220-702 objectives 3.1 and 3.2.

CHAPTER 16

Networking

A *network* is a group of computers, peripherals, and software that are connected to each other and can be used together. Special software and hardware are required to make networks work.

Two or more computers connected together in the same office are considered a LAN (local area network). LANs in different cities can be connected to each other by a WAN (wide area network). The Internet represents the world's largest network, connecting both standalone computers and computers on LAN and WAN networks all over the world.

At one time, it was necessary to use a network operating system (NOS), such as Novell NetWare, to enable networking. However, current operating systems, such as Windows, include the components needed for networking.

Windows 7, Vista, XP, and Windows 2000 include the following NOS features, enabling systems running these operating systems to be used either as network clients or as peer network servers:

- **Client software**—Enables systems to connect with other networks. Windows XP/2000 can connect to Windows and Novell NetWare networks, among others, and Windows 7 and Vista connect to Windows networks only by default.

- **Network protocols**—Windows XP/2000 can utilize TCP/IPv4, IPX/SPX, and NetBEUI. Windows 7 and Windows Vista use TCP/IPv4 and TCP/IPv6 by default.

- **File and print sharing**—Enables Windows systems to act as peer servers for Windows and Novell NetWare networks.

- **Services**—Enables specialized network services, such as shared printers, network backup, and more.

"Do I Know This Already?" Quiz

The "Do I Know This Already?" quiz allows you to assess whether you should read this entire chapter or simply jump to the "Exam Preparation Tasks" section for review. If you are in doubt, read the entire chapter. Table 16-1 outlines the major headings in this chapter and the corresponding "Do I Know This Already?" quiz questions. You can find the answers in Appendix A, "Answers to the 'Do I Know This Already?' Quizzes and Troubleshooting Scenarios."

Table 16-1   "Do I Know This Already?" Foundation Topics Section-to-Question Mapping

Foundations Topics Section	Questions Covered in This Section
Network Models	1
Internet Connectivity Technologies	2
Network Protocols	3
TCP/IP Applications and Technologies	4
Network Topologies	5
Network Types	6
Cable and Connector Types	7
Installing Network Interface Cards	8
Configuring Network Interface Cards	9
Switches and Hubs	10
Beyond LANs—Repeaters, Bridges, and Routers	11
Networking Configuration	12
Setting Up Shared Resources	13
Setting Up the Network Client	14
Using Shared Resources	15
Browser Installation and Configuration	16
Using Network Command-Line Tools	17
Network and Internet Troubleshooting	18

1. The Windows operating system uses two major types of networks. Which of the following are the two?

   a. Client/server

   b. Node server

   c. Peer-to-peer

   d. IP network model

2. One reason for implementing a network is to share the Internet. Which of the following methods can connect a network to the Internet? (Choose all that apply.)

   a. Dial-up modem

   b. ISDN modem

   c. DSL modem

   d. Cable modem

3. You are a technician for your company. You have been asked to determine which protocols are in use. You discover that the company is using TCP/IPv4. Which of the following network protocols might you also find on the network? (Choose all that apply.)

   a. TCP/IPv6

   b. ISP

   c. NetBEUI

   d. IEEE

4. Which of the following technologies are part of the TCP/IP suite? (Choose all that apply.)

   a. HTTP/HTTPS

   b. SSL

   c. TLS

   d. Ethernet

5. You have been asked to recommend a network topology to use in a new network. Which of the following are valid network topologies?

   a. Bus

   b. Star

   c. Ring

   d. Mesh

   e. All of these options are correct

6. The company you work for is using the oldest and most commonly used network today, Ethernet. Which of the following is another name for Ethernet?

    a. IEEE 1394

    b. IEEE 802.11b

    c. IEEE 802.3

    d. IEEE 802.11g

7. You have been asked by your company to create and install a network. You have decided that you are using Category 5e. Which of the following is the most common type of cable used by Cat5e? (Choose all that apply.)

    a. STP

    b. Coaxial

    c. UTP

    d. Thin-net

8. Which of the following devices would you need if a client asks you to connect his computer to a network? (Choose two.)

    a. A network interface card

    b. A wireless card

    c. An AGP adapter card

    d. A BNC connector

9. You are installing a network interface card. You have been instructed to configure the network card to send and receive data at the same time. Which of the following settings will you need to configure the network card to complete what has been asked of you?

    a. Half duplex

    b. Full duplex

    c. Super duplex mode

    d. Single duplex mode

10. You have been asked by your company to upgrade all hubs to switches. How would this upgrade change the existing network?

    a. The network will be slower

    b. There is no difference in speeds

    c. A switch creates a dedicated full speed connection

    d. You do not need to have NIC cards

11. You have been asked by a company to analyze their network. You find several hubs and switches within the network. Which of the following additional devices might you find in this network?

   a. Routers

   b. Bridges

   c. Repeaters

   d. VLAN technology

12. You have been contacted by a client that is having problems connecting to the Internet. Where would be a good place to start the troubleshooting process?

   a. File and Print Sharing

   b. Run the Ping command-line utility

   c. Configure the DHCP server

   d. TCP/IP configuration

13. You have been contacted by a client that is unable to access network printers and other shared resources. Which of the following should you verify is installed and enabled?

   a. Client services

   b. System monitor

   c. File and print sharing

   d. TCP/IP protocol

14. What is the name of the service that must be installed on a Windows computer to connect to a network?

   a. WINS

   b. AppleTalk Protocol

   c. Client for Microsoft Networks

   d. NDS

15. You need to connect to a server to use shared resources. Which of the following are ways to connect to the server? (Choose two.)

   a. Use the UNC path of the resource you need access to

   b. Contact the network administrator for help

   c. Use the map network drive tool

   d. Just walk over to the server and do what you need

16. Which of the following programs enables a user to browse the Internet? (Choose two.)

    a. Internet Explorer

    b. Firefox

    c. Windows Explorer

    d. The command prompt

17. A user with your company is having connectivity problems. You need to diagnose the problem as soon as possible. You call the client and walk her through finding the IP address. What should you do next?

    a. Run `ipconfig /release`

    b. Run `ipconfig /flushdns`

    c. Ping the IP address of the client's computer

    d. Walk her through how to ping the server

18. A user is unable to access the network. Which of the following could cause this to happen? (Choose all that apply.)

    a. Damage to cables

    b. A faulty network card

    c. The boot files are corrupt

    d. Connecting a high speed NIC to a low speed port

Foundation Topics

Network Models

As the network features found in Windows suggest, there are two major network models:

- Client/server
- Peer-to-peer

It's important to understand the differences between them as you prepare for the exams and as you work with networks.

Client/Server

Most departmental and larger networks are client/server networks, such as the one illustrated in Figure 16-1. The networks controlled by Windows Server 2008, Windows Server 2003, Windows 2000 Server, and Novell NetWare servers are examples of client/server networks.

The roles of each computer in a client/server network are distinctive, affecting both the hardware used in each computer and the software installed in each computer. In a client/server environment, there are many advantages including centralized administration, better sharing capabilities, scalability, and possibly increased security.

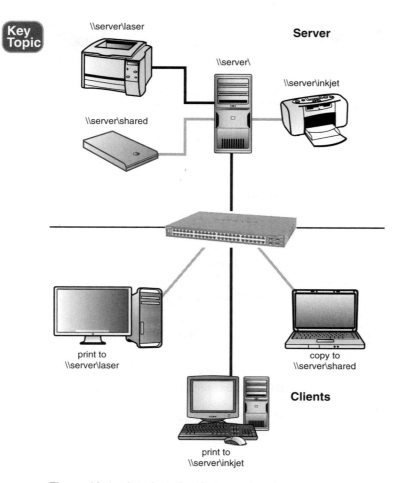

Figure 16-1   A typical client/server network.

Servers

A *server* is a computer on the network that provides other computers (called clients or workstations) with access to resources, such as disk drives, folders, printers, modems, scanners, and Internet access. Because these resources can be used by different computers over the network, they are called *shared resources*.

Servers can also be used for different types of software and tasks. For example, application servers run tasks for clients, file servers store data and program files for clients, and mail servers store and distribute e-mail to clients.

Servers typically have more powerful hardware features than typical PCs, such as SCSI or SATA RAID arrays or network-attached storage for hard disk storage, larger amounts of RAM, hot-swap power supplies, and server-optimized network adapters. However, because servers are not operated by an individual user, they often use low-performance integrated or PCI video and might be managed remotely rather than with a keyboard or monitor connected directly to the server.

Clients

A *client* is a computer that uses the resources on a server. Typical examples of operating systems used by client computers include Windows 7, Vista, XP, and 2000 (as well as Linux and MacOS). Depending on the network operating system in use, clients and servers can be separate machines or a client can act as a server and a server can act as a client. Clients can refer to servers either by assigning drive letters to shared folders (see the section "Mapped Drives" later in this chapter) or by using a Universal Naming Convention (UNC) path name to refer to the server, as shown earlier in Figure 16-1. See "The Universal Naming Convention (UNC)," later in this chapter.

Peer-to-Peer

The network features built into Windows allow for peer servers: Computers can share resources with each other, and machines that share resources can also be used as client workstations. As with client/server networking, resources on peer servers can be accessed via universal naming convention (as shown earlier in Figure 16-1) or by mapping drive letters and printer ports on a client to server resources.

As Figure 16-2 shows, if mapped drive letters and printer ports are used in a peer-to-peer network, the same resource will have a different name, depending on whether it's being accessed from the peer server (acting as a workstation) itself or over the network. In Figure 16-2, the system on the top shares its external hard disk drive with the system on the bottom, which refers to the shared hard disk drive as F:\. The system on the bottom shares its printer with the system on the top, which has mapped the shared printer to LPT2.

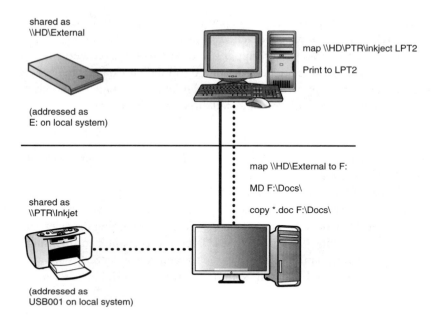

shared as
\\HD\External

map \\HD\PTR\inkject LPT2

Print to LPT2

(addressed as
E: on local system)

map \\HD\External to F:

MD F:\Docs\

shared as
\\PTR\Inkjet

copy *.doc F:\Docs\

(addressed as
USB001 on local system)

Figure 16-2 A simple two-station peer-to-peer network, in which each computer acts as a peer server to the other.

The peer server loads file and printer-sharing software to make printers and drives or folders available to others. Because a peer server is also used as a workstation, it is equipped in the same way as a typical workstation or standalone PC.

Internet Connectivity Technologies

One of the best reasons to create a network of any size is to provide access to the Internet. The many types of connectivity technologies that can be used for Internet access are discussed in the following sections.

> **TIP** As you review the following sections, try to determine which type of Internet connections you use at home and at your workplace.

Modems and Dial-Up Internet Connectivity

Until the late nineties, dial-up networking (DUN) had been the most common way for home and small businesses to connect to the Internet. Dial-up connections are often referred to as analog connections because the device used to make the connection is an analog modem, which connects to the Internet through an ordinary telephone line. Every time you connect to the Internet with a dial-up modem, you are making a network connection.

Modem Technologies and Types

A modem sending data modulates digital computer data into analog data suitable for transmission over telephone lines to the receiving modem, which demodulates the analog data back into computer form. Modems share two characteristics with serial ports:

- Both use serial communication to send and receive information.

- Both often require adjustment of transmission speed and other options.

In fact, most external modems require a serial port to connect them to the computer; some external modems use the USB port instead.

NOTE   Properly used, the term *modem* (modulator-demodulator) refers only to a device that connects to the telephone line and performs digital-to-analog or analog-to-digital conversions. However, other types of Internet connections such as satellite, wireless, DSL, and cable Internet also use the term modem, although they work with purely digital data. When used by itself in this book, however, modem refers only to dial-up (telephone) modems.

Modems come in six types:

- **Add-on card**—Add-on card modems for desktop computers, such as the one shown in Figure 16-3, fit into a PCI expansion slot.

- **External**—External modems plug into a serial or USB port.

- **PC Card**—PCMCIA (PC Card) modems are sometimes built in a combo design that also incorporates a 10/100 Ethernet network adapter.

- **Motherboard-integrated**—Many recent desktop computers have integrated modems, as do many notebook computers.

- **Mini-PCI card**—Some older-model computers that appear to have built-in modems actually use modems that use the mini-PCI form factor and can be removed and replaced with another unit.

- **Mini-PCIe card**—Many late-model notebook computers that appear to have built-in modems actually use modems that use the mini-PCIe form factor and can be removed and replaced with another unit.

To learn more about expansion slots, see "Expansion Slots" in Chapter 3, "Motherboards, Processors, and Adapter Cards." To learn more about mini-PCI cards, see "Mini-PCI" in Chapter 9, "Laptops and Portable Devices."

Although some high-end add-on card and PC Card modems have a hardware UART (universal asynchronous receiver transmitter) or UART-equivalent chip, most recent models use a programmable *digital signal processor* (DSP) instead. Modems with a DSP perform similarly to UART-based modems, but can easily be reprogrammed with firmware and driver updates as needed. Low-cost add-on card and PC Card modems often use *host signal processing* (HSP) instead of a UART or

DSP. HSP modems are sometimes referred to as Winmodems or soft modems because Windows and the computer's processor perform the modulation, slowing down performance. HSP modems might not work with some older versions of Windows or non-Windows operating systems.

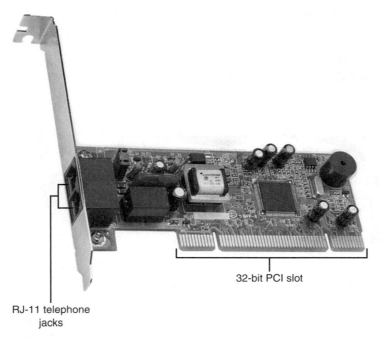

32-bit PCI slot

RJ-11 telephone
jacks

Figure 16-3   A typical PCI internal modem. Note two RJ connectors on the rear of the modem: They enable you to plug a phone into the modem, so you can use the modem or your telephone.

External modems, such as the one shown in Figure 16-4, must be connected to a serial or USB port. Serial port versions require an external power source (USB modems are usually powered by the USB port or hub), but the portability and front-panel status lights of either type of external modem make them better for business use in the minds of many users.

A typical PC Card modem is shown in Figure 16-5. The modem pictured here uses a *dongle*, a proprietary cable that attaches to one end of the PC Card to enable the modem to plug into a standard telephone jack or telephone line. If the dongle is lost or damaged, the modem can't be used until the dongle is replaced. Some PC Card modems use an integrated or pop-out RJ-11 jack instead of a dongle (it's one less thing to lose or break as you travel). To learn more about PC Card modems, see "PCMCIA (PC Card, CardBus)," in Chapter 9.

There have been various standards for analog modems used to make dial-up connections. Before the advent of so-called "56K" standards, the fastest dial-up connection possible was 33.6Kbps. Virtually all modems in recent systems or available for purchase support either the ITU v.90 or v.92 standards.

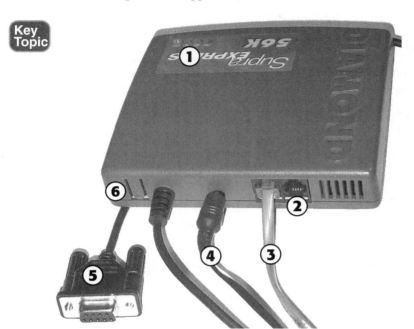

1. Status/activity lights
2. RJ-11 connector for telephone pass-through
3. RJ-11 telephone cable
4. Power cable
5. 9-pin serial cable
6. Reset switch

Figure 16-4 A typical external modem that connects to a serial port. Note the reset switch, which enables the user to reset the modem without turning off the computer.

PC Card connector   Dongle

Figure 16-5 A typical PC Card modem that uses a dongle (right). Many recent PC Card modems feature integrated or pop-out RJ-11 jacks instead of a dongle.

Note   Although v.90 and v.92 modems are all designed to perform downloading at up to 56Kbps, FCC (Federal Communications Commission) regulations limit actual download speed to 53Kbps. Speeds greater than 33.6Kbps apply only to downloads from Internet service providers (ISPs) and their special modems. If you make a direct connection between two PCs, the fastest speed you can have in either direction is just 33.6Kbps (if both modems can run at least that fast).

Analog Modem Installation

The method used for physical installation of the modem varies with the modem type. To install a PCI modem, follow these steps:

Step 1.   Take ESD precautions. (See Chapter 17, "Safety and Environmental Issues," for details.)

Step 2.   Open the system and locate an empty slot of the appropriate type.

Step 3.   Remove the screw holding the slot cover in place.

Step 4.   Remove the slot cover.

Step 5.   Install the modem into the slot and fasten it into place with the screw previously used to secure the slot cover.

Step 6.   Connect an RJ-11 telephone cable running from the telephone jack in the wall to the line connection.

Step 7.   If desired, plug a telephone into the telco jack.

Step 8.   Close the system and restart it.

Step 9.   Install drivers as required.

CAUTION   You can drive yourself crazy trying to make a connection with your modem if you plug the RJ-11 telephone cord into the wrong jack. There are actually three ways to make this mistake:

- Plugging the RJ-11 cord into the phone jack instead of the line or telco jack on the modem
- Plugging the RJ-11 cord into the slightly larger RJ-45 jack used for 10/100/1000 Ethernet networking
- Plugging the RJ-11 cord into a HomePNA network card (which also has two RJ-11 jacks) instead of the modem

If you use the now-rare (and obsolete) HomePNA network, check the network documentation for the correct way to connect your network card and your modem to the telephone line.

To install a PC Card modem, use these steps:

Step 1.   Slide the PC Card modem into an empty PC Card slot of the appropriate type (Type II or Type III; see Chapter 9 for details).

Step 2.   After the operating system indicates the modem has been detected, attach the dongle (if appropriate).

Step 3.   If the dongle has an RJ-11 plug, connect it to the telephone wall jack.

Step 4.   For modems with a pop-out RJ-11 jack, release the jack.

Step 5.   Connect an RJ-11 telephone cable between the RJ-11 connector on the PC Card or dongle and the wall jack.

Step 6.   Install drivers as required.

To install an external modem, follow these steps:

Step 1.   Connect the modem to a USB or serial port as appropriate.

Step 2.   Connect the modem to AC power and turn it on (if necessary).

Step 3.   If the modem is not detected automatically, use the operating system's modem dialog in the Control Panel to detect the modem and install its drivers.

See Chapter 9 for more information about mini-PCI modems.

Dial-Up Internet Service Providers

An Internet service provider (ISP) provides a connection between the user with an analog (dial-up) modem (or other connectivity device) and the Internet. ISPs that provide dial-up access have several modems and dial-up numbers that their customers can access. The ISP's modems are connected to the Internet via high-speed, high-capacity connections.

An ISP can be selected from many different sources:

- National companies

- Local or regional providers

- Specialized providers such as those that provide filtered, family-friendly access

Choose an ISP based on its rates, its reliability, or special services (such as content filtration or proprietary content) that are appropriate to your needs.

Creating a Dial-Up Connection

Windows Vista and Windows 7 create dial-up networking (DUN) connections within the Network and Sharing Center window. Windows XP and 2000 create DUN connections within the same window that stores other types of network connections:

- Windows XP stores all types of network connections in the Network Connections window.

- Windows 2000 stores all types of network connections in the Network and Dial-Up Connections window.

NOTE   If an ISP provides customized setup software, the software will usually create an icon for you in the folder used for DUN connections. This icon contains the settings needed to make your connection.

Requirements for a Dial-Up Internet Connection

All ISPs must provide the following information to enable you to connect to the Internet:

- Client software, including the preferred web browser, dial-up information, and TCP/IP configuration information
- Dial-up access telephone numbers
- Modem types supported (33.6Kbps, 56Kbps, v.90, v.92)
- The username and initial password (which should be changed immediately after first login)

Even if the client software provided by the ISP configures the connection for you, you should record the following information in case it is needed to manually configure or reconfigure the connection:

- **The dial-up access telephone number**—This might be different for different modem speeds. Users with a 56Kbps modem should know both the standard (33.6Kbps) and high-speed access numbers if different numbers are used.
- **The username and password**—Windows will often save this during the setup of a DUN connection, but it should be recorded in case the system must be reconfigured or replaced.
- **The TCP/IP configuration**—This is set individually for each dial-up connection through its properties sheet.

To determine this information, right-click the icon for the connection and select **Properties**.

For more information, see "TCP/IPv4 Configuration" later in this chapter.

ISDN Internet Connectivity

ISDN (Integrated Services Digital Network) was originally developed to provide an all-digital method for connecting multiple telephone and telephony-type devices, such as fax machines, to a single telephone line and to provide a faster connection for teleconferencing for remote computer users. A home/small office-based connection can also provide an all-digital Internet connection at speeds up to 128Kbps. Line quality is a critical factor in determining whether any particular location can use ISDN service. If an all-digital connection cannot be established between the customer's location and the telephone company's central switch, ISDN service is not available or a new telephone line must be run (at extra cost to you!).

NOTE   The telephone network was originally designed to support analog signaling only, which is why an analog (dial-up) modem that sends data to other computers converts digital signals to analog for transmission through the telephone network. The receiving analog modem converts analog data back to digital data.

ISDN Hardware

To make an ISDN connection, your PC (and any other devices that share the ISDN connection) needs a device called an ISDN terminal adapter (TA). A TA resembles a conventional analog modem. Internal models plug into the same PCI, ISA, and PC Card slots used by analog modems, and external models use USB or serial ports. External TAs often have two or more RJ-11 ports for telephony devices, an RJ-45 port for the connection to the ISDN line, and a serial or USB port for connection to the computer. For more information about these ports, see Chapter 7, "I/O and Multimedia Ports and Devices."

Setting Up an ISDN Connection

ISDN connections (where available) are provided through the local telephone company. There are two types of ISDN connections:

- Primary Rate Interface (PRI)
- Basic Rate Interface (BRI)

A PRI connection provides 1.536Mbps of bandwidth, whereas a BRI interface provides 64Kbps (single-channel) or 128Kbps (dual-channel) of bandwidth. BRI is sold to small businesses and home offices; PRI is sold to large organizations. Both types of connections enable you to use the Internet and talk or fax data through the phone line at the same time.

A direct individual ISDN connection is configured through the network features of Windows with the same types of settings used for an analog modem connection. Configuring a network-based ISDN connection is done through the network adapter's TCP/IP properties window. For more information, see "TCP/IPv4 Configuration," later in this chapter.

TIP   Most telephone companies have largely phased out ISDN in favor of DSL, which is much faster and less expensive for Internet connections.

Broadband Internet Services (DSL, Cable, Satellite)

Broadband Internet service is a blanket term that refers to the following Internet access methods: digital subscriber line (DSL), cable, and satellite. All of these methods provide bandwidth in excess of 300Kbps, and current implementations are two-way services, enabling you to use your telephone while accessing the Internet.

NOTE   Other types of broadband Internet service, including direct wireless (using microwave transceivers) and powerline, are not part of the A+ Certification exam domains, but you might encounter them in some areas.

DSL

DSL can piggyback on the same telephone line used by your telephone and fax machine, or it can be installed as a distinctly separate line. Either way, DSL requires a high-quality telephone line that can carry a digital signal. For home use, DSL is designed strictly for Internet access. But for business use, DSL can be used for additional services and can be used in site to site scenarios between organizations.

When it comes to connection speed, DSL leaves BRI ISDN in the dust. There are two major types of DSL: ADSL (Asynchronous DSL) and SDSL (Synchronous DSL). Their features are compared in Table 16-2.

Table 16-2   Common DSL Services Compared

Service Type	Supports Existing Telephone Line	User Installation Option	Typical Downstream Speeds	Typical Upstream Speeds	Typically Marketed To
ADSL	Yes	Yes	384Kbps to 6Mbps	128Kbps to 768Kbps	Home, small-business
SDSL	Not typical	No	384Kbps to 2.0Mbps	Same as down-stream speed	Larger business and corporate

NOTE   Downstream refers to download speed; upstream refers to upload speed. SDSL gets its name from providing the same speed in both directions; ADSL is always faster downstream than upstream.

A device known as a DSL modem is used to connect your computer to DSL service. DSL modems connect to your PC through the RJ-45 (Ethernet) port or the USB port. The rear of a typical DSL modem that uses an Ethernet (RJ-45) connection is shown in Figure 16-6.

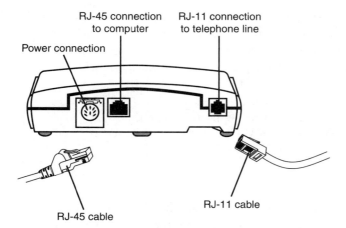

Figure 16-6 The rear of a typical DSL modem with a power port (top left), RJ-45 data port to the PC (top center), and an RJ-11 telephone line port (top right). The RJ-45 cable is shown at bottom left, and the RJ-11 cable is shown at bottom right.

As Figure 16-6 indicates, DSL uses the same telephone lines as ordinary telephone equipment. However, your telephone can interfere with the DSL connection. To prevent this, in some cases a separate DSL line is run from the outside service box to the computer with the DSL modem. However, if your DSL provider supports the self-installation option, small devices called microfilters are installed between telephones, answering machines, fax machines, and other devices on the same circuit with the DSL modem. Microfilters can be built into special wall plates, but are more often external devices that plug into existing phone jacks, as shown in Figure 16-7.

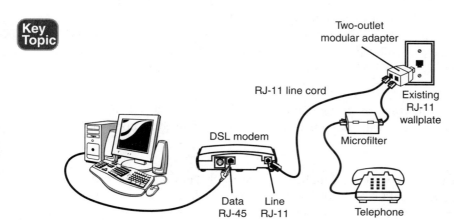

Figure 16-7 A typical self-installed DSL setup. The DSL vendor supplies the DSL modem (center) and microfilters that attach between telephones and other devices and the wall outlet (right).

Some DSL connections are configured as an always-on connection similar to a network connection to the Internet. However, many vendors now configure the DSL connection as a PPPoE (point-to-point protocol over Ethernet) connection instead. A PPPoE connection requires the user to make a connection with a user-name and password.

NOTE   Windows 7, Vista, and XP have native support through their Network Connection wizards. With older versions of Windows, the vendor must provide setup software.

Cable Internet

Cable Internet service piggybacks on the same coaxial cable that brings cable TV into a home or business. A few early cable ISPs used internal cable modems, which supported one-way traffic. (The cable was used for downloads, and a conventional telephone line was used for uploads and page requests.) Virtually all cable Internet service today is two-way and is built upon the fiber-optic network used for digital cable and music services provided by most cable TV vendors.

Cable Internet can reach download speeds anywhere from 2Mbps up to 50Mbps or faster. Upload speeds are typically about 10% of upload speed, but vary by vendor.

NOTE   You can have cable Internet service without having cable TV.

Some cable TV providers use the same cable that carries cable TV for cable Internet service, while others run a separate cable to the location. When the same cable is used for both cable TV and cable Internet service, a splitter is used to provide connections for cable TV and Internet. The splitter prevents cable TV and cable Internet signals from interfering with each other. One coaxial cable from the splitter goes to the TV or set-top box as usual; the other one goes into a device known as a cable modem. Almost all cable modems are external devices that plug into a computer's 10/100 Ethernet (RJ-45) or USB port. Figure 16-8 shows a typical cable Internet connection.

A cable Internet connection can be configured through the standard Network properties sheet in Windows or with customized setup software, depending upon the ISP.

Satellite

Satellite Internet providers, such as HughesNet (previously known as DirecWAY, and, before that, as DirecPC), StarBand, and WildBlue use dish antennas similar to satellite TV antennas to receive and transmit signals between geosynchronous satellites and computers. In some cases, you might be able to use a dual-purpose satellite dish to pick up both satellite Internet and satellite TV service.

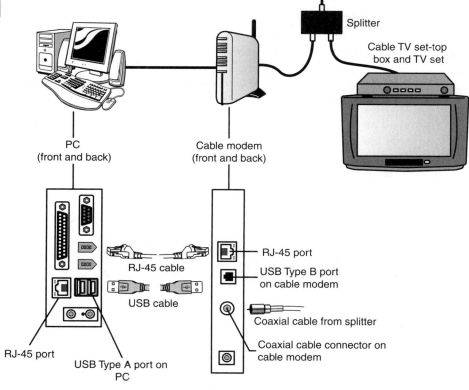

Figure 16-8   A typical cable modem and cable TV installation. The cable modem can be connected to the computer through an RJ-45 cable or a USB cable.

> **NOTE**   Geosynchronous satellites orbit the Earth's equator at a distance of more than 22,000 miles (approximately 35,000 kilometers). Because of their orbit and altitude, they remain in the same location in the sky at all times. In the Northern Hemisphere, you need an unobstructed view of the southern sky to make a connection. In the Southern Hemisphere, you need an unobstructed view of the northern sky to make a connection.

Satellite Internet services use external devices often called satellite modems to connect the computer to the satellite dish. They connect to the USB or Ethernet (RJ-45) port in a fashion similar to that used by DSL or cable modems.

The FCC requires professional installation for satellite Internet service because an incorrectly aligned satellite dish with uplink capabilities could cause a service outage on the satellite it's aimed at. Setup software supplied by the satellite vendor is used to complete the process.

LANs and Internet Connectivity

A LAN is an ideal way to provide Internet access to two or more users. However, a LAN by itself cannot connect to the Internet. Two additional components must also be used with a LAN to enable it to connect to the Internet:

- **An Internet access device**—This could be a dial-up modem, but more often a broadband connection such as DSL, cable, or satellite is used.

- **A router**—This device connects client PCs on the network to the Internet through the Internet access device. To the Internet, only one client is making a connection, but the router internally tracks which PC has made the request and transmits the data for that PC back to that PC, enabling multiple PCs to access the Internet through the network.

> **NOTE** As an alternative to a router, some small networks use a gateway, which is a PC configured to share its Internet connection with others on the network. Windows 2000 and later versions support this feature, known as Internet Connection Sharing. Note that wireless access devices known as gateways actually resemble routers.

Network Protocols

The 2011 A+ Certification Exams expect you to understand the major features of these network protocols:

- TCP/IP and how v4 and v6 compare in terms of address length differences and address conventions

- NetBEUI/NetBIOS

Although most current networks are based on TCP/IP, you might encounter others in some networks. The following sections cover the major features of these networks. For information about configuring these protocols, see "Networking Configuration," later in this chapter.

TCP/IP

TCP/IP is short for Transport Control Protocol/Internet Protocol. It is a multiplatform protocol used for both Internet access and for local area networks. TCP/IP is used by Novell NetWare 5.x and later and Windows 7/Vista/XP/2000 as the standard protocol for LAN use, replacing NetBEUI (used on older Microsoft networks) and IPX/SPX (used on older versions of Novell NetWare). Using TCP/IP as a network's only protocol makes network configuration easier because users need to configure only one protocol to communicate with other network clients, servers, or with the Internet.

> **TIP** Most networking you'll perform in the real world uses TCP/IP. TCP/IP is also the most complex network to configure, especially if you need to use a static IP address. Make sure you understand how it works before you take your exams!

NetBEUI/NetBIOS

NetBEUI (NetBIOS Extended User Interface), the simplest protocol, is an enhanced version of an early network protocol called NetBIOS (NetBIOS itself is no longer used for this purpose). Historically, NetBEUI was used primarily on peer networks using Windows, with direct cable connection between two computers, and by some small networks that use Windows NT Servers. NetBEUI lacks features that enable it to be used on larger networks: It cannot be routed or used to access the Internet.

> **NOTE** NetBEUI is not officially supported in Windows XP or later versions, although Microsoft provides the NetBEUI protocol on the XP distribution CD in the `Valueadd\MSFT\Net\NetBEUI` folder for use with older networks or for troubleshooting. For details on how to install NetBEUI in Windows XP, see Microsoft Help and article 301041 available at http://support.microsoft.com/kb/301041. NetBIOS can be used in conjunction with TCP/IP in Windows XP, Vista, and 7.

TCP/IP Applications and Technologies

TCP/IP actually is a suite of protocols used on the Internet for routing and transporting information. The following sections discuss some of the application protocols that are part of the TCP/IP suite, as well as some of the services and technologies that relate to TCP/IP.

ISP

An ISP (Internet service provider) provides the connection between an individual PC or network and the Internet. ISPs use routers connected to high-speed, high-bandwidth connections to route Internet traffic from their clients to their destinations.

HTTP/HTTPS

Hypertext Transfer Protocol (HTTP) is the protocol used by web browsers, such as Internet Explorer and Netscape Navigator, to access websites and content. Normal (unsecured) sites use the prefix http:// when accessed in a web browser. Sites that are secured with various encryption schemes are identified with the prefix https://.

> **NOTE** Most browsers connecting with a secured site will also display a closed padlock symbol onscreen.

SSL

Secure Socket Layers (SSL) is an encryption technology used by secured (https://) websites. To access a secured website, the web browser must support the same encryption level used by the secured website (normally 128-bit encryption) and the same version(s) of SSL used by the website (normally SSL version 2.0 or 3.0).

TLS

Transport Layer Security (TLS) is the successor to SSL. SSL3 was somewhat of a prototype to TLS and was not fully standardized. TLS was ratified by the IETF in 1999. However, many people and companies might still refer to it as SSL.

HTML

Hypertext Markup Language (HTML) is the language used by web pages. An HTML page is a specially formatted text page that uses tags (commands contained in angle brackets) to change text appearance, insert links to other pages, display pictures, incorporate scripting languages, and provide other features. Web browsers, such as Microsoft Internet Explorer and Netscape Navigator, are used to view and interpret the contents of web pages, which have typical file extensions such as `.HTM`, `.HTML`, `.ASP` (Active Server pages generated by a database), and others.

You can see the HTML code used to create the web page in a browser by using the View Source or View Page Source menu option provided by your browser. Figure 16-9 compares what you see in a typical web page (top window) with the HTML tags used to set text features and the underlined hyperlink (bottom window). The figure uses different text size and shading to distinguish tags from text, and so do most commercial web-editing programs used to make web pages.

Tags such as `<P>` are used by themselves, and other tags are used in pairs. For example, `<A HREF...>` is used to indicate the start of a hyperlink (which will display another page or site in your browser window), and `</A>` indicates the end of a hyperlink.

NOTE   The World Wide Web Consortium (http://www.w3c.org) sets the official standards for HTML tags and syntax, but major browser vendors, such as Microsoft and Netscape, often modify or extend official HTML standards with their own tags and syntax.

FTP

File Transfer Protocol (FTP) is a protocol used by both web browsers and specialized FTP programs to access dedicated file transfer servers for file downloads and uploads. When you access an FTP site, the site uses the prefix ftp://.

Windows contains `ftp.exe`, a command-line FTP program; type **FTP**, press **Enter**, and then type **?** at the FTP prompt to see the commands you can use.

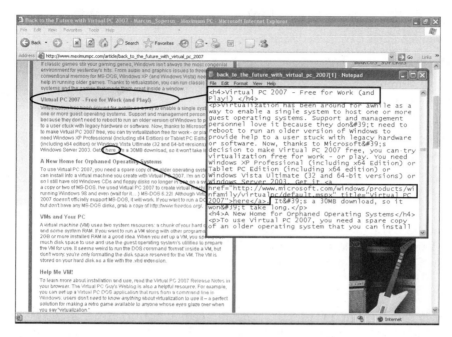

Figure 16-9   A section of an HTML document as seen by a typical browser uses the HTML tags shown in Notepad for paragraphs (**\<P>**) titles (**\<H4>**, **\</H4>**) and hyperlinks (**\<A HREF>**, **\</A>**).

FTP sites with downloads available to any user support anonymous FTP; if any credentials are required, it's typically the user's e-mail address as a password (the username is preset to anonymous). Some FTP sites require the user to log in with a specified username and password.

TIP   Although you can use Windows' built-in FTP client for file uploads and downloads with both secured and unsecured FTP sites, you should consider using third-party FTP products such as FileZilla (http://filezilla-project.org/) or WS_FTP Pro (http://www.ipswitchft.com/products/ws_ftp_professional/). These programs enable you to create a customized setup for each FTP site you visit and will store passwords, server types, and other necessary information. They also enable faster downloads than typical web browsers running in ftp:// mode.

Telnet

Telnet enables a user to make a text-based connection to a remote computer or networking device and use it as if he were a regular user sitting in front of it, rather than simply downloading pages and files as he would with an http:// or ftp:// connection.

Windows contains a command-line Telnet program. To open a connection to a remote computer, enter a command such as

```
telnet a.computer.com
```

To use other commands, open a command prompt, type **telnet** and press the **Enter** key. To see other commands, type **?/help**.

> **NOTE**   The remote computer must be configured to accept a Telnet login. Typically, TCP port 23 on the remote computer must be open before a login can take place.

SSH

Secure Shell (SSH) allows data to be exchanged between computers on a secured channel. This protocol offers a more secure replacement to FTP and TELNET. The Secure Shell server housing the data you want to access would have port 22 open.

DNS

The domain name system (DNS) is the name for the network of servers on the Internet that translate domain names, such as www.informit.com, and individual host names into their matching IP addresses. If you manually configure an IP address, you typically provide the IP addresses of one or more DNS servers as part of the configuration process.

> **CAUTION**   Can't access the site you're looking for? Got the wrong site? You might have made one of these common mistakes:
>
> - **Don't assume that all domain names end in .com**—Other popular domain name extensions include .net, .org, .gov, .us, .cc, and various national domains such as .uk (United Kingdom), .ca (Canada), and many others.
>
> - **Don't forget to use the entire domain name in the browser**—Some browsers will add the www. prefix used on most domain names, but others will not. For best results, spell out the complete domain name.

If you want a unique domain name for either a website or e-mail, the ISP that you will use to provide your e-mail or web hosting service often provides a registration wizard you can use to access the domain name registration services provided by various companies such as VeriSign.

A domain name has three major sections, from the end of the name to the start:

- The top-level domain (.com, .org, .net, and so on).

- The name of the site.

- The server type; www indicates a web server, ftp indicates an FTP server, mail indicates a mail server, and search indicates a search server.

For example, Microsoft.com is located in the .com domain, typically used for commercial companies. Microsoft is the domain name. The Microsoft.com domain has the following servers:

- www.microsoft.com hosts web content, such as product information.

- support.microsoft.com hosts the Microsoft.com support website, where users can search for Knowledge Base (KB) and other support documents.

- ftp.microsoft.com hosts the File Transfer Protocol server of Microsoft.com; this portion of the Microsoft.com domain can be accessed by either a web browser or an FTP client.

Many companies have only WWW servers, or only WWW and FTP servers.

NOTE Some small websites use a folder under a domain hosted by an ISP: www.ispname.com/~smallsitename

E-mail

All e-mail systems provide transfer of text messages, and most have provisions for file attachments, enabling you to send documents, graphics, video clips, and other types of computer data files to receivers for work or play. E-mail clients are included as part of web browsers and are also available as limited-feature freely downloadable or more-powerful commercially purchased standalone e-mail clients. Some e-mail clients, such as Microsoft Outlook, are part of application suites (such as Microsoft Office) and also feature productivity and time-management features.

TIP Users who travel away from corporate networks might prefer to use a web-based e-mail account, such as Hotmail or Gmail, or use Outlook Web Access to get access to e-mail from any system with a properly configured web browser.

To configure any e-mail client, you need

- The name of the e-mail server for incoming mail

- The name of the e-mail server for outgoing mail

- The username and password for the e-mail user

- The type of e-mail server (POP, IMAP, or HTTP)

Some e-mail clients and servers might require additional configuration options.

To access web-based e-mail, you need

- The website for the e-mail service
- The username and password

The following sections describe three e-mail protocols: SMTP, POP, and IMAP.

SMTP

The Simple Mail Transfer Protocol (SMTP) is used to send e-mail from a client system to an e-mail server, which also uses SMTP to relay the message to the receiving e-mail server.

POP

The Post Office Protocol (POP) is the more popular of two leading methods for receiving e-mail (IMAP is the other). In an e-mail system based on POP, e-mail is downloaded from the mail server to folders on a local system. POP is not a suitable e-mail protocol for users who frequently switch between computers because e-mail might wind up on multiple computers. The POP3 version is the latest current standard. Users that utilize POP3 servers to retrieve e-mail will typically use SMTP to send messages.

> **TIP**   For users who must use POP-based e-mail and use multiple computers, a remote access solution, such as Windows Remote Desktop or a service such as GoToMyPC, is recommended. A remote access solution enables a user to remotely access the system that connects to the POP3 mail server so she can download and read e-mail messages, no matter where she is working.

IMAP

The Internet Message Access Protocol (IMAP) is an e-mail protocol that enables messages to remain on the e-mail server so they can be retrieved from any location. IMAP also supports folders, so users can organize their messages as desired.

To configure an IMAP-based e-mail account, you must select IMAP as the e-mail server type and specify the name of the server, your user name and password, and whether the server uses SSL.

Ports

For two computers to communicate they must both use the same protocol. In order for an application to send or receive data, it must use a particular protocol designed for that application and open up a port on the network adapter to make a connection to another computer. For example, let's say you want to visit www.google.com. You would open a browser and type http://www.google.com. The protocol being used is HTTP, short for Hypertext Transfer Protocol, which makes the connection to the web server: google.com. The HTTP protocol would select an unused port on your computer (known as an outbound port) to send and receive data to and from google.com. On the other end, google.com's web server will have a specific port open at all times ready to accept sessions. In most cases the web server's port is 80, which corresponds to the HTTP protocol. This is known as an inbound port. Table 16-3 displays some common protocols and their corresponding inbound ports.

Table 16-3   Common Protocols and Their Ports

Protocol	Port Used
FTP	21
SSH	22
TELNET	23
SMTP	25
HTTP	80
POP3	110
HTTPS	443

Network Topologies

The physical arrangement of computer, cables, and network devices is referred to as a *network topology*. There are four different types of network topologies (see Figure 16-10):

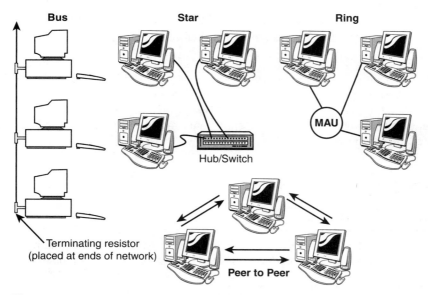

Figure 16-10   Bus, star, ring, and peer-to-peer topologies compared.

- **Bus—** Computers in a bus topology share a common cable. Connections in this topology are made largely with coaxial 10BASE2 and 10BASE5 cables.

- **Star**—Computers in a star topology connect to a central hub or switch (wired) or access point (wireless). This topology is used by 10BASE-T (10Mbps Ethernet), 100BASE-T (Fast Ethernet), and 1000BASE-T (Gigabit Ethernet) Ethernet networks and by Wireless Ethernet (Wi-Fi) when configured for the default infrastructure mode.

- **Ring**—Computers in a ring topology either connect as a physical ring, for example FDDI networks; or a logical ring, as is the case with Token Ring networks.

- **Peer-to-peer (Mesh)**—Computers in a peer-to-peer or mesh topology can connect directly to every other computer. This topology is used by computers with multiple network adapters, Wireless Ethernet (Wi-Fi) when configured for peer-to-peer mode, and Bluetooth.

The network goes down if a single computer on a bus-topology network fails, but the other network types stay up if one or more computers fail.

Network Types

The A+ Certification Exam expects you to be familiar with the key features of Ethernet and Wireless Ethernet. See the following sections for details.

Wired Ethernet Types

The oldest network in common use today is Ethernet, also known as IEEE-802.3. Most recent wired Ethernet networks use unshielded twisted pair (UTP) cable, but older versions of Ethernet use various types of coaxial cable.

> **NOTE**   Ethernet uses the Carrier Sense Multiple Access/Collision Detect (CSMA/CD) method of transmission access. Here's how it works: A station on an Ethernet network can transmit data at any time; if two stations try to transmit at the same time, a collision takes place. Each station waits a random amount of time and then retries the transmission.

Table 16-4 lists the different types of Ethernet networks and their major features.

Table 16-4   Wired Ethernet Networks

Network Type	Cable and Connector Type	Also Known As	Maximum Speed	Network Topology Supported	Maximum Distance Per Segment
10BASE-T	UTP Cat3 cable with RJ-45 connector	Ethernet	10Mbps	Star	100 meters

Table 16-4 Wired Ethernet Networks

Network Type	Cable and Connector Type	Also Known As	Maximum Speed	Network Topology Supported	Maximum Distance Per Segment
100BASE-TX	UTP Cat5, 5e, or 6 cable with RJ-45 connector	**Fast Ethernet**	100Mbps	Star	100 meters
1000BASE-T	UTP Cat5e or 6 cable with RJ-45 connector	**Gigabit Ethernet**	1000 Mbps	Star	100 meters

For more information about cables and connectors, see "Cable and Connector Types," later in this chapter. For more information about network topologies, see the earlier section "Network Topologies."

> **NOTE** Fiber-optic cables can also be used for Ethernet signaling. They are particularly common for long cable runs with Fast and Gigabit Ethernet.

Wireless Ethernet

Wireless Ethernet, also known as IEEE 802.11, is the collective name for a group of wireless technologies that are compatible with wired Ethernet; these are referred to as wireless LAN (WLAN) standards. Wireless Ethernet is also known as Wi-Fi, after the Wireless Fidelity (Wi-Fi) Alliance (www.wi-fi.org), a trade group that promotes interoperability between different brands of Wireless Ethernet hardware.

Table 16-5 compares different types of Wireless Ethernet to each other.

Table 16-5 Wireless Ethernet Standards

Wireless Ethernet Type	Frequency	Maximum Speed	Interoperable With
802.11a	5GHz	54Mbps	Requires dual-mode (802.11a/b or 802.11a/g) hardware; 802.11n networks supporting 5GHz frequency
802.11b	2.4GHz	11Mbps	802.11g
802.11g	2.4GHz	54Mbps	802.11b, 802.11n

Table 16-5   Wireless Ethernet Standards

Wireless Ethernet Type	Frequency	Maximum Speed	Interoperable With
802.11n	2.4GHz (standard) 5GHz (optional)	Up to 600Mbps (300Mbps max. is typical)	802.11b, 802.11g (802.11a on networks also supporting 5GHz frequency)

NOTE   Wi-Fi certified hardware is 802.11-family Wireless Ethernet hardware that has passed tests established by the Wi-Fi Alliance. Most, but not all, 802.11-family Wireless Ethernet hardware is Wi-Fi certified.

Wireless Ethernet hardware supports both the star (infrastructure) network topology, which uses a wireless access point to transfer data between nodes, and the peer-to-peer topology, in which each node can communicate directly with another node.

Bluetooth

Bluetooth is a short-range low-speed wireless network primarily designed to operate in peer-to-peer mode (known as ad-hoc) between PCs and other devices such as printers, projectors, smart phones, mice, keyboards, and other devices. Bluetooth runs in the same 2.4GHz frequency used by IEEE 802.11b, g, and n wireless networks, but uses a spread-spectrum frequency-hopping signaling method to help minimize interference. Bluetooth devices connect to each other to form a personal area network (PAN).

Some systems and devices include integrated Bluetooth adapters, and others need a Bluetooth module connected to the USB port to enable Bluetooth networking.

Infrared

Infrared is a short-range, low-speed, line-of-sight network method that can be used to connect to other PCs, PDAs, or Internet kiosks. Infrared networking is based on the Infrared Data Association (IrDA) protocol. Some laptops include an integrated IrDA port. IrDA can also be used for printing to printers that include an IrDA port or are connected to an IrDA adapter.

If you want to use a computer that does not have IrDA support with infrared networking, you can add an IrDA adapter. Many desktop motherboards include integrated IrDA support. To enable IrDA support, connect a header cable (available from various third-party sources) to the IrDA port and configure the system BIOS to provide IrDA support. On many systems with integrated IrDA support, one of the COM ports can be switched between its normal mode and IrDA support.

To add IrDA support to computers that don't include an IrDA port, use a third-party IrDA module that connects to the USB port.

Cellular

Digital cellular phone networks can be used for Internet access and remote networking, a feature that is extremely useful to mobile workers. To enable a laptop to use a cellular network for data access, you need to connect a cellular modem to your PC and purchase the appropriate data access plan from a wireless carrier.

Cellular modems can be connected to USB ports or installed into CardBus or ExpressCard slots. They can be purchased separately or as a bundle with a data access plan. If you purchase a cellular modem separately, make sure it supports the data access method used by your wireless carrier.

VoIP

Voice over IP (VoIP) is an increasingly popular method for providing home and business telephone access. VoIP routes telephone calls over the same TCP/IP network used for LAN and Internet access. Companies such as Vonage, Skype, AT&T, Verizon, and others provide VoIP services.

To add VoIP service to an existing Ethernet network, you can use either an analog telephone adapter (ATA) or a VoIP router. An ATA enables you to adapt standard telephones to work with VoIP services. It plugs into your existing router. A VoIP router can be used as a replacement for an existing wired or wireless router. Typical VoIP routers support most or all of the following features:

- **Quality of Service (QoS) support**—This feature prioritizes streaming media, such as VoIP phone calls and audio or video playback, over other types of network traffic.

- **One or more FXO ports**—An FXO port enables standard analog telephones to be used in VoIP service.

- **Real-time Transport Protocol/Real-time Transport Control Protocol (RTP/RTCP)**—Supports streaming media, video conferencing, and VoIP applications.

- **Session Initiation Protocol (SIP) support**—A widely used VoIP signaling protocol also used for multimedia distribution and multimedia conferences.

Cable and Connector Types

There are four major types of network cables:

- Unshielded twisted pair (UTP)
- Shielded twisted pair (STP)
- Fiber-optic
- Coaxial

Network cards are designed to interface with one or more types of network cables, each of which is discussed in the following sections.

> **NOTE**   Serial (RS-232) null modem and parallel (LPT) crossover cables can be used with direct parallel or direct serial connections (also known as direct cable connection), which are special types of two-station networking included in Windows that use standard network protocols but do not use network cards.
>
> Infrared (IR) ports built into many notebook computers can also be used with direct serial connection.

UTP and STP Cabling

UTP cabling is the most common of the major cabling types. The name refers to its physical construction: four twisted pairs of wire surrounded by a flexible jacket.

UTP cable comes in various grades, of which Category 5e (Cat5e) is the most common of the standard cabling grades. Cat5e cabling is suitable for use with both standard 10BaseT and Fast Ethernet networking and can also be used for Gigabit Ethernet networks if it passes compliance testing.

STP cabling was originally available only in Cat4, which was used by the now largely outdated IBM Token-Ring Networks. STP uses the same RJ-45 connector as UTP, but includes a metal shield for electrical insulation between the wire pairs and the outer jacket. It's stiffer and more durable, but also more expensive and harder to loop through tight spaces than UTP. Type 1 STP cable used by older token-ring adapters has a 9-pin connector. STP cabling is also available in Cat5, Cat5e, and Cat6 for use with Ethernet networks. It is used where electromagnetic interference (EMI) prevents the use of UTP cable.

Figure 16-11 compares the construction of STP and UTP cables.

Table 16-6 lists the various types of UTP and STP cabling in use and what they're best suited for.

> **NOTE**   The de facto standard for wire pairs in both UTP and STP cables is the EIA-568B standard. You can create a crossover cable by building one end to the EIA-568B standard and the other end to the EIA-568A standard. See http://www.incentre.net/content/view/75/2/ for a color-coded diagram.

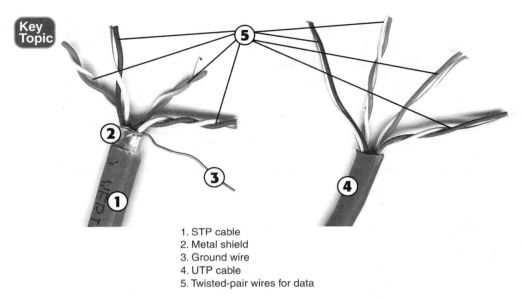

1. STP cable
2. Metal shield
3. Ground wire
4. UTP cable
5. Twisted-pair wires for data

Figure 16-11   An STP cable (left) includes a metal shield and ground wire for protection against interference, while a UTP cable (right) does not.

Figure 16-12 compares Ethernet cards using UTP (or STP), thin coaxial, and thick coaxial cables and connectors to each other.

The connector used by Ethernet cards that use UTP or STP cable is commonly known as an RJ45 connector. RJ stands for registered jack; the RJ45 has eight contacts that accept eight wires, also known as pins. It resembles a larger version of the RJ11 connector used for telephone cabling. UTP cabling runs between a computer on the network and a hub or switch carrying signals between the two. The hub or switch then sends signals to other computers (servers or workstations) on the network. When a computer is connected to a hub or switch, a straight through cable is used. This means that both ends of the cable are wired the same way. If a computer needs to be connected directly to another computer, a crossover cable, which has a different pin configuration on one end, is used. Keep in mind that between the computer and the hub or switch, there might be other wiring equipment involved, for example RJ45 jacks, patch panels, and so on. UTP and STP cable can be purchased in prebuilt form or as bulk cable with connectors, so you can build the cable to the length you need. Figure 16-13 compares RJ11 and RJ45 connectors.

NOTE   Although RJ45 is the common name for the UTP Ethernet connector, this is a misnomer; the proper name is 8P8C (8 position, 8 contact). Don't confuse it with the RJ45S connector, an eight-position connector, used for telephone rather than computer data. An RJ45S jack has a slightly different shape than the connector used for Ethernet and includes a cutout on one side to prevent unkeyed connectors from being inserted into the jack.

To see drawings of the RJ45S jack and other telephone jacks, see http://www.siemon.com/us/standards/13-24_modular_wiring_reference.asp.

Table 16-6   Categories and Uses for UTP and STP Cabling

Category	Network Type(s) Supported	Supported Speeds	Cable Type, Notes
1	Telephone, DSL, HomePNA	Up to 100 Mbps (Home-PNA)	UTP; one wire pair
2	LocalTalk	Up to 4Mbps	UTP; obsolete; one wire pair
3	10BASE-T Ethernet	Up to 10 Mbps	UTP; obsolete; Replace with Cat5, Cat5e, or Cat6; four wire pairs
4	Token ring	Up to 16 Mbps	Shielded twisted pair (STP); one wire pair
5	10BASE-T, 100BASE-T,	Up to 100 Mbps	UTP, STP; four wire pairs
5e	10BASE-T, 100BASE-T, 1000BASE-T	Up to 1000 Mbps	Enhanced version of Cat5; available in UTP, STP; four wire pairs
6	10BASE-T, 100BASE-T, 1000BASE-T	Up to 1000 Mbps	Handles higher frequencies than Cat5; available in UTP, STP
7	10BASE-T, 100BASE-T, 1000BASE-T	Up to 1000 Mbps	Uses 12-connector GG45 connector (backward-compatible with RJ45); available in UTP, STP

Hubs connect different computers with each other on the network. See "Switches and Hubs," later in this chapter for more information.

UTP and STP cable can be purchased in prebuilt assemblies or can be built from bulk cable and connectors.

Fiber-Optic Cabling

Fiber-optic cabling transmits signals with light rather than with electrical signals, which makes it immune to electrical interference. It is used primarily as a backbone between networks. Fiber-optic cable comes in two major types:

- **Single-mode**—Has a thin core (between eight and ten microns) designed to carry a single light ray long distances.

■ **Multi-mode**—Has a thicker core (62.5 microns) than single-mode; carries multiple light rays for short distances.

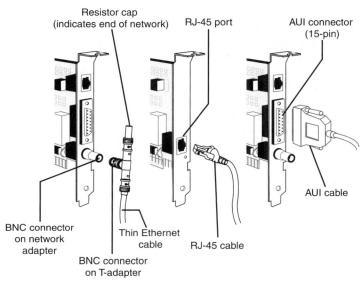

Figure 16-12 Combo UTP/BNC/AUI Ethernet network cards (left and right) compared with a UTP/STP-only Ethernet card (center) and cables.

Figure 16-13 RJ11 connector (left) compared to RJ45 connector (right).

Fiber-optic cabling can be purchased prebuilt, but if you need a custom length, it should be built and installed by experienced cable installers because of the expense and risk of damage. Some network adapters built for servers are designed to use fiber-optic cable. Otherwise, media converters are used to interconnect fiber optic to conventional cables on networks.

NOTE   When Ethernet is run over fiber-optic cables, the letter *F* is used in place of *T* (twisted pair) in the name. For example, 10BASE-F is 10Mbps Ethernet running on fiber-optic cable, 100BASE-F is 100Mbps Ethernet running on fiber-optic cable, and so on.

Coaxial Cabling

Coaxial cabling is the oldest type of network cabling; its data wires are surrounded by a wire mesh for insulation. Coaxial cables, which resemble cable TV connections, are not popular for network use today because they must be run from one station directly to another rather than to or from a hub/switch.

Coaxial cabling creates a bus topology; each end of the bus must be terminated, and if any part of the bus fails, the entire network fails.

The oldest Ethernet standard, 10BASE5, uses a very thick coaxial cable (RG-8) that is attached to a NIC through a transceiver that uses a so-called "vampire tap" to connect the transceiver to the cable. This type of coaxial cable is also referred to as Thick Ethernet or Thicknet.

Thin Ethernet, also referred to as Thinnet, Cheapernet, or 10BASE2 Ethernet was used for low-cost Ethernet networks before the advent of UTP cable. The coaxial cable used with 10BASE2 is referred to as RG-58. This type of coaxial cable connects to network cards through a T-connector that bayonet-mounts to the rear of the network card using a BNC connector. The arms of the T are used to connect two cables, each running to another computer in the network.

If the workstation is at the end of a network, a terminating resistor is connected to one arm of the T to indicate the end of the network (refer to Figure 16-12). If a resistor is removed, the network fails; if a station on the network fails, the network fails.

Two other types of coaxial cable are common in cable Internet, satellite Internet, and fixed wireless Internet installations:

- **RG-59**—Used in older cable TV or satellite TV installations; 75-ohm resistance. Also used by the long-obsolete Arcnet LAN standard.

- **RG-6**—Uses same connectors as RG-59, but has a larger diameter with superior shielding; used in cable TV/Internet, satellite TV/Internet, and fixed wireless Internet/TV service; 75-ohm resistance.

Plenum and PVC

The outer jacket of UTP, STP, and coaxial cable is usually made of PVC (polyvinyl chloride), a low-cost durable vinyl compound. Unfortunately, PVC creates dense poisonous smoke when burned. If you need to run network cable through suspended ceiling or air vents, you should use more-expensive plenum cable, which produces less smoke and a lower level of toxic chemicals when burned.

Connector Types

Most coaxial cables, including RG-58, RG-59, and RG-6 use a BNC (Bayonet Neill-Concelman) connector. RG-58 uses a T-adapter to connect to a 10BASE2 Ethernet adapter. RG-11 (Thicknet) cable is connected to an Ethernet card by means of an external transceiver, which attaches to the AUI port on the rear of older Ethernet network cards. The transceiver attaches to the cable with a so-called "vampire tap."

10BASE-T, 100BASE-T, and 1000BASE-T Ethernet cards using copper wire all use the RJ45 connector shown in Figure 16-13, as do newer token-ring, some ISDN, and most cable Internet devices. DSL devices often use the RJ11 connector shown in Figure 16-13, as do dial-up modems.

To attach a cable using RJ11 or RJ45 connectors to a network card or other device, plug it into the connector so that the plastic locking clip snaps into place; the cable and connector will fit together only one way. To remove the cable, squeeze the locking clip toward the connector and pull the connector out of the jack. Some cables use a snagless connector; squeeze the guard over the locking clip to open the clip to remove the cable.

Fiber-optic devices and cables use one of several connector types. The most common include

- **SC**—Uses square connectors

- **ST**—Uses round connectors

- **FC**—Uses a round connector

See Figure 16-14. If you need to interconnect devices which use two different connector types, use adapter cables which are designed to match the connector types and other characteristics of the cable and device.

SC cable   FC cable   ST cable

Figure 16-14   SC, FC, and ST fiber-optic cable connectors compared.

Installing Network Interface Cards

Although many recent computers include a 10/100 or 10/100/1000 Ethernet port or a Wireless Ethernet (WLAN) adapter, you sometimes need to install a network interface card (NIC) into a computer you want to add to a network.

PCI and PCI Express

To install a Plug and Play (PnP) network card, follow this procedure:

Step 1.   Turn off the computer and remove the case cover.

Step 2.   Locate an available expansion slot matching the network card's design. (Most use PCI, but some servers and workstations might use PCI-X or PCI Express.).

Step 3.   Remove the slot cover and insert the card into the slot. Secure the card in the slot.

Step 4.   Restart the system and provide the driver disk or CD-ROM when requested by the system.

Step 5.   Insert the operating system disc if requested to install network drivers and clients.

Step 6.   The IRQ, I/O port address, and memory address required by the card will be assigned automatically.

Step 7.   Test for connectivity (check LED lights, use a command such as ping, and so on), and then close the computer case.

USB

Although USB network adapters are also PnP devices, you normally need to install the drivers provided with the USB network adapter before you attach the adapter to your computer. After the driver software is installed, the device will be recognized as soon as you plug it into a working USB port.

NOTE If you are using a wireless USB adapter, you can improve signal strength by using an extension cable between the adapter and the USB port on the computer. Using an extension cable enables you to move the adapter as needed to pick up a stronger signal.

Most USB network adapters are bus powered. For best results, they should be attached to a USB port built into your computer or to a self-powered hub. Most recent adapters support USB 2.0, which provides full-speed support for 100BASE-T (Fast Ethernet) signal speeds.

PC Card/CardBus

PC Card network adapters work with both the original 16-bit PC Card slot and the newer 32-bit CardBus slot. However, CardBus cards work only in CardBus slots.

Both PC Card and CardBus cards are detected and installed by built-in support for these adapters in Windows 2000 and newer versions.

Some PC Card and CardBus network adapters often require that a dongle be attached to the card to enable the card to plug into a network port. See Chapter 9 for details.

Configuring Network Interface Cards

Although PCI, USB, PC Card, CardBus network adapters, and integrated adapters support PnP configuration for hardware resources, you might also need to configure the network adapter for the type of media it uses, for the speed of the connection, and with Wireless Ethernet adapters, the security settings that are used on the wireless network.

Hardware Resources

Typical network interface card hardware resource settings include

- IRQ
- I/O port address range

If the workstation is a diskless workstation, a free upper memory address must also be supplied for the boot ROM on the card. A few older network cards also use upper memory blocks for RAM buffers; check the card's documentation.

Media Type

Most recent Ethernet cards are designed to use only UTP Cat3 or greater network cabling. However, some older cards were also designed to use 10BASE5 (Thicknet) or 10BASE2 (Thinnet) cabling. Cards that are designed to use two or more different types of cabling are known as combo cards, and during card configuration, you need to select the type of media that will be used with the card. This option is also known as the Transceiver Type option. Depending upon the card's drivers, you might need to make this setting through the card's command-line configuration program or the card's properties sheet in Windows Device Manager.

NOTE   Some network adapters designed for use with UTP cable can automatically sense when the cable is not connected. Windows XP, Vista, and 7 might display an icon in the system area to indicate when a cable is not connected to a network adapter. To enable notification in Windows XP, open the Network Connections window, right-click the connection, select **Properties**, and make sure the option **Show Icon in Notification Area When Connected** is enabled.

Full/Half-Duplex

If the hardware in use on an Ethernet, Fast Ethernet, or Gigabit Ethernet network permits, you can configure the network to run in full-duplex mode. Full-duplex mode enables the adapter to send and receive data at the same time, which doubles network speed over the default half-duplex mode (where the card sends and receives in separate operations). Thus, a 10BASE-T-based network runs at 20Mbps in full-duplex mode; a 100BASE-T-based network runs at 200Mbps in full-duplex mode; and a 1000BASE-T-based network runs at 2000Mbps in full-duplex mode.

To achieve full-duplex performance on a UTP-based Ethernet network, the network adapters on a network must all support full-duplex mode, be configured to use full-duplex mode with the device's setup program or properties sheet, *and* a switch must be used in place of a hub.

Wireless Ethernet (WLAN) Configuration

Wireless Ethernet requires additional configuration compared to wired Ethernet, as shown in Table 16-7.

Most home and small-business networks using encryption will use a pre-shared key (PSK). When a pre-shared key is used, both the wireless router or access point and all clients must have the same PSK before they can connect with each other. WPA and WPA2 also support the use of a RADIUS authentication server, which is used on corporate networks.

Table 16-7 Wireless Ethernet Configuration Settings

Setting	What the Setting Does
Service Set Identifier (**SSID**)	Names the network. Windows XP, Vista, and 7 can detect SSIDs from unsecured networks and from secured networks that broadcast their SSIDs.
Channel	Specifies a channel for all stations to use. This option is required for ad-hoc (peer-to-peer) configurations and if the vendor's own software is used to configure the network. Windows XP's Wireless Zero Configuration service determines the channel to use automatically.
Wireless Equivalent Privacy (WEP)	Enable to prevent access by unauthorized users. Use this setting in place of WPA only if some hardware does not support WPA. WEP is not supported by 802.11n wireless network hardware. If WEP or WPA security is disabled (the default with most hardware), anybody can get on the network if they know or detect the SSID.
WEP Encryption Strength	Use the highest setting supported by both WEP and adapters for best security. Small-office home-office hardware might use 64-bit; business-market hardware often uses 128-bit encryption.
WEP Key	Use 10 alphanumeric characters for 64-bit encryption; use 26 characters for 128-bit encryption. All network devices must use the same WEP key and encryption strength if WEP is enabled.
Wi-Fi Protected Access (WPA)	Enable to prevent access by unauthorized users. WPA is much more secure than WEP. Disable this option and use WEP to secure your network only if some equipment on the network does not support WPA. A driver or firmware upgrade might be necessary on some older equipment to enable WPA support. Currently the latest version is WPA2, which is more secure than WPA.
WPA Key	WPA can use a variable-length alphanumeric key up to 63 characters. (Some WPA-compliant hardware might not work with a 63-character key.)
WPA Encryption Type	■ Temporal Key Integrity Protocol (TKIP) is a 128-bit encryption protocol that was developed for WPA to address weaknesses within WEP, but without the need to replace older equipment. This is the original version of WPA. ■ Advanced Encryption Standard (AES) is a 128–256-bit encryption protocol used in several technologies including wireless networking. It can be used exclusively or in conjunction with TKIP and is the recommended option. WPA using AES is often referred to as WPA2.

Switches and Hubs

Hubs connect different computers with each other on an Ethernet network based on UTP or STP cabling. A hub has several connectors for RJ45 cabling, a power source, and signal lights to indicate network activity. Most hubs are stackable, meaning that if you need more ports than the hub contains, you can connect it to another hub to expand its capabilities.

A hub is the slowest connection device on a network because it splits the bandwidth of the connection among all the computers connected to it. For example, a five-port 10/100 Ethernet hub divides the 100Mbps speed of Fast Ethernet among the five ports, providing only 20Mbps of bandwidth to each port for Fast Ethernet and 10/100 adapters, and only 2Mbps per port for 10BASE-T adapters. A hub also broadcasts data to all computers connected to it.

A switch resembles a hub but creates a dedicated full-speed connection between the two computers that are communicating with each other. A five-port 10/100 switch, for example, provides the full 10Mbps bandwidth to each port connected to a 10BASE-T card and a full 100Mbps bandwidth to each port connected to a Fast Ethernet or 10/100 card. If the network adapters are configured to run in full-duplex mode and the switch supports full-duplex (most modern switches do), the Fast Ethernet bandwidth on the network is doubled to 200Mbps, and the 10BASE-T bandwidth is doubled to 20Mbps. Switches can be daisy-chained in a manner similar to stackable hubs, and there is no limit to the number of switches possible in a network.

Beyond LANs—Repeaters, Bridges, and Routers

Hubs and switches are the only connectivity equipment needed for a workgroup LAN. However, if the network needs to span longer distances than those supported by the network cabling in use or needs to connect to another network, additional connectivity equipment is needed.

- **Repeater**—A repeater boosts signal strength to enable longer cable runs than those permitted by the "official" cabling limits of Ethernet. Hubs and switches can be used as repeaters.

NOTE   Windows 7/Vista/XP features built-in bridging capabilities. You can also use a wireless router with a built-in switch to create a single network with both wired and wireless clients. With Windows 7, you can use third-party software called Connectify (http://www.connectify.me/) to turn a computer with a wireless Ethernet card into a wireless access point that supports Internet and LAN access by other computers with wireless Ethernet adapters.

- **Router**—A router is used to interconnect a LAN to other networks; the name suggests the device's similarity to an efficient travel agent, who helps a group reach its destination as quickly as possible. Routers can connect different types of networks and protocols to each other (Ethernet, token ring, TCP/IP, and so on) and are a vital part of the Internet. Router features and prices vary according to the network types and protocols supported.

Switches and routers make up the basic infrastructure of most LANs. While other equipment is necessary for different types of connections and environments, these two are the most commonly found devices in a server room. Just remember that the switch generally connects one or more computers to each other. The router connects one or more networks to each other. In small home and office networks, it is common for routers to also incorporate switches.

Networking Configuration

Before a network connection can function, it must be properly configured. The following sections discuss the configurations required for the network protocols covered on the A+ Certification Exams: TCP/IP and NetBEUI.

Installing Network Protocols in Windows

Depending upon the network protocol you want to install and the version of Windows in use on a particular computer, you can install any of several different protocols through the normal Windows network dialogs, as shown in Table 16-8.

Table 16-8 Windows Support for Network Protocols

Network Protocol	Windows Version			
	7	Vista	XP	2000
TCP/IP	Yes	Yes	Yes	Yes
NetBEUI	No	No	*	Yes

*Not officially supported in Windows XP, but can be installed manually from the Windows XP CD-ROM's Valueadd\MSFT\Net\NetBEUI folder. See Microsoft Help and Support article 301041 for details.

> **NOTE** Windows operating systems support TCP/IPv4 and TCP/IPv6. TCP/IPv4 is still the most commonly used version. When TCP/IP is referred to in this book, it generally means TCP/IPv4.

To install a network protocol in Windows 7/Vista or XP/2000, follow this procedure:

Step 1. Open the **Network Connections** window.

- In Windows 7/Vista, click **Start, Control Panel**, and then double-click the **Network and Sharing Center** icon. Next, click **Manage Network Connections** under tasks.

- In Windows XP/2000, click **Start, Control Panel**, and then double-click the **Network Connections** (called Network in 2000) icon in Control Panel or right-click **My Network Places** and select **Properties**.

Step 2. Right-click the connection you want to modify and select **Properties**.

Step 3. Click the **Install** button.

Step 4. Click **Protocol**.

Step 5. Select the protocol you want to add.

Step 6. Click **OK**.

After the protocol is installed, select the protocol and click **Properties** to adjust its properties setting.

TCP/IPv4 Configuration

The TCP/IPv4 protocol, although it was originally used for Internet connectivity, is currently the most important network protocol for LAN as well as larger networks; in most modern business networks, TCP/IP v4 and v6 are used side by side. To connect with the rest of a TCP/IP-based network, each computer or other device must have a unique IP address. If the network connects with the Internet, additional settings are required.

There are two ways to configure a computer's TCP/IP settings:

- Server-assigned IP address
- Static IP address

Table 16-9 compares the differences in these configurations.

Table 16-9   Static Versus Server-Assigned IP Addressing

Setting	What It Does	Static IP Address	Server-Assigned IP
IP address	Identifies computer on the network	Unique value for each computer	Automatically assigned by DHCP server
DNS configuration	Identifies domain name system servers	IP addresses of one or more DNS servers, host name, and domain name must be entered	Automatically assigned by server
Gateway	Identifies IP address of device that connects computer to Internet or other network	IP address for gateway must be entered; same value for all computers on network	Automatically assigned by server
WINS configuration	Maps IP addresses to NetBIOS computer names; used with Windows NT 4.0 and earlier versions	IP addresses for one or more WINS servers must be entered if enabled	Can use DHCP to resolve WINS if necessary

All versions of Windows default to using a server-assigned IP address. As Table 16-9 makes clear, this is the preferable method for configuring a TCP/IP network. Use a manually assigned IP address if a Dynamic Host Configuration Protocol (DHCP) server (which provides IP addresses automatically) is not available on the network—or if you need to configure a firewall or router to provide different levels of access to some systems and you must specify those systems' IP addresses.

NOTE   Routers, wireless gateways, and computers that host an Internet connection shared with Windows's Internet Connection Sharing or a third-party sharing program all provide DHCP services to other computers on the network.

To configure TCP/IP in Windows, access the Internet Protocol Properties window; this window contains several dialogs used to make changes to TCP/IP. Note that these dialogs are nearly identical in Windows XP, Vista, and 7. To open the General tab of the Internet Protocol Properties window, open **Network Connections**, right-click the network connection, select **Properties**, click **Internet Protocol (TCP/IP)** in the list of protocols and features, and click **Properties**.

TCP/IP Configuration with a DHCP Server

Figure 16-15 shows the General tab as it appears when a DHCP server is used.

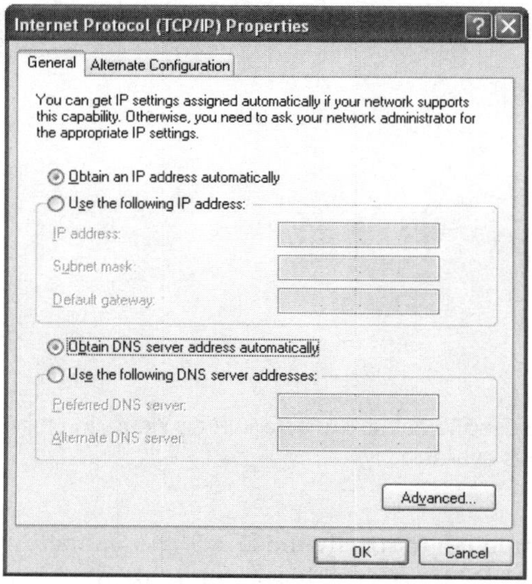

Figure 16-15   The General tab is configured to obtain IP and DNS server information automatically when a DHCP server is used on the network.

NOTE To determine the IP address, default gateway, and DNS servers used by a system using DHCP addressing, open a command prompt and enter the `ipconfig /all` command.

To learn more about using ipconfig, see "Using Ipconfig," in this chapter.

TCP/IP Alternate Configuration

The Alternate Configuration tab shown in Figure 16-16 is used to set up a different configuration for use when a DHCP server is not available or when a different set of user-configured settings are needed, as when a laptop is being used at a secondary location. By default, automatic private IP addressing (APIPA) is used when no DHCP server is in use. APIPA assigns each system a unique IP address in the 169.254.x.x range. APIPA enables a network to perform LAN connections when the DHCP server is not available, but systems using APIPA cannot connect to the Internet.

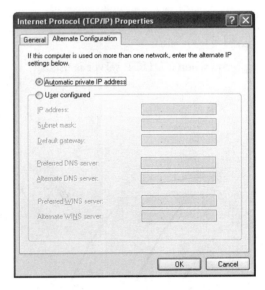

Figure 16-16 The Alternate Configuration tab is used to set up a different IP configuration for use on another network or when no DHCP server is available.

You can also use the Alternate Configuration tab to specify the IP address, subnet mask, default gateway, DNS servers, and WINS servers. This option is useful if this system is moved to another network that uses different IP addresses for these servers.

TCP/IP User-Configured IP and DNS Addresses

When a DHCP server is not used, the General tab is used to set up the IP address, subnet mask, default gateway, and DNS servers used by the network client. (The information shown in Figure 16-17 is fictitious.)

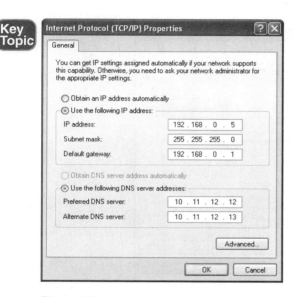

Figure 16-17 The General tab of the TCP/IP properties sheet when manual configuration is used.

TCP/IP User-Configured Advanced Settings

Click the Advanced button shown in Figure 16-17 to bring up a multitabbed dialog for adding or editing gateways (IP Settings), DNS server addresses (DNS), adjusting WINS resolution (WINS), and adjusting TCP/IP port filtering (Options). These options can be used whether DHCP addressing is enabled or not. Figure 16-18 shows these tabs.

Understanding IP Addressing, Subnet Masks, and IP Classes

An IPv4 address consists of a group of four numbers that each range from 0 to 255, for example: 192.168.1.1. IP addresses are divided into two sections: the network portion, which is the number of the network the computer is on, and the host portion, which is the individual number of the computer. Using the IP address we just mentioned as an example, the 192.168.1 portion would typically be the network number, and .1 would be the host number. A subnet mask is used to distinguish between the network portion of the IP address and the host portion. For example, a typical subnet mask for the IP address we just used would be 255.255.255.0. The 255s correspond to the network portion of the IP address. The 0s correspond to the host portion, as shown in Table 16-10.

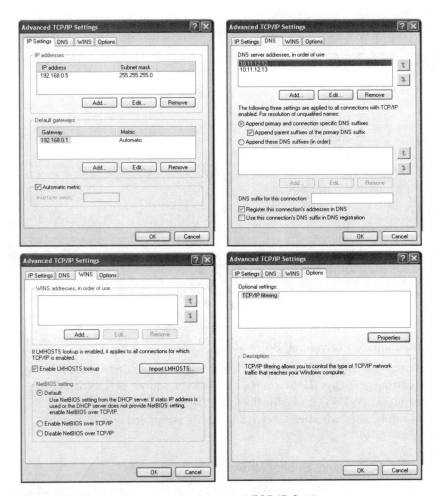

Figure 16-18   The tabs used for Advanced TCP/IP Settings.

Table 16-10   An IP Address and Corresponding Subnet Mask

IP Address/Subnet Mask	Network Portion	Host Portion
192.168.1.1	192.168.1	1
255.255.255.0	255.255.255	0

The subnet mask is also used to define subnetworks, if subnetworking is being implemented. Subnetworking goes beyond the scope of the A+ exam; if you would like more information on subnetworking, refer to *CompTIA Network+ (N10-004) Cert Guide* by Mike Harwood (Pearson Certification, October 2010).

Both computers and other networked devices, such as routers and network printers, can have IP addresses, and some devices can have more than one IP address. For example, a router will typically have two IP addresses—one to connect the router to a LAN and the other that connects it to the Internet, enabling it to route traffic from the LAN to the Internet and back.

IP addresses are divided into three major categories: Class A, Class B, and Class C, which define ranges of IP addresses. Class A is designated for large corporations, ISPs, and government. Class B is designated for mid-sized corporations and ISPs. Class C is designated for small offices and home offices. Each class of IP addresses uses a default subnet mask, as shown in Table 16-11.

Table 16-11 Internet Protocol Classification System

Class	First Octet Range	Starting IP	Ending IP	Default Subnet Mask
Class A	1–127	0.0.0.0	127.255.255.255	255.0.0.0
Class B	128–191	128.0.0.0	191.255.255.255	255.255.0.0
Class C	192–223	192.0.0.0	223.255.255.255	255.255.255.0

NOTE The 127 network is reserved for testing. This is known as the loopback, for example 127.0.0.1. The usable starting IP for Class A is actually 1.0.0.0.

In any given network, the first and last addresses are reserved and cannot be assigned to computers or other hosts. For example, in the 192.168.1.0 network, 192.168.1.1 through 192.168.1.254 can be assigned, but 192.168.1.0 is reserved for the network number, and 192.168.1.255 is reserved for something called the broadcast.

Each number in an IP address is called an octet. An octet is an eight-bit byte. This means that in the binary numbering system the number can range from 00000000–11111111. For example, 255 is actually 11111111 when converted to the binary numbering system. Another example: 192 equals 11000000.

NOTE To convert numbers from decimal to binary and vice-versa use the Windows calculator. Press **Windows+R** to bring up the Run prompt, then type **calc**. This will run the Windows Calculator. From there, click **View** on the menu bar and select **Scientific**. Now you will notice radio buttons on the upper left that allow you to change between numbering systems. Simply type any number, and then select the numbering system you want to convert it to.

In a Class A network, the first octet is the network portion of the IP address, and the three remaining octets identify the host portion of the IP address. Class B networks use the first and second octets as the network portion and the third and fourth octets as the host portion. Class C networks use the first three octets as network portion and the last octet as the host portion of the IP address. Table 16-12 gives one example IP address and subnet mask for each Class.

Table 16-12 Internet Protocol/Subnet Mask Examples for Classes A, B, and C

Class	IP Address/Subnet Mask	Network Portion	Host Portion
Class A	10.0.0.1	10	0.0.1
	255.0.0.0	255	0.0.0
Class B	172.16.0.1	172.16	0.1
	255.255.0.0	255.255	0.0
Class C	192.168.1.100	192.168.1	100
	255.255.255.0	255.255.255	0

See a pattern? The size of the network portion increases in octets, and the host portion decreases as you ascend through the classes. As time goes on, you will see more patterns like this within TCP/IP.

WINS Configuration

Windows Internet Naming Service (WINS) matches the NetBIOS name of a particular computer to an IP address on the network; this process is also called *resolving* or *translating* the NetBIOS name to an IP address. WINS requires the use of a Window Server that has been set up to provide the resolving service. If WINS is enabled, the IP addresses of the WINS servers must be entered.

If the IP address is provided by a DHCP server, or if a WINS server is used, you will need to enter the correct WINS settings (refer to Figure 16-18).

The network administrator will inform you of the correct settings to use on this dialog.

Gateway

A *gateway* is a computer or device (such as a router) that provides a connection between a LAN and a wide area network (WAN) or the Internet. Computers that use a LAN connection to connect to the Internet need to enter the IP address or addresses of the gateways on this tab (refer to Figure 16-17) if the computer doesn't use DHCP to obtain an IP address.

DNS Configuration

The Internet uses the domain name system (DNS) to map domain names, such as www.microsoft.com, to their corresponding IP address or addresses. A computer using the Internet must use at least one DNS server to provide this translation service. Use the DNS Configuration tab to set up the computer's host name, domain name, and DNS servers (refer to Figure 16-17) if the computer doesn't use DHCP to obtain an IP address.

NOTE   Most ISPs and networks have at least two DNS name servers to provide backup in case one fails. Be sure to enter the IP addresses of all DNS servers available to your network. In Windows, these are referred to as preferred and alternate DNS servers.

IPv6 IP Addressing

IP version 6 enables a huge increase in the number of available IP addresses for computers, smartphones, and other mobile devices. Windows Vista and 7 include IPv6. IPv6 uses 128-bit source and destination IP addresses (compared to 32-bit for IPv4), features built-in security, and provides better support for Quality of Service (QoS) routing, which is important to achieve high-quality streaming audio and video traffic.

IPv6 addresses starts out as 128-bit addresses that are then divided into eight 16-bit blocks. The blocks are converted into hexadecimal, and each block is separated from the following block by a colon. Leading zeros are typically suppressed, but each block must contain at least one digit.

Here is a typical IPv6 address:

    21DA:D3:0:2F3B:2AA:FF:FE28:9C5A

A contiguous sequence of 16-bit blocks set to zero can be represented by :: (double-colon). This technique is also known as *zero compression*. To determine the number of zero bits represented by the double-colon, count the number of blocks in the compressed address, subtract the result from 8, and multiply the result by 16. An address can include only one zero-compressed block.

Here is an IPv6 address that does use double-colon:

FF02::2.

There are two blocks (FF02 and 2). So, how many zero bits are represented by the double colon? Subtract 2 from 8 (8-2=6, then multiply 6 by 16 (6×16=96). This address includes a block of 96 zero bits.

The loopback address on an IPv6 system is 0:0:0:0:0:0:0:1, which is abbreviated as ::1. Thus, if you want to test your network interface in Windows Vista/7 where IPv6 is enabled by default, you can type ping ::1.

IPv6 supports three types of addresses: unicast, multicast, and anycast. There are five types of Unicast addresses:

■   Global unicast addresses are used in the same way as IPv4 public addresses. The first three bits are set to 001, followed by 45 bits used for the global routing prefix; these 48 bits are collectively known as the public topology. The subnet ID uses the next 16 bits, and the interface ID uses the remaining 64 bits.

■   Link-local addresses correspond to the Automatic Private IP address (APIPA) address scheme used by IPv4 (addresses that start with 169.254.) The first 10 bits are set to FE80 hex, followed by 54 zero bits, and 64 bits for the Interface ID. Using zero compression, the prefix would thus be FE80::/64. As with APIPA, link local addresses are not forwarded beyond the link.

■   Site-local addresses correspond to IPv4 private address spaces (10.0.0.0/8, 172.16.0.0/12, and 192.168.0.0/16).

■   Special addresses include unspecified addresses (0:0:0:0:0:0:0:0 or ::), which is equivalent to IP v4's 0.0.0.0 and indicate the absence of an IP address; loopback address (0:0:0:0:0:0:0:1 or ::1) is equivalent to the IPv4 loopback address of 127.0.0.1.

■   Compatibility addresses are used in situations in which IPv4 and IPv6 are both in use. In the following examples, w.x.y.z are replaced by the actual IPv4 address. An IPv4-compatible address (0:0:0:0:0:0:w.x.y.z or ::w.x.y.z) is used by nodes that support IPv4 and IPv6 communicating over IPv6. An IPv4-mapped address (0:0:0:0:0:FFFF:w.x.y.z or ::FFFF:w.x.y.z) represents an IPv4-only node to an IPv6 node. A 6to4 address is used when two nodes running both IPv4 and IPv6 connect over an IPv4 routing. The address combines the prefix 2002::/16 with the IPv4 public address of the node. ISATAP can also be used for the connection; it uses a locally administered ID of ::0:5EFE:w.x.y.z (w.x.y.z could be any unicast IPv4 address, either public or private); Teredo addresses are used for tunneling IPv6 over UDP through Network Address Translation (NAT); they use the prefix 3FFE:831F::/32.

Both IPv4 and IPv6 support multicasting, which enables one-to-many distribution of content such as Internet TV or other types of streaming media. IPv6 multicast addresses begin with FF.

Anycast addressing sends information to a group of potential receivers that are identified by the same destination address. This is also known as one-to-one-to-many association. Anycast addressing can be used for distributed services, such as DNS or other situations in which automatic failover, is desirable. IPv6 uses anycast addresses as destination addresses that are assigned only to routers. Anycast addresses are assigned from the unicast address space.

To see the IPv4 and IPv6 addresses assigned to a Windows Vista or 7 PC using both IPv4 and IPv6, use the command-line `ipconfig` utility. Here's an example of the output from a system using a wireless Ethernet adapter:

```
Wireless LAN adapter Wireless Network Connection:
   Connection-specific DNS Suffix  . :
   Link-local IPv6 Address . . . . . : fe80::5cf1:2f98:7351:b3a3%12
   IPv4 Address. . . . . . . . . . . : 192.168.1.155
   Subnet Mask . . . . . . . . . . . : 255.255.255.0
   Default Gateway . . . . . . . . . : 192.168.1.1
```

For more information, see http://technet.microsoft.com/en-us/library/dd392266(WS.10).aspx

NetBEUI Configuration

The only configuration required for a NetBEUI network is that each computer has a unique name and that all computers in a particular workgroup use the same workgroup name. To set or change the computer and workgroup names, use the Computer Name tab on the System properties sheet in Windows XP. In Windows Vista and 7, click **Change Settings** in the Computer Name, Domain, and Workgroup Settings section of the System properties sheet.

CAUTION   Windows XP also contains a Network Setup wizard, which is designed to automate various parts of the network setup process. Do *not* use this wizard if you have already configured network settings because the wizard might undo your changes.

Setting Up Shared Resources

Sharing resources with other network users requires the following steps:

Step 1.   Installing and/or enabling File and Printer sharing.

Step 2.   Selecting which drives, folders, or printers to share.

Step 3.   Setting permissions.

NOTE   Windows XP uses NTFS security permissions only on NTFS-formatted drives and only if simple file sharing is disabled.

The following sections cover performing these processes manually. However, the Network Setup wizard can also perform these steps for you.

Installing File and Printer Sharing

By default, File and Printer Sharing is installed in Windows. However, if you need to add it, File and Printer Sharing can be installed through the network connection's properties sheet. For Windows 7/ Vista/XP/2000, follow this procedure:

Step 1.   Open the properties sheet as described in "Installing Network Protocols in Windows," earlier in this chapter.

Step 2.   Click the **Install** button.

Step 3.   Click the **Service** icon.

Step 4.   Click the **Add** button.

Step 5.   Select **File and Printer Sharing for Microsoft Networks** and click **OK**.

Step 6.   Restart the computer.

Figure 16-19 illustrates a typical Windows XP network properties sheet after File and Printer Sharing is installed. The checkbox indicates this feature is enabled.

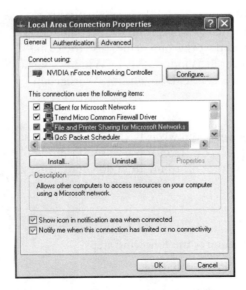

Figure 16-19   This network connection has File and Printer Sharing for Microsoft Networks installed and enabled.

Shared Folders and Drives

A shared folder or drive can be accessed by other computers on the network. Shares can be provided in two ways:

- On a client/server-based network, or a peer-to-peer network with peer servers that support user/group permissions, shares are protected by lists of authorized users or groups. Windows 7, Vista, XP, and 2000 support user/group access control. However, Windows XP supports user/group access control only when the default simple file sharing setting is disabled.

- A peer-to-peer network whose peer servers do not support user/group access control might only offer options for read/only or full access (as with Windows XP using its default simple file sharing setting).

When user/group-based permissions are used, only members who belong to a specific group or are listed separately on the access list for a particular share can access that share. After users log on to the network, they have access to all shares they've been authorized to use without the need to provide additional passwords. Access levels include full and read-only and, on NTFS drives, other access levels, such as write, create, and delete.

Sharing a Folder Using Simple File Sharing

To share a folder or drive in Windows XP with simple file sharing enabled, follow these steps:

Step 1.   Right-click the folder or drive and select **Sharing and Security**.

Step 2.   If you right-click a drive, Windows XP displays a warning. Click the link to continue.

Step 3.   Click the box **Share This Folder on the Network** to share the folder in read-only mode. To share the folder in read/write mode, click the box **Allow Network Users to Change My Files**. Click **OK**.

Figure 16-20 illustrates sharing a folder or drive when simple file sharing is enabled.

Sharing a Folder with User/Group Permissions in Windows XP

If you want to set up user/group permissions on Windows XP, you must first disable simple file sharing.

Step 1.   Open My Computer or Windows Explorer.

Step 2.   Open the Tools menu and click **Folder Options**.

Step 3.   Click the **View** tab.

Step 4.   In the Advanced Settings portion of the dialog, scroll down to **Use Simple File Sharing (Recommended)** and clear the checkbox.

Step 5.   Click **Apply** and then **OK**.

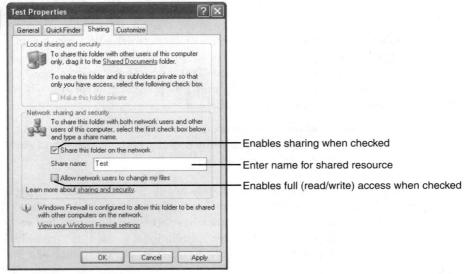

Figure 16-20   Setting up a network share in Windows XP using the default simple file-sharing option.

After simple file sharing is disabled, you can share a folder and control access with user/group permissions on any drive that uses the NTFS file system.

After simple file sharing is disabled, use this procedure to share a folder or drive:

Step 1.   Right-click the folder or drive and select **Properties**.

Step 2.   Click the **Sharing** tab (see Figure 16-21).

Step 3.   Click **Share This Folder** and specify a share name. (The default share name is the name of the drive or folder.) Add a comment if desired.

Step 4.   Specify the number of users or use the default (10).

Step 5.   Click **Permissions** to set folder permissions by user or group.

Step 6.   Click **Caching** to specify whether files will be cached on other computers' drives and how they will be cached.

> **NOTE**   If you need to convert a drive from a FAT-based file system to NTFS, you can use the command-line convert program. For example, if you were to convert the C: drive, the syntax would be
>
> ```
> convert c: /FS:NTFS
> ```

Step 7.   Click **OK**.

See "Operating System Access Control" in Chapter 10, "Security," for details.

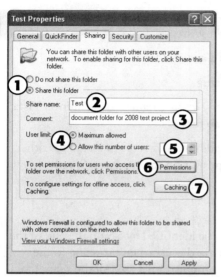

1. Enables/disables sharing
2. Share name
3. Comment (optional)
4. Specifies user limit
5. Specifies maximum number of users (1-10)
6. Configures permissions
7. Controls caching of offline files by other users

Figure 16-21   Setting up a network share in Windows XP when simple file sharing is disabled.

Sharing a Folder with User/Group Permissions in Windows Vista or Windows 7

To share a folder in Windows Vista or 7, follow these steps:

Step 1.   Ensure that file sharing is enabled. This is done by navigating to **Start**, **Control Panel**, and double-clicking the **Network and Sharing Center** icon. In Windows Vista, click the down arrow next to **File Sharing** and select the **Turn on File Sharing** radio button. (This window is also where you would enable printer sharing.) To access this dialog in Windows 7, click **Change Advanced Sharing Settings** after opening the Network and Sharing Center.

Step 2.   Click **Start**, then click **Computer**.

Step 3.   In the Computer window, navigate to a folder that you want to share.

Step 4.   Right-click the folder that you want to share, then click **Share**. The File Sharing window is now displayed.

Step 5.   If you have enabled password-protected sharing, use the File Sharing window and select which users will have access to the shared folder and select their permission levels. To allow all users, select the **Everyone** group within the list of users. If you disabled password-protected sharing, use the File Sharing window and select the **Guest** or **Everyone** account. This is the equivalent of simple file sharing in Windows XP.

Step 6.   When you are done configuring permissions, click **Share** and then click **Done**.

Shared Printers

To set up a printer as a shared printer, follow these steps:

Step 1.   Open the **Printers** or **Printers and Faxes** folder.

Step 2.   Right-click a printer and select **Sharing**.

Step 3.   Select **Share This Printer** and specify a share name. (In Windows Vista, you will have to click the **Sharing tab** first.)

Step 4.   Click **Additional Drivers** to select additional drivers to install for other operating systems that will use the printer on the network. Supply driver disks or CDs when prompted.

Administrative Shares

Administrative shares are hidden shares that can be identified by a $ on the end of the share name. These shares cannot be seen by standard users when browsing to the computer over the network; they are meant for administrative use. All the shared folders including administrative shares can be found by navigating to Computer Management > System Tools > Shared Folders > Shares. Note that every volume within the hard drive (C: or D: for example) has an administrative share (for example, C$ is the administrative share for the C: drive). Although it is possible to remove these by editing the Registry, it is not recommended because it might cause other networking issues. You should be aware that only administrators should have access to these shares.

Setting Up the Network Client

The client in both peer-to-peer networks and dedicated server networks is a computer that uses shared resources. To access shared resources, a client computer needs

- Network client software
- The name of the network and server(s) with shared resources
- The printer drivers for the network printers

To install network client software in Windows, open the **Properties** sheet of the appropriate network connection. To change the name of the network that the computer is a member of, open the **System Properties** window and click the **Computer Name** tab.

In Windows XP and 2000, My Network Places is used to locate shared resources and to provide passwords; in Windows 7 and Vista, it is simply called "Network." "Printers" is used to set up access to a network printer in all versions of Windows.

My Network Places, Network, and Printers can be accessed from the Start Menu or from within Windows Explorer.

Installing Network Client Software

Windows 7, Vista, XP, and 2000 incorporate network client software for Microsoft Networks.

If you need to install additional network clients, such as for NetWare, in Windows XP/2000, follow this procedure:

Step 1.   Open the Network Connections (Network in Windows 2000) icon in Control Panel or right-click **My Network Places** and select **Properties**.

Step 2.   Right-click the connection you want to modify and select **Properties**.

Step 3.   Click the **Install** button.

Step 4.   Click the **Client** icon.

Step 5.   Select the client you want to add.

Step 6.   Click **OK**.

NOTE   Windows 7 and Vista do not support Novell NetWare by default.

Installing a Network Printer

Follow this procedure to install a network printer:

Step 1.   Open the **Printers and Faxes** (or **Printers**) folder.

Step 2.   Click **Add a Printer** (or **Add Printer**). In some cases, you might need to alternate click anywhere in the white area and select **Add Printer**.

Step 3.   Click **Next** (Windows XP/2000), then select **Network Printer**. In Windows 7 and Vista, click the button to add a network printer. It will try to search for a printer automatically. To bypass this, click **The Printer I Want Isn't Listed**.

Step 4.   You can browse for the printer on a workgroup network, use Active Directory to search for a printer on a domain-based network or enter its name (*server**printername*). You can also specify the printer's URL. Click **Next**.

Step 5.   After the printer is selected, specify whether you want to use the new printer as the default printer. Click **Next**.

Step 6.   Specify if you want to print a test page. Printing a test page will allow you to verify if the correct print driver has been installed.

Step 7.   Click **Finish** to complete the setup process. Provide the Windows CD or printer setup disk if required to complete the process.

Using Shared Resources

With any type of network, the user must log on with a correct username and password to use any network resources. With a dedicated server, such as Novell or Windows 2000/Server 2003, a single username and password is needed for any network resource the user has permission to use. On a peer-to-peer network using user/group permissions, you must configure each peer server with a list of users or groups. In either case, you must then specify the access rights for each shared folder.

Information can be copied from a shared drive or folder if the user has read-only access; to add, change, or delete information on the shared drive or folder, the user needs full access.

Network printing is performed the same way as local printing after the network printer driver software has been set up on the workstation.

You can identify shared resources with Windows by using Explorer or My Computer. On a Windows XP or 2000 system that is sharing resources with other users, a shared drive, folder, or printer will use a modified icon with a hand, indicating that it is being shared (see Figure 16-22). In Windows Vista, there will be a small icon of two users indicating a share. In Windows Vista and Windows 7, the easiest way to see shared resources on a local or remote computer is to open the Network dialog and click the computer (see Figure 16-23).

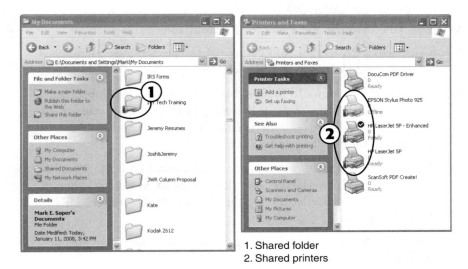

1. Shared folder
2. Shared printers

Figure 16-22   Viewing a shared folder and shared printers in Windows XP.

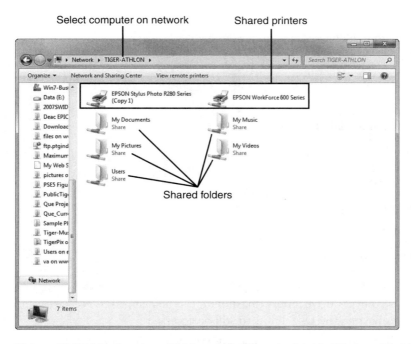

Select computer on network   Shared printers

Figure 16-23 Viewing shared folders and a shared printer in Windows 7's Network dialog.

> **NOTE**   On Windows 7 computers belonging to a homegroup, sharing is configured through the Homegroup option in Network and Sharing Center.

To use a shared resource on a peer server that uses share-level security, the user must provide the correct password for any password-protected share. To use a shared resource on a network that uses user/group permissions, the user must log on to the network. The administrator of the server or network has already assigned access levels and permissions to each user or group, so the user can immediately begin using shared resources as permitted.

Shared drives and folders can be referred to by a Universal Naming Convention (UNC) name, a fully qualified domain name (FQDN), or a mapped drive letter. Each of these is explained in the following sections.

The Universal Naming Convention (UNC)

The Universal Naming Convention (UNC) is designed to enable users to access network resources such as folders or printers without mapping drive letters to network drives or specifying the type of device that stores the file or hosts the printer. A UNC name has the following structure in Windows:

```
\\servername\share name\path\filename
```

A typical UNC path to a document would resemble

```
\\Tiger1\0\NetDocuments\this_doc.doc
```

A typical UNC path to a shared printer on the same system would resemble

```
\\Tiger1\Printername
```

What does this mean in plain English?

- `\\Tiger1` is the server.

- `\0` is the share name.

- `\NetDocuments` is the path.

- `\this_doc.doc` is the document.

- `\Printername` is the printer.

UNC enables files and printers to be accessed by the user with 32-bit Windows applications. Because only 23 drive letters (maximum) can be mapped, UNC enables network resources beyond the D–Z limits to still be accessed.

To display the UNC path to a shared folder with Windows XP, right-click the share in *My Network Places* (Network in Windows Vista) and select **Properties**. The Target field in the dialog lists the UNC path.

Some Windows applications will display the UNC path to a file even if the file was accessed through a mapped drive letter, and other Windows applications will refer to the UNC path or mapped drive letter path to the file, depending on how the file was retrieved.

Fully Qualified Domain Names (FQDNs)

TCP/IP networks that contain DNS servers often use FQDNs to refer to servers along with, or in place of, UNC names. The structure of an FQDN is

Name-of-server.name-of-domain.root-domain

For example, a server called "charley" in the informit.com domain would have an FQDN of

```
charley.informit.com
```

If you want to access the shared `Docs` folder on `charley.informit.com`, you would refer to it as

```
\\charley.informit.com\Docs
```

You can also use the IP address of the server in place of the servername. If 192.10.8.22 is the IP address of charley.informit.com, you can access the Docs folder with the following statement:

```
\\192.10.8.22\Docs
```

You can use either UNCs or FQDN along with the Net command-line utility to view or map drive letters to shared folders.

Mapped Drives

Windows enables shared folders and shared drives to be mapped to drive letters on clients. In Windows Explorer and My Computer (Computer in Windows 7/Vista), these mapped drive letters will show up in the list along with the local drive letters. A shared resource can be accessed either through Network/My Network Places/Network Neighborhood (using the share name) or through a mapped drive letter.

Drive mapping has the following benefits:

- A shared folder mapped as a drive can be referred to by the drive name instead of a long Universal Naming Convention path (see "The Universal Naming Convention [UNC]" earlier in this chapter for details).

- If you still use MS-DOS programs, keep in mind that mapped drives are the only way for those programs to access shared folders.

To map a shared folder to a drive in Windows 7/Vista/XP, follow this procedure:

Step 1. Click the shared folder in Network (7/Vista) or My Network Places (XP).

Step 2. Click **Tools**, **Map Network Drive**. (Note: In Windows 7/Vista, the menu bar might be hidden. To show it use the **Alt+T** shortcut. Alternatively, you can right-click the shared resource and select **Map Network Drive**.)

Step 3. Select a drive letter from the list of available drive letters; only drive letters not used by local drives are listed. Drive letters already in use for other shared folders display the UNC name of the shared folder.

Step 4. Click the **Reconnect at Login** box if you want to use the mapped drive every time you connect to the network. This option should be used only if the server will be available at all times; otherwise, the client will receive error messages when it tries to access the shared resource. See Figure 16-24.

Figure 16-24   The Map Network Drive dialog can be used to create a temporary or permanent drive mapping.

Step 5.   Click **Finish**.

Shared folders can be accessed by either their mapped drive letters or by their folder names in Windows Explorer.

Browser Installation and Configuration

A web browser, such as Microsoft Internet Explorer, Mozilla Firefox, or Google Chrome, is the main interface through which you navigate the Internet. Internet Explorer is a standard component of Windows. Updates and newer versions can be downloaded manually from the Microsoft website or via Windows Update. Other browsers can be downloaded in compressed form and installed manually.

Depending on how you connect with the Internet, you might need to adjust the browser configuration.

Typical options you might need to change include

- **Proxies for use with LAN-based or filtered access**—Users who access the Internet through a local area network might be doing so through a proxy server. A proxy server receives a copy of the website or content the user wants to look at and checks it for viruses or unapproved content before passing it on. The proxy server information is set through the browser's configuration menu (for example, Internet Options in Internet Explorer).

- **Automatic dial up for convenience**—Internet Explorer and most other browsers can also be set to dial up the Internet automatically whenever you start the browser to make Internet access easier. This option is useful for dial-up connections.

- **E-mail configuration**—Most browsers include an e-mail client; the settings for the e-mail server and other options must be made to allow e-mail to be seen and replied to within the browser.

- **Disable graphics**—Users with extremely slow connections who view primarily text-based pages can disable graphics for extra speed.

- **Security settings for Java**—Advanced features, such as Java and ActiveX, make sites more interactive, but might also pose a security risk; these features can be limited or disabled through the Security menu.

You can also adjust default colors and fonts and the default start page.

Generally, you should use all the features possible of the browser unless you have speed or security concerns that lead you to disable some features.

Setting Up Your Browser to Use Your Internet Connection

In most cases, users will want the Internet to be available as soon as they open their web browser. Because some users have dial-up connections and some networks use proxy servers to provide firewall protection or content filtering, you might need to adjust the browser configuration to permit Internet access.

To view or adjust the browser configuration for Internet Explorer, follow this procedure:

Step 1.   Open Internet Explorer.

Step 2.   Click **Tools**, **Internet Options**.

Step 3.   Click the **Connections** tab.

Step 4.   If the Internet connection uses a dial-up modem, select the correct dial-up connection from those listed and choose Always Dial (to start the connection when the browser is opened) or Dial Whenever a Network Connection Is Not Present. Click Set Default to make the selected connection the default.

Step 5.   If the Internet connection uses a network, click Never Dial a Connection, and click LAN Settings to check network configuration.

Step 6.   Ask the network administrator if you should use Automatically Detect Settings or whether you should specify a particular automatic configuration script.

Step 7.   Click **OK** to save changes at each menu level until you return to the browser display.

If a proxy server is used for Internet access, it must be specified by server name and port number (refer to Figure 16-25):

Step 1.   From the Connections tab, click **LAN settings**.

Step 2.   From the Local Area Network (LAN) Settings window, you have two options underneath Proxy Server. If a single proxy server address and port number is used for all types of traffic, click the **Use a Proxy Server** checkbox and enter the address and port number. However, if different proxy servers or ports will be used, click the **Use a Proxy Server** checkbox and click the Advanced button.

Step 3.   Specify the correct server and port number to use.

Step 4.   Click **OK** to save changes at each menu level until you return to the browser display.

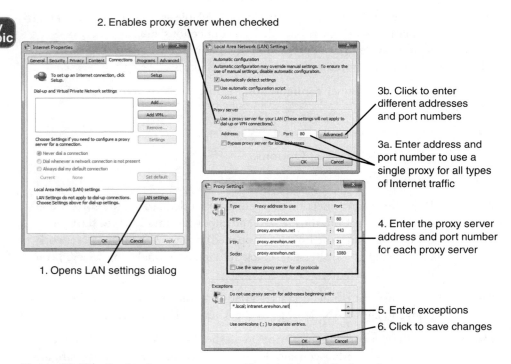

Figure 16-25   Configuring proxy server settings in Internet Explorer 8.

Enabling/Disabling Script Settings

Some networks use a separate configuration or logon script for Internet access. To specify a script with Internet Explorer, click **Tools**, **Internet Options**, **Connections**, **LAN Settings**, **Use Automatic Configuration Script**. Enter the URL or filename of the script and click **OK**.

TIP   You can also configure Internet Explorer to automatically detect the settings if your network is configured to provide them. However, if you enable this option and the network is not configured to provide them, Internet Explorer will not be able to connect to the Internet.

Configuring Browser Security Settings

You can configure Internet Explorer's default security settings for Java, ActiveX, and other potentially harmful content through the Internet Options' Security tab. Open the **Internet Options** tab with Control Panel, or click **Tools**, **Settings**, **Internet Options** within Internet Explorer.

Depending on the version of Internet Explorer, there will be four or five default security settings: High, Medium-High, Medium, Medium-Low, and Low. High blocks almost all active content and prevents websites from setting cookies (small text files that can track website usage). Medium (the default) enables some active content but blocks unsigned ActiveX controls. Medium-Low blocks unsafe content but downloads other content without prompts, and low has no safeguards.

Each setting is matched to a web content zone. By default, all sites not in other zones are placed in the Internet zone, which uses Medium-High security (Medium on older versions of Internet Explorer). The local Intranet zone uses Medium-Low security by default (medium in older versions). Trusted sites use Medium security by default (Low in older versions); restricted sites use High security by default.

To add or remove sites on the local Intranet, Trusted, or Restricted site list, select the zone and click Sites.

By default, local Intranet sites include all local sites, all sites that don't use a proxy server, and all UNC network paths. Remove check marks to restrict these options. Click Advanced to add or remove a specific site or to require a secured server. Trusted or Restricted sites display the Add/Remove dialog box immediately.

NOTE   Click Custom from the main Security tab to adjust the default settings for any security level. If the settings of any zone are misconfigured, one can return to default settings for an individual zone or reset security of all zones by clicking the Reset All Zones to Default Level button.

Using Network Command-Line Tools

Windows contains several command-line tools for troubleshooting and configuring the network. These include the following:

- **Net**—Displays and uses network resources
- **Ping**—Tests TCP/IP and Internet connections
- **Tracert**—Traces the route between a specified website or IP address and your PC
- **NSLookup**—Displays detailed information about DNS
- **IPConfig**—Displays detailed TCP/IP configuration about your Windows NT/2000/XP system

The following sections describe these tools.

Using the Net Command

Windows includes the Net command for use in displaying and using network resources from the command line. Some of the Net commands you can use include

- **Net Help**—Displays help for a Net option; for example, use Net Help View for help with the Net View command.
- **Net Use**—Maps a network drive to a shared resource on the network; for example, Net Use Q: \\Tiger1\shared. In this example, Q: will behave just like any other drive letter such as C:, D:, and so on. The only difference is that it will redirect to another computer on the network.
- **Net View**—Displays other hosts on the network.
- **Net Helpmsg *errorcode#***—Displays the meaning of any Microsoft error code.

To display a complete list of **Net** commands, type **Net /?** |**More** from the command prompt.

Using Ping

Windows can use the Ping command to test TCP/IP, check for connectivity to other hosts on the network, and check the Internet connection for proper operation. Ping is a more reliable way to check an Internet connection than opening your browser because a misconfigured browser could cause you to think that your TCP/IP configuration is incorrect.

To use `Ping` to check connectivity with another host on the network, follow this procedure:

Step 1.   Open a command-prompt window.

Step 2.   Type **Ping** *IPaddress* **or** *Ping servername* to ping another host on the network, then press **Enter**. For example, to ping a router, typical syntax would be **Ping 192.168.1.1**.

To use `Ping` to check your Internet connection, follow this procedure:

Step 1.   Start your Internet connection. If you use a LAN to connect to the Internet, you might have an always-on connection.

Step 2.   Open a command-prompt window.

Step 3.   Type **Ping** *IPaddress* or *Ping servername* and press **Enter**. For example, to ping a web server called www.erewhon.net, type `Ping www. erewhon.net`.

By default, `Ping` sends four data packets from your computer to any IP address or servername you specify. If your TCP/IP connection is working properly, you should see a reply from each ping you sent out indicating how quickly the signals traveled back from the target and the IP address or URL of the target. Note that some websites and servers are configured to ignore pings as a security measure. The replies indicate that the host is alive. Any other message would indicate a problem; for example, the "Request timed out" or "Destination host unreachable" messages would require further troubleshooting. Keep in mind that if it's the local computer that is configured incorrectly, you might not be able to "ping" anything! Also watch for the amount of time the ping took to reply back. A longer latency time could indicate network congestion. Conversely, the lower the time in milliseconds (ms), the faster your connection. Connection speeds vary a great deal due to various factors, such as Internet network congestion, server speed, and the number of relays needed to transfer your request from your computer to the specified server. To check relay information, use the `Tracert` command.

Using Tracert

The `Tracert` command is used by Windows to trace the route taken by data traveling from your computer to an IP address or website you specify. By default, `Tracert` will check up to 30 hops between your computer and the specified website or IP address. To use **Tracert** to check the routing, follow this procedure:

Step 1.   Start your Internet connection. If you use a LAN to connect to the Internet, you might have an always-on connection.

Step 2.   Open a command-prompt window.

Step 3.   Type **Tracert** IP address or Tracert servername and press **Enter**. For example, to trace the route to a Web server called www.erewhon.tv, type Tracert www.erewhon.tv. **Tracert** displays the IP addresses and URLs of each server used to relay the information to the specified location, as well as the time required.

To see help for the Tracert command, type **Tracert** without any options and press the **Enter** key.

Using NSLookup

NSLookup is a command-line tool used to determine information about the DNS. When NSLookup is run without options, it displays the name and IP address of the default DNS server before displaying a DNS prompt. Enter the name of a website or server to determine its IP address; enter the IP address of a website or server to determine its name. Enter a question mark (**?**) at the prompt to see more options; type exit, and then press **Enter** to exit the program.

Using Ipconfig

The IPConfig command-line utility is used to display the computer's current IP address, subnet mask, and default gateway (see Figure 16-26). Ipconfig combined with the /all switch will show more information including the DNS server address and MAC address, which is the hexadecimal address that is burned into the ROM of the network adapter.

TIP   If you're having problems seeing other computers on the network or connecting to the Internet on a network that uses server-assigned IPv4 addresses, type **IPConfig /release** and press **Enter**; and then type IPConfig /renew and press **Enter** to obtain a new IP address from the DHCP server on your network. The comparable commands for releasing/renewing an IPv6 address are **IPConfig /release6** and **IPConfig /renew6**.

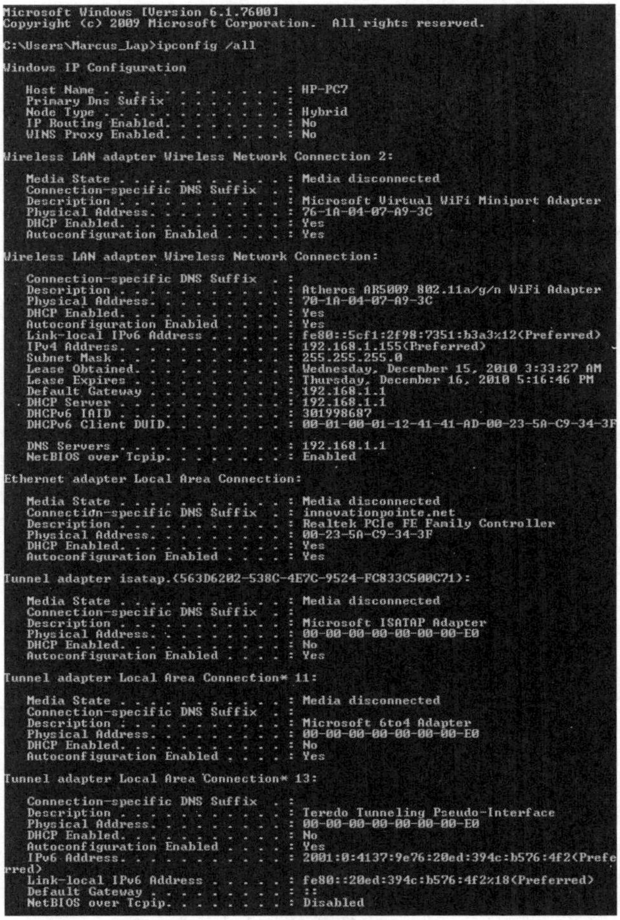

Figure 16-26   IPConfig /all displays complete information about your TCP/IP configuration.

Network and Internet Troubleshooting

Use this section to prepare for troubleshooting questions involving network hardware and software on the A+ Certification Exams and in your day-to-day work as a computer technician.

Can't Access Network Resources

If an error message such as Duplicate Computer Name or Duplicate IP Address is displayed during system startup, open the Network icon and change the name of the computer or the system's IP address. Contact the network administrator for the correct name or IP address settings to use.

Significant Drops in Network Performance

Significant drops in network performance can be traced to a variety of causes, including

- Damage to cables, connectors, hubs, and switches
- Expanding network capacity with hubs in place of switches
- Connecting high-speed NICs to low-speed hubs or switches
- RFI/EMI Interference with Wireless Networks

If network usage patterns remain constant but some users report lower performance, check cables, connectors, and other network hardware for physical damage. Dry, brittle, and cracked cables and connectors can generate interference, which forces network stations to retransmit data because it wasn't received correctly. Replace damaged cables and connectors.

Use diagnostic programs supplied with the network adapter if the same brand and model of adapter is used by multiple computers. These diagnostics programs send and receive data and provide reports of problems.

If all the users connected to a single hub or switch report slowdowns, check the hub or switch. Replace a hub with a switch to see an immediate boost in performance. Continue to use switches to add capacity.

Make sure that computers with Fast Ethernet (10/100) hardware are connected to dual-speed switches to get the benefits of 100Mbps performance. 10/100 cards will run at 10Mbps if connected to 10Mbps switches. Enable full-duplex mode if the cards and switches support it to boost performance to 20Mbps (with 10BASE-T) or 200Mbps (with 10/100 cards running Fast Ethernet).

Make sure that computers with Gigabit Ethernet (10/100/1000) hardware are connected to Gigabit Ethernet switches to get the benefits of 1000 Mbps performance.

Radio frequency interference (RFI) is closely related to EMI, and RFI/EMI interference can have a big impact on wireless network (WLAN) performance. For the A+ exam, some things to consider include cordless phone and microwave usage. Because these devices can also inhabit the 2.4GHz frequency range used by 802.11b, g, and n networks, they can interfere with the network signal. Because 2.4GHz cordless phones use spread-spectrum technology to help avoid eavesdropping, it is not possible to configure these phones to use a particular 2.4GHz channel.

To help avoid interference from other wireless networks, configure your 2.4GHz wireless network to use one of the non-overlapping channels (1, 6, or 11). Some anecdotal evidence suggests that channel 11 is less likely to receive RFI from 2.4GHz cordless phones.

You should also consider using cordless phones that use frequencies that will not interfere with 2.4GHz or 5GHz wireless networks, such as phones using DECT (1.9GHz) or DECT 6.0 (6.0GHz) frequency bands.

To avoid interference from microwave ovens or other microwave devices, make sure the oven or device is not physically near any wireless devices.

Unattended PC Drops Its Network Connection

Incorrect settings for power management can cause stations to lose their network connections when power management features, such as standby mode, are activated. Check the properties for the network adapter to see if the adapter can be set to wake up the computer when network activity is detected.

All Users Lose Network Connection

If the network uses a bus topology, a failure of any station on the network or of termination at either end of the network will cause the entire network to fail. Check the terminators first, and then the T-connectors and cables between computers. If you suspect that a particular computer is the cause of the failure, move the terminator to the computer preceding it in the bus topology. Repeat as needed to isolate the problem. Replace cables, connectors, or network cards as needed to solve the problem.

If the network uses a star topology, check the power supply going to the hub, switch, or wireless access point, or replace the device.

If only the users connected to a new hub or switch that is connected to an existing hub or switch lose their network connection, check the connection between the existing hub or switch and the new one. Most hubs and switches have an uplink port that is used to connect an additional hub or switch. You can either use the uplink port or the regular port next to the uplink port, but not both. Connect the computer using the port next to the uplink port to another port to make the uplink port available for connecting the new hub or switch.

If the uplink port appears to be connected properly, check the cable. Uplink ports perform the crossover for the user, enabling you to use an ordinary network cable to add a hub or switch.

TIP If you use a crossover cable, you must connect the new hub or switch through a regular port, not the uplink port.

Users Can Access Some Shared Resources But Not Others

Users who need to access shared resources on a network using user/group permissions must be granted permission to access resources; different users are typically allowed different access levels to network resources. Contact the network or system administrator for help if a user is prevented from using a resource; the administrator of the network or peer server will need to permit or deny access to the user.

Can't Print to a Network Printer

Problems with network printing can also come from incorrect print queue settings and incorrect printer drivers.

When you configure a network printer connection, you must correctly specify the UNC path to the printer. For example, if the printer is shared as LaserJ on the server Xeon3, the correct UNC path to specify in the printer properties sheet would be

```
\\Xeon3\LaserJ
```

> **TIP**   If a shared printer connected to a Windows system is available at some times, but not at other times, open the printer's properties sheet and adjust the Scheduling Option settings. See Chapter 11, "Printers," for details.

Ping and Tracert Work, But User Can't Display Web Pages with Browser

If Ping and Tracert receive output from the specified websites but the web browser cannot display web pages on those or other sites, the browser configuration might be incorrect.

If the browser doesn't use the correct configuration for the connection type, no pages will be displayed. With dial-up Internet connections, either the user must manually open the connection or the browser should be set to dial the connection. If a proxy server or special network configuration is needed, this must be configured in the browser.

See "Setting Up Your Browser to Use Your Internet Connection," earlier in this chapter for details.

Overview of Creating a Small Office/Home Office (SOHO) Network

Use the following information to help you understand the "big picture" of creating a Small Office/Home Office (SOHO) network that can be used to share an Internet connection and provide shared resources:

Step 1.   Decide on the type of Internet connection you will use. For best performance, use a cable or DSL connection with at least 6Mbps minimum download speed. Choose higher speeds to enable more users to share the connection with acceptable performance.

Step 2.   Determine how users will connect to the network: wired Ethernet, wireless Ethernet, or a mixture of wired and wireless devices.

Step 3.   Select a cable or DSL modem (depending upon your connection type) and a router. You have more flexibility if you use separate modem and router devices.

Step 4.   Have the cable or DSL modem installed by the ISP (or order a self-install kit from the ISP; a self-install kit contains the modem and other hardware needed for installation). You can also purchase cable modems at computer and electronics stores.

Step 5.   Place the router where it will be most convenient for connections, such as a wiring closet or shelf. Make sure the modem and the router can connect to each other via a suitable network cable (CAT5e or better quality). If you plan to connect with wireless clients, try to choose a central location for the router.

Step 6.   Configure the router to connect to the modem and, if you are using wireless clients, select the most appropriate wireless security settings.

Step 7.   Connect each client to the router. If you are using wireless Ethernet, you must configure each client to use the same SSID, encryption type, and encryption key as those you used when setting up the router.

Step 8.   Configure each client to be part of the same workgroup.

Step 9.   Set up file and printer sharing on each client which has resources you want to share.

Step 10.   Test the Internet connection on each client.

Step 11.   Test the ability to access shared resources. Depending upon the version(s) of Windows in use, you might need to set up additional user accounts on systems with shared resources or change password settings to enable remote users to access shared resources.

Exam Preparation Tasks

Review All the Key Topics

Review the most important topics in the chapter, noted with the key topics icon in the outer margin of the page. Table 16-13 lists a reference of these key topics and the page numbers on which each is found.

Table 16-13   Key Topics for Chapter 16

Key Topic Element	Description	Page Number
Figure 16-1	A server with three workstations, each of which is using a different shared resource.	806
Figure 16-4	A typical external modem that connects to a serial port.	811
Figure 16-7	A typical self-installed DSL setup.	817
Figure 16-8	A typical cable modem and cable TV installation.	819
Table 16-4	Wired Ethernet Networks	828
Table 16-5	Wireless Ethernet Standards	829
Figure 16-11	An STP cable (left) includes a metal shield and ground wire for protection against interference, while a UTP cable (right) does not.	833
Table 16-6	Categories and Uses for UTP and STP Cabling	834
Figure 16-13	RJ11 connector (left) compared to RJ45 connector (right).	835
Figure 16-14	SC, FC, and ST fiber-optic cable connectors compared.	838
Table 16-7	Wireless Ethernet Configuration Settings	841
Table 16-9	Static Versus Server-Assigned IP Addressing	844
Figure 16-15	The General tab is configured to obtain IP and DNS server information automatically when a DHCP server is used on the network.	845
Figure 16-17	The General tab of the TCP/IP properties sheet when manual configuration is used.	847
Table 16-10	An IP Address and Corresponding Subnet Mask	848
Table 16-11	Internet Protocol Classification System	849
Figure 16-20	Setting up a network share in Windows XP using the default simple file-sharing option.	856

Table 16-13   Key Topics for Chapter 16

Key Topic Element	Description	Page Number
Figure 16-21	Setting up a network share in Windows XP when simple file sharing is disabled.	857
Figure 16-24	The Map Network Drive dialog can be used to create a temporary or permanent drive mapping.	864
Figure 16-25	Configuring proxy server settings in Internet Explorer 8.	866

Complete the Tables and Lists from Memory

Print a copy of Appendix B, "Memory Tables," (found on the CD), or at least the section for this chapter, and complete the tables and lists from memory. Appendix C, "Memory Tables Answer Key," also on the CD, includes completed tables and lists to check your work.

Definitions of Key Terms

Define the following key terms from this chapter, and check your answers in the glossary.

LAN, WAN, Client, Server, Client/Server, Peer-to-Peer, Modem, DUN, DSL, ADSL, SDSL, TCP/IP, NetBEUI, NetBIOS, HTTP, HTTPS, SSL, TLS, HTML, FTP, DNS, Domain name, SMTP, POP3, IMAP, 10BaseT Ethernet, 10/100/1000 Ethernet, 802.11a, 802.11b, 802.11g, 802.11n, IrDA, VoIP, SSID, WEP, WPA, Star Topology, Repeater, Hub, Switch, Router, WINS, DHCP

Troubleshooting Scenario

You have a computer that has an issue connecting to network resources such as a printer or share on a server. What are some of the tests you can perform to fix this problem so the user can continue working?

Refer to Appendix A for the answer.

This chapter covers the following subjects:

■ **Recycling and Disposal Issues**—Recycling is important and can have legal ramifications for a company. In this section you learn the proper way to recycle toner cartridges and batteries and how to dispose of chemical solvents, monitors, and other computer hardware.

■ **Using an MSDS (Material Safety Data Sheet)**—The MSDS determines how to handle and store chemicals safely. It also identifies what to do in the case of an emergency, as is explained in more detail within this section.

■ **Electrostatic Discharge (ESD)**—This section demonstrates how to protect your computer equipment from ESD by using various tools and methods, for example an antistatic wrist strap. It also talks about the proper ways of storing and otherwise protecting computer equipment.

■ **Hazards**—Here you learn how to deal with high voltage within printers, power supplies, and CRT monitors, and how to protect components from electrical shock. This section also covers mechanical, liquid, and other hazards.

■ **Environmental and Accident Handling**—Finally, you need to know what to do in the event of an emergency. This section briefly explains who to contact and what to do in the unlikely case of an emergency.

This chapter covers the CompTIA A+ 220-701 objective 6.1.

CHAPTER 17

Safety and Environmental Issues

When dealing with computers, power, networking, and anything else in IT, remember to put safety on the top of your priority list. Computer equipment is not a toy and should be treated with care. Another issue to consider is how you dispose of your technology, since this will affect the environment. Most companies have procedures in place that specify what to do with computers, monitors, batteries, and other technology equipment after it has outlived its usefulness to the company. This chapter discusses some of the more common practices when it comes to environmental issues, and it identifies what to watch out for when working on computers. Finally, it demonstrates how to keep yourself and the computer protected and safe.

"Do I Know This Already?" Quiz

The "Do I Know This Already?" quiz allows you to assess whether you should read this entire chapter or simply jump to the "Exam Preparation Tasks" section for review. If you are in doubt, read the entire chapter. Table 17-1 outlines the major headings in this chapter and the corresponding "Do I Know This Already?" quiz questions. You can find the answers in Appendix A, "Answers to the 'Do I Know This Already?' Quizzes and Troubleshooting Scenarios."

Table 17-1 "Do I Know This Already?" Foundation Topics Section-to-Question Mapping

Foundations Topics Section	Questions Covered in This Section
Recycling and Disposal Issues	1, 2
Using an MSDS (Material Safety Data Sheet)	3, 4
Electrostatic Discharge	5–7
Hazards	8–10
Environmental and Accident Handling	11, 12

1. One of your clients is in need of a replacement laptop battery. What should you do with the failed battery?

   a. Throw it in the trash can

   b. Make sure it has been discharged completely and then throw it away

   c. Keep it just in case it is still good

   d. Send the battery to a recycling center

2. The company you work for has purchased all new computers. Your boss wants you to get rid of all the older equipment. Which of the following are the best alternatives to throwing away the older equipment? (Choose all that apply.)

   a. Donate it to a charity

   b. Give it to an electronics trade school

   c. Bring it to a recycling center

   d. Bring it to a municipal incinerator

3. Which of the following are uses for the material safety data sheet (MSDS)? Choose all that apply.

   a. Determine safe storage practice

   b. Determine treatment if a product is accidentally swallowed or contacts the skin

   c. Determine safe disposal methods

   d. Determine how to deal with spills, fire, and other hazards

   e. Determine safe storage and safe disposal methods only

4. You are working in the shop with a co-worker. You notice that he has just spilled a substance on the floor. What should you tell your co-worker to do at this point?

   a. Mop up the chemical

   b. Use a wet vac to vacuum up the material

   c. Check the MSDS for instructions

   d. Leave it on the floor until it evaporates

5. You are working on a client's computer. You are about to install a new video card in the computer. When you reach to open the case you get a small shock. What is this known as?

   a. MSU

   b. GUI

   c. ESD

   d. ESDT

6. You have just completed a computer upgrade on a client's computer. What should you do with the components that you have taken out of the system?

   a. Place them in the antistatic bags that came with the new hardware

   b. Put them in the boxes that the new hardware came in

   c. Throw them in the trash because you don't need them anymore

   d. Sell them to a computer store

7. Which of the following is the most effective way to prevent ESD from happening to you when working on a computer?

   a. Make sure you are free of static before starting to work

   b. Wear rubber-soled shoes

   c. Be sure to work with both hands inside the computer

   d. Use an antistatic work mat equipped with a wrist strap

8. Which of the following can be considered hazards in your computer area? (Choose all that apply.)

   a. High voltage sources

   b. Printers

   c. Cable locations

   d. Atmospheric hazards

   e. All of these options are correct

9. You are the lead technician for your company. You walk in the office one morning and notice a co-worker is servicing a computer with the power cable still plugged in. What should you tell your co-worker to do?

   a. Tell her to be careful

   b. Tell her to use an antistatic wrist band

   c. Tell her that she shouldn't have the power plugged in while working on the computer.

   d. Tell her nothing, because it is her choice to do this

10. You are walking into the work area and notice that a technician is lifting a heavy server by himself. What should you say to your co-worker? Choose all that apply.

   a. Tell him to wear a back brace

   b. Let him do it alone

   c. Use the team lift method

   d. Watch him to make sure he doesn't drop the server

11. You are working for a company as a support technician. You walk into a work area and see a co-worker lying on the floor. She is not responsive. What should you do first as quickly as possible?

   a. Bring her to the hospital

   b. Call 911

   c. Contact the manager

   d. Ask other co-workers if the person takes special medications

12. You are the lead technician for your company. You have hired a new technician to help you. Which of the following should the new person be aware of in case of injuries, chemical spills, or fires? (Choose all that apply.)

   a. Know who to contact in case of emergency

   b. Show him the break room

   c. Have him review and follow procedures

   d. Let him know where the MSDS information is

Foundation Topics

Recycling and Disposal Issues

Nothing lasts forever in the computer business. Whether it is a worn out real-time clock battery, an obsolete monitor, or an empty toner cartridge, there's a right way to get rid of it or to recycle it. Generally, the more "durable" a computer-related item is, the more likely it is that it should be recycled when it reaches the end of its useful life, instead of simply being discarded.

NOTE To prepare for the A+ Certification exam, you should know which items are suitable for disposal, which should be recycled, and the proper methods for handling each type of item.

Disposing of Batteries

Batteries no longer contain significant amounts of mercury, a highly toxic chemical that can cause memory loss, vision impairment, and other health issues in high exposures, but today's batteries still contain chemicals that should not go into landfills.

Depending on the type of battery that you have replaced, you might find more than one option for disposal of the old ones:

■ Some stores have drop-off bins for watch and calculator batteries; the popular 3.0V lithium CR-2032 or equivalent battery used on motherboards to maintain the CMOS and RTC settings could be disposed of this way.

■ Hardware stores and home centers often feature drop-off bins for Ni-Cd, NiMH, or Li-ion rechargeable batteries, such as those found in computer, PDA, or cell phone power supplies or power tools.

■ To recycle alkaline or other types of dry or wet-cell batteries, including batteries used in UPS battery backup systems, as well as rechargeable, watch, and calculator batteries, contact companies that specialize in safe battery disposal or recycling. To locate companies, check your local telephone directory or perform a web search using search terms such as "battery recycling."

Recycling Toner and Printer Cartridges

As you learned in Chapter 11, "Printers," many manufacturers of laser toner and inkjet printer cartridges want you to recycle the empty cartridges; these companies provide postage-paid envelopes or mailing labels to help you return the empty product.

Otherwise, contact local rebuilders of laser toner or inkjet cartridges. Some of these companies might pay you a small fee per empty toner cartridge for popular printer models or might offer other inducements.

Disposing of Chemical Solvents and Cans

When you've used the contents of a cleaning product container, check the label for container-disposal instructions. Depending on the product, you might

- Be able to recycle the plastic container in household recycling; this is most often true for citrus-based and other mild cleaners

- Be required to follow toxic material disposal procedures; check with your local EPA office for a "Tox-Away Day" and store your empty containers for safe disposal at that time

If you need additional information about disposing of a particular type of container, check the product's material safety data sheet (MSDS). See the section "Using an MSDS (Material Safety Data Sheet)," later in this chapter for details.

Disposing of Obsolete Monitors and Computer Hardware

If you send your obsolete PC, printer, or monitor to a landfill, it will have plenty of company. Millions of old units go there every year; it's legal, but it's also a waste of equipment that could teach somebody something or still be useful to someone. Here are some better ways to deal with obsolete computers and peripherals:

- If possible, try to dispose of your working, cast-off computer equipment by giving it to a school or charity. These organizations might be able to wring an additional year or two of useful life out of the equipment and are usually grateful for the opportunity.

- To dispose of non-working equipment, see if an electronics trade school is willing to take the equipment for classroom use. Some electronic and computer service facilities will allow you to drop off defective monitors with payment of a small disposal fee.

- Use "computer" and "recycling" in a major search engine such as Google.com to find options for constructive disposal of both working and non-working equipment.

CAUTION   Hard disk drives in castoff machines can be a treasure trove of confidential information for the recipients, even if you format or repartition the drives. Many off-the-shelf data recovery programs such as Norton Unerase, Norton Unformat, Ontrack Easy Data Recovery, and others can pull all kinds of information from an intact hard disk, including credit-card, bank, and proprietary company data.

Norton WipeInfo and other programs that overwrite data areas of the drive repeatedly are designed to help prevent easy data recovery. However, forensic data-recovery tools intended for use by law-enforcement organizations can be purchased and used by anyone to retrieve data, even if it has been overwritten with Norton or other programs.

For maximum security for your personal or company data, take the hard disks out of any machine you're disposing of and physically destroy them. Open the cover of each hard disk drive and destroy the platters with a hammer.

Using an MSDS (Material Safety Data Sheet)

What happens if a toddler decides to taste the ink in a printer cartridge? The Material Safety Data Sheet (MSDS) knows. Many consumable products such as cleaners and printer cartridges have an MSDS. In more and more cases today, this information is available from the manufacturer's website on the Internet.

The MSDS can be used to

- Determine safe storage practice

- Determine treatment if the product is accidentally swallowed or contacts the skin

- Determine safe disposal methods

- Determine how to deal with spills, fire, and other hazards

The MSDS is divided into sections 1 through 16. For example, to determine first-aid measures in case of ingestion or inhalation, you would view section 4; to view fire-fighting information, go to section 5 (see Figure 17-1).

For easy reading, many manufacturers use the Adobe Acrobat (.pdf) format; documents in this format can be read by anyone with the free Adobe Reader program, obtainable from www.adobe.com.

Electrostatic Discharge (ESD)

Anyone who works with electronics, especially disassembled components, needs to be very concerned about ESD. ESD is the static electricity discharge that happens when two differently charged objects (such as your body and a computer component) come in contact with each other. ESD is an invisible killer of memory modules, interface cards, hard disks, and other computer components, because ESD buildup and discharge happens long before you actually notice it.

You might dread shaking hands with a new acquaintance in the winter because you'll get a shock, but ESD discharges far below the 3,000V level that you can actually feel can still destroy chips. As little as 30V of ESD is enough to destroy the current generation of low-powered chips, and you can build up as much as 20,000V of ESD from walking across a carpeted room in the winter if you shuffle along.

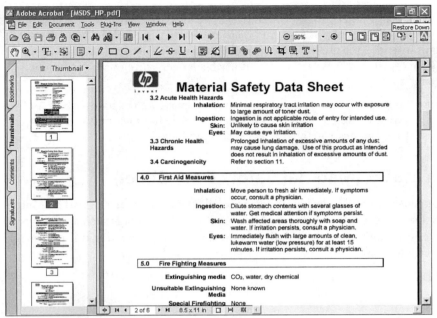

Figure 17-1   A portion of an MSDS for a typical HP laser printer toner cartridge, viewed with Adobe Acrobat.

ESD damage is "invisible" for another reason: It leaves in its wake equipment that has no visible damage but simply won't work reliably.

ESD damage is a major cause of intermittent failures, which are the bane of computer technicians everywhere. An intermittent failure is the classic "it wasn't working when I called you" kind of problem that "goes away" when you examine the system but recurs from time to time later.

Preventing ESD

You can prevent ESD by taking proper precautions when you do the following:

- Install or remove components

- Store and transport components

- Use computers

One way to prevent ESD is to equalize the electric potential of your body and the components on which you're working.

Unequal electrical potential between you and the device on which you're working is the major cause of ESD. When your body has a higher electric potential than the device or component with which you're working, an ESD from your body to the device or component equalizes the potential—but at the cost of damage or destruction to the component.

> **NOTE**   Although the greatest danger of ESD occurs when you have the system open and are working with components, PC users can also cause ESD problems when working with closed systems. I once delivered such a big static shock to a keyboard after a coffee break that I couldn't save my document and had to power down and restart the computer to restore my keyboard to working order.

Power Diagnostics, ESD, and Safety

The following items enable you to perform electrical testing on power entering the system (AC) and power levels inside the system (DC), prevent ESD damage to components, and prevent electrical shock caused by worn insulation on power cables. Figure 17-2 shows most of these products.

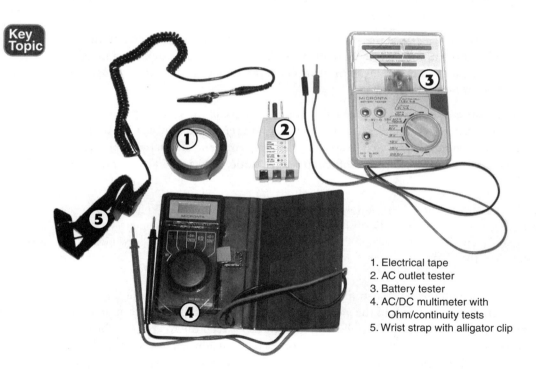

1. Electrical tape
2. AC outlet tester
3. Battery tester
4. AC/DC multimeter with Ohm/continuity tests
5. Wrist strap with alligator clip

Figure 17-2   ESD, electrical, and safety products used by computer technicians.

- **AC/DC multimeter with Ohm and Continuity options—**Tests power inside the system and at wall outlets

- **Grounded AC circuit tester—**Fast testing for wall outlets; many offices and homes are incorrectly wired, and the tester will help you determine whether this is the problem

- **Antistatic mat and wrist strap**—Prevents ESD, which can damage parts and systems

- **Electrical tape**—Temporarily repairs worn spots in the insulation of AC and DC power cables until replacements can be obtained

- **Battery tester**—Helps determine the condition of batteries used in motherboards and other components

Protection Devices

You can best equalize the electrical potential of a computer or component that is being serviced by placing the computer or component on an antistatic work mat equipped with a wrist strap; attach your wrist strap to the mat. This will help place you and the component at the same level of electrical potential, and thus eliminate the "need" for ESD to occur to equalize the potential.

For additional safety, use the alligator clip on the antistatic mat to attach to the component or computer you are working on. Attach the clip to unpainted metal on the chassis, such as the frame. This provides superior equalization for the mat, you, and the hardware on the mat.

Table mats connected to a grounded power supply are useful tools for preventing ESD on working computers, especially if users are reminded to touch the mat or grounded keyboard strip first. Antistatic cleaning spray and antistatic carpet spray should be used in any carpeted office to reduce static, especially in the winter when dry heat causes buildup.

CAUTION   Do *not* leave the computer plugged in while you work. This does *not* minimize the chances of ESD, and you could damage equipment if you attach or remove it. This is because virtually all modern computer systems still draw power even when they have been shut down.

A typical commercial wrist strap and a grounded work mat are shown in Figure 17-3. Both the wrist strap and the work mat include alligator clips that are attached to the system chassis to equalize electrical potential between the wearer and the computer. Wrist straps use hook and loop or other types of adjustable closures; it's important to wear the wrist strap comfortably snug so that the metal plate underneath the resistor touches the skin to provide proper conductivity.

CAUTION   You should use a commercial wrist strap for most types of computer service, but there is one major exception: *Never* ground yourself when you are working with high-current devices, such as when you discharge a CRT monitor. Grounding yourself to such devices could cause your body to receive a fatal high-current electrical charge.

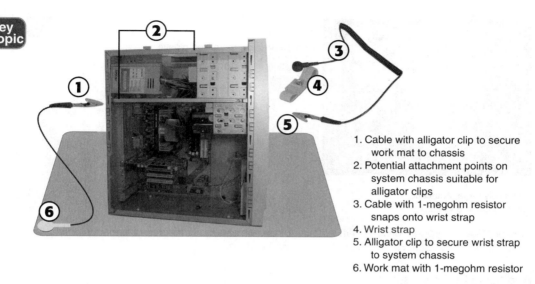

1. Cable with alligator clip to secure work mat to chassis
2. Potential attachment points on system chassis suitable for alligator clips
3. Cable with 1-megohm resistor snaps onto wrist strap
4. Wrist strap
5. Alligator clip to secure wrist strap to system chassis
6. Work mat with 1-megohm resistor

Figure 17-3   A typical ESD kit includes a grounded work mat and wrist strap. Both have 1-megohm resistors to protect the user from electric shock and alligator clips to connect the mat and wrist strap to unpainted metal parts on or inside the system.

Correct Storage for Equipment

Correct equipment storage should have two goals:

- Eliminating the possibility of ESD
- Protecting equipment from impact damage

To protect equipment from ESD, store equipment in the Faraday cage antistatic bags originally supplied with the equipment; retain bags for installed equipment for reuse. Faraday cage antistatic bags feature a thin metallic layer on the outside of the bag, which is conductive and prevents ESD from penetrating to the components inside. Thus, metalized metallic bags should never be used for temporary mats for components; if you lay a component on the outside of the bag, you're laying it onto a conductive surface. Colored antistatic bubble wraps also work well for parts storage and can also be used as a temporary mat, too. If you use bubble wrap, make sure it is antistatic (see Figure 17-4).

All work mats and wrist straps should have a 1-megohm resistor, as shown in Figures 17-3 and 17-4, to stop high voltage that comes through the ground line from injuring the user.

Store components in appropriate boxes to avoid physical damage. If the original boxes have been discarded, use cardboard boxes that have enough room for the component, the Faraday cage bag around the component, and antistatic padding.

Faraday cage: metalized plastic

1-megohm resistor for protection against high voltage

Faraday cage: antistatic bubble plastic with a pocket

Figure 17-4 A grounded work mat, suitable for use on either a work area or under an office computer in a high-static area, and antistatic Faraday bags.

Additional ESD Precautions

A grounded wrist strap can help prevent ESD, but you should also follow these additional precautions:

- If you must handle expansion cards and other devices with chips without suitable antistatic protection, *never touch the chips*! Most current products use a **CMOS (Complementary Metal-Oxide Semiconductor)** design, which has practically no resistance to ESD; as little as 30V of ESD can damage CMOS-based devices.

- Hold expansion cards by the brackets, never by the gold edge connectors, chips, or circuitry.

- Wear natural fibers, such as cotton and leather-soled shoes, instead of synthetics, to avoid ESD buildup.

- Use an antistatic spray (commercial or antistatic fabric softener/water mixture) to treat carpeting to reduce ESD.

- Use antistatic cleaning wipes on keyboards, monitors, and computer cases to reduce static buildup. Turn off the power, and if you use a liquid cleaner, always spray the cloth, never the device!

Hazards

Computer equipment and supplies can pose a number of potential hazards for the technician (and, in some cases, for computer users):

- High voltage sources, such as computers, and peripherals, such as printers and monitors

- Mechanical devices, such as printer mechanisms

- Power or data cables running across floors or other locations where users could trip and fall

- Liquids, such as those used for cleaning or refilling inkjet cartridges

- Situational hazards, such as unsafe temporary equipment or cabling locations

- Atmospheric hazards, such as those created by the use of toxic cleaners or the discharge of computer-room-rated fire suppression chemicals

- Moving heavy equipment, such as laser printers, servers, large UPS systems, or print/scan/copy devices

CAUTION   Computers and their peripherals can *kill* or *injure* you if you don't take reasonable precautions. This section discusses typical dangers of computer maintenance and the precautions you can take against these dangers.

High Voltage Hazards

The number-one hazard created by computer equipment is high voltage that can be present while devices are turned on and plugged in and even when some devices are unplugged and turned off. The major sources of potentially dangerous voltage include

- Printers

- Power supplies

- Monitors

- Systems in suspend or sleep modes

Printers also pose laser and mechanical hazards to technicians. All these risks are covered in the following section.

Printers

Unlike computers, printers normally do *not* run on safe, low-voltage DC (direct current). Although laser printers typically do use DC current, it is at a high voltage. Most impact and inkjet printers also use high-voltage AC (alternating current).

Any printer should be turned off and unplugged before being serviced. In the event of ink or toner spills, water or other liquids should *not* be used to clean up the mess unless the printer is turned off and disconnected, due to the risk of a potentially fatal electric shock.

The Power Supply

The exterior of practically every power supply is marked something like this:

CAUTION! Hazardous area! Severe shock hazards are present inside this case. Never remove the case under any circumstances.

See Figure 17-5 for a typical example.

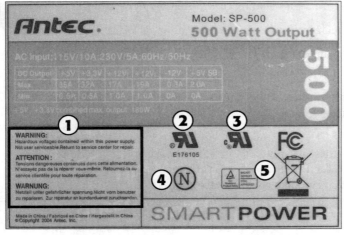

1. Hazard warning
2. UL rated for safety - US
3. UL rated for safety - Canada
4. Nemco (N-Mark) rated for safety - Norway
5. TÜV rated for safety - Germany

Figure 17-5 Hazard warnings and safety certifications on the label for a typical power supply.

> **CAUTION** Believe it. You can see the danger if you understand what is in the "cage" at the back of the typical power supply. Past the cooling fan it contains, you'll see capacitors (which resemble small cans). These capacitors retain potentially lethal high voltage levels for a long time.
>
> Because any power supply you buy as a replacement is likely to have a higher wattage rating and can also have a quieter fan than your current power supply, don't go cheap and wind up dead. Heed the warnings and replace the power supply without opening it to find out why it is broken. Make sure you purchase a UL-rated power supply.

CRT Monitors

As with the power supply, the outside of the monitor is safe. However, if you remove the cover of a CRT monitor for servicing or adjustments, you expose the danger. The high voltage anode (a metal prong covered with a red insulator, found on the wide top of the CRT) holds dangerously high voltage for days after the power is turned off.

Disassembled monitors also pose the following hazards:

- X-rays coming from the unshielded neck of the CRT when the monitor is on

- Dropping the monitor and breaking the CRT

Replace the shielding around the neck of the CRT before using the monitor, and use padding and carefully balance CRTs and monitors during storage and transport to avoid damage. See "Discharging CRTs" later in this chapter for additional information.

Systems in Suspend Mode

Systems based on the ATX, BTX, or NLX standards typically go into a deep suspend mode rather than a true "off" condition when shut down by Microsoft Windows. Some ATX and BTX systems have power supplies with a separate on/off switch on the back of the unit, but some do not. For these reasons, you should disconnect the power cord from the system.

NOTE I learned about this feature of ATX systems the hard way: I reached down into a system that was supposedly "off" and received a nasty tingle from a modem.

As with other devices, the power can be on unless you disconnect it at the source.

Precautions Against Electric Shock

This section discusses the precautions you should take to avoid the hazards covered in previous sections.

To work with electricity safely, follow these simple precautions:

- Remove jewelry, including rings, bracelets, and necklaces. Metal jewelry provides an excellent path for current.

- Use rubber gloves for extra insulation—rubber gloves prevent your hands from touching metal parts; however, they do not provide sufficient insulation to enable you to work on a live system.

- Work with one hand out of the system if possible, to avoid electricity passing through your chest if your arms complete a circuit.

- Keep your hands and the rest of your body dry; your body's natural shock resistance drops to virtually nil when your skin is damp.

Regardless of the level of service you will provide to a component, devices such as printers, computers, monitors, and so on should be disconnected from power as well as turned off before service. This will help prevent shock hazards as well as mechanical hazards.

Do *not* leave the computer plugged in while you work inside it. At one time, an acceptable practice was to leave the computer plugged in but shut down and keep one hand on the power supply as a ground. This is no longer appropriate because ATX, BTX, and other modern computers aren't really "off"; they're in a suspend mode and power is still running through memory, expansion cards, and so on.

Discharging CRTs

Do not service CRT-based monitors as a first choice today; most companies are rapidly replacing their remaining CRTs with LCD displays to save power and desk space. You should not service any monitor unless you are a certified technician. However, if you must open a CRT-based monitor for service, discharge the high voltage anode following this procedure:

Step 1. Turn off and unplug the monitor.

Step 2. Remove the housing carefully.

Step 3. Attach a large alligator clip and wire from a long, flat-bladed, *insulated* screwdriver to the metal frame surrounding the monitor.

Step 4. Slide the flat blade of the screwdriver under the insulator until the tip touches the metal anode clip (see Figure 17-6).

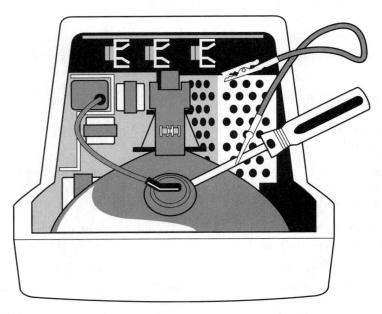

Figure 17-6   Discharging the high voltage anode on a typical CRT. Note the ground wire clipped between the metal monitor frame and the screwdriver.

Step 5. Be prepared for noise—anything from crackling to a loud pop—as the anode discharges its stored electricity. Keep the screwdriver in place for several seconds to fully discharge the anode.

Step 6. Slide the screwdriver out without twisting it; you could damage the CRT.

This process must be repeated after each time the monitor is powered up until the housing is replaced.

Mechanical Hazards

Although computers and their peripherals are primarily electronic and electrical devices, they can pose various mechanical hazards to users, including

- Impact and inkjet printers can pinch or crush fingers in their gears and paper feeders if the cover is removed while the printer is in operation.

- CD and DVD trays can pinch fingers or damage cables when retracting.

- Pins in serial, parallel, VGA, and DVI cable connectors can cause puncture wounds.

- Sharp edges on metal computer cases, card brackets, and drive rails can cause minor cuts.

To avoid mechanical hazards like these, take the following precautions:

- Turn off printers before attempting to remove paper or label jams.

- Follow the manufacturer's recommended procedure for changing ink cartridges to prevent the printer from attempting to print, move the printhead, or advance paper during the process.

- Make sure fingers, cables, and other potential obstructions are out of the way before closing CD and DVD trays.

- Don't touch the pins in cable connectors to avoid potential harm to yourself or ESD risks to connected equipment.

- Handle chassis components such as computer cases, card brackets, and drive rails with care. Avoid sliding your hands along the edges of these and similar sheet-metal parts to avoid cuts and scrapes.

- Have antibiotic ointment and appropriate bandages, including finger and knuckle bandages, handy in case of injury to hands or fingers.

Tripping Hazards

Watch out for loose cables! Whether it's a temporary setup while you are repairing a balky PC or printer or a "permanent" office setup, power or data cables running across floors or other locations where users could trip and fall are accidents waiting to happen. When someone trips or falls because of power or data cables, both the individual and the connected equipment can be harmed.

Avoid trip/fall hazards by controlling cable sprawl. Use the following tools and techniques to manage cables:

- Cable ties are an inexpensive way to keep overlength cables out of the way. They use Velcro or similar hook-and-loop material to provide self-adhesive properties, and come in a variety of colors you can use for color-coding or to assure that the cable tie is the same color as or a contrasting color to the cable.

Cable ties are available at electronics and computer stores, as well as fabric and hobby stores.

- To manage bundles of cables running to a particular PC or other equipment, consider cable wraps or cable trappers.

- For temporary cable runs across floors, such as in a repair situation, a trade show, or a training class, use gaffers' tape or duct tape to tape the cables to the floor. These types of tape leave little or no residue when used for short periods of time and can be used to hold down network, power, video, or other types of cables.

- For long-term cable installations, use cable management systems to keep cables out of the way. These can be as simple as a floor cable concealer, which protects cables on the floor from damage, or as elaborate as cable trays, which carry cables over a suspended ceiling, or cable raceways, which conceal cable runs along wallboards or crown molding. The Cable Organizers website, www.cableorganizer.com, is a good place to start your search for permanent cable organizing solutions.

Liquid Hazards

Liquids, such as those used for cleaning computer equipment or refilling inkjet cartridges, pose a variety of hazards, including

- Electric shock hazard when used to clean ink or toner spills in a printer
- Carpet or clothing stains when refilling inkjet cartridges

To avoid electric shock hazards caused by liquid cleaner, make sure the printer or other component is turned off and unplugged before using a liquid cleaner. To clean up spilled toner, use a toner-rated vacuum cleaner.

To avoid carpet or clothing stains when refilling inkjet printer cartridges, be sure to follow the vendor's instructions carefully.

Situational Hazards

When you are setting up computer equipment on a temporary basis, such as for a repair or configuration before permanent installation, it might be tempting to take shortcuts that you would not consider for a permanent installation. Watch out for the following:

- Don't overload a worktable or bench with equipment. If the legs collapse or the tabletop gives way, both you and the equipment could be harmed. Check the rating for the furniture before piling it up with heavy printers, UPS systems, all-in-one units, 19-inch or larger CRT monitors, or similar heavyweights.

- Avoid using chairs, tables, or other surfaces as replacements for stepstools or ladders. You can fall and hurt yourself—and break equipment in the process.

- Don't use empty boxes as temporary stands for equipment. If you must use boxes until the furniture arrives, use boxes that still contain equipment—and don't put heavy components atop lightweight boxes.

- Watch out for trip/fall hazards from power and data cables, surge suppressors, and the like. See "Tripping Hazards," earlier in this chapter, for methods to avoid tripping hazards during short-term computer setups.

Situational hazards can also pose potential threats during permanent computer or peripheral installation:

- Don't overload tempered-glass desktops or other furniture. These items usually have clearly-marked load limits. Exceed them, and watch the monitors or printers crack the glass as they fall.

- Tag power and data cables to make it easy to tell which cables go with what equipment.

Atmospheric Hazards

The major atmospheric hazard for computer users is the use of Halon in the fire-extinguisher systems of computer rooms. Halon is toxic to humans (it can cause cardiac problems), although it is safe for computer equipment. If you work in a computer room or other area that uses Halon-based fire extinguishers or sprinkler systems, make sure you do not breathe in Halon fumes. Exit the area immediately in case of fire.

DuPont FE-36 is a safe alternative to Halon, providing comparable fire suppressant control for Class A, B, and C fires, while being far less toxic. To learn more about FE-36, see the DuPont FE-36 information page at http://www2.dupont.com/FE/en_US/products/fe36.html.

Heavy Equipment Hazards

Laser printers, workgroup-grade all-in-one units, high-capacity UPS battery backup systems, and servers are potential hazards because of their weight and bulk. Take the following precautions to avoid injury and damage

- Move equipment in its original cartons and packaging whenever possible.

- Use wheeled freight dollies or carts to move equipment.

- Use "team lift" methods to move heavy and bulky items.

- Wear a back brace.

Environmental and Accident Incident Handling

Even with the best of precautions, environmental issues and accidents involving computers and related technologies can and do happen. Use the following procedures to handle problems safely and professionally

- Know who to contact in case of injuries to personnel, damage to equipment, fires, or chemical spills.

- Know how to reach an outside phone line to call 911 in case of serious emergency.

- Review and follow procedures for cleaning up chemical spills, retrieving damaged computer equipment, or other problems.

- Have MSDS information available for computer-related supplies and chemicals.

- Write up the incident in a professional manner, noting time, place, personnel involved, and other important information.

- Work with other personnel to solve problems resulting from the incident.

- Learn from the incident to help avoid future problems.

Exam Preparation Tasks

Review All the Key Topics

Review the most important topics in the chapter, noted with the key topics icon in the outer margin of the page. Table 17-2 lists a reference of these key topics and the page numbers on which each is found.

Table 17-2   Key Topics for Chapter 17

Key Topic Element	Description	Page Number
Figure 17-1	A portion of an MSDS for a typical HP laser printer toner cartridge, viewed with Adobe Acrobat.	886
Figure 17-2	ESD, electrical and safety products used by computer technicians.	887
Figure 17-3	A typical ESD kit includes a grounded work mat and wrist strap.	889
Figure 17-4	A grounded work mat, suitable for use on either a work area or under an office computer in a high-static area, and antistatic Faraday bags.	890
Figure 17-5	Hazard warnings and safety certifications on the label for a typical power supply.	892

Definitions of Key Terms

Define the following key terms from this chapter, and check your answers in the glossary.

ESD, MSDS, AC, DC, Suspend mode, Faraday cage antistatic bags

Troubleshooting Scenario

You are a technician for your company. You walk into work one morning and turn on the lights. You notice that one of your co-workers worked late the night before and left many electrical cables stretched across the floor. What should you do in this scenario?

Refer to Appendix A for the answer.

This chapter covers the following subjects:

■ **Troubleshooting Methods Overview**—Here you learn about the six-step CompTIA A+ troubleshooting process, as well as how to interview clients and how to evaluate their environment.

■ **Determining Whether a Problem Is Caused by Hardware or Software**—This section discusses a computer's subsystems, and components, in an effort to help you differentiate between hardware and software-related issues. It also covers important topics such as backing up data, recording configurations, and more.

■ **Where to Go for More Information**—Information related to technical issues can be found in many places including the manufacturer's website, PC books, online computer magazines, and search engines. Be sure to read through this section to find out where to go for those technical solutions!

■ **Useful Hardware and Software Tools**—This section describes the various hardware and software tools used for diagnosing, repairing, and cleaning PCs and their components.

■ **Professional Behavior**—In this final section, you read about how to talk to and treat customers, focusing on respect for the customer. After all, this is where all PC repair business comes from!

This chapter covers a portion of the CompTIA A+ 220-701 objectives 2.1, 2.2, and 6.2.

CHAPTER 18

Troubleshooting and Communications Methods

Two factors make for successful troubleshooting: extensive computer knowledge and an understanding of human psychology. You must understand how hardware and software work to troubleshoot them. That's what the preceding chapters of this book were all about. You also must treat customers with respect. By combining these two factors, you can quickly detect and solve computer problems.

"Do I Know This Already?" Quiz

The "Do I Know This Already?" quiz allows you to assess whether you should read this entire chapter or simply jump to the "Exam Preparation Tasks" section for review. If you are in doubt, read the entire chapter. Table 18-1 outlines the major headings in this chapter and the corresponding "Do I Know This Already?" quiz questions. You can find the answers in Appendix A, "Answers to the 'Do I Know This Already?' Quizzes and Troubleshooting Scenarios."

Table 18-1 "Do I Know This Already?" Foundation Topics Section-to-Question Mapping

Foundations Topics Section	Questions Covered in This Section
Troubleshooting Methods Overview	1–3
Determining Whether a Problem is Caused by Hardware or Software	4, 5
Where to Go for More Information	6, 7
Useful Hardware and Software Tools	8, 9
Professional Behavior	10–12

1. You have been contacted by a client. You arrive at her location and find that she is unable to work on her computer due to a malfunction. You need to find out what has happened. What should you do first?

   a. Walk in and tell the user you will handle it from here

   b. Learn as much as possible when speaking to the client

   c. Tell the client you will have to run some tests

   d. Look to see if anything has come unplugged

2. You are sent out on a tech call. You arrive at the client's desk. He seems to know what the problem is during the interview. Which of the following should you *not* do during the interview?

   a. Use clear, concise statements

   b. Allow the customer to complete statements

   c. Use tech jargon to make you look smarter

   d. Listen to the customer until he is finished

3. A client has asked you to look at her computer. She is telling you that the system will not boot or power on. You then ask if she gets any error codes or messages and she says no. Which of the following could be the cause of the problem?

   a. Power problems

   b. Motherboard is not working

   c. The memory chip has come loose

   d. The video card has stopped functioning

4. A client calls and needs to see you about a computer issue he is having. Once you arrive at his desk, he tells you that his computer is unresponsive. You ask if anything has changed on the computer. The client informs you that he has changed out the NIC. What do you need to do before you begin?

   a. Remove the NIC card

   b. Uninstall the NIC card

   c. Try to determine whether it is a hardware or software problem

   d. Boot the computer in safe mode

5. Which of the following should you do on a client's computer before you start making any changes that might affect the computer's settings or performance? Choose all that apply.

    a. Back up the customer's data

    b. Create an image of the machine

    c. Use an anti-static strap

    d. Change the size of the virtual memory file

6. You have just purchased a new video card for your computer. You notice that the device does not have an installation CD with it. Where would you go to get the installation information?

    a. A popular search engine

    b. The manufacturer's website

    c. Look on the newsgroups

    d. Windows Update

7. You have just completed work on a client's computer. You spent a long time troubleshooting this issue. What should you do to expedite the troubleshooting process? (Choose all that apply.)

    a. Note symptoms

    b. Note any other problems

    c. Document final resolutions

    d. Document any workarounds

8. You have just achieved your A+ certification. You are in need of a kit to help you in your work. Which of the following should you have access to?

    a. Screwdrivers

    b. Pliers

    c. Tweezers

    d. Penlight

    e. All of these options are correct

9. A client has contacted you about a boot system error. Which of the following will you need to restore the missing files and get the user back up and running? Choose all that apply.

    a. A bootable disk

    b. A floppy drive

    c. An external hard drive with all system files

    d. An installation CD

10. Your client is having problems with his computer. He is under a tremendous amount of stress and is very hostile. What should you do to prevent a confrontation with him?

    a. Tell the client to leave the area while you work

    b. Tell them you don't have to listen to them talk like that and leave

    c. Avoid having a defensive attitude

    d. Call your supervisor and have them speak with the customer

11. You are at the home of one of your main customers. Since she knows and trusts you, she leaves you alone to work. Which of the following should you *not* do while at her home? (Choose all that apply.)

    a. Look around her hard drive

    b. Print personal information

    c. Use her equipment for your personal tasks

    d. Make her sorry she called you

12. You have been notified to work on a client's workstation. You ask who it is and you find out it is someone who is very difficult to deal with. What should you do when you arrive at the client's desk?

    a. Go in knowing you will be confronted by the client

    b. Take your time in getting to their desk

    c. Try your best to smile

    d. Maintain a positive attitude

Foundation Topics

Troubleshooting Methods Overview

To become a successful troubleshooter, you need to

- Learn as much as possible during the client interview

- Evaluate the client's environment

- Use testing and reporting software to gather information about the system

- Form a hypothesis (a theory you will try to prove or disprove)

- Use the troubleshooting cycle and the CompTIA six-step troubleshooting process to isolate and solve the problem

It is necessary to approach computer problems from a logical standpoint. To best accomplish this, PC technicians will implement a troubleshooting methodology (or maybe more than one). There are several different troubleshooting methodologies available; CompTIA has included its own six-step process within the 2009 and 2001 A+ objectives. Memorize the steps in Table 18-2 for the exam.

Table 18-2   The Six-Step CompTIA A+ Troubleshooting Methodology

Step	Description
Step 1	Identify the problem
Step 2	Establish a theory of probable cause (question the obvious)
Step 3	Test the theory to determine the cause
Step 4	Establish a plan of action to resolve the problem and implement the solution
Step 5	Verify full system functionality and, if applicable, implement preventative measures
Step 6	Document findings, actions, and outcomes

As you attempt to troubleshoot computer issues, think in terms of this six-step process. Plug the problem directly into these steps.

For example, in Step 1 you might identify an issue; maybe the computer won't turn on. For Step 2, a possible theory could be that the computer is not plugged in to the AC outlet. To test the theory in Step 3, you would plug the computer in. If it works, then great, but if it doesn't, you would go back to Step 2 and establish a new theory. When you have reached a theory that tests positive, move on to Step 4 and establish the plan of action based on that theory, and then implement your solution. (Keep in mind that many plans of action will be more complicated than just plugging the computer in! Perhaps the AC outlet was loose, which would require a licensed electrician to fix it.) Next, in Step 5 you want to *test*. Always test and verify that the system is functioning correctly. If need be, implement preventative measures; for example, re-route the power cable so that it is out of the way and can't be disconnected easily. Finally, in Step 6, you want to document your findings and the outcome. In many companies, documentation begins right when you first get a troubleshooting call (or trouble ticket), and the documentation continues throughout the entire process. You can track documentation on paper, or in an online system; it depends on your company's procedures. Be sure to keep track of what happened, why it happened, and how you fixed the problem.

Because computer failures happen to the customer (who usually is less technically aware than you of the possible causes for the problem), you must work with the customer to create a complete list of symptoms so that you can find the right solution quickly and accurately. To do this, you need to

- Carefully observe the customer's environment to look for potential causes of computer problems, such as interference sources, power problems, and user error.

- Ask the customer what (if anything) has changed recently about the computer or its environment. Anything from new hardware or software being installed, new telephone or network being installed, or even a new coffee maker or air-conditioning unit could be at the root of the problem. A simple way to ask this would be to say, "What has changed since the last time it (the PC) worked?"

- Determine what tasks the customer was performing on the PC. You can determine this not only by asking the customer questions, but by reviewing system log files, browser history, and so on

- Ask the customer detailed questions about the symptoms, including unusual system behavior, such as noises or beeps, office events taking place around the same time, onscreen error messages, and so on.

TIP Windows generates several log files during routine use that can be useful for determining what went wrong. Many of these can be viewed through the Event Viewer. To view the contents of the Event Viewer, right-click **Computer/My Computer**, click **Manage**, and click **Event Viewer**. The Event Viewer captures three types of information: Application errors, security audits, and system errors. See Chapter 18, "Troubleshooting and Maintaining Windows," for typical examples.

Because some types of computer problems aren't easy to replicate away from the customer site, your customer might see system problems you never will, even if you attempt to reproduce the problem.

> **TIP**   Remember, troubleshooting is the art and science of quickly and accurately determining what is wrong with a customer's system. Troubleshooting is an art because every technician will bring his or her own experience and personality to the task. Troubleshooting is also a science because you can apply a definite method that will bring you a great degree of success.

The Client Interview

The client interview is the all-important first step in solving any computer troubleshooting situation. During the client interview, you need to ask questions to determine the following information:

- **What hardware or software appears to have a problem?**—The user might have an opinion about this, but don't be unduly swayed by a statement such as "the printer's broken"; the device or software the user believes to be at fault might simply reflect a problem coming from another source.

- **What other hardware or software was in use at the time of the problem?**—The user probably will answer these types of questions in terms of open applications, but you will also want to look at the taskbar and system tray in Windows for other programs or routines that are running. Pressing **Ctrl+Alt+Del** will bring up a task list in Windows that has the most complete information about programs and subroutines in memory. To determine the exact version of a Windows-based program in use, click **Help, About**. View the System properties sheet to determine the version of Windows in use.

- **What task was the user trying to perform at the time of the problem?**—Ask the questions needed to find out the specific issues involved. You want to know which computer was in use, what operating system was in use, what task was being performed, and whether any peripheral hardware was being used (printer, multifunction device, etc.). Don't forget to check the Event Viewer in Windows for details about the software running at the time of the error. Refer to Chapter 15 for more information.

- **Is the hardware or software on the user's machine or accessed over the network?**—If the network was involved, check with the network administrator to see if the network is currently working properly. If the hardware and software are not networked, your scope for troubleshooting is simpler.

- **What were the specific symptoms of the problem?**—Some users are very observant, but others might not be able to give you much help. Ask about the approximate time of the failure and about error messages, beeps, and unusual noises.

- **Can the problem be reproduced?**—Reproducible problems are easier to find than those that mysteriously "heal" themselves when you show up. Because power and environmental issues at the customer's site can cause computer problems, try to reproduce the problem at the customer's site before you move the computer to your test bench, where conditions are different.

■ **Does the problem repeat itself with a different combination of hardware and software, or does the problem go away when another combination of hardware and software is used?**—For example, if the user can scan photos directly to the hard disk but cannot scan them into the Adobe Photoshop workspace, this means that the scanner or multifunction device is working, but there might be a problem with the Photoshop program's configuration. If the user can't scan anything, there might be a general problem with the scanner or multifunction device's hardware or drivers.

Tips for Conducting the Client Interview

During the client interview, you will make an impression on the client. Will it be "this tech knows what's going on and wants to fix my problem" or "this tech's a blowhard know-it all that just won't listen!" If you want to come across as someone who's competent and caring, and not as a blowhard who won't listen, follow these guidelines:

■ **Use clear, concise, and direct statements**—Clients appreciate it when you use language they can understand.

■ **Allow the customer to complete statements**—Don't interrupt. You might *think* you know what they're going to say next, but you could be wrong. If you don't allow the customer to complete their statements, you might miss some vital information or clues about the problem.

■ **Clarify customer statements—ask pertinent questions**—Whether you think you understand what the customer said or are totally at sea, make sure you ask the questions that will help keep you on the right track. Try rephrasing what they said and ask them to agree or clarify: "If I understand you correctly, what you're saying is...."

■ **Don't baffle the customer with technobabble**—Avoid using jargon, abbreviations, and acronyms. Explain what you mean in plain language. Remember, if you can't explain a problem or solution in everyday language, you don't understand it either.

■ **Who saw the problem? The customer!**—So, listen to your customers; they may be the best way to find the solution, especially if the problem refused to show up when you're around.

Sometimes, the client interview alone will reveal the answer. More often, however, you'll need to go to the client's work area and evaluate the hardware and software that are involved. For additional tips on talking to customers and working with customer property, see "Professional Behavior" later in this chapter.

How to Evaluate the Client's Environment

Depending on the clues you receive in the initial interview, you should go to the client's work area prepared to perform a variety of tests. You must look for three major issues when evaluating the customer's environment:

- Power issues

- Interference sources

- Symptoms and error codes—this might require that you try to reproduce the error

You can select from the tests listed in Table 18-3 based on your evaluation of the most likely sources of problems. You might need to perform several tests to rule out certain problems.

Table 18-3   Troubleshooting Tests and Requirements

Test	Requires
Power	Multimeter, circuit tester
BIOS beep and error codes	List of BIOS codes, POST card, or display device
Printer self-test	Printer and paper
Windows bootlog	Start Windows with Bootlog option enabled
I/O Port	Connect Loopback plugs and run third-party diagnostics
Video tests	Run third-party diagnostics
Hardware resources	Windows Device Manager
Device drivers	Windows Device Manager

For more information about the requirements listed in Table 18-3, see "Useful Hardware and Software Tools" later in this chapter.

Testing Power

Systems that won't start or that have lockups or shutdowns with no error messages could be the victims of power problems. To determine whether power problems are located inside the computer or are coming from outside the system, use the tests and tools described in Chapter 5, "Power Supplies and System Cooling." If a system malfunctions at a customer site but works properly at your test bench, power problems due to improper wiring might be to blame.

Looking for Sources of Interference

Power problems also can be caused by interference from other devices, such as copiers, vacuum cleaners, elevators, and alarm systems. If a system performs properly when moved away from its normal work area, but malfunctions when it is returned to its normal location, or if it works during the business day but not after hours (when an alarm system is activated), interference might be to blame. See the section "Power Conditioning Devices" in Chapter 5 for suggestions on dealing with sources of interference.

If the problem is network-related, it might be necessary to reroute UTP (unshielded twisted-pair) cabling away from interference sources or connect the cable to a different port on the hub or switch.

Recording Symptoms and Error Codes

If your tests rule out power and interference, you must proceed to tests that focus on the hardware or software that appears the most likely cause of the problem.

Which test or diagnostic routine is the best one to start with? Before you perform any specific tests, review the clues you gathered from the client. Examples of places where symptoms and error codes can be found include

- **Event Viewer**—The System log records error information regarding drivers and system files, while the Application log records information and errors about applications within the operating system.

- **Device Manager**—If a device in Device Manager is disabled it will be marked with a red x (Windows XP) or a down arrow (Windows 7/Vista); if it is not configured properly there will be an exclamation point against a yellow background (Windows XP, Vista, and 7). Device Manager also displays codes in the Properties window of a device indicating particular issues.

- **On screen messages**—Various messages can popup on the screen while a user is working in Windows. Sometimes these messages can be helpful in finding out what the problem is. If the computer fails completely, a stop error (BSOD) will be displayed offering further information as to why the system halted.

- **The BIOS**—The BIOS can indicate errors by way of onscreen messages and beep codes. Use the particular system's motherboard documentation to discern what these codes and messages mean.

- **Printer Displays**—The small LCD panel or LED array found on many printers is used to indicate the status of the printer. From this display you can verify whether the printer is online, if there is a paper jam, identify error codes, and so on.

Determining Whether a Problem Is Caused by Hardware or Software

The oldest dilemma for any computer technician is determining whether a problem is caused by hardware or software. The widespread use of Windows operating systems makes this problem even more acute than it was when MS-DOS was the predominant standard, because all hardware devices in a Windows system are controlled by Windows device drivers.

A troubleshooting cycle is a method that you can use to determine exactly what part of a complex system, such as a computer, is causing the problem. The troubleshooting cycle used in this section goes into more depth than the CompTIA six-step troubleshooting process. The first step is to determine the most likely source of the problem. The client interview will help you determine which subsystem is the best place to start solving the problem. In the previous example, the printing subsystem was the most likely place to start.

A *subsystem* is the combination of components designed to do a particular task, and it can include hardware, software, and firmware components. Use Table 18-4 to better understand the nature of the subsystems found in any computer.

Table 18-4   Computer and Peripheral Subsystems and Their Components

Subsystem	Hardware	Software	Firmware
Printing	Printer, cable, parallel or serial port	Printer driver in Windows application	BIOS configuration of port
Display	Graphics card, monitor, cables, port type, motherboard (integrated video)	Video drivers in Windows	Video BIOS, BIOS configuration of video type, boot priority
Audio	Sound card, microphone, speakers, speaker and microphone cables, CD analog and digital cables to sound card, motherboard integrated audio	Audio drivers in Windows	BIOS configuration of integrated audio
Mouse and pointing device	Mouse or pointing device, serial or mouse port, USB port	Mouse driver in Windows	BIOS port configuration, USB legacy configuration
Keyboard	Keyboard, PS/2, or USB port	Keyboard driver in Windows	BIOS keyboard configuration, USB legacy configuration
Storage	Drives, data cables, power connectors, USB, IEEE-1394 or SCSI cards, or built-in ports	Storage drivers in Windows	BIOS drive configuration, BIOS configuration of built-in PATA, SATA, USB, IEEE-1394 ports, RAID functions

continues

Table 18-4   Computer and Peripheral Subsystems and Their Components

Subsystem	Hardware	Software	Firmware
Power	Power supply, splitters, fans, cables	Power-management software (Windows)	BIOS power-management configuration
CPU	CPU, motherboard	System devices	BIOS cache and CPU configuration
RAM	RAM, motherboard	(none)	BIOS RAM timing configuration settings
Network	NIC, motherboard, USB port (for USB devices), cable	Network configuration files and drivers	BIOS PnP and power management, BIOS configuration of integrated network port or USB port
Modem	Modem, motherboard or serial port or USB port, cable	Modem drivers, application	BIOS PnP, power management, BIOS port configuration

You can see from Table 18-4 that virtually every subsystem in the computer has hardware, software, and firmware components. A thorough troubleshooting process will take into account both the subsystem and all of its components. The following steps are involved in the troubleshooting cycle:

Step 1.   Back up customer data (if possible). Before you do anything to a customer's system, you should ensure that the system's data has been backed up. The easiest way to ensure that you can restore the system to its "as-was" configuration is to use a disk-imaging program such as Symantec Norton Ghost or Acronis True Image. The current versions of these programs perform disk-imaging to preserve the contents of the system drive (and other specified drives) at both a data and operating system level. However, if you need to restore specified files only, the current versions of these programs also permit file-level restoration. For speed and convenience, use an external hard disk connected to a USB 2.0, FireWire, or eSATA port as the destination for the image (note that eSATA ports might not be supported by some older disk-imaging programs).

Step 2.   Find the most likely cause. Based on the client interview and the information from Table 18-4, determine the subsystem that is the most likely cause of the problem.

Step 3.   Record the current configuration of the subsystem. This includes items such as the driver version, BIOS settings, cable type and length, and hardware settings. Before you change anything, record the current configuration. Depending on the item, this might include recording jumper or DIP switch settings, printing the complete report from Windows Device Manager, recording BIOS configurations, and backing up the Windows Registry. If you perform an image backup as recommended in the previous step, the Windows Registry is included as part of the backup. If you don't record the current configuration of the system's hardware and software before you start the troubleshooting cycle, you will not be able to reset the system to its previous condition if your first change doesn't solve the problem.

Step 4. Change one component or setting at a time. Change a single hardware component or hardware/software/firmware setting you suspect is the cause of the problem. If you replace hardware, use a replacement that you know to be working. No matter how concerned your client is and no matter how heavy your workload, change only one component before you retest the system. Examples of changing a single component or configuration setting include swapping a data or power cable, removing the device from Windows Device Manager, changing a device's IRQ or other hardware resource setting, reinstalling a device's driver software, and reinstalling or repairing an application. Performing two or more of these types of tasks before you retest the system can make matters worse, and if you fix the problem you won't know which change was the correct change to make.

Step 5. Retest after a single change and evaluate the results.

Step 6. Reconfigure or reinstall. If the problem persists, reconfigure or reinstall the device or hardware/software/firmware setting to its original condition and repeat Steps 4 and 5 with another component in the same subsystem.

Step 7. Continue until all subsystem components have been tested. Repeat Steps 4–6 until the subsystem performs normally or until you have tested all components in the subsystem. If the problem stops occurring after a change, that item is the cause of the problem. Repair, replace, or reload it as appropriate to solve the problem.

Step 8. Move on to another subsystem. If changing all components or settings in a particular subsystem does not solve the problem, move on to another subsystem that you think might be the culprit. Choose from one of the subsystems in Table 18-4. You will find that some problems can be deceiving; they will appear to be caused by one subsystem when in reality they are caused by another.

There are a few other techniques to consider when troubleshooting, including which components to check first, common points of failure, the fact that a device is known to be working doesn't necessarily mean it's new, and to keep track of your solutions.

What Components to Check First

As the previous subsystem list indicated, there's no shortage of places to start in virtually any subsystem. What's the best way to decide whether a hardware, software, or firmware problem is the most likely cause? Typically, hardware problems come and go, whereas software and firmware problems are consistent. Why? A hardware problem is often the result of a damaged or loose wire or connection; when the connection is closed, the component works, but when the connection opens, the component fails. On the other hand, a software or firmware problem will cause a failure under the same circumstances every time.

Another rule of thumb is to consider the least expensive, easiest-to-to-replace item first. In most cases, the power or data cable connected to a subsystem is the first place to look for problems. Whether the cable is internal or external, it is almost always the least-expensive part of the subsystem, can easily come loose, and can easily be damaged. If a cable is loose, has bent pins, or has a dry, brittle, or cracked exterior, replace it.

When new software or new hardware has been introduced to the system and a problem results immediately afterward, that change is often the most likely cause of the problem.

Hardware conflicts such as IRQ, I/O port address, DMA channel, and memory address, or conflicts between the software drivers in the operating system are typical causes of failure when new hardware is introduced. New software can also cause problems with hardware, because of incompatibilities between software and hardware or because new software has replaced drivers required by the hardware.

Points of Failure on the Outside of the Computer

The front of the computer might provide valuable clues if you're having problems with a system. In case of problems, check the following common points of failure for help.

- **Can't read CD, DVD, or Blu-ray media**—The drive door on the Blu-ray, DVD or CD drive might not be completely closed or the media might be inserted upside down; press the eject button to open the drive, remove any obstacles, reseat the media, and close the drive.

> **TIP** You can also eject optical media with Windows Explorer/My Computer. Right-click the drive and select **Eject**. If the drive doesn't eject the media, there could be a problem with the drive's data cable, cable connection, or power connection.

- **Can't shut down the computer with the case power switch**—The case power switch is connected to the motherboard on ATX, BTX, and other modern desktop systems, not directly to the power supply as with older designs. The wire might be loose or connected to the wrong pins on the motherboard. Keep in mind that most systems require you to hold in the power button for about four seconds before the system will shut down. If the computer crashes, you might need to shut down the computer by unplugging it or by turning off the surge suppressor used by the computer. Some ATX and BTX power supplies have their own on-off switches.

- **Can't see the drive access or power lights**—As with the case power switch, these lights are also connected to the motherboard. These wires might also be loose or connected to the wrong pins on the motherboard.

- **Can't use USB, IEEE-1394, or other ports on the front of the system**—Some systems have these ports on the front of the computer as well as the rear. Front-mounted ports are connected with header cables to the motherboard. If the cables inside the case are loose, the ports won't work. If the ports are disabled in the system BIOS, the ports won't work.

As you can see from this section, in many situations, you will need to open the case to resolve a problem, even though the symptoms might first manifest themselves outside the computer.

"Known-Working" Doesn't Mean "New"—Best Sources for Replacement Parts

To perform parts exchanges for troubleshooting, you need replacement parts. If you don't have spare parts, it's very tempting to go to the computer store and buy some new components. Instead, take a spare system that's similar to the "sick" computer, make sure that it works, and then use it for parts. Why? Just because it's new doesn't mean it works.

I once replaced an alternator on my van with a brand-new, lifetime-warranty alternator that failed in less than a week. Whether it's a cable, a video card, a monitor, or some other component, try using a known-working item as a temporary replacement rather than brand-new.

TIP   Rather than give away, sell, or discard working video cards, hard disks, and other components you have replaced with faster, bigger, better upgrades, keep at least one of each item to use as a replacement for testing purposes or as a backup in case the upgrade fails.

If you don't have spare parts, use a spare system if possible rather than knocking another working system (and user) out of action by "borrowing" parts from an operational system. Use the same brand and model of system for known-working spares if possible, because the components inside are more likely to be identical to the "sick" system you are diagnosing.

Swapping from an identical or nearly identical system is especially important if the system you are diagnosing uses proprietary components or is a laptop computer.

Keeping Track of Your Solutions

Make a practice of keeping detailed notes about the problems you solve. If your company has a help-desk system with tracking capabilities, use it. Even if the best you can do is write up your findings, you can use desktop search tools to find the answers to the same problems that might arise later.

Be sure to note symptoms, underlying problems, workarounds, and final resolutions. To help capture the information you need:

- Use Windows' Screen Capture feature (press the **PrtScn** button and copy the clipboard contents into Paint or another image editor) to grab screens.

- Use the Save As Web Archive feature in Internet Explorer to grab web pages complete with text and links as one file.

Where to Go for More Information

After you've gathered as much information as possible, you might find that you still need more help. User manuals for components often are discarded, software drivers need to be updated, and some conflicts don't have easy answers. Use the following resources for more help:

- **Manufacturers' websites**—Most system and component manufacturers provide extensive technical information via the World Wide Web. You'll want to have the Adobe Reader program in its latest version available to be able to read the technical manuals you can download (Adobe Reader itself is a free download from www.adobe.com). These sites often contain expert systems for troubleshooting, specialized newsgroups, downloadable driver updates, and other helps for problems.

- **Printed manuals**—Although many vendors have switched to web-based or Adobe Reader (PDF) manuals, some vendors still provided printed manuals or quick-reference diagrams. Be sure to file these in a way that permits quick access when needed.

- **Web-based or PDF manuals on disc**—Many vendors, especially those that use CDs or DVDs to distribute device drivers or utility programs for hardware, now put their user or reference manuals on the same medium. To view a web-based manual, open the file with your web browser. To view a PDF manual, open the file with Adobe Reader, Adobe Acrobat, or other PDF viewer/editor.

- **Help for "orphan" systems and components**—It's frustrating to need information about a system whose manufacturer is no longer around. Sites such as http://download.cnet.com and www.windrivers.com provide information and drivers for orphan systems and components.

- **Online computer magazines**—If your back-issue collection of major computer magazines is missing some issues, or even if you've never subscribed to the print versions, you can find a lot of technical content from the major magazine publishers online: www.pcmag.com (*PC Magazine*), www.pcworld.com (*PC World*), and www.maximumpc.com (*Maximum PC*) are just three of my favorite resources.

- **Third-party news and information sites**—Tom's Hardware (www.tomshardware.com), AnandTech (www.anandtech.com), The Register (www.theregister.co.uk), and iXBT Labs (http://ixbtlabs.com/) are just a few of the websites I rely on for product reviews, news, and insights.

- **Book series**—With over 2.2 million copies sold, Scott Mueller's *Upgrading and Repairing PCs* (www.upgradingandrepairingpcs.com) is still the single best source of information about desktop computer hardware, old and new. Other books in the series include *Upgrading and Repairing Laptops* and *Upgrading and Repairing Windows*.

- **Search engines**—Google (www.google.com), Yahoo! (www.yahoo.com), Goodsearch (www.goodsearch.com), Bing (www.bing.com), and others and aggregators such as Dogpile (www.dogpile.com) are among the fastest ways to locate specific resources for further research. Currently, of these, my favorite is Google. Google is fast, finds text in many types of online content (not just HTML web pages, but also PDF, Microsoft Word, and others), can search newsgroups, and finds image and video files as well. Use its Advanced Search feature to narrow your search; you can even search a particular website only. Click the Cached button to see the site as Google last saw it if the current contents aren't what you need or the website is down. Go to http://groups.google.com to search or browse Usenet newsgroups.

With so many sources of information available in print and online, there's no reason to stop learning. To succeed and enjoy yourself, take every opportunity to learn more.

Useful Hardware and Software Tools

The A+ Certification test's troubleshooting content expects you to know the use of basic diagnostic devices, so a review of this section will be useful before your exam. The following list of items also provides you with a handy reference for what you should bring on service calls.

Hardware Diagnostics

Hardware diagnostic tools can help you determine what components inside of a bootable system are not working correctly. Testing software used as part of the diagnostic process can also be used to perform burn-in tests on new hardware to help find problems before systems are put into service. Figure 18-1 shows some typical products.

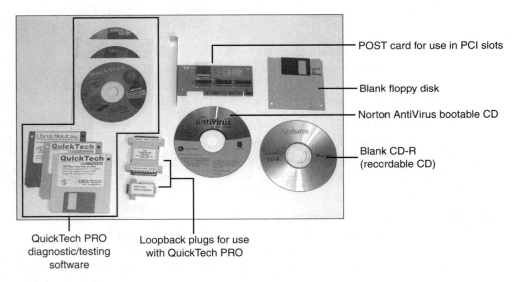

Figure 18-1   Typical hardware diagnostic tools.

- **Testing software**, such as BurnIn Test Professional Edition (www.passmark.com), CheckIt Diagnostics (www.smithmicro.com), or Ultra-X QuickTech for Windows or Professional, (www.ultra-x.com)—Tests RAM, hardware configuration, motherboards, serial ports, parallel ports, and drives; some also check USB ports.

- **Loopback plugs for USB, network, serial and parallel ports**—These "loop back" transmit lines to receive lines during diagnostic testing.

NOTE   If the testing software you choose doesn't include the loopback plugs you need, make sure you use compatible loopback plugs (these can be ordered from the software vendor or various online or mail-order hardware vendors). Mixing and matching serial and parallel loopback plugs and testing software can provide inaccurate results because different brands of testing programs use various wiring designs for their loopback plugs.

USB 2.0 loopback plugs (also compatible with USB 1.1 plugs) are available from PassMark Software (www.passmark.com); they are compatible with PassMark's USB2Test and BurnIn Test Professional programs.

SuperLooper loopback plugs for various Ethernet and telecom interfaces are available from the Smartronix Store (www.smartronixstore.com).

- **POST card**—Displays hex POST codes during system startup to find boot errors that don't have matching beep codes. To display POST codes on systems that don't have PCI, mini-PCI, or ISA expansion slots but have parallel ports, use a parallel-port based POST code displayer, such as Ultra-X's MicroPost.

- **Blank media (floppy disk, USB flash drive, recordable CD and DVD media)**— These can be used to transfer drivers from a working machine to a similar machine that is not working. Note that you must use a floppy disk to provide a mass storage (RAID, SCSI, or SATA) driver for Windows XP during installation. On Windows Vista and Windows 7, you can load a mass storage driver from USB, CD, or DVD.

- **A preinstalled Windows environment on CD or DVD matching the Windows version in use**—The most famous of these is BartPE (www.nu2.nu/pebuilder/). A BartPE disc can be used to recover files, perform maintenance, and other rescue tasks on a system running Windows XP; it is created from a licensed Windows XP CD with the PE Builder program.

- **Virus/malware scanning software**—An up-to-date copy of a major anti-virus and anti-malware program helps find and remove viruses and Trojan Horse programs that affect systems. If you don't have a licensed anti-virus program available to scan a system, but it has a working Internet connection, use free online scanning services, such as Trend Micro's HouseCall (housecall.trendmicro.com), Symantec's Norton Security Scan (http://security.symantec.com), Panda's ActiveScan (www.pandasecurity.com), BitDefender Online Scanner (www.bitdefender.com), or others to scan the system. Many antivirus vendors now offer bootable CDs that can be used to scan for problems and fix them before Windows starts. You can also add antivirus programs to a BartPE disc; see the BartPE website for details.

Cleaning and Maintenance Tools

Some of the items listed in this section clean computers and peripherals to help prevent failures and keep systems in top condition. Other items can be used as spares for replacement testing or to replace missing components. Figure 18-2 shows many of the products in both categories.

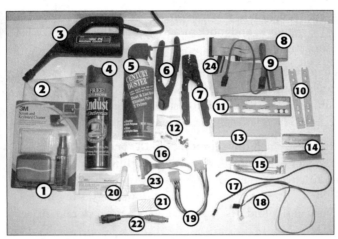

1. Screen and keyboard cleaning kit
2. Microfiber cleaning cloth
3. PC vacuum cleaner
4. Endust for Electronics antistatic cleaner
5. Compressed air
6. Wire cutter
7. Wire stripper
8. Floppy drive ribbon cable
9. Serial ATA (SATA) cable
10. Drive rails (one pair)
11. I/O shield
12. Screws and jumpers
13. Drive bay covers

14. Drive bay adapter kit
15. Slot covers
16. Serial port header cable for Baby-AT motherboards
17. Two-wire (digital) audio cable from optical drive to sound card
18. Four-wire (analog) audio cable from optical drive to sound card
19. Internal drive power splitter cable
20. Foam wands for cleaning keyboards
21. CAT5 cable coupler
22. PS/2 port to USB keyboard adapter
23. PS/2 port to USB mouse adapter
24. 80-wire ATA/IDE ribbon cable

Figure 18-2 Typical cleaning supplies and replacement/testing components used by computer technicians.

- **Compressed air**—Cleans gunk out of cases, fans, and power supplies

- **Keyboard key puller**—Safely removes keys to allow effective keyboard cleaning

- **Computer-rated mini-vacuum cleaner**—Cleans gunk out of cases, fans, power supplies, and keyboards and dust off motherboards and add-on cards

- **Wire cutter and stripper**—Used to build network cable

- **Extra case, card, and drive screws (salvage or new)**—Used as spares to replace missing or defective screws

- **Extra card slot covers (salvage or new)**—Used to replace missing covers to maintain proper system cooling

- **Extra hard disk and motherboard/card jumper blocks (salvage or new)**—Used to replace missing or defective jumper blocks when needed to configure devices

- **Antistatic cleaning wipes**

- **Replacement ATA/IDE (40-wire and 80-wire), floppy, USB, IEEE-1394, Serial ATA, parallel, SCSI, CAT 5 network, and modem/serial cables**—Customize list as needed for your organization

Recommended Equipment Cleaning Products

To clean equipment safely, don't reach under the kitchen sink and grab the first cleaner you see. Instead, use materials designed especially for electronics and computer use, or general-purpose cleaners proven to work well on electronics and computer equipment. Some useful cleaning materials include

- **Antistatic electronic wipes**—Use antistatic electronic wipes for monitor cases and glass surfaces, keyboards, LCD screens, and all types of plastic and metal cases for computers and peripherals. This type of product combines effective cleaning and **antistatic** properties, which protect your computer investment. You can also use these wipes to clean up gunk after it's been loosened by compressed air.

- **Glass and surface cleaners**—Glass and surface cleaners can be used on monitor glass and LCD screens and on other surfaces. However, they are not the preferred choice because they usually lack any antistatic properties. Endust for Electronics in pump or aerosol sprays is preferred for this use because it cleans and has antistatic properties.

CAUTION   With any spray cleaner, always spray the product onto the cleaning cloth, and never on the product to be cleaned. Spraying any kind of cleaner directly onto a keyboard or monitor can damage or destroy the device.

- **Isopropyl alcohol**—Isopropyl alcohol can be used along with foam (not cotton!) cleaning swabs to clean tape drive heads, floppy disk drive heads, and some keyboards. Some cleaning swabs are pre-moistened for convenience.

- **Specialized device cleaning kits for mechanical mice, tape drives, floppy disk drives, inkjet and laser printers, and CD/DVD cleaning discs**—Specialized device cleaning kits, as I have recommended in other chapters, are good ways to clean the devices they are built for. These device cleaning kits enabled me to avoid repairing or replacing at least one floppy disk drive and one inkjet printer.

- **Compressed air**—Compressed air is a powerful but "brainless" cleaner. Unlike the cleaners mentioned previously, compressed air cannot trap dirt and dust. Instead, dirt, dust, grit, and assorted fuzz are expelled violently out of their hiding places. If you use compressed air, put plenty of old newspapers under and around the device you are cleaning to catch the gunk compressed air expels from the device being cleaned. Use liquid cleaners or cleaning wipes to pick up residue left behind after using compressed air.

- **Stabilant-22a**—Stabilant-22a (sold by D. W. Electrochemicals; www.stabilant.com) is often recommended for use when assembling or reassembling a system for use in memory module sockets and expansion slots. It cleans the sockets and provides a more effective electrical connection.

Selecting and Using a Computer-Compatible Vacuum Cleaner

Vacuum cleaners are great for cleaning homes and offices, but typical models use plastic parts that can build up harmful static electricity. So, instead of using an ordinary office or home vacuum cleaner to clean a computer, purchase a model especially suited for computer use.

Computer-compatible vacuum cleaners have features such as

- Small-sized tips and brushes perfect for cleaning keyboards and working around motherboards and add-on cards

- Antistatic construction

- Hand-held with an adjustable neck for easy use inside a system

TIP   Use a vacuum cleaner as an alternative to compressed air whenever possible, especially when working at the client's site because it's neater—there's no flying gunk that can land in awkward places.

Professional Behavior

Passing the A+ Certification exams isn't an end in itself—it is designed to help start (or advance) your Information Technology (IT) career. In most IT careers, how you deal with customers, whether they're people you see day after day in your company or clients you might see only once or twice, can have as much of an impact on your career progress as your knowledge of hardware, software, firmware, and operating systems. The following sections will help you master the "soft skills" you need to move up in the computing world.

How to Talk to Customers

According to pop-culture references like the Dilbert comic strip and innumerable others, computer techs are incapable of relating to "normal" people in either social or professional situations. Unfortunately, these comic stereotypes are based on a lot of real-world data. Here's how to reverse the stereotype, one customer interaction at a time:

- No matter how difficult the problem, **maintain a positive attitude and tone of voice**—Your job is to make possible the seemingly impossible. As discussed earlier in this chapter, there are abundant resources available from Microsoft, hardware vendors, and numerous forums and newsgroups to help you solve problems.

- No matter how tough the problem (or the customer), **avoid arguing with customers—and drop the defensive attitude too**—Your job is to solve the customer's problem. To do that, you need to work *with* the customer. Get it? Got it? Good!

- No matter how many times you've seen the same problem show up, **do not minimize customers' problems**—Sure, you might have seen a couple of dozen instances of drive failure, for example, but keep in mind that every person with a dead drive has lost valuable personal or business data—maybe even enough of a loss to wipe out a business. You wouldn't want your handyman or mechanic acting as if your house or car problems were trivial—don't act as if your customers' problems are trivial, either.

- No matter how incorrect their actions or poor their judgment, **avoid being judgmental of your customers—and while you're at it, drop the insults and name-calling**—Declaring "war" on your customers just adds to everyone's stress level and doesn't get you any closer to a solution. Even if the customer decides to call your ancestry or intelligence into question, avoid responding in kind. "Fight the real enemy"—the computer problem!

- Don't let your cell phone, the big game on the big-screen TV, or the view out the corner office window get between you and a solution: **avoid distractions and/or interruptions when talking with customers**—Stay focused on what your customer is telling you, and the solution will be easier to find.

How to Treat Customers' Property

The old Aretha Franklin song said it best: "R-E-S-P-E-C-T." Whether it's the device you're servicing (laptop or desktop PC, PDA, printer, monitor, or other peripheral) or the telephone, respect it. Here's how:

- **Don't use customer equipment for personal tasks.** Make personal phone calls with your own phone (you *do* have a cell phone, don't you?).

- **Don't go poking around their hard disk or mobile device folders** unless it's necessary to solve the problem.

- **Don't "test" the printer by printing personal information.** Use your own printer to print your resume or a pinup of your favorite movie star, sports figure, or car.

- **If you need to reset the resolution on the display for testing, change it back when you're done.** Ditto with any other changes necessary for troubleshooting.

- **Don't make the customers sorry they called you or your company for help.** Customers who become ex-customers have a way of helping potential customers call somebody else for help.

Exam Preparation Tasks

Review All the Key Topics

Review the most important topics in the chapter, noted with the key topics icon in the outer margin of the page. Table 18-5 lists a reference of these key topics and the page numbers on which each is found.

Table 18-5   Key Topics for Chapter 18

Key Topic Element	Description	Page Number
Table 18-2	The Six-Step CompTIA A+ Troubleshooting Methodology	905
Table 18-3	Troubleshooting Tests and Requirements	909
Table 18-4	Computer and Peripheral Subsystems and Their Components	911
Figure 18-2	Typical cleaning supplies and replacement/testing components used by computer technicians	920

Complete the Tables and Lists from Memory

Print a copy of Appendix B, "Memory Tables," (found on the CD), or at least the section for this chapter, and complete the tables and lists from memory. Appendix C, "Memory Tables Answer Key," also on the CD, includes completed tables and lists to check your work.

Troubleshooting Scenario

You have been asked by your supervisor to help a user in the Human Resources area at work. HR is known for keeping a close eye on employee behavior. What should you do (or avoid doing) when working at the user's desk?

Refer to Appendix A for the answer.

Answers to the "Do I Know This Already?" Quizzes and Troubleshooting Scenarios

Chapter 2

1. **A, B, C, D.** The essential computer components listed here are a motherboard (no motherboard means no computer), a CPU or processor (the brain of the computer), memory, and video output (by means of a video card or a video port integrated into the motherboard).

2. **A, B, C.** You might find all of the listed devices on either the front or back of a computer. Some, such as a USB port, are on both front and back.

3. **A, B, C, D.** An overheated processor can shut down the computer or cause an unrecoverable error. A loose video card causes a blank display. Hard drive failure results in a non-bootable operating system. And if the additional memory is incompatible with the original memory or the motherboard, it could stop the computer from booting.

4. **A, B, C, D.** Even though some people still use Windows 98 on their computers, it is not considered a major player among the operating systems of today.

5. **A, C.** Use CHKDSK and Disk Defragmenter to help prevent your computer from possible hard drive failure. Keeping your hard drive defragmented is a very important part of maintaining a computer.

6. **A.** When installing a new PCI card, the first thing you should do is shut down the computer and unplug the system. You should always make sure there is no power going into the system to prevent electrostatic discharge (ESD).

7. **A.** You should look at the system manual before opening the case. Make sure that you are not voiding the service warranty or violating any other service terms by opening the computer case yourself.

8. **A, D.** Wearing an antistatic wrist strap is highly recommended when working on the inside of the computer. If you do not have one, you can touch the unpainted part of the computer before touching the components.

9. C. The floppy drive uses a 34-pin cable that has a twist at one end. This end of the cable connects to the floppy drive (A:) drive. The middle connector is used for B: drive (if it's present; it's not supported on some machines).

10. D. Turn the thumbscrews so they are completely retracted. If they are not completely retracted, the VGA cable might not make a proper connection with the video card.

Chapter 3

1. A, B, C, E. The motherboard is essential to computer operation in large part because of the two major buses it contains: the system bus and the I/O bus. Together, these buses carry all the information between the different parts of the computer.

2. A, C. Motherboards use expansion slots to provide support for additional I/O devices and high-speed video/graphics cards. The most common expansion slots on recent systems include PCI, AGP, and PCI-Express (also known as PCIe). Some systems also feature AMR or CNR slots for specific purposes.

3. A, B, C, D. SCSI (Small Computer Systems Interface) is a more flexible drive interface than PATA (ATA/IDE) because it can accommodate many devices that are not hard disk drives. Devices are high performance hard drives, image scanners, and removable media, as well as laser printers and CD-ROM/DVD-ROM drives.

4. A, B, C. The ATX family of motherboards has dominated desktop computer designs since the late 1990s. ATX stands for Advanced Technology Extended, and it replaced the AT and Baby-AT form factors developed in the mid 1980s for the IBM PC AT and its rivals. The ATX family includes Mini-ATX and FlexATX.

5. G. Motherboards in both the ATX and BTX families feature a variety of integrated I/O ports, including serial, parallel, USB, PS/2, audio, and Ethernet. These are found in as many as three locations. All motherboards feature a rear port cluster, and many motherboards also have additional ports on the top of the motherboard that are routed to header cables that are accessible from the front and rear of the system.

6. D. The Pentium III processor was the last Intel processor produced in both a slot-based and socket-based design. Slot-based versions use Slot 1, the same slot design used by the Pentium II and slot-based Celeron processors. Socketed versions use Socket 370, which is mechanically the same as the socket used by the first socketed Celeron processors. However, some early Socket 370 motherboards are not electrically compatible with the Pentium III.

7. A. AMD's first dual-core processor was the Athlon 64 X2, which uses a design that permits both processor cores to communicate directly with each other, rather than using the North Bridge (Memory Controller Hub) as in the Intel Pentium D.

8. B. Hyperthreading is a technology developed by Intel for processing two execution threads simultaneously within a single processor. Essentially, when HT Technology is enabled in the system BIOS and the processor is running a multithreaded application, the processor is emulating two physical processors.

9. C. If the processor has a removable heat sink, fan, or thermal duct that is attached to the motherboard, you must remove these components before you can remove the processor.

10. E. A system that overheats will stop operating, and with some older processors, serious damage can result. Most processors today are fitted with active heat sinks that contain a fan. If the fan stops working, an overheated processor follows.

11. A, C. Heat sink fans don't have to stop turning to fail; if they turn more slowly than they are specified to run, they can cause processor overheating. So keep them clean. If the heat sink is incorrect for the processor model or if the heat sink is not attached correctly, it can also cause overheating.

12. D. After installing a sound card, you must connect 1/8-inch mini-jack cables from speakers and the microphone to the sound card. Most sound cards use the same PC99 color coding standards for audio hardware that are used by onboard audio solutions.

Troubleshooting Scenario

You have recently purchased a 500GB storage device. You plug it in to your system and nothing happens. What could be the cause of the problem, and how would you correct this?

Answer: In this case you should verify whether the port you have plugged into has been disabled in the system BIOS configuration. If it will not connect, try enabling the port and retry the device.

Chapter 4

1. **B.** CMOS memory, also referred to as non-volatile memory, is used to store BIOS settings and should not be confused with system memory (RAM). CMOS stands for complimentary metal-oxide semiconductor.

2. **A.** If the CMOS battery fails it will lose all information, such as time/date, CPU information, and drive types.

3. **A.** Most motherboards use either a function key, the delete key, or a combination of keys to enter the BIOS setup program. Which key you use depends on the manufacture of the motherboard. F2 is a common key when entering the BIOS, as are F1, F10, and Delete. The F8 key is not used by BIOS programs; it is used by the Windows Advanced Options Boot menu when accessing options such as Safe Mode.

4. **A, B, C.** Many BIOS versions enable you to automatically configure your system with a choice of these options from the main menu.

5. **D.** Usually, you do not have access to the mouse when you are configuring the BIOS setup. You must use the keyboard.

6. **A, B, C, D, E.** The type and speed of the processor, amount of RAM, amount of cache memory, and the details of the BIOS program can all be viewed from within BIOS setup. Feature settings refers to the ability to configure various features of the operating system.

7. **A, D.** When accessing the BIOS advanced settings, some of the features available are quick boot, which will skip memory and drive test to enable faster startups, and also protection against boot sector viruses.

8. **C.** The Hardware Monitor screen (sometimes referred to as PC Health) is a common feature in most recent systems. It helps you make sure that your computer's temperature and voltage conditions are at safe levels for your computer, and it sometimes also includes the Chassis Intrusion feature.

9. **E.** Security features of various types are scattered around the typical system BIOS dialogs. All of the features listed can be used to secure your computer systems from hackers or unauthorized personnel.

10. **B, C.** When you are in the BIOS and are not planning on making any changes, be sure to click Discard Changes after clicking ESC to prevent accidental changes.

11. **B.** Each and every time you start your computer it goes through a test known as POST or power-on self test. If the BIOS finds any errors with the system, it notifies you by error messages known as beep codes.

12. A, C. Beep codes are used by most BIOS versions to indicate either a fatal error or a serious error. A fatal error is an error that is so serious that the computer cannot continue the boot process. A fatal error includes a problem with the CPU, the POST ROM, the system timer, or memory. Serious error beep codes report a problem with your video display card or circuit. Although systems can boot without video, you do not want to boot without video because you can't see what the system is doing.

13. A. Sometimes the BIOS does not support newer technologies. When making changes to the systems, such as adding a faster CPU or a larger SATA or PATA drive, you might need to update the BIOS.

14. C. When it is time for a BIOS update, go to the computer or motherboard manufacturer's website to see if a new update has been released. Flashing the BIOS is the act of erasing all of the BIOS's current contents and writing a new BIOS to the BIOS chip. You can do this by booting off of a special floppy disk, from CD-ROM, and from within Windows. This process is now much easier than it used to be, but to be safe you should still backup your BIOS settings before performing this task

Troubleshooting Scenario

You have just started up your computer. It gives off a series of loud beeps and will not boot. What would you need to do to determine what the beeps mean and how to fix the problem?

Answer: First you will need to determine who the manufacturer of the motherboard or the particular BIOS is. Then you should go to the website and download the manual for the motherboard or a copy of the beep codes for the BIOS. Reboot the computer and count the beeps and compare with the chart. It could be as easy as re-seating the RAM memory modules, or it could be a video problem.

Chapter 5

1. A, C. To keep your power supply up and running and to help prevent damage from power surges, you should use a surge protector. The UPS will supply power for a short period of time to the computer system in case of total power outage.

2. C. Power supplies are rated in watts, and the more watts a power supply provides, the more devices it can safely power.

3. D. Most newer computers have 500 watt or larger power supplies in them because of the greater number of drives and expansion cards that are available now.

4. A, C. Standard North American power is 115 volts and European power is 230 volts. Some power supplies have a slider on the back to switch between the two voltages.

5. D. All of the listed reasons can cause damage to the power supply as well as overheating your computer.

6. A. Most of the newer power supplies in use today have 24 pins. Older motherboards have a 20-pin connection.

7. D. All of the listed answers are correct. You must disconnect from the wall first, then once inside the computer unhook the connection to the motherboard, drives, and other devices.

8. A, B. The capacitors inside the power supply retain potentially fatal voltage levels. To prevent shock you should not disassemble power supplies or stick in a metal object such as a screwdriver.

9. B. A UPS (uninterruptible power supply) will keep a standard desktop up and running in case of a complete power outage.

10. D. UPSs are designed to supply power to a computer long enough for you to complete a formal shutdown.

11. A, C, D. When an SPS is used there is a momentary gap, usually about 1ms or less, between when the power goes off and when the SPS starts supplying power. SPSs are also less expensive and are not used at all times.

12. A, B, C, D. When turning on a system that shows no signs of life you must consider all of these as potential problems.

13. A, C. All processors require a heat sink. A heat sink is a finned metal device that radiates heat away from the processor. An active heat sink (a heat sink with a fan) is required for adequate processor cooling on current systems. Some older systems used a specially designed duct to direct airflow over a processor with a passive heat sink (a heat sink without a fan). Most motherboards' northbridges use passive heat sinks.

14. A. Thermal compound (also known as thermal transfer material, thermal grease, or phase change material) provides for the best possible thermal transfer between a component (for example a CPU) and its heat sink. This prevents CPU damage. The fan and adapter cards should not have thermal compound applied to them. As a side note, most northbridges do not have fans.

Troubleshooting Scenario

You are working on a computer that is overheating. What steps should you take to make sure the power supply is not being overloaded?

Answer: First you should get out a calculator and add up the wattage ratings for everything that is connected to your power supply. If the wattage exceeds 70% you should upgrade your power supply to a larger one. Refer to Table 5-2, "Calculating Power Supply Requirements," for more information.

Chapter 6

1. C. Random access memory (RAM) loses its contents when the computer shuts down. Hard disk drives, USB flash drives, and read-only memory (ROM) are designed to retain their contents even if they are not receiving power.

2. B. SRAM or Static RAM is bulkier and more expensive than DRAM because it does not require electricity as often as DRAM.

3. D. Rambus memory that uses 32-bit RIMMs must use pairs, and unused sockets must be occupied by a continuity module.

4. B. SDRAM was the first memory type that was in sync with the motherboard's memory bus.

5. A, C. These two methods have an additional memory chip added for parity.

6. A. Unbuffered memory is used in most desktop computers sold in the market. This kind of memory is also used in some servers and workstations.

7. A. ECC memory enables the system to correct single-bit errors and notify you of larger errors.

8. A, B, C. To correctly insert the memory modules, you should follow all the steps listed. You might also have to use a fair amount of pressure to securely lock these modules in place.

9. B. Overclocking is the process in which you can set the speeds of the CPU or memory to run at a faster rate than normal. It can lead to overheating and system crashes.

10. A, D. The two types of metal that are used as contacts on SIMMs are gold and tin. Placing gold connectors in a tin socket and vice versa are most likely to see corrosion and eventual system lockups.

11. D. CheckIT, AMIDiag, and RAMExam can all be used to test memory.

12. D. All of these can be done to help prevent any memory issues, such as overheating.

13. B. DDR3 and DDR2 both use 240-pin connectors is the only correct answer. While DDR3 and DDR2 both use 240-pin connectors, the connectors use different pinouts and are keyed differently to avoid installing DDR3 in a DDR2 slot or vice-versa. DDR3 uses lower voltage than DDR2. DDR3 memory uses 1.5V DC power, compared to 1.8V DC for DDR2.

Troubleshooting Scenario

You are asked to help a user overclock his system memory. What should you tell him?

Answer: Tell him no. Overclocking can cause the components to overheat and the system to crash. You should also tell him that overclocking could damage the hardware and could also void the warranty.

Chapter 7

1. **A, B.** High-performance hard drives, image scanners, removable-media drives—such as most tape backups and Iomega REV—and other devices use SCSI interfaces.

2. **A, C.** When using the daisy-chain method, each device must have a unique ID number and needs to be terminated to prevent device slowdowns.

3. **B.** A PC's serial ports are usually called COM ports. Serial ports can also be used to connect docking stations and digital cameras.

4. **B.** A parallel port can be used to hook up all the items listed in the question. Most motherboards still come with this port even though USB is much faster and more popular.

5. **C.** FireWire is Apple Inc.'s brand name for the IEEE 1394 standard. IEEE 1394 is a family of high-speed, bidirectional, serial transmission ports that can connect PCs to each other, digital devices to PCs, or digital devices to each other.

6. **D.** In some ATX/BTX port clusters, the bottom PS/2 port is used for key-boards, and the top PS/2 port is used for mice and pointing devices. On sys-tems and devices that use the standard PC99 color coding for ports, PS/2 keyboard ports (and cable ends) are purple, and PS/2 mouse ports (and cable ends) are green.

7. **B.** The 1/8-inch audio mini-jack is used by sound cards and motherboard-integrated sound for speakers, microphone, and line-in jacks. Also, to avoid confusion, most recent systems have color-coded jacks.

8. **A, D.** USB 1.1 and USB 2.0 are the two common standards for USB ports. USB 2.0 is the newer and faster of the two.

9. **A, B, C.** If you need more ports for USB devices, your options are mother-board connectors, USB hubs, and add-on cards.

10. **D.** The keyboard remains the primary method used to send commands to the computer and enter data. There are many shortcuts that can take the place of actions that would be otherwise accomplished with the mouse, for example Ctrl+X is cut, Ctrl+C is copy, and so on. You can even use it to maneuver around the Windows Desktop if your mouse or other pointing device stops working.

11. **A.** Touch screen monitors enable the user to transfer data into the computer by pressing on-screen icons. Touch screen monitors are very popular in public-access and point-of-sale installations.

12. D. All listed devices are considered multimedia devices. The webcam, sound card, and microphone give you the ability to make Internet phone calls, for example.

13. C, D. The mini-jacks for the speaker and microphone are identical in shape and are not always color coded. If you plug the speaker in to the wrong jack you will hear nothing from the sound card.

14. C. The Universal Serial Bus (USB) connector is by far the most common keyboard and mouse connector in today's computers. Unlike older DIN or Mini-DIN jacks you do not have to turn off the PC's power to connect the keyboard. To install a USB keyboard you just plug it in to an empty USB port. Most of the newer computers only have USB ports. PS/2 ports have become very rare on new computers.

15. A, B, C. These are mostly simple causes that can occur. You will also want to make sure that you never plug a PS/2 keyboard in while the power is on. It could destroy the motherboard.

16. C. When more than one USB device is not recognized by Windows, one possible reason is that the USB ports have not been enabled in the BIOS program. Disabling the device in Windows only makes Windows ignore the device regardless of what you do in the BIOS, thus making the problem worse. Reinstalling the driver could be a possible solution if only one USB device is malfunctioning or is not recognized properly by Windows. Flashing the BIOS isn't necessary in a scenario like this and is definitely not the first thing to check.

17. A, B, C, D. All of the listed solutions are correct. You open the access cover and remove the ball. Then you shake it out to remove any dust. You can also wipe out the rollers and then put the ball back in and close the mouse.

Troubleshooting Scenario

You have been asked about a printing issue on a specific computer. You have looked in the Windows Control Panel Printers and Faxes folder and determined that the printer is installed correctly. What procedure would you use to try to fix the problem?

Answer: After determining that the printer is installed correctly, check the cable. If the cable is damaged it will either not print or print out garbage. Try replacing the cable with a cable that you know to be working and try again.

Chapter 8

1. A, B, D. Currently, video cards use the following bus types: PCI, AGP, and the newer PCI Express.

2. A, C, D. Cooling can be provided through passive heat sinks or through cooling fans and fan shrouds. Passive heat sinks on older video cards typically cover only the graphics processing unit (GPU), but newer ones provide cooling for both the GPU and memory. Video cards with passive heat sinks are good choices for home theater PCs, such as those running Windows XP Media Center Edition, because these PCs need to run as quietly as possible. The material used to transfer heat between heat sinks and cooling fans is known as thermal paste or phase-change material, not thermal glue.

3. A, B, D. With the addition of the plug and play BIOS, most of the time you will be able to skip the BIOS configuration. But some cards might not be recognized and you must configure the BIOS manually.

4. B. Without the device driver installed, you will not be able to use all the features that come with it. Most of the time you get an install disk when you purchase a new card.

5. A, B, C. The three main types of display devices in use today are LCD monitors (the most common), CRT monitors, and data projectors.

6. A, B, C. VGA, DVI, and HDMI are the three main types of connectors you will be dealing with. You can also use S-Video for a connection.

7. C. The DVI port is the current standard for digital LCD monitors. The DVI port comes in two forms: DVI-D supports only digital signals and is found on digital LCD displays. DVI-I provides both digital and analog output and supports the use of a VGA/DVI-I adapter for use with analog displays.

8. B. Right-clicking on the desktop and selecting Properties opens the Display Properties window. Select the Settings tab to modify the display resolution.

9. A. The three steps listed are all ways to install a monitor; however if you have a monitor that your video card does not support, you must either get another cable or a new video card that supports the cable you have.

10. C. Most of the time if you see the colors flickering on the monitor, you can turn off the monitor and the system, tighten the cable, and restart the computer.

11. D. When installing a new monitor it might not accept the current settings, so using the buttons on the front of the monitor, you can adjust your picture size.

12. A, B, C, D, E, F. It is recommended that you use all of the solutions listed to help prevent problems with your monitor as well as with your video card.

Troubleshooting Scenario

Your client is experiencing problems with the display on his monitor. He informs you that the screen is blurry and will not provide a display over 800 by 600. What would you tell the client to try?

Answer: First you would want your client to find out what kind of video card he is using. You should then tell your client to check whether he has the correct driver installed by going into the Windows Device Manager.

Chapter 9

1. **B.** To assist in saving space, laptops without a numeric keypad use the Fn key to perform tasks.

2. **D.** Generally, portable systems have only one or two connectors for additional memory. Older portable systems might use proprietary memory modules, whereas recent systems use SODIMMs (a reduced-size version of a DIMM module).

3. **B.** Smaller form factors for laptop and portable systems use 2.5-inch or 1.8-inch hard disks, instead of the 3.5-inch hard disks found in desktop computers; also, laptop and portable systems use slim line optical drives, rather than half-height drives that are used in desktop computers.

4. **A.** A docking station expands the capability of a portable computer by adding features such as expansion slots and I/O ports. Examples of expansion slots include PCMCIA and Express Card. Examples of I/O ports include serial, parallel, VGA, component video, SPDIF digital audio, and USB 2.0.

5. **D.** Laptop and portable computers don't use the PCI, AGP, or PCI Express expansion slots designed for desktop computers, but feature expansion slots especially designed for portable use. Examples of PCMCIA cards are wireless cards or NIC cards.

6. **A, B, C.** The stylus, keyboard, and mouse are all examples of input devices. They can be used to enter data on to a computer.

7. **C.** Processor throttling is a feature of recent processors from both Intel and AMD. Some processors also reduce the front side bus speed during time periods when processor loads are light.

8. **A, B, C, D.** All of the listed technologies are installed on most of the newer laptops available in today's market.

9. **B.** The built-in touch pad is the most common mouse equivalent used in laptops. Some laptops might also use a pointing stick (for example, Lenovo ThinkPads) or other technologies instead of or in addition to the touch pad.

10. **D.** To configure user alerts and automatic actions to take when the system reaches low or critical battery power levels, use the Alarms tab of the Power Options Properties window in Windows XP. The Advanced tab configures actions the computer will perform when the lid is closed or the power or sleep buttons are pressed. The Power Schemes tab controls how long the system is idle before the monitor and hard disks are turned off or the system goes into standby or hibernation modes. The Suspend tab does not exist.

11. C. The Windows Wireless Zero Configuration can automatically locate wireless networks and start a connection. Ethernet is a type of network and can be wired or wireless (though most people will refer to Ethernet as a wired network). The Bluetooth devices applet in the Control Panel enables the user to configure Bluetooth devices such as a Bluetooth Anycom networking device, or a Bluetooth printer. WPA2 is a type of encryption used in wireless networks.

12. A, D. Look for an ejector button next to the PC Card slot. On some systems, the button is folded into the unit for storage. Unfold the button and remove any connected cables or dongles from the card.

13. A. When troubleshooting power problems, use a multimeter to check to see if the outlet is working properly. Make sure the multimeter is set for DC power.

14. D. An overheated system might quit, display STOP errors (also known as Blue Screen of Death, or BSOD), or throttle down the processor to very low clock speeds. Overheating can be caused by a blocked cooling fan outlet, cooling fan failure, or damage to the heat sink.

Troubleshooting Scenario

You have been asked to change out the hard drive in a laptop computer. The laptop is a small compact model. How would you change the hard drive without removing the keyboard?

Answer: Most laptops in use today have an easier access method in place for hard drives:

Step 1. Turn off the laptop.

Step 2. Unplug the AC power.

Step 3. Remove the battery.

Step 4. Remove the four screws that hold the drive cover in place on the bottom of the laptop. You will then have easy access to remove the hard drive. Remove the drive.

Step 5. Install the replacement drive and screw in the drive cover.

Step 6. Restore the original system or install a new operating system to the new hard drive. If whole disk encryption was used on the original drive, be sure to use it on the new drive.

Chapter 10

1. **A.** A smart card contains user information and when used with a pin number to secure workstations gives you better security.

2. **B.** Biometrics is a technology that can use fingerprints, voice, and retina scans as an authentication method.

3. **D.** All of the listed products can help in the prevention of viruses, malware, and phishing scams. These need to be turned on and kept up to date to be effective.

4. **C.** A software firewall is a program that examines data packets on a network to determine whether to forward them to their destination or block them. Firewalls can be used to protect against inbound threats only (one-way firewall) or against both unauthorized inbound and outbound traffic.

5. **A, B, D.** The three standards are WEP, WPA, and WPA2. All are used to encrypt data on wireless networks.

6. **D.** All wireless routers come with default SSID names, and passwords. You should change these, and hide the SSID name, to prevent a hacker from looking up the information about what type of WAP you are using.

7. **B.** Windows 7, Vista, XP, and 2000 have a built-in encryption protocol called the Encrypting File System. Once applied, it can be accessed only by the user who created it and administrator or the EFS key holders.

8. **C.** Windows 7 Enterprise includes the option to use BitLocker Drive Encryption, which can encrypt an entire hard disk drive without a user's knowledge.

9. **A.** Social engineering is a simple and very easy way to get information from someone inside a company. By simply calling on the phone and pretending to be someone else, they can get information that should not be given out. Training users is the best way to prevent this kind of attacks.

10. **B.** User Account Control (UAC) is a security component of Windows 7 that keeps every user (beside the actual Administrator account) in standard user mode instead of as an administrator with full administrative rights even if they are a member of the administrators group.

11. **D.** If the BIOS setup program is protected by a password and the password is lost, you can clear the password on most desktop systems by using the BIOS clear jumper on the motherboard or by removing the battery for several seconds.

12. C. After configuring a WAP or wireless router to provide WEP, WPA, or (preferably) WPA2 encryption, you must configure wireless clients with the same encryption information. You can set up clients manually or automatically. Note that each wireless client connecting to a WAP or wireless router must use the same encryption standard and passphrase and specify the SSID used by the WAP or wireless router.

Troubleshooting Scenario

You are called to a customer's computer. She is complaining of pop-up messages redirecting her to undesired websites. You must fix this problem as soon as possible. What would you need to do to get the computer back up and running?

Answer: First you would determine what operating system the client is using. If she is using Windows 7, Vista, or XP SP2, you can run Windows Defender to clean the obvious malware (Windows Defender is not included in Windows XP by default but can be downloaded from Microsoft's website). You can also use a third-party software program to remove the spyware from the computer. After the problem is resolved, be sure to install an anti-malware product to the computer. This will help to prevent the problem from happening again.

Chapter 11

1.   A, D. The essential difference between a laser and an LED printer is in the imaging device. The laser printer uses a laser to transfer the image to the drum, whereas an LED printer uses an LED array to perform the same task. Otherwise, these technologies are practically identical.

2.   B. If you try to print a page to a laser printer that requires more memory than the laser printer contains, the laser printer tries to print the page but stops after the printer's memory is full. The printer displays an error message or blinks error status lights, at which point you must manually eject the page. Only a portion of the page is printed.

3.   C. Generally, printer drivers provided by the printer vendor offer more configuration options and utilities for cleaning and maintenance than the drivers provided by Microsoft.

4.   A. To determine the firmware revision installed in a printer, use its self-test function to make a test printout. Firmware can be implemented in a flash-upgradeable chip built into the printer, or in a special memory module sometimes called a "personality" module.

5.   A, B, C. A laser printer (and its close relative, an LED printer) is an example of a page printer. A page printer does not start printing until the entire page is received. At that point, the page is transferred to the print mechanism, which pulls the paper through the printer as the page is transferred from the printer to the paper.

6.   B, C. Interface types used by printers and scanners include USB and parallel. USB 2.0 is used by most inkjet, dye-sublimation, thermal, and laser printers, either when connected directly to a PC or connected to a network via a print server. The parallel interface works for older inkjet and laser printers.

7.   B. To add support for Ethernet local area networking to a printer that does not have built-in networking capability, connect it to an Ethernet print server. Print servers are available in versions that support USB or parallel printers and enable the printer to be accessed via the print server's IP address.

8.   C. The easiest way to assure compatibility for a device is to visit the vendor's website and look for the drivers for that device. Get the driver you need for your device and your operating system, and you're ready to continue.

9.   A. You can find the print spool settings in computer management. You select Services and Applications, Services and then scroll down to the print spooler, right-click it, and go to Properties.

10. C. Most recent printers with upgradeable memory use the DIMM memory module form factor, but printers do not use the same types of DIMMs as desktop or laptop computers.

11. B, C, D. By printing or scanning a test page you might be able to discern what is causing the problem with the device. Being able to identify symptoms, such as slow printing, can help you speed up the time that it takes to troubleshoot. If your device has an LCD display, it probably came with error codes that can save you some time.

12. B. The first step in printing is that an application program in the computer sends a print request to the Windows operating system, which relays the command to the printer. It will then send it to the queue and proceed with the other steps.

13. D. To add support for the Bluetooth short-range wireless network to a printer with a USB 2.0 port without built-in Bluetooth capabilities, connect a Bluetooth printer adapter. Note that the best results are usually obtained when the adapter is made especially for your printer.

14. A, D. You should install the drivers provided by the vendor, either from the CD that is packaged with the device or by downloading the latest version from the manufacturer's website.

Troubleshooting Scenario

You have just purchased a new printer. You have set up the printer where it needs to be. Once you have completed the setup and try to print a test page, you notice that the page is unreadable. What process should you complete to correct the problem?

Answer: Most of the time, when a test page is unreadable there is a problem with the printer driver. When you buy a printer you get an installation disc with it. Sometimes the drivers on the disc are not the correct ones for your operating system, or they might not be the latest versions. To correct this problem, visit the manufacturer's website to download and install the most recent driver for your printer. This should correct this problem.

Chapter 12

1. B. Floppy disks are used primarily for backups of small amounts of data, for bootable diagnostic disks, and for the creation of bootable emergency disks with some versions of Windows.

2. C. Hard disk drives are the most important storage device used by a personal computer. Hard disk drives store the operating system (Windows, Linux, or others) and load it into the computer's memory (RAM) at startup. Hard disk drives also store applications, system configuration files used by applications and the operating system, and data files created by the user.

3. C. Hard disk drives use one or more double-sided platters formed from rigid materials such as aluminum or glass. These platters are coated with a durable magnetic surface that is divided into sectors. Each sector contains 512 bytes of storage along with information about where the sector is located on the disk medium.

4. A, C. SATA and PATA are the two correct answers, (ATA/IDE) is the 40-pin interface used by most CD and DVD drives and a few early Blu-ray drives. SATA is the seven-pin high-speed serial interface used by late-model high-performance DVD drives and most Blu-ray drives. PATA and SATA are also used by hard disks and some types of removable-media drives. IrDA is an infrared (IR) interface used for line-of-sight printing and data transport between some computers (mostly older laptops) and printers. USB (Universal Serial Bus) is used for almost all external devices, from printers and multi-function devices to hard disks, optical drives, and flash memory devices. Although some USB adapter cards feature a single internal port, that port is intended for use by drive-bay mounted USB hubs or card readers.

5. B. If you want to play music CDs through your sound card's speakers, you might need to connect a CD audio patch cable. One end connects to the CD-ROM drive and the other end connects to the CD audio port on the sound card or motherboard. Older drives support a four-wire analog cable, whereas newer drives support both the four-wire analog and newer two-wire digital cable. If the power cable wasn't connected, the drive wouldn't have opened when you inserted the disc. CD-ROM drives normally don't need drivers installed; they are installed automatically by Windows. However you might need a soundcard driver. If the CD was faulty, Windows Media Player would not have played the song, and you wouldn't have seen the song title or the elapsed time of the song.

6. A, B, D. Zip drives have capacities of 100MB, 250MB, and 750MB due to the size limitations that go along with the rigid cartridges.

7. D. Tape drives use various types of magnetic tape. Some tape drive mechanisms can be incorporated into autoloaders or tape libraries for large network backup and data retrieval. Tape drives are mostly used on servers but are still considered removable storage.

8. B. To install a flash card reader on Windows 2000, XP, or Vista, connect it to an available USB port. The system will automatically detect the reader, assign drive letters as required, and display a notification at the end of the installation process.

9. A. USB flash memory drives have largely replaced floppy drives for transfers of data between systems or for running utility programs. USB flash memory drives, like flash memory cards, use flash memory, a type of memory that retains information without a continuous flow of electricity.

10. C, D. USB flash memory drives are preformatted with the FAT16 or FAT32 file system and are ready to use. Simply plug one into a USB port, and it is immediately assigned a drive letter. You can copy, modify, and delete information on a USB flash memory drive, just as with a hard disk or floppy drive.

11. A, B, C. Most external hard disks connect via the USB or IEEE-1394 ports, but some can connect to external SATA ports, or to the network via RJ45 External USB or IEEE-1394–based hard disks, are preformatted (typically with the FAT32 file system), and are ready to work. Plug in the drive, and it appears in My Computer or Windows Explorer. PCIe is an internal expansion bus used by video cards and other secondary adapter cards.

12. A. Floppy drive data cables that are reversed (pin 1 to pin 33) at either the floppy drive interface on the motherboard/floppy controller card or at the drive itself will cause the drive light to come on and stay on. To correct this, turn off the system, remove and reattach the data cable correctly, and restart the system.

Troubleshooting Scenario

You are working on a computer. You plug up your external hard drive and for some reason it does not show up in the Explorer window. You then happen to notice that this computer is actually running a server-based operating system. What would be the steps you would need to take to fix this problem?

Answer: Once you have discovered that the computer is running a server operating system, you should take these simple but necessary steps to allow the operating system to see the external drive. First you will need to open the computer management console. Then you will need to select disk management under the storage list, and then you will right-click on the unrecognized drive and select a drive letter. The operating system will then recognize the drive and you will be able to do the work you need to complete your task at hand.

Chapter 13

1. **B.** Windows Aero is Microsoft's new visual experience. It features translucent windows, window animations, three-dimensional viewing of windows, and a modified taskbar. You can make modifications to the look of Aero by right-clicking the desktop and selecting Personalize. Then select Windows Color and Appearance. There you can modify features such as the transparency of windows. Note: Aero is not available in Windows Vista Home Basic.

2. **C.** To enable applications written for older versions of Windows to run properly on Windows Vista/XP, you can use the Program Compatibility wizard that is built into Windows, or the Compatibility tab located on the executable file's properties sheet. XP Mode uses Windows Virtual PC to run older applications under a virtualized copy of Windows XP rather than running them in Windows 7.

3. **B.** The Windows Registry acts as a central database for Windows, applications, and user settings. When you install a program, update Windows, or even change the color of the desktop, a part of the Windows Registry changes.

4. **D.** If you run short of money, you can borrow some from the bank (assuming your credit's in decent shape). However, there's a penalty: interest. Similarly, if your system runs short of memory, it can borrow hard disk space and use it as virtual memory. The penalty for this type of borrowing is performance: Virtual memory is much slower than real RAM memory. However, you can adjust how your system uses virtual memory to achieve better performance.

5. **A.** If you are using a Windows-based operating system, you have used this at one time or the other. You can view all files on the system as well as view network drives.

6. **C.** Windows XP uses My Network Places to manage dial-up and local area network connections. When you open My Network Places, you see a list of network connections and shared folders on the network, including those located on the local computer and on remote computers.

7. **A, B, C, D.** The boot files have changed with the newer operating system. Bootmgr has taken the place of NTLDR and determines which operating system to boot. Boot Configuration Data store (BCD) tells Bootmgr the operating systems that can boot and their method of booting. Hardware Abstraction Layer (Hal.dll) allows applications to access devices without the application having to understand a specific protocol used by any one device. Ntoskrnl.exe is the kernel image for 7 (and Vista, XP, 2000), and is responsible for services such as process and memory management and hardware virtualization among other things.

8. B. The Boot.ini file is a specially formatted text file that configures the startup process for Windows XP. It resides in the default boot drive, even if Windows is installed on another drive.

9. A, C. While you install the Windows operating system to the new drive, you must go through the partitioning and formatting steps. Hardly any drives are ready to accept an operating system right out of the box.

10. B, D. You can start a command-prompt session in Windows 7 by clicking on the **Command Prompt** option in the Start menu; it's located in the Accessories menu. However, it's faster to use the Search box.

11. C. /E is needed to copy the files, directories, subdirectories, *including* empty subdirectories. /S will copy files, directories, and subdirectories, but *not* empty subdirectories. If you add /T on to the end, you will get just the empty directories copied. \T is not a valid switch.

12. C. For you to view the installed devices you need to instruct the user to go in to Device Manager and see if there are any errors on the display adapters.

13. A. You can use the performance monitor by going to the Run command (Windows XP, 2000) or Search box (Windows Vista, 7) and typing **perfmon**. This utility can help you diagnose memory bottlenecks.

14. D. Windows 7 requires at least a 1 GHz processor, although faster processors will improve performance.

15. C. 1024MB (1GB) of RAM is the minimum needed for the 32-bit version of Windows 7. However, 2048MB (2GB) is the minimum needed for the 64-bit version of Windows 7.

16. D. To manage network connections while in the Network window, click the **Network and Sharing Center** button. Once that window opens, click the link for **Manage Network Connections**.

Troubleshooting Scenario

You have a client who is having problems with network connectivity. She is complaining that things work fine for a while, and then there is no connectivity at all. What steps could you take to verify that there is a problem?

Answer: First you can ping the server that the client is connected to. If the ping is successful, you can use the ping with the -t switch and see if packets are being lost. If you see a lot of time outs, the NIC may be failing or a wire in the network cable may have been cut or broken.

Chapter 14

1. **C.** When using the newer hardware, there would not be a problem. However with older hardware, before you even try to install the operating system, you should verify the computers are capable of running the new OS by checking the Windows 7 Logo'd Products List.

2. **A, B, C, D.** All the listed methods are valid ways to install an operating system. The most common ways are to use the distribution CD or DVD, or the recovery disc that comes with your system. You can also install from a network share, or by imaging the drive.

3. **A, B, D.** When creating an unattended installation disk for Windows XP or Windows 2000 you must have these files. The unattend.txt provides all answers if you want to use a share or command line. Systprep.inf provides answers for a mini-setup and Winnt.sif is used to boot from a floppy disk.

4. **A, B, D.** FAT16, FAT32, and NTFS are the three file systems that are supported. You can use FAT32 and NTFS. The operating system can support FAT16, but it is only supported so Windows can access devices such as memory sticks or older hard drives. exFAT support is not included in Windows XP, but an update from Microsoft can be installed to provide exFAT support. exFAT support is standard in Windows Vista SP1 and later and in Windows 7.

5. **B.** In Windows Vista, device drivers are added within the same screen where partitioning was done by clicking Load Driver. These could be drivers for SATA or SCSI controllers, or other special hard disk controllers. These drivers can come from floppy disk, CD, DVD, or USB flash drive.

6. **B.** For the log files for the XP install you will need to go to the system root directory and look for `setuperr.log` along with `setuplog.txt`. There are several more you can look at as well.

7. **C.** Some older systems might require processor, memory, or hard disk upgrades to be qualified to run Windows 7. You should make sure your computer meets or exceeds these standards before you start the upgrade process.

8. **A.** Windows 7 Upgrade Advisor checks your existing hardware and software to determine if it is compatible with 32-bit and 64-bit versions of Windows 7.

9. A, B, C, D. Before you replace Windows XP with Windows 7, you should also download any new device drivers or new application updates that you need. Create a folder for your updates on your system and uncompress them if necessary so they can be used during the upgrade process. And, of course, back up any important files, email, and settings: for example, Internet Explorer favorites, your email program's blocked sender list, or download and run Windows Easy Transfer to back up the bulk of the files and settings on your computer.

10. B. During the upgrade process, you can convert the file system to NTFS. Do this to save space on your hard disk (NTFS is more efficient than FAT32) and if you want features such as encryption, file/folder compression, and better security.

11. C. You need at least 15GB free for Windows 7 (32-bit) or at least 20GB free for Windows 7 (64-bit); more is better.

12. B, C, D, E. If you encounter any of these problems you will be unable to do the upgrade. You should check this before you try the upgrade.

Troubleshooting Scenario

You are a technician for a company that is in the process of upgrading the operating systems from Windows XP to Windows 7. You have a mixture of newer and older computers. To be more effective during this process you need to make sure that the Windows 7 operating system will install without any problems. What should you do to minimize the time to determine if the upgrade will work or not?

Answer: You should first get a list of all the older computers. Start with them by running the Windows 7 Upgrade Advisor. This should give you a better idea of which of the newer computers will accept the upgrade. This will help save you time and make this process run much smoother.

Chapter 15

1. A. If you are unable to start Windows 7/Vista/XP but don't see an error message, the problem could be caused by a driver or startup program, video driver problems, or problems with the system kernel. When pressing F8, Windows 7, Vista, and XP display the Advanced Boot Options menu, which includes various options, such as Safe Mode, VGA Mode, and Last Known Good Configuration, which will help you correct startup problems.

2. D. WinRE is a set of tools included in Windows 7, Windows Vista, and Windows Server 2008. It takes the place of the Recovery Console used in Windows XP/2000. Also known as System Recovery Options, WinRE's purpose is to recover Windows from errors that prevent it from booting.

3. B. The Windows Recovery Console is a special command-line interface that is designed for copying files and performing disk repairs. It is used by Windows XP and 2000. In Windows 2000, you can use the Recovery Console as an alternative to the Emergency Repair process, such as if you need to restore only one system file. Windows XP lacks the Emergency Repair provision, so understanding how to use the Recovery Console is even more important.

4. A. The Automated System Recovery (ASR) option in NTBackup enables you to restore the system state (user accounts, hard disk configuration, network configuration, video settings, hardware configuration, software settings, operating system boot files). The Emergency Repair Disk (ERD) is used in Windows 2000, and Complete PC Backup is used in Windows Vista. Windows XP Professional does not include a true disaster-recovery backup program like Complete PC Backup.

5. B. Windows 2000 has a feature called Emergency Repair that can fix some startup problems. The Windows 2000 Emergency Repair Disk (ERD) is created with the Windows 2000 NTBackup program.

6. D. All the listed options are valid for recovering an operating system if the system will not boot. WinRE is the Windows 7 and Vista Recovery Environment, which has several options to repair boot failure. The Last Known Good Configuration is one of the Advanced Boot Options that can be accessed by pressing F8 in any version of Windows. You can install the recovery console from the Windows XP CD-ROM. After it's installed, it becomes part of the boot selection in the boot.ini file.

7. A, C, D. To keep a computer updated you should install the latest service pack, which can be downloaded from the Internet or installed from CD; install any hotfixes and security updates through Windows Update; and install anti-virus updates, which is usually accomplished by setting the AV updates to download and install automatically.

8. C. In this case you will need to go to the windows update site and download the latest service pack and any additional patches and hotfixes that are listed on the update webpage.

9. A. To modify settings regarding how updates are downloaded and installed in Windows XP go to Control Panel\Automatic Updates. From here a user can decide whether to download and install updates automatically and can schedule the time of download. In Windows 7 and Windows Vista this can be accomplished by accessing Control Panel\Windows Update\Change Settings.

10. B. You should always have some sort of backup schedule for your user documents to prevent permanent loss of their data. You can use the NTBACKUP tool to setup these backups.

11. C. If you create an image backup of the system, you can easily restore the computer back to its original state in about 20 minutes or so. This has become a great tool for technicians to use if a hard drive fails or you are unable to bring the system back up online.

12. C, D. Modern image backup programs such as recent versions of Norton Ghost and Acronis True Image make it possible to restore an entire computer to an earlier state. They can also be used to create incremental backups, enabling the image backup program to work as both an image and file/folder backup.

Troubleshooting Scenario

You are a technician for your company. You have been having problems with a user's computer hard drive. The user is losing her data. You need to come up with a solution that will keep the user's documents from being deleted. You do not have a network server to store the user's data. What should you do to prevent this from happening?

Answer: First you might want to run some sort of diagnostic program on the user's hard drive. If you find the drive is good, you will then want to set up some type of backup strategy using the backup utility provided with the version of Windows in use (or a third-party backup utility). Because you don't have a network server to store the user documents, you should back the data up to a USB hard disk or flash drive. This will help keep the user's data safe from deletion and make her very happy.

Chapter 16

1. **A, C.** The Windows operating system uses two types of networks. One is a client/server network, meaning that client computers will need to contact a domain controller to work. A peer-to-peer network is used in smaller networks where the expense is a factor, no centralized administration is necessary, or if the organization doesn't have the resources to support a client/server network.

2. **A, B, C, D.** Although the older dial-up modems are going by the wayside, they are still used. The newer technologies such as an ISDN, cable, and DSL more commonly connect today's networks to the Internet.

3. **A, C.** Although most current networks use TCP/IPv4, you can also find the TCP/IPv6 and in some situations you might even find the older NetBEUI protocol.

4. **A, B, C.** The TCP/IP protocol suite includes many protocols including the Hypertext Transfer Protocol (HTTP), HTTP Secure (HTTPS), Secure Sockets Layer (SSL), and its successor Transport Layer Security (TLS). Ethernet is a network architecture commonly used, upon which TCP/IP runs.

5. **E.** Bus, star, ring, and mesh topologies are used in the field today. You can use these techniques to supply network connectivity to your client computers.

6. **C.** The oldest network in common use today is Ethernet, also known as IEEE-802.3. IEEE 1394 refers to the PC version of FireWire cable. 802.11b and 802.11g are wireless networking technologies.

7. **C.** UTP cable comes in various grades, of which Category 5e is the most common of the standard cabling grades. Category 5e cabling is suitable for use with both standard 10BaseT and Fast Ethernet networking, and can also be used for Gigabit Ethernet networks if it passes compliance testing. STP is a form of cabling also available in Cat5e, but is used only when shielding from EMI/RFI is necessary, as it is more expensive, bulkier, and harder to work with than UTP.

8. **A, B.** Although many recent computers include a 10/100 or 10/100/1000 Ethernet port or a wireless Ethernet adapter, you might need to install a network interface card (NIC) into a computer you want to add to a network. For desktops, the card would be installed into a PCIe x1 or a PCI slot; for laptops, the card would be installed into an ExpressCard or CardBus slot. A USB network adapter could be used by both types of computers.

9. B. If the hardware in use on an Ethernet, Fast Ethernet, or Gigabit Ethernet network permits, you can configure the network to run in full-duplex mode. Full-duplex mode enables the adapter to send and receive data at the same time, which doubles network speed over the default half-duplex mode.

10. C. A switch resembles a hub but creates a dedicated full-speed connection between the two computers that are communicating with each other. By doing this it will upgrade the speed of the existing network.

11. A, B, C. Hubs or switches are the only connectivity equipment needed for a workgroup LAN. However, if the network needs to span longer distances than those supported by the network cabling in use or needs to connect to another network, additional connectivity equipment is needed. A repeater is used to carry the signals even farther than normal. You can also use a bridge to connect two networks together. A router can be used to connect two or more networks.

12. B. Ping is a command-line utility used to check Internet connectivity. Ping is already included in Windows.

13. C. On a Windows operating system, to be able to share printers and resources with other users, you must make sure that the file and print services are installed and enabled in the Properties window of a network connection.

14. A. WINS is the Windows Internet Naming Service. WINS is already installed as part of Windows' TCP/IP support.

15. A, C. The Universal Naming Convention (UNC) is designed to enable users to access network resources, such as folders or printers, without mapping drive letters to network drives or specifying the type of device that stores the file or hosts the printer. If you are using a Windows operating system, you can also use the map network drive tool and provide the UNC path.

16. A, B. A web browser, such as Microsoft Internet Explorer or Mozilla Firefox, is the main interface through which you navigate the Internet. Internet Explorer is a standard component of Windows. Updates and newer versions can be downloaded manually from the Microsoft website or via Windows Update. Other browsers can be downloaded in compressed form and installed manually.

17. C. After you have discerned the IP address of the client's computer, ping that IP address to see if it is alive. If you get replies, then the client computer has network connectivity. If your ping times out, then you will need to troubleshoot the issue further.

18. A, B. If a user reports that he or she cannot connect to the network, check cables, connectors, and other network hardware. A disconnected cable is a common culprit. A faulty connector or network card could also be the cause. Replace any damaged cables and connectors.

Troubleshooting Scenario

You have a computer that has an issue with connecting to network resources such as a printer or share on a server. What are some of the tests you can perform to fix this problem so the user can continue working?

Answer: First you would need to make sure the file and print sharing is turned on for the system. If that is turned on, the next thing would be to check the permissions to see if you are even allowed to connect to the resource. After you have determined that one of these issues has been fixed, you can then recheck to see whether the access is working.

Chapter 17

1. **D.** To recycle alkaline or other types of dry or wet-cell batteries, including batteries used in UPS battery backup systems, as well as rechargeable, watch, and calculator batteries, contact companies that specialize in safe battery disposal or recycling. To locate companies, check your local telephone directory or perform a web search using search terms such as "battery recycling."

2. **A, B, C.** You can and should see if charities and schools could use this old equipment. If not, make sure it is recycled properly. It is illegal to incinerate computer parts, and as such municipalities will refuse them.

3. **A, B, C, D.** The MSDS can be used to determine safe storage practices. It can also be used to determine what you should do if a product is swallowed or splashed on skin. It also describes safe disposal methods and how to deal with the different types or hazards.

4. **C.** Check the MSDS. Many consumable products such as cleaners and printer cartridges have an MSDS, or material safety data sheet. In more and more cases today, this information is available from the manufacturer's website.

5. **C.** By just walking across a carpeted floor, you build up static electricity, which can be discharged to computer components, possibly damaging them and leading to data loss. This discharge is called electrostatic discharge (ESD).

6. **A.** To protect equipment from ESD, store equipment in the Faraday cage antistatic bags originally supplied with the equipment; retain bags for installed equipment for reuse. Faraday cage antistatic bags feature a thin metallic layer on the outside of the bag, which is conductive and prevents ESD from penetrating to the components inside.

7. **D.** You can best equalize the electrical potential of a computer or component that is being serviced by placing the computer or component on an antistatic work mat equipped with a wrist strap. Attach your wrist strap to the mat. This will help place you and the component at the same level of electrical potential, and thus eliminate the "need" for ESD to occur to equalize the potential.

8. **E.** You must always be aware of the hazards in your computer shop. High voltage sources, printers, cables, and atmospheric hazards such as those created by the use of toxic cleaners or the discharge of computer-room–rated fire suppression chemicals can become a hazard and cause bodily harm to you or your co-workers.

9. C. Do *not* leave the computer plugged in while you work inside it. At one time, an acceptable practice was to leave the computer plugged in but shut down and keep one hand on the power supply as a ground. This is no longer appropriate because even if the computer is shut down, ATX and BTX power supplies still send +5 volts of standby power to the computer if it is plugged into an AC outlet.

10. A, C. Lifting heavy equipment can be hazardous to your health. You should tell him to stop and go help him. For extra protection, wear a back brace.

11. B. If a co-worker is lying on the floor and is unresponsive, call 911 immediately. Afterwards, contact the worker's manager. Stay with the person until help arrives.

12. A, C, D. There should always be some type of procedures available for the new person to review. He should have a copy of the MSDS as well just in case he cannot get to the manual.

Troubleshooting Scenario

You are a technician for your company. You walk into work one morning and turn on the lights. You notice that one of your co-workers worked late the night before and left many electrical cables stretched across the floor. What should you do in this scenario?

Answer: First you need to remove the cables from the walkways on or around the walking area. You would then want to speak with the person who left the shop in a hazardous condition. You should explain to him that people could come in and trip, fall, and hurt themselves, or cause a fire or chemical spill. You should let him know to be more cautious when placing cables across the walkways.

Chapter 18

1. B. You should always gather as much information as possible before you start working on the client's computer. You should also document the details so that in the future you will have this information readily available.

2. C. Avoid using jargon, abbreviations, and acronyms. Explain what you mean in plain language. Remember, if you can't explain a problem or solution in everyday language, you don't understand it either.

3. A. Systems that won't start or that have lockups or shutdowns with no error messages could be the victims of power problems. To determine whether power problems are located inside the computer or are coming from outside the system, use the tests and tools described in Chapter 5, "Power Supplies and System Cooling."

4. C. One of the most common problems you will face is determining whether the problem is a hardware issue or a software issue. In this question you should check Device Manager to see if there are any hardware issues.

5. A, B. Before you do anything to a customer's system, you should back up the system's data. The easiest way to ensure that you can restore the system to its previous configuration is to use a disk-imaging program such as Symantec Norton Ghost or Acronis True Image.

6. B. Even if an installation CD came with the device, it might not include up-to-date drivers. It is always a good practice to go out to the manufacturer's website for drivers or installation CDs.

7. A, B, C, D. Make a practice of keeping detailed notes about the problems you solve. If your company has a help-desk system with tracking capabilities, use it. Even if the best you can do is write up your findings, you can use desktop search tools to find the answers to the same problems if you encounter them again.

8. E. All tools listed should be in a technician's toolkit and should be used when working on a client's computer. You should also have some software tools such as drivers and an update disk.

9. A, D. Operating system bootable disks and installation CDs help you restore systems with missing system files or other problems to working condition. They can also be used to prepare hard disks, check and fix partition problems, and view the contents of an existing hard disk in a non-working system or a hard disk that has been pulled from storage for re-use.

10. C. No matter how tough the problem (or the customer), avoid arguing with customers—and drop the defensive attitude, too. Your job is to solve the customer's problem. To do that, you need to work *with* the customer.

11. A, B, C, D. You must learn to respect other people's property. You should never use customers' equipment for personal tasks or look at their personal information, such as documents or pictures.

12. D. No matter how difficult the customer might seem, maintain a positive attitude and tone of voice. Your job is to make possible what is seemingly impossible. As discussed in this chapter, there are abundant resources available from Microsoft, hardware vendors, and numerous forums and newsgroups to help you solve problems.

Troubleshooting Scenario

You have been asked by your supervisor to help a user in the Human Resources area at work. HR is known for keeping a close eye on employee behavior. What should you do (or avoid doing) when working at the user's desk?

Answer: You should always try your best not to use a lot of tech jargon. It makes people feel you are talking down to them or making them feel they are stupid. You should avoid this at all costs. You need to develop a way of talking to your clients in a way that does not make them feel degraded in any way.

You should also speak clearly to the customer and maintain a positive attitude. Avoid interruptions and distractions. You must also treat the customer's property with respect.

Index

X-Y-Z

PEARSON IT Certification

Your Publisher for IT Certification

Pearson IT Certification is the leader in technology certification learning and preparation tools.

Apps

Articles & Chapters

Blogs

Books

eBooks

eBooks (Watermarked)

Cert Flash Cards Online

Newsletters

Podcasts

Question of the Day

Rough Cuts

Short Cuts

Videos

Visit **pearsonITcertification.com** today to find

- **CERTIFICATION EXAM** information and guidance for IT certifications, including

CISCO CompTIA Microsoft

- **EXAM TIPS AND TRICKS** by reading the latest articles and sample chapters by Pearson IT Certification's expert authors and industry experts, such as
  - Mark Edward Soper and David Prowse – CompTIA
  - Wendell Odom – Cisco
  - Shon Harris – Security
  - Thomas Erl – SOACP

- **SPECIAL OFFERS (pearsonITcertification.com/promotions)**

- **REGISTRATION** for your Pearson IT Certification products to access additional online material and receive a coupon to be used on your next purchase

Be sure to create an account on **pearsonITcertification.com** and receive member's-only offers and benefits.

Connect with Pearson IT Certification

pearsonITcertification.com/
newsletters

 twitter.com/
pearsonITCert

 facebook.com/
pearsonitcertification

 youtube.com/
pearsonITCert

 pearsonitcertification.
com/rss/

MARK EDWARD SOPER
SCOTT MUELLER
DAVID L. PROWSE

Includes Coverage of Windows 7

Cert Guide
Learn, prepare, and practice for exam success

▸ Master every topic on both new 2011 A+ exams.
▸ Assess your knowledge and focus your learning.
▸ Get the practical workplace knowledge you need!

CompTIA **A+**
220-701
220-702
Second Edition

DVD FEATURES 2 COMPLETE SAMPLE EXAMS

From Scott Mueller author of *Upgrading & Repairing PCs*
More than 2.2 million copies sold!

PEARSON

FREE Online Edition

Your purchase of **CompTIA A+ 220-701 and 220-702 Cert Guide** includes access to a free online edition for 45 days through the Safari Books Online subscription service. Nearly every [imprint] book is available online through Safari Books Online, along with more than 5,000 other technical books and videos from publishers such as Addison-Wesley Professional, Cisco Press, Exam Cram, IBM Press, O'Reilly, Prentice Hall, Que, and Sams.

SAFARI BOOKS ONLINE allows you to search for a specific answer, cut and paste code, download chapters, and stay current with emerging technologies.

Activate your FREE Online Edition at
www.informit.com/safarifree

> **STEP 1:** Enter the coupon code: ZPVEQGA.

> **STEP 2:** New Safari users, complete the brief registration form.
> Safari subscribers, just log in.

If you have difficulty registering on Safari or accessing the online edition, please e-mail customer-service@safaribooksonline.com

 Addison Wesley
 Adobe Press
 ALPHA
Cisco Press
 FT Press
 IBM Press
 lynda.com
 Microsoft Press
New Riders

O'REILLY
 Peachpit Press
 PRENTICE HALL
 QUE
 Redbooks
 SAMS
 SAS Publishing
 Sun microsystems

 WILEY